C000109477

Malcolm

Soldier, Diplomat, Ideologue of British India

Sir John Malcolm in 1824, while visiting Sir Walter Scott at Abbotsford.

Malcolm

Soldier, Diplomat, Ideologue of British India

The Life of Sir John Malcolm (1769–1833)

John Malcolm

John Donald

First published in Great Britain in 2014 by
John Donald, an imprint of Birlinn Ltd

West Newington House
10 Newington Road
Edinburgh
EH9 1QS

www.birlinn.co.uk

ISBN: 978 1 906566 73 9

British Library Cataloguing-in-Publication Data
A catalogue record for this book is available on request from the British Library

Typeset by Mark Blackadder

Printed and bound in Malta by
Gutenberg Press Limited

Contents

List of Illustrations

In-text illustrations

p. ii Sir John Malcolm (Chalk drawing by William Bewicke. Reproduced by permission of the Scottish National Portrait Gallery.)

p. 32 View of Seringapatam from the north-east, 1791. (Drawing by I. Smith, included in A Dirom, *A Narrative of the Campaign in India*, 1791. Reproduced by permission of the National Library of Scotland.)

p. 37 Henry Dundas, Viscount Melville (1747–1811). (Painting by Henry Raeburn, reproduced by permission of the Lloyds Banking Group, Bank of Scotland.)

p. 41 General Sir Alured Clarke (1745–1832). (Engraving by unknown artist. Private collection.)

p. 60 James Achilles Kirkpatrick (1764–1805). (Portrait by Chinnery, 1805. Private collection.)

p. 92 Jonathan Duncan (1756–1811), Governor of Bombay. (Drawing by Mesquerier. Reproduced by permission of the Scottish National Portrait Gallery.)

p. 110 Persepolis carving made by Malcolm and his party in 1800. (Photograph by Julian Lush.)

p. 113 Fath Ali Shah (1772–1834). (Engraving by C. Heath, from an original Persian painting. Reproduced by permission of the National Library of Scotland.)

p. 159 Mahratta Cavalry. (Drawing by unknown Indian artist, included in A. Dirom, *A Narrative of the Campaign in India,* 1791–2. Reproduced by permission of the National Library of Scotland.)

p. 162 Colonel (later Major General) Sir Barry Close (1758–1813). (Painting by an Indian artist, copied by Moore. Reproduced courtesy of the Oriental Club, London.)

p. 206 John Leyden (1775–1811). (Ink drawing 1811. Frontispiece of John Reith's *Life of Dr John Leyden,* 1908. Reproduced by permission of the National Library of Scotland.)

p. 216 General Sir Gerard (later Viscount) Lake (1744–1808). (Painting by an unknown artist. Reproduced courtesy of the Oriental Club, London.)

p. 239 Gilbert Elliot, 1st Earl of Minto (1757–1814). (Painting by Chinnery, 1811. Reproduced by permission of the Scottish National Portrait Gallery.)

p. 248 Sir Harford Jones Bt (1764–1847). (Painting by Sir Thomas Lawrence. Reproduced by permission of the Bridgeman Art Library, London.)

p. 273 Sir George Barlow Bt (1762–1846). (Painting by an unknown artist. Reproduced by permission of the National Portrait Gallery, London).

p. 282 Charles Grant (1746–1823). (Chalk drawing by an unknown artist. Frontispiece of Henry Morris's *The Life of Charles Grant,* 1904. Reproduced by permission of the National Library of Scotland.)

p. 306 Abbas Mirza (1789–1833). (Drawing by R. Ker Porter, included in his *Travels in Georgia, Persia etc 1817–1820*. Reproduced by permission of the National Library of Scotland).

p. 310 Claudius James Rich (1787–1821). (Painting by an unknown artist. Reproduced by permission of the British Library.)

p. 548 Obelisk on Whita Hill, Langholm. (Photograph by Bini Malcolm. Private collection.)

Plates

1 Burnfoot and Douglen farms in the eighteenth century. (Unknown artist, Private collection.)

2 River Esk, near Burnfoot. (Photograph: Bini Malcolm.)

3 George Malcolm (1729–1803), father of John Malcolm. (Painting by Henry Raeburn c.1800. Private collection.)

4 Margaret, 'Bonnie Peggy', Malcolm (1742–1811), mother of John Malcolm. (Painting by Henry Raeburn c.1800. By permission of the Courtauld Gallery, London.)

5 Douglen Cottage, where John Malcolm was born. (Reproduced by permission of the National Gallery of Scotland.)

6 Westerkirk Schoolhouse. (Photograph: Bini Malcolm.)

7 Fort St George, Madras, from the sea. (Painting by G. Lambert and S. Scott. Reproduced by permission of the British Library.)

8 Tipu Sultan, Ruler of Mysore, 1782–1799. (Drawing by an unknown Indian artist. Reproduced courtesy of the Oriental Club, London.)

9 Lord Cornwallis and the sons of Tipu, 1792. (Painting by Mather Brown. Reproduced courtesy of the Oriental Club, London.)

10 Richard Wellesley (1760–1842). Bust by Noellekens. (Reproduced by permission of the Provost and Fellows of Eton College.)

11 Meer Alam (?1760–1809), c.1799, the Nizam of Hyderabad's *vakeel* to the British. (Painting by an unknown Indian artist. Reproduced by permission of the Salar Jung Museum, Hyderabad.)

12 The Nizam and his durbar on a hunting expedition. (Painting by Venkatchellam. Reproduced by permission of the Salar Jung Museum, Hyderabad.)

13 William Kirkpatrick in Madras, c.1799, with his assistants and Persian munshis. (Painting by Thomas Hickey. Reproduced by permission of the National Gallery of Ireland.)

14 Persepolis – a contemporary view. (Drawing by James Morier, c.1811. Reproduced by permission of the National Gallery of Scotland.)

15 Government House Calcutta. (Engraving by James Baillie Fraser, from *Views of Calcutta,* 1821. Reproduced by permission of the National Gallery of Scotland.)

16 Baji Rao II, Peshwah of Poona (1775–1851). (Painting by an unknown Indian artist. Reproduced courtesy of Wellcome Images.)

17 Sir Arthur Wellesley and his favourite charger Diomed. (Painting by John Hoppner in 1806. Reproduced courtesy of the Trustees of the Stratfield Saye Preservation Trust.)

18 Dowlat Rao Scindiah (1781–1827). (Painting by an unknown Indian artist. Reproduced courtesy of Her Highness Shrimant Maharani Sir Jivaji Rao Scindia Museum, Gwalior.)

19 Tiger Hunt in India, c.1795 (Painting by an unknown artist. Reproduced by permission of the British Library.)

20 British Envoys at the Persian Court, 1808–1811. (Painting by an unknown Persian artist. Reproduced by permission of the Bridgeman Art Library, London.)

21 Lady Charlotte Malcolm and her children in 1815. (Drawing by George Hayter, 1815. Private collection.)

22 Sword of the Maharajah Holkar. (Reproduced courtesy of the Victoria and Albert Museum, London.)

23 The Fortress of Asirgarh. (Photograph by Bini Malcolm.)

24 Nalcha, near Mandu. (Photograph by Bini Malcolm.)

25 Mehmet Ali, Pasha of Egypt (1769–1849). (Painting by Thomas Brigstock. Reproduced courtesy of the Oriental Club, London.)

26 Hyde Hall, Hertfordshire. (Drawing by J. P. Neale 1819. Reproduced by permission of Cambridge University Library.)

27 Malcolm's meeting with Sahajanand Swami. (Painting by an unknown Indian artist. Reproduced courtesy of Bochsanawasi Shri Akshar Purushottam Swaminarayan Sanstha (BAPS).)

28 The Duke of Wellington, elder statesman. (Painting by H. W. Pickersgill. Reproduced courtesy of the Oriental Club, London.)

29 India House, Leadenhall Street, London, headquarters of the East India Company. (Print from Ackermann, *Views of London*. Reproduced by permission of the British Library.)

30 Lady Charlotte Malcolm in 1840. (Painting by Sir Francis Grant. Private collection.)

List of Maps

Preface

In August 1967 my employer, Royal Dutch Shell, appointed me to be its representative in an oil refining/marketing joint venture in Iran. By way of background briefing, I attended a function at the Middle East Association in London. There I met its Director, Richard Goddard Wilson. He murmured, 'Dear boy, that name will be very useful to you in Iran. Are you related to Sir John Malcolm?' I had no idea what he was talking about, and my immediate family had no idea either. But eventually the elderly wife of a Scottish cousin explained that Sir John came from a Dumfriesshire offshoot of my Fife Malcolm family.

Goddard Wilson had worked in Iran and I suspect might once have been a spy. He urged me to study Malcolm, and sent me a handwritten reading list (which I still have) comprising 59 numbered items, the first one instructing me to 'read Curzon with care'. Shortly afterwards he produced a bound volume of handwritten letters which Malcolm had written from Persia in 1808 to his newly wedded wife in Bombay. He had acquired the volume, he said, in 1956, when he was travelling north by car past Langholm on his way to Edinburgh. On a whim, he decided to make a detour and call at Burnfoot, the home of the Malcolm family since the eighteenth century. The descendant living there at the time, John Palmer-Douglas, welcomed him, ushered him into a rather dilapidated library/museum, and left him there. After an hour or two Palmer-Douglas returned, and found him reading the bound volume mentioned above. 'Take it,' said Palmer-Douglas, cheerfully, 'I'm not interested in this stuff.' So, after mild protestations, he did so. I am glad to report that in 2008 this volume of letters was reunited with the rest of the Malcolm of Burnfoot papers in the National Library of Scotland.

When I got to Tehran I was further intrigued to find that my Persian co-directors of the joint venture were two brothers – Abdolali and Cyrus Farmanfarmaian – direct descendants of the Qajar ruler Fath Ali Shah, who had signed the 1801 Treaty with Malcolm as the representative of the East India Company. I was far too busy with work and a young family to follow up on Goddard Wilson's reading list, but I did read Malcolm's *Sketches of Persia*, and was impressed by his sharp but affectionate insights into the Persian character. And when I left Iran for Australia in 1972 I was touched by Abdolali and Cyrus's leaving present – a first edition of Malcolm's *History of Persia*, published in 1815.

I also read a weighty two-volume biography of Malcolm by the military historian Sir John Kaye, published in 1856. It is an imposing work, but written in the style and reflecting the mores of mid-Victorian Britain. I made a resolution that one day, when I had more time, I would delve further into Malcolm's life, and perhaps write a memoir from a twenty-first century perspective. The idea of a short memoir was however pre-empted in 1982, when an 80,000 word work (*'Send Malcolm!'*) by a Malcolm kinsman, Sir Rodney Pasley, was published. This was a skilful essay, but Pasley used mainly secondary source material. A more thorough work was still needed. Eventually, after I retired in 1996, I was free to pursue Malcolm, and that is what I have been doing, on and off, ever since.

Kaye had written in the preface of his biography that when he was given the task by Malcolm's widow, he had at his disposal 'literally, a roomful of materials' (i.e. manuscript correspondence). Sadly, many of these 'materials', which Kaye had described as 'the very best biographical materials at my command' were lost through damp and a fire in the 1860s, among them all Malcolm's letters to his wife (apart from the 1808 letters found by Goddard Wilson).

My quest for Malcolm has taken me to archives all over Britain, especially to the National Library of Scotland in Edinburgh and the British Library in London. In India, from a base at Mahabaleshwar, the hill station founded by Malcolm in 1828, I have followed in his footsteps throughout southern and western India, and also in Iran. Thanks to Malcolm, these travels have been fascinating and rewarding experiences. My wife and I have been helped by literally hundreds of people whom we would never have met as mere tourists.

At first, conscious of how much the history of the British in India seemed to have been told from a British viewpoint, from British source material, I looked for Indian source material and for alternative interpretations from Indian historians. The results in the English language were, however, slightly disappointing, especially when compared with the undoubted mastery of English in contemporary Indian fiction. With a few exceptions Indian historians appeared either to confine themselves to a mere chronicling of events, or, in recent years, to bang a nationalist drum in which fantasy and wishful thinking overrode inconvenient facts. On the other hand, with the vernacular languages I dithered between Hindi and Marathi and, regrettably, mastered neither. So, sadly, this work remains largely an interpretation from Western sources.

Most educated Indians (and Persians) seem to have heard of Sir John Malcolm. He is part of their direct history, in the same way that William the Conqueror is part of British history. And they appear to me to have a remarkably balanced view of the British Raj. By contrast, today's British public (I speak here as an Australian) appear quite indifferent to the history of British India, especially to its earlier years. They seem to have persuaded themselves that because *some* aspects of the British imperial story warrant justifiable censure, the *whole* should be treated as shameful, or at least dotty, and ignored. Malcolm's memory in Britain is confined to a life-size marble statue in Westminster Abbey, and an obelisk standing lonely at the top of Whita Hill, above Langholm, in Dumfriesshire, Scotland.

But as time has passed I have found myself becoming more and more enthralled by the story of how a few intrepid fellows somehow bluffed their way into dominating a huge subcontinent; and how some of them, including Malcolm, tried very hard to rule for the benefit of the people who came under their control.

In the end, though, this is not primarily a thesis about imperial governance in British India. It is the story of one very talented and ambitious man, living in an exciting era of British and Indian history. Echoing the words of Iris Butler, in the preface to her biography of Richard Wellesley (*The Eldest Brother*, 1973), I have tried to present John Malcolm as a human being, and not only as an imperial symbol, a marble statue gathering dust.

Acknowledgements

This book has taken me many years to research and write, in many countries. I have been helped along the way by literally hundreds of people. I am hugely grateful to them all, but there are too many to list all of them individually.

Professor Jim Masselos of Sydney University started me off. Derrick Mirfin (who had corrected my history essays at Cambridge over half a century earlier) waded through the whole of my unwieldy first draft. Professor M. E. Yapp stimulated my thinking about Malcolm as an 'ideologue'. In Australia John Blay read successive drafts, and Mark O'Connor commented on Malcolm's poetry. But most of all I must thank Martha McLaren, in Canada, who read through my second draft and made many pertinent suggestions.

Descendants of the extended Malcolm family – Mrs Jean Crossley, Napier Malcolm, Heather and Bruce Osborne and Dr Walther Frhr von Marschall – all provided valuable private material.

For the Eskdale dimension Terence Waters, Shirley Rodden, Ann Little (who let me use the Little family archive), Arthur Bell, Professor Tom Scott and John Packer were supportive throughout.

For Malcolm's friendship with the Duke of Wellington I was helped by Anthony Bennell, and latterly by Rory Muir; also by Chris Woolgar and Karen Robson of the Hartley Library at the University of Southampton, and by the Stratfield Saye archivist. For Malcolm's relationship with Richard Wellesley I was greatly encouraged by Iris Portal.

For the Persian chapters I took advice from Sir Denis Wright, and later from Michael Noel Clarke, Charles Drace Francis and Soraya

Tremayne, who read and commented on my draft.

In India many people helped in various ways; among them Bittu and Dilnaar Ahmadullah, Manohar Awati, Gunvanthi Balaram, Vasant Bawa, Dr N. K. Bhide, Gavan Bromilow, Shyam Chainani, William Dalrymple, Arunkanti Dasgupta, Amol Divkar, Amar Farooqui, Sanjay Godbole, Richard Holkar, Dilip and Jaya Kibe, Professor A. R. Kulkarni, Dr Uday Kulkarni, Colonel Mini Mohite, Sadhu Mukundcharandas (historian of BAPS Swaminarayan), Chanda Nimbkar, Pranay and Anjali Patwardhan, Shoba Shirke, Farrokh and Statira Wadia, and dozens more.

At Birlinn, Hugh Andrew turned my vague aspirations into practical reality, while Mairi Sutherland took me, as an eighty-year-old beginner author, through the process of turning a rough draft into a published book.

Lastly, my wife, Bini Malcolm. I thought of dedicating the book to her, but she has been an active partner in the project from the start, really a co-author. So I will just thank her for travelling with me so enthusiastically throughout this whole Odyssey.

Introduction

> The great Empire which England has established in the East will be of wonder to succeeding ages. That a small Island in the Atlantic should have conquered and held the vast Continent of India as a subject Province is in itself a fact which can never be stated without exciting astonishment. But the surprise will be increased, when it is added, that this great conquest was made, not by the collective force of the Nation, but by a Company of Merchants, who, vested with a charter of exclusive commerce . . . were in a few years hurried – by the enterprise and ambition of their agents; [by] the hostile and rival spirit of the other nations of Europe; and [by] the weakness and perfidy of the Princes of Asia – into the possession of Royal power; and actually found themselves called upon to act in the character of Sovereigns over extended kingdoms, before they had ceased to be the mercantile directors of petty factories.[1]

These words were written, not by an academic historian a hundred years later, but by an active participant in the events as they unfolded.

John Malcolm was born in 1769, one of seventeen children of the same mother, the wife of an impoverished tenant farmer living in the Scottish Borders. He left school, family and country at the age of thirteen, and achieved distinction in the East India Company over the next half-century, as a soldier, diplomat, administrator and scholar. A spirited character, he was nicknamed 'Boy' Malcolm, for throughout his life he retained a youthful enthusiasm for field sports and fun and games. But behind this boisterous exterior lay serious intellectual ability and a considerable talent for government. As a soldier he became a General, leading the Company's troops to victory in 1817 against the Mahratta Chieftain Holkar at the battle of Mehidpoor. As a diplomat he acted as troubleshooter to successive Governors-General, leading three Company missions to Persia. As an administrator, he pacified Central India (roughly, today's Madhya Pradesh) and later became Governor of Bombay (ruling a large part of western India). As a scholar, he wrote nine books, including *The History of Persia*, which remained the standard English-language history of that country for nearly a century. As a linguist, he spoke at least eight languages. He was known, too, as an expert judge of Arab horses and as an enthusiastic amateur poet.

Though a patriotic Scot, he appears to have been entirely free of racial prejudice or cultural chauvinism. Above all, he had a warmth of heart and a generosity of spirit which enabled him to make friends with the humblest and the greatest in the land – Indian and British alike. One distinguished historian has even claimed that Malcolm was the Duke of Wellington's 'best and lifelong friend'.[2]

Why should Malcolm concern us today?

First, as a man, who came from an impoverished Scottish rural background to achieve distinction in many countries, in many fields, through sheer ability and effort, despite many setbacks; in short, in contrast to these days of narrow credentialists, as a quintessential all-rounder.

Second, as a major participant during a crucial period of British and Indian political history.

Third, as a steadfast servant of the East India Company, one of the world's first multinational corporations, during the critical half-century when it was transformed from a purely commercial venture into an agent of imperial government.

Fourth, as one of the earliest players of the Great Game of diplomatic rivalry between Britain and Russia in Persia and Central Asia during the nineteenth century.

Fifth, and perhaps most importantly, as one of a trio of eminent Scotsmen – the other two being Thomas Munro and Mountstuart Elphinstone – who worked out a philosophical basis for British rule in India, a unique form of imperialism.

British political involvement in India was relatively short lived. The 190 years between the battle of Plassey in 1757 and Indian independence and partition in 1947 were no more than a short episode in the nearly 3,600 years of recorded Indian history. Yet they were also dramatic and decisive.

The current perception of the British Raj tends to be of Curzon, Kipling, E.M. Forster and memsahibs and the Freedom Struggle; of a complacent and apparently immovable imperial edifice being outmanoeuvred by the non-violent tactics of the saintly Mahatma Gandhi. And before that, of evangelically minded British Generals in the nineteenth century, crushing brave but pathetic Indian resistance with superior weaponry.

Yet there was an earlier period – the half-century from 1783 to 1833, roughly beginning with the Governor-Generalship of Lord Cornwallis and ending with that of Lord William Bentinck – when the East India Company achieved political hegemony over the whole subcontinent, the first time that this had ever been done.

In 1783, when Malcolm arrived in India, the East India Company was still a Joint Stock Company which had been founded in 1600, with a licence from Queen Elizabeth I to trade between Britain and the East Indies (technically as a monopoly, a status it retained until 1813). Its headquarters were in London, with an elected Court of Directors, though only a few of the Directors ever went to India. The Company's activities were not confined to the Indian subcontinent; it also operated at one time or another in China, Indonesia, Singapore, the Persian Gulf and the Arabian Peninsula. For the first 150 years of its existence its activities had been purely commercial. Then came Robert Clive, the battle of Plassey, and the Company's acquisition of territorial power in Bengal. Surprisingly, most of the Company's profits came from its China trade (buying tea and selling opium). It made hardly any profit from its Indian operations, although some of its employees certainly did – often by misappropriating the Company's assets, especially in the twenty years after Plassey, when they were able to use their dual status as both government magistrates and private merchants to indulge in disgraceful exploitation of the local populace.

In 1784, through William Pitt's India Act, the British Government belatedly set up a Board of Control under a senior Government Minister to oversee the Company's governmental functions, and attempted to separate them from its trading activities. Both these London-based bodies – the Company's Court of Directors and the Government's Board of Control – opposed territorial expansion by the Company, for different reasons. The Directors wanted dividends, and territorial expansion usually involved war, which was expensive. The Government was not interested in India. It looked to North America and the West Indies for overseas expansion and settlement.

'British' India was ruled by a Governor-General, appointed in theory by the Court of Directors, but in practice by the British Government. The issues that the Company's management faced have many parallels in the management of multinational corporations today: for instance, the tensions between head office and a distant 'man on the spot'; and the relationship between businesses and governments. For the Governor-General, the management structure was a nightmare. He reported to two masters in London, the Board and the Court, each with its own very different agenda. And he had only loose control over the Governors of Madras and Bombay. Letters between London and Calcutta took four to six months each way. As a result Governors-General often had to take major decisions on the spot, and hope that in due course they would be approved retrospectively; if not, they might be recalled in disgrace. Of course enterprising Governors-General could also exploit these delays, making use of the time lags to do what they wanted to do anyway, and presenting *faits accomplis* to their London masters; trusting that, if they were successful, London would forgive them for having acted without prior approval. It was a risky game, but as long as he kept 'winning', the 'man on the spot' could usually circumvent the rules laid down by head office.

The key figure in this period was Richard Wellesley, first Marquess Wellesley (eldest brother of the Duke of Wellington), Governor-General from 1798 to 1805, for whom Malcolm worked as Private Secretary and general troubleshooter. It was Wellesley who had the clarity of vision to see that the chaotic state of India at that time could only be cured by a single controlling power; and that of the various candidates – the Mahrattas in the west, Tipu Sultan, the ruler of Mysore in the south, the remnant of the Mughal Empire in the north, and the Company in Bengal (with outposts in Madras and Bombay) – only the Company had the will, the discipline and above all the necessary wherewithal to succeed. From the date of his arrival he set out to do so, with breathtaking audacity; and moreover, against the wishes of his two employers, the Company and the British Government. Seven years later, when he was within sight of achieving his aim, he suffered the fate which has overtaken many a successful proconsul of the British Empire – he was (effectively) recalled; and when he returned to Britain, nearly impeached. The commercially minded Directors in London were understandably alarmed by the size of the negative cash flows which Wellesley's wars had generated. His project was put on hold. But it was reluctantly resumed twelve years later, and by 1818, largely achieved. Wellesley is mostly forgotten today, but his imperial achievement can reasonably be compared with that of his contemporary, Napoleon Bonaparte. Napoleon's career of conquest was spectacular, but within his own lifetime it ended in defeat and humiliation for France; Wellesley's, for better or for worse, lasted for 140 years.

Between 1783 and 1833 Malcolm was a leading player in British India – a man of action in war and peace; and, through his books, a leading ideologue in the fierce contemporary debates about how British India was to be governed.

This book tells his story.

PART ONE

Scotsman

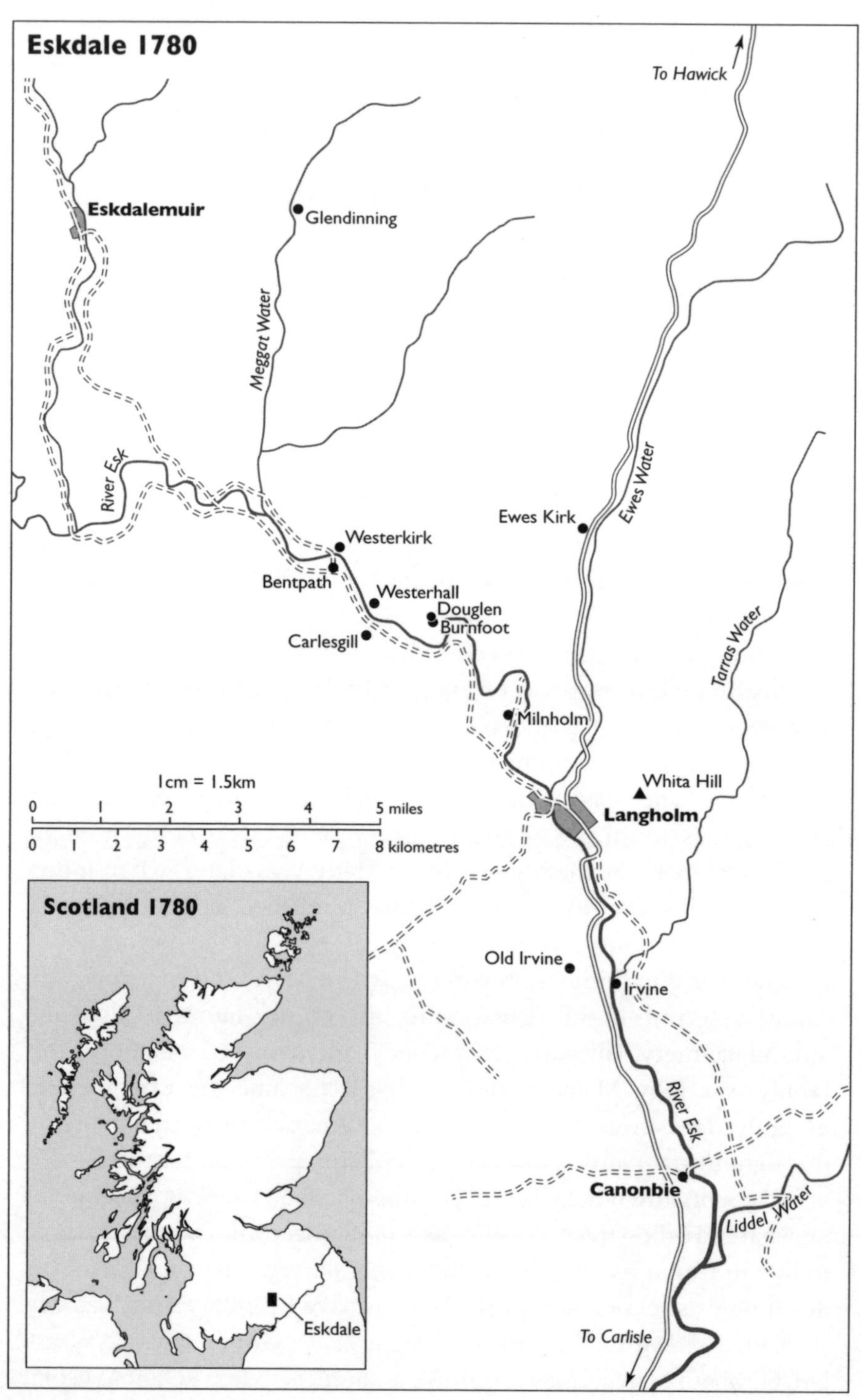
Eskdale 1780
To Hawick
Eskdalemuir
Glendinning
Meggat Water
River Esk
Ewes Water
Ewes Kirk
Westerkirk
Bentpath
Westerhall
Douglen
Burnfoot
Carlesgill
Tarras Water
Milnholm
1cm = 1.5km
0 1 2 3 4 5 miles
0 1 2 3 4 5 6 7 8 kilometres
Whita Hill
Langholm
Scotland 1780
Old Irvine
Irvine
River Esk
Canonbie
Liddel Water
Eskdale
To Carlisle

CHAPTER ONE

Eskdale Childhood, 1769–1782

John Malcolm was born on 2 May 1769 at Douglen farmhouse, on the bank of the Esk river, four miles upstream from the small town of Langholm in the Scottish Border country. He was the seventh child and fourth son of George and Margaret Malcolm. By his fourth birthday three more children had been born; by his tenth he had thirteen siblings. As a visitor described the scene many years later, 'the noise was intolerable, everyone talked at once'.[1] John was one of the noisiest.

He was 'cheerful, mischievous, uninhibited and full of spirit, from an early age'. The village schoolmaster, Archibald Graham, later remembered him as an unruly pupil. Whenever pranks were committed, he would say 'Jock's at the bottom of it'. Many years later, when John's magnum opus, *The History of Persia*, was published, he sent a copy to Graham, with an inscription on the flyleaf, 'Jock's at the bottom of it'.[2]

The Malcolm family came originally from Fife, and first appear in surviving records in the early seventeenth century, living in Cupar and around Ballingry. The patriarch and most distinguished member of this family was John Malcolm (1611–1692). He became the Chamberlain (roughly, Treasurer) of Fife in 1641, and gradually acquired property throughout the county. His cousin, William Malcolm (1617–1707), was born at Scottstown near Aberdeen, and married Elizabeth, daughter of Sir Charles Forbes, from a distinguished Aberdeenshire family. He came to live in Cupar as a Writer to the Signet (lawyer). By the time of his death he was sufficiently prosperous to have his own family vault in the Cupar kirkyard. His third son David, also a lawyer, married a local girl, Elizabeth Melvill, and sired nine children, including Robert Malcolm

(1687–1761), the grandfather of John Malcolm, the subject of this book.

Robert Malcolm achieved an MA at St Andrews University in 1707, and became a tutor to the sons of Sir Hew Dalrymple of Haddington, East Lothian. He was ordained as a Presbyter, and in 1717 Sir Hew probably spoke to the Duke of Buccleuch about finding his young tutor a 'living' somewhere on the huge Buccleuch estates in Dumfriesshire; perhaps, too, Robert's maternal uncle, John Melvill, the Duke's factor at Langholm, pressed his case with the Duke. The Reverend Robert was duly nominated as Minister to the parish of Ewes, and on 29 August 1717 he was elected by the elders of the Ewes kirk. He took up residence at the Ewes manse, next door to the kirk, and there he remained until his death forty-four years later. In 1722 he married Agnes Campbell, daughter of the redoubtable George Campbell (1636–1701), Professor of Divinity at the University of Edinburgh.

Robert and Agnes had four children, but only Wilhemina (1727–1806) and George (1729–1803) survived to maturity. It was a poor clerical family, with a limited stipend and practically no capital. Again Uncle John Melvill came to the rescue. One of the perquisites of his job was the possession of the 'tack' (lease at nominal rental) of the Burnfoot farm in Eskdale, four miles upstream from Langholm on the north bank of the Esk, and about three miles over the hills from Ewes. In 1730 Melvill was able to persuade the Duke to let him pass on the 'tack' of Burnfoot to his nephew Robert.

Burnfoot lay in the rural Dumfriesshire parish of Westerkirk, with a population of 700, mostly engaged in subsistence agriculture and running white-faced Cheviot sheep. The 'heritors' (major landowners) in the area were the Dukes of Buccleuch, the Johnstones of Westerhall and the Pasleys of Craig and Mount Annan.

The Buccleuchs owned (and still do) a great deal of land in the parish, and indeed all over southern Scotland and parts of England.

The Johnstones lived at Westerhall, immediately to the west of Burnfoot. In the second half of the eighteenth century four Johnstone brothers, all contemporaries of George Malcolm, became Members of Parliament, and only intermittently returned to Westerhall. Sir James Johnstone, the eldest, and 4th baronet, was a highly independent MP, 'cast . . . in the Herculean mould, of an uncouth aspect, rude address and almost gigantic proportions . . . who concealed under unpolished manners great integrity directed by common sense'.[3] He was no respecter of persons, and in 1785 supported the impeachment of Warren Hastings and Sir Elijah Impey: 'We have beheaded a King, we have hanged a peer, we have shot an admiral, we are now trying a Governor-General, and I can see no reason why we should not put on trial a judge and a chief justice.' While advocating religious toleration, he himself favoured Presbyterianism, as 'the least expensive road to Heaven'. The second brother, William, who succeeded to the baronetcy on Sir James's death in 1794, was clever or lucky enough to meet and marry Frances Pulteney, the niece and heiress of the Earl of Bath, said to be the richest man in Britain, and worth over £1 million. The condition for approving her marriage was that William should change his surname to Pulteney, which he did with alacrity. A third brother was George 'Governor' Johnstone. After serving in the Royal Navy he was appointed Governor of West Florida at the age of thirty-three. He later became an MP, and later still a director of the East India Company. The fourth brother was John Johnstone, who went to Bengal in 1750, aged sixteen; was captured and imprisoned by Suraj-ud-Dowla (the Nawab of Bengal); commanded the artillery at the Battle of Plassey; made a fortune as a 'shrewd and unscrupulous businessman'; was dismissed by the Company; opposed Clive on the Bengal Council in 1765; resigned and came back to Scotland; bought estates with his *nabob* fortune; managed to avoid prosecution through the support of Sulivan faction in the East India Company directorate; and entered Parliament in 1774, making the estate of Alva, near Stirling, his base.

The Pasleys owned the farm of Craig, barely half a mile across the Esk from Burnfoot. In the eighteenth century it was the home of James Pasley of the Eskdale branch of the family. James's wife Magdalen was descended from the Elliots of Minto, about twenty-five miles away – 'the Border Elliots' – a tough lot. One of Magdalen Elliot's ancestors was 'little Jock Elliot, and wha daur meddle wi' me?' After several centuries of clan feuds and cattle raiding, the Elliot family gained greater respectability by public service abroad – Gilbert Elliot becoming Governor-General of India in 1807, and first Earl of Minto. James and Magdalen Pasley had seven sons and four daughters including John (1729–1804), a London merchant; Thomas (1734–1808), a naval officer who at the Battle of Glorious First of June in 1794 'lost a leg and won a baronetcy', later becoming Admiral Sir Thomas Pasley Bt; Charles, a wine merchant based for many years in Lisbon and later in London; and

Gilbert, who joined the East India Company and later became Surgeon-General at Madras. But in some ways the most remarkable child was their daughter Margaret ('Bonnie Peggy') Pasley (1742–1811), who lived her whole life within a mile of her birthplace at the Craig farmhouse.

George Malcolm was meant to become a clergyman, but he had a slight speech impediment, so he became a farmer instead. As soon as he reached maturity he was made manager of the Burnfoot farm. There was no proper house at Burnfoot, so he 'commuted' daily, riding over the hills to and from the Ewes manse. In 1758 the Duke of Buccleuch allowed George to join his ageing father in the Burnfoot 'tack'. The Esk was easily fordable for most of the year, and George had plenty of opportunities to meet Bonnie Peggy Pasley, 'the girl next door' at Craig farm. When the Reverend Robert died in March 1761, George inherited the full 'tack' of Burnfoot. He married Bonnie Peggy in August that year, and set up house a couple of hundred yards north of Burnfoot at Douglen Cottage and its farm, which he rented from John Johnstone of Westerhall.

George was straightforward, outgoing, charming and a bit of a dandy; 'honest but naïve', was his reputation. Margaret was breezy, rough and uneducated, strong but kind; the perfect foil for George. Both were popular in the district. Over the first twenty-one years of their marriage Bonnie Peggy gave birth to no fewer than seventeen children – an astonishing feat of fecundity. Throughout this entire period she must have been either pregnant or lactating. Inevitably the cottage at Douglen – a standard two-storey farmhouse, sixty feet by twenty feet – became inadequate for their growing family. Around 1772 (by which time they had produced eight children), they built and moved into a larger house on Burnfoot farm itself. In such an atmosphere there was little room for shrinking violets. The children needed to shout to make themselves heard. They would be pushed out of the cottage after breakfast, and told to go and play all day in the open air on the surrounding hills, or on the banks of the river. In the damp climate of the Borders there was plenty of rain in the summer, and snow in the winter. Despite these harsh conditions, all but one survived to maturity. They were a hardy lot.

Bonnie Peggy ruled firmly over this cacophonous throng. Despite being almost continually pregnant, she was catering, from 1780, for eighteen mouths at every meal, every day. Yet she still found time to write several cooking recipe books, which have survived.[4] Her attitude to illness is demonstrated in a letter she wrote to her youngest son, Charles, a midshipman at sea aged thirteen at the time, who had complained to her of a stiff neck. 'The Allmighty can protect you as well at sea as on Land. Put your trust in him, fear God and keep his commandments, and my dearest boy need have no other fear . . . I hope you will have no more wry necks and loom limbs, but be a brave, stout fellow.'[5] As each child reached the age of six, he or she would walk or ride for about two miles through the Johnstone property of Westerhall, to the one-room parish school just up the hill from the Westerkirk kirk.[6]

In the 1760s and 1770s George farmed Burnfoot (rented from the Duke of Buccleuch); Douglen (rented from John Johnstone); and Craig (for his father-in-law, James Pasley, already sixty-six when George married Bonnie Peggy). He had inherited no more than £1,200 from his father, 'a narrow capital, as times now are, to support a large family'.[7] He also became a farming consultant and factor, supervising the tenant farmers on the farms belonging to gentry who were living away from Eskdale. In particular he acted as joint factor with his brother-in-law John Maxwell, the laird of Broomholm farm, for William (Johnstone) Pulteney on the Pulteney estates at Solwaybank (about three miles south of Langholm) and Dornock (on the shore of the Solway Firth). But consulting work did not bring George much money – he was paid a fee of only £20 per annum by Pulteney. He looked around for some way to increase his income. Some of his Pasley in-laws were in the wine business, owning vineyards at Tenerife in the Canary Islands. So in 1768 he set up a wine-importing venture based at Longtown, just over the English border on the road to Carlisle, in partnership with his brother-in-law John Maxwell, and Maxwell's cousin Sir William Maxwell. George supervised the business, which was financed largely by borrowings secured by George's guarantee. Somewhat unwisely, he also signed promissory notes in his own name to purchase stock. At first, all went reasonably well. But around 1775 things started to go wrong. Farming was in the doldrums, the wine trade was in recession, and cash flow problems became acute. By September 1779 the business was effectively bankrupt, partly 'through the unpardonable neglect of the [partnership's] agent' at Longtown. There were mutual recriminations.

Further disaster then struck George's family. He wrote to William Pulteney: 'My family is at present in the utmost distress. Mrs Malcolm has been at the Gates of Death in a Fever. She is recovering but is still in a very critical situation. I have lost my youngest child [a baby daughter, aged one month] and this day my eldest is no more [a daughter aged seventeen], as amiable a Girl as ever lived. My two eldest sons have had the fever, but are now thought to be recovering.' And, two weeks later: 'My fourth son [John] just now lyes at the Point of Death. It is a malignant spotted Fever which has attacked us. I hope my good God will not permit it to spread any farther. We are using every precaution to prevent the Infection. I make all the children eat Garlic and wash their Faces and Hands with Vinegar, and it is often sprinkled in the room where the sick boy lyes.'[8]

On 1 August 1780 George publicly declared himself insolvent. His estate is said to have paid out only 7/7 in the pound (38 per cent), though this may have been an interim payment.

George remained in debt to the Maxwells until the end of his life. Some of this debt was paid off by his brother-in-law Gilbert Pasley, and the balance was finally cleared by his sons (Pulteney and John), immediately after his death in 1803. These events illustrate several aspects of George Malcolm's character: his optimism, his poor business judgment, his naivety, yet also his obvious integrity and determination to repay – or rather inspire his family to repay – his creditors. These qualities were later reflected in some of his sons.

By 1780 George and Bonnie Peggy had already produced thirteen surviving children – eight sons and five daughters (two daughters had died in 1779) – with two more sons to come. In his insolvent situation George could not feed them. The daughters might be married off, but could never be expected to earn a living. The only hope was to put his sons out to work as soon as possible. There were no competitive examinations in those days. 'Places' could be 'bought', but this required an investment of capital, which he did not have. 'Nominations' could, however, be obtained through patronage. Fortunately George had lots of charm and some excellent contacts, and now he went to work to call up his credit with his patrons. The Johnstone brothers in particular were keen to help. Bonnie Peggy's brothers John Pasley, the London merchant, and Thomas Pasley, the Royal Navy Captain, were also called upon.

Through the influence of the Johnstones George secured a writership in the East India Company for his eldest son Robert, who sailed to

Madras in 1779 (aged fifteen). His second son James was found a place in the Marines in 1780 (aged thirteen). His third, Pulteney, joined the Royal Navy as a midshipman in 1778 (aged ten), his first posting being on HMS *Jupiter*, commanded by his uncle Thomas. Of the five surviving daughters only one, Margaret, was ever married – to a cousin – and she returned to Burnfoot three years later as a childless widow. So the five sisters lived on at Burnfoot for the next half-century.

John was eleven years old when a nomination came to Burnfoot for him to join the Madras Army, courtesy of the Johnstone family. John Johnstone wrote to George: 'The enclosed, from my worthy brother, the Governor, is fresh proof of his never ceasing attention to his friends. He thinks that John, the eldest of your boys now at home, if I have not mistaken his name . . . though young, should nevertheless accept of this appointment.'[9] Not for the last time in his life, John had caught the eye of a grandee, in this case 'Governor' George Johnstone. And he had also impressed John Johnstone, who in correspondence with George Malcolm about farming matters, wrote in July 1781 that 'in regard to the balance of the price of cattle when you receive it, I think it cannot be so well bestowed as in paying my debt to your son John, and you will accordingly carry £100 to his credit and employ it as you think most for his benefit.'[10]

Nomination was one thing, but the actual appointment would depend on passing an oral examination in front of a committee of Directors in the boardroom at the India House in Leadenhall St, London – a daunting prospect for anyone, but positively terrifying for an eleven-year-old country boy who had never left the Scottish Borders. During the first six months of 1781 the family could not decide what to do about George Johnstone's nomination. Then in July Bonnie Peggy's brother John Pasley visited Eskdale. A prosperous and respected London merchant, and a bachelor, he had already come to the aid of the Burnfoot family in 1780, auditing the books of the failed wine venture, and giving his assurance to William Pulteney that George Malcolm's conduct 'stands fair in terms of honour and integrity.'[11] He had already paid off enough of George's debts to allow the family to continue to live in reasonable style at Burnfoot. His strong advice was to let John take the oral examination without further delay, regardless of the likely outcome. So, at the end of July 1781 the boy set off with his uncle in the stagecoach on the two-day journey to London. He stayed at John Pasley's house in Gower St, and ten days later Pasley wrote to his sister at Burnfoot: 'I allowed him to remain with me all the week, that he might see and become better acquainted with this immense city. His time was fully employed in traversing its streets, and during those few days he saw everything almost that was curious, and was delighted beyond expression. His ideas began to open, his behaviour is much altered, and on the whole, hitherto, I have a very good opinion of him.'[12] On 7 August Pasley brought in a tutor, Mr Allen, to build on the rudimentary education that John had received from Archibald Graham at the Westerkirk parish school.

Time went by, and John Pasley found a Captain Tod, master of the East Indiaman *Busbridge*, who was prepared to take John to India free of charge – a major consideration, since passages in those days were very expensive. Yet he still hesitated to put John through the interview at the India House. He wrote to George Malcolm: 'Johnny, though tall for his age, I don't know how to dispose of. He certainly will not pass at the India House, and Tod will sail in March. If he loses this opportunity, next year he may have his passage to pay for. In two or three weeks Tod is expected in town. I will consult him on the subject, and endeavour, if possible, to get him out. Another year at the Academy would not hurt him: but though he would be by that means better qualified for his employment, the delay will be attended with many disadvantages, which I wish to guard against.'[13] The crucial interview took place shortly afterwards. The Directors were unhappy about his extreme youth (he was still only twelve), and the interview was heading towards a rejection. Then the Chairman asked him, half in jest, a final trick question. At that time the scourge of the British in Southern India was Hyder Ali, the Sultan of Mysore. 'My little man,' he asked, 'what would you do if you were to meet Hyder Ali to-morrow?' Quick as a flash came the reply: 'Do, Sir? I'd out wi' my sword and cut off his heid.' This spirited answer produced laughter. The Chairman looked round, and saw that the mood of the committee had suddenly changed. 'You'll do,' he said, 'Let him pass.'[14]

The *Busbridge*'s departure was delayed until the autumn of 1782, and John got a year's intensive education at the expert hands of Mr Allen. By the time he embarked he was probably not much worse educated than the majority of thirteen-year-old British boys setting out for the East. He was, nevertheless, facing an extraordinary adventure. He had already been parted from his parents for a year, but at least letters to and from Scotland took only a few days. From India letters home would take up to six months, with a further six months for the reply. But, as his mother would have wanted, he was quite prepared to put his trust in God, 'and be a brave stout fellow'.

PART TWO

Soldier

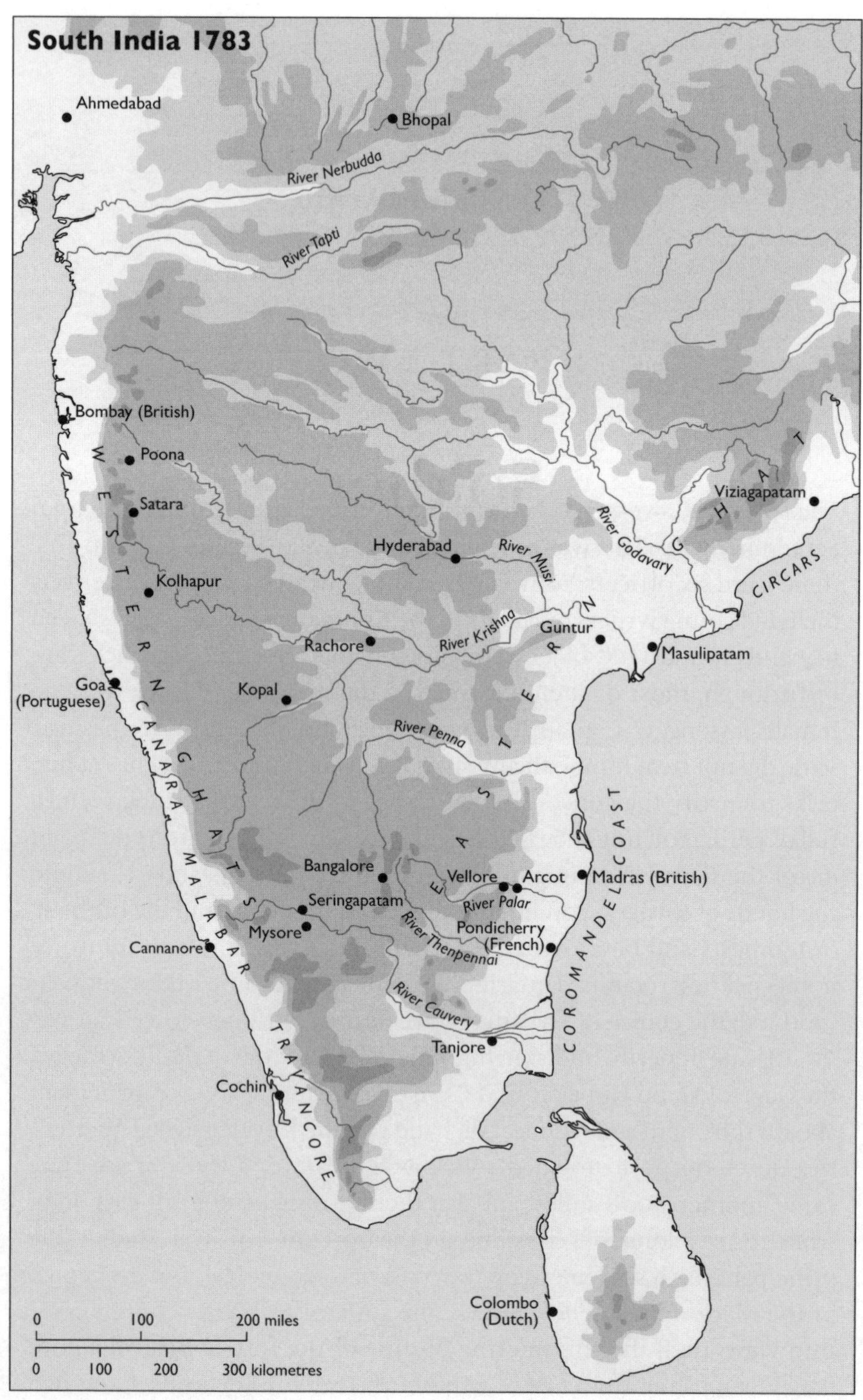

South India 1783
Ahmedabad
Bhopal
River Nerbudda
River Tapti
Bombay (British)
Poona
Satara
Kolhapur
Goa
(Portuguese)
WESTERN GHATS
CANARA
MALABAR
TRAVANCORE
Hyderabad
River Musi
River Godavary
Viziagapatam
GHATS
CIRCARS
Rachore
River Krishna
Guntur
Masulipatam
Kopal
EASTERN GHATS
River Penna
COROMANDEL COAST
Bangalore
Vellore
Arcot
Madras (British)
River Palar
Seringapatam
Mysore
Pondicherry
(French)
River Thenpennai
Cannanore
River Cauvery
Tanjore
Cochin
Colombo
(Dutch)
0
100
200 miles
0
100
200
300 kilometres

CHAPTER TWO

The Madras Army, 1783–1794

The *Busbridge*, a vessel of 755 tons, finally sailed from Portsmouth on 11 September 1782.[1] This was only its second voyage. Besides Captain Tod, there were six officers: four mates, a surgeon, and a purser. Passengers included young writers or cadets in the Company's service, aged sixteen to eighteen, and a few older Company servants returning after sick leave or furlough, most of them destined to die in Madras. There were no female passengers. Captain Tod was giving John Malcolm a free passage, so he did not treat him with any special consideration; in fact he set him tasks to justify the concession. 'A voyage to India at that time seemed full of perils. You might be taken by the French or the pirates; you might die of the scurvy. You might be wrecked on a desert island or fall into the hands of savages; you might meet contrary winds and die of thirst, or tempests and be drowned . . . There was sea-sickness to reinforce home-sickness; cramped quarters to emphasise the uncertainty of your foothold; the choice of freezing above deck or stifling below.'[2]

Passing Tenerife and skirting Rio de Janeiro, the *Busbridge* reached the Cape of Good Hope around Christmas. After the long confinement aboard ship, with a salted meat diet and cramped, overcrowded quarters, the Dutch outpost provided a welcome break for a week or so. Then came another 5,000 miles, and, on the morning of 16 April 1783, John woke to see a long low coastline on the horizon. This was Madras, the principal British settlement on the coast of Coromandel, and the capital of the Madras Presidency. Slowly the spire of St Mary's church came into view, then the shimmering outline of the fort, appearing above dark green palms and a line of white surf. The ship anchored about two miles offshore, and was immediately surrounded by dark-skinned boatmen manoeuvring their *masula* boats, made of 'rude planks, sewn together with coir rope, and much resembling a walnut shell . . . so constructed that, when struck by a surge, and even dashed to the ground, it yields to the blow, spreads out for a moment, and then resumes its original shape, without losing its buoyancy.'[3] John jumped into one of these *masula* boats and was rowed through the surf, then carried to the beach on the shoulders of a half-naked boatman. Stumbling up the beach to the fort gate into the town, his senses were assailed by a cacophony of sounds; by sights and smells and jostling merchants hawking their wares, women in saris of every colour imaginable, beggars, pariah dogs, bullock carts, stray cattle, all in the overpowering heat and glare of southern India in April.

He was just a month short of his fourteenth birthday.

Madras was already a city of 300,000 people, of whom no more than a few thousand were European – mostly officers and men of the European regiment. It was the oldest of the three British Presidency towns, older than Bombay or Calcutta.

John's maternal uncle, Dr Gilbert Pasley, had arrived at Madras in 1754, aged twenty-one, as a 'surgeon's mate' to the 39th regiment of Foot, and the following year became a 'lieutenant fireworker' in the Madras artillery. In 1761 he became a surgeon, exchanging, as *Hicky's Bengal Gazette* put it, 'the sword, spunge and ramrod for the lancet, gold headed cane and snuffbox'. He did well, and by 1778 had been appointed Surgeon General of the Madras Presidency, a loved and respected pillar of the small British community. Later records are more coy about the fact that he took up with an Indian lady, 'a native woman of Madras'. She bore him three children; the eldest, Gilbert, later becoming a lawyer in Madras, the second, Charles, a Lieutenant in the Royal Navy, and the third, Elizabeth, being married to Robert Campbell, a successful Madras merchant who later became a director, then Chairman of the East India Company, and a baronet. In 1778 Dr Pasley married Hannah Dashwood. It is not clear whether the Indian lady had by this time died, or whether the two ladies overlapped, or even conceivably that in the late eighteenth century Hannah and the Indian lady were one and the same. What it does illustrate is that the children of such liaisons – stable relationships, in modern parlance – between the races, were not disadvantaged in seeking a career or a marriage.

The Burnfoot family's original plan had been for Uncle Gilbert to take John under his wing at Madras. He had done this for John's eldest brother Robert, when Robert had arrived at Madras in 1780. But unfortunately Uncle Gilbert had died in September 1781, and his widow Hannah had since married a local merchant, a Mr Ogilvie. The Ogilvies were now based at the fort of Vellore, about ninety miles inland from Madras.[4] They came down to the coast to meet John, and after a short stay in Madras took him back to Vellore with them.

On 5 July Mrs Ogilvie wrote dutifully from Vellore to Bonnie Peggy at Burnfoot, to tell her how John – nicknamed Jack – was getting on:

> by this conveyance you will receive letters from your son Jack, who, I suppose, will tell you of our journey up here, and of the wonders he had seen in India . . . Jack came to us immediately on his landing from Captain Tod's ship, and happy was I, dear sister, to receive your son, and to do all in my power to make him happy. He was too young to go to the field, so we brought him up here and got him appointed to the troops in this garrison. He is a very old ensign, though a very young lad. He is grown a head and shoulders, and is one of the finest and best tempered young lads I ever saw, and very much liked by everybody.[5]

John had probably not thought too much about his future as a cadet in the Madras Army. He would have been carried along by the sheer novelty and adventure of each successive day. But now, as he settled down to the routine of cantonment life in Vellore, he may have started wondering what he was letting himself in for.

At the time of his arrival in India the political position of the Company was not good, though better than it had been a couple of years earlier. Following the gradual decline of the Mughal Empire during the course of the eighteenth century, there were three main contenders for power and influence on the subcontinent. First, the Company, dominant in Bengal and on the Coromandel Coast (the Bombay Presidency comprised no more than a small enclave surrounding Bombay itself); second, the Mahrattas, the dominant people of most of western India, but divided among themselves; and third, the Sultanate of Mysore in the south. Between them lay the lands of the Nizam of Hyderabad, the former Mughal *subhadur* (proconsul) of the Deccan.

In the 1760s, control of Mysore had been wrested from its Hindu Rajah by Hyder Ali, an illiterate Muslim officer in the Rajah's army. Hyder Ali was a brilliant General. In the first Anglo-Mysore War (1767–69) he attacked the Company's possessions on the Coast, and although beaten back, won the respect of the British for his military capability. Hyder's army, like many native Indian armies of the period, was not vastly different from the Company's Madras or 'Coast' army. Like the Company, Hyder employed European officers to command his native troops, known as sepoys. In 1782 his army had 700 European (mercenary) officers, compared to the Company's 400,[6] and his weaponry was also broadly similar. His infantry were hardy, but lacked the steadiness and discipline of the Company's sepoys.

There were other differences. The 50,000-strong Company army included several 'European' regiments, where the rank and file as well as the officers were European – a motley lot, mainly British, but also some German, Swiss and Portuguese (Eurasian) mercenaries, to provide, in theory, 'stiffening and dash in battle' and to act as an insurance policy against any possible disloyalty of 'native black troops'. The Company army had very little cavalry, which was considered expensive to maintain, and it had hitherto relied on the cavalry of allied native princes. Hyder's cavalry on the other hand was numerous (over 40,000 at the Battle of Porto Novo in 1781) and 'singularly mobile and efficient . . . [while] the Mysorean Light Horse was superlatively excellent for purposes of partisan warfare'.[7]

In 1780 war had broken out again between the Company and Hyder (the second Anglo-Mysore War). Hyder, annoyed by the British seizure of Mahe (Malabar) from the French, attacked the Company's territory on the Coromandel Coast, and in September 1780 inflicted a severe defeat on Colonel Baillie's detachment of Company troops. Many of them were captured and imprisoned at Hyder's capital, Seringapatam. The officers were allegedly chained together in pairs and kept underground. Among them was a King's Army Colonel called David Baird, a huge and rather testy individual. On hearing of his capture and shackling, his mother remarked that 'she pitied the man who was shackled to our Davie'.[8] They were given an allowance to pay for food and minor services such as *dhobie* (laundry). Their officers' mess menu followed an unvarying weekly cycle: 'Monday: Ketcheree: Tuesday: Fowl curry:

Wednesday: Mutton Curry: Thursday: Mutton, baked: Friday: Dholl pepper water [mulligatawny soup?]: Saturday: Fowl curry: Sunday: Mutton curry.'[9]

Hyder died in December 1782, and was succeeded by his son Tipu. At the time of Malcolm's arrival at Vellore the Company army was besieging, in a desultory way, the French coastal settlement of Cuddalore. Peace with the French in Europe (and with the colonists in America) came in 1783, and was followed by peace between the respective British and French armies in India. The war with Tipu dragged on, but peace was eventually negotiated early in 1784 with the Treaty of Mangalore.

Now came Malcolm's first recorded military assignment. Prisoners were exchanged as part of the Treaty. Major Dallas of the Company army was sent into Mysore territory to collect the 3,000 sepoy and 1,200 European prisoners. On their return to the border they were met by a detachment of 200 sepoys, to act as escort for the journey across Company territory to Madras. A boy from the sepoy detachment rode forward on a pony to meet them. Major Dallas greeted him, and asked to be taken to the commanding officer.

'*I* am the commanding officer,' the boy replied. The boy was Ensign John Malcolm, just short of his fifteenth birthday.

Peace brought respite for the Coast Army, but not prosperity. The Madras Government was in a sorry state. 'The moral atmosphere of Madras at this time appears to have been pestilential . . . Within seven years two Governors had been dismissed from office by the Court of Directors and a third suspended by the Governor General; while Lord Pigot, who had been sent out to restore the Rajah of Tanjore, was actually deposed and imprisoned by his subordinates, for the necessary though tactless opposition he had made to their dishonest dealings. The unhappy man died in prison in 1777.'[10]

Many years later John Malcolm himself had to admit, when writing about Warren Hastings (Governor-General, 1772–1785) that 'his most strenuous advocates . . . while they defend his personal integrity, are forced to acknowledge that the whole system over which he presided was corrupt and full of abuses.'[11] While Hastings's authority was largely limited to Bengal, the Madras and Bombay Presidencies suffered from similar abuses. 'To join the Company's army was not so much to enter a profession as to take a speculative risk. A cadet gambled his health against the hazards of life in India, and the odds were that he would lose his venture. The return, where there was one, was status and affluence, modest in most cases, spectacular in a few. Eighteenth-century Indian army officers were mercenary adventurers, men on the make . . . climate and disease, not the weapons of his opponents were the deadliest enemies that an Indian army officer encountered in the eighteenth century.'[12]

Young officers' pay was low, and often in arrears for up to twelve months; moreover it was paid in promissory notes on Bengal, cashable only through the Madras *shroffs* (moneylenders), at a considerable discount.[13] The pay of a Captain was about £30 per month. Out of this, one officer complained, he was expected to maintain a *dubash* (interpreter); a cook; four bullocks, with two bullock drivers, to carry his baggage; a palanquin, and nine palanquin bearers; a horse, a 'horse-keeper' and a 'grass cutter'; and to pay for all his food, drink, clothes and other necessaries. The one 'luxury' on his list was alcohol – two dozen brandy and rum, plus two dozen bottles of wine per month, 'often necessary', he asserted defensively, 'in case of sickness in this hot climate'.[14]

Despite this entourage of servants, officers generally lived in fairly Spartan conditions. Malcolm's later great friend Tom Munro, also an officer in the Coast Army, wrote from Vellore in 1789 to his sister in Scotland, wishing that she could 'be transported for a few hours to my room, to be cured of your Western notions of Eastern luxury, to witness the forlorn condition of old bachelor Indian officers . . . walking in an old coat, and a ragged shirt, in the noonday sun, instead of looking down from my elephant, invested in my royal garments . . . I never experienced hunger or thirst, fatigue or poverty, till I came to India – that since then, I have frequently met with the first three, and that the last has been my constant companion.'[15]

Of Malcolm's first five years in India, no records survive. But he seems to have been a boisterous youth – full of 'animal spirits . . . adept at all games and a capital shot';[16] and 'an idle and wild cadet'.[17] He was growing fast – he eventually stood six feet five inches tall, and weighed fifteen stone. This was the period when he acquired – and kept for the rest of his life – the nickname, 'Boy Malcolm'.

With little serious fighting, regimental life in peacetime was far from stimulating. Besides, 'a regiment, was not, at that time, the best school for either industry, morals or sobriety'.[18] Malcolm was far from home, at an impressionable age. His only relative on the same continent was his elder brother Robert, based at Masulipatam, 300 miles north of Madras, and they would only have met when his battalion happened to be stationed nearby. Not surprisingly, he got into scrapes. His particular scrape during this period was gambling, and losing, and getting into debt; and not earning enough to pay his way out of trouble.

Gambling had long been a vice of the Coast settlements. As early as 1721, the Court of Directors in London had voiced its concern: 'we hear the itch of Gaming hath spread itself over Madras, that even the gentlewomen play for great sums' and thirty years later the Court was still complaining that 'the pernicious vice of gaming has spread like a contagion among all ranks and degrees of our servants'.[19]

Malcolm had no assets of his own, and had to pay off his debts by instalments from his meagre salary. This left him barely able to afford to eat. An old woman from the bazaar is said to have supplied him with food, and was content to wait indefinitely for payment. News of his plight reached Britain, and although no funds were forthcoming from Burnfoot, his wealthy uncle John Pasley sent him £200 via Robert. But Robert did not pass on the money, nor did he even tell John of the remittance. He wrote to their mother: 'Do not blame John, poor fellow. Nothing but distress led him to what he did. It was even unknown to me until I received my uncle's letters, which I suppressed, and wrote to John in a different style than his uncle had done. Had he got the money my uncle ordered – viz £200 – he would effectually have been ruined. But I knew too well his situation to give him a shilling. He has now cleared himself from debt, and is as promising a character in his profession as lives.'[20] Although Robert was five years older than John, this elder-brother-knows-best line may appear presumptuous. But it was a first indication of the attitude taken for many years afterwards by John's brothers. They did not entirely trust his judgment about money. They thought him extravagant, an opinion later shared by several East India Company Directors.

At that time Robert had spent nearly eight years as a Company civil servant at Masulipatam, the port at the mouth of the great Krishna river at the northern end of the Coromandel Coast, known as the Northern Circars. In the mid 1780s Robert took an Indian mistress (perhaps following the lead of his uncle Gilbert Pasley), Nancy Moor Noman, a lady of Muslim origin who presumably acquired the name Nancy when she became Robert's mistress. She seems to have come from a well-to-do family, because she owned property in her own right. She bore him seven children, all of whom were acknowledged and in due course provided for by the Malcolm family.

Meanwhile, things were looking up for John. He wrote from Masulipatam to his father at Burnfoot: 'I expect promotion [to Lieutenant] every day, and with it a removal. I am at present doing duty as adjutant of that part of my regiment stationed here. Though I receive no pay for doing that duty, it is a great recommendation for a young man to act, as it gives him a chance, when any vacancy happens in the staff line, to be appointed and receive the allowances annexed.'[21] This is the earliest surviving letter written by Malcolm, the first tiny trickle of what over the next forty-five years became a thundering torrent of material from his pen. For a boy of eighteen who had left school at thirteen, it was already decidedly literate. It gave, too, an early hint of his future attributes – his optimism, his ambition and his interest in local politics.

In 1786 Lord Cornwallis arrived in India as Governor-General, the first to be armed with the greatly increased powers granted by Pitt's India Act of 1784.[22] Several years before, the Company and the Nizam of Hyderabad had signed, but not implemented, a treaty, whereby the Company undertook to supply the Nizam with a 'Subsidiary Force' to help him defend his territory against the Mahrattas and Mysore. This was a forerunner of the arrangement which later became known as the system of subsidiary alliance, under which the Company would raise and maintain a force of troops in a Native State, to provide protection against external attack. The ruler would pay for the upkeep of these troops, either directly in cash or by ceding territory to the Company with an estimated (tax) revenue equivalent to the cost of maintaining the force. It seemed like a good deal for both parties – the ruler got a relatively efficiently led and reliable army, and the Company got reimbursed for its services. In practice the arrangement effectively gave the Company a veto over the ruler's defence and foreign policy, at no net cost to itself.

Lord Cornwallis now proceeded to implement the Treaty. As the first British Resident at the Nizam's Court he appointed Captain John Kennaway, who had been his ADC since his arrival at Calcutta. Kennaway, from a prominent Devonshire family, had come to India at the age of fourteen, and had served in the Madras Army until 1786. Arriving at Hyderabad in mid-1788, he succeeded in winning Nizam Ali's trust, and put the Treaty into effect. One part of the Treaty was the creation of two new Madras Army battalions to form the Nizam's 'auxiliary force'. One of them, the 29th Madras Native Infantry (29 MNI), was raised at Ellore (near Masulipatam) by Captain James Dalrymple. On 1 November 1788 John Malcolm transferred to the 29 MNI, and took up residence at Ellore.[23]

As part of its Treaty with the Nizam, the Company acquired the Guntur District, near the north-eastern boundary of Mysore. This annoyed Tipu Sultan. He was further annoyed when the Rajah of Travancore, whom the British considered an ally, sold two of his principalities, one of which Tipu regarded as his feudatory vassal, to the Dutch. In retaliation he assembled 30,000 men at Coimbatore, and in April 1790 invaded Travancore.

Lord Cornwallis treated this act as a *casus belli*, and immediately set out to invade Mysore from all sides simultaneously. He negotiated alliances with the Nizam, and with the Peshwah (Prime Minister) of Poona, the senior Chieftain of the Mahrattas, by which they were each to invade Mysore from the north. A force from the British Presidency of Bombay was to threaten Tipu from the Malabar coast in the west, while the main Madras Army was to overrun the rich Coimbatore district and carry the war to the heart of Mysore.

For Malcolm, just twenty-one and a newly promoted Lieutenant, this was an exciting prospect. After seven years of cantonment life, interspersed by occasional punitive raids against bandits, here at last was a full-scale war, and the chance for glory, prize money and accelerated promotion. The immediate reality, however, was more sobering. He wrote home to his eldest sister Agnes (Nancy) at Burnfoot from Rachore (Raichur):

> it is five hundred miles from Masulipatam. We marched here about ten days ago. Our road was terrible – all rocks and deserts, in the hottest season that perhaps was ever known. The thermometer at 115 degrees for nearly a month . . . I walked nearly the whole way, as my horse was sick; and we frequently marched at twelve o'clock at night, and did not arrive at our ground till 2 pm next day. We were sometimes greatly distressed

> for provisions – often forty or fifty hours without any – but that was little compared to the dreadful want of water on the road. Officers in general supply themselves, and have a servant for the purpose; but, in some of our long marches, I have seen men raving mad, go into high fever, and die in a few hours. We are going on service in a few days.[24]

At Bhuspore, the two battalions of the auxiliary force met the main body of the Nizam's army coming from Hyderabad, which was described as: 'a gorgeous mass, numerically sufficient for the conquest of the whole peninsula'. The cavalry was numerous but ill disciplined; while the infantry 'under Monsieur Raymond, an intelligent and enterprising Frenchman, was as good as, with indifferent arms and extremely imperfect means of enforcing discipline, he could expect to make them'.[25] The actual fighting force was not more than 20,000, but with camp followers there were said to be up to 500,000 people, covering an area of country ten miles long and three miles wide.[26] 'After laying waste the whole country . . . the grand army sat down before the fortress of Capool [Kopal].'[27] Malcolm was impressed by Kopal, later describing it as 'the strongest fortress I have seen in India'.[28] They settled into a lengthy siege, the main activity being systematic artillery bombardment to create breaches in the wall of the fort. At last, on 18 April 1791, the defenders of Kopal capitulated, apparently more influenced in their decision by the news of the main Company army's capture of Bangalore on 21 March, than by the efforts of the Nizam's besieging force.

The campaign was a salutary lesson. 'Six tedious months,' Malcolm wrote, 'were spent opposite the fortress, and some valuable lives were lost before it was finally carried.'[29] He was shocked by the ill-discipline, rapacity and cruelty of the Nizam's troops towards the local people, even in the Nizam's own territory. He also came to realise at first hand that the movement of armies under war conditions is more often a scene of chaos, breakdowns, failures in communication and panic, than the smoothly planned sequence of events that one reads about in military manuals or in the memoirs of retired Generals.

Following Cornwallis's capture of Bangalore in March 1791, the main Company army advanced steadily southwards. On 15 May it was within nine miles of Tipu's capital at Seringapatam. But by that time the lines of communication were lengthening, and supplies were running short.

Neither the Mahratta nor the Hyderabad contingents had arrived from the north, nor the Bombay contingent from the west. The monsoon was due in a month, and it was too late in the season to begin what might be a long siege. Prudently, Cornwallis decided to make a tactical retreat; to spend the monsoon near Bangalore, then clear several hostile forts along his line of communications, and return the following year to attack Seringapatam.

Sometime in April 1791, shortly after the capture of Kopal, Malcolm fell ill, and had to go to the coast to recuperate – perhaps to stay with Robert at Masulipatam. From Travancollah he wrote to Kennaway.[30] The tone of this letter is respectful – there is little of the familiarity which later characterised their relationship. Yet it indicates that Malcolm had spent some time with Kennaway, and had got on well with him. Nor was life in Kennaway's camp too Spartan. His shopping list for procurement in Madras included: '4 chests claret: 6 doz cherry or raspberry brandy: 6 hams: 1 Parmesan cheese: 4 Gloster cheese: 1 dozen of large stone or 4 doz small white pots of raspberry jam.'

Malcolm had been studying Persian (the language of the Native Courts since Mughal times), since 1788, and by 1790 he was considered sufficiently proficient to be paid a special allowance of 300 rupees per month to act as Persian interpreter to the two battalions of the Nizam's auxiliary force.[31] Many years later, Graeme Mercer, Kennaway's Persian language assistant at the Hyderabad Residency, wrote of meeting Malcolm for the first time: 'Our acquaintance commenced in 1791, when I was attached to the Residency at Hyderabad, and John joined us as an ensign in the detachment of Madras troops which was settled by treaty to be stationed in the Nizam's country. He soon became a favourite with us all, and particularly with Sir John Kennaway, the Resident. He was then a careless good humoured fellow, illiterate, but with pregnant ability. He took a fancy to learn Persian, and I made over to him my moonshee (munshi, teacher), under whom he made rapid improvement.'[32] And again, in another letter: 'He was quite illiterate when he joined us, but . . . in short, possessed an intellect which only needed to be set a-going, either for good or evil. He had been accused of gambling before I knew him; but I never heard of his exercising his talents in that way after he had been engaged in any employment of any consequence. His overflowing spirits made him riotous, and he was generally known by the name "Boy Malcolm".'[33]

Malcolm was off sick again at the Coast – this time at Madras – for two months from early November 1791 to early January 1792. He stayed at the garden house of David Haliburton, a well known merchant who had been Mayor of Madras in 1790; it was a surprising acquaintance for a young army officer who had spent most of his military career 'upcountry'.

The Mahratta force had joined Cornwallis's Company army just before the 1791 monsoon, while the Nizam's army, after the capture of Kopal in April 1791, had moved steadily east, then south, finally joining up with Cornwallis near Ootradroog on 25 January 1792. The combined force set off on 1 February, covering the 120 miles to Seringapatam in a week. Malcolm's battalion, the 29 MNI under Captain Dalrymple, was in the order of battle of Lord Cornwallis's army before Seringapatam, but held in reserve. Tipu's army was defeated in battle, and Seringapatam itself besieged. By 25 February Tipu was suing for peace.

Sir John Kennaway led the Company delegation in the Seringapatam peace negotiations, which lasted from 13 February to 21 March. Malcolm attended the negotiations as interpreter representing the Nizam's auxiliary force, probably on the recommendation of Kennaway.[34] It was a fascinating first experience of high-level diplomacy. To any Westerner who has carried on diplomatic negotiations

View of Seringapatam from the north-east, 1791.

with Asians (and vice versa), the journal makes familiar reading. Throughout, there are the unfailing civilities, the mutual compliments, the superficial air of calm concealing inner turmoil, the tactical sallies, the protestations of undying friendship if only a particular point can be conceded, the last minute try-ons. Kennaway may have had problems with Tipu's *vakeels* (emissaries), but he also had to contend with the sideshow antics of the Mahratta Chieftains, who 'took care to support their dignity by being constantly late in all their appointments; and his Lordship (Cornwallis) had occasion to exert all his patience to keep them in humour, and all his talents and diligence to make arrangements for the further prosecution of the war.'[35]

At long last the Treaty was signed. Approximately half of Tipu's territories, by revenue value, were ceded to the three allies, in roughly equal shares, despite the fact that the Company had borne the lion's share of the burden of the war – and the Mahrattas hardly any. For Tipu it was a crushing blow, from which he never fully recovered.

By May 1793 Malcolm was back near Kopal. Under the terms of the Treaty Kopal had been ceded to the Nizam, but the inhabitants had been plundered by the Nizam's officers and had rebelled. 'We are to be sent to reduce them – poor wretches! – to obedience, and to be the instruments of oppression.'[36]

But his health still refused to mend. He was again advised that the only solution was to travel home by sea. Kennaway himself was going home in the cold season of 1793–94, also for his health, and urged Malcolm to go with him on the same ship. The prospect of spending several months at sea with such a patron as Kennaway probably persuaded him to go. They embarked from Madras in February 1794.

As their ship sailed south, past Ceylon, then west into the Indian Ocean, the first priority for both men was to recover their health. In India at that time there was an extraordinarily high death rate among Europeans. Life there was 'a great lottery, and many drew a blank'.[37] They died of fevers, of cholera, of plague, of rabies, of smallpox and of heatstroke. They were also very vulnerable, at least in their first five years or so, until they became 'salted' like the local population, to water-borne diseases like typhoid and dysentery, and to malaria – and one of these was likely to have been the trouble with Malcolm and Kennaway.[38] Moreover, treatment was crude and inadequate, delaying recovery; mercury was administered for liver complaints. In practice the patient often preferred to wait for nature to take its course, meanwhile seeking solace in liquor or opium; fifteen drops a day of laudanum (a solution of opium) was a favourite prescription.

Sea air was the acknowledged panacea for most Indian ills, despite the living conditions of a passenger on an East Indiaman – cramped quarters, lack of fresh meat and vegetables, lack of exercise – and so it soon proved for Kennaway and Malcolm. Though still barely twenty-five, Malcolm was by now a veteran soldier – he had completed nearly eleven years of active service – and the disciplined habits of a soldier were there to stay. The career of a regimental officer involved a few hours of adrenalin-pumping terror and exultation, interspersed with long years of stultifying routine, obeying orders, some of them mindless, because instinctive obedience in battle was what converted an enthusiastic rabble into a disciplined fighting force. But in the last two years he had had a glimpse of the diplomatic life. He had seen Kennaway at work; he had even been briefly 'noticed' by Lord Cornwallis at Seringapatam. He yearned to do more than soldiering. He wrote home from Madras, just before boarding his ship: 'My favourite amusement, is reading; and being assisted with a good memory, I seldom have occasion to read a work twice. Of all reading I prefer history. It pleases most upon reflection, and the impressions it makes are more lasting.'[39]

There was plenty of time on board ship for reading, and for discussion with Kennaway of politics and the diplomatic life. They became friends for life, though there was always a note of deference in Malcolm's approach to the older man. What Kennaway had stirred in Malcolm was ambition – ambition to rise above and beyond regimental soldiering; ambition to raise his family out of the genteel rural poverty which was Burnfoot; ambition for his country, and pride in its new Empire of the East; above all, ambition for himself, to become a famous man. Fame was the spur which drove him, but his too blatant pursuit of it was eventually to curb its full achievement.

Meanwhile their ship bore them slowly towards England. Malcolm had spent nearly twelve long years dreaming of home and family, and constantly putting the dream aside as absurdly distant. But as the ship turned into the English Channel on the last leg of its journey, he was suddenly able to count the remaining distance in days rather than years.

CHAPTER THREE

Britain, the Cape and Madras, 1794–1798

The Britain he returned to in July 1794 was a very different place from the Britain he had left twelve years before. In 1782 the country had been in the final throes of losing the American colonies; a war with France was also coming to an end. Warren Hastings was the Governor-General of India. In the intervening years, revolution had come to France, which was now ruled, not by the civilised but effete Louis XVI, but by 'a nest of democrats' in Paris. Robespierre's reign of terror was about to end with his own execution, but the new French revolutionary armies were seeking conquest abroad. The British governing classes felt that French aggression, and the accompanying spread of revolutionary ideas, had to be stopped, and war had broken out in February.

For the moment, however, all Malcolm wanted was to be reunited with his family. After a short stay with Uncle John Pasley in Gower St, he headed north to Eskdale, where he spent most of August and September 1794 – incidentally the best months of the year to be in Scotland.

At Burnfoot he found his ageing parents and his five surviving sisters. The Burnfoot family doted on John, and the tender care that was lavished on him went some way to making up for the lack of it in the previous twelve years. He was well again, and relished the chance to meet his childhood friends in Eskdale. But, as he demonstrated during the rest of his life, he was not the sort of person who could bear to take things easy for long. Within six weeks he had taken the stagecoach back to London.

The issue which captured his enthusiasm and brought him to London was the state of the Company's Indian armies, and more particularly the conditions of service of its European officers. After many years of procrastination, these problems were about to be determined in London by the Government and the East India Company's Court of Directors.

The problems stemmed primarily from the way in which the three Presidency armies had expanded, on a somewhat ad hoc basis, since their formation fifty years earlier. The combined armies had comprised 18,000 troops in 1763, 115,000 in 1782, and were destined to rise to 155,000 by 1805, and to 225,000 by 1827. And since they were separately commanded, anomalies in the conditions of service between each army had grown up, causing jealousy and resentment.

Promotion was strictly by seniority; in some ways desirable, because it obviated the considerable opportunities for nepotism and abuse of patronage. However, the highest rank to which an officer in the Company armies could aspire was Colonel. There were no provisions for retirement pensions, nor allowances for sick and wounded officers on furlough, nor even for free passages to Britain at the end of an officer's service. As a result, older officers postponed their retirement as long as they could, and many never returned to their native land. By the 1790s this situation had caused a logjam in promotions; on average, officers would have to serve thirty-three years to reach the rank of Colonel.

On top of all this, there was the superior position of the King's, i.e. British Army officers serving with their British regiments in India. Not only did the King's Army provide all the Generals commanding combined King's and Company forces in India, they also took automatic precedence over Company officers of equivalent rank in an army unit. Thus a Company veteran of twenty years' tough campaigning sometimes had to give way to a young officer fresh out from England, with no knowledge of local conditions or languages.

In 1788 the unsatisfactory conditions of service prevailing in the early 1780s had been mildly alleviated, but the situation was increasingly unacceptable. Lord Cornwallis, who commanded universal respect as a soldier, had been well aware of these problems during his period as Governor-General, and had corresponded regularly on the subject with Henry Dundas, the President of the Board of Control for India. Dundas was an advocate of bringing the Indian Army directly under the control of the Crown, and Cornwallis agreed with him. This was common knowledge in Calcutta military circles, and there were hopes – and some apprehension – about the nature of the reforms which might follow. Cornwallis prepared a major reform plan during his sea voyage home, and on arrival in England in early 1794, duly presented it to Dundas.

Unfortunately Dundas was hopelessly overworked. When war with France was declared in February 1794 he was already responsible for the Home Office, Scotland and Indian affairs. He had then been given additional responsibility for the war effort against France, and was formally appointed Secretary of State for War in July. Only on 1 September did he get around to asking Cornwallis for a copy of his reform plan.

This delay gave rise to frenzied lobbying by interested parties in London, and when Malcolm arrived from Scotland in late September, he joined in with enthusiasm. He wrote to a newspaper, supporting Cornwallis's proposed reforms (signing himself 'Mulligatauny');[1] and sent a letter, containing similar sentiments, via a Colonel Wood,[2] to Dundas, who apparently found time to read it, and commend its author 'in tones', as Malcolm later put it, 'flattering to my feelings'.[3]

Henry Dundas, Viscount Melville (1742–1811), President of the Board of Control for India in William Pitt's ministry, 1793–1801.

Regardless of the outcome of this lobbying, Malcolm's part in it had been useful in building his career. As a very junior officer his views would not normally have been given much weight. But in London, wide-ranging decisions had to be made, based on claims and counter claims by military officers and civil servants who might once have served in India, but were now out of touch. Here was an articulate young officer straight from the front line. For the first time he was 'noticed' in London. Moreover, his mentors were able to put in favourable words for him in the right places. Probably the most important were Sir John Kennaway, Colonel Wood and Colonel Ross (Cornwallis's Military Secretary at Seringapatam). Ross recommended him to General Sir Alured Clarke, recently appointed as Commander-in-Chief of the Madras Army. Sir Alured was looking for a Military Secretary, and interviewed Malcolm in London in October or November. The interview went well, but at this stage no definite offer was made. Besides, Malcolm himself had not yet made a firm decision to go back to India.

By the beginning of December, having done all he could in London on the Indian Army reform issue, and having tentatively secured the offer of Military Secretary in Madras with Sir Alured Clarke, he headed north again to spend Christmas and Hogmanay at Burnfoot. Once again he was doted upon by his sisters. He had an almost infinite capacity for soaking up praise, but even he must soon have felt quite overwhelmed by the attentions of his five adoring sisters. He left Burnfoot for Edinburgh in early January, aiming to use his time in Edinburgh to make up for the shortcomings in his academic education. He had studied Indian languages, but he regretted not having mastered mathematics and science, and nine years of regimental soldiering in the Deccan could not have been conducive to academic learning. Kennaway and Mercer had tried to interest him in intellectual pursuits, but in the remote locations where his regiment was stationed he had access to only a few odd books, and lacked tutors to guide him. He had never had the opportunity to discuss the books he was reading with scholars. Now he came to Edinburgh at the very peak of the Scottish Enlightenment. One historian has suggested that Malcolm's philosophy of government and his later approach to writing history were influenced by his time in Edinburgh, absorbing the thought of such men as David Hume, Adam Smith, William Robertson, Adam Ferguson and John Millar.[4]

He stayed two months in the city, and loved it. As a country boy who had spent the whole of his adult life in India he had very few contacts – his parents usually made their city excursions to Glasgow rather than to Edinburgh – but he somehow managed to locate and attend public lectures, and to seek out some of the most eminent intellectual figures of the time. He wrote to his brother Gilbert:

> It is in my opinion one of the most agreeable [towns] I ever was in. There is no place in the world where such encouragement is given to the literary man, so I believe there are nowhere to be found men of more deep learning and science . . . independent of the medical line, the law, and some others, the numerous professors' chairs hold out rewards both of fame and fortune to the aspiring youth . . . I have been both instructed and entertained by attendance at some of their classes. I have given up a good deal of my time to the Oriental Professor, a sensible, modest man. His name is Mudie. I have read Persian with him whenever I have had a leisure hour, and have found him grateful to a degree for the little instruction I could give him.[5]

Malcolm had the obsessive drive of a person with a good brain who has been prevented from developing it through lack of opportunity. Yet his enthusiasm alone could not have been enough to capture the attention of such high calibre intellectual figures. There must have been considerable intellectual capacity as well. The secret probably lay in his prodigious memory. As he had written to his mother, 'I seldom have occasion to read a book twice.'[6]

One contact he was able to follow up was his old patron John Johnstone, now living on his large estate at Alva near Stirling. Since being forced by Clive to return from India in 1765, Johnstone had bought several large estates in Scotland and had entered Parliament, where he sought to revenge himself on Clive by leading a faction attacking him. Mostly, though, he had been content to live a quiet life in Scotland. He had followed Malcolm's career with interest, and George Malcolm, who had grown up at Burnfoot next door to Westerhall, kept him regularly informed about his son. By 1795 Johnstone was an old man – he was to die in December that year – but he must have been delighted to discuss Indian developments with his young protégé, who was stranded at Alva for a week when heavy snowfalls blocked the road back to Edinburgh.

During this period Malcolm resolved to return to India. His family were worried about his health, and Uncle John Pasley at first advised him against going. But he saw the job with Sir Alured Clarke as a great opportunity for escaping from the tedium of regimental life and building his career in the diplomatic field. The family saw that there was no point in trying to dissuade him. By April he was back in London making final preparations. 'My departure is yet uncertain, but I am determined the arrangement of my little matter shall not be put off to the last day, and am therefore dispatching my trunks for Portsmouth.'[7]

Now came an intriguing development. The ship in which he was to sail with Sir Alured was part of a fleet carrying a large body of European troops. 'I have this moment received orders to go on board, as our ship is getting under weigh. I am appointed Secretary to General Clarke, on a secret expedition. My prospects are very flattering.'[8] Rumours abounded about the destination. As John Johnstone wrote later to George Malcolm, '[John] thinks the expedition was meant against the Cape, which was John's first wish. His mind is all on fire.'[9]

The Cape of Good Hope had been a Dutch colony since Jan van Riebeck had arrived there in 1652. It was a vital port of call for European traders on the way to the Indian subcontinent and the East Indies, providing a healthy climate, good water, animals for slaughter, fresh produce, ship's supplies and Dutch efficiency. In the early years of European trade with the East via the Cape, the Dutch East India Company had been more powerful than the English Company, and even after the English had become the larger operators, Dutch control of the Cape was tolerated. But the possibility of the French taking over was another matter. In 1795 French revolutionary forces were causing alarm all over Europe. In Holland the nation was split between the 'Orange' party of the King, and the 'Patriot' party which supported the aims of the Republican French revolution. In April the 'Patriot' party seized power and formed the Batavian Republic. The Colonial administration at the Cape was similarly divided. The officials, led by the Stadtholder and his military commander, Colonel Gordon, a Scot, were for the Orange party, while the colonists and the military rank and file were for the pro-French Patriot party.

The British Government sent a small naval expeditionary force of about 2,000 men (mostly seamen) to the Cape under Sir George Elphinstone (later Admiral Lord Keith). This force landed at Simon's Bay, on the eastern side of the Cape Peninsula, on 17 June but, failing to persuade the Dutch to surrender, Elphinstone judged that he did not have the military strength to overcome their resistance. So he camped at Muizenburg, seven miles north of Simon's Bay, and waited for reinforcements.

Sir Alured Clarke's expeditionary force sailed from Ports-mouth on 14 May and on 4 September anchored off Simonstown. Malcolm had guessed correctly about the purpose of the expedition. As Sir Alured's Military Secretary he had an insider's view of the subsequent capture of the Cape from the Dutch, and he described it in a long report written two months later.[10]

When the fighting was over and law and order restored, Malcolm set out to discover and record all he could about the colony. In little more than a month he had produced a sort of Government Almanack or Gazetteer, seven pages long, listing facts under such headings as 'Climate; Towns; Inhabitants; Government; Revenue'.

General Sir Alured Clarke (1745–1832), Commander-in-Chief, Madras Presidency 1795–1797, Bengal 1797–1801.

He went on to describe the Cape as of great value to the Company:

> The Cape, while we retain such a communication as we have at present with India, must be of great value to us for two reasons. In the first place it furnishes in profusion every refreshment for our Ships, and in the second place we might suffer severely from its situation were it in the hands of a Powerful Enemy . . . Commissioners should be sent to settle its law and to give it a government on as economical principles as possible. This Government, excepting the immediate Heads of Departments, to consist of natives of the Cape. All subordinate offices to be exclusively held by them. This measure is indispensably necessary, as it is meant they should forget that they are a conquered people and become attached Loyal Subjects.

On and on he went, with boyish enthusiasm. Here we see the first blossoming of his philosophy of government in a conquered territory – riding with a very light rein, letting the local people themselves run things as far as humanly possible.

But he also found time for social pursuits. In a letter to his sister Nancy he described Cape Town as

> a charming place – not very large, but uncommon neat and clean. The appearance is like the best part of Glasgow. Their meat, vegetables and fruit are superior to [those of] any country I ever was in: and their wines, of which they have great variety, are excellent. Had I been rich enough, I would have purchased some Constantia; but it is very dear, so I must therefore postpone for a period sending a pipe to Burnfoot.
>
> The inhabitants of the town are a cheerful, good-humoured people – rather too phlegmatic; not so mad as I could wish them, but on the whole make an agreeable society for sober minded people. The 'Dyong-Frows' are some of them very pretty – play on the harpsichord, and danse bien tolerable . . . I have got an honourable, but troublesome, employment in recruiting men out of the prisoners of war for the service of the Company in India. A set of finer fellows I never knew – all Germans.[11]

By the end of November he was on his way to Madras, bringing 200 German recruits for the Coast Army.

Malcolm landed at Madras in January 1796, in very different circumstances from his first arrival thirteen years earlier. He was now part of the 'family' of Sir Alured Clarke. The Commander-in-Chief in each of the three Presidencies was an important figure, ranking second after the Governor in the five-member Governor's Council, and standing in for the Governor when he was away. A Governor's or a Commander-in-Chief's 'family' comprised not only his wife and children (if they were with him), but his Private Secretary, Military Secretary and aides-de-camp (ADCs) as well. They generally lived with their master in the Governor's or Commander-in-Chief's house (though during 1796 Malcolm moved into a house of his own). This was an agreeable arrangement for the 'family'. Not only were they privy to affairs of state at the highest level; they were also housed and fed in considerable comfort at no personal cost. Moreover – and this would have been of crucial importance to Malcolm – the nature of their job meant that they rubbed shoulders with the greatest in the land on a daily basis. To 'get on' in those days the great thing was to be 'noticed', and as Military Secretary Malcolm had a much greater opportunity to make himself noticed than if he were a young Lieutenant living in a regimental cantonment.

For the next two and a half years he was based in Madras, one of the longest consecutive periods in his career of being 'static'. But the period was important for his development, and he was happy. He was busy – 'my employment is of that nature as to leave me hardly one idle moment' – but relatively carefree. A secretary or ADC had in many ways the best of both worlds; he was in the midst of the affairs of state, but was not a participant. 'He sees history, but does not act it. He has all the excitement, but none of the responsibilities of greatness. He shares the pomp, but not the troubles of office.'[12] His health was good, and he had 'two fine prancing horses, fellows that beat the air and paw the ground. They are both grey. One of them was born at the source of the Indus, and the other within a few miles of Ispahan, in Persia. I could not wish a wife with a sweeter disposition than that they both possess – nor one with more fire and spirit.'[13]

Sir Alured Clarke, a bachelor in his fifties, had been a soldier since the age of fourteen. He had served in the later stages of the Seven Years' War on the Continent, and in the first four years of the American War.

From 1782 to 1790 he had been Lieutenant Governor of Jamaica, acting as Governor for a year, and had then spent two years in Quebec. He was a very experienced old soldier and imperial proconsul. To Malcolm, perhaps used to the rougher, more pedestrian style of most Coast Army officers, Sir Alured's gentlemanly character was a revelation. Before he left the Cape he had already written glowingly to Burnfoot: 'He is a man of a stamp not often met with – mild and gentlemanlike in his manners, clear and just in his own conduct . . . I never was a swearer; but I can now venture to say, I never now, even in an unguarded moment, let slip an oath. He abominates the practice.'[14] In Madras he went further, describing Clarke as 'without exception, one of the best men I ever knew.'[15]

A year later, in early 1797, Sir Alured was appointed Commander-in-Chief of Bengal (effectively of British India), a considerable promotion, since the position reported directly to the Governor-General. Moreover, in the Governor-General's absence, the Commander-in-Chief would stand in for him (as in fact happened in 1798 for a few months). For a short time this opened up the possibility of Malcolm moving with him to Calcutta. He was urged to do so by George Johnstone, a friend based in Lucknow, who pointed out to him the very considerable financial perks of office as Secretary to the Commander-in-Chief in Bengal. But for some reason Sir Alured was not in a position to offer him the job. This left Malcolm worrying about whether Sir Alured's successor as Commander-in-Chief, Madras, General George Harris, would keep him on as Military Secretary. Sir Alured finally left Madras on 6 March 1797. 'I never felt more than in parting with him. His attention to me was excessive, and I have every reason to believe that he was as sorry to leave me as I was to stay.'[16] He was right. But all was well. Harris came from Calcutta, and on arrival at Madras later in March, immediately reappointed him to the same job.

Harris was a different character. Now in his early forties, he had served, like Clarke, in the American War, and later in Ireland, before coming to Madras in 1790 as Military Secretary. He fought in the Mysore War of 1790–92, and probably met Malcolm at Seringapatam. After the peace he went home, but returned to India in 1794 with a wife and one daughter, to become Commandant of Fort William at Calcutta. Although his biography describes him as 'of unaffected bearing, kindly disposition and simple manners' and 'though economical . . . never penurious',[17] his portrait belies this somewhat ascetic picture. Heavy jowled, he looks like a man who enjoyed his claret. Malcolm wrote: 'The family I am now in is an uncommon pleasant one. The General appears everything that is honest and worthy – Madame, an amiable good woman; and Madamoiselle, sensible, pleasing and unaffected.' But the role of ADC has always had its drawbacks. 'I am not fond of going visiting at night. The truth is, I get sleepy. I fear that this is a symptom of age. To-night I am on duty, having the honor of attending Mrs and Miss Harris to return about a dozen visits. I wish it were over.'[18]

The European population of Madras comprised no more than 1,000 civilians and army officers, plus a few thousand 'Other Rank' soldiery in the Company's European regiments. It was a frontier town, full of adventurers, lacking refinement and the solid background of a long established community. At the upper levels, between the Nawabs and the Princes on the one hand, and the Governors and senior Company officials on the other, there was more contact on a more or less equal basis. But at the ordinary level there was little social intercourse between Europeans and Indians. Each side had its reasons.

Despite the limitations of the social scene, Malcolm made several friends for life, including Tom Munro, Josiah Webbe and Stephen Lushington, while Colonel Ross, his mentor at the time of his visit to Britain in 1794, returned to Madras in 1797. Among merchants he resumed his friendship with David Haliburton, with whom he had stayed in 1792. He met Thomas Cockburn, who later distinguished himself in organizing supplies for the Grand Army at the time of the second Seringapatam campaign in 1799; and his younger brother Alexander Cockburn, elected Mayor of Madras in the same year.

Tom Munro had been born in Glasgow, and unlike most Company officers, had completed school and university before coming to Madras in 1780 as an eighteen-year-old military cadet. He served as an officer in the second and third Anglo-Mysore Wars, but from 1792 he became a civil administrator, settling the Baramahal region (around Krishnagiri) which had been ceded to the Company as part of the 1792 Peace Treaty with Tipu Sultan. Here he began to form ideas for revenue raising which later developed into the celebrated '*ryotwari* system'. In the Bengal system, peasant proprietors paid land tax to *Zamindars* (large proprietors/landlords), who were effectively tax farmers for the government. In the *ryotwari* system they paid taxes direct to the state, via village headmen. Munro and Malcolm had met in 1792, during the Mysore War (possibly even earlier) and they became firm friends, with shared views on most issues.

Josiah Webbe had come to Madras as a writer (a junior civil servant in the East India Company) in 1784, aged sixteen, and had worked ever since in the Madras revenue department, becoming Secretary to Government in 1796. He was one of those admirable public servants who combine great administrative ability with unimpeachable integrity (a rare quality in the Madras Government of the day), and was understandably liked and respected by all. He popped in and out of Malcolm's life for several years thereafter.

Stephen Lushington had arrived in Madras in 1792, aged sixteen, as a civilian cadet. He rose through various jobs at the Revenue Board, and acquired sufficient fluency in Persian to become the official translator to the Board. In early 1797, at the time of General Harris's arrival in Madras, he held the position of 'Under-searcher at Sea Gate'. This could not have been too taxing a job, because he also took on the role of Private Secretary to General Harris, which brought him into daily contact with Malcolm (as General Harris's Military Secretary) and with the Harris family.

Apart from these friends, several Malcolm brothers were in the region at the time. Robert was based at Masulipatam, but they could not find time to meet – 'I would give the world for a month's leisure to go and see him'[19]. Pulteney, who had taken command of the frigate HMS *Fox* in late 1794, appeared on the Indian scene in late 1796, still commanding the *Fox*. He had with him his youngest brother Charles as a fourteen-year-old midshipman, and, as passengers, his brother Thomas (Tom), and his first cousin Gilbert Briggs (son of Bonnie Peggy's sister Magdalen). Tom had been a 'problem' son in Scotland. Back in 1789 he had been involved in some 'unfortunate business' with his uncle John Pasley (the family benefactor, hence not a man to get on the wrong side of). Various jobs had been lined up for him over the years, including a position in his uncle Charles Pasley's wine business in Tenerife, but none had worked. Eventually Uncle John Pasley managed to obtain a commission for him in the Bombay Army, and Pulteney brought him to India. But the Bombay Army did not appeal to him; by early 1797 he had resigned his commission and arrived in Madras, whence he was sent up the coast to stay with Robert at Masulipatam.

Despite being the eldest of the Malcolm brothers, Robert had been isolated on the Coromandel Coast for many years. Pulteney, although only the third brother, and spending most of his time at sea, was a naturally bossy character, and thought and acted much like an eldest brother. Until the late 1790s his career was more distinguished than John's. He had taken part in some daring exploits in the West Indies, and had achieved the ambition of every young naval officer – command of his own ship – at the age of twenty-six. He had plenty of dash, and in late 1797 jointly led a daring raid on Manila harbour, then held by the Spanish, who were allied with revolutionary France at that time.[20]

Pulteney wrote to his sisters at Burnfoot from time to time with character assessments of his brothers. In June 1797, after spending a fortnight with John in Madras, he wrote to his sister Wilhemina (Mina) from Penang:

> I was ordered from Madras in such a hurry that I had not time to write you to go by the first ship, but I shall enclose this to John who will forward it . . . On my arrival in Madras . . . John introduced me to everyone and fourteen days seemed but as one; everyone loves and respects him – his conduct is so truly proper it can't be otherwise. I now confess, Mina, that you knew John better than I did when we were wont to describe the busyness, but yet he has his faults and I may chance to tell you of them in the course of this letter, but they are so trifling when compared to the truly good points that it is with difficulty I find them out. His oversanguine temper is fixed in his nature, and although now and then he will be led into disappointments by it, yet it is I fancy the source of much pleasure to him. His finances are now tolerable; his income is about £1,500 a year, a very large sum, but his expenses are unavoidably large, and he is of all his brothers the one who knows least how to render them smaller.[21]

'Oversanguine!' Time and again this was the word used by John's admirers (and detractors) to describe his temperament. He seemed to recognise this in describing himself, in a letter to his sister: 'You know I can be the most serious man on earth when I assume that character. I have not found it necessary for more than five hours of my life, and I hope that I may laugh through the remainder as happily. Laughing or crying, I am always your affectionate brother.'[22]

And what about female company? Was he now – aged twenty-eight – thinking of marriage? There was one potential opportunity very close by. In mid-1797 he wrote further on the Harris family ménage to Stephana:

> My situation continues agreeable. General Harris is a good man & sincerely my friend. Mrs Harris is a character I admire more and more every day I see her. She has a disposition like our mother's, and is like her actively benevolent – can I say more for her? Miss is sensible & plays and sings well – you may hear reports, sister, but though it will probably never be my fate to take by the hand so fine a girl as Miss, and you may rest assured no change is likely to take place in my situation . . . I must fight my way through life for some years first without encumbering another with my cares, then God willing the sooner the better.[23]

When this letter reached Stephana (visiting Glasgow with Helen) in February 1798, it produced a buzz of speculation among the sisters. Could this be a classic example of the Governor's daughter falling in love with the ADC? Stephana wrote from Glasgow to Nancy at Burnfoot: 'John has the most sanguine hopes of his success, and that he will be an honour to his family . . . his own words tell you what he says of the Harrises, from which Helen concluded he is in love with Miss H; I say he is not . . . Now Nancy, what do you think? To be sure he praises her warmly in the end, but . . . I am sure the eulogy he begins with is not lover-like. What says Pulteney? We shall be most anxious to hear his news.'[24]

Perhaps John knew which way the wind was blowing in the Harris household, or perhaps he just wanted to tease his sisters. For, unknown to them, their question had already been answered, without any help from Pulteney. On 9 December 1797, at St Thomas's Church Madras, Miss Anne Elizabeth Harris was married to Stephen Lushington, General Harris's Private Secretary. The Burnfoot sisters had guessed the wrong man. Miss Harris probably made a sound choice, because Lushington, though a somewhat earnest and uninspiring fellow, had a successful career. Returning to England in 1807, he became a long-serving MP, and was later appointed Governor of Madras. They had six sons and two daughters.

There is scanty contemporary information about the romantic and sexual environment in which Malcolm lived, as a young European officer at Madras. For most of the Victorian era and the first half of the twentieth century open discussion of the subject was taboo. We need not be concerned with the 'licentious soldiery'. Housed in cantonments separated from the Indian cities, their material needs were satisfied in the regimental bazaar, and their sexual needs in the lal bazaar, an unofficially sanctioned regimental brothel. These brothels continued to operate right through to the twentieth century, despite the best (and in terms of health, counter-productive) efforts of evangelical Christian priests and missionaries.

For Company servants, cohabitation with a *bibi* [mistress], was perfectly normal until the early nineteenth century. Job Charnock, the founder of Calcutta in 1690, rescued a Hindu widow from a *sati* (funeral pyre), made her his mistress and had three children by her. Warren Hastings's first wife was Eurasian. Sir John Shore (Governor-General 1793–98), had a liaison with an Indian woman. And such an easy-going attitude to mixed marriages was not confined to India. Lord Liverpool, the British Prime Minister (1812–27), had an Indian grandmother. As late as 1800, a third of the Company's servants had Indian wives or mistresses.[25] As we have seen, John's uncle Gilbert Pasley's first mistress was Indian, and his brother Robert had been living with Nancy Moor Noman since the early 1780s. It was said that a favourite after-dinner toast was to turn the traditional lament 'Alas and alack-a-day' into 'A lass and a lakh a day!', an aspiration natural to men who saw a lakh (100,000 rupees), as a proper object of ambition and a *bibi* as a fitting companion.[26]

But towards the end of the eighteenth century the situation was changing. 'As the Company began to concern itself more with government than with commerce, its officials were transformed from merchants into diplomats, administrators and judges. This change was completed by Lord Cornwallis . . . as Governor-General between 1786 and 1793. The Company's officials were assured of a good salary . . . and had to abandon all thought of private profit.'[27] Lord Cornwallis's main motive was admirable. He wanted to clear out corruption, and he feared that the presence of Indian mistresses in the households of British officials would be interpreted by other Indians as giving them the chance of unfairly favouring their families and hangers-on. Another motive was fear. Cornwallis had been through the American War, and he feared that these liaisons could produce a mestizo community of settlers, who might eventually try to seize the government of the country. He had also heard with alarm of the slave uprising in the Caribbean island of Santa Domingo in 1791, where 500,000 black slaves had risen and massacred 30,000 whites and 30,000 half-castes. Unfortunately Lord Cornwallis's measures largely solved one problem – corruption – only to exacerbate another, the widening of the social gulf between Europeans and Indians.

A young man's prospects of regular sex with young and marriageable European women were not good. The opportunities were few and far between. Those women who came to India to look for a husband, later known as the 'fishing fleet', congregated mainly in Calcutta, where there was a much larger pool of available bachelors than in Madras. And they were not generally available for sex.

The primary source materials for Malcolm's private life were mainly put together in mid-Victorian times by his spinster sisters, and are understandably uncommunicative about his sex life. We can only speculate. He had left Scotland and the stabilising influence of his parents before puberty. When he arrived in Madras in 1783 he was immediately introduced to the mores of Madras Army officers. The nearest model he had of how to behave was his elder brother Robert, who had taken up with Nancy Moor Noman. Nor, as later events were to confirm, was he motivated by strong religious conviction. He was a fine, strapping athlete. But more importantly, he was a warm-hearted extrovert and a natural linguist who got on famously with Indians of all classes. There can be little doubt that he met his youthful sexual needs with happily compliant Indian women.

All in all, this was a delightful period for Malcolm. He had his own house, where his younger brother Charles would come to stay when on shore leave from the Royal Navy.[28] In early February 1798 his young cousin Charles Pasley (son of Bonnie Peggy's brother Charles, the Lisbon wine merchant, and his wife Jean) arrived in Madras, aged sixteen, as an ensign in the Madras Army, and came to stay at the house. Charles Pasley had a half-brother William, of almost the same age, who had also been sired by the Lisbon wine merchant, probably via a domestic servant at Eskdalemuir. William had been brought up at Burnfoot, and was treated as part of the Malcolm family. He was destined to have a highly distinguished military career. Writing to William, Charles described his life with John: 'I live very pleasantly here with Capt. Malcolm who is very good to me . . . Lord Hobart is going away in a few days, when General Harris will be Governor. When Harris is Governor [Captain Malcolm] will be made Town Major, the best military preferment in India.'[29]

The Town Major of Madras acted as a sort of liaison officer between the Governor (the civilian supreme commander), and the military garrison. It was said to be highly lucrative, a plum job. The offer to Malcolm came about as a result of a reshuffle of Governors. Lord Hobart left Madras in February 1798, but his successor, Lord (Edward) Clive (son of the great Robert, Lord Clive of Plassey fame) was not due to arrive until the end of August. So General Harris, as the Commander-in-Chief, became interim Governor. The Town Major job was in the gift of the Governor, and Harris offered it to Malcolm, whom he knew and liked. But there was no certainty that Lord Clive would allow Malcolm to continue in the role. In fact it was highly unlikely, since such plum jobs were eagerly sought after, and Governors often reserved them for relations or others for whom they wished to do favours. Nevertheless, as Malcolm pointed out in a letter to his mentor, General Ross, it put him in line for other possible jobs on the staff.

In his spare time he amused himself by translating the odes of Hafez from the Persian,[30] and writing poetry of his own. Despite all his apparently carefree social activities, he was taking life much more seriously. He read Adam Smith's *Wealth of Nations*, the definitive economic textbook of the day. He was steadily improving his Persian, and managed to get himself made Persian interpreter to General Harris.

At the same time he was sending regular bulletins of political analysis to his mentors in England. In August 1796, he sent Kennaway a four-page general letter, plus a thirteen-page dissertation on Indian politics. In a significant insight, he asserted that 'we gave the Nizam up at a moment [in 1795] when we could have saved him without risk of an immediate rupture, because "had we acted with spirit we would have irritated the Marhattas and drawn their revenge on some future occasion"!! They will never want pretences when they find it convenient to attack us, and the more prompt we on all occasions show ourselves to face them, the less liable we will be to their insults.'[31] He acquired this information by employing agents at the Native Courts, and this led him on to the idea of setting up a sort of Intelligence Coordination Department at Madras:

> I employ people in both the Nizam's and Tipoo's country, and your friend Colonel Kirkpatrick [Resident at Hyderabad] has been kind enough to let me have the daily papers . . . I have at times imagined I should be able to point out to the Government at some future period the serious advantages likely to result from an Intelligence Department fixed at Madras, where the information that comes in from different quarters from want of being regularly digested and arranged, and from want of those who receive it being properly acquainted with the Native Courts or the characters in them is entirely lost. It is a study that I conceive must require the sole attention of the person who undertakes it, and if he was capable the most serious important advantages would result. There does not appear to have been any consideration given to this point and entre nous the general ignorance of the subject is disgraceful.[32]

In intelligence-gathering, as in so many aspects of governance, he was ahead of his time.

But by April 1798 he realised that he had to look for a new career opportunity. Lord Clive, the incoming Governor of Madras, was due to arrive in August, so he could not expect the Town Major job to last for more than a few months. He knew that his strengths were a fascination with Indian politics, a gift for languages and an extraordinary ability to get on with all sorts of people, both Indian and European. He rightly saw the role of Political Officer (i.e. diplomat) at Native Courts as the natural outlet for his talents. And he was relentlessly pushy, urging his supporters in England to advance his claims with Lord Clive.

He did not have long to wait. On 26 April 1798, Richard Wellesley, second Lord Mornington and the new Governor-General of India, arrived at Madras on the frigate HMS *Virginie*, on his way to Calcutta. He brought with him as his Private Secretary his youngest brother, Henry Wellesley. Another brother, Arthur Wellesley, the Colonel of the 33rd Regiment of Foot (and future Duke Of Wellington), was already in Calcutta, awaiting his arrival. In the seven years that followed, Richard Wellesley was to change the map of India, from Cape Comorin in the south to the Punjab in the north. From that moment, and for the rest of his life, Malcolm's destiny became entwined with that of the Wellesley family.

CHAPTER FOUR

Hyderabad, 1798

Although Malcolm met the new Governor-General during his stopover at Madras he was not, as Town Major, sufficiently senior in the local hierarchy to claim much of Mornington's time. Instead, he set out to befriend and impress Mornington's younger brother, Henry Wellesley. Henry was upper-class, an old Etonian, much grander socially than Malcolm, but at only twenty-three (to Malcolm's twenty-eight) he appreciated and shared Malcolm's youthful high spirits. Besides, though overshadowed in India by his illustrious elder brothers, Henry was an able man, and later achieved distinction as a diplomat. Malcolm slipped into Henry's hand some of the papers which he had written on the local political situation, based on the intelligence he had acquired over the previous twelve months while acting as Persian interpreter to General Harris. He correctly anticipated that Henry would pass them on to Mornington.

Richard Colley Wellesley, Lord Mornington, was a scion of the Anglo-Irish Protestant ascendancy, the peerage of the Pale (and beyond). Born in 1760 at Dangan Castle, County Meath, the eldest of the five sons of Garret, first Viscount Wellesley and Earl of Mornington, his education was first at Harrow, then at Eton, and finally at Christ Church Oxford. His friends at school and university included such precocious political aspirants as William Grenville (Foreign Secretary at thirty-one), who introduced him to his cousin, William Pitt (Prime Minister at twenty-four). Many portraits depict him as about five feet seven inches tall, with a neat, delicate figure and large piercing eyes. Those eyes enabled him to dominate men, and to captivate women. He was sensitive, vain, and could be a bully. His acute intelligence, which did not suffer fools gladly, coupled with his upper-class detachment, combined to give him a wholly justified reputation for arrogance.

In May 1781 his father died, and he inherited his father's title and his debts, together with responsibility for 'placing' his four younger brothers and his sister. With characteristic decisiveness, he promptly left Oxford without taking a degree and returned to Ireland to try to restore the family finances. When visiting Paris in 1786, he met and fell in love with a French woman, Hyacinthe Roland, who came back to live with him in London, and gave birth to no fewer than five children before he finally married her in 1794. In late 1790 he and Hyacinthe went on a Grand Tour of the Continent, and when in Paris called on the King and Queen (Louis XVI and Marie Antoinette), at that time under a sort of house arrest at the Tuileries Palace. It may have been during this visit that he formed his intense antipathy to the principles of Jacobinism – an antipathy that was to have profound consequences when he reached India in 1798.

His intellect and political ambitions were far too intense to be satisfied by estate management in Ireland. He became a member of the House of Commons in 1786 by purchasing a rotten borough, and held increasingly senior Government posts in Pitt's ministry. His background and his friendships with Grenville and Pitt later made him a staunch supporter of 'the King's Government', but he also held distinctly liberal views on some issues, notably his support for Roman Catholic emancipation in Ireland, and for Wilberforce in his fight against the slave trade. Even when serving in Tory governments, he never wavered in his support for these objectives.

In 1793 Pitt appointed him to the six-man Board of Control for India. The Board was dominated by the Secretary of State, Henry Dundas, and there was not a great deal for Richard (now Lord Mornington) to do, but it was a valuable introduction to the politics of India and the East India Company. The Governor-General in Calcutta was the chief executive of British India, but the Governors of Madras and Bombay, though subordinate, could take advantage of slow communications to wield considerable independent authority. In 1797 the positions of both Governor-General and Governor of Madras were becoming vacant. Lord Cornwallis was earmarked to return for a second spell as Governor-General, so Mornington canvassed hard to be made Governor of Madras.

His brother Arthur, who had reached Calcutta in early 1797 with his regiment, advised him to accept that position, if offered. However, Lord Cornwallis was then appointed Lord Lieutenant of Ireland, so the much more prestigious role of Governor-General was suddenly available, and Mornington got it. At thirty-seven, his dreams of power and glory as an imperial proconsul, not to mention lavish financial emoluments, were about to be fulfilled.

He sailed from Southampton in November 1797, with his youngest brother Henry in tow as his Private Secretary. He had to wait at the Cape for six weeks while his ship was being repaired. The enforced delay was useful, for he found there several Company officers in transit who were able to brief him about the latest situation in India. The forty-four-year-old Colonel William Kirkpatrick, on sick leave from the position of Resident at the Nizam's Court in Hyderabad, was among them. Mornington was so impressed with Kirkpatrick's grasp of the issues that he asked him to become his Military Secretary as soon as he was well again. Kirkpatrick duly returned to Calcutta in early September 1798, and acted as Mornington's right-hand man for the next three years.

Thus when Mornington arrived at Madras on 26 April 1798, en route to Calcutta, he was already well briefed on Indian affairs. He made good use of the two weeks he stayed there, interviewing all the key figures in the Madras Government, and judging most of them incompetent or corrupt, or both. In a later note from Calcutta to Lord Clive, he wrote what amounted to 'staff reports' on those few Company officials whom he deemed to be of some potential value to the Company. These included Barry Close, Josiah Webbe and John Malcolm. Of Malcolm he wrote: 'Captain Malcolm, the Town Major, deserves every degree of countenance and protection. He is an officer of great worth, of extremely good sense, and well acquainted with the country [i.e. local] languages. He has turned his attention particularly to the study of the political system of India . . . He has also the advantage of very pleasing and amiable manners.'[1]

Some late twentieth-century historians – both Indian and European – have denigrated Mornington, emphasising his imperialist outlook, his arrogance, his vanity and his inability to get on with his peers. By today's standards he seems to have been a personally unattractive character – vain, bullying and philandering – with some slightly ridiculous posturing. Yet in judging his performance as Governor-General, we should beware of falling into the *post hoc ergo propter hoc* trap. We know how things turned out over the next seven years; in April 1798 neither Mornington nor anyone else could have known. To be fair to him, we should stand beside him and look at the daunting problems which faced him on arrival; and consider how we, as armchair Governors-General, would have tackled them.

This was the political situation that awaited him when he reached Calcutta in late May 1798. In Mysore, Tipu Sultan was planning revenge for his humiliation in 1792, building up his military and economic forces, and in touch with France. The Mahrattas, though once more torn by dissensions of their own, were encouraged by their victory over the Nizam in 1795, and had large armies, mostly officered by mercenary Frenchmen of Jacobin leanings. The Nizam was strengthening the Hyderabad army under French influence, disappointed by the British not having come to his aid in 1795, and losing confidence in them. The the Native State of the Carnatic was bankrupt, wide open to attacks from the Mahrattas and Mysore. Oudh [Awadh], with its administration and economy in chaos, was threatened by invasion from the north and west. The Mughal Emperor at Delhi was now a negligible pawn of the Mahrattas, with the threat of an Afghan invasion hanging over him. Finally, the Company had debts of more than £8 million.[2]

Mysore was clearly the most dangerous of these problems. Urgent decisions had to be made about how to deal with Tipu. Some historians see the post-1792 Tipu as essentially non-belligerent; but the British of that period were sure that he was incorrigibly hostile, and most of the evidence now available points to that conclusion.

What was to be done? There were two opposing factions, a 'Peace' (or 'Ring Fence') party, and a 'War' (or 'Forward Policy') party.

The 'Peace' party's case, most eloquently expressed by Josiah Webbe, the Chief Secretary at Madras, was that the objectives of the 1792 Treaty of Seringapatam had been to maintain Tipu as 'a Power of India', but to balance his power with that of the Mahrattas, the Nizam and the British. Since then, and despite losing half his territory, Tipu's position had been relatively strengthened – the Nizam's defeat by the Mahrattas in 1795 had weakened Hyderabad, the Mahrattas were having internal dissensions, and the British were distracted by the European war with France. In a war against Tipu, neither the Mahrattas nor Hyderabad could be relied upon as allies of the British. In 1790–92 it had taken the combined forces of the British, the Nizam and the Mahrattas acting in concert over two seasons to defeat him, using more seasoned Company troops than were currently available. And Tipu had learned from his mistakes in 1792. He now had shorter lines of communication, and had taken the precaution of destroying Bangalore, depriving the Company of its use as a base. In 1792 he had had no help from the French. This time, even if only a few French troops were to arrive on the battlefield, they would make a significant difference to Tipu's fighting capacity. There would be huge logistical difficulties in supplying sufficient grain and other materials to the Company's army in time for it to reach and storm Seringapatam before the onset of the next monsoon in June 1799. Finally, the Madras treasury was empty – the Government could hardly afford to pay the existing army, let alone fund a military campaign.[3]

The counter-argument of the Forward Policy camp was expressed in Malcolm's paper entitled 'Reflections on a Policy of forming a more intimate alliance with the Nizam'.[4] It contained the classic general argument for any forward policy: that the best way to achieve peace, at least in unsettled situations such as existed in India in 1798, was to prepare for war, and that to put up a 'ring fence' and retire behind it was to invite the enemy to attack you. Many years later, in discussing Sir John Shore's policy of neutrality in 1795 (when Shore had refused to go to the aid of the Nizam against the aggression of the Mahrattas) Malcolm wrote: 'It was proved, from the events of this administration, that no ground of political advantage could be abandoned without being instantly occupied by the enemy; and that to resign influence, was not merely to resign power, but to allow that power to pass into hands hostile to the British government.'[5] He conceded that to some extent close connections with Native States often involved the Company in more disputes and wars; that treaties generally favoured the native powers; and that 'experience has proved that the Natives are faithless, and that they will break, or make, a Treaty when convenient'. But he pointed out that this was the inevitable result of the extent of territory which the Company had already acquired, while the breaking of treaties which were no longer in a party's favour, was unfortunately 'the principle by which all Nations are in a greater or lesser degree governed.' He fell back upon Robert Clive's well known advice to the Court of Directors 'by calling to their mind that they were no longer Merchants, but Sovereigns of a vast Empire which must take the course of past Empires.

"To stop", he [Clive] had added, "is dangerous, to recede ruin". What may be denominated schemes of ambition by men whose minds are incapable of embracing so wide a subject, might by those who saw clearer be reduced to prudent plans for future security.' He agreed that there had been an increase in the Company's military expenditure, but ascribed this chiefly to the fact that some native powers had modernised their armies, and that additional expenditure was unfortunately inevitable if the Company's army was to maintain its superiority in defence of its existing territories. He saw no reason why an alliance, as such, should necessarily produce any net additional expenditure by the Company.

When Malcolm wrote this paper in April, he would not have been aware that Mornington had already come to similar conclusions while he was waiting at the Cape. A possible connecting link might have been William Kirkpatrick, who would have discussed the issues with Malcolm before he left Madras in late 1797, before briefing Mornington at the Cape. In any case, Malcolm's paper impressed Mornington, who, in a letter to Dundas, noted the similarity of its conclusions with his own, and commented 'I have annexed to this letter two papers drawn up by Captain Malcolm, late Town Major of Fort St George, one on the state of Tipu's army, the other a general view of our present political situation. The latter is curious, as Captain Malcolm had not seen any of my letters or minutes on the same subject, and only knew that a detachment was ordered to Hyderabad. I had no knowledge of Captain Malcolm, nor was he recommended to me before I met him at Fort St George.'[6]

But despite his consistent view about what should be done, Malcolm was sceptical about a new Governor-General having the courage to seize the opportunity. Writing to Hobart (now back in England) in April, he voiced his doubts: 'This is a period, my Lord, when a Governor-General of energy might give the fatal blow to that alarming power which the French have gained in the Deccan [i.e. Hyderabad] . . . But an effectual interference is a step of too much responsibility for a new Governor-General to take, unless he possesses uncommon nerve.'[7]

Whatever we might think of the propriety of Mornington's (and Malcolm's) policy, we can only marvel at Mornington's clarity of analysis and decisiveness in action. He knew exactly what he was trying to do. Very soon after arriving at Calcutta, he had clarified his objectives, his strategy and his tactics for dealing with the situation that confronted him. His aim, not yet fully divulged to his masters in London, and certainly not approved by them, was to make the Company the pre-eminent power in India, and in doing so to snuff out any possibility of a French resurgence. He realised that the *sequence* of steps to achieve this aim was vitally important: (1) to remove the French Corps from Hyderabad and bring the Nizam into a subsidiary alliance with the Company, while concurrently putting the Madras Army on a war footing; (2) with the support of the Nizam and his Subsidiary Force, to bring Tipu under control – preferably by threats alone, but if necessary by actual force; (3) to bring order to Oudh, the Carnatic and Tanjore; (4) to deal with the Mahrattas, either through an alliance with the Peshwah to bring the other Chieftains under his control, or by dealing directly with each Chieftain so that none of them could dominate the others. It was a breathtakingly ambitious vision, but in the following seven years, he very nearly brought it off. And Malcolm played a key role in each step of the journey.

Turning to the specific case for a closer alliance with the Nizam, Malcolm contended that Hyderabad could no longer defend itself against aggression, either from the Mahrattas or from Mysore, without outside assistance. Its army, defeated by the Mahrattas in 1795, would certainly not be able to withstand them now. Tipu would only come to Hyderabad's assistance against the Mahrattas in exchange for restoration of the territory he had lost to Hyderabad by the Treaty of Seringapatam in 1792, and that would be unacceptable: 'As it is certain that the Deckan [i.e Hyderabad] must depend on some power or other for support, he [Aristu Jah, the Prime Minister, also known as Azeem-ul-Amrah] chuses that which can give the most efficient aid, and from whom least danger is to be expected. He knows well that the English wish more to preserve and consolidate their present power than to extend it, and that while they will not give aid without deriving advantage, yet that they are more easy to be satisfied than either the Marhattas or Tippoo.' A further concern of the Chief Minister was the possibility of a coup against him, led or fomented by the French Corps.

For the British, 'the enemy that we must be ever jealous of is the Sultaun [i.e. Tipu]. From the Sultaun we need to expect nothing but inveterate enmity.' But a campaign against him without the support of the Nizam, and more particularly access to the Hyderabad grain supply, would be impracticable. In short, 'if we ever go to war on this coast without an ally, that war will be ruinous, and the Nizam is the only power with whom we can form an alliance with a well grounded hope of durability'.

Elimination of the Nizam's French Corps would also serve an additional British objective, in preventing the Nizam becoming too powerful for the Company's liking: 'Though it is in our interest to support the Nizam, I am well convinced it is equally if not more in our interest to prevent his becoming formidable, as on his weakness rests the policy of our connection. From it he is now our natural friend. Discipline and recruit his army, and he may prove the most dangerous of enemies. His situation enables [him] to be either with effect.'

A copy of Malcolm's paper on relations with the Nizam was sent to James Kirkpatrick, the acting Resident at Hyderabad at the time. He marked it in handwriting 'Jack Malcolm's Policy for a connection with the Nizam', and made comments in the margin, mostly supporting Malcolm's arguments.[8]

James Achilles Kirkpatrick (1764–1805), British Resident at Hyderabad (1797–1805).

William and James Kirkpatrick[9] were half-brothers, the sons of Colonel James Kirkpatrick of the Madras Cavalry. 'The Handsome Colonel', as their father was known, obtained cadetships in the Madras Army for William in 1771, and for James in 1779. The two half-brothers eventually met for the first time in 1784 or 1785, and quickly built up a close and affectionate relationship. William attended the Peace negotiations at Seringapatam in 1792, conducted on the British side by Sir John Kennaway, and acted as Lord Cornwallis's Persian interpreter. In December 1793 William took over from Kennaway as Resident. Protective of his young half-brother and eager to help him, he managed to get him assigned to a military post at Hyderabad. And later, on the death of the Assistant Resident in October 1795, he successfully lobbied for James to be his successor. But in the middle of 1797 William's health deteriorated to such an extent that he was forced to go to the Cape to recuperate. It was there that he met Mornington. At the end of June 1798, Mornington, thoroughly briefed by William Kirkpatrick on the options available for dealing with the Hyderabad problem, instructed James Kirkpatrick, still only acting Resident, to begin negotiations with the Nizam for the replacement of the French Corps by a Company force.

Malcolm had also attended the 1792 peace negotiations, acting as interpreter for the Nizam's auxiliary force, and Kennaway would have introduced him to William Kirkpatrick at that time. During 1796–97 Malcolm and the Kirkpatrick brothers corresponded frequently about the developing political situation at Hyderabad, and when William had to go on sick leave in 1797, he suggested that if he were not able to return, his brother James should become the Resident, and Malcolm his assistant. James welcomed the idea, and wrote to William that 'I am delighted at the prospect of Malcolm being my assistant. He is good natured, diligent, and has a tolerable share of sagacity with a decided turn for politics.'[10]

Malcolm, too, was excited by the idea – as William knew he would be. He was desperate to become a 'Political'. William may also have floated this idea with Mornington at the Cape, especially after Mornington had told William that he wanted him to be his Military Secretary in Calcutta, thus creating a vacancy at the Hyderabad Residency. But Mornington bided his time. Meanwhile, the arrival of Lord Clive as the new Governor of Madras was imminent. With the Town Major job being almost certainly earmarked for someone else, Malcolm was becoming frantic to secure a new appointment.

Lord Clive duly arrived at Madras on 21 August, and a week later Malcolm resigned as Town Major, with no confirmed new appointment. But he did not need to be too anxious. As Pulteney wrote home from his ship, 'He is known and respected by every one in the settlement, and in his publick capacity has given universal satisfaction to all his brother officers, and everyone is interested in his welfare.'[11]

The first step of Mornington's strategy – an alliance with the Nizam and the replacement of the French Corps with Company troops paid for by Hyderabad – was an entirely logical *realpolitik* strategy. But its implementation – getting the Nizam's agreement and actually disbanding the French Corps – was a different matter. This was the challenge that faced James Kirkpatrick, the man on the spot. The political situation in Hyderabad at the time was full of problems. At the centre there was Nizam Ali (Asaf Jah II) himself. Aged sixty-four, he had already ruled Hyderabad for thirty-six years – no mean feat of survival in the (almost literally) poisonous atmosphere of eighteenth-century Indian Courts. Even his own immediate family were not to be trusted. He had come to power by dethroning his brother Salabat Jung, who had been thrown into a dungeon and was later found strangled. One of his sons, Ali Jah, had rebelled against him in October 1795 and afterwards apparently committed suicide. A son-in-law, Dara Jah, had led a revolt in March 1796, and disappeared. Nizam Ali maintained his position through an extensive and lavishly financed intelligence network of spies, covering every city, village, fort, palace and shrine in his territory, including the British Residency. Nor was his the only intelligence network: similar networks were maintained by the British, by Tipu, by the Mahrattas, and by M. Raymond, the mercenary General commanding the French Corps.

In early 1798 the Nizam's army comprised about 25,000 infantry – more than half in Raymond's French Corps, 2,000 in the Subsidiary Force supplied by the Company under Colonel Hyndman, and about 10,000 under other mercenary officers – plus a large number of irregular cavalry. By far the most formidable and best trained (apart from the Company's small Subsidiary Force), was Raymond's force. Raymond himself was much more than a mere mercenary adventurer. In a few years he had built up the French Corps from virtually nothing into a disciplined body which had performed well in the war with the Mahrattas and later put down the revolt of the Nizam's son. For this the Nizam had rewarded him with large estates and two Persian titles. But what really worried the British was that the Corps was officered by 'Frenchmen of the most notorious principles of Jacobinism'. Raymond was in touch with revolutionary French elements in Pondicherry, Mauritius and Seringapatam (Tipu's capital). The Corps fought under the French revolutionary tricolor banner rather than the Nizam's standard, and was well funded, even managing to lure Company sepoys to desert and join it by offering better pay.

Even more apprehensive about Raymond's rise in influence was Aristu Jah, the Nizam's Prime Minister. In the Nizam's war with the Mahrattas in 1795, Sir John Shore, had not allowed the two Company battalions attached to the Nizam's army to take part. The Nizam was understandably furious, questioning the value of paying for these troops if they were not available when he needed them most. After the battle of Khardla in 1795, the victorious Mahrattas had taken Aristu Jah hostage, and he was only allowed to return to Hyderabad in 1797. In the meantime the pro-French and pro-Tipu factions at the Nizam's Court gained in influence at the expense of the British. Naturally enough the French faction, led by Raymond, were able to exploit this state of affairs to their advantage. So when Aristu Jah was reinstated as Prime Minister, he saw that Raymond was in a strong position to overwhelm the two Company battalions and mount a pre-emptive coup to replace the Nizam and/or his Prime Minister with others more sympathetic to the French. Aristu Jah had therefore a strong incentive to form an alliance with the British to oust the French. He realised that they would exact a price for doing so, but he reasoned that the price was worth paying. He immediately set out to engineer Raymond's downfall, and cut the French Corps down to size.

Late in 1797 he delivered the first blow, by removing some estates from Raymond. Then, on 25 March 1798 Raymond was found dead, aged forty-three. The circumstances were suspicious; poison was suggested. Aristu Jah immediately confiscated his remaining estates. Raymond's successor as commander of the French Corps was an Alsatian officer called Jean-Pierre Piron, a rough character who had little of Raymond's charm and influence at Court.

In June Aristu Jah opened secret negotiations with James Kirkpatrick for a revision of the Treaty – in essence the disbandment of the French

Corps and a threefold increase in the size of the Company's Subsidiary Force. Kirkpatrick had to conduct these negotiations under the detailed supervision of Mornington, who laid down the terms that he wanted – and allowed Kirkpatrick virtually no leeway for compromise. In mid-July, in anticipation of a treaty being signed, orders were given for a detachment of four battalions of the Madras Army under Colonel Roberts to be assembled at Guntur, fifty miles inland from the Circar coast and the nearest point to Hyderabad in Company-controlled territory.

Throughout this period Kirkpatrick was confidently anticipating his own confirmation as Resident, and Malcolm's appointment as his assistant. Mornington, however, had still not made up his mind about this. In fact he started losing his nerve. Meanwhile Malcolm, realizing that the crisis in Hyderabad would soon reach a climax, was now more determined than ever to get there as soon as possible, by hook or by crook. He contrived to have himself appointed as Persian interpreter to Roberts's detachment. The Nizam finally signed the Treaty on 1 September. It was secret, but it was inevitable that news of its terms would soon leak out. Colonel Hyndman's 2,000 Company troops were already at Hyderabad, but it was vital that Roberts's 4,000 additional Company troops should reach Hyderabad before a pre-emptive coup could be organised by opposing forces, using the French Corps under Piron. By early September Roberts's detachment was ready to march from Guntur to Hyderabad.

With the signing of the Treaty Mornington's confidence in Kirkpatrick was restored. In mid-September he made the formal announcement that William Kirkpatrick was to become his Military Secretary in Calcutta; that James Kirkpatrick was to be confirmed as Resident at Hyderabad; and that Malcolm was to be James's Assistant. Arthur Wellesley, who had recently arrived at Madras, saw additional roles for Malcolm. Worried that the appointment of Colonel Roberts to command the detachment going to Hyderabad might cause trouble, 'when it was well known that there was an old quarrel between him and Kirkpatrick', he asked Malcolm to act as peacemaker.[12] He also remained hopeful that the crisis might be resolved without bloodshed. He wrote to Malcolm on 2 October: 'Respecting the Hyderabad negotiations; that I believe it will end peaceably yet.'[13]

On 20 September Mornington wrote formally to Malcolm:

> the office of Resident of Hyderabad having become vacant by the resignation of Colonel Kirkpatrick, I have this day appointed Captain Kirkpatrick to succeed him; and it affords me great satisfaction at the same time to have it in my power to nominate you Assistant at that Court, having learnt from my brother that, in a letter to him, you had stated that such an appointment would be acceptable to you . . .
>
> I wish to see you previously to your proceeding to Hyderabad . . . I therefore hope that you will contrive to visit Calcutta soon after the receipt of this letter.[14]

Mornington clearly felt that his appointment of Malcolm was important, for at the end of a long letter to Henry Dundas in London, he wrote: 'He [Malcolm] is a very promising young man. I have appointed him assistant to the resident at Hyderabad.'[15]

Mornington's letter reached Malcolm about 7 October, while he was on the road to Hyderabad with Roberts's detachment. He was thrilled. He had of course hoped and expected that he would land the job, but there was always the possibility that it would fall through. Even more exciting was that the Governor-General had asked him to come to Calcutta to 'learn from me [i.e. Mornington] . . . many circumstances relative to the political system of India'. Considering that Malcolm had had fifteen years' direct experience of Indian politics and Mornington had had four months, this was an interesting way of putting it. But despite all his years of Indian service he had never been to Calcutta, the seat of the Supreme Government. And to go there now, specifically to meet the Governor-General himself, a Governor-General who seemed to have the vision and the determination to carry into effect the policies which Malcolm had been advocating for years – this exceeded his wildest dreams. He was tempted to break away from Roberts's detachment and set off immediately for Calcutta. But he was within two days' march of Hyderabad, so it seemed sensible to complete the journey first. On 9 October, he galloped on ahead, and that night dined with James Kirkpatrick at the Residency. When Kirkpatrick explained the latest situation, it became clear that the climax was imminent, and Malcolm was soon persuaded not to depart for Calcutta until the outcome was clear. He was badly needed right there in Hyderabad. Moreover, he was acting with rather wider terms of reference than Kirkpatrick may have realised.

In addition to his role as Assistant Resident, he was also supposed to be an interpreter to Roberts's detachment; to dampen down any latent hostility between Roberts and Kirkpatrick; and to act as an agent for the Wellesleys in Hyderabad, reporting to Mornington in Calcutta and to Arthur Wellesley in Madras.

James Achilles Kirkpatrick was a complex character. Outwardly handsome, easy-going and charming, underneath he was sensitive, longing for reassurance, wary of people's motives. Like his older half-brother (and Malcolm) he had a gift for languages, and this had helped him to escape from the army into the 'political line'. His interest in things Indian had been encouraged by his relationship for many years with an Indian *bibi*, by whom he had a son. And it was to deepen over time, until in 1801 Mountstuart Elphinstone could describe him as 'a semi-Indianised Englishman who . . . led a half-Oriental life. He is a good-looking man; seems about thirty, is really about thirty-five. He wears mustachios; his hair is cropped very short, and his fingers are dyed with henna. In other respects he is like an Englishman. He is very communicative, and very desirous to please; but he tells long stories about himself, and practices all the affectations of which the face and eyes are capable.'[16] It was not surprising therefore that Kirkpatrick, while appreciating Malcolm's talents, should have been a little jealous of the brash and ambitious young officer, and a little suspicious of his motives. As time went on, his suspicion increased. Malcolm was probably unaware of this, or chose to ignore it. He liked Kirkpatrick, as he liked practically everyone; he was not by nature a suspicious man.

The next fortnight was destined to be the most exciting of Malcolm's life so far. The British reinforcements under Colonel Roberts marched into Hyderabad the next day (10 October). With all 6,000 Company troops now in place, the stage was set for the showdown with the French Corps. All that remained was for the Nizam to give the order to dismiss its officers and disband the Corps. But now a new crisis arose. The Nizam and Aristu Jah began to get cold feet.

Sure enough, as Kirkpatrick had anticipated, the realisation began to sink in with the Nizam and his Minister, that the replacement of the French Corps by Company troops, while improving Hyderabad's defences against Tipu and the Mahrattas, would expose them to another, possibly greater danger. They would be delivering themselves into the hands of the Company. Would they be going from the French frying pan into the English fire? Were the English likely to be more reliable friends than the French? At this crucial moment some astonishing news came in from Europe. Bonaparte had landed in Egypt and had taken possession of Alexandria and Cairo. Right now he might be preparing to take his army to the Malabar coast, join up with Tipu, defeat the English and move on to Hyderabad. Were they backing the wrong horse? Naturally enough, the pro-French faction at Court was making the most of all this. The Hyderabadis were not the only ones to be alarmed by the news from Egypt. James Kirkpatrick wrote to William: 'The more I think of this damned Egyptian expedition of the French, the more uneasy it makes me.'[17] Nor, had they all known it, were their various alarms without foundation. From Cairo, Bonaparte had written to Tipu, answering Tipu's pleas for help against the English, assuring him that he was 'full of the desire of releasing and relieving you from the iron yoke of England . . . May the Almighty increase your power, and destroy your enemies! Yours etc. etc. Bonaparte.'[18]

To understand the various military movements that took place over the following ten days, we need to have a picture of the Hyderabad landscape. The old walled city was near the south bank of the Musi river, which runs from west to east. The British Residency was on the north bank 'lodged in the house of a native nobleman, which was pleasant from being surrounded with small gardens and fountains, and had been sufficiently modified by improvements to be rendered a tolerably convenient European residence'.[19] It was later described by Mountstuart Elphinstone as 'laid out partly in the taste of Islington and partly in that of Hindustan'.[20]

On Aristu Jah's orders the 13,000 men of the French Corps had been concentrated into one body, and were camped on the flat ground on the south bank of the Musi, a little less than two miles to the east of the city.[21] The French camp faced southwards, towards a low ridge running parallel to the river. From a parapet on the southern wall of the Residency, Kirkpatrick was able to look across the river Musi southwards to the city, and eastwards to the French camp.

The 4,000 men of Colonel Roberts's detachment were placed on arrival in a camp on the south side of the low ridge, about a mile to the south of the French Corps. There was concern, however, that the Residency needed better protection from a possible French attack. So Colonel Hyndman's two battalions were brought southwards from their

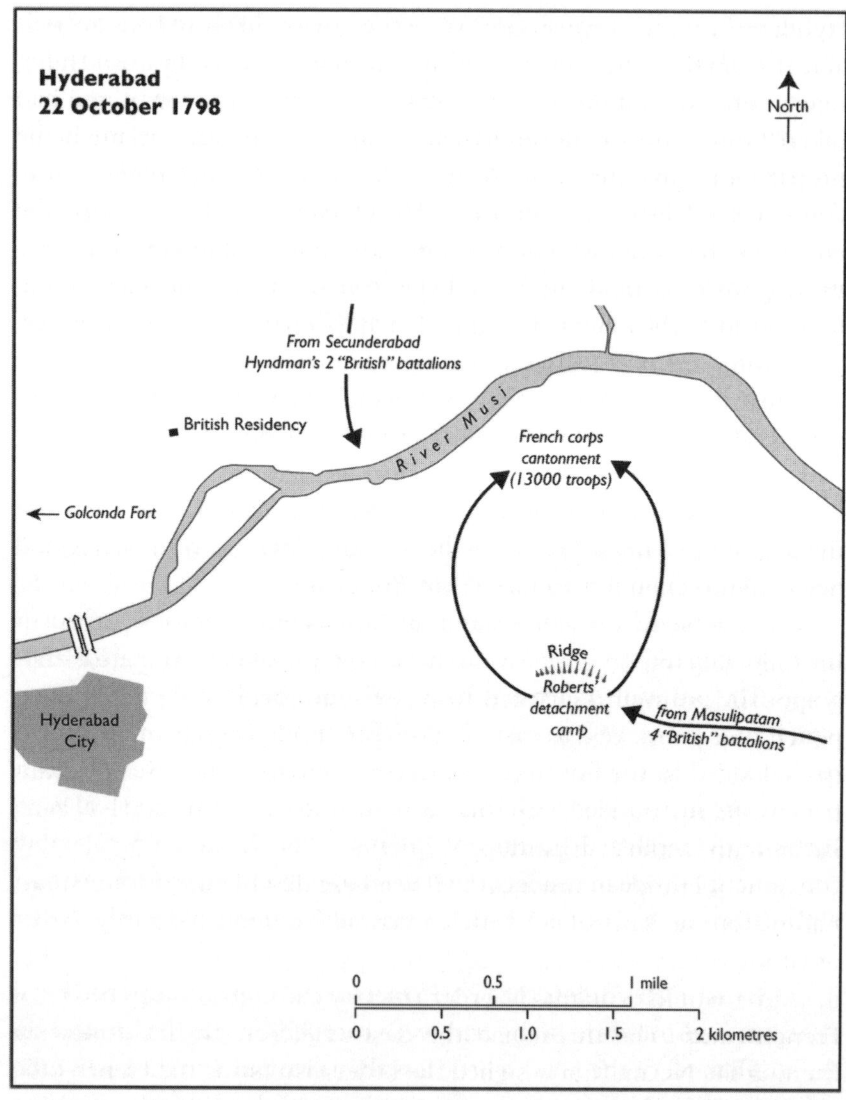

cantonment at Secunderabad to a new camp near the Residency, on the north bank of the river, and opposite the French Corps.

Despite having only 6,000 men at their disposal, the British were confident of overcoming Piron's 13,000 French-officered troops. But on the evening of 14 October heavy rain made the river virtually impassable to troops, and Kirkpatrick became concerned that the already outnumbered British force should be further divided by the turbulent river into two groups: Roberts's 4,000 being south of the river and

Hyndman's 2,000 being north of it. He was reassured by both Roberts and Hyndman. As Malcolm put it, 'it was concerted that Colonel Hyndman's corps should move . . . to a position about 400 yards in the rear of M. Piron's camp, between which and him was the river; there being no ford for guns, those with Colonel Hyndman's corps were to play from the bank he was encamped upon, which they could with excellent effect, on the principal magazine and storehouses of the French camp. Whilst these battalions attacked the rear of their centre and right, Colonel Roberts was to advance his whole corps and guns to attack [from the south] the front of their centre and left.'[22]

Meanwhile, there was no sign of the Nizam giving the order to dismiss the French officers and disband the sepoys of the French Corps. Instead, he retired in fear to the old fortress of Golconda, several miles south-west of the city. The pressure on Kirkpatrick was now intensifying. He wrote daily letters to Aristu Jah, imploring him to take action before Piron should discover the definitive terms of the Treaty. At the same time he was being bombarded by letters from Calcutta. His brother William, no doubt himself being harassed by an increasingly anxious Mornington, wanted to know why action kept being postponed. But James kept his nerve. He wrote back to William, deploring the delay, but pointing out the enormous long-term diplomatic advantage to the British if the decision was seen to be taken by the Nizam, rather than by the Company.

By 19 October no answer had been received from the Nizam or Aristu Jah, and Kirkpatrick's patience finally ran out. That evening he went to Golconda, and delivered an ultimatum. If there was any further delay, he would unilaterally order the Company troops to attack the French camp. The threat had the desired effect. On the following evening the Nizam finally signed the order dismissing the French officers and disbanding the troops. To Kirkpatrick's considerable surprise, as soon as Piron received the Nizam's order, he sent two officers over to the Residency, reaching it about midnight, with the message that he was ready to surrender, asking only that he and his officers should be taken into custody by the Company rather than by the Nizam.[23]

Early in the morning of 21 October, Piron (in Malcolm's words): 'requested an officer might be sent from the Residency to the French lines, to take charge of articles of public and private property'.[24] Malcolm continued:

> As it was very hot, I went in my palanquin, and my horse was led after me. Just after I entered the lines a violent mutiny broke out. Several battalions came round my palanquin; which they took from the bearers, hoisted me on their shoulders, and endeavoured with it to force the gate of Perron's [Piron's] garden, which was defended by the first, or Pondicherry battalion. I expostulated in vain against the violence with which I was treated. Though they did not mean to kill me, I was in imminent danger, as several balls fired in the confusion of the mutiny struck the palanquin.[25]

At that moment two soldiers who had been with him years before in the 29th Madras Native Infantry, but had been lured to the French Corps by an offer of better pay, appeared on the scene, and saved his life. He pressed them to return with him to the Residency, but they declined, saying their object was only to place him in safety and rejoin their comrades.[26] It was a narrow escape for Malcolm, but he got back to the Residency unscathed. Later that evening Piron and some of the French officers turned up at Colonel Roberts's camp, having managed to escape from their confinement, 'though not without a scuffle, in which several were wounded'.

Daylight on 22 October saw the French camp in chaos. Roberts had moved his detachment of 4,000 men to the crest of the hill overlooking the camp from the south. Hyndman was across the river to the north, his guns trained on the French powder magazine. By agreement between Kirkpatrick and Aristu Jah, Malcolm had been put in command of 2,000 of the Nizam's cavalry. He sent 500 of them to the east of the French camp, and remained himself with 1,500 to the west. The French troops, now without their French officers, were surrounded and virtually defenceless. Around midday the endgame began. As Malcolm later described it:

> The Resident sent instructions to Colonel Roberts . . . to give the men one quarter of an hour to stack their guns, and march off to a cowle [safe conduct] flag, which was pitched by one of the Nizam's principal officers, about half a mile to the right [i.e. west] of their camp. If they did not comply with the terms of this summons, they were immediately to be attacked, and on

> such commencing, Colonel Hyndman was to advance also [from the north bank] . . . As I reached the ground [about one o'clock] two hours before Colonel Roberts came up, and observing they were extremely alarmed, I ventured near, though cautiously . . . Four or five *subadars* [native officers] came to meet me, and after I had explained the intention of Colonel Roberts, they returned to explain it to their corps, from whom they instantly brought me a message that they were ready to comply with all the conditions, but trusted the Company's Sepoys would be sent to take possession of their lines, as the Nizam's horse, if admitted, would plunder everything. On observing this favourable aspect, I advanced, and found that they were completely disunited, and terrified, and ready to obey my orders, and as a proof of their return to their senses, they released all the officers they had confined.
>
> I went to meet Colonel Roberts, to inform him of this favourable turn; he took immediate possession of the heights, and [about three o'clock] advanced eight Grenadier companies to take possession of the grand magazine, store-houses, and cannon, while the natives of the French Corps moved off in a deep column to the appointed flag, and the Europeans [124 of them] all joined our camp, the latter full of spirits; for the fears they had experienced from the fury of the men made them view us, not as belonging to a nation who had by its policy ruined all their prospects, but as men who had exerted themselves to save their lives. At five o'clock their whole lines were in our possession.

And then, barely able to contain his excitement, he ended, 'and a corps consisting of sixteen thousand men in all, had been annihilated in six hours, without shedding one drop of blood'.[27]

Nor was this all. Colonel Roberts reported to the Madras Government that 'by seven o'clock that evening my troops were in complete possession of every part of the extensive lines, their guns, arms and all their military stores to a considerable amount. Upwards of 12,000 stand of arms and 27 pieces of cannon mounted have already been collected. Their force consisted of 13,000 men.'[28]

By any standard it was a brilliant coup. Malcolm was well aware of the implications. In a letter to Lord Clive he wrote: 'This Government is now strictly speaking dependent on us, and we have by this measure secured an alliance, the value of which we would have confessed had we ever lost it.'

As a result, the people of Hyderabad got peace and prosperity, at least compared with their Mahratta neighbours. But they also became dependent on the British – for 150 years. James Kirkpatrick, who had watched the events of the afternoon from the Residency with his spy glass, wrote to his brother William that night: 'I think the march of Roberts' Detachment over the heights near the French cantonments, and his unopposed possession of the cantonments themselves, together with the disarming and turning adrift of ten or eleven thousand of Raymond's troops . . . was the finest sight I ever saw in my life.'[29] And the next day he wrote to Neil Edmonstone in Calcutta that 'only three days ago matters wore a very dismal appearance.'[30] On 19 October, while the Nizam was wavering and procrastinating, the French Corps might easily have attempted a coup, or an escape, with bloody consequences whether it succeeded or not. The news of Napoleon's landing and conquest of Egypt had given heart to the pro-French faction at Court, and had induced some misgivings among the British. All these fears had been banished in a single day. And just for good measure, news had just come in of Nelson's destruction of the French fleet at Aboukir Bay, thus wrecking Napoleon's plans for using Egypt as a base to launch an attack on British India.

The disarming of the French Corps was a major personal triumph for James Kirkpatrick. It was he who had built up warm personal relations with the Nizam and Aristu Jah over the previous year; it was he who had patiently negotiated the Treaty of 1 September, and had kept his nerve in the seven weeks that followed, despite erratic wavering at the Court, and harassment from Calcutta; it was he who had finally applied just enough diplomatic pressure on the Nizam to get him to act, while maintaining the public perception that the Nizam had acted of his own volition; finally, it was he who had masterfully engineered the mutiny of the French sepoys, and the timing of the movement of the Company's troops.

But for Malcolm, too, it was a triumph. Many months before, he had advocated the action that had been taken. He had been at least partly instrumental in strengthening the case for action with the Governor-

General. He must have been a huge help to Kirkpatrick in the twelve days leading up to the denouement. Last but not least, he had played a central and crucial role in the action itself. He had been brave to enter the lines of the mutinous sepoys on 21 October; and just as brave – and resourceful – the next day, in seizing a favourable moment to accost the five *subadars* and convince them that they could safely surrender; and then, to address the mutineers (in Telugu, their native language) to lay down their arms.

As the news spread, congratulations poured in from all sides. Most immediately relieved were the Nizam and Aristu Jah. Kirkpatrick was named *Hushmat Jang* ['Glorious in battle' or 'Lion of War']. As soon as Mornington heard the news, he wrote to congratulate Kirkpatrick, formally confirming his substantive appointment as Resident; he also wrote to Dundas in London, recommending that Kirkpatrick should be given 'a mark of Royal favour', in other words a baronetcy, as Kirkpatrick's predecessor, Sir John Kennaway, had received.

Malcolm's thoughts now turned back to the Governor-General's summons to Calcutta. He asked Kirkpatrick for permission to leave immediately, in compliance with the Governor-General's order. Kirkpatrick had no choice but to let him go. But he did so with some reluctance. In the aftermath of the action, he needed all the diplomatic help he could get in sorting out the loose ends, and no one was better qualified than Malcolm to supply it: 'As Malcolm is certainly very anxious to proceed to Calcutta I shall let him go in a day or two though very inconvenient to me, and much against my judgement.'[31]

But there was also the first hint of a jealousy, which was to develop over the next five years into distrust, and finally to hatred. He wrote a few days later to William: 'I cannot help thinking it very cruel of Malcolm to have left me here to drudge by myself, while he goes on his wild goose chase to Calcutta.'[32] He could anticipate only too clearly that this brash young man was going to arrive at Calcutta and accept all the accolades for the success of the action, which belonged more appropriately to him.

At the end of October Malcolm set off on horseback for the 150-mile journey to the coast. He took with him three of William Kirkpatrick's former Hyderabad servants, who wanted to rejoin their master, and also William's fur coat – the nights could be quite chilly at Calcutta in the cold season. But his most cherished pieces of baggage were the colours of the French Corps. To present the colours of the vanquished foe to headquarters would be a thrill for any young officer – like a gun dog placing a shot pheasant at the feet of its master.

In mid-November Malcolm sailed up the Hooghly. It would have been exciting to arrive for the first time at Fort William in any circumstances, but now he was arriving in triumph, as a hero, carrying the French colours directly to Government House. And, despite his junior status, he had friends at Court. William Kirkpatrick, his mentor from Hyderabad days, was Military Secretary to the Governor-General, and probably his most influential adviser. Henry Wellesley, whose friendship he had cultivated at Madras back in May, was Private Secretary. His former boss, Sir Alured Clarke was the Commander-in-Chief. But above all there was the Governor-General himself.

Mornington was by now in a state of euphoria. The ousting of the French from Hyderabad, step one in his grand design, had been triumphantly executed. And, he felt, it had been done almost entirely on his own personal initiative, against the misgivings of his advisers. To his French wife, Hyacinthe, he wrote candidly: 'You will enjoy my gentle conquest of an army of fourteen thousand men under the command of French officers for the service of the Nizam. My dispatches do not mention a curious fact, that the standard of this army was the Tricolour Flag; the only one of this description erected on the continent of India. This standard has fallen into my hands; and I shall send it home as the best comment upon the whole policy of making an effort to crush the French influence in India.'[33]

And send it home he did, directly to Henry Dundas in London: 'You will receive with this letter a box containing the standards of the late French party at Hyderabad. I beg you particularly to remark the emblems upon the top of the standards; the sword bearing the cap of liberty, the meaning of which is too obvious to need any explanation.'[34] The bearer of all this good news, its physical embodiment, was John Malcolm. With his tall frame and his cheerful, loud, self-confident manner, he was immediately accepted into the Government House circle. He had indeed 'landed on his feet'.

Moreover, he brought with him further evidence that the hand of the Paris Directory was involved in the intrigues of the French Corps at Hyderabad. In a 'Memorandum relative to the late French Corps in the Deccan', written shortly after his arrival at Calcutta, he set out the evidence that the French Corps had been in touch with the French Government in Paris. 'It was generally reported and believed that Raymond had a General's commission with the Directory . . . There was found in store when our troops took possession of the French lines, small arms and clothing for 12,000 men beyond the force then serving under Mons. Piron.'[35] This report was music to the ears of Mornington.

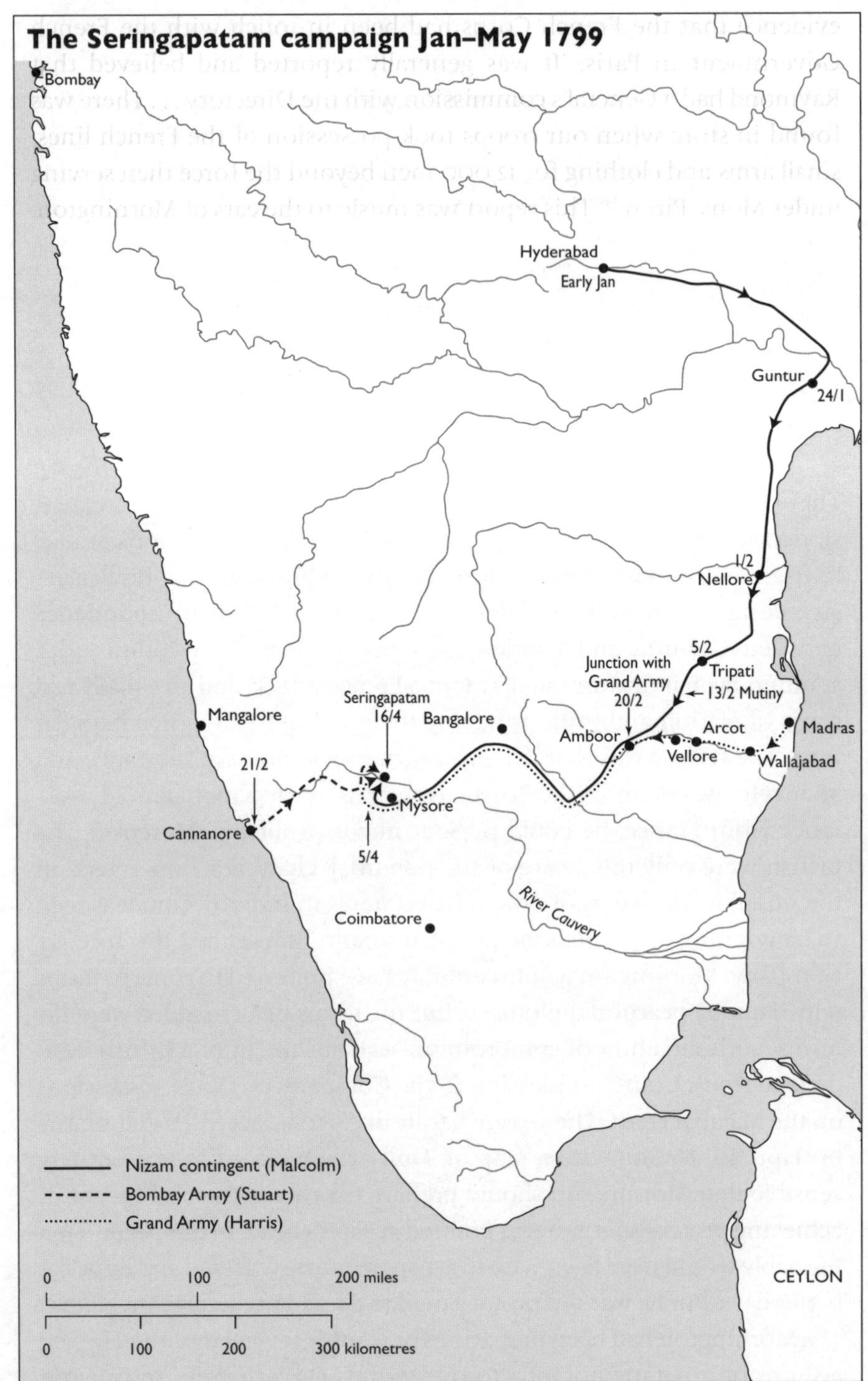
The Seringapatam campaign Jan–May 1799
Bombay
Hyderabad
Early Jan
Guntur
24/1
1/2
Nellore
5/2
Tripati
Junction with Grand Army
20/2
13/2 Mutiny
Seringapatam
16/4
Bangalore
Mangalore
Amboor
Arcot
Madras
Vellore
Wallajabad
21/2
Mysore
Cannanore
5/4
River Cauvery
Coimbatore
Nizam contingent (Malcolm)
Bombay Army (Stuart)
Grand Army (Harris)
0
100
200 miles
0
100
200
300 kilometres
CEYLON

CHAPTER FIVE

Mysore, 1799

There is a view among some historians that Mornington (and by extension Malcolm), deliberately exaggerated the French threat to British India, to frighten his masters in London into letting him carry out his aggressive designs against Tipu Sultan in Mysore. But the correspondence between Calcutta and London over this period clearly points to a genuine, even if unwarranted, fear of a French attack, and an equally real sense of elation and pride at having thwarted it, for the time being at least. The feeling was that if Tipu, a man of real military substance and an inveterate enemy of the British, were to get even a modicum of assistance from France, he could present major problems. Moreover, the British were only too aware of the potential 'chain reaction' effect on the minds of the rulers of other Native States in India. If Tipu was seen to be winning, they might be tempted to join him against the 'foreign' Company. Mornington would certainly have preferred to come to terms with Tipu by peaceful diplomacy, but the terms he demanded were his terms, without a hint of compromise – establishment of a British Resident at Tipu's Court, and cession to the Company of Tipu's possessions on the Malabar coast. These were hardly likely to be accepted voluntarily by Tipu. In dealing with a man of Tipu's track record, it was entirely sensible that Mornington should prepare for war as the best means of achieving peace. But a gun was pointed at Tipu's head. In hindsight, Tipu probably would have been wise to accept the terms offered and hope for better days. But he was too proud a man to do so. War became inevitable.

Mornington had been preparing for war for several months. He sent a series of crisp memoranda to the Madras Government, setting out what he required of them. Previously, there had been opposition to these preparations. But since the arrival of Lord Clive at Madras in late August and Arthur Wellesley in September, the Madras Government had been doing its utmost to cooperate with the Governor-General. Mornington's greatest worry was timing. Letters between Seringapatam and Calcutta took several weeks, depending on wind and weather. He knew that Tipu had plenty of opportunity to procrastinate in the hope that the British would not have time to attack Seringapatam before the next monsoon started in June 1799. And he certainly wanted to avoid the fate of Cornwallis, whose army had reached the gates of Seringapatam in May 1791 only to have to destroy its siege train and retreat because of lack of food and the imminent arrival of the monsoon. Delay until the following dry season would give Tipu time to receive French assistance. It would also give Mornington's opponents in London a chance to veto his grand design.

In late December 1798 Mornington took ship for Madras, to be closer to the scene of action when, and if, hostilities began. Meanwhile he asked Malcolm to prepare an updated paper, what we might today call an 'options paper', on the Mysore situation. Malcolm produced a thirty-four-page document, just as the Governor-General and party (which now included Malcolm) were about to embark.

Malcolm's paper discussed Tipu, and concluded that he was unlikely to get outside aid – definitely not from the Nizam; probably not from the Mahrattas (who would most likely sit on the fence until they could see who was winning); and not, in the short term at least, from the French. He was in a poor negotiating position. Yet his power rested on his prestige; he could not afford the humiliation of compromise. The Company's objective was to neutralise Tipu as an enemy. This could be done by establishing a Resident at Seringapatam; cession of some land to the Company (probably on the Malabar coast); and expulsion of non-British Europeans from his Court. This should be achieved by diplomacy if possible, by war if necessary. Not surprisingly, the action recommended was similar to what had been successfully applied at Hyderabad. But it was unrealistic – Tipu Sultan was a very different man from Nizam Ali.

The voyage from Calcutta to Madras was quick, and the party arrived at Fort St George on 30 December 1798. Mornington went to stay at a house lent by Mr Petrie, a member of the Madras Presidency Council. Here he sat in spacious gardens under the shade of a *peepul* tree and dictated long letters to every corner of India as well as to London. Malcolm was no longer part of the Government House circle, but Madras was his old stamping ground and he had plenty of friends there. In any case, within a week he was called in by Mornington and given an important new assignment. He was to join the Nizam's army as his liaison officer on political matters and General Harris's liaison officer on military matters.

At this time, the Madras Army (the 'Grand Army'), under the command of General Harris, was assembling at Vellore, in preparation for the march westwards towards Seringapatam. The Bombay Army, under General Stuart, was meanwhile on its way from Bombay to the Malabar coast. The Nizam had agreed to join the Company in confronting Tipu; and a large part of his army (known as the 'Nizam's Contingent') had set off southwards from Hyderabad on 13 December.

The Nizam's Contingent comprised the six infantry battalions (6,000 men) of the Company's Subsidiary Force, plus artillery, 4,000 other infantry – mostly from the former French Corps, but now with Hyderabadi officers – and about 10,000 cavalry: over 20,000 fighting men in total. In addition there would have been about 20,000 camp followers.

All these troops were under the command of Meer Alam, a protégé of the Nizam's Chief Minister, Aristu Jah. He had been appointed by Aristu Jah as the Nizam's *vakeel* to the British some years before, and had led a successful diplomatic mission to Calcutta. He was an able man and had steadily grown in stature and influence at the Nizam's Court. He was not, however, a professional soldier. While Malcolm's official brief was to act as chief liaison officer between the British and the Hyderabadi armies, in practice it also meant providing professional military advice to Meer Alam. The task was to get this sprawling host from Hyderabad to Amboor, the agreed rendezvous with General Harris's Grand Army, and then to proceed together to Seringapatam.

Starting on 6 January, and for the next four months, Malcolm kept a daily journal and sent a copy to Mornington.[1] A journal written with the boss as a potential reader is likely to be circumspect. It does however provide a valuable record of Malcolm's part in the fourth (and last) Anglo-Mysore War.

Leaving Madras on 7 January, he rode along the coast, and met the Nizam's Contingent on 19 January, about 220 miles north of Madras. The logistical problems of moving an army across country have taxed Generals since the days of Alexander the Great. In India in 1799, food, water and firewood (for cooking and heating) had to be provided, day in, day out, for the men and their horses. Together with camping equipment and ammunition, they had to be carried, and the guns dragged, by bullocks, which also had to be fed and watered. At one time the Nizam's Contingent had 25,000 pack and draft bullocks in camp, and a further 25,000 on their way to and from the camp. Some armies, particularly the Mahratta irregular cavalry, managed to live off the land. Their needs were satisfied by plunder, and they passed through districts like a plague of locusts. By contrast, the Company's policy was to pay for everything it took. Payment was a form of enlightened self-interest, because it generally kept the local inhabitants friendly. Unlike many Native rulers, the Company could afford to pay, and generally did so. The only 'plunder' allowed was prize money following victory in battle. Wages could only be paid in *specie* (coins), so the *specie* had to be carried too, in this case on fifty elephants supplied by Meer Alam.

To complicate matters, while food (mainly sacks of rice) could be bought in advance for a campaign of, say, three months, it could not be carried – three weeks' supply was the maximum that could be handled at any one time by the available bullocks. This meant that army quartermasters were continually having to search for replenishment stocks. Water was another problem. January to May is the dry season in South India. Well water was always available, but for 40,000 people and, say, 15,000 horses, drawing water from wells was far too slow. The army relied on tanks (reservoirs) lying at intervals across the country. But in dry years these tanks were sometimes empty. Moreover, a retreating enemy could empty the tanks as part of a 'scorched earth' strategy.

Malcolm and Meer Alam got along well: 'I pass two or three hours each day with Meer Alam, and find him always equally high in spirits and zealous to promote anything recommended';[2] but there were inevitable problems in smoothing diplomatic relations between allies with such fundamentally different approaches to military campaigns. One difference, already mentioned, was in getting supplies. Another was soldiers' pay: the Company sepoys were paid slightly more, and more regularly, than the Nizam's troops. So there was jealousy. Malcolm tried to persuade Meer Alam to go some way to matching the pay of both parts of the Contingent, but was told that only the Nizam and Aristu Jah could sanction such a change. Then there was the problem of dealing with the British officers of the Subsidiary Force, some of them considerably senior to Malcolm. The Hyderabadi commissariat arrangements seemed haphazard, and they directed their complaints squarely at Malcolm as the liaison officer: 'There was yesterday a very great scarcity of grain in Camp and a similar scarcity prevails to-day. I this day received a publick representation on the subject from Colonel Roberts.'[3]

Malcolm was quick to respond, recommending that Roberts should set up a Regimental bazaar, as the Commander-in-Chief had ordered. Considering that Roberts was a full Colonel, three ranks senior to him, this was cheeky. He also had to keep headquarters informed: Mornington himself, of course; General Harris, the Commander-in-Chief; and Colonel Kirkpatrick, the Military Secretary. In theory he could write letters addressed only to the Governor-General, with copies to the others. But his previous experience at Government Houses had taught him that men of elevated station were sensitive of their dignity and did not like receiving copies of letters addressed to others. They wished to be addressed directly. So, after completing each day's march and dealing with local problems, he would usually have to sit down in his tent with a candle and write to Mornington, and to Harris or Kirkpatrick as well. He also had to bear that perennial cross of commanders in the field – helpful suggestions from headquarters. A greater worry was the mood of the former French Corps troops. The replacement of French officers by Hyderabadi officers had not worked well. Soon after Malcolm joined the Contingent, he raised this issue with Meer Alam. The Meer's view was 'that the Corps would be useless unless European officers were immediately appointed to it, and it had better be left behind, either in the Nizam's or in Company districts'.[4] Malcolm agreed that either European officers should be put in charge or the Corps should be dispersed. But action to implement this was postponed.

Early on the morning of 13 February, he received a rude shock. The officers of the French Corps announced that they would refuse to march unless they 'were assured that European officers were not to be introduced among them'. All day long Meer Alam parleyed with them to no avail. At midnight, when the order to march was given, they refused to move. Malcolm asked for and received Meer Alam's permission to take control. Then:

> I rode into the Lines and after ordering the Sepoys to fall in, I directed one Corps [to go] with the Stores and three [others] to Major Grant's Line, and was immediately obeyed. The remainder I placed under Captain Schohey.
>
> The ready obedience of the Men convinced me they had been misled by [a] designing person, and on my reporting my success to Meer Alam he requested me to . . . take charge of the Corps for the present. I immediately attached about 800 of these men to Major Grant, and with his own people to form the whole into two Corps and distribute his officers equally between the two. The other four Corps I have put under command of Captain Schohey, and shall trust to the General [General Harris] for some more officers.[5]

A few days after this mutiny the Nizam's Contingent reached Amboor, the appointed meeting place with the Grand Army. In fact, it arrived ahead of schedule, and had to wait a couple of days for the junction of the two armies. The meeting between Meer Alam and General Harris now took place in a series of formal ceremonies. From Malcolm's point of view the most useful immediate outcome of this meeting was General Harris's agreement to second about twelve British officers to the former French Corps. This enabled Malcolm to dismiss the recalcitrant *subadars* of that force, though not without further drama.[6]

On 21 February, the British and Hyderabadi forces moved off ponderously towards the Mysore border. The armies marched in two parallel columns about three miles apart, with the cavalry at the front and rear of each army. On the right marched the Grand Army, comprising 3,000 cavalry, 5 regiments of European infantry and 11 sepoy battalions – 20,000 fighting men, plus 50 cannon. On the left marched the Nizam's Contingent of around 20,000 men. Between them marched up to 100,000 camp followers, including merchants, coolies, plunderers and sepoys' families. In addition there were at least 100,000 bullocks, plus elephants, camels, carts, a huge battering train and an arsenal of 1,200 rounds of shot and powder for each of the 50 cannon. The combined column was about 6 miles across and covered an area of 18 square miles.

Moving a maximum of 10 miles a day, it started at 6 a.m. and usually arrived at its camping spot around midday, halting for a day every four or five days. Some distance away to the south were the 5,000 men of the Madras Army's Baramahal force, and another 5,000 men of the Coimbatore force. By now, too, the 6,000 men of the Bombay Army under General Stuart had landed on the Malabar coast, and were making their way up the western *ghats*.

Over the next few days, Malcolm laconically recorded two events in his journal that were to have a profound effect on rest of his life. First, on 27 February, he 'received a letter from Lord Mornington'.[7] Mornington was concerned that delicate political decisions would probably need to be taken in final negotiations with Tipu before (and possibly after) a final showdown, and that he was too far away in Madras to direct them with sufficient speed. He respected Harris's military skills, but doubted his political competence. So he set up a 'Mysore Commission', comprising Arthur Wellesley, Barry Close, John Malcolm and Captain Agnew (Harris's Military secretary), and gave them considerable scope to act on their own.

Second, on 3 March he wrote: 'This day His Majesty's 33rd Regiment of Foot [King's Army] joined the Contingent under the Honble Colonel Arthur Wellesley, who assumed the Command of it, and Colonel Roberts was directed to proceed and join the Grand Army, in which he was appointed to the command of a Native Brigade.'[8] For some time it had been agreed that the Nizam's Contingent needed to be 'stiffened' by a battalion of European troops. Arthur Wellesley's appointment was controversial, because he was superseding several other more senior British officers. But since Meer Alam remained the nominal, and in many respects, the actual commander, the job required diplomatic tact. Arthur Wellesley, supported by his battalion of King's troops, was considered the best candidate for the job. Malcolm had met Mornington and his youngest brother, Henry Wellesley, during their stopover in Madras in April/May 1798. But earlier in that year he had also met Arthur Wellesley.

There was nothing particularly distinguished about Arthur Wellesley at that time; nothing to suggest that over the next fifty years he would become, as the Duke of Wellington, one of the most famous men in the world. He had been sent to Eton, but removed at fifteen after 'showing no sign of academic distinction'. He went to live with his mother in Brussels for a year. Then from January 1786 he learned the rudiments of soldiering as a cadet at the Royal Academy of Equitation at Angers in France. His mother's view was that he was 'food for powder and nothing else'. He was a quiet youth who played the violin and kept a devoted white terrier dog. He spent some years in Ireland as ADC to the Lord Lieutenant. Then at the start of the war against revolutionary France in 1794, his family bought him a majority in the 33rd Regiment of Foot, and a few months later he became, at the age of twenty-three, its Colonel and commanding officer. He acquired a modest military reputation during an unsuccessful British expedition to the Continent in 1794. In the spring of 1796, the 33rd was ordered to India, but Wellesley was convalescing from illness at the time and had to stay behind. By the end of June he had recovered and boarded a Royal Navy frigate, hoping to catch up with the regimental convoy by the time it reached the Cape of Good Hope. The frigate was HMS *Fox*, commanded by Captain Pulteney Malcolm.

Arthur Wellesley arrived at Calcutta in February 1797 and spent the rest of the year there with his regiment, apart from a short, abortive expedition to Penang. Little of his correspondence survives but he does seem to have gained a reputation for having an extremely strong head for drink. The diarist, William Hickey, a lawyer who worked as a Supreme Court clerk in Calcutta, met Wellesley through his friendship with Colonel Sherbrooke, also of the 33rd Foot, and described some epic drinking sessions with him.[9]

But Wellesley was becoming more serious about his profession. While on the ship coming to India he had waded through a heavy diet of improving books. On arrival at Calcutta he had found himself taken up by the Governor-General, Sir John Shore, partly because he was considered an authority on warfare in Europe. Shore was a competent civil servant who had risen through the ranks of the Company by hard work and his local expertise on revenue collection. But he was a man of limited vision and cautious outlook, and moreover, had hardly any powerful contacts in the Government at home. Arthur Wellesley described him as 'a good man, but cold as a greyhound's nose'. At the beginning of 1798 Wellesley took three months leave to visit Madras. He must have met Malcolm and spent some time with him during the visit, though neither mentions the other in correspondence. He went back to Calcutta in early April, and was on hand to welcome Mornington on his arrival there in mid-May.

Arthur Wellesley's appointment in February 1799 as, effectively, the commander of the Nizam's Contingent altered Malcolm's position. On the one hand he was subordinate to Wellesley in a way that he had not previously been to Roberts. On the other hand, as an experienced Madras Army officer, he was in a position to influence the relatively inexperienced King's Army officer. Wellesley had only briefly been in battle in Europe, and not at all in India. He had no experience of dealing with Indian rulers and their *vakeels*. In all this, Malcolm had experience in abundance. So it was to him that Wellesley turned for professional military and diplomatic advice. For the next four months, the two men, both under thirty and born within a day of each other, were in daily contact and worked closely together.

But there was much more to the relationship than that. From the start, the two men became friends. Despite his later reputation as the 'Iron Duke' – General, Prime Minister and European statesman – Wellesley was in fact rather shy, taciturn and introverted. This may perhaps explain why he was fond of women's company. 'Boy' Malcolm, on the other hand, was a typical extrovert: '[he] brought a special lighthearted flavour to Arthur's rather sombre . . . camp. Around him there was always a buzz of lively conversation, an unfailing flow of animal spirits. He got on well with everyone, whether Indian, British, Persian or Afghan. With his amusingly squeaky voice, he was a constant source of fun, always arriving in camp with "a brisk explosion of jokes", and not surprisingly became Arthur's best and lifelong friend.'[10] However, the relationship was not without its tensions. After the campaign was over, Arthur Wellesley wrote to Mornington: 'I do not [insinuate] that Malcolm and I are not upon the very best of terms; but what I mean is that upon one or two occasions he sent me orders which he said came from Meer Allum & which never could have entered into his [Meer Alam's] head, excepting from his own suggestions . . . This is between ourselves.'[11]

The march continued. Arthur Wellesley wrote to his brother Henry in Madras that 'Malcolm is indefatigable. He leads the life of a canister at a dog's tail.'[12] So far the two armies had not had to cope with the enemy. But when they crossed the Mysore border on 5 March, the Mysore cavalry began to make an appearance. The armies moved inexorably on, with occasional dramas, skirmishes, shortages, and conflicting intelligence about Tipu's whereabouts. On 6 March Tipu's main army attacked the Bombay Army contingent, which had just reached the top of the Western Ghats, about thirty miles west of Seringapatam, but was driven off. On 27 March he moved against the Grand Army at Malavelly, to the east, and was again repulsed, with heavy losses. He then retreated to his fortress at Seringapatam, and the combined forces were able to move towards it with relative ease, arriving in the vicinity on 5 April.

The story of the siege of Seringapatam, which lasted until the final assault and the death of Tipu Sultan on 4 May, has been told a hundred times.[13] Malcolm faithfully recorded the daily developments in his journal, but the Nizam's Contingent (apart from Wellesley and his 33rd Regiment, and 200 men from Meer Alam's army) were held in reserve throughout the action. One anecdote, however, does illustrate Malcolm's effervescent bumptiousness: 'On the morning of the final assault on Seringapatam, he entered General Harris's tent in high spirits, and with his accustomed hilarity of manner [anticipating victory and glory for Harris] addressed the Commander-in-Chief as "Lord Harris". The General gravely answered that it was too serious an occasion for a jest.'[14]

At the end of that day he made one triumphant final entry in his journal:

> This day will ever be celebrated in India for the accomplishment of one of the grandest and most important achievements, whether considered in a military or political point of view that has ever occurred. It is the storm and capture of Seringapatam. In a military point of view [when] it is considered that this Army with all its immense equipment left Madras only [three] months ago, and is now in possession of Seringapatam, a Fort so prodigiously strong both by art and nature, the highest [acclaim] must be bestowed on the Valour and Skill of the troops who achieved it . . . In a political point of view its advantages are incalculable as it affords us the means of securing and confirming our Power and Influence in the Deckhan beyond the chance of risk.[15]

And Harris did him proud in his official report to the Governor-General. He extolled Malcolm's conduct, and in particular praised 'his peculiar talent for conciliating the *Sirdars* of the allied force, and directing their exertions to objects of general utility in a manner foreign to their habits of service'.[16]

The 'Mysore Commission', which had clarified the political strategy and smoothed the diplomatic path between the allies during the march and the siege, was now replaced by a 'Peace Commission' to supervise the settlement of the conquered territories. Its nominal head was General Harris, but its working membership comprised Arthur Wellesley and Barry Close from the previous commission, with William Kirkpatrick and Henry Wellesley joining them from Madras at the end of May. John Malcolm and Thomas Munro were made joint secretaries to the Commission. The members have been described as 'the largest number of men of genius ever assembled at the same board in India, before or since'.[17] This was probably going a bit far, but they were perhaps the ablest half dozen men in British India at the time.

Their task was a little easier than in 1792, because this time Tipu was dead, the Nizam's forces had played only a subordinate role, and the Mahrattas had contributed practically nothing (apart from refraining from attacking Hyderabad in the absence of most of the Nizam's army). Nevertheless, the Commission took only five weeks to complete the process – an amazing achievement, given the need to report back to Madras and Hyderabad with the slow means of communication available at the time. The chief issues were how Mysore should be governed in future and how to divide the spoils of victory. The Commission, with Mornington's approval and Meer Alam's acquiescence, decided that the Hindu Wadeyar dynasty, which had been ousted by Tipu's father, Hyder Ali, in 1760, should be restored to the *musnud* (throne). Purneah, the *Brahmin* who had been Tipu's Treasurer and right-hand man, was made the *Dewan* (Chief Minister). The division of the spoils involved delicate negotiations with Meer Alam, acting on behalf of the Nizam's government. The British, still obsessed with the fear of a French invasion, took the Canara region on the Malabar coast, and the fertile Baramahal district. The Nizam was given some more territory adjoining Hyderabad, and the Mahrattas, the smaller areas of Bednore and Soond (though on certain conditions which they understandably refused to accept so the area was later taken back by the British).

Throughout June 1799 Malcolm was heavily occupied, acting as the Commission's de facto liaison officer with Meer Alam. Every few days he wrote to Mornington at Madras, apprising him of the latest developments in the Meer's reaction to the Commission's proposals. By early July the Commission had completed its work and disbanded. Arthur Wellesley was left in overall control of Seringapatam and Barry Close was appointed British Resident to the new Maharajah.

Meer Alam was keen to travel to Madras to meet Mornington before returning to Hyderabad. As the commander of the Nizam's army in the victorious Mysore campaign, he knew he had gained tremendous kudos; a meeting with the Governor-General would give him even more. He set off for Madras on 3 July, leaving the Contingent to make its own way slowly back to Hyderabad. But soon after reaching Madras he fell ill, and when Malcolm joined him there a few days later his condition was so serious that his formal introduction to Mornington had to be postponed. His illness may have been the first sign of the leprosy which gradually consumed his body over the next ten years. Malcolm assumed that as soon as the Meer's meeting with Mornington had been completed, he and the Meer would go on together to Hyderabad, and he would resume his duties as the Assistant Resident. So did James Kirkpatrick.[18] But, unknown to Kirkpatrick and to Malcolm himself, the Governor-General had other plans for him. On 1 August, Mornington called him in and told him that he was appointing him to lead a diplomatic mission to the Court of Fath Ali Shah, ruler of Persia.

PART THREE

Diplomat

CHAPTER SIX

Envoy to Persia, 1799

Malcolm's was in many ways a suitable appointment. He had dealt with the Courts of oriental Muslim rulers for several years. He had mastered Persian,[1] the Court language in Hyderabad. But above all he had that vital ingredient for the leader of any negotiating team: the complete confidence of his boss back at headquarters. Despite his autocratic ways, one of Mornington's great attributes as a leader was to give wholehearted support to his trusted lieutenants and allow them considerable room for manoeuvre in their negotiations. No doubt wanting to test Malcolm's mettle, he asked him to prepare a paper outlining the recent history of Persia. Three weeks later Malcolm duly submitted a memorandum entitled 'The Rise and Progress of Baba Khan' (an alternative name for Fath Ali Shah).[2]

For Malcolm the appointment was hugely exciting. Hitherto he had been given roles of considerable and increasing responsibility. But now, aged just thirty, he was to be the Company's fully accredited leader of a major diplomatic mission to the Court of the Shah of Persia. 'John is in the clouds,' wrote Pulteney (whose ship was in Madras at the time) to their sister Nancy at Burnfoot. 'A Persian Envoy. Myself and friends have been using our best endeavours to convince him that it is incompatible with the diplomatick character to laugh and play the Boy, but [our] advice is thrown away, and we in our turns are laughed at – he is the most extraordinary man – his spirits and good humour never forsake him.'[3]

He wrote ecstatic letters to two of his old mentors: to General Ross[4] and to Sir John Kennaway, now living in retirement in Devon. To Kennaway he talked of his opportunity, and said that if the mission was successful, 'it will be attended with more reputation than I could hope to attain in this quarter. To relieve India from the annual alarms of Zirman [Zaman] Shah's invasion which is always attended with serious expenses to the Company . . . [and] to counteract the possible attempts of those villainous but active Democrats the French.'[5] To Jonathan Duncan, the Governor of Bombay, who had direct oversight of the Company's commercial activities in Persia, he wrote: 'I am now at

Jonathan Duncan (1756–1811), Governor of Bombay (1794–1811).

liberty to acquaint you that Lord Mornington has named me Envoy to the Court of Persia – a distinction which I hope to merit by zealous exertions.'[6] To William Kirkpatrick, who was to be his 'head office' contact at Calcutta, he submitted a draft budget for the mission, estimating that 'the additional expenses of personnel will be Rs 8780 per month'.[7] And of course he also wrote home to Burnfoot. He told Mina that he was taking full advantage of the opportunity to include on his mission staff as many of his own family and fellow Scottish Borderers as possible. His first choice was his young cousin Charles Pasley.[8] Charles had stayed with him in 1798 for his first few months in Madras,[9] and had taken part in the Mysore campaign, acting as Malcolm's assistant on the Seringapatam Peace Commission before being appointed Brigade Major to the Nizam's Contingent at Seringapatam.[10] Malcolm also chose Gilbert Briggs[11] as the mission's surgeon. From outside the family he chose Captain William Campbell as first assistant; Lieutenant John Colebrooke, a cavalry officer in the Madras Army, as commander of the Escort; William Hollingbery as writer; and Richard Strachey as assistant. Hollingbery was a protégé of William Kirkpatrick, and later wrote frequent letters to him from Persia. Strachey was one of the many Stracheys to serve in India, and extremely well connected. His father, Sir Henry, was an East India Company director, and had been Robert Clive's secretary in 1764. Malcolm was the oldest member of the mission team. Four were in their twenties, and Pasley and Strachey were only nineteen.

By early September, the delightful pastime of pencilling in mission staff appointments for friends and relations came to an end. It was time to proceed to Bombay to board a ship to Persia. On 5 September the Governor-General set sail for Calcutta in the *Chiffone*,[12] and two days later Malcolm and his party set off overland for Hyderabad with Meer Alam. He had left Hyderabad a year earlier in a hurry; much of his heavy baggage had been left there, and he had unsettled personal accounts to clear. Moreover, there were issues relating to the Nizam's Contingent in the Mysore War, such as distribution of prize money. These matters needed clearing up in Hyderabad before he could proceed to Bombay and board a ship for Persia.

Meer Alam, accompanied by Malcolm and his party, reached Hyderabad on 11 October. The Meer, as expected, received a hero's welcome. 'The Nizam ordered a reception party to greet him outside the city, and sent his personal elephant for him to make a triumphal entry.' As a local chronicler put it, 'when Mir Alam returned from Seringapatam his fame reached the skies'.[13]

But beneath the surface 'the moment of triumph was also the beginning of his downfall, as courtiers itched with envy and started plotting his downfall'.[14] Much more important than the envy of mere courtiers, however, was that the Meer was beginning to incur the jealousy of his erstwhile mentor, the Prime Minister, Aristu Jah, and even of the Nizam himself.

After the victory at Seringapatam, these two had seen themselves enjoying up to half of the spoils of the whole state of Mysore – after all, had not Hyderabad provided half the army? While they waited for the results of the Peace Commission negotiations, their expectations soared beyond the dreams of cupidity. But in the event the British allocated only a small portion of the Mysore State to themselves and to the Nizam; and left the bulk to the restored Hindu Wadeyar Maharajah. Although this might ostensibly have seemed fair, the British had cunningly arranged the terms so that the Maharaja would be under their influence and, indirectly, under their control. The Nizam and Aristu Jah regarded this as a British trick and blamed Meer Alam for acquiescing in the arrangement; and moreover for doing so without prior reference back to Hyderabad (the Meer had signed the Treaty with his own seal). Besides, they had learned that the British had rewarded the Meer with a substantially increased pension, which they considered to be a bribe for his acquiescence. Aristu Jah felt that he too should have received a pension (the drawback with bribes is that they so often excite envy in those who have *not* received them). Finally, there were dark rumours that the Meer had got his hands on some of Tipu's jewels; this again excited their envy. James Kirkpatrick had anticipated these developments, and had written to his brother about it. Malcolm, too, had noticed the Meer's apparently 'insatiable thirst for gold, that led him to peculate to an enormous amount during his command of the Contingent'.[15]

A year earlier, when Malcolm had left Hyderabad, he could hardly have anticipated that it would take him all those months to get back to his base. And now he was going off again, probably for good this time, first to Persia, and then – who knew? A letter from William Kirkpatrick in Calcutta set out his instructions for the Persian mission in more detail, urging him in no uncertain terms to get moving.[16] He answered respectfully, but a little testily, that:

> I am as desirous of getting forward as soon as possible, but when you consider that my late situation not only occasioned my having accounts to settle with your brother [i.e. James Kirkpatrick] to the amount of six or seven lakhs of rupees, but with this Circar [*sirdar*] for double the sum, and with three thousand men [the Hyderabad contingent in the Mysore War] for their prize money and clothing, you will allow, that if I leave Hyderabad in twelve days after having satisfied all parties, and with a clear reputation, I shall have made my escape from the complicated concerns in which I have been engaged in as speedy and as happy a manner as could be expected.[17]

There were other complications. Accompanying Malcolm and Meer Alam in the march to Seringapatam earlier in the year had been the Meer's first cousin, Baqar Ali Khan, whom the Meer had appointed paymaster to the Nizam's Contingent. Baqar was an elderly Persian, originally from Shushtar,[18] 'a very jolly conversible man, and . . . a mighty pleasant companion, since he has all the anacreontic tribe [of Persian poetry] at his finger ends. He drinks (under the rose) three glasses of wine after dinner, provided there be no black-visaged lookers on; and among the ladies is a very gallant fellow.'[19] Malcolm had made friends with Baqar and thought he would be just the right person to take with him on his Persian mission. At first Baqar had been enthusiastic, but when he heard that Mehdi Ali Khan, the Company's Resident at Bushire (a seaport on the south coast of Persia), was going to be involved, he backed off quickly. Mehdi, originally a Persian from a distinguished Khorasan family, had fled to India in the late 1770s, first to Hyderabad, then to Lucknow, then to Benares, where he became a protégé of Jonathan Duncan. At Hyderabad he had been involved in a robbery scandal, and had been banished by Aristu Jah.

Thus Mehdi, the Company's current envoy to the Shah, representing in effect the British nation, had been found, on evidence from an impeccable source, to be an absolute rogue, though not unlike quite a few rogues, he was also a man of 'ability, charm and vanity'.[20] Not only was Malcolm's first choice as Persian 'adviser' (Baqar Ali) not available, but the hitherto obvious second choice (Mehdi) was not respectable.

Another problem to be sorted out in a hurry was the question of Malcolm's salary and allowances during the period of the mission. There were virtually no precedents for his situation.

Despite these frantic preparations there was still time for entertainment. During the Mysore campaign Malcolm had become very friendly with both Meer Alam and Baqar Ali. Indeed, the Meer had Malcolm to thank for much of his military success. So, on 18 October, Meer Alam arranged a grand *nautch* party at his house. Malcolm was guest of honour. Performing at the *nautch* was the Meer's current mistress, Mah Laqa Bai Chanda. 'A most remarkable woman', as Malcolm later described her. She was a celebrated dancer and courtesan and the first major female Urdu poet at the Hyderabad Court. At one time or another, her lovers had allegedly also included Aristu Jah and even Nizam Ali himself – the first of his two strokes in 1801 was said to have been precipitated by his becoming overexcited by Chanda's dancing.

In the middle of her dance, Chanda approached Malcolm and presented him with a *diwan* (book) of her poems.[21] What would Meer Alam have thought of such a gesture? Perhaps he had asked her to make it, as a compliment to Malcolm. Perhaps he had even asked her to make a public gesture which was meant to be followed up later in private. Perhaps the gesture came entirely from Mah Laqa herself – her standing at Court was quite sufficient for her to act on her own. It is tempting to speculate that Malcolm may at one time or another have been her lover. Although she was five years older than him, they had both been around in Hyderabad between 1790 and 1794. But any such intimate liaison during Malcolm's short stay in Hyderabad in 1799 seems highly unlikely.[22] The Shustari family bestowed another mark of honour on Malcolm, when Baqar Ali invited him to his *deori* (courtyard house) and introduced him to the women of the family. This made him a sort of honorary member of the family.

Having cleared up his affairs at Hyderabad (more or less), and incidentally polished off another forty-page report to the Governor-General on 'The Background and History of Hyderabad, mainly from 1786 to the Present',[23] it was time for Malcolm and his party to resume the journey to Bombay.

He took a month to cover the 500-odd miles to Bombay, pausing briefly at Poona en route. When he reached Poona, the Mahratta capital and seat of the Peshwah, he found it to be a virtual armed camp. The current Peshwah, Baji Rao II, may have been nominally in charge, but he was surrounded by Mahratta Chieftains with their own armies. Dowlat Rao Scindiah of Gwalior was camped nearby with 8,000 infantry and 10,000 cavalry; Jaswunt Rao Holkar of Indore had 9,000–12,000; while Lurchman Bhye of Baroda was about thirty miles away with a further 12,000 horse. Malcolm stayed with the Company's Resident, General William Palmer, and his Delhi *Begum* wife, Fyze Baksh, in the Residency compound at the *sangam* (confluence) of the Mula and Musa rivers. Palmer took him to meet the Peshwah, with whom he was to have such a fateful relationship over the following eighteen years. After a few days he pressed on to Bombay, as usual engaging in animated conversation with anyone he met, from local Chiefs to palanquin carriers. His curiosity was insatiable.

Arriving at Bombay on 1 December, he was met by Governor Duncan's mountain of briefs on the Company's political and commercial affairs in Persia and the Gulf, and further elaborate instructions from Calcutta. There were the usual logistical problems to be sorted out – ships, stores and presents for the Persian Court. Then there were rumours, the most worrying being that Fath Ali Shah had died. This rumour had reached Fort William, prompting a message from the Governor-General that if this proved correct, Malcolm was not to embark. Another rumour, from Persia, was that the Company's representative in Bushire, Mehdi Ali Khan, was dead. They both proved false.

By 26 December, Malcolm was able to write to William Kirkpatrick that he had completed his preparations and was intending to embark the following day in the frigate *Bombay*, accompanied by his staff of six officers. The brig *Harrington* was to follow, carrying most of the escort, the servants and the baggage. They were held up by last-minute repairs to the ship, but on 29 December 1799 they finally sailed out of Bombay harbour.

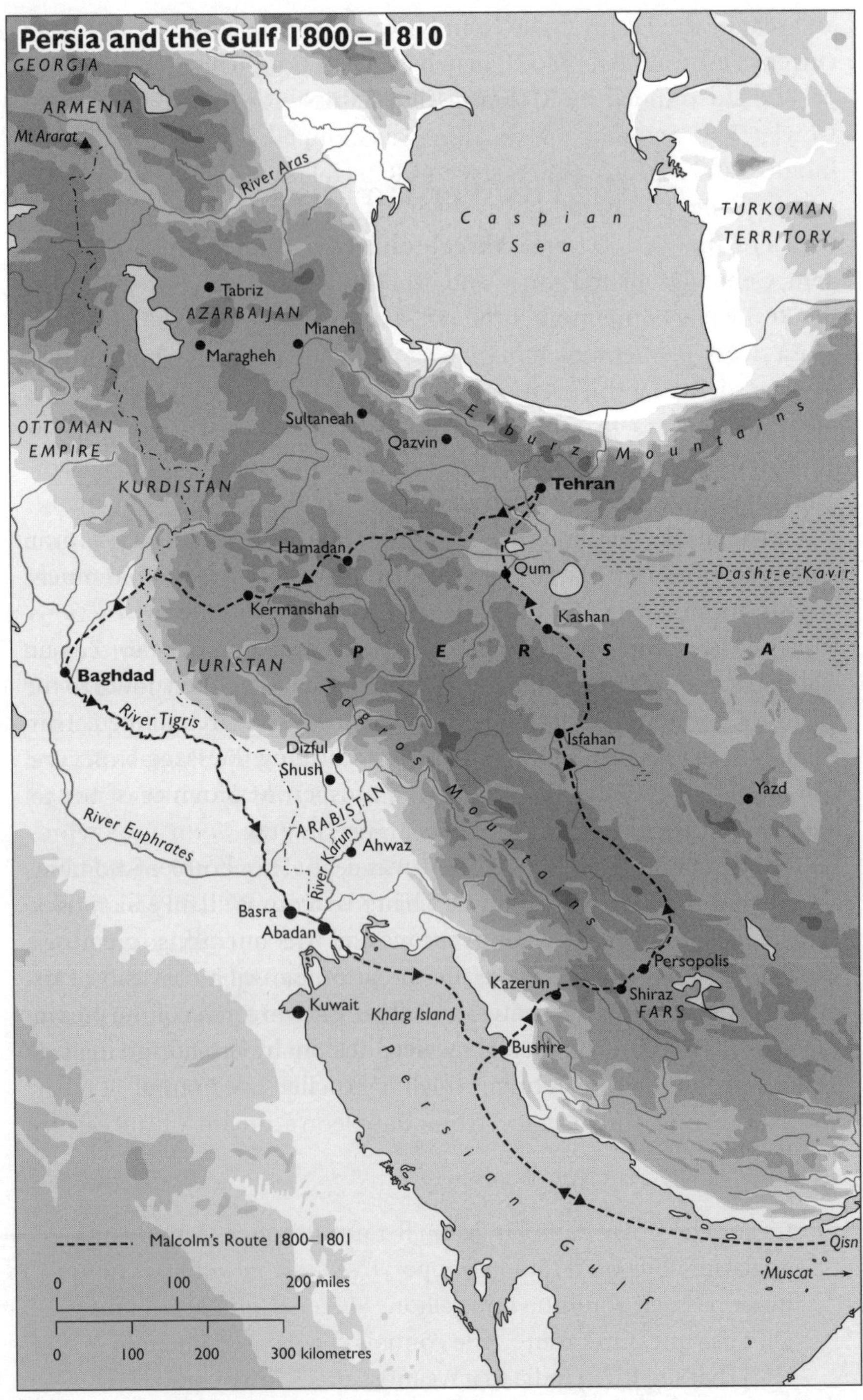
Persia and the Gulf 1800 – 1810
GEORGIA
ARMENIA
Mt Ararat
River Aras
Caspian Sea
TURKOMAN TERRITORY
Tabriz
AZARBAIJAN
Mianeh
Maragheh
Sultaneah
Qazvin
Elburz Mountains
OTTOMAN EMPIRE
KURDISTAN
Tehran
Hamadan
Qum
Dasht-e-Kavir
Kermanshah
Kashan
PERSIA
Baghdad
LURISTAN
Zagros Mountains
River Tigris
Isfahan
Dizful
Shush
Yazd
River Euphrates
ARABISTAN
River Karun
Ahwaz
Basra
Abadan
Persopolis
Kazerun
Shiraz
FARS
Kuwait
Kharg Island
Bushire
Persian Gulf
Malcolm's Route 1800–1801
0 100 200 miles
0 100 200 300 kilometres
Qisn
Muscat

CHAPTER SEVEN

The First Persian Mission, 1800–1801

Until the 1790s, the Company's interest in Persia had been mainly commercial. Thereafter, however, as the Company's political power in India increased, it became concerned about perceived external threats to its position.

The most immediate threat came from the Afghan ruler, Zaman Shah. For centuries the Afghans had periodically swooped down to the plains of Hindustan in search of plunder. Between 1792 and 1797 Zaman Shah had crossed the Indus three times, ravaging the Punjab. Beyond the Punjab to the east, the Company's prosperous province of Bengal made an enticing prospect for these Afghan raiders.

In September 1798, Jonathan Duncan, the Governor of Bombay, sensing the danger, sent Mehdi Ali Khan to encourage the Persian ruler, Fath Ali Shah, to attack Herat in the west of Afghanistan, so creating a diversion which would reduce the threat of an Afghan invasion eastwards over the western frontier of Bengal.[1] Mehdi arrived at Bushire in December 1798, and eventually received the Shah's *farman*, giving him permission to travel to Tehran, which he reached late in 1799.

The second threat came from Napoleon's dream of an eastern empire.

> C'est cela! C'est dans l'Inde qu'il faut attaquer la puissance anglaise! Voila ou il faut la frapper. La Russie ne veut pas nous livrer passage pour que nous allions en Perse. Eh bien, il faut y aller par une autre route. Je le connais et je la prendrai, moi.
>
> [That's it! It's in India that we must attack British power. This

> is how we'll hit them. The Russians won't give us passage through to Persia. So we will have to go by another route. I know it, and I will take it.][2]

So cried Napoleon, in 1797 or early 1798, when the French expedition to Egypt was being planned. About the same time Talleyrand, the French Foreign Minister, suggested to the Directory that with Egypt occupied and fortified, they could sail from Suez with a force of 15,000 men to India, and there join forces with Tipu Sultan of Mysore to fight the British. Soon afterwards the French successfully invaded Egypt, and the Calcutta Government thought it possible that Napoleon might try to invade India via Persia. We now know that he did indeed have such an ambition, and although we also now know that such an expedition would have been wildly impractical, the ignorance of the British about the geography and climate of Persia at that time was enough to make them fearful. After the French fleet was destroyed by Admiral Nelson at Aboukir Bay on 15 August, the French army was stranded, cut off from its base in France. Napoleon may have been shattered, but he nevertheless still dreamt of expelling the British from India. He rallied his troops: 'Nous n'avons pas de flotte; eh bien! Il faut rester ici ou en sortir grands comme les anciens!' [We haven't got a fleet. Very well, we must either stay here, or leave here in style, like the Ancients!][3] Imagining himself as a reincarnation of Alexander the Great, he planned to march in Alexander's footsteps through Palestine, Syria, Mesopotamia and Persia, en route to India. He left Cairo on 20 February, but when he reached the fortress of St Jean d'Acre in Palestine a month later, he was held up by a Turkish army, supported by a British naval force under Commodore Sidney Smith. After two months the French army had failed to storm the fortress, and was suffering from the plague. Napoleon was forced to call off the siege and return to Egypt. His dream of an overland expedition to India was finished.

These two threats – from the Afghans and the French – had persuaded the Governor-General to send a fully fledged diplomatic mission to Tehran. In October 1799 Malcolm had received detailed instructions for his mission from Calcutta. The ostensible objectives were similar to those given earlier to Mehdi Ali Khan, namely to promote goodwill and improve trade between Persia and the Company. But in reality they were, firstly, to prevent Zaman Shah of Afghanistan from invading Hindustan and, secondly, to get the Shah to 'act vigorously and heartily' against the French in the event of their 'attempting at any time to penetrate to India by any route in which it may be practical for the Shah to oppose their progress'.[4] He was to persuade the Shah to invade Afghanistan from the west, thus hopefully preventing Zaman Shah from invading the Company's territory in Hindustan. In consideration of this, the Company would renounce any claim to a portion of Afghan territory annexed by Persia, and would provide an annual subsidy of three lakhs.[5] The method of payment of the subsidy and the handling of the French issue was left to Malcolm's discretion. A political treaty with a duration of three years and a commercial treaty of indefinite duration should be negotiated. Significantly, preventing the Afghans from invading Hindustan was considered far more urgent and important than stopping the French. While en route to Persia, Malcolm was to call briefly at Muscat and get the Imam, Sultan Ibn Ahmed, to renounce all connection with the French.

The *Bombay* and the *Harrington*, carrying the mission party, arrived at Muscat on 7 January 1800. Ibn Ahmed was away at sea, chasing pirates. Malcolm first sought advice from the Company's resident Indian broker, 'a shrewd old Banian, with all the interested selfishness of his tribe',[6] who told him that Ibn Ahmed had flirted with the French but was now more favourably disposed towards the British. He then exchanged visits with the Governor, Seyyid Seif Mohammed, who had visited Bombay many times and knew the British well. Aware that Calcutta wanted him to ensure that the Imam would renounce any connection with the French, and perhaps interpreting his instructions a little too enthusiastically, Malcolm launched into a rather hectoring lecture, pointing out to the Governor how much stronger the British in India had become in the last few years; how the French had been ousted from the entire Indian Ocean apart from Mauritius; and how Tipu Sultan of Mysore had flirted with the French, in contravention of his 1792 treaty obligations with the Company, and had been dethroned and killed as a consequence. The Governor assured him that all was well and that the Imam would respond favourably to his overtures.

A few days later the mission party left Muscat and sailed up through the mouth of the Gulf in search of the Imam. They eventually found him anchored at a small island between Qishm and Anjam. 'The Imam has a navy which is by no means contemptible – five cruisers, three of which have more than twenty guns, and twenty more at Muscat. He has taken possession of almost every island in the Guelph that can facilitate the commerce of his country.'[7] Malcolm was received by the Imam on the quarterdeck of his frigate. He presented formal letters from the Governor-General, and produced presents: 'an elegant watch set with diamonds, a silver ornamented clock, a gold enamelled creese [dagger], a double barrelled gun, a pair of pistols [and] a spying glass'; and for the Imam's two sons, aged ten and eight, 'a model of a 50 gun ship, a curious hunting knife and a tortoise-shell case, containing instruments and a hunting knife'.[8] The Imam was quite happy to agree to all the Company's proposals and a suitable treaty was signed on 18 January. Its most tangible outcome was the placing of a British Resident at Muscat. The man chosen was a young Bombay physician, Dr Bogle (but the Muscat climate proved unkind to Dr Bogle, and he died there a year later). Malcolm proudly reported the news of the Treaty to the Governor-General and to William Kirkpatrick in Calcutta; also directly to Henry Dundas, and to the Company's Secret Committee in London. He then chose to sail up the Gulf coast to Bushire and to travel overland to Tehran via Shiraz and Isfahan, rather than via Basra and Baghdad, as originally planned.

Persia had hitherto been regarded by the British as

> a remote, fabulous country, difficult of access, of some commercial but minor political importance . . . Little was known of Persia's immense size and her great contrasts of scenery and climate. The country lay isolated behind the high walls of the Zagros mountains to the south and west and of the Elburz range to the north. To the east the desert and stark hills merged with the sands of Afghanistan and Baluchistan. A traveller entering the country by way of Russia and the Caspian Sea would be impressed by the dense jungle and forests that clothed the hills along the Caspian shore; if he first landed in the south at one of the Persian Gulf ports he would note the barrenness and immense heat of the palm fringed coastal plains. Only after climbing steep mountain passes to the high central plateau would he find himself in the heart of Persia. Here he would discover a great expanse of salt and sandy desert around whose edges lay oasis towns and villages of sun-dried brick and flat

> roofs, against which the green of slender poplar and tall walnut and plane trees stood in vivid contrast. Water, a perennial problem, was brought to them in long underground conduits or *qanats*, whose lines, like a series of giant ant-heaps, ran across the desert from the surrounding hills where the water had accumulated. In summer the heat was great everywhere but on the plateau the air was dry and the nights cool; in winter snow fell and blocked the mountain passes. The sun seemed to shine through the year in a cloudless sky and gave a crystalline quality to the light of the plateau.[9]

Bushire was inhabited almost entirely by Arabs and presided over by an Arab, Sheik Nasser, who was only loosely under the control of the central government in Tehran and the Governor of the Fars province based at Shiraz.

They 'were met on the beach by the whole population',[10] and the mission set up a tented camp outside the town. Its first task was to acquire horses, both for the envoy and his suite and for the detachment of Indian cavalry which had come unmounted, knowing that they could find Gulf Arab and Persian Galloway horses (also called *yaboos*) of better quality than in the whole of India. For some weeks the camp 'looked like a fair for horses and mules'.[11]

Although Malcolm's destination was Tehran, 768 miles further north, he could not just set off; he had to wait at Bushire for an invitation from the Shah. The whole exercise took more than three months. The practice of the Persian Court was to attach an official, called a *mehmandar*, a diplomatic 'meeter and greeter', to such missions, to make sure that it was properly looked after; also, incidentally, to obtain intelligence about it and report back. The *mehmandar* attached to Malcolm's mission was Mohamed Sheriff Khan, Chief of the Burgashattees, a small Turkish-speaking tribe. Malcolm quickly realised that Persians were quite ignorant about Europeans, but were 'a very keen and observing people, and full of curiosity. In the absence of books, they will peruse us, and from what they hear and see, form their opinion of our country.'[12] His strategy was therefore to ensure that the *mehmandar* formed an impression of the British as a hardworking, tireless and persistent people so that the Persians would never feel that they could wear them down or, in their impatience to achieve tangible results, lead them to make unnecessary concessions in negotiation. The success of this strategy may be gauged from a report prepared by Mohamed Sheriff Khan which many years later he showed to Malcolm:[13]

> The *Elchee* [envoy, i.e. Malcolm] and the English gentlemen with him rise at dawn of day: they mount their horses and ride for two or three hours, when they come back home and breakfast. From that time till four o'clock, when they dine, the *Elchee* is either looking at horses, conversing, reading, or writing; he never lies down, and, if he has nothing else to do, he walks backwards and forwards before his tent door, or within it. He sits but a short time at dinner, mounts his horse again in the evening, and when returned from his ride, takes tea, after which he converses, or plays cards till ten o'clock, when he retires to rest; and next day pursues nearly the same course.
>
> What I chiefly remark is, that neither he nor any of the gentlemen sleep during the day, nor do they ever, when the weather is warm, recline upon carpets as we do. They are certainly very restless persons; but when it is considered that these habits cause them employing so much more time every day in business, and in acquiring knowledge, than His Majesty's subjects, it is evident that at the end of a year they must have some advantage.[14]

While cooped up at Bushire, there was plenty of time for discussion of diplomatic strategy. Malcolm corresponded with the Company's three representatives in the region –Samuel Manesty in Basra, Harford Jones in Baghdad, and Mehdi Ali Khan, now on his way back to Bushire from Tehran via Baghdad and Basra.

Manesty had joined the East India Company as a writer in 1779. He was sent to Basra in 1781 and became the Company's Resident there in 1784. He was assisted by Harford Jones, then a twenty-year-old Company writer transferred from Benares. Jones was descended from two prominent families in the Welsh border country – the Harfords from Herefordshire and the Joneses from Radnorshire. Before coming to India he had trained briefly as a jeweller in London. Like Manesty, he acquired an Armenian mistress, Maria Goorjee, who bore him three daughters, but unlike Manesty, he did not marry her. In the 1780s he twice visited

Persia, with Mohammed Nabee Khan[15] as his *munshi*. In late 1795 he became ill and had to return to England. In London he was lucky enough to meet Henry Dundas, the Secretary of State for War and the all-powerful President of the Board of Control from 1793 to 1801, at a very opportune moment – just after Napoleon's invasion of Egypt in 1798. Dundas was worried about eastern ambitions. Impressed by Jones's knowledge of the region, he appointed him to the new post of Resident at Baghdad to watch and report on the developing situation there and to counter French influence with the Turkish Pasha. Dundas did this entirely on his own initiative without consulting the Court of Directors or the Governor-General. Jones thus became a personal protégé of Dundas and later of Dundas's son Robert, who was President of the Board of Control from 1807 to 1811. This was a major step forward in Jones's career, but the manner of his appointment was to store up future trouble for him. Manesty was understandably miffed at being superseded by his junior, and thereafter worked relentlessly to undermine Jones's position. Meanwhile Calcutta Government officials, though for the time being treating 'Baghdad Jones' with amused disdain, became in due course intensely jealous of his direct line of communication to Dundas in London. Jones returned to Baghdad in late September 1798.

Both Manesty and Jones opposed the Calcutta Government's strategy of encouraging Persia to attack Afghanistan as a way of diverting the Afghans from plundering India. They felt that a direct approach and subsidy to Zaman Shah would be cheaper and more likely to succeed. They were also sceptical of the Shah's willingness, let alone his ability, to do as the Governor-General wanted. Manesty felt that the Persian Government was not worth much British time or money. Malcolm had been aware of Jones's views before he left India and had strongly opposed them.[16] With Manesty he was more circumspect, acknowledging his arguments but rejecting his case for an embassy to Kabul, chiefly on the ground that Afghan rulers were compulsive plunderers and thus impossible to hold to any agreement. But when he closed with the observation about the Governor-General that 'my recognition of his extraordinary judgment has always led me to be more solicitous about carrying out his orders than investigating their propriety',[17] Manesty responded bravely that 'really great men listen to all suggestions with attention and frequently benefit very essentially from the wisdom of their conduct in doing so'.[18] Events were to prove Jones and Manesty wrong about the relative strength and stability of the Afghan and Persian governments. Zaman Shah of Afghanistan was driven from his throne in 1801 and anarchy ensued, while the Qajar dynasty in Persia lasted, more or less, for another 125 years.

Mehdi Ali Khan arrived back at Bushire on 3 May. He had left Tehran at the end of December and stopped en route at Baghdad and Basra. In some ways Mehdi had done well. He had persuaded the Persian Government to act against the Afghans without having to give away any of the financial inducements which he had been authorised to offer. The trouble with Mehdi as an envoy representing a European government in Persia was that he was a Persian, using Persian methods of diplomacy. The result was confusing to both sides in the negotiations. The British did not trust him because he was a Persian (there was an element of racial prejudice here), likely to be prone to 'intrigue, falsehood and collusion . . . ever disposed to sacrifice the public interests to views of private ambition and individual profit'.[19] They were also dismayed by his 'phenomenal mendacity, though faithfully executed in his employer's interest'.[20] The Persians did not trust him either – precisely *because* he was a Persian. An example of the confusion this could cause was when Mehdi carried a letter to the Shah from Jonathan Duncan. Fearing that Duncan's letter was too candid and might encourage the Persians to increase their demands for financial assistance, he decided that the wording of the letter should be revised. He managed to open the envelope without breaking the seal, and to substitute a letter of his own which he thought more appropriately worded. This sort of initiative may have improved the British negotiating position, but it hardly appealed to British officials. Nor did his behaviour at Shiraz in September 1799 when he came upon two envoys from Tipu Sultan of Mysore. Not realising that Tipu was already dead, he arranged to have the envoys assaulted and severely flogged, and even threatened to remove an eye from one of them. This might have produced the desired effect of 'shock and awe' among the Persians of Shiraz but, as Jonathan Duncan rather pompously pointed out, it was 'inconsistent with the decorum due to your public character and exceeded the bounds of moderation and humanity for which the English nation have ever been conspicuous, more especially towards a subdued and prostrate enemy'.[21] Malcolm was already becoming aware of this Persian characteristic of embroidery and exaggeration, remarking, half-jokingly, in a letter to William Kirkpatrick 'I never was so sensible of the Beauty of Truth as since I entered this land of Falsehood.'[22] To Mehdi's great disappointment, Malcolm decided not to include him in the party going to Tehran.

For the next three months there was a battle of wills with the Governor of Fars Province in Shiraz over Malcolm's status as envoy. The Governor claimed to regard the East India Company as merely 'a Company of Merchants' and of subordinate status to the Shah. Malcolm, on the other hand, was determined to be received as the representative of a sovereign power. When the Persian reply came back from Shiraz in early March, Malcolm returned it, politely observing that it was in the form of a *farman*, such as a ruler would issue to his subjects. He pointed out that the Shah had been prepared to correspond with Tipu Sultan of Mysore as an equal and that the Governor-General ruled over a much larger territory than Tipu ever had. A lengthy debate by correspondence was only brought to an end by the return of Malcolm's *munshi* on 13 May with an appropriately welcoming letter of authority from the Shah, which he 'received . . . with great state'.[23]

By 23 May the mission party was at last able to leave Bushire. The envoy's suite that set off on the road to Tehran was several times larger than the party that had arrived at Bushire four months previously, and now amounted to 498 people.[24] The party made its way across the barren coastal plain, then climbed through the mountains to Kazeroon where, as the erudite Hollingbery described it, they came upon

> several streams of water which rush from the Mountains, and which are strongly impregnated with naptha. We were informed that the inhabitants apply the oily mineral, which they skim off the stagnate part of these streams to medicinal purposes, and also use it in their lamps.
>
> Such are the lamps, according to our immortal poet, that illuminate the infernal regions:
>
> From the arched Roof,
> Pendent by subtle magic, many a row
> Of starry lamps and blazing cressets, fed
> With Naptha and Asphaltes; yielded lights
> As from a sky.[25]

An early indication of Iran's oil wealth to come, a century later.

They reached Shiraz on 15 June, and were met 'five miles from the city by several chiefs, and attended . . . to my tents, where I had the honour of entertaining them'.[26] Malcolm had been offered accommodation in a palace, but preferred to stay in a tented camp on the outskirts. This grand reception convinced Malcolm that the Shah wanted to cultivate the British; partly, he wrote to the Governor-General, to 'fix his wavering subjects to obedience.'

The Governor of Shiraz, Fath Ali's twelve-year-old son Hussein Ali Mirza, was surrounded by a retinue of tutors and other advisers. Before Malcolm could be received by the Prince in audience, there were more petty disputes over ceremonial – what was termed *Kyda Nushest-oo-Berkust* ('the art of sitting and rising').[27] Malcolm insisted on being treated with the courtesies due to the representative of a sovereign power, and when these were not at first forthcoming, threatened to leave Shiraz without an audience and to report the matter to the Shah in Tehran. At this point the Court gave in and received Malcolm with fulsome compliments and lavish entertainment. This insistence on being treated correctly may seem petty, but Malcolm's reasoning was that it was better to insist on his rights at the first opportunity; otherwise the same silly disputes would follow him round the country

Six days later he was again received by the Prince. Now was the moment that the courtiers had been waiting for – the distribution of presents. To the Prince, Malcolm gave 'watches and pistols; mirrors and telescopes; shawls and table lustres; knives and toothpicks; filigree boxes and umbrellas; cloths and muslins; chintz; and an unlimited supply of sugar [27,000 pounds] and sugar-candy [two tubs]'.[28] The Persian courtiers treated these presents like money: before Malcolm had even left the room, the Prince was redistributing some of the presents to the courtiers, who 'had a habit of asking the price of every article'.[29]

From the outset a problem troubling Malcolm was how much money he should spend in fitting out the mission party, and how lavish the presents distributed to Persian dignitaries should be. The difficulty was that 'face' was the key to success in oriental diplomacy. Magnificence did matter for the Persians. Still, he was enjoying himself. Apart from the constant 'forms, feasts and intrigues . . . I am trying to get some good books, but the task is difficult. There are few modern writers of celebrity, and the ancient authors are to be procured both cheaper and better in India. If this country ever again enjoys repose, it will overflow, as usual, with poetical productions. The men appear to me all poets. Their conversation is elegant, pointed and witty; and was it not too often spoilt by flattery, would be the pleasantest in the world.'[30]

Persians have always been great *raconteurs* and Malcolm loved noting down and retelling the endless comic anecdotes he heard. Their chief misfortune was the continuing despotism under which they suffered. As he later phrased it:[31]

View millions by a Despot kept in awe
His nod their mandate, and his will their law:
Ne'er on that land has Freedom shed one ray,
By Fate decreed to feel tyrannic sway.

He was also beginning to acquire a taste for Persian history. He wrote to his father at Burnfoot: 'I employ every leisure hour in researches into this extraordinary country, with which we are but little acquainted. Of the little information we have received respecting its ancient history from the Greeks you will form an idea, when I assure you that, with the exception of Alexander's conquests, which is related by both authors (though in a very different manner), there is no fact recorded by the Greeks of which Persian histories make the least mention, nor is there one name which the Greeks have given, to either the Persian Generals or towns that can be understood by any Persian.'[32]

Several of the party made a day trip to the ruins of Persepolis, about forty miles north of Shiraz. Persepolis (Takht-e-Jamshid) had been the ceremonial capital of the Achaemenid Empire, built by Darius the Great around 500 BC and burnt down by the Macedonian Emperor Alexander the Great in 330 BC. In 1800 the ruins were partly covered by dust and sand but the upper parts of the buildings were still visible, including the Grand Staircase and Xerxes' Gateway (the Gate of all Nations). Here the 'English gentlemen' carved their names. The carvings have survived to this day.

CAP JOHN MALCOLM ENVOY &
CAPT WILLIAM CAMPBELL
CAPT J COLEBROOKE
G BRIGGS

Persepolis. In 1800 Malcolm and several of his party made a 'tourist' visit to the ruins and carved their names on the ancient gateway.

Such graffiti may be frowned upon today, but at that time it was a widely practised custom of European travellers coming upon famous ruins. Ninety years later, the celebrated George Curzon visited Persepolis and took a more favourable view of Malcolm's name-carving:

> From this proud memorial it is, I believe, with affected disgust that most travellers turn to the records of many generations of European visitors, who have either cut or painted their names on the lower surfaces of this gateway, in some cases even on the bodies of the bulls. I confess that I do not share this spurious emotion. A structure so hopelessly ruined is not rendered the less impressive – on the contrary, to my thinking, it becomes the more interesting – by reason of the records graven upon it, in many cases by their own hands, by famous voyagers of the past . . . It was with no irritation therefore, but with keen interest, that I read here in large characters the name of 'Cap. John Malcolm, Envoy Extraordinary, Pleni-Potentiary'.[33]

During his stay at Shiraz, Malcolm received periodic intelligence about the progress of Persian military operations against the Afghans. In late June there were reports of Zaman Shah suing for peace; in July, of unexpected Afghan resistance; in September, of negotiations; in early October, of peace. Malcolm lingered in Shiraz until early September – there was no point in his arriving at Tehran before the Shah returned from the scene of battle in the north-east – and then set off at a leisurely pace for Isfahan.

There was further delay. The Tehran Government had offered to provide, free of charge, the mission's requirements of labour and materials, with the cost being reimbursed to the local authorities by the central government. In practice, as Malcolm soon became aware, the local authorities would extort these services from the local population along the route with minimal reimbursement, thus creating extremely bad feeling towards the mission. He refused the offer, determined that the mission should pay its own way. But this in turn did not please the local authorities, since it would remove their chances of pocketing a percentage of the reimbursement paid to them by the Tehran Government.

Arriving at Isfahan on 23 September, Malcolm wrote to the Governor-General in Calcutta that, 'it is difficult to give your Lordship an adequate idea of the splendid manner in which I have been received and treated in this City'.[34] He was offered the choice of two Safavid royal palaces. By this time, after ceaseless battles with what he saw as local chicanery and greed, his infectious enthusiasm for everything he came across was beginning to show signs of wear and tear: 'The more I see of this parade and nonsense, the more I desire to escape with honor and reputation from the strange bustle.'[35]

He had intended to spend only a few days at Isfahan, but news came through that Fath Ali, though back from Khorasan, had gone to Qazvin (about a hundred miles west of Tehran) for the wedding of one of his sons. So the mission party waited for nearly a month in Isfahan, until Fath Ali was on his way back to Tehran. They left Isfahan on 28 October, pausing briefly at Kashan, and pressed on to Tehran, arriving at the outskirts on 13 November.

Tehran lies on the southern foothills of the Elburz range of mountains, which run east-west for several hundred miles. At 5,000 feet above sea level, the dry air is invigorating, as is the backdrop of the snow-capped ridge of Kuh-i-Tochal at 12,000 feet and the distant prospect of Kuh-i-Demavand, eighty miles to the east, at 18,400 feet. When the first Qajar monarch, Aga Mohamed Khan, made Tehran his capital in 1795, it had a population of no more than 15,000, and at the time of Malcolm's arrival it had little of the grandeur of Isfahan or even of Shiraz. But as the capital and centre of government, it was growing rapidly. Once again, the ceremonies attending the entry of the mission party to the city were a matter of seemingly endless negotiation. 'Letters and notes passed every minute; secretaries and confidential messengers went to and fro without intermission.'[36] The most propitious moment for entry through the city gate had already been fixed at 'forty five minutes past two o'clock, p.m., on the 13th of November 1800' after consultation with the Chief Astronomer of Isfahan, 'a man with the most imposing beard I ever saw. It is whiter than the snow that covers the lofty Demavand, and almost as long as the mountains of Alburz'.[37] Six hundred horsemen, headed by Nou Ruz Khan Qajar, the Lord of Requests and Commander of the King's Guard, came out several miles to meet them. The mission party sounded their trumpets and beat their drums. After ritual introductions, they all rode together towards the city. The mission's chronometer had been entrusted to Mirza Aga Meer, Malcolm's Persian secretary, who rode in the procession 'sufficiently near the Elchee to prompt him when to go a little faster or slower, in order that the gate of the capital might be entered at the exact moment . . . "You have ten minutes – a little slower". "Quicker!" . . . Again, "Slower!" Then, "Now!" and the charger of the Elchee put his foot over the threshold of the gate of Tehran. *"Al hamd-ool-illah!"* [Thanks be to God!] said the Meer, with a delighted countenance; "it was the very moment – how fortunate!"'[28]

They were accommodated at the house of the elderly Prime Minister, Haji Ibrahim Khan, who announced that he personally would be their *mehmandar* for the rest of their stay. Originally from Shiraz, Haji Ibrahim had been no more than a humble magistrate when he caught the eye of Karim Khan, the Zend ruler of the day, who made him his Chief Minister. Later, when the Zends appeared to be losing the struggle with the Qajars for control of the country, he changed sides and joined Aga Mohamed Khan, who became the first Qajar Shah in 1785. A man of formidable ability and guile, he had helped Aga Mohamed to secure control of the whole country, and probably advised him in the policy of killing off many members of his Qajar family, in order to make the succession secure for his nephew, Fath Ali.[39]

The mission's next task was to work out the protocol for their reception by the Shah – how to approach him, where and when to sit, etc. One problem was dress. A messenger from Haji Ibrahim came to

Fath Ali Shah (1772–1834), the second Qajar Shah of Persia (1796–1834).

ask them politely what dress they were proposing to wear for the audience. When Malcolm replied that they would wear their military uniforms,

> the [messenger] smiled, and said that they were better informed upon such subjects than the Elchee imagined. He then produced a parcel; and after opening a number of envelopes, he showed some pictures of ambassadors who had visited Persia two centuries ago. One, which was called the painting of the English representative and believed to be Sir Anthony Shirley, was dressed in the full uniform of the time of Queen Elizabeth. 'This,' said the Meerza, 'is the pattern which it is hoped you will adopt, as his Majesty desires to follow in all points the usages of the Saffavian kings, since they well understood what was due to the dignity of the throne of Persia.'[40]

The royal audience had to be fitted into the Shah's extraordinary daily routine, described some years later by an English doctor who had access to the Shah's *zenana* to attend to the health of high-born ladies:

> He rises at daybreak, as all Mahometans do, for the Matins; his prayers are said in the seraglio; after them three or four of his female valets wash, comb, perfume and dress him. He then holds a levee for the ladies of the seraglio, who are about four hundred, with each a large female establishment. As much state is observed here as at public levees; he is seated on a throne, and two of his wives are allowed to sit on chairs, one of whom has this honour from her high birth; the other, from being the mother of Abbas Mirza, the Heir Apparent. The two principal female officers of state are the Lady of Requests and the Superintendent of Punishments; the former presents to his Majesty, first the band of virgins, dressed in white and covered with jewels; then the Georgian slaves and mistresses of every colour and rank. The female levee is then broke up, and his Majesty leaves the seraglio at eight o'clock; he then goes to a private hall, where he receives the Princes and favourite courtiers, called the Companions. At ten he breakfasts in great state. The nauzur or steward, sees everything prepared in the kitchen, and is respon-

sible for its goodness and *safety*; he sees the dishes put into a large covered tray, which he locks and seals; he breaks the seal in the King's presence, and places the dishes before him; the hakin bashee, or chief physician, must also be present. A council is then held, at which all the ministers attend; after this, a public levee and parade of the troops, which terminate about noon. Soon after, he retires to the seraglio, amuses himself by exhibitions of female singers and dancers etc etc, and sleeps for three hours in the afternoon. About an hour before sunset he comes out, and holds a second levee, less formal and numerous, attended chiefly by the princes, ministers and favourite courtiers. He sometimes rides out in the evening, and dines between eight and nine, with the same ceremony of the trays brought under lock and seal as in the morning. At eleven o'clock he retires.[41]

The first audience finally took place on the morning of 16 November:

Everything being arranged, we proceeded towards the 'Threshold of the World's Glory' . . . We were all dressed in our best attire. A crowd had assembled near the house of Hajee Ibrahim, and the streets were filled with gazers at the strangers . . . Many persons whom we saw in the first square of the citadel, before we entered the palace, were richly dressed, and some of the horses were decked out with bridles, saddles and trappings of great value; but it was not until we passed into the garden in front of the king's hall of audience, a highly ornamented and spacious building, that we could form any idea of the splendour of the Persian court . . . There was not one person in all this array who had not a gold-hilted sword, a Cashmere shawl round his cap, and another round his waist. Many of the princes and nobles were magnificently dressed, but all was forgotten, as soon as the eye rested upon the king.

He appeared to be above the middle size, his age little more than thirty, his complexion rather fair; his features were regular and fine, with an expression denoting quickness and intelligence. His beard attracted much of our attention; it was full, black, and glossy, and flowed to his middle. His dress baffled all

> description. The ground of his robes was white, but he was so covered with jewels of an extraordinary size, and their splendour, from his being seated where the rays of the sun played upon them, was so dazzling, that it was impossible to distinguish the minute parts which combined to give such amazing brilliancy to his whole figure.
>
> The two chief officers of ceremonies, who carried golden sticks, stopped twice, as they approached the throne, to make a low obeisance, and the Elchee at the same time took off his hat. When near the entrance of the hall the procession stopped, and the lord of requests said, 'Captain John Malcolm is come, as envoy from the governor-general of India to your majesty.' The King, looking to the Elchee, said, in a pleasing and manly voice, 'You are welcome.'
>
> We then ascended the steps of the hall, and were seated, as had been previously arranged. The letter from the governor-general, which had been carried in the procession on a golden tray, was opened and read. His majesty inquired after the health of the king of England and the ruler of India. He desired particularly to know how the Elchee had been treated in his dominions, and whether he liked what he had seen of Persia?[42]

A second audience took place eleven days later. On this occasion, the ceremony of handing over presents took place. A Minister announced the gifts, reading from a list. Though the meeting began just as formally, Fath Ali soon enlivened it:

> 'I have heard a report, which I cannot believe, that your king has only one wife.'
>
> 'No Christian prince can have more.'
>
> 'O, I know that! But he must have a little lady.' ['Amma Keneezekee']
>
> 'Our gracious king, George the Third, is an example to his subjects of attention to morality and religion in this respect, as in every other.'
>
> 'This may all be very proper, but I certainly should not like to be a king of such a country.'[43]

But at later, more private audiences, they got down to brass tacks. Malcolm's difficulty was that his political instructions had been received more than twelve months previously, and had largely been overtaken by events.

Zaman Shah of Afghanistan was now in full retreat. Faced with a rebellion by his elder brother Prince Mahmud, the ruler of Herat, he had at first forced Mahmud into exile in Persia. But Mahmud had struck back and, supported by the Persians, had forced Zaman to flee eastwards. Later, in 1801, Zaman was captured, blinded and imprisoned in Bala Hissar fortress in Kabul for the remaining forty years of his life; Afghanistan was, and remains, no place for losers. At least for the time being, therefore, there was no remaining threat from Afghanistan to the Company's position in Hindustan, and there was no need for Malcolm to offer a subsidy to the Persian Government to induce them to carry on the war with Afghanistan.

By November 1800 it was also clear that the French threat had receded. The fact remained, however, that there was still a formidable French army in Egypt and no one knew quite what mischief it might get up to. There followed a game of diplomatic bluff. The Calcutta Government was scared of the French threat, but feared that if the Persians came to realise this, they would drive a harder diplomatic bargain. Mehdi Ali Khan had told the Persian Ministers that the British were not in the least apprehensive about the French. But he was a Persian, they concluded, and he *would* say that, wouldn't he? Fath Ali decided to put Malcolm to the test:

> 'Are the French', he asked, 'a powerful people?'
>
> 'Certainly,' replied the Elchee; 'they would not otherwise deserve to be mentioned as enemies of the English.'
>
> 'There again,' said the king, turning to his ministers, 'you know we were told the French were a weak and contemptible nation, which was incredible; the Elchee, by telling the truth, has done them justice, and raised his own country at the same time.'[44]

Malcolm now doubted the need for a political treaty. He soft-pedalled, but the Persians took a different view for reasons which were unclear. They were possibly hoping that by signing a political treaty with the

British, they could draw them in as allies against their real enemy, Russia. The Russians had annexed Georgia in 1798 and the Persians feared that they had designs on the rest of Persia. Yet entanglement in a Persian war with Russia was precisely what the British were anxious to avoid.

With a political treaty becoming rather a dead letter, attention now turned to the commercial treaty. Again, there was not much scope for development. Persia imported chintzes, Bengal muslins, cotton, sugar, sugar-candy, iron and metals of various sorts from India, worth about £1.6 million; and exported drugs, rosewater and dried fruits worth £1.5 million, the balance being made up in specie (coins).[45]

There was, however, one suggestion which Malcolm took up enthusiastically – that the Company should acquire an island off the Persian coast as a site for a factory which might, in time, become an emporium of trade in the Gulf.[46] This idea was not new – Mehdi Ali Khan had floated it with the Persian Government the previous year – but Malcolm perceived strategic potential in the idea as well as commercial advantage. In seeking security for the Company against the Afghans, the French, the Ottoman Empire and in due course, the Russians, Mornington and Malcolm were early exponents of a forward defensive policy; of the Company being active participants in the diplomatic games played by neighbouring states rather than standing aloof from them. To do this they needed to find ways of exerting diplomatic pressure on the countries bordering the Gulf. This meant having credible military and naval forces in the region to back up diplomatic moves. The Ottomans would never allow a British military garrison to be stationed at Basra or Baghdad, and the Persian Government would be exceedingly reluctant to allow a foreign military base on its territory. In any case, Bushire would not be a suitable place to house a military garrison, since the Company would inevitably be drawn into purely domestic and local political disputes, and possibly into a Persian war with Russia too.[47] On the other hand, acquiring sovereignty over an island in the Gulf and turning it into a garrisoned fortress would enable the Company to influence the foreign policies of the countries in the region without overtly interfering in their domestic affairs. Moreover, the usual military vulnerability of an island fortress (that it could be blockaded) no longer applied. The British Navy now dominated the Indian and Arabian seas. Furthermore, a naval base in the Gulf would facilitate the destruction of the Jaswanee pirates operating out of Ras al Khaima, who had hitherto made life and commerce in the Gulf so difficult and dangerous.

The purely commercial arguments in favour of an emporium were not strong. The Portuguese had run a successful trading operation out of Qishm Island in the sixteenth century, but closed it down in the eighteenth century. The Dutch had once had a factory on Kharg Island but had abandoned it in 1766. In Baghdad, Harford Jones, who knew a lot more about trade in the region than Malcolm, was strongly opposed to the idea. In a survey of trade in the region, he pointed out that the volume of trade between Persia and India had fallen substantially in the last hundred years. India had lost market share to French goods coming via Aleppo, and Russian goods via the Caspian Sea.[48] Manesty, too, was lukewarm on the idea of annexing an island in the Gulf.

Nevertheless, despite these difficulties and with the benefit of 200 years of hindsight, these critics would surely not have been quite so sure today that the commercial proposal was such a bad one. Singapore in 1819, Aden in 1839 and Hong Kong in 1841 all started in fairly unpromising circumstances, yet grew into triumphant commercial successes lasting well into the second half of the twentieth century – and even later – under British control. The rule of law, security of property, protection from piracy, and low and predictable taxes provided a magnet for merchants from far and wide, and more than outweighed any additional costs of double handling of cargoes.

The real drawback to Malcolm's proposal was that no single island in the Gulf seemed suitable as a combined fortress and emporium. Qishm, at the mouth of the Gulf, was in the right place for an emporium but had little water and a rotten climate. Kharg was in the right place for a fortress but lacked a decent sheltered harbour and was too close to Basra to be competitive as an entrepot port (though in the second half of the twentieth century it emerged as one of the largest oil-storage depots in the world). On this occasion, there was a further tactical reason for Malcolm to push hard for an island in the Gulf – to make the Persian Government believe that this was the Company's prime objective, rather than forming an alliance with it against the French.[49]

But in the end the Persian Ministers could not be persuaded. They knew that Kharg Island was of absolutely no use to them and that Qishm was anyway under the control of the Imam of Muscat. They were also suspicious about the Company's reputation in India – that they would come first to trade; then they would set up a colony/trading station; and finally they would take over the country. They were understandably apprehensive that the Company might try to work the same sort of trick in Persia. So (as reported by Mehdi Ali Khan), while their initial reaction to the general idea of selling an island in the Gulf to the Company was favourable, when it got down to brass tacks with Malcolm, they demurred. The likely explanation is that Mehdi raised the matter in general terms and the Persian Court expressed its willingness in principle to consider the proposition, but later, when negotiations got down to detail, thought better of it.

By late January it was clear that the Persians were not going to agree to cede Kharg or Qishm. The Shah declared that he needed more time to consider it and would give his answer via the Ambassador whom he would be sending to India in due course. The Calcutta Government was relatively unconcerned, but for Malcolm personally it was disappointing. He continued to press the case for a Company emporium and garrison on Kharg Island unremittingly for the next thirty years. He never succeeded in getting approval from the British authorities to implement it. Nevertheless, it is difficult not to be impressed with the breadth and magnitude of his strategic vision.

By mid-December all the main points of both the political and the commercial treaties, apart from the Gulf island issue, had been agreed between Malcolm and Haji Ibrahim. So the Treaties were signed without mentioning the Gulf. The signing ceremony took place on 28 January with Haji Ibrahim acting for the Shah and Malcolm for the Governor-General.

The political Treaty made no mention of relations with the Afghans, and nowhere was there any mention of Anglo-Persian cooperation against Russia. As for the French, Article 5 in its final form stated, quite mildly, that 'should it ever happen that an army of the French nation . . . attempts to settle, with a view to establishing themselves on any of the islands or shores of Persia, conjunct force shall be appointed by the two high contracting states, to act in cooperation, and to destroy and put an end to the foundations of their treason.' Pending ratification by the Governor-General in Calcutta, the Treaty was issued as an annexe to a *farman* issued independently by the Shah to his Ministers and governors. The *farman* was couched in much more belligerent language towards the French than the Treaty itself (though this was probably no more than Persian hyperbole): 'And should ever any persons of the French nation attempt to pass your ports or boundaries, or desire to establish themselves either on the shores or frontiers, you are to take means to expel and extirpate them, and never to allow them to obtain a footing in any place; and you are at liberty to disgrace and slay them.'[50]

There now remained only the taking of leave. The Shah had become genuinely fond of Malcolm. In the stifling atmosphere of an Oriental despot's Court, surrounded by terrified courtiers by day and a compliant harem by night, he probably enjoyed the novelty of exchanging badinage with someone of almost the same age, so self-confident, so jovial, so quick-witted in repartee.

The taking of leave from Haji Ibrahim, with whom Malcolm had worked closely in negotiating the Treaties, was a less happy event. The Haji told Malcolm candidly that he anticipated his own downfall and death very soon. He spoke of the envy and hostility of a large number of people, who had sought revenge by fabricating charges against him. The Haji's fears proved only too accurate. Not long after Malcolm's departure, the Shah was persuaded that the Haji had been plotting against him with other former supporters of the Zend faction. His death was gruesome – first his eyes were gouged out then he was thrown into a cauldron of oil and boiled alive. His family were slain or blinded as well (including his five-year-old son whom Malcolm had played with) and their property confiscated. Ten years later, when Malcolm returned to Tehran, 'he directed . . . that the sightless youth, who had enjoyed such favour as a child, might meet [us] on our advance, and receive . . . all the consolation which could be administered to one in his melancholy condition.'[51]

Immediately after taking leave, the mission party set off towards Baghdad. At the end of January there was heavy snow and by the time they reached Hamadan on a high plain dominated by Mount Alvand (11,600 feet), Malcolm was snow-blind and Charles Pasley, who had been ill when they left Tehran, had a high fever. They lingered for a fortnight at Hamadan, then pressed on, reaching the Ottoman frontier on 15 March and entering Baghdad a week later. Here Malcolm met Harford Jones, the British Resident, for the first time. The two had corresponded for over a year. The atmosphere must have been rather tense, for it was clear that they had profoundly different views about how to deal with the political challenges facing the Company. They were now to discover that they also had profoundly different characters and backgrounds. Jones, five years older than Malcolm, able, quick-tempered, not easily charmed and a bit 'difficult', would have recoiled at Malcolm's extrovert exuberance. The tension shows in the letters they subsequently wrote to each other. Malcolm's were full of slightly forced joviality; Jones's were stiffly formal. They got along well enough in the short time they were together on this occasion, but they were later destined to have a major falling-out.

Malcolm spent the week in Baghdad writing letters: to the Secret Committee in London; to Kirkpatrick in Calcutta; and to Lord Elgin, the British Ambassador in Constantinople, with whom he had been corresponding for several months. In these letters he discussed the possibility (and feasibility) of a Russian (as opposed to French) attack on British India.[52] He wanted the mission to pay its way in Turkish territory, just as it had in Persia, and for the same reason. And, as he put it to Harford Jones, 'I was an ambassador in Persia, but [am] only a traveller in the Turkish dominions.' But the Pasha insisted on paying the mission's expenses, even supplying his personal barge for the journey down the Tigris to Basra a week later. The party was met at the junction of the Tigris and the Euphrates by the Governor's state barge, but they chose instead to travel on Samuel Manesty's Company barge. They arrived at Basra on 9 April and stayed for a few days at Manesty's country house before embarking on the Company ship, *Governor Duncan*. Bad weather delayed them on their voyage down the Gulf and forced them to take shelter for a short period at Kharg Island, the very place which Malcolm had envisaged as a possible trading emporium and military base. They were back in Bombay on 13 May, seventeen months after they had left.

The signing of the Treaties and the completion of the mission were a huge relief to Malcolm. For a whole year, he had been under great stress. Now at last, as far as he was concerned, he had carried out his brief successfully. But there was still a nagging concern that the Governor-General might think differently. The latest letters from Calcutta were several months old. Although he had met all the Governor-General's objectives, which in due course Mornington generously acknowledged, the mission did not receive unalloyed praise from Calcutta or London. During the course of 1799 and 1800, external events had conspired to achieve the main political objectives without the need for diplomacy. This made it easier for critics to question the need for the mission. This was unfair – like criticising the purchase of fire extinguishers on the ground that no fire occurred.

A more valid criticism of Malcolm's mission (and of some later British missions to Persia as well) was that it cost too much. Malcolm was blamed for setting a bad example with his alleged extravagance on this first mission (although to some extent, Mehdi Ali Khan had already set an expensive precedent which Malcolm, with more formal credentials from Calcutta, was bound to exceed). It was claimed that he encouraged the Persian Court to expect and demand extravagant presents whenever a British embassy arrived in Tehran. With hindsight, it is fair to say that Malcolm's first mission probably did cost more than it should, even though Malcolm had the Governor-General's authority for the level of expenditure incurred. But even in hindsight, it is difficult to judge just how much the mission *should* have cost – is an expensive mission which achieves its objectives better than a cheap mission which does not? Striking an appropriate balance between achieving optimum results for minimum cost is not easy. Most diplomatic missions, but especially first missions to unfamiliar countries, tend to spend lavishly to create a suitably favourable impression of the power and wealth of the governments they represent. Malcolm was well aware that it was a delicate issue, proved by his frequent letters to Mornington, Kirkpatrick and Edmonstone in Calcutta, worrying about the costs he was incurring.[53]

What was not so fully appreciated at the time – certainly not by the Directors in Leadenhall Street – was the very favourable public relations effect which Malcolm's mission achieved for the Company. Edward Scott Waring, a Bengal civil servant of the Company, passed through Shiraz in 1802 and had this to say:

> The names of Major Malcolm, and the gentlemen who accompanied him, are mentioned in the liveliest terms of Oriental panegyric . . . The success with which Major Malcolm's embassy is universally supposed to have terminated, may be in a great manner attributed to his transacting everything himself; to his being capable of conversing alike with the peasant and the King; and to his rejecting the intervention of Persian or Indian agency . . . The Persians were astonished at the information, courtesy and generosity of the Europeans who had appeared amongst

> them, so different from what they had observed in their intercourse with the Russians on the borders of the Caspian Sea.[54]

Even allowing for some exaggeration, this was a flattering report from someone who had never met Malcolm and had no particular reason to praise him.

CHAPTER EIGHT

Private Secretary – 'Send Malcolm', 1801–1802

A letter from Henry Wellesley greeted Malcolm at Bombay on his way back from Persia. Henry had been sent back to England in August 1799 to explain in person the series of great events that had occurred in India, and, more importantly, to assess the reaction of the Government, a task almost impossible to achieve by letter. Now Henry was back in Calcutta in his old job as Private Secretary. The message was that Malcolm should come to Calcutta as soon as possible; the Governor-General wanted to see him.

In the seventeen months that Malcolm had been away from India, much had changed. In London, William Pitt had resigned as Prime Minister in February 1801 in favour of Addington, and Dundas had been replaced as President of the Board of Control by Lord Lewisham (later Earl of Dartmouth). The new ministry had much less weight with the Directors of the East India Company (the cry was that 'Pitt is to Addington as London is to Paddington'), and Mornington's critics among the directors seized their chance to castigate him. They did so, firstly, by obstructing his thoroughly admirable project for a College at Fort William to train young writers in Indian languages and learn about Indian culture from learned Indians; and, secondly, by thwarting his plan to loosen the Company's shipping monopoly and thereby liberalise trade between India and Britain. To a man with as short a fuse as Mornington, these were exasperatingly retrograde steps.

Mornington had been rewarded for his conquest of Mysore with a Marquessate – but, to his rage and disgust, an *Irish* Marquessate.[1] His wife, Hyacinthe, had accepted the Marquessate on his behalf, plus

£100,000; especially the latter, as a heaven-sent opportunity to pay off his debts. But as a Frenchwoman she had not appreciated the lower status of an Irish Marquessate compared to an English one. When the news reached Calcutta, there was an explosion of anger. He wrote to Hyacinthe to 'express the rage and indignation in my heart against my so-called friends who, with their Irish honours, have made me the laughing stock of India', and turned down the £100,000.[2]

This reaction illustrates Mornington's extraordinary character: brilliant, arrogant, petulant and vain, but in a strange way faithful to his aristocratic conception of honour. He must have been a difficult person to live with, yet he seems to have inspired an extraordinary level of devotion in his closest subordinates. For them, he became, as Charles Metcalfe later described him, 'The Glorious Little Man'.

After a few days in Bombay, writing despatches and thank-you letters to Harford Jones and others, Malcolm sailed for Madras and Calcutta. Calling at Trincomalee, the naval base on the east coast of Ceylon, he came upon Pulteney, now Flag Captain of the *Suffolk*, Admiral Rainier's flagship. Pulteney wrote home that 'John was here a few days in high health and spirits. He is gone to Bengal. What is to become of him is not known.'[3] At Madras he stayed long enough to catch up with old friends and the local gossip. William Kirkpatrick had been appointed earlier in the year to the Poona Residency in succession to William Palmer, who was over sixty and did not get on with the Governor-General. But while in Madras en route to Poona, he had fallen ill, and after a long period of convalescence, he had finally decided to return to England for good. Malcolm wrote from Madras to Arthur Wellesley, still the military commander at Seringapatam, and Arthur wrote back: 'I wish you joy in the termination of your mission [to Persia]. I am convinced that it will be approved of, and I hope that you will be sent upon another to a place where your presence is much wanted, and where you will do much good.'[4]

After surviving a severe storm in the Bay of Bengal, he reached Calcutta on 7 July. He went straight to Government House to report to the Governor-General. With the successful Persian mission under his belt, he could hope to be appointed to one of the Residencies at the Native Courts. The three 'plum' posts at this time were Hyderabad, Mysore and Poona. James Kirkpatrick at Hyderabad and Barry Close at Mysore were firmly entrenched, but with William Kirkpatrick unable to take up the Poona job, there was speculation that it might be offered to Malcolm. In the event, Barry Close was transferred from Mysore to Poona, and Malcolm was nominated to the Mysore post as Close's replacement. Meanwhile, as he wrote to his father: 'You will learn with pleasure that Marquis Wellesley has honoured my conduct in Persia with his most unqualified approbation, and has assured me that the moment the rains will admit of my travelling, I shall either be nominated to Poonah or some other Residency equal to it both in rank and emolument. In the interim the Marquis has appointed me acting Private Secretary in the absence of his brother, Mr Henry Wellesley – a nomination at once honourable and flattering in the extreme.' To his parents, scratching a living as tenant farmers in the Scottish Borders, the progress of their son was astonishing. His father wrote back: 'the account of your employments is like fairy tales to us'.[5]

The Governor-General's appointment of Malcolm as his Private Secretary, in succession to his brother Henry (whom he was sending to Lucknow) was indeed a great compliment. Now Malcolm had 'brilliant prospects'. Apart from its political aspects, the job also involved a whole new social learning curve for him. His modest Scottish background had been followed by eleven years of the rudimentary social mores of a Madras Army officers' mess. He had then graduated to Government House in Madras, and since then mastered the etiquette of the Courts of Hindu rajahs, Muslim nawabs and the Shah of Persia. Now he was going to have to act as the factotum for a prickly nobleman and his Etonian hangers-on at Fort William. To anyone less self-confident than Malcolm, it might have been a daunting prospect.

His first task was to report on the Persian mission, and at the end of July he submitted a copy of his Persian journal,[6] together with a covering letter making the rather obvious point that the mission had been 'attended by complete success'.[7] The whole report was encapsulated in a despatch from the Governor-General to the Secret Committee in London in late September.[8]

His next task was to write a memorandum summarising the events leading up to the settlement of the Carnatic state, following the death of the Nawab Omdut-ul-Omrah in July 1801. The affairs of this State had been in chaos for many years. The Nawab, through incompetence and corruption, had run into debt, and had taken out loans, including private loans at enormous interest rates from certain Company employees, so the Company was at least partly to blame. Probably the only practical solution was for some form of Company takeover. But the way in which the Marquess went about it – first advancing his claim by implying (from documents discovered in Tipu's palace after the fall of Seringapatam) that the Nawab had been in collusion with Tipu, and then questioning the legitimacy of the Nawab's chosen successor – smacked of the bullying tactics which were to cloud his whole term of office. Malcolm had not been involved in the negotiations, but his long experience of dealing with the problems of the Carnatic probably made him the best informed, or the least ill-informed, man in Calcutta on the subject.

A much bigger issue that had been exercising the Marquess's mind over previous months was the chaotic situation in the Native State of Oudh. Having made a tentative settlement with the Nawab Vizier in early 1801, the Marquess sent his brother Henry to Lucknow to finalise it. Now he decided to visit Oudh himself, taking his new Private Secretary with him. On 15 August 1801, 'His Excellency the Most Noble the Governor-General . . . attended by the officers of his suite and by a detachment of the bodyguard . . . embarked on board the *Soonamooky* yacht between 5 and 6 in the morning, and proceeded up river, the ships in the Port saluting as he passed.'[9] The great Ganges was navigable up to Cawnpore (Kanpur), 650 miles from Calcutta. From Cawnpore, a fifty-mile trip across country led to Lucknow, the seat of the Nawab Vizier.

Also accompanying the Governor-General on the *Soonamooky* was his new Military Secretary, Captain Merrick Shawe. Shawe had been an officer in the 76th Foot, and had lived in India since 1790. He later succeeded Malcolm as the Marquess's Private Secretary, then accompanied the Marquess back to Britain, and remained with him as his trusted aide for the rest of his life. A man of charm and tact, but 'without ideas of his own', he was the perfect servant to the Marquess.[10]

The viceregal party took eight months to complete the round trip to Lucknow and back. At first the *Soonamooky* passed through Company-administered Bengal. Every few days the Governor-General and his entourage, consisting of up to 200 boats, would come to a town. They would be welcomed by the local military commander or the local Company judge, and pay formal visits to the local ruling family: at Murshedabad, to the Nawab of Bengal; at Benares, to the grandsons of the Mughal Emperor (now an old man in Delhi, living under the 'protection' of the Mahratta Chieftain, Dowlat Rao Scindiah). As they progressed upriver, Malcolm and Shawe wrote frequent private letters to Henry Wellesley in Lucknow in the bantering style of self-confident young men, conscious that they were at the centre of events.

There were lighter moments. After a month on the river, Malcolm described a tiger shoot: 'after an action of four hours, not very desperate but sufficiently dangerous to be interesting, we returned, after having killed two enormous tigers – the smallest of which was eight feet long'.[11]

There were no women on the *Soonamucky*, and having not much to do between mail deliveries from Calcutta, the Governor-General and his aides amused themselves by indulging in jocular rivalry for whatever ladies they might come across at the places where they stopped. At Muslim Courts they might visit the Begums, but protocol put any flirtations with them out of the question. So they had to fall back on the wives and daughters of the officers in the local British communities. At Patna they came upon the wife of the Collector of Benares, a Mrs Barton. Shawe had previously had some emotional liaison with her, from which he now professed himself recovered. During their ten-day stay at Patna, Malcolm and Shawe both wrote letters about her to Henry Wellesley. Meanwhile, possibly unknown to them, the 'Great Man' himself had cast a lascivious eye upon her, writing a teasing letter to Hyacinthe in England that he had fallen in love with her.

At Mirzapore they were joined by Henry Wellesley, who had come from Lucknow to report on his negotiations with the Nawab Vizier. The whole deal had in fact been finalised and only needed the Governor-General's formal ratification, which he gave ten days later. They stayed with Henry Colebrooke, a 36-year-old judge and magistrate. At this time Colebrooke was hard at work completing his translation of the massive *Hindu Digest of Laws*, left unfinished by Sir William Jones.[12]

In mid-December 1801, when the party reached Allahabad, the Marquess again decided to 'Send Malcolm' – this time to Madras. He had wanted to extend to Madras the revenue collection and judicial systems which Lord Cornwallis had introduced in Bengal. Lord Clive was due to return to England at the end of 1801, thus leaving a lengthy interregnum until the arrival of a new Governor of Madras. But the Marquess was confident in the ability of the Chief Secretary, Josiah Webbe, and the Revenue

Member of the Madras Council, Thomas Cockburn, to implement the reforms competently, without a Governor in place. In August, however, as he was setting out on his up-country tour, he heard that the Court of Directors in London apparently wanted to dismiss Webbe and Cockburn, replacing them with their cronies from London. This, the Marquess felt, would result in chaos. After consulting Malcolm, he concluded that they should try to persuade Clive to postpone his departure, and somehow retain the services of Webbe and Cockburn at the Presidency. This had to be done in a hurry because Clive was about to leave. They tried drafting letters to the three people involved – Clive, Webbe and Cockburn – but soon decided that only face-to-face meetings would have any chance of achieving the desired end. Malcolm was the obvious person to undertake this task. To get to Calcutta and then sail to Madras would take him at least a month, so in the meantime they used William Kirkpatrick, still recuperating at Madras, as a go-between. With the Governor-General's approval, Malcolm wrote Kirkpatrick an urgent private letter, asking him to sound out Webbe and Cockburn discreetly, without informing Clive, It was a delicate task, but Kirkpatrick was well qualified to carry it out.

With his penchant for dramatising situations, just before leaving Allahabad Malcolm wrote to George Barlow, the Chief Secretary of the Calcutta Government, who had been left behind in Calcutta: 'Lord Wellesley has directed me to request you to take measures to secure me a passage to Madras . . . that will prevent delay. I expect to leave this on the 23rd [December] . . . and shall be at Calcutta on the 1st or 2nd of January. I can leave Calcutta with convenience in four or five hours after I reach it, if the vessel is ready to sail.'[13]

Malcolm reached Calcutta in ten days, but Barlow was not a man to be rushed, by Malcolm or by anyone else, as later events were to confirm. He made him wait for four days before sending him off on the *Mermaid* schooner, and just for good measure, gave him the task of taking the two Barlow children with him on the ship.

Arriving at Madras early on 26 January, protocol dictated that Malcolm should report immediately to the Governor. He indulged in a little subterfuge: 'After breakfast, I requested Lord Clive would be so indulgent as to permit me to read my despatches from Bengal, and to sort my papers, that I might be fully prepared to communicate next morning all I had to say to his Lordship on the part of his Excellency the

Governor-General. By this I gained sufficient time to discuss with Mr Webbe and Colonel Kirkpatrick the question of Lord Clive's remaining in India till next season.'[14]

At the interview next morning, Malcolm easily persuaded the dutiful Clive to postpone his departure until the following October. Cockburn was determined to go home, and nothing would dissuade him. Webbe, on the other hand, accepted the offer of the Residency at Mysore, in succession to Barry Close (now on his way to Poona). In fact he never went to Mysore, although he drew the Resident's salary. He was instead 'seconded' back to the Presidency at Madras to implement the new revenue and judicial settlement arrangements. The Mysore Residency had been promised to Malcolm, but he had offered to forego the appointment in favour of Webbe to solve the Madras staffing problem. This was a considerable financial sacrifice for Malcolm, whose salary and allowances as Private Secretary were worth about £2,000 per annum, while as Resident at Mysore he could hope to *save* up to £2,000. But since the effective result was that he remained Private Secretary and right-hand man of one of the most active Governor-Generals in British Indian history, it was not much of a sacrifice of career prospects.

Having secured most of what he wanted at Madras, Malcolm rushed back to Bengal as quickly as he had come. Leaving Madras on 8 February, he reached Calcutta on 27 February, travelled upstream by *dawk* towards the Governor-General's party, now on its way downstream, and met them on 7 March, just above Benares.

CHAPTER NINE

Private Secretary – Scandal in Hyderabad

A Private Secretary's job is often messy. He is there to make sure that the mind of the Great Man is concentrated upon Great Issues, not frittered away on small ones. So the Secretary must try to gather in the small issues and attend to them himself, on the Great Man's behalf. One such issue came up shortly after Malcolm took over as Private Secretary in August 1801 – the case of James Kirkpatrick, the British Resident at Hyderabad.

Malcolm had last met Kirkpatrick in October 1799, when he was passing through Hyderabad en route to Bombay and Persia. At that time a mood of euphoria prevailed at the Nizam's Court. Their great rival, Tipu Sultan, was no more. Hyderabad had acquired some Mysore territory, albeit not as much as the Nizam and his Prime Minister had hoped for. Meer Alam, the commander of the Nizam's Contingent in the Mysore War, had received a hero's welcome on his return from Seringapatam. Accompanying him had been his cousin and fellow member of the Persian Shustari family, Baqar Ali Khan, the *Bakshi* (paymaster) to the Company's Subsidiary Force at Hyderabad. Kirkpatrick's standing was high, both in Hyderabad and Calcutta. But within six months the scene had changed dramatically. The story can be told on two levels: as a passionate love affair between James Kirkpatrick and Khair un Nissa, the young granddaughter of Baqar Ali Khan; or as a tale of political intrigue at the Nizam's Court.

First, the love affair. Baqar Ali's daughter Sharaf un Nissa was a widow with two daughters. Baqar Ali took responsibility for arranging their marriages. He found suitable husbands from the Hyderabadi nobility for both of them, and the wedding of the elder sister took place in December 1798. But for some reason, Sharaf un Nissa and her mother did not approve of the potential husband whom Baqar had found for his younger granddaughter Khair. They reckoned that they could find a much better match for her – none other than the British Resident, James Kirkpatrick. This may sound far-fetched, in view of the differences of age, of race and especially of religion. Yet perfectly respectable marriages were not uncommon at that time between senior British officials and upper-class Indian ladies at Native Courts. There would, nevertheless, be huge difficulties in surmounting the major obstacle – untying the existing betrothal knot between Khair and her Hyderabadi fiancé. Soon after the wedding of the elder granddaughter in December 1798, Baqar had to leave Hyderabad to accompany Meer Alam to Mysore with the Nizam's Contingent, and while he was away the two ladies plotted to prevent Khair's marriage. They did so by a 'honey trap', putting the beautiful young Khair 'in the way of' James Kirkpatrick. At first he resisted her charms but eventually, in the middle of 1799, he succumbed.

Kirkpatrick said nothing about the affair, even privately to his brother William. But rumours began to fly around in Hyderabad. In late January 1800 two scurrilous *akhbars* (newsletters) appeared, one accusing Kirkpatrick not merely of seducing Khair un Nissa, but of raping her, and another woman as well; the other, of conniving at the death in a firearms accident of Khair's uncle, who had allegedly been opposed to Kirkpatrick's relationship with Khair. The news reached Calcutta, and Kirkpatrick received an icy note from the Marquess, demanding that he should obtain statements from both Nizam Ali and his Chief Minister, Aristu Jah, that the allegations were false. With very little delay, Kirkpatrick was able to forward to Calcutta statements from both of them, and also from Baqar Ali, that there was no truth in the rumours.

But William Kirkpatrick privately suspected that his brother was not 'coming clean' with him, and pressed him repeatedly to tell him the truth. Eventually, in May 1800, James wrote him a long, anguished letter, admitting that he had slept with Khair un Nissa, but tried to excuse himself on the ground that the initiative for the seduction had come from the female side.[1]

Still, the affair continued, and Baqar Ali became more and more distressed and embarrassed by it. For a while the lovers were separated but miserable. But as so often happens, the pull of love outweighed discretion. At the end of December 1800, the truth came out – Khair had become pregnant in June. Now all present agreed that the only way out was for the existing engagement to be broken off, and for Khair and Kirkpatrick to marry. But this inevitably meant that, to preserve any sort of propriety, he would first have to convert to Islam. Although no written record survives, he almost certainly did so. The marriage went ahead in January 1801, with the blessing not only of Baqar Ali and the Shushtari clan, but also of Aristu Jah and the Nizam himself. Aristu Jah, in fact, is said to have taken the place of Khair's dead father and provided her with a substantial dowry, while the Nizam made Kirkpatrick his adopted son. Khair remained in the Shushtari *zenana* until a baby boy was born to her on 4 March 1801.

That was the love story. But this extraordinary sequence of events can equally be told as a tale of political intrigue at the Nizam's Court. When Meer Alam made his triumphal return to Hyderabad in October 1799 at the head of the Nizam's Contingent, accompanied by Baqar Ali Khan, he was not received with unalloyed joy by Aristu Jah and the Nizam. They felt that he was getting 'too big for his boots'. So he was given the job of administering the southern provinces, which had been ceded by Mysore to Hyderabad as part of the Peace Treaty. It was a big job, but it was well away from the centre of influence and intrigue at the Court in the city of Hyderabad. Reluctantly, he set off southwards in January 1800. Aristu Jah then set out to destroy him. He realised that as long as the Meer was supported by the British he would be more or less inviolate. His tactic was therefore to blacken the Meer's name in the eyes of the British. His first move was to 'leak' the two *akhbars* referred to above, which accused James Kirkpatrick of raping Khair un Nissa (the Meer's cousin) and engineering the death of her uncle. Meer Alam, now in the southern provinces, had heard vague rumours about the affair, but he was too far away to obtain definitive information. Rising to Aristu Jah's bait, he believed the worst, and overreacted. He wrote a letter of protest to the Governor-General about the behaviour of Kirkpatrick, thus occasioning the Marquess's stern letter to Kirkpatrick in early March 1800.

When Kirkpatrick, as instructed, passed on the Marquess's letter to the Chief Minister for his comments, Aristu Jah saw his opportunity. He offered to write a letter to the Governor-General, exonerating Kirkpatrick of all the charges – but, on condition that Meer Alam be replaced by himself as the Nizam's *vakeel* to the British.[2] So a letter went off to Calcutta from Aristu Jah, countersigned by the Nizam, to the effect that Kirkpatrick was entirely innocent of the charges brought by Meer Alam. Not surprisingly, Calcutta replied that if the Nizam was still content to have Kirkpatrick as Resident, that was all right by Calcutta; and regarding the Meer, of course the Nizam was free to select whomever he liked as his *vakeel* to the English, so long as the Meer's life, property and honour remained safe. Whereupon Aristu Jah immediately stripped the Meer of both his position as *vakeel* to the English and his position as administrator of the southern provinces, and put him under house arrest in Rudrur fort, in the south-western extremity of the Nizam's dominions. In terms of political intrigue, Aristu Jah had scored a double header – simultaneously ruining his rival Meer Alam and setting up the British Resident for future blackmail. As Arthur Wellesley commented a little later: 'if it were true that he [Aristu Jah] had told a falsehood to screen Kirkpatrick from disgrace, he [Kirkpatrick] must be a most convenient Resident to the Nizam's government'.[3]

Despite this, the Marquess took no further action. As far as he was concerned, the Nizam seemed to be happy with the Resident. He had indulged in a diplomatically unfortunate love affair, but all that was now apparently forgiven and forgotten. James Kirkpatrick said not a word to the Governor-General about his marriage, let alone his conversion to Islam in January 1801. But when Khair un Nissa produced a baby boy in March 1801, it was virtually impossible to keep the fact secret. Once again, rumours began to circulate, and unfortunately for James Kirkpatrick, they had willing purveyors. During early 1801, he had become concerned about irregularities and corruption among British officers in the Hyderabad Subsidiary Force. Quite rightly, he initiated an investigation. This made him unpopular in some quarters, and by way of revenge, certain officers sent fresh reports about the Khair un Nissa affair to Calcutta.

This was the confused state of the Kirkpatrick saga that awaited Malcolm when he arrived at Calcutta from Persia in early July 1801. William Kirkpatrick was still convalescing in Madras, waiting for a ship to take him back to England. Henry Wellesley set off in early August for Lucknow. At that point the Marquess, considering Malcolm to be well informed about Hyderabadi affairs, called him in to explain what he knew about the affair. He faced a distressing moral dilemma. He owed a lot to James Kirkpatrick, who had taken him on as his assistant at Hyderabad in 1798, but he owed even more to William, who had been his mentor for several years, had supported his candidacy for the Hyderabad job as Assistant Resident and later for the Persian mission, and whose guidance he had constantly sought when in Persia. The Marquess warned him that he must be totally frank, despite his previous links with the Kirkpatrick brothers. Malcolm admitted that he had heard reports about the affair, but that he had considered them scurrilous, 'arising from that Envy which ever attends distinguished merit'. This response was disingenuous, especially since he went on to tell William Kirkpatrick in a 'private and confidential' letter: 'My situation in this affair has been rendered still more delicate and distressing by Lord Wellesley's intimating his intention (if he should remove your brother) to send me to Hyderabad. That station, however great and key in my hopes, will have no charms for me under such circumstances. I shall be still more unhappy if my conduct throughout this affair does not meet your entire approbation. I do not know another man in the world on whose impartiality I could so much rely, upon so trying an occasion.'[4]

He wrote again, a fortnight later, in the same spirit:

> The evidence Lord W has received appears very positive and must have obliged him to some proceeding – though I confess I was averse to the mode he has pursued. I wish to God you had been here and I wish I had been five thousand miles distant . . . If you think under the possible event of your brother's removal, I should not accept Hyderabad – write me & I will re-urge the objections I have already stated to Lord W upon the subject. Rest assured that this is no sacrifice. I have no fear of my rise, or of my obtaining a fortune – I wish to preserve my reputation & my friends.[5]

Opinion in the Governor-General's entourage about the James Kirkpatrick saga was divided. Neil Edmonstone, the Persian Secretary, felt that he should be removed; Malcolm favoured delay. A further complication was that Kirkpatrick, hitherto a staunch supporter of the Marquess, was gradually becoming disillusioned with the way in which the Marquess was bullying the rulers of Hyderabad and Oudh. In September he wrote a letter to Malcolm, strongly critical of the

Marquess's policy. As a general rule, letters (even private ones) from Residents at Native Courts to members of the Governor-General's staff were passed on to the Marquess to read. But on this occasion Malcolm held back Kirkpatrick's letter, fearing that it might enrage the Marquess, who was averse to the mildest criticism, and might lead him to take intemperately drastic action against Kirkpatrick. Suppressing letters, however, even for the best of motives, was a dangerous game – if the Marquess later discovered that his Private Secretary had been deliberately withholding facts from him, that would be the end of the Private Secretary.

But the anonymous Hyderabad correspondents knew how to stir up the Marquess – by effectively calling him a wimp. As Malcolm reported to William Kirkpatrick, 'some subsequent communications . . . reached him. These not only contained more serious allegations, but insinuated that Lord Wellesley's character suffered by the passive line he had taken; and that the fact that your Brother having debauched the girl and having a child by her, was known to almost every person in the country except the Marquis. These communications, which were (considering previous circumstances) certainly of a nature to impress Lord Wellesley's mind with the truth of some of the allegations, [and] made his Lordship resolve upon the line he has adopted.'[6]

The 'line he has adopted' was prompt and decisive. In early October the Marquess set up an inquiry, to be held in Madras and chaired by Lord Clive, to look into the whole scandal. The inquiry was to be held without James Kirkpatrick's participation or even knowledge. The choice of Madras as a location was presumably to preserve secrecy. The Marquess asked William Kirkpatrick to remain in India until the outcome of the case was known because, as he pointed out, the Government and the Court of Directors in London were probably ignorant of all the facts and might not realise that, whatever James had done, William was totally innocent of any wrongdoing. In other words, William needed to have his own name cleared officially before he sailed for home.[7]

The Clive Inquiry duly took place in Madras, and issued its report on 7 November.[8] Its conclusion was to exonerate Kirkpatrick completely of the rape and murder charges; to agree that the 'seduction' had been initiated from the female side, and that no offence appeared to have been taken by the Nizam and his Prime Minister, nor for that matter, in the end, by Baqar Ali Khan. The one remaining charge, from which it seemed impossible to exonerate Kirkpatrick, was that he had failed to inform his superiors about what was going on; that he had, in fact, prevaricated when questioned about the affair on several occasions over many months. For a diplomat such a failure of trust must usually be fatal.

At this point William Kirkpatrick hatched a plot to save his brother's career. Somehow he had to deflect the charge that James had not reported the affair to his boss. He did so by claiming that he had received letters from James giving full details of the affair, in the belief that he, William, would convey the information to the Governor-General. He had failed to do so – it was therefore his fault, not James's. He was thus offering to sacrifice his own reputation to save his brother's. It was a remarkable piece of brotherly solidarity, and it worked. James had undoubtedly told outright lies at various stages in the affair, not only to the Marquess, but even to his own friends and confidants. Frankly, he should have told his superiors the whole story at a much earlier stage, and offered to resign. Despite this, there was a general feeling of relief at Calcutta, from the Marquess down, that a way had been found to let James 'off the hook'. He was an able official and had done a magnificent diplomatic job at the Nizam's Court. Nobody wanted to lose his services. In the end, this was probably the deciding factor. Whatever one might think of the Marquess's character in general, he handled this difficult case in exemplary fashion.

Before the inquiry the Marquess had sworn William to secrecy – he was not to mention it to his brother. This prohibition also applied to Malcolm. This meant that throughout the period of the inquiry, the two people from whom James Kirkpatrick could most easily seek sympathy and advice – his brother William, of course, but also Malcolm, his former friend, assistant, and now the Governor-General's Private Secretary – were unable to be completely open and honest with him about what they knew, and what he should do. The unfortunate effect of this situation was that James, already feeling beleaguered at Hyderabad, gradually developed a persecution complex, suspecting even his friends of betraying him for their own selfish motives. During November and early December 1801 several letters passed between the Kirkpatrick brothers. In one, William, while sticking to his promise to keep silent, hinted to his brother that 'he had enemies' and warned him to be discreet in what he said. Malcolm could only write to James that 'there are many parts of your letter to which I cannot give you any satisfactory answer, for reasons that I will explain hereafter'.[9] Malcolm kept William informed of developments, writing on 30 November that the Governor-General had accepted the inquiry's conclusion that James had been guilty of no more than 'indiscretion', but still thought that James should go because of his failure to be candid.

Sadly, James Kirkpatrick was less than appreciative of what had been done for him. He quite unjustly suspected the Marquess of being out to 'get' him. He also felt, even more unjustifiably (although he was not to know this at the time) that Malcolm was angling to take over his job as Resident at Hyderabad, and therefore wanted him to be dismissed. It is understandable that a man in the grip of a romantic passion, which he must have known was highly controversial, should feel beleaguered and rather paranoid. But he had only himself to blame.

Despite his arguably undeserved exoneration by the Governor-General, James Kirkpatrick became increasingly disenchanted with the Calcutta authorities. Malcolm in particular he suspected of being out to ruin him. Some time later he wrote to his brother William, now back in England, that he had asked Malcolm to get 'certain unfulfilled assurances', but the reply was 'as usual brief, reserved and evasive'.[10] He went on to say that, now he had found out about Malcolm's 'secret enmity', he would be discreet, and only hoped that Malcolm would not be given the Residency in the event of him (Kirkpatrick) being summoned to Calcutta, as 'nothing would be left undone by him at the expense of truth for which he has proved he possesses so little regard, to fasten such accusations upon me, which might be made a pretext for my removal'.[11]

As for Malcolm, after 1801 he seems to have lost respect for James Kirkpatrick, although maintaining professional cordiality. Such episodes – being caught in the middle of a controversy without being able to defend one's actions publicly – are the 'downside' of a Private Secretary's job. James Kirkpatrick died in 1805 while on a visit to Calcutta.

CHAPTER TEN

Private Secretary – Lord Wellesley's Factotum, 1801–1802

When Malcolm rejoined the *Soonamooky* near Benares on 7 March 1802, he found the Marquess in sombre mood, in fact ready to resign. The Court of Directors seemed to be implacably against him. Resenting his alleged attempts to dilute the Company's shipping monopoly and encourage the so-called 'Private Trade' by non-Company merchants, the 'Shipping Interest' at Leadenhall Street (a faction of the Company's 'proprietors' or shareholders who owned ships used by the Company and who naturally wanted to preserve the Company's monopoly) had vented its anger in a way which they knew would upset him, by campaigning to scupper his pet project, the College at Fort William.[1] They had also railed against his extravagance, with some justification. The resignation of Pitt and Dundas had left him, he thought, bereft of friends in the Government and at the Board of Control, which had the power to override the Court of Directors. So he decided to send in his resignation before they could ask for it.

In 1802 a Governor-General's resignation would not have been like such a resignation today. For a start, the resignation letter might take up to six months to arrive, and anything might happen in the interim. Sometimes a resignation was used as a lever to extract greater freedom of action from the Government or the Court of Directors, though this was risky – more than one Governor had sent in his resignation, and been mortified to find out, up to a year later, that it had been immediately accepted. In the event, when the Mahratta situation was deteriorating later in 1802, he withdrew his resignation.

Meanwhile the *Soonamooky* continued on its way down river. On 14

April the viceregal party reached Barrackpore, the Governor-General's country retreat, seven miles upriver from Calcutta. It was met by members of the Council and senior civil and military officers. The Marquess stayed there for a few days before finally entering Calcutta. He had been away for over eight months.

In Calcutta for the first time as the Governor-General's Private Secretary, Malcolm came into his own. The Marquess's management style was despotic, to put it mildly. He did not merely chair meetings of the Supreme Council; he dominated them, treating the other members of Council as rubber stamps. He did not lightly give audiences to anybody, British or Indian, though he could be full of charm if he deemed it politic to be so. With such a person in command, the role of the secretaries was crucial. They alone had the ear of the Governor-General, but were approachable on a daily basis. The Marquess's trait of giving his secretaries a lot of latitude in carrying out his instructions further increased their status.

As Private Secretary, therefore, Malcolm wielded a great deal of power, and just about everyone in Calcutta knew it. Some months later, a newly arrived young officer, Lieutenant James Young, described the scene in a letter to his parents in Scotland.

> Major Malcolm . . . sent for me to see him, and told me in the most sincere and friendly manner his intention to befriend me: 'My old father has asked me to befriend you, Young. Anything that he wishes is a *firman*, which I put on my head as a Turk does the Grand Seigneur's, and which I will obey at all hazards.' Since then I have frequently been at Major Malcolm's house . . . he has treated me in the kindest and most affectionate manner – this, too, when he was Lord Wellesley's factotum, and the *greatest* man in all Calcutta . . . I mention this that you may all, with one voice, thank the old gentleman, and delight his heart with hearing of his son's filial piety and kindness to me.[2]

Malcolm and Shawe gradually worked their way through the outstanding business which had piled up while they had been away (though incoming correspondence had been forwarded to the *Soonamooky*). They laughed scornfully, as head office men can, at reports submitted by Jonathan Duncan ('Old Jonathan', as they called him), the Governor of Bombay, on his negotiations with the Gaekwad of Baroda, one of the Mahratta Chieftains. 'I send you Extracts that will show in what a preposterous stile the *Honorable Jonathan* is proceeding', wrote Malcolm to Henry Wellesley.[3]

There was, of course, another side to this. Sir James Mackintosh, shortly after his arrival in Bombay as Recorder (Chief Justice) in 1804, compared Duncan and the Marquess thus: 'the Governor [Duncan] is indeed an ingenious and intelligent man; but every Englishman who resides here very long has, I fear, either his mind emasculated by submission, or corrupted by despotic power. Mr Duncan may represent one genus, the *Brahminised* Englishman; Lord W[ellesley] is indisputably at the head of the other, the *Sultanised* Englishman.'[4]

When the viceregal party reached Calcutta, their first desire was to view the progress in building the new Government House. From the day of his first arrival at Calcutta, the Marquess had complained about the inadequacy of the Calcutta residence to accommodate his 'family' of secretaries and ADCs. Within a year he had started to design and build a magnificent new Government House, without bothering to obtain prior approval from the Court of Directors. By the time Malcolm arrived in Calcutta in July 1801, it was in an advanced stage of construction and the first public function was held there at about this time. But the Marquess and his family were not able to move into the new accommodation until late in 1802.

They also caught up with the latest gossip:

> The male part of the Calcutta Nobility is in better temper than usual and both sexes seem to rejoice at the return of the Court. But the women have been under no controul during its absence and are become licentious in all vices of scandal, malicious untruth & Billingsgate dialogue. Mrs Barlow [wife of George Barlow] & Lady A[nstruther] [wife of Sir John Anstruther, Chief Justice of Bengal, 1798–1806] generally spar whenever they meet. Two to one in favour of Mrs B, at [Lady A] starting – 'I am not Irish, Mrs Barlow.' 'Your ladyship may deny it if you please. But Sir Alured Clarke assured me he saw the Hovel you were born in.'[5]

At a house party held at the Governor-General's country residence at Barrackpore in early June, a contemporary visitor found that:

> the situation of the house is much more pleasing than anything I have yet seen. It is considerably elevated above the Hoogly river, on a very extended reach of which it stands: directly opposite it is the Danish settlement of Serampore: on the sides are pagodas, villages and groves of lofty trees. The water itself is much clearer than at Calcutta, and covered with state barges and cutters of the Governor-General. These, painted green and ornamented with gold, contrasted with the scarlet dresses of the rowers, were a great addition to the scene. The park is laid out in the English style; and the house, at present unfinished, is well adapted to the climate, having a beautiful verandah on every side, and the rooms being on a very ample scale. This place originally belonged to the Commander-in-Chief; but Lord Wellesley took possession of it on being appointed Captain-General, and has improved it with his usual taste. Several of the bungalows belonging to the lines have been taken into the park, and are fitted up for the reception of the Secretaries, Aides-de-Camp and visitors.

On 9 August 1802, a fresh crisis arose. Edward Strachey arrived from Bombay with the alarming news that the newly arrived Persian Ambassador, pausing en route to Calcutta, had been killed there in a shooting affray on 20 July.

The Persian Government's appointment of an Ambassador to the East India Company's Government at Calcutta had been one result of Malcolm's mission to Persia in 1800. The man chosen as Ambassador was Haji Khalil Khan, a rich merchant based at Bushire, who had trading interests with India. The Haji left Bushire in April 1802 with a following of about 120 people, plus horses, camels and presents, in three ships. He arrived at Bombay on 21 May, to be welcomed with elaborate ceremonial. On 4 June, King George III's birthday, he was entertained at a ball and firework display organised by Edward Strachey, who had been appointed his *mehmandar* (guide). On the voyage from Bushire one of the three ships had been wrecked in a storm, and he had lost a lot of property. He became rather demanding in his claims on the Governor for compensation. On 20 July, fighting broke out in the courtyard of the Haji's residence between the Haji's bodyguard and the sepoy guards provided by the Company. The Haji, hearing the commotion, attempted to stop the trouble, but he and his nephew Agha Husain were caught in the crossfire. He was killed and Agha Husain wounded; four of the Haji's staff were also killed and five wounded. The cause was not clear, but since only Persians were killed, it seems likely that the sepoys fired first. The Governor was away at the time, and there was considerable confusion. Edward Strachey was sent in a fast frigate to Calcutta to report the event to the Governor-General.

The reaction in Calcutta was consternation, particularly for Malcolm: 'It brings sorrow to us all. To me it brings the most severe distress. I see in one moment the labor of three years given to the winds (and that by the most unexpected and unprecedented of all accidents) just when it was on the point of completion.'[6] Malcolm certainly knew Haji Khalil Khan and may have been quite sincere in mourning his death. But he was also acutely aware that if the Shah chose to blame the Company for the Haji's death, the diplomatic consequences could be potentially disastrous. And, as the architect and prime mover of the Persian diplomatic connection, he must have feared that this would in turn halt his own advancement in the Company. Rapid action was needed to prevent the whole affair getting out of hand. He managed to convey his fears so forcefully to the Marquess that between them they reacted with a touch of panic. On 11 August the Governor-General issued a special edition of the *Calcutta Gazette*, giving details of the affray; and a fortnight later he published a public letter of condolence to the Haji's surviving family, expressing his sorrow at 'this dreadful, unforeseen and uncontrollable calamity'. Neither of them trusted Jonathan Duncan in Bombay to deal with the situation satisfactorily, so they reverted to the now well-worn policy of 'Send Malcolm!' As the acknowledged expert in Calcutta on Persia, and as the Governor-General's right-hand man, Malcolm was the logical choice to offer official condolences and hand out compensation to the bereaved relatives of the Haji.

So, on 30 August Malcolm set off on yet another troubleshooting mission for the Marquess. As Shaw wrote to Henry Wellesley: 'his departure . . . took place yesterday at 10 a.m., accompanied by every species of noise and confusion. All the bores of Calcutta, from Mr Justice Louis to Padre Perthenio were assembled at his door to take leave, or rather huzza him off. He is in confident expectation of being here again in the first week of November, for which I will pray devoutly, for in the present state of Calcutta he cannot be spared.'[7]

As his ship sailed down the Hoogly, Malcolm wrote frantic notes, including the draft text of a letter of condolence from the King George III to the Shah of Persia, and gave them to the pilot to take back to Government House. His ship took the party down the coast to Masulipatam, where they landed and went by *dawk* to Hyderabad, arriving there on 24 September. While the primary purpose of Malcolm's journey was to get to Bombay as soon as possible, he was incidentally passing en route through the capitals of the Nizam and the Peshwah, and as the Governor-General's special and trusted representative, he could hardly avoid being received in *durbar* at each place. At Hyderabad he was treated with considerably more deference than when he had arrived there as James Kirkpatrick's assistant five years before. 'I am loaded with attention. Hushmat Jang [James Kirkpatrick] has made every arrangement for my reception at Hyderabad, which a sense of propriety and respect for the Governor-General could dictate . . . No man was in such a bustle.'[8]

He found the Nizam's government in complacent mood:

> exulting in that foresight which had led them to form a treaty of defensive alliance with the British Government. On a visit I paid to the Minister Azim-ool-Omrah [Aristu Jah], he told me that I should find all in confusion at Poonah, and 'before you return,' he added, 'we shall have war.' 'I hope not,' said I. 'It is quite impossible to avoid it,' returned the Minister. 'You know how exhausted the countries around Poonah are, from the large armies that have been constantly encamped in the vicinity of that city for several years. The temporary absence of Scindiah and Holkar has permitted them to recover a little; but both these chiefs are now hastening towards this quarter with hordes of plunderers, and you are bound to defend us and the Rajah of Mysore; and supposing these Mahratta chiefs were to abandon that policy by which they exist and desist from plundering their neighbours, the situation into which they are bringing their armies makes it impossible they should persist in so virtuous a resolution. The country into which they are coming cannot

> support them, and if they mean to keep their lawless bands together, they must lead them to plunder. I am not sorry,' he concluded, 'things are coming to this crisis. These Mahratta gentlemen want a lesson, and we shall have no peace until they receive it.[9]

Not recorded is how Malcolm and James Kirkpatrick got on with each other during the visit, which lasted about a week. It was the first time they had met since the Khair un Nissa affair, and the atmosphere was probably rather tense. Khair un Nissa was by now living with her two babies in the special *zenana* quarters which Kirkpatrick had built for her in the Residency garden.

Malcolm now hurried on to Poona, the Mahratta capital, where he was greeted on arrival by his old friend Barry Close, who had taken over as Resident from General Palmer, with a brief from the Governor-General to try to negotiate a 'Treaty of Subsidiary Alliance' with the Peshwah, similar to the ones with Mysore and Hyderabad. But the Mahrattas were an entirely different proposition. In October 1802 the Peshwah held only nominal suzerainty over the Mahratta territories. Real power was now held by the four major Chieftains. Two of them – Dowlat Rao Scindiah of Gwalior and Oujein, Jaswunt Rao Holkar of Indore – had recently arrived in the vicinity of Poona with large armies, both of them intent on overawing the Peshwah and defeating each other in battle. Malcolm accompanied Barry Close to Durbar with the Peshwah: 'Soon after I had paid my respects in the public hall of audience, he, with much apparent earnestness, requested the Resident and myself to accompany him to another room, in order to have a secret conference, from which he pointedly excluded his most confidential advisers. The moment we were in private he commenced his enquiries after the Governor-General's health.' It became clear to Close and Malcolm that the Peshwah was stalling. 'See how he winces at the least touch,' said Close as they left the meeting.[10]

Malcolm left Poona on 7 October, on the last stage of his journey to Bombay. Fifty miles down the road, a bizarre incident occurred – he was kidnapped.

> It was dark before I arrived at Keroli [Karli]. My palanquin was waiting there. I went into it, and, being fatigued with my ride

> in a hot sun, I had fallen into a very profound slumber, when I was suddenly awoke by the noise of a number of armed men on foot and horseback, and the light of twenty or thirty flambeaux. Springing out of the palanquin, I demanded to know why I was so surrounded. 'You are our prisoner,' said a man, who appeared to be the leader of two hundred pikemen, who now encircled me. 'And who are you?' I asked; 'and by what right do you detain an English officer proceeding on the affairs of his Government?'

Resistance was useless, but he managed to send a message about his predicament to Barry Close in Poona. He was sent with a guard to a village in the mountains a few miles off the main road. Here he was held hostage for two days. Typically, he made the most of it. He got on so well with the villagers that on the second day they put on an 'entertainment' for him – comic dances imitating 'fowls' and 'sheep'. One man had been a post office runner many years before, and had witnessed Europeans dancing. Dressed as 'an English lady', he mimicked a minuet. On the third morning a detachment of 1,500 cavalry sent by the Peshwah rescued him. The local Chief was alarmed, fearing fatal retribution from a furious Peshwah, but Malcolm wrote to the Peshwah to say that he had been treated with kindness; it was a matter of mistaken intelligence. The Chief was let off with a fine.[11]

Malcolm arrived in Bombay at last on 9 October, more than eleven weeks after the death of the Persian Ambassador. In the meantime Jonathan Duncan had attempted to conciliate the Ambassador's party. Sensing their opportunity, they had begun to escalate their claims for compensation, with ever more outrageous demands. Duncan had written a letter of apology to the Shah, but Mehdi Ali Khan, the Company's Resident at Bushire, had considered the letter too detailed, and lacking 'two or three paragraphs adapted to the understanding of the natives of this country'. He had therefore taken it upon himself to substitute a letter of his own, falsely accusing the Haji of being to blame for his own death, claiming that this would serve to 'indispose the King's mind against Haji Khalil Khan, that his Majesty may the less regret his being killed'; and justifying this approach in a letter to Duncan by airily remarking that 'falsehood is a common thing in this country'.[12] Such conduct was in due course to prove Mehdi's downfall. Malcolm was furious, and later made sure that Mehdi was pensioned off and an

Englishman appointed to succeed him as Resident at Bushire. Taking immediate control, he wrote a few days later to Edmonstone in Calcutta that 'The Hadjee's body will be conveyed aboard a ship in a day or two, and it will be accompanied to Kirbalah [Karbala] by Abdul Luteef, who will *now* behave *as he ought*, and about forty Persians. The others (about eighty) will remain here until his Majesty's pleasure is known.'[13] He soon got the Persians to calm down and agree to these terms. Luckily, he knew many of them and they knew him. He then wrote a series of letters of abject apology to the Shah and various Persian dignitaries whom he knew. The letter to the Shah was suitably florid.

The saga of the Ambassador's death demonstrates some of Malcolm's strengths and weaknesses as a diplomat. The Governor-General, largely through Malcolm's influence as the acknowledged 'expert' on Persia, grossly overreacted to the event. The Haji was no more than a rich merchant, and the Shah and his Court were not particularly upset by his death. The compensation paid was much more than they expected or needed. The Persians joked that the British might kill ten ambassadors if they would pay for them at the same rate. And the idea of sending Charles Pasley (a Christian) to accompany the Haji's corpse was criticised many years later by Harford Jones (admittedly a man with a long-standing grudge against Malcolm) as certain to be seen by the Persians, not as 'a high compliment', as Malcolm claimed, but (in Muslim terms) as defiling the corpse. On the other hand this is 'hindsight judgment'. Malcolm may have been ignorant of the level of importance which the Persians would give to the incident, but he correctly judged that it could easily escalate out of control (which it nearly did), and took urgent and decisive action to ensure that the diplomatic damage was minimised. He spent too much, but he succeeded.

By the end of October he had sorted out the problem of the Ambassador and was ready to return to Calcutta. Meanwhile, however, a major crisis had erupted in Mahratta country. In a pitched battle at Hadapsar, just north of Poona on 25 October, Holkar's army had defeated the combined armies of Scindiah and the Peshwah; Holkar had entered Poona, and the Peshwah had decamped. This unrest meant that Malcolm could not return to Calcutta overland via Poona. He had to wait for a ship, which finally sailed on 17 November, taking him to Mahe on the Malabar coast. From there he travelled overland to Madras. On the way, he stayed for a few days at Seringapatam with Arthur Wellesley.

They discussed the likelihood of the Company going to war with Holkar and/or Scindia, ostensibly in order to restore the Peshwah to his throne in Poona, but in reality to safeguard the territories of the Company and its allies, Hyderabad and Mysore, against Mahratta plundering.[14]

In Calcutta again after three months away, he found that the magnificent new Government House had at last been completed. It was modelled on Kedleston, the mid-eighteenth century home of the Curzon family in Derbyshire, except that it was built primarily in brick plastered over in white rather than in Derbyshire sandstone, and it had four detached wings or pavilions emanating from the central block (as originally planned by Robert Adam at Kedleston) rather than two. A hundred years later, George Curzon, who had grown up at Kedleston, was to occupy this Government House as Viceroy. He said that it had been his ambition 'from an early age to pass from a Kedleston in Derbyshire to a Kedleston in Bengal'.[15]

Malcolm had organised the first public function at the new Government House while it was still under construction in early May 1802, and several others had been held during the course of the year. Now, on 26 January 1803, there was a grand ball, ostensibly to celebrate the signing of the Peace of Amiens with France; in practice, to celebrate the completion of the new building. Lord Valentia, a travelling British peer, arrived at Calcutta on the morning of the ball, and was immediately invited. He provided a detached view of social life at Calcutta in the time of the Marquess:

> The state rooms were for the first time lighted up. At the upper end of the largest was placed a very rich Persian carpet, and in the centre of that, a *musnud* of crimson and gold, formerly composing part of the ornaments of Tippoo Sultan's throne. On this was a rich chair and stool of state, for Lord Wellesley; on each side, three chairs for the members of council and judges. Down to the door on both sides of the room, were seats for the ladies, in which they were placed according to the strict rules of precedency, which is here regulated by the degree of seniority of the husband in the Company's service. About ten, Lord Wellesley arrived, attended by a large body of aid-de-camps, etc, and after receiving, in the northern verandah, the compliments

> of some of the native princes, and the vakeels of the others, took his seat. The dancing then commenced, and continued till supper. The room was not sufficiently lighted up, yet still the effect was beautiful. The row of chunam [a kind of stucco] pillars, which supported each side, together with the rest of the room, were of a shining white, that gave a contrast to the different dresses of the company. Lord Wellesley wore the orders of St Patrick and the Crescent in diamond. Many of the European ladies were also richly ornamented with jewels. The black dress of the male Armenians was pleasing from the variety; and the costly, though unbecoming habits of their females, together with the appearance of officers, nabobs, Persians, and natives, resembled a masquerade . . . About 800 people were present, who found sufficient room at supper, in the marble hall below; thence they were summoned about one o'clock to the different verandahs to see the fireworks and illuminations.[16]

This ball was Malcolm's swansong as Private Secretary. As far back as 1801, when Barry Close moved to Poona, it had been intended that he should succeed him as Resident at Mysore. But the Calcutta Government had used the offer of the Mysore Residency to retain the services of Josiah Webbe. Now Webbe had returned to Madras, and Arthur Wellesley, at Seringapatam, was pressing the Marquess to release Malcolm for Mysore. In October 1801, Arthur had written to Henry: 'I still have thoughts of going home, particularly if there is to be peace; but I won't leave this country [i.e. Mysore], at all events till Malcolm arrives.'[17] A week after the ball at Government House, Malcolm packed his bags once more and headed south. He was held up at the mouth of the Hoogly by adverse winds and had time to reflect on the last four years, and especially on the heady events of the past eighteen months as Private Secretary to the Marquess.

As his ship, the *United Kingdom*, dropped its pilot, he wrote a highly emotional letter to Henry Wellesley: 'A few days before we parted at Allahabad [in December 1801] you told me that there was no one event in your Indian life with which you were better satisfied than that of having promoted my advancement. I know not what answer I made at the instant, but I never heard an expression which made so deep an impression on my mind.'[18]

He wrote in equally emotional terms to the Marquess: 'Among the various feelings which at this moment occupy my breast, I recognise with exultation that of a personal attachment to your Lordship to be predominant; and I shall glory in every opportunity I may have of showing the nature of the zeal which that attachment inspires, and how far it places me above the common motives which influence men who are busy in the self-interested pursuit of fortune.'[19]

For a man from Malcolm's relatively humble background, to have been 'noticed' by a grandee like the Marquess was genuinely appreciated, as well as being extremely useful to his future career. The relationship, however, always remained one-sided, with Malcolm seeking praise and the Marquess not always making much of an effort to give it. But the Marquess was not releasing Malcolm simply to let him mark time as Resident at Mysore. As so often, he had a deeper motive. He wanted him to play a leading role, alongside Arthur Wellesley and Barry Close, in the upcoming struggle with the Mahrattas. The successful Seringapatam team of 1799 was being reassembled.

CHAPTER ELEVEN

Private Secretary – The College of Fort William, 1801–1802

Hitherto we have followed the Marquess as he devised and implemented his strategy for the Company to achieve paramountcy over the whole of India. And Malcolm was his trusted aide throughout the process. But the Marquess was not content merely to annex provinces and bully Native rulers. His grand imperial vision foresaw that the vastly increased territories which the Company was acquiring could not continue to be run by the ramshackle system developed over the previous forty years. The system was a hangover from the Mughal era of despotic rule.

Warren Hastings had done his best to understand the local scene and adapt Western methods of government to oriental traditions in the directly British-ruled part of the subcontinent. Cornwallis had introduced the so-called 'Permanent Settlement' or *zamindari* system of revenue collection in Bengal, but it was still an inconsistent mess – understandably so, because the Court of Directors were commercial men, more concerned with return on investment than with government administration. The Marquess was sure that an English form of representative democracy could not be introduced, at least not for a very long time, in such a variegated collection of nations with a long tradition of despotic government, and with a government of foreigners holding power, in the last analysis, by the sword. But at least, he felt, the Company's Indian subjects could have some indirect protection against despotic tendencies in their governors, by ensuring that the governors appointed by the Company were accountable to their own King and Parliament back in Britain. His solution envisaged the Governor-General being effectively 'controlled' in his legislative activity by the British government, leaving him with a fairly free hand in his executive role. Answering the obvious objection that British voters were unlikely to be the most efficient agents for promoting the interests of the native population of India, he merely made the lame assertion that: 'at the same time that we excluded our native subjects from all participation in the legislative authority, abundant security was afforded to them, that the exercise of that authority would always be directed to their happiness and comfort'. But he was more 'modern' about the accountability of the executive arm: 'no effectual controul can be exercised over him [the Governor-General] in the administration of the laws, and he may render the laws altogether nugatory by abuses, omissions, or delays in their administration'. This being so, the Governor-General should have no say in the judiciary, which should be independently controlled from London. Again, no local voice.

He went on to argue that if there was no alternative to government administered by expatriate British officers, it was essential for efficiency and fairness that the best possible British officers should be recruited and thoroughly trained for the job. He pointed out the huge change in the scope and complexity of government in British India in the previous twenty years:

He had already complained, in a letter to Dundas, about the quality of government, that:

> the state of the administration of justice, and even of the collection of revenue throughout the provinces, affords a painful example of the inefficacy of the best code of laws to secure the happiness of the people, unless due provision has been made to secure a proper supply of men qualified to administer those laws in their different branches and departments. The evil is felt in every part of this government, and it arises principally from a defect at the source and fountain head of the service, I mean the education and the early habits of the young gentlemen sent hither in the capacity of writers. My opinion . . . is decided, that the writers on their first arrival in India should be subjected for a period of two or three years to the rules and disciplines of some collegiate institution at the seat of government . . . and habits of activity, regularity, and decency, formed, instead of those of sloth, indolence, low debauchery, and vulgarity, now

> too apt to grow on those young men, who have been sent at an early stage into the interior of the country.[1]

Coupled with the plan for this 'collegiate institution' at Calcutta to train young administrators, he proposed compulsory retirement and a pension scheme for Company staff to eliminate ageing and incompetent officials.

His formal proposal for a College of Fort William was put to the Court of Directors in July 1800 at great length. In setting out the curriculum for the College, the Marquess's tremendous imagination went into overdrive. The subjects covered were to be:

> Languages – Arabic, Persian, Shanscrit, Hindoostanee, Bengal, Telinga, Mahratta, Tamil, Canara; Mahomedan law, Hindoo law, ethics, civil jurisprudence, and the law of nations; English law; the regulations and laws enacted by the Governor-General in Council, or by the Governors in Council at Fort St George and Bombay respectively, for the civil government of the British territories in India; political economy, and particularly the commercial institutions and interests of the East India Company; geography and mathematics; modern languages of Europe; Greek, Latin, and English classics; general history, antient and modern, the history and antiquities of Hindoostan and the Deccan; natural history, botany, chemistry and astronomy.[2]

He planned to gather together learned men, both British and Indian, from all parts of India, to staff the College. He saw himself as the reincarnation of the Mughal Emperor Akbar, holding periodic *durbars* 'composed of natives of rank and learning, pundits and moonshees, rajas and foreign ambassadors'.[3] So obviously self-evident did the excellence of the project seem to him, that he did not feel any need to wait nearly a year for the Court's formal approval to come back from London. He went straight ahead and started it.

Viewed with the wisdom of hindsight, the great defect in this concept was that it continued the Cornwallis doctrine of not allowing native participation in the higher ranks of executive government. But it would be a mistake to accuse the Marquess of racial prejudice; his was an advanced form of class prejudice. Throughout his long life, he looked down with aristocratic disdain on just about everybody.

When Malcolm arrived on the Calcutta scene in July 1801, the College was already in full operation. Not surprisingly, he was enthusiastically in favour of it. For someone who had left school at twelve, and had never himself been given the chance to study in a systematic way, the Marquess's vision stood in marked contrast to what he saw as the mean-spirited attitude of many of the Directors. But, as a soldier and administrator rather than a commercial executive, he suffered some of the same defects as the Marquess, chiefly an inability to understand that boards of directors sometimes have a duty to pour cold water on grand projects to safeguard their shareholders' funds.

The Marquess should have realised that his project was in trouble when Dundas, hitherto his great supporter in London, expressed reservations in a letter which reached him as early as September 1800. Dundas and the Board of Control were prepared to support him against the Court of Directors – up to a point. But they were hesitant about overruling the Directors on an issue of spending shareholders' funds on what was, after all, a civic project. In any case, Dundas resigned in early 1801. By January 1802 the new President of the Board of Control had given in to the Court of Directors, who notified the Governor-General that the College should be wound up. The letter was received at Fort William on 15 June 1802, causing consternation.

Malcolm wrote a long letter to Henry Wellesley at Bareilly, with a copy to Arthur at Seringapatam: 'The Directors have ordered the College to be abolished. They praise its institution, and give Lord Wellesley's ability and genius credit for the conception; but their circumstances do not admit of such an appropriation of cash.' Of course, as Malcolm went on, no one was in any doubt that the real force behind the veto was the Shipping Interest, intent on preserving its monopoly of shipping between India and Britain.

The rejection of the College was highly embarrassing and potentially humiliating for the Marquess. He must have been tempted to offer his resignation, but in the end he decided to abide by the Directors' instructions and officially abolish the College, rather than argue the toss with them. He did however seek and gain their permission to wind it down slowly, so that its existing students could complete their courses over the following few years.

Whether Malcolm shared his master's views on the governance of India at this time is a moot point. He certainly supported him to the hilt. That was his job. But his own vision, as it developed over the following years, diverged considerably from that of the Marquess. For instance, together with Tom Munro, he was always a strong advocate of the employment of Indians in the upper levels of government administration.

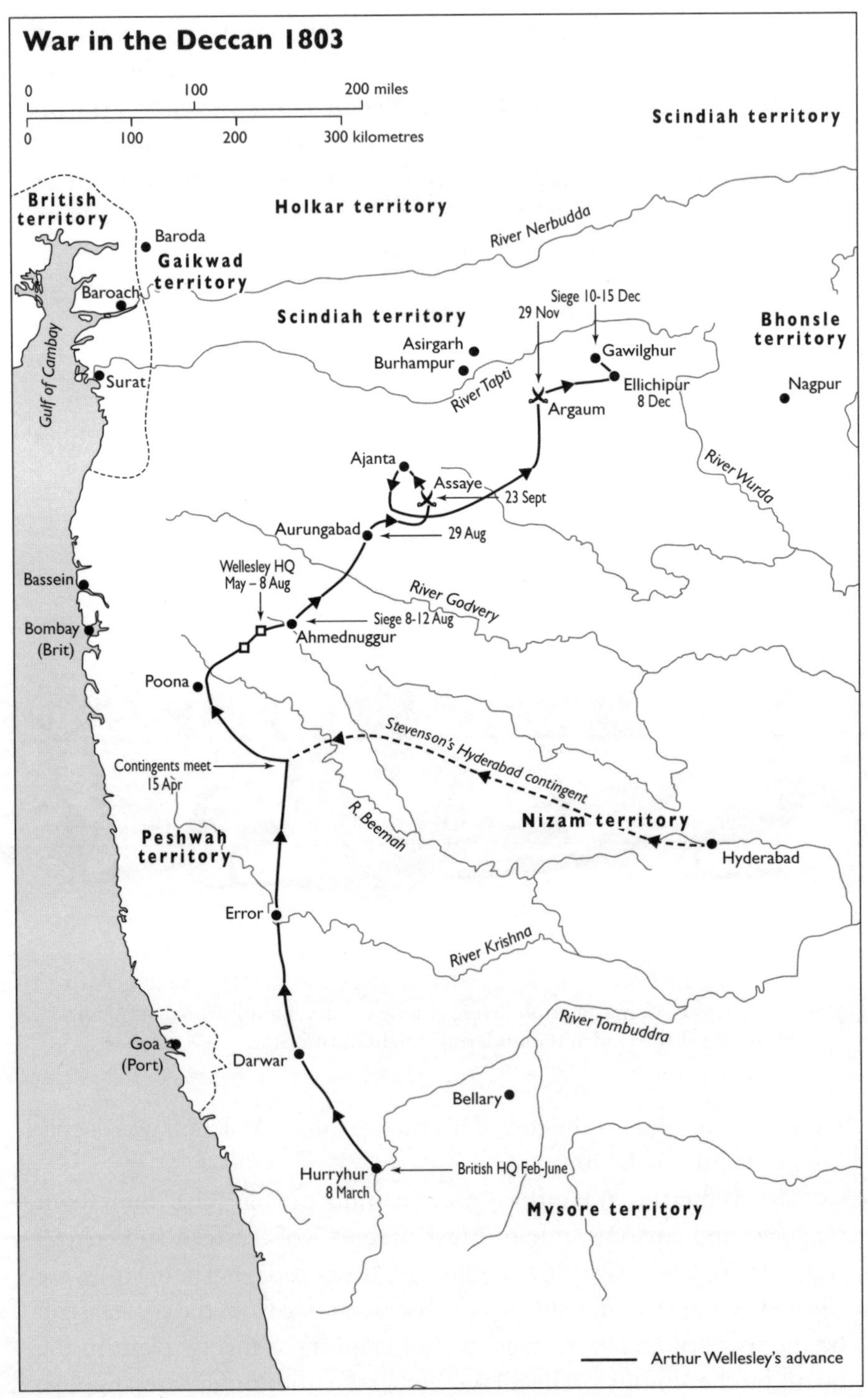
War in the Deccan 1803
0
100
200 miles
0
100
200
300 kilometres
Scindiah territory
British territory
Holkar territory
Baroda
Gaikwad territory
River Nerbudda
Baroach
Scindiah territory
Siege 10-15 Dec
29 Nov
Bhonsle territory
Asirgarh
Burhampur
Gawilghur
Gulf of Cambay
Surat
River Tapti
Ellichipur
8 Dec
Nagpur
Argaum
Ajanta
Assaye
23 Sept
River Wurda
Aurungabad
29 Aug
Wellesley HQ
May – 8 Aug
Bassein
River Godvery
Bombay
(Brit)
Siege 8-12 Aug
Ahmednuggur
Poona
Stevenson's Hyderabad contingent
Contingents meet
15 Apr
R. Beemah
Nizam territory
Peshwah territory
Hyderabad
Error
River Krishna
River Tombuddra
Goa
(Port)
Darwar
Bellary
British HQ Feb-June
Hurryhur
8 March
Mysore territory
Arthur Wellesley's advance

CHAPTER TWELVE

The Mahrattas – Peace and War, 1803

Mahratta Cavalry. Mahratta armies were chiefly cavalry: lightly armed, moving swiftly, living off the land and plundering neighbouring States.

From now on, and for the rest of his Indian career, Malcolm was deeply involved with the Mahrattas.

The Mahrattas (Marathas) are a Hindu people with their own language and customs, inhabiting a large part of western and central India (there are nearly 100 million of them today). Their lands are centred on the Deccan plateau, which is separated from the coastal strip by the western and eastern *ghats,* and from the Gangetic plain in the north by the Vindhya range. Fine horsemen and tough campaigners, they were nevertheless conquered by the Mughals in the sixteenth century, though they retained some elements of independence. In the middle of the seventeenth century they were galvanised into rebellion by their charismatic leader Shivaji, first against the Adilshahi dynasty of Bijapur, and later against the Mughal Emperor Aurangzeb. Shivaji managed to form a roughly cohesive empire which eventually stretched across the subcontinent from the Ganges plain in the north to Mysore in the south.

A Hindu community can be roughly divided into four main castes, namely: *Brahmins* (priests and teachers), *Kshatriyas* (warriors and rulers), *Vaisyas* (farmers, merchants, artisans etc), *Sudras* (labourers), plus 'outcastes' (untouchables). Shivaji and his descendants were *Ksatriyas.* His Chief Minister or Peshwah was, however, a *Brahmin*. On Shivaji's death in 1680, his descendants, the Rajahs of Satara, remained nominal overlords, but central power passed to their *Brahmin* Chief Ministers, the Peshwahs of Poona. In 1761 the combined Mahratta forces suffered a massive defeat at the hands of the Afghan King Ahmed Shah Durrani at Panipat, near Delhi. Over 200,000 men were said to have been killed in the battle. The Mahratta Empire never really recovered after Panipat. It became a loose federation, dominated by four great feudal Kshatriya Chieftains in the northern Mahratta country, and by the Peshwahs themselves in the south. In the late eighteenth century, these northern Chieftains resembled the mediaeval robber barons of Europe, living largely by plundering their neighbours or by exacting *chauth* (protection money) for refraining from doing so. There were no clear-cut boundaries between the lands controlled by each Chieftain; neighbouring villages might belong to different Chieftains.

In the confrontation with the Company from 1803 onwards, the chief Mahratta players were the Peshwah of Poona, Baji Rao II, and the four northern Chieftains. Baji Rao had succeeded to the *musnud* in 1795, aged eighteen. He directly controlled the lands around Poona, and in the south received the somewhat reluctant fealty of several minor Chiefs, known as 'the southern *jaghirdars*', the most important of whom were the Patwardhans and the Rajahs of Kolhapur. Confusingly, despite acting as rulers rather than as priests/teachers, these southern *jaghirdars* were *Brahmins* like the Peshwah. Baji Rao, a rather weak young man, was dominated by an able but elderly Minister, Nana Phadnarvis (or Furnavese), until Nana's death in 1800. Thereafter the dominant influence over Baji Rao was Dowlat Rao Scindiah. Originally from Gwalior and Oujein, the Scindiahs were easily the most powerful of the northern Chieftains. Dowlat Rao's father, Mahadji Scindiah, ruled territories stretching north into Hindustan as far as Delhi where he held the old Mughal Emperor Shah Alam as a virtual prisoner. His large army was partly officered by European mercenaries, and his leading General, in charge of his northern army in Hindustan and operating semi-independently, was a Frenchman called Perron.[1] Raghuji Bhonsle, the Rajah of Berar, based at Nagpur, controlled the eastern part of the Mahratta country all the way across to the Carnatic coast. Jaswunt Rao Holkar, based at Indore, another young man in his twenties, was a fine soldier, but a plunderer rather than a governor. The territory under his control was comparatively small, but he was hungry for more. Lastly, there was Anadrao, Gaekwad of Baroda, based around the Gulf of Cambay.

In 1780, the Mahrattas had fought an indecisive war against the Company. In 1790–92 they had joined with the Company and the Nizam to defeat Tipu Sultan, though their participation had been half-hearted. Technically, their relationship with the Company was governed by the 1792 Treaty following the Mysore War. But they had shown scant regard for the terms of the Treaty, and regularly threatened to plunder the territories of both the Company and the Nizam (for whose defence the Company had become responsible in 1798). The Marquess rightly judged that the Company and its allies could never relax unless some definitive settlement could be made with the Mahrattas. His preferred solution was a subsidiary alliance with the Peshwah, along the lines of the treaties with Mysore, Hyderabad and Oudh. But the Mahratta set-up – with no single ruler in undisputed charge – did not lend itself to this formula, as he was soon to find out.

In October 1802, when Holkar defeated the combined armies of Scindiah and the Peshwah at Hadapsar, his objective was not to dethrone the Peshwah, but to replace Scindiah as the power behind the Peshwah's throne. Baji Rao, however, did not accept Holkar's overtures, preferring to flee to the coast and seek British help to restore him as paramount ruler.

This presented a major dilemma for the British. In a paper written while he was in Bombay in November 1802, Malcolm asserted that the Peshwah would 'never enter into Subsidiary Engagements with the English until he is reduced to a state in which he dreads either the loss

Colonel (later Major General) Sir Barry Close (1758–1813) was British Resident at Mysore (1799–1802) and Poona (1803–11). In December 1802 he signed the Treaty of Bassein with the Peshwah.

of his life or of his liberty, and cannot indulge a hope of being extricated by any other Powers.' He went on to discuss the desirability of the Company signing a treaty with the Peshwah, and concluded that while there were considerable risks attached, they were worth taking.

After wandering for a few weeks around the coastal region to the south-west of Poona, Baji Rao sailed to Bassein, an old Portuguese coastal town just north of Bombay, escorted by a Company ship. Barry Close came from Poona to meet him at Bassein, and on 25 December 1802 they signed a 'Treaty of Subsidiary Alliance'. By this treaty the British undertook to restore the Peshwah to his *musnud* at Poona and to his nominal headship of the Mahrattas. In return the Peshwah was to become a protected Prince, like the rulers of Mysore, Hyderabad and Oudh – in other words he acknowledged British suzerainty. Meanwhile Holkar, having failed to persuade Baji Rao to return to Poona, replaced him on the *musnud* with the younger son of Amrit Rao, an adopted son of Baji Rao's father, and made Amrit Rao himself the Chief Minister.

Restoring the Peshwah might therefore mean ousting Holkar by force from Poona, and quite possibly taking on two other Mahratta Chieftains, Scindiah and Raghubi Bhonsle, as well. It was a risky prospect, especially if these three Chiefs decided to join forces. But the British correctly judged that they were too jealous of each other to cooperate. For this task, the Marquess had decided to appoint Arthur Wellesley to lead the military force and Malcolm to act as the Governor-General's representative and Arthur's political adviser.

In February 1803, as Malcolm sailed down the Carnatic coast to Madras on the *United Kingdom*, the Marquess was putting these staffing arrangements into effect, using the curiously oblique etiquette of the time. The military force being assembled by Arthur at Hurryhur in north-west Mysore (near the frontier with the south Mahratta country) was part of the Madras Army, of which General Stuart was now the Commander-in-Chief. Stuart in turn reported to the Governor in Madras, Lord Clive. At the end of a long letter to Lord Clive, the Marquess wrote, almost as a throwaway line, that: 'Your Lordship may be disposed to avail yourself of the services of Major Malcolm, whose extensive information with regard to the general political system of India, and whose intimate knowledge of my sentiments on this particular branch of policy, will furnish peculiar advantages in accomplishing the measures which your Lordship may pursue, for the purposes of securing the support of the Marhatta feudatories.'[2] Lord Clive passed this message on to General Stuart, in camp at Hurryhur,[3] and Stuart replied to Clive that: 'I have informed Major-General Wellesley of your Lordship's wishes regarding the employment of Major Malcolm.'[4]

Arriving at Madras on 27 February, Malcolm made straight for Fort St George to brief Lord Clive on the Governor-General's strategy:

> A detachment of eight thousand men will move with the Nizam's army towards Poonah, to countenance the Peshwah's return to the capital; and another corps of equal, or superior, strength[5] will advance in cooperation with the Southern Mahratta Jageerdahs, and in communication with the army from Hyderabad, along the Tangabudra,[6] until they are joined by the Peshwah, who will march from some part of the Coast near Bombay, protected by his own followers and a small corps from that settlement.

> Whilst these armies are proceeding towards Poonah to reinstate the Peshwah in his authority, the main body of the Coast army will occupy a position on the frontier of Mysore, for the purpose of covering that country and the Carnatic from the inroads of freebooters, and preserving open the communications with its advanced detachments.[7]

A week later Malcolm was on his way to the Madras Army's camp at Hurryhur. 'I am getting into my palanquin', he wrote, 'and shall be on the frontier in five or six days; and then for the *nusseeb* [destiny]! I cannot tell you the state of my mind, but honest hope, thank God! is uppermost!'[8] After a two-day stop to brief General Stuart, Malcolm hurried on, finally catching up with Wellesley's 'detachment' – really an army – at Hubli, near Dharwar, on 19 March. Wellesley was away for the day but had left instructions that 'a salute of fifteen guns [is] to be held in readiness in the park, to be fired on the arrival at Major General Wellesley's tent of Major Malcolm, the Resident of Mysore'.[9]

The two friends were delighted to be together again on campaign. Apart from Malcolm's brief stopover at Seringapatam in the previous November, they had not seen each other for nearly four years. During that time both of them had matured; Malcolm with the Persian mission, followed by Government House Calcutta; Wellesley as the military supremo of Mysore. Wellesley was now a Major-General and Malcolm still only a Major, despite being exactly the same age, and having more military experience. As well as being friends, they had considerable respect for each other's military and diplomatic abilities.

The plan was for Wellesley's detachment to march on Poona and restore the Peshwah, by peaceful means if possible, by force if necessary. The detachment comprised about 15,000 troops (4,200 cavalry, 9,500 infantry and 1,300 artillery). They were to be supported by the 8,000 troops of the Company's Hyderabad Subsidiary Force, commanded by Colonel Stevenson. The combined contingent had to be large enough to take on Holkar's army, if it came to that point. There were potentially very long lines of communication and supply. The country around Poona had been plundered so thoroughly that no army could survive there for long by living off the land. While in theory the southern *jaghirdars* were supporters of the Peshwah, in practice most of them had some sort of axe to grind with him. In fact his main motivation in signing the

Treaty was to secure the Company's help in subjugating, and in some cases revenging himself upon, these Chiefs. Bad behaviour by Company troops, or any sign of them suffering a setback in the confrontation with Holkar, might tempt these Chiefs to change sides, attack the Company army's extended supply lines and plunder its provisions. Besides, Baji Rao had shown himself again and again to be unreliable. He had only signed the Treaty of Bassein because he was desperate. If the situation changed, he could well turn against the Company. On top of all this, there was the genuine fear of being harried by the formidable Mahratta irregular cavalry.

Just such a situation brought out Arthur Wellesley's military genius, which made his later career so illustrious. He was lucky in his superiors. His elder brother, the Marquess, completely trusted his judgment. But his immediate superior, General Stuart, had also come to know and trust his professional ability during the eighteen months that they had worked together. More importantly, both the Marquess and Stuart were excellent delegators. Over the following few months they gave Arthur complete authority to control the Hyderabad contingent led by Colonel Stevenson, the Bombay Army operating in Gujerat, and even the small force operating out of Ganjam towards Cuttack on the east coast.[10] Stuart had the right to take command of the detachment himself, and could easily have assumed it. Nevertheless, he gave Wellesley virtual *carte blanche* to act in military and political matters as he thought fit, short of actually starting a full-scale war.

Wellesley had prepared for the coming campaign with great care. While accepting that a Company army could never move as fast as the Mahrattas, he was determined to improve its mobility. One problem was that it was firm Company policy not to live off the land, as the Mahrattas tried to do, and 'a part-European army had to carry, among other things, salt beef, biscuit, *arrack* and medicines as well as ammunition'.[11] The army also had to carry rice for the sepoys, who were rice-eating south Indians; and even the horses needed a different type of grain to that available locally. Despite Wellesley's slimming-down, the baggage train was still enormous, and the army's provisions would have to be replenished on its way to Poona from ever-lengthening supply lines. Another problem was water. The climate on the Deccan plateau was different to that of south India. The western *ghats* were well forested and watered but the central plain had thin soil and only occasional water. This water shortage would severely limit the mobility of infantry columns except during the three monsoon months (July to September). Traditionally, campaigning ceased during the monsoon because rivers in spate could not be crossed, even by Mahratta cavalry. Wellesley's answer was to deliberately campaign during the wet season, thus guaranteeing water for his mainly infantry army, and to build basketwork boats to ferry the troops across rivers.

It was thus absolutely vital that the southern *jaghirdars* should be kept friendly. Here Malcolm played a major role. His task was to keep the Chiefs happy, and if possible persuade them to support the Peshwah's restoration, occasionally by the judicious use of bribes. Some of them did so in the hope that the British could bring pressure to bear on the Peshwah to settle their long-standing claims against him. The difficulty was that hardly anyone trusted Baji Rao.

Officially Malcolm was only meant to have joined Wellesley's detachment on a temporary basis, to brief him about the Governor-General's strategy, and then to return to Mysore to take up his post as Resident. But Wellesley wanted him to stay, and Malcolm also soon realised that he was providing valuable service. He wrote a careful letter to Lord Clive, his official boss, intimating that General Wellesley had 'asked him to stay on, as political questions of a serious magnitude seemed likely to arise, and to press for decision as this force approximated Poonah'.[12] He added that he was intending to do so, and hoped Clive would not mind. Of course, the pliant Clive did not mind. Both he and Malcolm knew perfectly well that this was what the Marquess wanted Malcolm to do. Nevertheless, no official directive had been published and over the next few months his status and thus his authority to make decisions remained unclear.

As the detachment neared Poona, they heard from Barry Close (now at Bassein) that the new Peshwah, Amrit Rao, intended to wait until the British were in the vicinity of Poona, then burn down the city and withdraw. Wellesley's reaction was prompt. He wrote to General Stuart that 'I shall move forward briskly to prevent the execution of this horrid plan.'[13] His next letter, dated 21 April, was from 'Camp at Poonah': 'I determined to march to Poonah in the night of the 19th, with the cavalry and a battalion of native infantry. Accordingly, I arrived here yesterday about three o'clock, and found the city in safety. Amrit Rao heard of the movement in the morning, and marched off with some precipitation.

He is now at Juneer with a small force. It is generally believed that Amrit Rao did intend to burn Poonah, but that the city has been preserved by the arrival of the British troops. The infantry of the detachment under my command will arrive here to-morrow.'[14]

This Wellingtonian terseness understates an astonishing feat of endurance. On 19 April the detachment marched, as usual, about twenty miles between 6 a.m. and 1 p.m. and stopped to rest. At 6 p.m., Wellesley, Malcolm and the cavalry, with one battalion of infantry, set off as night fell. They marched all night (it was a full moon) and throughout the next morning. Leaving the infantry battalion at the bottom of the *ghat* just outside Poona, the cavalry arrived in the city in the early afternoon. This was in late April, one of the hottest months of the year. Malcolm wrote a letter to Lord Clive three days later, in more triumphalist tones: 'I have much satisfaction in informing your Lordship of the arrival of the whole of the force under the Honorable Major-General Wellesley at Poonah; which city, there is every reason to believe, was saved from total destruction by a rapid movement of the cavalry under the General's command, who actually marched near sixty miles in thirty-two hours to its relief.'[15] Wellesley and Malcolm billeted themselves in Barry Close's Residency building. The city's inhabitants appeared to be relieved that the city was still intact, and that the threats of the various northern Chieftains had so far come to nothing. The operation had been a success.

The next task was to bring Baji Rao back to Poona, without unduly upsetting the Chieftains. This was easier said than done. Close wrote to Arthur Wellesley from Bassein with increasing exasperation:

> You see that you can conquer a kingdom under the most menacing circumstances, in less time than I can move the Peshwa to re-accept his crown . . . [16]
>
> . . . the misfortune is that all the chieftains that are hostile to the Peshwa sting him constantly with reproaches for his having united with us, by which they say he has shown himself a traitor to his nation, has abdicated his government, degraded himself from the rank of a brahmin and a Maratha, and become literally an outcast. This you see may make peacekeeping a difficult task . . . Hitherto I have thought that I have done much in keeping the Peshwa staunch to the alliance. His mind is so timid and unsteady and his temper so capricious that I could not be

> certain of him, and Scindiah's hopes turned for a long time on the probability that he could be drawn off from us . . . he is slow and indolent and averse to business, unless it is conducted in his own crooked and sinister way . . . At political lying the Marathas are a match for the world.[17]

It is hard not to feel some sympathy for Baji Rao. He had only signed the Treaty of Bassein as a last resort because he could not reach an acceptable deal with Scindiah or Holkar and because he thought the British could bring the southern *jaghirdars* to heel for him. But the British viewed the Treaty differently and they meant business. Rather unrealistically, they expected him to assert his authority (with their help) over Scindiah, Raghuji Bhonsle (Berar) and Holkar; and to reach a compromise with the *jaghirdars*. They felt that they were upholding their end of the bargain by restoring him to his throne and doing their best to conciliate Amrit Rao and the *jaghirdars*, and they now expected him to do his bit in dealing with the northern Chieftains. But, as they soon discovered, he did not have the power to do this, even if he had wanted to. And he did not want to. Any ruler who takes on a foreign ally to help him subjugate his own countrymen must be deeply hurt by the taunts that he is a puppet of the *feringhees* (foreigners). But Baji Rao's handling of the situation was so inept that he managed to lose the confidence not only of the Chieftains but of the British as well.

The Peshwah's party reached the vicinity of Poona in early May, and at last arrived in the city on 13 May, to be met by his increasingly exasperated liberators. The next three months saw an elaborate game of diplomatic bluff. Baji Rao, while not hostile to the British, was in their view thoroughly unreliable and uncooperative. He resisted efforts to conciliate his brother-by-adoption Amrit Rao, and to separate him from Holkar by giving him a *jaghir* and some role in the government. And he remained vindictive towards some of the southern *jaghirdars*, whom the British desperately needed as active allies when they came to confront the northern Chieftains. He actually remained in secret touch with Scindiah, thus giving Scindiah some hope that if he continued to resist the British, the Peshwah might eventually change sides again.

Ostensibly Scindiah was still on good terms with Baji Rao. In October 1802 they had been on the same losing side at the battle of Hadapsar, and immediately after that battle he had welcomed the Company's intention to restore the Peshwah. Moreover, there was a British Resident, Colonel Collins, at his Court to explain the Company's latest negotiating position. But after the Treaty of Bassein, Scindiah had realised that the British were effectively intending to replace him as the power behind the Peshwah's throne. During the first half of 1803, he pursued two parallel policies: to cajole the Peshwah into separating himself from the British alliance while concurrently trying to form a confederacy of northern Chieftains to oust the British by force. He needed time to achieve these objectives, and his tactic was to procrastinate for as long as he could.

Holkar retreated northwards, then wandered around looking for plunderable land, partly to feed the army, partly to intimidate the Nizam and partly to keep Colonel Stevenson's Hyderabad contingent tied up in protecting the Nizam's fertile territory from his attacks. To further complicate matters, the Nizam was expected to die at any moment, which might mean that Colonel Stevenson's contingent would be needed at Hyderabad to maintain order until the Nizam's succession was settled. Raghuji Bhonsle moved his army westwards towards Scindiah's camp, trying to create the impression in British eyes (and in Baji Rao's too) that he was on the point of establishing a 'confederacy' with Scindiah to oppose the British (and the Peshwah, if he continued to support the British).

This was the extremely volatile situation facing Wellesley, Close and Malcolm. They were slowly coming to realise that the Peshwah was not going to honour his side of the bargain which they thought he had made by the Treaty of Bassein. They were playing for high stakes. At worst, the Company army was in potentially hostile foreign territory with lengthening lines of communication and supply problems. The expected support of the southern *jaghirdars'* cavalry was not forthcoming; and there was a strong possibility that the northern Chieftains would combine to oppose the Company in battle. Meanwhile, as time went by, the enormous cost of maintaining the army in the field was mounting alarmingly. Cool nerves were called for and no one had cooler nerves than Arthur Wellesley. And in Malcolm and Close, he had two brilliant and highly experienced soldier-diplomats at his side. Malcolm had anticipated this situation when he wrote to General Stuart in March: 'A political agent is never so likely to succeed as when he negotiates at the head of an army; and in a crisis like the present, it appears indispensable to speedy and complete success, that the military operations and political negotiations should be conducted from the same point. Otherwise, we never can take full advantage of the various events which we must expect to arise in the course of an affair which involves such complicated interests as at present.'[18]

Malcolm, in short, was in his element. But in the first week of May, he was struck down by fever. He became quite seriously ill, and his illness was to persist, on and off, for nearly eighteen months. Arthur wrote to General Stuart that 'Major Malcolm is sick, and is gone into Poona',[19] and was sufficiently worried about him to suggest to the Marquess that he should be sent to Bengal to brief him about the Mahratta situation; and in the process recuperate on the sea voyage. But Malcolm was not to be deterred. A few days later he wrote to Merrick Shawe and Edmonstone in Calcutta, saying that he was too sick to write, but was doing so anyway. He worked from his sickbed, compiling a long memorandum to the Governor-General, concluding: 'I am still sanguine in the hope that the great measure of settling the Peishwah's government will be accomplished without even the appearance of war.'[20]

The British policy now was to make the northern Chieftains retreat into their own territories and to accept the suzerainty of the Peshwah. This was the only way that the territories of the Company and its allies, Hyderabad and Mysore, would be safe from plundering freebooters, and some semblance of peace and prosperity restored to the Mahratta territories. Colonel Collins was instructed to tell Scindiah to agree to retire to his own territories and accept some sort of subsidiary alliance arrangement with the Company. Scindiah played for time, with ambiguous answers to Collins's demands. A similar approach was made to the Bhonsle. Holkar's attitude was not known, but since he did not seem to be threatening anyone, he was left alone for the time being.

On 4 June Wellesley led his army northwards from Poona and camped outside Ahmednuggar. The plan was that, if war was declared with Scindiah, Wellesley's first objective would be to take possession of Ahmednuggar and use it as his base for further operations. Malcolm stayed behind in Poona, partly because he was too ill to travel, partly because he and Close had their work cut out trying to get the Peshwah to settle with Amrit Rao and the southern *jaghirdars*, and to procure carriage bullocks, which were in desperately short supply. He wrote to Wellesley on 18 June enclosing a long memorandum analysing the situation, which he copied to Calcutta, ending despondently: 'I have lost all faith, God knows I never had much, in this court . . . If we place any dependence whatever in the aid of this court we shall be liable to constant disappointment, and we ought not to engage in hostilities unless we are prepared to take their weight on our own shoulders.'[21] Wellesley replied immediately, agreeing 'almost entirely' with Malcolm's opinions, and candidly admitted how much they had misread the Mahratta situation: 'We have been mistaken entirely regarding the constitution of the Marhatta empire. In fact the Peshwah never has had exclusive power in the state. It is true, that all treaties have been negotiated under his authority, and have been concluded in his name; but the chiefs of the empire have not consented to them; and the want of this consent in any one of them, or of power in the head of the empire, independent of these chiefs, is the difficulty of the case at the present moment.'[22]

Wellesley was by this time totally exasperated with Baji Rao. He wrote to Malcolm: 'I wish with you that the Peshwah would act as he speaks; but he is a terrible fellow, and I have no hopes from him';[23] and to Close that 'the only principle of [Baji Rao's] conduct is his insincerity'.[24]

By 24 June, Malcolm felt sufficiently recovered to struggle out to Wellesley's camp near Sanghvi, about forty miles north of Poona, and a week later he wrote another long memorandum to Calcutta, describing the 'very strong remonstrance' which he and Close had delivered to the Peshwah on 23 June. By now, Baji Rao's lack of cooperation led Malcolm to suggest that the Company might unilaterally conciliate Amrit Rao with 'a scheme of gift of territory', from the lands allocated to the Company under the Treaty of Bassein; and if this led to Baji Rao fleeing Poona and joining Scindiah or Raghuji Bhonsle, so be it. It would enable the Company to 'substitute a more efficient local authority at that city' (i.e. Poona). And as a parting shot he concluded that if Baji Rao changed sides 'there cannot exist a doubt but that he would be found to the full as impotent as an enemy as he has hitherto proved himself as an ally'.[25]

But in early July he fell sick again with 'a severe relapse'. He told Shawe that 'you will hardly be able to read this letter; I write in pain. To add to my other ills, I have some symptoms which make me think that my liver is affected.' To Close in Poona he wrote that 'I have been very unwell with liver-complaint, for which I have begun a course of mercury. I have had a bowel complaint – my spirits begin to fail me. I feel incapable of holding out much longer in Camp against an accumulation of such disorders.'[26] For the first time, he began to talk of going to Bombay for a couple of months to recuperate.

Throughout July he lay sick in camp. He did some useful minor jobs such as drawing up a draft agreement with Amrit Rao, which envisaged Amrit Rao joining the British side, in return for lands with an estimated annual income of seven lakhs of rupees.[27] But he was unable to play any active part in the negotiations with Scindiah, which were now reaching a climax. Wellesley had asked the Marquess for full powers to wage war, if necessary, against Scindiah and Raghuji Bhonsle, and on 17 July, he got them.[28] The next day he wrote to Colonel Collins, instructing him to deliver an ultimatum to Scindiah to withdraw his troops from the Hyderabad frontier within a time limit, or face attack. With no answer forthcoming, Wellesley wrote to Scindiah on 6 August what was in effect a declaration of war, concluding: 'I offered you peace on terms of equality, and honourable to all parties; you have chosen war; and are responsible for all consequences.'[29]

The next day Wellesley set out for Ahmednuggar. Malcolm dragged himself along. He was less feverish but not much use. To add insult to injury, he received from Calcutta letters delivering a 'wigging' (ticking-off) from the Marquess. Although the situation had been changing on a daily basis, Malcolm had been sending updates to Calcutta about once a week. One quite significant development, about the shortage of bullocks, had led them to plead with the Peshwah to provide some more. News of this had first come to Calcutta in a letter from Close rather than from Malcolm. The Marquess was not impressed. 'His Excellency', wrote Shawe, 'requests that you contrive to write daily from General Wellesley's camp. A few words will be sufficient.' The letter went on to provide that most exquisite form of torture which head office staff can inflict on officers in the field – treating them as complete idiots. 'His Lordship doubts the policy of informing the Peishwah that the British army is at his mercy.'[30] The insinuation that three such experienced diplomatic operators as Wellesley, Close and Malcolm would have lacked the elementary nous to realise that such a danger existed was insulting. Malcolm would probably like to have sent an equally insulting reply. But displeasing his hero, the Marquess, was his worst nightmare, and now, in his weakened state, he probably took it all far too seriously. 'I by no means deny that the weakness of my judgment in one instance, and my culpable negligence in another, did not fully merit the censure which I have received.'[31] When his letter was received at Government House, there was general hilarity at his earnestness.

Malcolm was still in camp when Ahmednuggar was stormed on 12 August. He was present at the signing of the surrender document by the *vakeels* of the enemy, but complained that: 'I am reduced so low that the General has joined the pack of doctors who insist on my retiring to the sea coast for a short time'[32] He left camp next day, travelling slowly – about ten miles a day – by palanquin to Bombay, arriving in late August. There he stayed for nearly two months. It was a time of intense frustration for him. He had been waiting and preparing for several years, both as a soldier and as a diplomat, for this climactic moment of confrontation with the Mahrattas. Now all he could do was to sit on the sidelines like an athlete who has trained for years for the Olympic Games, only to hurt himself just before the big race.

Nevertheless, his health had started to improve on the journey and after a week in Bombay he was back at work writing letters. Despite being unable to use him in the campaign, Wellesley still found time to write frequent letters to him from camp (at least fifteen during Malcolm's two-month stay in Bombay). He used Malcolm as his trusted confidant and sounding board, to float and clarify his own developing military strategy and political ideas.

Malcolm's presence in Bombay did also help to solve one problem for Wellesley: the chain of command in the Gujerat region. In July he had been given command of that part of the Bombay Army which covered the Gujerat region, and which was normally answerable to the Governor of Bombay. The idea was to provide a unified command to face any possible westward attack by Holkar on Baroda, or to threaten Holkar's rear if he were to march eastwards to attack Hyderabad. The Resident at the Gaekwad's Court was a Colonel Walker. Governor Duncan was alarmed by the order from Calcutta to make the local military commander, Colonel Murray, report directly to Wellesley, rather than through the Resident. Malcolm calmed him down, and persuaded him to authorise the change by agreeing to accept the buck of responsibility passed to him by the risk-averse Duncan.[33] It was an attractive trait in Malcolm's character, but a potentially rash one, as future events were to show.

In September, letters from Wellesley tracked his progress northward, searching all the time for Scindiah's army so that he could bring it to battle. Malcolm continued to write letters to all and sundry. He also tried to keep his contacts in England informed of events. Then came the news of Welleseley's tremendous victory over the combined armies of Scindiah and Raghuji Bhonsle at Assaye on 23 September. The story of Assaye has been told many times. The battle, viciously fought, was over in less than two hours, with great heroism and appalling losses on both sides. But the British were left in charge of the field and of most of Scindiah's ninety guns.

Arthur wrote to Malcolm on 26 September:

> Colonel Close will have informed you of our victory on the 23rd. Our loss has been very severe, but we have got more than 90 guns, seventy of which are of the finest brass ordnance I have ever seen. The enemy, in great consternation, are gone down the ghauts. Stevenson follows them to-morrow. I am obliged to halt, to remove my wounded to Dowlatabad.
>
> PS The bay horse was shot under me, and Diomed[34] was piked, so that I am not now sufficiently mounted. Will you let me have the grey Arab? I must also request for you to get for me two new saddles and bridles.[35]

Two days later Wellesley wrote again: 'our victory of the 23rd has been very complete. The enemy lost 1200 killed, and their wounded and dying are on all parts of the road from here to Adjuntee [Ajanta]. All agreed that the battle was the fiercest that has ever been seen in India. Our troops behaved admirably; the sepoys astonished me.'[36]

Malcolm was, of course, thrilled with this news. But he was also hugely relieved. No one knew better what risks he and the Wellesleys had taken from the outset of the campaign. No one knew better that victory over Scindiah's forces was anything but inevitable. It was not just a matter of numbers, although the Mahratta army outnumbered the Company's by six to one. The core of Scindiah's army was well trained, led by professional European mercenary officers, and at least as well equipped as the Company's forces. Assaye was about five hundred miles (about eighty days' bullock march) north of the Company's headquarters and supply base at Hurryhur. They knew that the country in between was controlled by the southern *jaghirdars*, who gave only fickle acquiescence to the Peshwah, who in turn, despite his treaty obligations, was communicating secretly with Scindiah. Both were watching to see which side would win. For the Company, to lose such a battle (or any battle) would therefore be a disaster – the one thing which might unite the disparate Mahratta Chieftains in waging war against it.

But his joy was heavily tempered; he had not been on the field of battle. 'My fate did not permit that I should share in the honors which every individual on that field has acquired. During life I shall regret my absence.'[37] By 'honors', he meant not only battle honours, but the more mundane reward of prize money as well. He was becoming increasingly desperate to rejoin Wellesley's camp before the next battle. During October, he spent some time trying again to smooth relations between Wellesley and Jonathan Duncan on the issue of Wellesley's takeover of the Gujerat command. Duncan had written to Wellesley that he 'acquiesced' in this, but he did not 'approve' of it. Wellesley became uncharacteristically tetchy, telling Duncan that if that was his attitude, he (Wellesley) would refuse to become directly involved in the Gujerat campaign.

Meanwhile Malcolm's health was slowly improving. He left Bombay on 27 October and reached Poona on 5 November, but suffered a recurrence of headaches and had to rest there for a further fortnight. On 17 November, he finally set off on the 250-mile trek north from Poona to Wellesley's camp, escorted by a small cavalry detachment. En route, he heard the news of General Lake's victories over Scindiah's Hindustan army, the taking of Delhi on 18 October, the battle of Laswarrie on 1 November; and in the Deccan, the fall of Burhampur and the fort of Asirghar to Colonel Stevenson's Hyderabad troops, followed by Wellesley's second great victory, over Raghuji Bhonsle of Berar at Argaum on 29 November. By 15 December, when he was within a few miles of Wellesley's camp, outside the great hill fortress of Gawilghur, he heard a distant sound of gunfire. Guessing that Gawilghur was being stormed, he sent a note asking what was happening. It was answered by Wellesley himself, scribbling on the back of the envelope: 'We have taken the fort without much loss. I am this instant back from thence . . . I don't detain the bearers one instant, and send them back to you. God bless you, my dear Malcolm. I long to see you.'[38] It was the last major engagement of the campaign and he was rejoining the army, a few hours too late to be a participant.

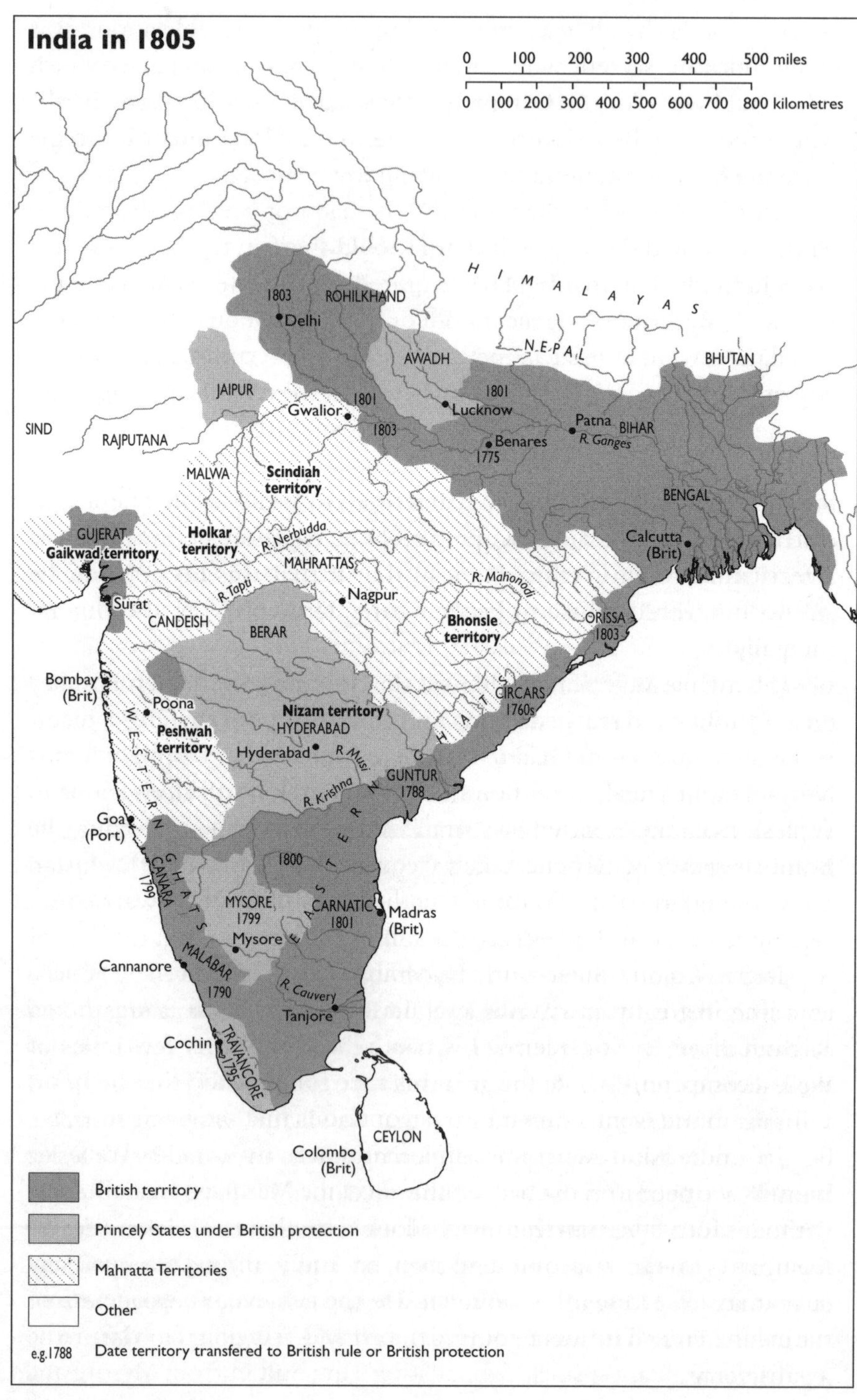

India in 1805
0
100
200
300
400
500 miles
0
100
200
300
400
500
600
700
800 kilometres
HIMALAYAS
NEPAL
BHUTAN
1803
ROHILKHAND
Delhi
AWADH
JAIPUR
1801
Lucknow
1801
Gwalior
1803
Patna
BIHAR
R. Ganges
Benares
1775
SIND
RAJPUTANA
MALWA
Scindiah territory
BENGAL
GUJERAT
Gaikwad territory
Holkar territory
R. Nerbudda
MAHRATTAS
Calcutta (Brit)
R. Mahonadi
R. Tapti
Nagpur
Surat
CANDEISH
BERAR
Bhonsle territory
ORISSA 1803
Bombay (Brit)
Poona
Peshwah territory
Nizam territory
HYDERABAD
Hyderabad
R. Musi
CIRCARS 1760s
GUNTUR 1788
R. Krishna
WESTERN GHATS
EASTERN GHATS
Goa (Port)
CANARA 1799
1800
MYSORE 1799
CARNATIC 1801
Madras (Brit)
Mysore
Cannanore
MALABAR 1790
R. Cauvery
Tanjore
Cochin
TRAVANCORE 1795
CEYLON
Colombo (Brit)
British territory
Princely States under British protection
Mahratta Territories
Other
e.g.1788
Date territory transfered to British rule or British protection

CHAPTER THIRTEEN

The Mahrattas – Scindiah, 1804

When he reached Wellesley's camp next morning, Malcolm found the staff in gloomy mood. After months of campaigning, marching up to twenty miles a day, living constantly in tents, searching for the enemy, skirmishing and fighting bloody battles, they were physically and mentally exhausted. For Wellesley, Malcolm's absence had been particularly hard, because he had had to act as chief diplomatic negotiator as well as military commander. Malcolm's arrival was, therefore, 'like a sudden burst of sunshine'.[1] He brought much-needed supplies of wine and beer and brandy, and news from the outside world, and 'a brisk explosion of jokes'. He showed off the Arab horses he had brought from Bombay, and generally cheered everyone up. He was as delighted to be back among his friends as they were to receive him. Despite his uncertain health, he was 'Boy Malcolm' again.

There was no time to settle in. Mountstuart Elphinstone had been standing in for him as Wellesley's liaison officer with Scindiah and Raghuji Bhonsle. Considering his youth (he was twenty-four), he had done a competent job. But now it was time for Malcolm to take up the reins again. He went straight into negotiations that same morning.

To understand Malcolm's diplomatic activity over the next six months, we need to backtrack. In June 1803, the Marquess was still sticking to his four-stage strategic plan, adopted back in 1798, envisaging the Company as the paramount power in India through a series of subsidiary alliances with local rulers. He had achieved stage one, eliminating the French influence at Hyderabad and bringing the Nizam into a subsidiary alliance; stage two, ousting Tipu Sultan from Mysore and replacing him with a compliant Hindu rajah; and stage three, annexing the Carnatic and converting Oudh and Tanjore into tributary states. But stage four, dealing with the Mahrattas, was always going to be the most formidable challenge. By the Treaty of Bassein in December 1802 he thought he had brought the Peshwah under control, and through him the whole Mahratta Empire. But Baji Rao and the Mahrattas were proving to be quite unlike the Nizam or Tipu. As Sir John Shore, the Marquess's predecessor, had put it: 'the Maratha dominion is an aristocracy, which connects many discordant individuals; but avarice, ambition and rapacity are the ruling principles, not only of the paramount government of Poona, but of all the feudal chieftains'.[2]

As time went by, however, it became increasingly clear to the key Company men on the ground – Wellesley, Close and Malcolm – that the Peshwah could not control Scindiah or Raghuji, let alone Holkar. Only the much weaker Gaekwad of Baroda had been brought more or less under control in 1802. So the Marquess had to modify his plan and deal with these three Chieftains separately.

Immediately after the Battle of Argaum, Raghuji Bhonsle sued for peace. From Raghuji the Company demanded the cession of the whole province of Cuttack, thus cutting off Berar from direct access to the sea, and incidentally giving the Company direct control of the entire Indian sea coast from Calcutta to Gujerat, apart from Travancore and the small enclave of Goa. By the time Malcolm arrived at Wellesley's camp on 16 December, Raghoji's *vakeel*, Yeetal Punt, 'a little plump man', had largely completed negotiations, and Elphinstone was left to draft the treaty document. In a letter to Edward Strachey, he described what happened: 'Next day [16 December] Major Malcolm came, and that day passed in negotiation, and the night in copying the Treaty. The moonshees wrote in my tent, and I woke every now and then and looked over them. Next morning Major M talked to me about the Nagpur secretaryship [Nagpur was the capital of Berar]. I said I should like to stay with the army; he said somebody must go before Webbe can come. I said I would; he hinted that he would; I said I should be extremely glad to go with him. You know he talks diffusely and indistinctly, but this was *al ghurruz* [the gist].'[3] A week later, Yeetal Punt came back to the camp to finalise the Treaty. An eyewitness, Captain James Welsh of the Madras Army, described the occasion:

> At noon, Bonsala's [Bhonsle's] vakeel, Yeetal Punt, arrived without any state, and all the officers having assembled at the door of the General's tent, he came out with Major Malcolm. They saluted the *vakeel*, and each taking a hand, conducted him to a seat between them. As soon as compliments had passed, he pulled a bundle of papers out of his pocket, and the General, at the same time, ordering a similar one to be brought from his sleeping tent; they then exchanged them, the vakeel declaring that such and such marks in Mahrattah were the Rajah's bone fide personal signature, with the date correct. The band immediately struck up 'God Save the King' . . . the company departed, without much ceremony, to meet again in the evening.[4]

Not long after the Battle of Assaye, Scindiah's *vakeels* had made overtures for peace, but in Wellesley's view they had not carried sufficiently strong credentials from their Chieftain. This was not surprising, for Scindiah, a vacillating young man, was finding it hard to come to terms with the consequences of his military defeat.

From Scindiah, the Company demanded the cession of Broach and all of his territory in Gujerat; all of his territory north of an imaginary line stretching east-west through Jaipur; all of his territory south of the Nerbudda (Narmada) river; the Rana of Gohad to become a tributary chief of the Company; Gwalior to be occupied by the Company;[5] and, finally, his acceptance that the Mughal Emperor's person would fall under Company protection.[6] On 16 October, the Company amplified these terms by demanding that Scindiah should accept a British Resident at his Court on a permanent basis; ban all other Europeans (especially Frenchmen) from serving in his government or army, except with the Resident's approval; admit responsibility for starting the war;[7] and accept the terms of any treaties which might be made between General Lake and Scindiah's northern tributary Chieftains in Hindustan.

On the same day (23 December) that the Treaty with Raghuji Bhonsle was ratified, the preliminary skirmishing with Scindiah's lesser *vakeels* also gave way to more substantial negotiations. Scindiah's *Dewan* arrived at the British camp. Again, Welsh was there:

> At three o'clock, p.m., our light companies arrived at the

> General's tent, to wait the arrival of Scindiah's Dewaun, who made his appearance in great state, about five p.m, attended by the General, Major Malcolm, and all the English officers, Eswunt Row Goreporee [a Mahratta representative of the Peshwah at the camp] and other respectable natives; and followed by state elephants, camels, horses, etc, and two hundred of his master's chosen cavalry, as an escort. We saluted him with presented arms, and the 'Grenadiers March'; the park also resounding its shout of welcome.
>
> A decrepit old Brahmin, whose nose and chest almost met each other, and dressed in a coarse white cloth, without a single ornament, yet the Prime Minister and chief ruler of a most extensive kingdom, now stood before our astonished eyes. He was conducted into the tent by the General [Wellesley] and Political Agent [Malcolm], as usual, and seated between them.[8]

The 'decrepit old Brahmin' was Bapu Wattel Punt, whose inscrutable demeanour led Malcolm to nickname him 'Old Brag' after Brag, the poker game.[9] Wattel Punt was accompanied by Munshi Kavel Nyn. Over the next four months, and again a year later, these two men were to be Malcolm's regular counterparts in negotiations.

The next day negotiations started in earnest, and on Christmas Day Malcolm wrote to Shawe in Calcutta that it had been agreed that there should be two agreements: a Treaty of Peace (which came to be known as the Treaty of Surji Anjangaon); and a Treaty of Defensive Alliance (the British sometimes referred to such treaties, more accurately, as 'Treaties of Subsidiary Alliance').[10]

The Treaty of Peace was duly signed on 30 December. Since neither side knew what commitments might have been made in negotiations between General Lake and Scindiah's feudatory Chiefs to the north in Hindustan, the Articles relating to the cession of Scindiah's territory were necessarily vague. This appeared to Scindiah's *vakeels* to be an open-ended commitment, and right up till the last moment they were understandably unhappy about it. In the end Wellesley and Malcolm persuaded Scindiah to sign the Treaty of Peace, by assuring his *vakeels* that he could rely on British good faith, plus a personal assurance from Wellesley that there was no intention to deprive Scindiah of any territory which had not already been ceded. In other words, they fell back on the slogan, 'Trust Us'. Both Wellesley and Malcolm were sincere in giving these assurances. But they had reckoned without the Marquess; and as events turned out, this ambiguity was to generate an almost fatal breakdown in mutual trust in the months to come.

Malcolm's next task was to negotiate a Treaty of Defensive Alliance with Scindiah at his *durbar* (camp) at Burhampur, and to clarify the way in which the Treaty of Peace would be implemented, as soon as the facts became clear. He left camp on 7 January, armed with a lengthy brief from Wellesley. It was a critical mission. If Scindiah and Raghuji Bhonsle could be signed up to defensive alliances, only Holkar would remain outside the British embrace. The Marquess had put Wellesley in overall charge of the negotiations with Scindiah, covering his Gujerat and his Hindustan territories as well as the Deccan. And Wellesley was now trusting Malcolm to bring the negotiations to a successful conclusion. He was the point man for a major diplomatic enterprise.

Negotiating such a treaty with Scindiah should have been straightforward. The Company would effectively assume responsibility for the foreign affairs and defence of the Maharajah's state. Six thousand Company infantry, plus proportionate artillery and cavalry, would be held ready to defend Scindiah's frontiers. They would be maintained from the revenues of the territories ceded to the Company under the Treaty of Peace. The treaties of defensive alliance with Mysore and Hyderabad, and even with the Peshwah, were examples of what was required. But in Mysore and Hyderabad the Company was dealing with a single ruler of a contiguous territory. Scindiah's pre-war territories, on the other hand, were a scattered hotchpotch stretching all the way from Delhi in the north to near Poona in the south, over 800 miles.

Moreover, the Company's chain of command was awkwardly dispersed. The Marquess in Calcutta had authorised Wellesley (and Malcolm) in the Deccan to negotiate with Scindiah on the whole range of his territories, but he had concurrently authorised General Lake to negotiate with Scindiah's feudatory Chiefs in Hindustan. As Commander-in-Chief, Lake was senior to Wellesley and understandably unhappy to defer to a junior officer. Communication was slow. It took three weeks for letters from the Deccan to reach Calcutta. The distance to Lake was much shorter but messages had to go through hostile territory so their passage was unreliable. In the critical months of December and January, Wellesley and Malcolm had little idea about what terms were being negotiated by Lake and Scindiah's feudatory Chiefs in Hindustan.

Malcolm arrived at Scindiah's Burhampur camp on 11 January. He was feeling ill again. The next day he was presented to the young Maharajah. The event was described in a letter Wellesley later forwarded to the Marquess:

> at the first meeting Scindiah received him with great gravity, which he had intended to preserve throughout the visit. It rained violently; and an officer of the escort, Mr Pepper, an Irishman . . . sat under a flat part of the tent which received a great part of the rain that fell. At length it burst through the tent upon the head of Mr Pepper, who was concealed by the torrent that fell, and was discovered after some time by an 'Oh Jasus!' and an hideous yell. Scindiah laughed violently, as did all the others present; and the gravity and the dignity of the durbar degenerated into a Malcolm riot – after which they all parted on the best terms.[11]

The state of affairs in Scindiah's camp was dire. Beaten in battle, his army's morale was low. The troops had not been paid for months. Opportunities for further plunder were limited. Desertion, not only of individual soldiers but of tributary Chiefs and their followers, was increasing. The monsoon had failed in 1803. This was bad enough for a Company army, because there was no grass for the carriage bullocks bringing grain from the south. But for a Mahratta army, which lived off the land, it was catastrophic. The waterholes were drying up. And in late January plague struck the camp.

As for Scindiah himself, he had no personal desire to make a Treaty of Defensive Alliance with the British, and he later took every opportunity of avoiding his treaty obligations. But he did have one overriding motive for seeking British protection. He was terrified of another beating by Holkar, still at large with a fully intact army. In the short term, only the British could prevent that. And, like most Mahratta rulers, he took an opportunistic approach to policy.

Within a week Malcolm had put together a draft treaty document[12] for Scindiah's *vakeels* to consider. To make it more attractive to the leading figures in Scindiah's Court, he inserted 'inducements' for certain *sirdars*, payable only when the Treaty was implemented. At the end of January, Scindiah fell ill, delaying discussion for three weeks. Eventually the Mahratta response came back, and Malcolm reported that 'I received yesterday the fruit of their long consultations in the draft of a treaty of nineteen articles; so great a jumble of nonsense was never collected into a regular form.'[13] This response was probably what we would today call an 'ambit claim'. One can imagine Wattel Punt and Kavel Nyn allowing Scindiah's nobles to have their say, knowing full well that their suggestions would have no chance of being accepted, but preferring that 'the English' should be the ones to incur the odium of turning them down.

Scindiah had only one significant objection to Malcolm's draft treaty document. Calcutta had laid down that the Subsidiary Force should be stationed at or near the capital city of the ruler,[14] as in the Hyderabad and Mysore treaties, and Malcolm's draft had followed this policy. Scindiah objected, understandably fearing that it would lessen his personal authority. Arthur Wellesley was disposed to concede the point. As it turned out, the Marquess weakened just enough to enable Malcolm to negotiate a compromise. The final wording was that 'the force is to be stationed at such place, near the frontier of Dowlet Rao Scindiah, as may hereafter be deemed most eligible by the British Government'. The necessary amendments to the original draft were made, and the Treaty of Defensive Alliance was signed on 27 February, subject to ratification by the Governor-General within seventy days.

The immediate reaction on both sides was relief followed by euphoria: 'I am to deliver the treaty to-day, and after that ceremony is over, to play hooley [a traditional Indian spring festival, during which red powder and coloured water are thrown at passers-by], for which I have prepared an old coat and an old hat. Scindiah is furnished with an engine of great power by which he can play upon a fellow fifty yards distance. He has, besides, a magazine of syringes, so I expect to be well squirted.'[15] The drenching did him no good. He wrote to Shawe that 'the cursed hooley play' had given him a sharp recurrence of fever.

As he waited for reactions to the Treaty from Calcutta, Malcolm began to worry. The Marquess, under pressure from the Directors in London, had become increasingly irritable and difficult to please. And neither Shawe, his Private Secretary, nor Edmonstone, his political secretary, had the strength of personality or the character to question his judgment. He was surrounded by greedy British officials in Bengal, trying to stretch the legal wording of treaties to grab as much territory as they could. Arthur Wellesley had become exasperated: 'In fact, my dear Malcolm . . . there is no person about the Governor-General to take an enlarged view of the state of our affairs, and to resist the importunities of the local [British] authorities to force on the treaties a construction which will tend to increase their own petty power and authority.'[16] But a few days later, good news started to flow in. Wellesley (now in Bombay) wrote, on 18 March: 'I sincerely congratulate you upon the success of your negotiations with Dowlut Rao Scindiah. The treaty which you have concluded appears to me to embrace all important objects, and it secures the tranquillity of the possessions of the Company, and those of their allies.'[17]

And in early April he received what he had been waiting for – much desired pats on the back from Calcutta, in a letter from Shawe: 'The duplicate of your subsidiary treaty was received this morning through Hindustan. I have the most sincere pleasure in telling you that it meets his Excellency's approbation in every point.'[18]

The Treaty of Defensive Alliance had thus been brought to a successful conclusion.

Meanwhile the Treaty of Peace, signed on 30 December, had left several loose ends to be tied up; and since they involved cessions of territory, they were of more immediate importance to Scindiah and his *vakeels* than the Treaty of Defensive Alliance. Malcolm's task was to clarify the effect of Article 9 of the Treaty on Jodhpur, Jaipur, Gohad (including Gwalior) and some other feudatory territory. Jodhpur and Jaipur posed no problem – Scindiah readily accepted their loss since they were in any case already largely independent. But he did not expect to lose the territory of Gohad, and especially the fort of Gwalior.

Gohad and Gwalior had a troubled history. Captured from the Mughals in 1760 by the Rana of Gohad, a petty Jat prince named Chhatria Singh, it was later annexed by Mahadji Scindiah, Dowlat Rao's father. In mid-December 1803, Dowlat's Rao's military commander, Ambaji Inglia, playing a double game, negotiated secretly with General Lake, whereby in exchange for becoming a Company tributary, he would obtain the *jaghir* of Gwalior and some surrounding country. At this point, just to further complicate the issue, Kirat Singh, a purported descendant of the Rana of Gohad, appeared on the scene and, encouraged by the British, seized part of the Gohad territory from Ambaji Inglia. He then signed a treaty with General Lake, ceding Gohad and Gwalior to the British in exchange for recognition of himself as a tributary, independent of Scindiah (and presumably of Kirat Singh as well). But Ambaji then refused entry to the Gwalior fort to the British. The British declared that any treaty they might have had with Ambaji was now null and void, and took possession of the fort anyway, on 5 February. When the Treaty of Peace between Scindiah and the British had been signed on 30 December 1803, neither the British negotiators (Arthur Wellesley and Malcolm) nor Scindiah's *vakeels* (Wattel Punt and Kavel Nyn) knew of these Gwalior developments, partly because the most crucial element – the British occupation of the Gwalior fort – had not yet happened.

Wattel Punt had first expressed concern about the fate of Gwalior in December. In February, having probably heard about the approach of British troops to Gwalior, he again sought assurance from Malcolm that if and when they occupied Gwalior, the fort would be returned to Scindiah in due course. He cited Article 2 of the Treaty of Peace which stated that Scindiah would retain his territories south of the line running eastwards from Jaipur (and Gwalior and Gohad were south of this line). Malcolm responded by pointing out that under Article 9, Scindiah would accept any treaties between the British and his feudatories in Hindustan which might involve Gwalior. The trouble was that neither side knew what commitments might have been made under Article 9 and whether they were in conflict with Article 2. Malcolm sought clarification from Arthur Wellesley.[19] Wellesley, none the wiser, wrote in turn to Calcutta. Meanwhile, he sensibly advised Malcolm to avoid making any further response on Gwalior until the situation was clarified.

A fundamental difference in strategy between the Marquess in Calcutta (supported to some extent by Lake and his political assistant Graeme Mercer in Hindustan), and Wellesley and Malcolm in the Deccan, was now emerging. As far as the Marquess was concerned, Scindiah had been thoroughly defeated in battle. Advantage should be taken of his weakened state to reduce his power as much as possible. Wellesley and Malcolm, on the other hand, thought that if Scindiah were 'conciliated', and allowed to retain at least enough military power to resist attacks by Holkar, he might become more amenable and even be a useful ally of the Company, like the Nizam. As to the possibility of Scindiah and Holkar combining militarily against the Company, Wellesley was 'convinced that both of these Chiefs will always be occupied by the gratification of their mutual envy and revenge, and that they will never unite'.[20] As to the fort of Gwalior itself, the Marquess was adamant that the Company should hold it. Malcolm doubted its military worth: 'I am not one of those who attach much consequence to a hill fort in the hands of a Maratha. It can never give such an advantage in a contest with the English nation, though it adds greatly to the menace of one Maratha power against another.'[21]

But both Wellesley and Malcolm could see at first hand that the loss of Gwalior would be a huge psychological blow for Scindiah. They were inclined to return Gwalior to him in the interests of retaining his goodwill and maintaining good faith. As Wellesley put it: 'I would sacrifice Gwalior or every frontier of India ten times over, in order to preserve our credit for scrupulous good faith, and the advantages and honor we gained by the late war and the peace; and we must not fritter them away in arguments drawn from overstrained principles of the laws of nations, which are not understood in this country. What brought me through many difficulties in the war, and the negotiations of peace? The British good faith, and nothing else.'[22]

Scindiah's *vakeels* were meanwhile bringing increasing pressure to bear on Malcolm. They raised the issue of Gwalior at the meeting of 21 February and they kept returning to it at regular intervals during March and April. They had a powerful case. Gwalior and Gohad had been in Scindiah's hands for over twenty years; they had not been specifically mentioned in Article 9 of the Treaty of Peace; the Rana of Gohad had not existed before the war and Scindiah could not therefore have recognised him as a feudatory Chief, like the Maharajahs of Jodhpur and Jaipur; the Treaty with the Rana had not been signed until 29 January 1804, i.e. a month *after* the Treaty of Peace. What also lent a personal edge of anxiety to the *vakeels*' arguments, Malcolm realised, was that back in December they had persuaded Dowlat Rao to sign the Treaty of Peace by assuring him that he would not lose Gwalior as a result. Now they were alarmed by the possibility that they might have given their ruler the wrong advice – a dangerous mistake for a Minister in a Mahratta Court.

To add to his troubles, Malcolm was sick again, as he had been, on and off, throughout his stay at Scindiah's camp. He was due to be relieved by Josiah Webbe. But Webbe had only set out from Madras on the long overland route in February and was not due to arrive at Burhampur until May.

Unaware of the prevailing attitude in Calcutta, Malcolm continued to fire off public despatches describing, perhaps a little too sympathetically, the objections of the *vakeels* to the Company's stance. Moreover, he backed these up with private letters to Shawe and Edmonstone (and also to his old friend Mercer at General Lake's camp), frankly stating his personal preference for compromise on Gwalior. He remembered the informal debates he used to have with them and even with the Marquess himself when he was in Calcutta as Private Secretary. He knew that Arthur Wellesley agreed with him, and wrote blithely that 'I shall get *praised* for the Treaty [of Peace] but abused both privately and publicly for anything I have said or done about Gwalior and Gohud.'[23] As usual, he was sticking his neck out in a way that the more cautious Arthur Wellesley was not. He was in for a rude surprise.

The first intimation of trouble came in mid-April, with a short warning note from Shawe: 'the Governor-General [was] by no means satisfied with your arguments in favour of the restoration of Gwalior and Gohad to the authority of Dowlat Rao Scindiah. These possessions ought to have been specifically secured by the Treaty.'[24] Otherwise Bapu Wattel Punt would be seen to 'triumph' over Wellesley. It was followed by a despatch from Edmonstone, detailing the Marquess's righteous indignation at the 'insolence' of the Maharajah's *vakeels*, the 'fraud' that they were trying to foist on Malcolm, and the pristine fairness, justice and moderation of the Company's position. Malcolm, it seemed, had not rebutted the calumnies and insults to the British name with sufficient vigour. He was ordered to state in detail what had been his replies to certain specific claims made by the *vakeels* which he had mentioned in his despatches. He was ordered, furthermore, to point out to Scindiah that, even if all his arguments were valid, in the last resort the Company could lay claim to Gwalior/Gohad on the basis of the 'right of conquest'.[25] The whole despatch reflected the worst aspects of the Marquess's character – arrogant, bullying and petulant.

Malcolm received this broadside with relative equanimity. He complained to Arthur Wellesley that:

> It is full of anathemas against Bappoo Wattill, who is the most insolent presumptuous old dog that ever lived. I am considered in some part of it, as a man who is not so much alive as he should be to the honor of the country. I am directed to assert

> the right of the British Govt to maintain the Treaty with the Ranah, with all the subsidiary appendages and to insist upon a full recognition of that Treaty etc etc. With all this [vinegar] there is not one drop of [sweet]. The letter indeed maintains that substantial policy requires Scindiah should be conciliated, and that something may be done for him hereafter, of which I shall in due time be informed. In short, that if he [Scindiah] proves himself a good boy he shall have the jam plums.
>
> I am far from well; indeed, I was confined to my bed yesterday but this letter has roused me, and I shall not shrink from the Duty it imposes upon me.[26]

In fact, since late March he had already begun to take heed of the uncompromising attitude in Calcutta and to stiffen his public defence of the Company's case. He was even complimented by Shawe on the strong line he had taken with the *vakeels* in a meeting at the end of March. And in late April he wrote to Kavel Nyn, complaining about the 'objectionable nature' of a memorandum on Gwalior by Bapu Wattell Punt.[27] But he still had not changed his private views, and could not resist putting them forward.

The Marquess's mood towards Malcolm darkened further and in late April he demanded that Shawe and Edmonstone should show him all Malcolm's recent private letters to them. An embarrassed Shawe handed them over. On 3 April, after completing his official despatch to the Governor-General, Malcolm had felt the need to let off steam in a private letter to Shawe. The Marquess seized upon this letter and wrote furious comments in the margin (his comments are shown below underlined):

> My public letter of to-day says enough of the unpleasant subject of Gwalior and Gohud . . . Mr Chisholm at the Court of Proprietors, who used to begin his eloquent harangues by saying the question lay in a nutshell – the present question certainly lies in a nutshell – do you wish the alliance with this chief to be cordial, sincere and useful, or is that a consideration of which you are independent? ['shameful imbecility of mind. W'] If the former you must make an arrangement that will satisfy this government on the point at issue. No arrangement will I fear do

> that which does not include the cession of Gwalior. ['scandalous ignorance'] If you do not want this man's aid, and mean to have no hold but that on his apprehension, why the way is clear. ['impertinent and false insinuation'] Keep what you have got, and make haste to get more. ['absurd and false'] . . . I am a little unwell again – I must visit the Governor at Prince of Wales island and you at Bengal, but when I am to escape from this, God only knows. Let me get through my work here with credit and defy fate. ['the sooner he quits Scindiah and Mr Wittal [Wattal Punt], the better for his country. W'][28]

Although this letter survives, Malcolm presumably never came to know of these derogatory comments. Nor would he have seen the Marquess's comments on another private letter he wrote to Edmonstone: 'God knows, throughout this troubled scene my attention has been exclusively directed to one object – the promotion of the public interest.' The last two words were underscored, and in the margin was written: 'Major Malcolm's duty is to obey my orders and to enforce my instructions. *I* will look after the *public* interests. W.'[29]

Malcolm certainly did, however, see a letter dated 30 April from Shawe, which enclosed 'a Short Note' from the Marquess (actually a long letter) addressed, not to him personally, but to 'the Resident with Dowlat Rao Sindiah'.[30] The 'Short Note' contained a paragraph-by-paragraph dissection and demolition of the contents of Malcolm's despatches of 3 and 10 April. Some of his comments practically burn the paper they are written on. For example:

> Para 2.– Munshee Kavel Nyn states an apprehension that the recognition of the title of the Rana would alienate the territory of Gohud and fortress of Gwalior from Scindiah – Major Malcolm.
>
> Undoubtedly. This most extraordinary and even insolent declaration, appears to have been received without any particular remark or expression of surprise and disapprobation. – Wellesley.

There follows a long tirade listing Malcolm's 'errors', which 'cannot have proceeded from want of information . . . His error seems to be in suffering his judgment to be perverted by the sophistry of the ministers.' The note concludes: 'It may be hoped [by the Ministers] that . . . the appearance of so many causes of discontent concurring to disturb the temper of Scindiah's councils may alarm me for the stability of the peace, and may terrify me into the cession of Gwalior and Gohud, and into a general system of concession and submission, conformably to Major Malcolm's principles. In this expectation, however, Scindiah's friends and advisers will be disappointed; they will not move me as easily as they have shaken Major Malcolm. I am perfectly ready to renew the war to-morrow, if I find the peace is not secure.'

Shawe realised only too well how upset Malcolm would be by the Marquess's note, and the following day he wrote an explanatory letter, outlining the underlying causes of the Marquess's displeasure:

> You have shown a great disposition to admit the justice of Scindiah's right [claim] to Gwalior and Gohud which is likely, Lord Wellesley thinks, to give his enemies in Leadenhall Street room to found an accusation against Lord Wellesley of injustice and rapacity in insisting on retaining those possessions, contrary to the opinion of the Resident [i.e. Malcolm] . . . Lord Wellesley thinks the restoration of Gwalior and Gohud to Scindiah would be a breach of his public duty. But in retaining them, he is apprehensive that the countenance you have given to Scindiah's pretensions will induce common observers to believe that the right is with Scindiah, and that it has been trampled on by Lord Wellesley.[31]

The arrival of the 'Note' from the Marquess hit Malcolm very hard; and even Shawe's explanation that the real cause of the Marquess's anger was to do with his battles with Leadenhall Street, rather than with Malcolm himself, was small consolation. The fact was that Malcolm's 'ardent attachment' to the Marquess, as Shawe had called it, was an understatement. He hero-worshipped the Marquess, and to be castigated in this way was almost more than he could bear. He wrote back immediately to Shawe that 'I am perfectly heart-broken from these communications – in reply to which, neither the state of my mind nor my body will admit my saying much at present. I may trouble you hereafter.'[32]

Meanwhile, the Gohad and Gwalior affair dragged to a close. Possibly frustrated by Malcolm's more spirited defence of the Company position, Scindiah decided to play one final card. He wrote, in early May, a personal letter directly to Arthur Wellesley, now in Bombay, despite Malcolm warning him that he would not receive any more favourable treatment from Wellesley – the decision had been made in Calcutta, and that was that – although the Marquess had made one further concession, promising Scindiah a share of Holkar's territories if and when they should be acquired by the Company in war.[33] Arthur Wellesley's reply was masterly. Scrupulously polite, it recapitulated the facts of the case, regretted the misunderstandings, set out the options open to each party, and recommended that acceptance of the de facto situation would be the least bad course for both parties.[34] Scindiah, no doubt now also being pressed by his *sirdars*, impatient to take up the 'inducements' promised to them in the Treaty, realised that the game was finally up, and confirmed his acceptance of the loss of Gwalior and Gohad.

Wellesley was nevertheless honest enough to admit privately to Malcolm that 'although I am convinced that I should not have made the peace [i.e. the Treaty of Peace on 30 December] if I had insisted upon Gwalior, I wish that I had had that point clearly explained before the treaty was signed.'[35] Writing to his brother Henry in England, Wellesley was even more explicit:

> Scindiah's government, although it has concluded the defensive alliance, is not satisfied with us; and the misfortune is that, between ourselves, I think we are in the wrong. The difference relates to the fort of Gwalior, which Scindiah thinks ought to belong to him, and the Governor-General will not give it up. I differ in opinion with the Governor-General both as to the right and [the] policy of keeping this fort; I have delivered my opinion to him regarding the latter, but have said nothing upon the former, as the question turns upon a nice point of the law of nations, which the Governor-General has argued with his usual ingenuity; but I acknowledge I differ from him entirely . . .
>
> In fact, my dear Henry, we want at Calcutta some person who will speak his mind to the Governor-General. Since you and Malcolm have left him, there is nobody about him with capacity to understand these subjects, who has nerves to discuss them

> with him, and to oppose his sentiments when he is wrong. There cannot be a stronger proof of this want than the fact that Malcolm, and I, and General Lake, and Mercer and Webbe, were of opinion that we had lost Gwalior with the treaty of peace.[36]

Malcolm's only relief from all this misery and sickness was the arrival on 12 May of Webbe, who took over as Resident on 20 May. Malcolm hung around for a few days, before setting off southwards on the 300-mile journey to Poona. As he lay in his palanquin – he was too sick to ride a horse for the first part of his journey – he must have reflected on the cruelty of fate. All the effort he had put in trying to do the right thing by his superiors and his country had only brought him abuse and professional obloquy.

He wrote to Arthur Wellesley en route: 'I am almost exhausted. The rains will probably do me good. If you see a copy of Lord Wellesley's notes under date 30th April on my conduct at Scindiah's Durbar you will have an idea of the state of my mind. If you have not seen these notes I will shew you them when I arrive at Poona . . . I trust it is not impossible but the day may yet come when Lord Wellesley may be sensible that he has treated me with unnecessary and unmerited harshness.'[37]

Arthur Wellesley at least remained his stout supporter. After a two-month stay in Bombay, he had returned to the camp near Poona. He wrote, on 29 May: 'I can easily conceive that you must have been rendered very uncomfortable by everything that has been written in Bengal relative to affairs at Scindiah's Durbar.' On 6 June: 'I have just received your letter of 30th May. I saw the notes to which you allude, and think them quite shocking. You did not deserve such treatment, positively, and I am not astonished at its having distressed you.' And on 9 June: 'I am rejoiced to hear that you are so near us again. I will go to see you at Poonah if you cannot come here; but you can have no idea what a fine healthy camp I have got. What do you mean to do? Do you stay with me, or go to Mysore, or go to Bombay and to sea?'[38] The letter then reverted to their favourite subject – horses.

Malcolm reached Poona on 12 June and stayed with Close at the Residency. Together they visited Arthur at his camp a few miles north. The three men, who had worked together and achieved so much over the previous five years, and especially during the last year, had much to discuss. Ostensibly, they felt, the Marquess had got what he wanted –

the military neutralisation of Scindiah and Raghuji – leaving him relatively free to tackle Holkar, the last Mahratta Chieftain to openly oppose the Company's suzerainty. But this apparent victory had been bought at considerable diplomatic cost. Scindiah thought that he had been both bullied and duped. As an ally he remained sulky, like the Peshwah, though with more justification. He never thereafter felt any compunction to adhere to the terms of the treaties he had signed, if they happened in any way to go against his immediate advantage. In fact, he conspired with the enemies of the Company on a continuing basis. To what extent this attitude was caused by the Company's treatment of him, or was inherent in his nature, is unclear. But it certainly cost the Company dear over the next few years.

Malcolm's top priority now was to recover his own health before resuming as Resident at Mysore. Although he had been appointed to the job more than a year earlier, he had never been able to take it up. Rather than undertake another exhausting journey overland to Madras, he decided to travel down to Bombay and take a ship. Sea air was regularly cited at the time as the best remedy for his sort of liver complaint. By modern standards those ships were hardly models of hygiene, but compared to a city or a military tented camp, the air was cleaner, the drainage more complete, and there was plenty of salt water to kill bugs. He spent about ten days waiting for a boat at Bombay, then a fortnight at sea.

Arriving at Madras on 22 July, he was greeted by something which did more than any medicine or sea air to revive his spirits – a letter, a long letter, from, of all people, the Marquess. Moreover, it contained, amazingly for a man of the Marquess's character, something very close to an apology for his treatment of Malcolm over the Scindiah negotiations. Of course, the word 'sorry' never appeared in the letter; rather, it was couched in terms of patiently explaining to Malcolm where he (Malcolm) had gone wrong. First, there was concern, then praise; then a lecture; then forgiveness, followed by handsome good wishes; and finally a PS: 'General Wellesley has not told me whether he ever received the horse which I sent him. Or how that horse turned out; somebody told me that he had suffered the same fate as "Old Port", who was shot under General Lake at Laswaree. – W.'[39]

In the main body of the letter, the Marquess, despite trying to be conciliatory, was still tending to sit on his high horse – and how high that horse could be. The postscript was saying, between the lines, 'don't worry, you're still my friend'.

A day or two later Arthur Wellesley arrived at Madras, having come across country from Poona. The Marquess had summoned him to Calcutta, probably meaning to send him on to Hindustan to help Lake. There was talk of Malcolm sailing with Wellesley, but he felt that his health was not up to the Calcutta climate in September; nor was he yet fit enough to return to work at Mysore.[40] He decided instead to take a ship up the coast to Vizagapatam, and stay for a while with his brother Robert. To say that he needed a holiday would be an understatement. For six years, he had been continuously at work on the most exhausting assignments. The only mild respite had been the sea voyages to and from Persia and around the Indian coast from Bombay to Madras. He had been ill, at times seriously, with a persistent liver complaint for the last year. It was time to rest.

CHAPTER FOURTEEN

The End of the Wellesley Era, 1805

Early in 1804, when Malcolm was in Scindiah's camp at Burhampur, news came from Burnfoot that his father had died, aged seventy-four. Malcolm was deeply upset. He had left home aged twelve and had only seen his father for a month or two over the previous twenty-three years. But to the restless and romantic expatriate, thirty-five years old and still unmarried, Burnfoot represented an emotional anchor, and his father the venerated patriarch. He shared his grief with his friends even though most of them could not have known his family. Leaving Madras at the end of July, he arrived a few days later at Vizagapatam on the coast. There he stayed for the next seven weeks with his brother Robert and caught up with family news.

Robert had been living at Vizagapatam since 1799, first as the Company's Commercial Resident, now as the 'Second Judge of the Circuit Court of Appeal'. Government in late eighteenth-century British India was a simple business, restricted to revenue collection for defence and peace-keeping, and the administration of justice. Following Robert Clive's conquest of Bengal and the acquisition of the Northern Circars from the Nizam in the 1760s, the servants of the Company simply tacked their government duties on to their existing commercial activities (which included a monopoly of trade with Britain). The resulting opportunities for graft and corruption can be imagined. This was the period of the *nabobs*, of scandalous behaviour and bloated fortunes. Pitt's India Act of 1784 and Cornwallis's reforms in 1788–94 separated responsibility for government and commerce, and banned private trading by Company servants. But it took some further years for these measures to be enforced in outlying stations like Masulipatam and Vizagapatam. By the time that Robert became a judge in 1802, he should have amassed a sizeable nest egg from quite lawful private trading. But somehow his 'investments' had gone wrong and he was only moderately well off. By now Nancy had produced six children, ranging in age from seventeen to five, and he was living a comfortable and apparently happy domestic life. But according to John, he had been 'very ill, and his old Circar habits had perhaps, in some degree, contributed to his bad health'.[1] 'Old Circar habits'? He may have had a weakness for 'the Dyse' (dice), but this would not have caused serious illness. More likely they meant the bottle. One can imagine endless sultry days and months spent in that flat, mosquito-ridden river delta, bereft of the company of fellow Europeans. It was said of Masulipatam in 1799 that 'only a Dutchman, a frog or an alligator would have chosen it as an abode'. Only a man of the strongest character could have withstood it for more than twenty years, and Robert does not seem to have had as much strength as some of his brothers. Boredom and loneliness probably got the better of him.

Another Malcolm brother was living in the Circars at the time, Thomas ('Tom') Malcolm. Born in 1770, Tom's early life had been chequered; he had quarrelled with his parents and got into trouble more than once. In 1796 he was given a commission in the Bombay Army and travelled to India as a passenger on Pulteney's frigate, *Fox*. But within a year he resigned his commission and came to live with Robert, then at Masulipatam. Though 'a very clever fellow', according to Pulteney, he seemed to have been 'a bit of a trial' to Robert. Possibly the bottle was a problem for Tom as well as for Robert. But by 1804 things seemed to be looking up. Tom had set up in business as a private trader at Bimilpatam, just up the road from Vizagapatam, 'and with the patience of a Spaniard is waiting until the Company is obliged to relinquish some of their privileges to Private Merchants, which sooner or later must be the case'.[2] In August 1804 Tom became engaged to Frances (Fannie) Deane, an eighteen-year-old Scottish girl living nearby. The shortage of chaplains in remote areas meant that marriage ceremonies were sometimes performed by Political Officers. So John, as a Resident (at Mysore), officiated at Tom's marriage to Frances at Bimilipatam on 9 September. He wrote to Josiah Webbe that 'I have married Thomas to a charming young woman who is sincerely attached to him, and the couple proceed in a month to Bombay, under circumstances of such advantage as secure his making a speedy fortune.'[3] The 'circumstance of such advantage' was a job offer from John Leckie, a Bombay merchant. When the bride and groom sailed to Bombay they took with them Robert's eldest daughter, Anne, aged seventeen. Within a few months of their arrival at Bombay, John Leckie made Tom a partner in his firm, which was renamed Leckie and Malcolm, and he married Anne. Leckie was reputed to have an annual income of £4,000 (worth at least £250,000 today, tax free), so he must have been mightily impressed by Tom to make him his partner; and even more so by Anne, to make her his wife. For Anne, a Eurasian girl who had presumably never previously left the Northern Circars, this would have been a tremendous 'catch'. The marriage was successful; Anne produced seven children and went to England with John Leckie when he retired in 1827.[4]

For his first six weeks at Vizagapatam Malcolm did practically nothing. He wrote a letter of condolence to his mother about the death of his brother William in Scotland, and gave the Calcutta secretariat his mail forwarding addresses. But he did not entirely stop thinking about Indian politics. And letters from Arthur Wellesley, in Calcutta, continued to flow in. In the middle of September John and Robert moved up the coast to Ganjam. He wrote to Wellesley that this put him only seven days' sailing time away from Calcutta and he could get there quickly if he was needed. A more likely explanation for abandoning the relative comfort of Robert's house at Vizagapatam to go to Ganjam was that it was the site of the Company's premier horse stud in India – an irresistible lure to Malcolm as a judge and breeder of horses.[5]

By the end of September he was getting back some of his old energy. He boasted to a friend in Calcutta that he was 'growing stout' and had acquired a 'corporation' (paunch). He spent three days examining a paper (dated March 1804) by an anonymous author (in fact Lord Castlereagh, the newly appointed President of the Board of Control in London), entitled 'Observations on the Treaty of Bassein'. Attached to the paper was a lengthy commentary by an anonymous author in Calcutta, probably the Marquess. Malcolm's own commentary[6] called Castlereagh's paper 'an unprincipled compound of false facts and false reasoning' – rash words about the views of his ultimate boss, who later became one of Britain's most distinguished Foreign Secretaries.

Castlereagh's paper was a 'think piece' written shortly after his appointment, probably in response to a rising chorus of disapproval from the Directors in Leadenhall Street of the Marquess's Indian policy. He attempted to evaluate whether the Marquess had implemented the Company's strategic objectives and whether he had exceeded his authorities, as claimed by some of the Directors. Castlereagh's tentative conclusion was that Calcutta had exaggerated the French threat; that the Treaty of Bassein with the Peshwah seemed to have alienated the other Chieftains; that the Company's aim should be to unite, not divide, the Mahratta Chieftains, and to turn them into allies of the Company; that the Company should perhaps have teamed up with the Rajah of Berar to mediate between Scindiah and Holkar; and that if peace with and among the Mahrattas could only be achieved by the sword, the effort was not worthwhile and should be abandoned.

This line of thought was, of course, anathema to Malcolm (and to the Marquess). Malcolm's paper fired a powerful broadside against Castle-reagh's arguments, and in the process gave the first full outline of his ideology of the Company State. In dealing with Native rulers, especially Mahrattas, he asserted, a Forward Policy was the only effective approach; a Ring Fence policy would be regarded by them as a sign of weakness, and tempt them to attack the Company's territories. While the Company might seek peace and tranquillity for its territories, in the end its power came from the sword, and it should face this fact squarely. The only sure way to achieve ultimate peace would be readiness to go to war. In dealing with Mahratta rulers, whose *modus operandi* was to plunder their neighbours, 'divide and rule' was the most effective and least expensive policy. The system of subsidiary alliances was not perfect and would only work properly if and when it covered the whole subcontinent. He brushed aside the idea that the Mahrattas might become good neighbours: 'Was it likely that the Marhattoes would at once abandon all those objects for which they had contended since the first rise of their nation – and altering their very nature become to the English (what they had been to no other power in India) quiet, friendly and unambitious neighbours?'

He then set out what he considered to be the Company's strategic objective in India, an objective certainly not shared by a majority of the Directors in London: 'The Treaty of Bassein is founded upon principles calculated for the support of a great system of policy which has in view a defined end: the maintenance of the tranquillity of India through the means of the general establishment of the power and influence of the British Government.' He admitted that the system of subsidiary alliances could well lead to the acquisition of more territory by the Company and ultimately to paramountcy – against stated Company policy. But 'it appears to my mind certain, that both the measures of preventive policy which the intrigues and ambition of the native powers must continually lead the English Government to adopt, and the wars into which the latter must occasionally be forced by the rapacity and violence of the former, will not only gradually tend to the increase of the British Dominions, but ultimately to the paramount establishment of the influence and power of that nation over all the continent of India.' He defended what he considered the enlightened actions of the Calcutta Government against criticism from a narrow-minded 'head office' in London:

> This Empire has originated in commerce, and many of the principles and institutions of its Government must therefore have been framed with the view of promoting its commercial [rather] than its political Interests, and in fact a prevalent sense of the advantages to be derived from the commerce with India; and the apprehension entertained of danger from Territorial Possessions or political connections in that quarter, has almost invariably led the superior authority in England to mark by censure and disapprobation every measure by the local government in India which appears calculated to increase our Territories or to extend our political relations, nor has the extraordinary wisdom and energy which has been often displayed in the formation and execution of their plans always secured to the Government abroad that full portion of applause which their great services merited.

He ended with a grand flourish: 'by substituting in the place of narrow maxims of policy those just and liberal principles which are suited to the form and magnitude of our present Power, we shall succeed in rendering our Empire in India an inexhaustible source of riches and of strength to the mother country. We shall at the same time, through the means of our political connections and by the influence of our authority and example, make nations whom we found a prey to all the evils attendant on a rude and barbarous state of continual warfare, peaceable and industrious.'[7] The egg of the liberal imperialist was beginning to hatch.

The current political hot topic was the war with Holkar, which was not going well. Holkar was a fine soldier, but his *modus vivendi* was to plunder the territories of his neighbours rather than govern his own people. He was never likely to be a willing candidate for the Marquess's concept of a subsidiary alliance with the Company. Arthur Wellesley, not a man easily intimidated, referred to 'the violent ferocity and superstition of Holkar' and 'the ferocious and suspicious nature of his disposition'.[8] He had stood aloof from Scindiah's and Raghuji Bhonsle's campaign against the Company in 1803, perhaps shrewdly judging that he was unlikely to beat the Company armies in pitched battle. He was also a man of considerable spirit. In answer to a conciliatory letter from Wellesley thanking him for his non-participation in the war of 1803, and suggesting that, if both parties kept strictly to their own territory, they could live in peace with each other, he had replied that 'a saddle on my horse's back is my house',[9] and later to Lake, 'my country and my possessions are on my horse's saddle. Please God, to whatever country I turn the reins of my horse, it shall be brought under subjection.'[10] This defiant talk did not go down well with the Marquess. In March 1804 when the treaties with Scindiah and Raghuji were more or less in place, he concluded that the only way of bringing Holkar into line was to destroy his army.

Holkar's army was primarily cavalry, which gave it extreme mobility and the ability to harass the supply lines of an infantry column. But its weakness was that it lived entirely off the land and derived its income from plunder. If pursued relentlessly, allowing no respite, it would begin to disintegrate. The Marquess had set out his plan of campaign against Holkar in April 1804. Lake was to pursue Holkar from Delhi in the north, Wellesley from the Deccan in the south and Colonel Murray from Gujerat in the west. He hoped, too, that a detachment from Scindiah's army would also approach from the east.

This strategy did not work out as planned. Famine in the Deccan had made it necessary for Wellesley's army to retire southwards. Murray advanced from Gujerat but heavy monsoon rains and perhaps timidity in the face of Holkar's military reputation delayed his progress. The force sent by Scindiah did not cooperate with Murray. With the coming of the monsoon season in June, Lake put his main force into cantonments, sending only a small detachment led by Colonel Monson to secure the Mukhandra Pass near Kotah. In early July Monson unwisely ventured further south. He was caught by a large force of Holkar's cavalry and badly mauled, then beat a desperate retreat all the way back to Agra. It was a severe military defeat but, worse still for the Company, a tremendous psychological boost for Holkar and, indeed, for all the wavering Mahratta rulers. The Company's army, hitherto considered invincible, now seemed beatable.

Malcolm heard of Monson's retreat while recuperating at Vizagapatam. He answered Arthur Wellesley's letters from Calcutta in typically grandiose style, urging him to stay on in India. 'What renders every war a subject of alarm to my mind, is neither our want of troops nor of resources (we have sufficient of both) but the want of commanders. I know only two – General Lake and yourself – to whom armies could be entrusted. On the other hand he felt that the Marquess should not delay his return to England:

> the risks incurred by his departure are serious, but not half so much so, as far as I can judge, as those incurred by his stay. A coalition has been formed by weak and designing men, which, if not stifled in the birth (as it will be, [with] Lord Wellesley in England), may subvert our empire in India. It will, I fear, be in vain to combat this coalition at a distance . . . upon Lord Wellesley's personal efforts the fate of India now rests – not as that is likely to be affected by the desultory invasion of Jeswunt Rao Holkar, or the ravages of a Mahmoud Shah (these can be resisted and repelled by his agents), but as it is likely to suffer from the more serious attacks of a presumptuous and ignorant President of the Board of Control [Castlereagh], or an illiberal and prejudiced Chairman of the Court of Directors [Charles Grant]. It is therefore against these that the great effort must be made, and the action which is to decide the destiny of our Indian Empire must be fought upon the banks of the Thames, not on the banks of the Ganges.[11]

Such thoughts seem more appropriate to a Governor-General, or even a Prime Minister, than from a middle-ranking officer in a Company army. But that was Malcolm's nature – a soaring imagination and an ability to think 'outside the box'.

Wellesley replied from Calcutta with his usual *douche* of common sense. He was prepared to go back to the Deccan but not to stay for a moment longer than it took to defeat Holkar. He did not fancy serving in 'a subordinate situation, contrary to my inclination' for several years. There was also an element of pride. The Marquess had put his name forward to General Lake, but Lake had not taken up the offer of his services. He could not see himself taking over from Colonel Murray in Gujerat, and he did not know whether it would be feasible for his Deccan army to attack Holkar from the south until he had examined the situation on the ground.

It was probably just as well that Arthur Welleseley did not leave Calcutta to join Lake in Hindustan as originally planned, for the Marquess was suffering symptoms of a nervous breakdown. His brother's presence at Government House provided a reassuring public front for him. The crisis was kept secret in Calcutta, but Wellesley probably told Malcolm about it.[12]

In early November 1804, with no prospect of Lake inviting Arthur Wellesley to join him in Hindustan, the Marquess allowed his brother to return to Seringapatam and resume command of the Deccan and Gujerat armies. He would then stand ready to advance northward if necessary to assist Lake in his pursuit of Holkar. But by this time Wellesley had already tentatively decided to return to England. It was time, too, for Malcolm to take up his post as Resident at Mysore. Although not fully fit, he felt well enough to carry on 'in a quiet way'. Wellesley came by sea to Ganjam, and they sailed on together to Madras, and thence continued to Seringapatam.

Over the next few months, until Wellesley's final departure for England in March 1805, they remained together, and the friendship between the two men reached its apogee. They had been through so much as comrades. They had seen triumphs – the Seringapatam campaign in 1799, the Mahratta campaign of 1803, the negotiation of the treaties with Scindiah – and setbacks, particularly the recent disagreements with the Marquess. They had made a wonderful team, usually agreeing but being completely open and honest about it when they did not. Their skills complemented each other: Malcolm, the brains trust, full of imaginative ideas; Wellesley, the superb judge of people. Wellesley commented: 'you and I have frequently had discussions upon military and political subjects, the result of which has generally been that we don't much differ in opinion. You generally see what is right and what is desirable, I what is practicable.'[13]

At Madras Malcolm met the new Governor, Lord William Bentinck. The third son of the Duke of Portland, Bentinck was barely thirty years old, and had never been to India before. His previous career had been twelve years as an officer in the Coldstream Guards, rising to Colonel in 1803. He had seen active service in the Napoleonic Wars, being present at the Battle of Marengo in 1800, so he was not entirely without qualifications for the job. He and Malcolm took to each other from the outset, forming a friendship which lasted until Malcolm's death nearly thirty years later.

At Madras they also heard the sad news that Josiah Webbe had fallen seriously ill in Scindiah's camp at Burhampur (in fact, unknown to them, he had already died, on 9 November). A replacement would have to be found. Malcolm had a moment of dread that he might be told to return to that most insalubrious place. Fortunately Wellesley could see that this was not sensible, and wrote, rather desperately, to Shawe: 'For God's sake send Sydenham [Captain Benjamin Sydenham, Military Secretary to the Governor-General in Calcutta at the time] off as soon as possible. There is no other mode whatever of providing for that Residency. Malcolm, although to some degree recovered, is neither in health nor strength sufficient to enable him to bear the journey, or the fatigues to which he would be liable at that durbar. He cannot go into the sun at all.'[14]

This did not prevent Wellesley from asking the Marquess's permission to take Malcolm with him to visit the Deccan army in camp near Poona. By now, it seemed, the pair could not bear to be parted. But the trip to the Deccan never took place, because Wellesley himself fell sick. Even his iron constitution was faltering. It had taken him through nearly two years of campaigning and was in future to take him unscathed through the Peninsular War, and would enable him to go virtually without sleep for three nights during the Waterloo campaign. Many years later, asked how he had acquired his astonishing stamina, especially since he had been a rather sickly youth, he replied 'Ah, that was all India.'[15] Asked also how he managed to get through such an immense volume of correspondence, he famously replied 'My rule always was to do the business of the day in the day.'[16] The same could largely be said about Malcolm. Perhaps Malcolm learned his self-discipline from Wellesley's example; perhaps it was the other way round.

For the next three months Malcolm divided his time between hanging about with Wellesley at Seringapatam and commuting to Mysore, twenty miles down the road. A Residency was a plum job for aspiring Company servants. The British Resident at a Native ruler's Court was expected to demonstrate the power and prestige of the Company. He lived in the style of an Ambassador, far above that of a regimental officer or even a senior commercial representative of the Company. He was given allowances on top of his normal salary and was able to save substantial sums. He was housed in a suitably grand building, erected, in the case of Hyderabad and, later, of Mysore, at the local ruler's expense.[17] During Wellesley's stay at Calcutta earlier in the year, he had secured two important concessions for Malcolm from the Marquess; first, that the Resident at Mysore should report directly to the Governor-General rather than through the Governor of Madras; and second, that a Residency building should be erected for him at Mysore (previously the Resident had been based at the Company's military camp at Seringapatam). The work of the Resident at Mysore was not especially taxing for a man of Malcolm's energy. On the restoration of the Wadeyar Rajah, Purneah, the *Brahmin* who had been Tipu's Treasurer, became *Dewan* and turned out to be an excellent administrator. Interference by the Company in Mysore affairs, apart from the strictly military role of the Subsidiary Force, was seldom required.

By now Arthur Wellesley had firmly decided to return to England. He was sick and needed a change. After some setbacks, the war with Holkar was going reasonably well again. He knew that his presence in the Deccan was useful, but he pointed out that 'the same state of affairs which renders my presence in the Deccan desirable, will exist for the next seven years. I certainly do not propose to spend my life in the Deccan.'[18] He felt that he could be more useful to the Marquess's political cause in London. 'But', he wrote to Shawe, 'I have not come to this determination without consulting Malcolm, who agrees in opinion with me on every part of the subject.'[19]

Malcolm saw Wellesley off from Seringapatam on 9 February. He realised that he was losing not only a friend but his chief career sponsor. He sent him a resumé of his service to date, hoping that Wellesley might be able to promote his career through his contacts in England. He also asked him to send a picture or bust of himself as a memento, and Wellesley agreed.[20] As the moment for departure approached, Wellesley too became quite sentimental about his years in India. From Madras, in the month before he boarded his ship, he wrote at least eleven letters to Malcolm. He pleaded with Malcolm to keep him informed of events. On the way home he wrote a long letter from St Helena ending 'I beg that you will remember me to Purneah and Bistnapak and all my friends, black, white and grey at Seringapatam and elsewhere within your reach. God bless you, my dear Malcolm.'[21]

Arthur Wellesley had also given Malcolm the delicate task of keeping him informed about a certain Mrs Freese, the wife of an officer in the garrison at Seringapatam, of whom he had become very fond during his time there. He might have had an affair with her – certainly he became godfather to her son, born in 1802 and christened Arthur Freese. Little Arthur was sent home in 1806 to live with an aunt, but when the child arrived, the aunt was dead. Wellesley, as his godfather, was asked to take him in and of course he did. Two years later Malcolm wrote to Wellesley that: 'I never saw Mrs Freese better, and your accounts of Arthur which she read to-day have made her mad with joy. Why do you shave the poor boy's eyebrows – and endeavour to alter God's works – in Scotland red hair is a Beauty, at least it was five centuries ago.'[22]

Meanwhile, Malcolm settled down to what he imagined was going to be a quiet life at Mysore. There were the usual perquisites of office, the first of which was the choice of staff. He put in an immediate request for his cousin Charles Pasley to act as his assistant. He sent off to Calcutta the latest plans for the new Residency building at Mysore. Nervous about his reputation for extravagance, his accompanying letter was quite defensive: 'If his Lordship thinks I am too magnificent, I will circumscribe my plan, but I conscientiously think the house is such as the station requires. However, you have only to mention that I am to spend so much more, and your orders will then be obeyed – *gildee gildee* [very quickly].'[23] All to little avail. Unfortunately for him, the continual military operations over the previous two years had caused a cash crisis, and capital expenditure on such relative luxuries as Residency buildings was postponed, even when the funding was, in this case, to come from the Maharajah. He was allowed to build a modest bungalow at Mysore and told to retain the dilapidated house at Seringapatam which he had

John Leyden (1775–1811), Scottish poet, oriental scholar and linguist.

hoped to pull down. The grand Mysore building was eventually approved and completed three years later.

During this period he met John Leyden, the Scottish poet, oriental scholar and linguist, an event which was to have a profound and lifelong effect upon him. Leyden, a shepherd's son from Denholm in the Teviotdale district of the Scottish Borders, was born in 1775. From childhood, he displayed an extraordinary memory and facility for languages. Taught to read and write in a shepherd's cottage by his grandmother, he somehow managed to get to Edinburgh University at the age of fifteen. He spent seven years there studying philosophy, theology and medicine in term time, and in the vacations, presumably by way of relaxation, mastering 'Scandinavian and modern languages, besides Hebrew, Arabic and Persian'.[24] He then turned to literary and poetic pursuits and, through the patronage of the great bibliophile Richard Heber, came to the notice of Walter Scott. In 1802 he collaborated with Scott in the production of the *Border Minstrelsy*. In late 1803, armed with a medical degree from St Andrews University (obtained in six months), he arrived in Madras. He started work at the General Hospital there but within a few months was recruited by Major Colin Mackenzie to help with a survey of Mysore, an area of 40,000 square miles. Leyden set out with Mackenzie's party, but after a few months fell seriously ill and reached Seringapatam in late November 1804 'in a state one's greatest enemy would wish one to be in'.[25] 'When I was ill at Seringapatam, the Persian Ambassador, Colonel Malcolm, arrived from Bengal. As soon as he heard that I was a Border man, he instantly came to see me without any ceremony, and as soon as I was able to move, carried me out to his palace at Mysore, where I stayed with him until he was called to Bengal again. He has acted towards me in the kindest manner, and like a true friend.'[26]

Leyden was a fanatical scholar. Malcolm described an incident shortly after he had brought Leyden to Mysore: 'He was so ill at Mysore . . . that Mr Anderson, the surgeon who attended him, despaired of his life; but though all his friends endeavoured at this period to prevail upon him to relax in his application to study, it was in vain . . . he actually continued, under the depression of a fever and a liver complaint, to study more than ten hours each day.'[27]

Later in his stay with Malcolm at Mysore, Leyden lent Malcolm his narrative poem *Scenes of Infancy*, telling of his childhood in the Scottish Border country. When Malcolm returned it one morning, he noticed that Malcolm had pencilled a twenty-line poem on the flyleaf beginning:

Thy muse, O Leyden, seeks no foreign clime,
For deeds of fame, to twine her brow with bays,
But finds at home whereon to build her rhyme,
And patriot virtues sings in patriot lays.

The significance of these verses lies not in their quality (or lack of it) but in the fact that they are the first evidence of any specifically literary output by Malcolm. Years of writing letters and despatches had sharpened his prose; and he had privately dabbled in poetry. But this was the first public expression of it.

He showed Leyden the journal of his travels in Persia in 1800, and Leyden's immediate reaction was encouraging enough to inspire Malcolm to tell the Marquess in Calcutta that he was intending 'to gather my Persian materials into a framework'.[28] Realising that Malcolm had accumulated a great deal of knowledge about Persia and had some raw literary talent, Leyden continued to encourage him. By March Malcolm was settling down in Mysore with enthusiasm for his new literary hobby and the prospect of a quiet, well-ordered life. Leyden can be credited with being his first inspiration.

But at the end of March 1805 this pleasant interlude came to an abrupt end. Letters came from both Edmonstone and Shawe. The Marquess wanted Malcolm to come to Calcutta immediately, to advise him about the latest developments at Scindiah's Court. He responded immediately. Within a week he had packed up at Mysore (leaving Leyden to recuperate at the Residency for several more weeks). He reached Madras on 1 April, and by 17 April he was sailing up the Hoogly.

The atmosphere at Government House had changed profoundly since the day he had left it more than two years earlier. The Marquess and his old colleagues Shawe and Edmonstone were still there, but they were tired and dispirited. The war against Holkar was going better again, but it was not going to be over before the monsoon. Cash was short, and to pay for the war the Government was having to divert bullion that had been intended for the China trade. Much more damaging than this, however, was the news coming from London. A majority of the Court of Directors had always been against the Marquess, and for the past two years had waged a relentless campaign against him. His main supporter, David Scott, had retired in 1802 and died in 1805. The Marquess was an aristocrat who saw the governance of India in political terms. In his view, if peace could be achieved, prosperity and profits would inevitably follow. The Directors were merchants, looking for a reasonable return on their investment in the short and medium term. They were not interested in territorial acquisition and were worried about the heavy cost of the Marquess's wars. The Marquess, moreover, was an advocate of breaking the Company's monopoly of trade between India and Britain. The Directors felt that the monopoly was justified by the fact that the Company was shouldering almost the full cost of government in addition to its commercial activities. Above all, they were understandably worried by the Company's escalating debt, which had risen from £4.5

million in 1784 to £14.4 million in 1800, to £18 million in 1802 and was to rise to over £30 million by 1808.[29] In late 1804 the Court issued a document called an 'Animadverting Despatch', largely put together by Charles Grant, a director since 1794 and about to become the Chairman: 'This was a man utterly antagonistic to Richard Wellesley [the Marquess]. A pious, inflexible, power-loving merchant who returned from Bengal with a fortune in 1790. Although older than Wellesley, he represented the new world of the nineteenth century, the rising middle and mercantile class, the dogmatic, evangelical interpretation of Christianity. He presaged the empire builders who went to India with the sword in one hand and the Bible in the other; he had their conviction of a direct mandate from God.'[30] We shall hear more of Charles Grant.

Arthur Wellesley saw the 'Animadverting Despatch' shortly after his return to Britain, and wrote to his brother that: 'I never saw such a paper in my life. In this the Court entered into a discussion of all the measures of your government since the settlement of Mysore, excepting the treaty of Arcot, each of which they censured in the grossest and least candid terms.'[31]

Against this rising clamour from the Court of Directors, Pitt (now back as Prime Minister) and Castlereagh (President of the Board of Control) had indeed weakened. They had at last accepted that they would have to recall the Marquess. In his place they reappointed the 66-year-old Lord Cornwallis, whose high reputation from his previous tenure in the job and his unimpeachable integrity made him acceptable to all factions. He could be trusted as 'a safe pair of hands' who would do exactly what he was told. His appointment was an understandable but unfortunate compromise. At his age and state of health he was mad to take on such a stressful assignment. Only his strong sense of public duty swayed him into acceptance.

By the time Malcolm arrived at Calcutta, it was already known that the Marquess had received the Government's permission to return home, and that Cornwallis had been appointed to succeed him. It was a lame-duck government. Gone was the 'glad, confident morning' of the Marquess's earlier years at Fort William. Now he was dispirited, broken in health and longing to go home. For Malcolm, to whom the Marquess was such a hero, the mood must have seemed especially bleak. Still, even with only a few weeks of his regime remaining, there was work to be done.

Monson's failure in July 1804 had been offset to some extent by the successful defence of Delhi and Lake's victories over Holkar at Deeg and Farruckabad in December. But despite three attempts, Lake had failed to storm the Jat fortress at Bharatpoor. This military failure was even more damaging to the Company's aura of invincibility than Monson's retreat because it had involved the full force of Lake's army. Scindiah, humiliated by what he conceived as the Company's bad faith over Gwalior, had come more and more under the baleful influence of one of his courtiers, his father-in-law, Surgee Rao Ghautka. Ghautka had always been against the connection with the Company and now his prestige at Scindiah's Court steadily increased. About this time came the death of Scindiah's aged *Dewan,* the wily Bapu Wattel Punt, who had negotiated the Treaties of Peace and Defensive Alliance with Malcolm a year earlier; and the removal from power of Wattel's veteran colleague Munshi Kavel Nyn, who had fled to Delhi. Far from allying himself with the Company against Holkar as the Treaty of Defensive Alliance had laid down, Scindiah now made secret contacts with Raghuji Bhonsle, with the Rajah of Kolhapur and with the Patwardhans, and even indirectly approached the Peshwah, trying to persuade him to abrogate his treaty with the Company.

Hostility to the Company was expressed in other ways. Richard Jenkins, the young acting Resident at Scindiah's Court, who had taken over on the death of Josiah Webbe in November 1804, was subjected to deliberate insults and harassment. In January 1805 the Residency was attacked and plundered, probably on Ghautka's orders. Later that month, when Jenkins asked for permission to leave Scindiah's camp, it was refused; he was held under house arrest. Holkar, meanwhile, flushed with his success against Monson, but smarting and increasingly desperate after successive defeats by Lake, canvassed the possibility of forming a confederacy to fight the British on an even wider scale. Letters were even sent to the Portuguese Governor of Goa inviting him to send 6,000 European troops, with the prospect of taking a share of territory as a reward for success, and to the Afghans and the French. But none of them came forward to help. In March Scindiah at last swallowed his pride and marched towards Bharatpur, blithely informing the British Resident that he was going there to broker a peace settlement between the British and Holkar. In reality, his two days of talks were spent in mapping out an alliance with Holkar to fight the Company. But the long-standing mutual suspicion and antagonism between the two princes meant that this alliance lasted only two months.

Back in Calcutta, the setbacks in the war with Holkar had also eroded the certainties of the Marquess and his Secretariat. They were uncomfortably aware that Arthur Wellesley and Malcolm had probably been right about how to deal with Scindiah in early 1804 – a much greater effort should have been made to 'conciliate' him over the Treaty of Peace. So, when a sort of apology was received from Scindiah for the plundering of the Residency at his camp, the Marquess sent a conciliatory reply, stating that either Malcolm or Graeme Mercer (Lake's political assistant) would be sent on a special embassy to the Maharajah to help him implement the takeover of part of Holkar's territory. This was to be conditional, however, on Scindiah moving back southwards to his own territorial heartland.

Once again – and for the last time – the Marquess decided to 'Send Malcolm'. On 1 May, after barely a fortnight at Calcutta, with instructions largely advocated and drafted by himself, Malcolm set out to join General Lake's camp at Muttra (Mathura), a hundred miles south of Delhi. The journey up the Ganges took a month; a mixture of boat, horse and palanquin. Malcolm's large frame was a trial to the palanquin bearers. He reported to Shawe on arrival at Murshedabad that: 'Both Cole [Arthur Cole] and I are too substantial to be carried by the eight [palanquin carriers] that are accustomed to transport your Bengal Parchment from one station to another.'[32]

He was thoroughly depressed by the portents from England. The hostile attitude of the Directors and the weakness of the Government seemed likely to result in a new policy, and a reversal of all that he and the Marquess had been striving for, just when they were on the point of achieving their goal. Moreover, with the monsoon season approaching, nothing could be done about Holkar for several months. He wrote to Shawe of 'the villainy of the directors, and the weakness of the Board . . . My ambition is dead.'[33]

At this point, he received an extraordinary proposal from the Marquess, conveyed through Shawe, that he should accompany them back to England. Though tempting and flattering to his ego, Malcolm realised that it was a silly idea, and was sensible enough to reject it. He did so in a most carefully drafted letter: 'Colonel Shawe communicated to me your Lordship's wish that I should, if possible, accompany you to

England; and no circumstance in life would have made me so happy, but the peculiar situation of my private finances and the urgent nature of my public duties, made it difficult for me to arrange for so early a departure from India. I wrote most earnestly to the Colonel on the subject, that he might satisfy your Lordship that no slight causes could induce me to decline a proposition so flattering to my feelings and so perfectly accordant with my views in life.'[34]

Lord Cornwallis had left Britain in February 1805. He arrived at Calcutta on the evening of 29 July and disembarked the next morning. The Marquess was at Government House to receive him. The contrast in style between the two men is vividly described in William Hickey's account of their meeting:

> Lord Wellesley, with his customary attention to parade and show, sent down all his carriages, servants, staff officers and general establishment to receive his noble supercessor at the waterside. Lord Cornwallis upon landing looked surprised and vexed at the amazing cavalcade that were drawn up, and turning to Mr George Abercrombie Robinson (. . . his Lordship's confidential Secretary), he said, 'What! What! What is all this, Robinson, hey?' . . . Mr Robinson answered, 'My Lord, the Marquis Wellesley has sent his equipages and attendants as a mark of respect and to accompany you to Government House.' To this Lord Cornwallis replied, 'Too civil, too civil by half. Too many people. I don't want one of them. I have not yet lost the use of my legs, Robinson, hey? Thank God I can walk very well, Robinson, hey? Don't want a score of carriages to convey me a quarter of a mile; certainly shall not use them,' and he accordingly did walk, accompanied by Doctor Fleming, also formerly of the Bengal Establishment, and who with Mr Robinson were the only persons his Lordship brought out with him . . . We were all greatly shocked to see how ill his Lordship looked and what a wreck of what he had been when formerly in Bengal.[35]

The Marquess sailed for England on 14 August, accompanied by Merrick Shawe, who was to remain with him as his faithful secretary for the rest of his long life.

Malcolm, 900 miles away at Muttra, felt utterly bereft at the departure of the Marquess. Not only was he losing his chief sponsor, who had in the last seven years transformed his life, he was facing the prospect of a complete change of policy and the undoing of all that he and his colleagues had fought so hard to achieve.

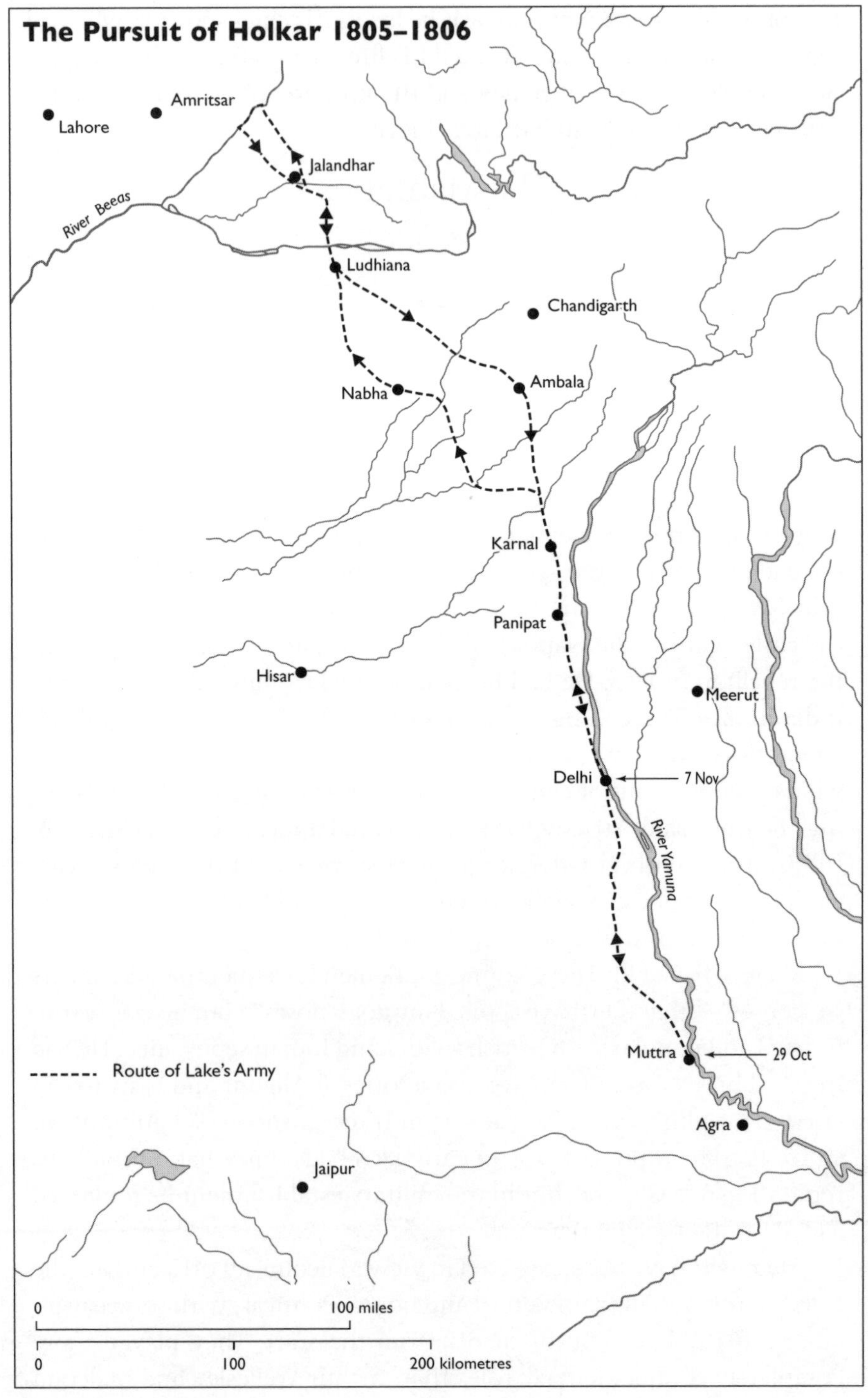
The Pursuit of Holkar 1805–1806
Lahore
Amritsar
Jalandhar
River Beeas
Ludhiana
Chandigarth
Ambala
Nabha
Karnal
Panipat
Hisar
Meerut
Delhi
7 Nov
River Yamuna
Muttra
29 Oct
Agra
Jaipur
Route of Lake's Army
0
100 miles
0
100
200 kilometres

CHAPTER FIFTEEN

The Mahrattas 1805–1807

General Gerard Lake was sixty years old when Malcolm joined him at Muttra. An immensely experienced veteran soldier, he had joined the Grenadier Guards at the age of fourteen, fought in Europe in the Seven Years' War, in America in the War of Independence, in Europe again in the early years of the Napoleonic Wars, and in Ireland, putting down the rebellion of 1798. He had been appointed Commander-in-Chief in India in 1801, succeeding Sir Alured Clarke. He was a fighting soldier, straightforward, brave, dashing, uninterested in diplomacy, and somewhat contemptuous of civilians: 'Damn your writing, mind your fighting', he once said. Strictly formal, he would appear every morning in full uniform with powdered wig. The story is told that many years earlier he was one of several young bucks hunting in Lincolnshire: 'the old huntsman of the pack . . . exclaimed in a passion, "No wonder the pack has behaved ill. These young gentlemen have their handkerchiefs so scented . . . that they have spoiled my dogs' noses!"'[1] But he was warm-hearted and popular with British soldier and Indian sepoy alike. He had inspired his troops to tremendous victories at Alighur and Laswarry in late 1803. Failure with heavy losses in three unsuccessful attempts to storm the Bharatpur fortress in early 1805 had somewhat dimmed his reputation as a General, but in the military establishment he remained a loved and respected figure.

He might have been expected to view Malcolm, an officer from the Deccan rather than from Bengal and now a 'Political', with some suspicion. But the two men hit it off from the start. They played more completely complementary roles than Arthur Wellesley and Malcolm

General Sir Gerard (later Viscount) Lake (1744–1808) was Commander-in-Chief of the Bengal Army (1801–7).

had done in the Deccan. Unlike Wellesley, Lake did not seek to act as chief diplomat as well as military commander. Lake's letters to the Governor-General were mostly in Malcolm's handwriting.

This was Malcolm's first direct contact with the Bengal Army, and there were many new faces, military and civil, to get to know. One of them was the twenty-year-old civilian, Charles Metcalfe, son of Sir Theophilus Metcalfe Bt, a long-time director of the East India Company.

At Eton he had shown 'remarkable powers of application, and a great distaste for athletic sports'. He had arrived at Calcutta in 1800 and was one of the first students at the Marquess's Fort William College, where he studied oriental languages. After an unsatisfactory stint as assistant to Colonel Collins at Scindiah's Court, he worked in the secretariat at Government House in Calcutta, where he attracted the eye of the Marquess. In late 1804 he was sent as a political assistant to Lake's headquarters. A short, squat, ugly young man, he abhorred the Philistine 'hunting and shooting' atmosphere of Lake's entourage. By June 1805 when Malcolm arrived in Lake's camp, he had half-decided to return to administrative duties in Calcutta (also to pay his farewell respects to the departing Marquess, whom he hero-worshipped). But Malcolm sought him out and befriended him. As Metcalfe put it in a letter to a friend: 'He laid open to me the various plans which were in contemplation, gave me admission to all his papers, and by appearing to interest himself in my welfare, prepared me to listen to him with attention. He expatiated on the great field of political employment now open in Hindostan, the necessity of many appointments and missions, the superiority, as he seems to think, of my claims . . . It is my intention to cultivate his intimacy zealously.'[2] Thus Malcolm, with his uncanny knack for spotting youthful talent, seduced the young Metcalfe into pursuing a career which ultimately led him to become, successively, Governor-General of India, Jamaica and Canada.

The diplomatic challenge facing Lake and Malcolm was daunting. Holkar was down but not yet totally defeated. The monsoon was about to arrive, suspending further active military operations until October. Scindiah, now under the thumb of his father-in-law, Surgee Rao Ghautka, was waiting to see which way the wind would blow; meanwhile he was holding Richard Jenkins as a virtual hostage. Back in Calcutta, the Company's credit with the *shroffs* (moneylenders) was running out. On top of all this there was the disturbing prospect of the Marquess's successor, Lord Cornwallis, arriving from London with orders to implement a new and different policy. And indeed that was just what happened.

It was a classic rerun of the old policy clash between the Ring Fencers and the Forwarders. During the Wellesley years the Ring Fencers at the Court of Directors had been overridden by the Forwarders at the Board of Control (i.e. the Government). In the long run the Forwarders were probably right. Peace and political stability across the subcontinent was a necessary prerequisite to prolonged economic prosperity. The fact that the Marquess may have allegedly misused his powers did not invalidate this argument. The trouble was that he was careless and arrogant in his relations with the Court. He conveniently ignored the fact that even the Company's financial resources were finite. During his tenure there had been a dangerous outflow of cash. The commercial men at the Court understandably feared that bankruptcy might overtake the Company before it could reach the nirvana of paramountcy. And the Marquess signally failed to keep the Directors informed about what he was up to, knowing full well, of course, that if he were completely honest and open with them they would probably stop him in his tracks. The Ring Fencer argument for the more modest and short-term objective of maximising the Company's commercial returns was beginning to prevail.

Lord Cornwallis quickly revealed himself as an enthusiastic Ring Fencer. Within days of his arrival he wrote to Lake, worrying that as 'my opinions may differ very widely from those of some of the gentlemen in the political line who attend upon you, I feel myself obliged, in the very responsible situation in which I stand, seriously to require that you will take no step without a reference to me . . . Lord Wellesley assured me yesterday (to my great satisfaction) that the Rajah of Jainagar [Jaipur], had by his conduct, forfeited all claim to our protection. Would to God we could get rid of the Rana of Gohud, and many more of our burthensome allies or dependants.'[3]

A few days later he set off up the river towards Muttra, taking Edmonstone with him, but leaving Barlow to hold the fort at Calcutta. The Court of Directors had appointed him Commander-in-Chief as well as Governor-General, and his journey was officially to take over command from Lake, who would revert to Commander-in-Chief of the Bengal army. Lake was understandably miffed at being thus demoted. He had served with Cornwallis in the American War, and they were together in the surrender at Yorktown which took them out of that war. Cornwallis wrote Lake a friendly letter, trying to soothe his ruffled feelings. He also wrote to Malcolm, probably sensing that Malcolm was the most ardent and articulate Forwarder. The letter was polite enough, praising Malcolm for a paper he had written for the Marquess, but went on to put forward his own very different views:

> I think that no success could indemnify us for carrying on this ruinous war one moment longer than the first occasion that may present itself for our getting out of it without dishonour; and there is no acquisition that we could obtain by it that would not be productive of the greatest inconvenience to us. We are apparently now waging war against two chieftains who have neither territory nor army to lose. Our prospects, surely, of advantage or losses are not equally balanced. Our treasury is now completely emptied; we can send home no investment; and I am reduced to the necessity of taking the very disagreeable step of stopping the treasure destined by the Court of Directors for China, in order to have a chance of being able to get rid of a part of our irregular forces . . . I deprecate the effects of the almost universal frenzy which has seized even some of the heads (which I thought the soundest in the country) for conquest and victory. I need only add, that I shall come to the army with a determination not to submit to insult or aggression, but with an anxious desire to have an opportunity of showing my generosity.[4]

Cornwallis's letter implied a policy which was a reversal of all that Malcolm had been advocating over the previous seven years. Nevertheless he responded immediately that: 'the same sense of duty which has invariably led me to give my opinions, when they were required, with freedom and honesty, has also taught me to submit on every occasion with the most implicit respect and deference to the better judgment of my superiors.'[5]

Was he being sincere? In a way, yes. He was a soldier; he knew that orders had to be obeyed. But he had underestimated the strength of Cornwallis's conviction. He imagined that Cornwallis was merely outlining his personal inclinations rather than issuing a directive for immediate implementation. Surely, he thought, a man of Cornwallis's immense experience and practical disposition would wait at least until he had met Lake and Malcolm on the ground, before making decisions and issuing orders. And he was probably confident that after a few days of debate, his own persuasive powers could modify the elderly Governor-General's views. Unfortunately he no longer had any close friends at Court to keep him closely informed. He respected Barlow, but he did not really like him, and the feeling was mutual. Edmonstone, now coming up the river with the new Governor-General – earnest, plodding, immensely hard-working Edmonstone – was the nearest thing to a confidant, but hardly a soulmate to a man of Malcolm's flamboyant nature.

Meanwhile, unknown to Lake and Malcolm, Cornwallis was becoming ever more adamant in his opposition to the Forward policy. His letters to Castlereagh and the Directors in August and September reveal that he opposed the whole idea of subsidiary alliances, and would have liked to find some way of escaping from all of them, even those with Hyderabad and Mysore. Edmonstone passed this information on to Malcolm, causing him increasing consternation. He expressed his fears in a letter to the Marquess, now on the high seas.[6] He also wrote to Barry Close in Poona, who responded with this bitter commentary on the 'new principles', i.e. the Ring Fence policy: 'The tenour of Lord Cornwallis's letter to you agrees much with the principles expressed in his public dispatch to me; that is, we are encumbered with alliances, and all we have obtained is a burden to us . . . But, in truth, I am sick when I think of present principles!'[7]

As August gave way to September and as Edmonstone's letters revealed the full extent of the change in direction of Company policy, Malcolm's mood became ever more depressed. He wrote candidly to Edmonstone setting out his view of what should be done, believing that Edmonstone privately agreed with him on most points. He asked to be spared the humiliation of having to implement a policy which he could not believe in.[8]

When Edmonstone tried to calm him down, saying that he was equally distressed but felt it his duty to carry on obeying orders, Malcolm pointed out that

> your station and mine are, my dear friend, widely different. As an officer of Government acting immediately under the Governor-General, you have, in fact, only to obey orders, and are never left to the exercise of your own discretion and judgement . . . Now look at my situation. Placed at a great distance from the Governor-General, and acting upon instructions of a general nature – obliged constantly to determine points upon my own judgment, as there is no time for reference – liable to be called

> upon by extraordinary exigencies to act in a most decided manner to save the public interests from injury, it is indispensable that the sentiments of my mind should be in some unison with the dictates of my duty, and if they are unfortunately contrary to it, I am not fit to be employed, for I have seen enough of these scenes to be satisfied that a mere principle will never carry a man through a charge where such discretionary powers must be given, with either honor to himself or advantage to the public.[9]

But as September progressed, Lord Cornwallis's health, which had been frail from the outset, steadily deteriorated. Barlow, as senior member of the Supreme Council, was alerted. He came up-country by *dawk* and arrived at Ghazipur just in time to receive a deathbed briefing from Cornwallis before he expired on 5 October. His Lordship was buried on the banks of the Ganges.

Malcolm wrote fulsome tributes to Cornwallis both at the time and later in his *Political History of India*. He genuinely admired him as a man, and looked back to his previous Governor-Generalship from 1786 to 1794 rather than to these last three sad months. But he also saw a faint glimmer of hope in the succession of Sir George Barlow, who had now become the interim Governor-General. Surely Barlow, who had been the faithful and trusted servant of the Marquess and knew the Mahratta situation intimately, would use his discretion to apply some common sense to the negotiations with Scindiah and Holkar? Surely he would see the folly of trying to woo them by returning territory without any conditions; surely he would not abandon the Rajput rulers to be ravaged by the Mahrattas? He also knew, with some embarrassment, that his letters to Edmonstone seeking to resign or be transferred rather than carry out Cornwallis's policy, had been passed on to Barlow. So he wrote to Barlow, pledging his loyalty and backtracking on the resignation threat, hinting that he was confident that Barlow would interpret his instructions in a way which would be in the best interests of the Company.

But, unfortunately for Malcolm, Barlow was not that kind of man. He was able, industrious and of unimpeachable integrity, a very safe pair of hands. As Vice-President of the Council he had served the Marquess very well. The Marquess, in return, was grateful to have such a reliable chief of staff and recommended Barlow as his substantive successor. It is a curious weakness of great and visionary leaders that they so often choose pedestrian successors. Perhaps it is vanity – if their successor is dim, their own light may seem to have shone more brightly.

William Hickey, who had known Barlow for twenty years, wrote acidly about his succession to the Governor-Generalship:

> A grievous change was experienced upon the succession of Sir George Barlow (so different a man in every respect) to the situation Lord Wellesley had so recently filled, the one all dignity and possessed of the most shining talents, the other a compound of meanness and pride without a particle of genius. Sir George Barlow was the son of a silk mercer of King St, Covent Garden, and nature had certainly intended him for nothing more elevated in Society than a measurer of lute strings from behind a counter; although that fickle jade, Madam Fortune, with her usual unsteadiness, threw him into so much more exalted a sphere. His manner in Society was cold, distant and formal. I do not believe he had a single friend in the world, nor one individual person about whom he cared, or in whose welfare he felt at all interested.[10]

Meanwhile Malcolm had been spending the monsoon season with Lake's army at the splendid though decayed Mughal palaces at Fatehpore Sikri, to the west of Agra and Muttra.[11] He was not, however, quiescent. Diplomatic activity continued. His personal inclination had always been to 'conciliate' Scindiah, to allow him enough territory to finance the maintenance of a civil government and defence force, without having to resort to plundering neighbouring states, but to keep him out of Hindustan. On the other hand he felt that Holkar was incorrigible and should be utterly destroyed. The new policy that was emerging from Calcutta made conciliating Scindiah a relatively easy diplomatic task. The first priority was to patch up personal relations with him. A firm letter, signed by Lake but undoubtedly drafted by Malcolm, was sent to him, demanding the unconditional release of Jenkins from his Court as a prerequisite to any further negotiation. After considerable toing and froing, this finally happened in mid-September.[12] Malcolm then looked around for someone trusted by both sides to act as a reliable intermediary. Bappu Wattel Punt had died earlier in the year but his second-in-command, Munshi Kavel Nyn, was still living in exile in Delhi. In June, Scindiah, disillusioned with the Holkar alliance, had expelled Ghautka from his Court. In August Holkar's army left Scindiah's camp at Midnapur. Scindiah now gave Kavel Nyn plenipotentiary power to negotiate a new treaty with the Company. In early October negotiations began between Kavel Nyn in Delhi, and Malcolm with Lake's army as it moved northwards from Muttra. When the army passed through Delhi in late October, Kavel Nyn joined it. By 23 November Malcolm and Kavel Nyn had hammered out the terms of the Treaty of Mustafapur. It largely reaffirmed the original 'Treaty of Peace',[13] but with some vital differences, namely that Gohad and Gwalior were to be restored to Scindiah. To save British face, this was presented as a gesture of goodwill, but the effect was the same as if it had been recognised as Scindiah's by right. The Rana of Gohad was to be paid off in cash by the Company; the boundary between the territories of Scindiah and the Company was to be the Chumbul river; and both parties were to be at liberty to negotiate separately with Holkar.

Malcolm was, of course, more than happy with this arrangement. The return of Gwalior and Gohad was what he and Arthur Wellesley had advocated in early 1804, when he had got into such trouble with the Marquess. More importantly, it detached Scindiah from Holkar, thus isolating Holkar from his last potential ally among the Mahrattas. Lake was delighted, and paid extravagant praise to Malcolm's diplomatic skills in a letter to the Governor-General: 'You can perfectly judge how much his experience and ability have contributed to its favourable conclusion and . . . greatly augmented his claim on the Hon'ble Company and his country.'[14]

Attention could now be concentrated on tracking down Holkar. Lake's army moved as soon as the rains ceased in early October. But there was a dire shortage of cash. Pay for the troops was several months in arrears. Over the previous year, Lake had recruited large numbers of freebooting soldiers as 'irregular cavalry'. By retaining their services and paying them, he had prevented them taking up service with Holkar, who would pay them in plunder. In the short term this was tactically shrewd but hugely expensive. With the Company's finances in such desperate straits, Cornwallis had rightly judged that it would be a lesser evil to pay them off, and bring the regular troops' pay up to date. Malcolm worked hard throughout the wet season to scrape up loans wherever he could, and largely succeeded.

But where was Holkar? After leaving Scindiah's camp at Midnapur in August, he had retreated into Rajput country. Failing to get a promise of cooperation from the Rajputs, he decided to march northward to the Punjab and seek shelter with the Sikh Paramount Chieftain, Ranjit Singh. Skirting the Rewari hills on the edge of the desert, he eluded Company detachments sent to cut him off, and proceeded north towards Ranjit Singh's capital at Lahore, in the Punjab. Lake's army passed through Delhi on 7 November 'in the afternoon of which day Lord Lake paid a visit to the Emperor, attended by his staff [which presumably included Malcolm], and all the brigadiers in camp.'[15] Shah Alam, the Mughal Emperor who received them, was a pathetic 77-year-old blind man sitting under a tattered canopy in the Red Fort, presiding benevolently but powerlessly over his Court. In late 1803, with the ousting of Dowlat Rao Scindiah from Hindustan, the British had replaced the Mahrattas as Shah Alam's protectors/jailers. Despite all his humiliations, both the Mahrattas and the British still paid deference to him as the Great Mughal. Officially he still ruled Delhi. In practice, the British Resident, David Ochterlony, now pulled the strings.

Lake and Malcolm spent only two days at Delhi, pushing on northwards in pursuit of Holkar. They followed the route taken through millennia by conquerors of Hindustan from the north and west. Between the Himalayas to the north and the desert to the south is a narrow corridor through which all these armies had passed. They passed Panipat about eighty miles north-west of Delhi, the scene of three great battles: the victories of Babur, the first Great Mughal, in 1526; of Akbar over the Hindu General Hemu in 1556; and of the Afghan Ahmed Shah Durrani over the Mahrattas in 1761.

About this time, Malcolm suffered a curious accident. 'I write in pain. A horse which a gentleman was riding alongside of me seized me by the thigh, which he held for some minutes, and has crippled me for the moment.'[16] For some time he had to conduct business lying on a couch.

Lake hoped to catch up with and corner Holkar on the eastern bank of the Beas river, thinking Holkar would not be able to cross it. But cross it he did, on 1 December, reaching the Sikh city of Amritsar on 10 December. All this time he had been sending messages to the Sikh

Chiefs, pleading with them to help him against the British, and promising them monetary rewards, even undertaking to embrace the Sikh religion. At the same time, he threw in the implied threat that if they did not join him he would be forced to seek the protection of the Afghan ruler, Shah Shuja al Mulk, possibly becoming Muslim himself in the process. At first the minor Chiefs were inclined to support Holkar, but Maharajah Ranjit Singh, ruler since 1801 and still only twenty-five years old, remained sceptical. He knew that Shuja al Mulk was too preoccupied with his own internal troubles to take on Holkar. He sent his *vakeels* to the British camp, where they were warmly received by Malcolm, though they might have been surprised by his sometimes unorthodox negotiating style. On one occasion, when an officer rushed into the negotiating tent to announce that two large tigers had been seen in the neighbourhood, Malcolm seized his gun, cried, *'Baug! Baug!'* (Tiger! Tiger!), ordered his elephant, and went in search of the tigers. He returned some time later, having shot the animals, and resumed the discussions. The Sikh *vakeels* thought him mad.

Lake's army reached the Beas river on 10 December, about thirty miles upstream from the place where Holkar's army had crossed it ten days earlier, but could not find a way over it. Malcolm had already been in touch by letter with Ranjit Singh, trying to persuade him by a mixture of incentives and threats to withhold support from Holkar, and then sent an agent, Bhag Singh, to Ranjit's Court. This had the desired effect on Ranjit, who confirmed that he would 'send Holkar out of his territories very soon'. He also offered his services as mediator in any negotiations the Company might have with Holkar. Holkar now realised that he was cornered. Cursing every Indian leader who was 'trying to save his own skin', he sent his *vakeels* to Lake's camp. They arrived on 20 December, professing Holkar's desire to negotiate a peace treaty.

In late November Barlow had sent Lake and Malcolm general guidelines for negotiation with Holkar.[17] Holkar was to be deprived of territory south of the Tapti river and north of the Chumbul river, including Tonk and Rampura, and limits were to be placed on the size of his army. He was to refrain from hiring Europeans or Americans without the Company's prior knowledge. Significantly, Holkar's future relationship with the Rajput territories was left unclarified. This was an easy negotiating brief for Malcolm, since he knew that Holkar would probably be expecting a much less generous offer. Nevertheless, when he put a draft treaty in front of Holkar's *vakeels* and asked for their comments, they protested bitterly (in line with the best traditions of oriental diplomacy) about the sacrifices which their Chief was being asked to make, especially the cession of Tonk and Rampura. Malcolm remained implacable, although he did concede that if all other points in the Treaty were adhered to, the position on Tonk and Rampura might be reconsidered after eighteen months. A treaty (the Treaty of Rajghat) based on the guidelines he had received from Calcutta was provisionally agreed on 24 December, subject to Holkar's ratification: 'After a lapse of several days, Holkar's *vakeel* returned; when it appeared, that instead of presenting the intended ratification of the Treaty on behalf of his master, he had recourse to objections and evasions; in consequence of which he was ordered to quit the camp immediately, as all intercourse was at an end. On hearing this, the ambassador pulled out a paper in the handwriting of Holkar, instructing him to get better terms if he could, but if not, to accept what was offered.'[18]

The formal signing ceremony took place on 7 January 1806 on the banks of the Beas river:[19] 'On the right of his Lordship [Lake] were seated several of the Seik [Sikh] chiefs, whose joy at the event was visibly marked in their countenances; and on his left were Colonel Malcolm and the *vakeels* of Holkar. A silk bag was first presented, containing a letter from Holkar, expressive of his pacific disposition, the sincerity of his professions, and his desire to live in amity with the English government.'[20]

The Sikh Chiefs' 'joy at the event' may have been partly influenced by a parade and show of European military tactics, which Lake had put on for them a few days earlier on the bank of the river. Here they saw the manoeuvres of disciplined Company troops and the superior firepower of the Company's artillery and firelocks compared with the Sikhs' own matchlocks. They were allegedly heard to whisper to one another, 'thank God we did not go to war with the English'.[21] Another intriguing feature of this parade was that 'his Lordship placed himself opposite the centre, where also stood the Seiks, with Colonel Malcolm as their interpreter, mounted on elephants.' Can Malcolm have somehow mastered Punjabi in addition to his other Indian languages, despite having only entered Sikh country a few weeks earlier? Or was he speaking a neutral language, the description of 'interpreter' meaning merely that he was explaining the movements on the parade? What is certain is that he used the three weeks that he was in direct contact with the Sikhs to find out an astonishing amount of information about them, which he later included in his first book, *Sketch of the Sikhs*.

The military and diplomatic operations over the previous six months had so far been an unqualified success for Lake and Malcolm. They had restored relations on honourable terms with Scindiah and put the marauding Holkar firmly back in his box.

Young Metcalfe was sent to Holkar's camp to deliver the Treaty. He was greeted by a salute of fifty guns and enthusiastic crowds. 'Ek-chusm-oo-doula's [One-eyed governor's] appearance [Holkar had only one eye] is very grave, his countenance expressive, his manners and conversation easy. He has not at all the appearance of the savage that we know him to be. A little lapdog was on the musnud – a strange playfellow for Holkar! The jewels on his neck were invaluably rich.'[22] In fact, by this time Jaswunt Rao Holkar had become thoroughly unstable.[23] By 1808 he was certified as completely mad and was deposed, finally dying in 1811.

But now the heavy hand of Sir George Barlow intruded. No doubt he was mindful of the Court of Directors' instructions passed on to him by the dying Cornwallis, to disengage from alliances with native princes. As a conscientious civil servant he believed in strict adherence to orders from above, and he may have felt that the arrangements made by Lake and Malcolm had not followed the instructions of the Court with sufficient precision. He proceeded to make two decisions which seriously compromised the success of the arrangements worked out by Lake and Malcolm.

First, in ratifying the Treaty of Raghat with Holkar, Barlow unilaterally added an extra 'declaratory article' by which the Company immediately relinquished all claim to the districts of Tonk and Rampura. This was a direct reversal of his instruction of 20 November whereby he had urged Malcolm not to give up these two districts. Why did he change his mind? Apparently he wished 'to create confidence in the Maratha Chief's mind about the moderate and amicable view of the British Government'. He told Lake and Malcolm that this would ensure the 'friendship and goodwill of Holkar'. In fact, it had three adverse effects: first, in weakening the principle that Holkar should cede all lands north of the Chumbul river (Tonk and Rampura were north of that river); second, in Lake's words, giving 'a decisive blow to the system of political and military defence' of the western approaches to Hindustan;[24] and third, in removing the one surety the Company had that Holkar would uphold the Treaty by returning peaceably to his base and actually cede the lands which he had agreed to surrender before the restoration of Tonk and Rampura took place. For Malcolm, an opportunist ruler like Holkar would interpret such unsolicited generosity as weakness; it would only encourage him to try to wring some more concessions out of the Company. If the Company really wanted to make further concessions, the time to do so would be at some future date in exchange for some new concession from Holkar. Next, and more seriously, Barlow confirmed Holkar's and Scindiah's right of protectorate over the Rajput states. He insisted that Lake should dissolve the Company's alliance with the Rajah of Jaipur[25] and wrote to the Rajah directly, pointing out that during the war with Holkar, the Rajah had remained inactive, contrary to his treaty obligations; hence the Company no longer considered itself committed to protect him. Technically this was true, although the Rajah had later been helpful to the Company; but in reality Barlow was simply finding an excuse to follow the Directors' desire to be rid of as many subsidiary alliances as possible. A similar line was later taken with Jodhpur.

The Rajput princes protested vigorously to Lake and Malcolm. They had taken the side of the Company in the war with Holkar and and incurred Holkar's enmity. Now they were to be put at his mercy. The Company had a moral obligation to protect them. Of course Lake and Malcolm privately agreed with them but what could they do? There is nothing more galling to the front-line negotiator than to insist on a particular point at issue and get it accepted, only to watch 'head office' nonchalantly give it away again. Professionally, he feels that a mistake is being made; personally he feels humiliated, knowing that the negotiators on the other side no longer take him seriously.

Despite his training as a soldier, it was not in Malcolm's nature to accept without question measures that he felt were wrong. Confident, perhaps overconfident, in his powers of persuasion, he went on arguing his case with Calcutta. This had almost been his undoing with the Marquess in 1804 when he had opposed the annexation of Gohad and Gwalior. Now his mutterings about the unilateral concessions to Holkar and the abandonment of the Rajput princes reached the ears of Barlow. It was left to the faithful Edmonstone to pass on to him the Governor-

General's displeasure. Edmonstone delivered the message to Malcolm as gently as he could: 'it will be satisfactory to you to know that your services have been represented to the Court of Directors in strong terms of approbation. Sir G Barlow entertains a high sense of your zealous exertions, and only laments that they should occasionally have been directed by principles of policy in which he could not conscientiously concur. For my own part, I will only say that I have a just conception of the astonishing labours you have gone through, and the arduous nature of your situation.'[26]

He then went on to apologise for letting Malcolm down, to bemoan his own situation and to cry out for release from it in such anguished terms that Malcolm felt obliged to respond at length. He agreed with Edmonstone that he had been deeply hurt by the way his views had been 'treated with neglect, and on some occasions with severity; and this disappointment has been increased from your being the medium of communications which were [in] every way unpleasant and unexpected'. But he reassured Edmonstone that 'my regret, . . . though extreme . . . has no ways impaired my friendship for you, nor lessened (as you seem to think) my esteem and regard for your character'.[27]

Lake's army started its march back eastwards from the Punjab on 9 January. It reached Delhi in mid-February and most of the troops were back in their cantonments at Cawnpore by the end of that month. Lake was acutely conscious of how much money the war was costing and how straitened were the Company's financial resources. It was essential to get back to cantonments and disband and pay off as many irregular troops as soon as possible. He largely deputed this mundane but exacting task to Malcolm, who responded with his usual vigour. By early April the monthly outgoings on these troops had been reduced more than tenfold from 400,000 to 35,000 rupees. The only remaining irregular troops whom Lake and Malcolm wanted to retain were Colonel James Skinner's cavalry corps, later to become famous as Skinner's Horse. Skinner was the son of Hercules Skinner, a Scots Colonel in the Company's Bengal army, who had taken under his protection a Rajput landowner's daughter. She had borne him six children. Educated at a Calcutta boarding school, James Skinner joined Scindiah's Mahratta army led by General de Boigne in 1796. In 1803, when the Mahratta army under General Perron was being attacked by Lake near Delhi, Skinner and some of his fellow officers were dismissed and joined Lake's army.

In the 1805 campaign against Holkar, it was Skinner who had guided the Company army over the Sutlej river. So they felt a considerable obligation to reward him. But Barlow would have none of it, insisting that Skinner's corps should be disbanded, and when Malcolm suggested as an alternative that Skinner might instead be given a *jaghir*, Barlow promptly overruled him, on the ground that Skinner was a British subject.

While the main body of the troops were stationed at Cawnpore, Lake and Malcolm spent much of March and April in Delhi. There they relaxed and had a good time. The weather at Cawnpore in late April and May was becoming impossibly hot. Malcolm and Charles Pasley, who had been with him throughout the Punjab campaign, travelled to Lucknow, fifty miles away, to escape some of the heat. Finally, in early July, they took a boat and sailed down the Ganges, reaching Calcutta at the end of the month.

There were plenty of old friends to catch up with. Malcolm stayed for a while with Henry Colebrook, now a judge of the Court of Appeal and already celebrated as a Sanskrit scholar. Later he moved in with John Adam, ten years his junior but already Deputy Secretary of the Secret and Political Department. When he reported to Government House he was greeted cordially but rather stiffly by Barlow. As he put it in a letter to the Marquess: 'I have received every polite attention from Sir G Barlow since I came here. He has however limited his communications to points on which he could refer to no other with equal hope of information . . . he has promised attention to the suggestion I have stated regarding Mysore, where, I can collect from his manner, he wishes me to be as soon as possible.'[28] The feeling was mutual. The two men were such utterly different characters that they felt uneasy in each other's company.

As he waited for a ship to take him to Madras, Malcolm also wrote several memoranda on the Hindustan situation, and felt that he had succeeded in getting Barlow to deviate a little from strict adherence to the Cornwallis strategy. By the middle of September, he wrote to Bentinck in Madras, 'All my baggage was embarked, and I meant to leave in a few hours, when I received a message from Sir G Barlow, the purport of which was that he wished I would defer my departure. This I of course received as a command.'[29]

What had changed Barlow's mind was the latest news from Hindustan. Just as Lake and Malcolm had feared, Holkar had failed to withdraw according to the terms of the Treaty of Rajghat. He was hanging around in the general vicinity of the Company's new provinces, and threatening them. Reluctant as he was to involve Malcolm, Barlow badly needed informed advice as to how to deal with the situation, and Malcolm was the obvious person to provide it.

He was called in again to deal with the saga of the new Persian Ambassador. After the first Persian Ambassador, Haji Khalil Khan, had been killed in Bombay in 1802, the Shah had appointed Haji Khalil's brother-in-law, Mohamed Nabee Khan, as his replacement. After interminable delays, Mohamed Nabee had arrived at Bombay in October 1805 with a retinue of 230 people, determined to outdo his predecessor in grandeur. After four months of making outrageous demands of Governor Duncan, he sailed on to Calcutta, arriving in early April 1806. Despite severe warnings by the Calcutta Government about his behaviour, Mohamed Nabee continued to complain about his treatment. He seems to have been a tiresome fellow, demanding special privileges for himself and in no hurry to get down to work. And, as a British officer later remarked: 'he amused himself writing verses on the personal charms of some of the beautiful European women he met with. These amatory flights of fancy can hardly be wondered at when we take into consideration that during the whole course of his life he had never seen a woman's face unveiled except that of his own wife in the haram apartments.'[30]

The Governor-General, unable to humour this importunate man, called in Malcolm, an assignment for which Malcolm was uniquely well-fitted, both in his experience of Persia and in his warmth of manner in dealing with Persians. He managed to get Nabee to admit that he had no claim against the Calcutta Government, but he presented Nabee's case sympathetically, recommended that the Company should make a virtue of necessity by forgiving Nabee the debts that he owed the Company as a result of his mission's extravagant expenditure. Nabee was eventually put on a ship and sent back to Persia in early 1807.

But Malcolm's advice was only asked for intermittently. As a 'Wellesley man' he was out of favour in government circles, and he resented it. He became rather sorry for himself and petulant. He was tired of life on the periphery in Calcutta. He thought longingly of a quiet and remunerative existence as the Resident at Mysore, where he could put together a more substantial literary work based on his experiences in Persia. At the end of 1806 Barlow released him. But before he left there was one last event which raised his spirits. The universally popular General Lake was about to return to England, and Malcolm attended a farewell dinner for 400 people given in Lake's honour. Lake called Malcolm forward and sat him down on his right, observing: 'Malcolm, that has been your place through all our late hard work in Hindostan, and I see no reason why you should not occupy it at a moment of gratification like the present.'[31]

Within a year of the old General's return to England, he caught a violent chill and died.

In the Punjab in late 1805 Malcolm had negotiated with the Sikhs, 'a Singular Nation who inhabit the Provinces of the Punjab situated between the rivers Jumna and Indus' as he later termed them, and had acquired whatever information he could about their history and religion. After arriving in Calcutta, he obtained a copy of the Sikh 'bible', the *Adi Granth,* from a Sikh priest, and with his help was able to put together a paper on the Sikhs, the first available in English. He wrote to the Marquess that 'I have almost finished a long and detailed paper on the Sikhs, of whose history and religion and present critical state I have been enabled by circumstances to collect considerable information.'[32] This was Malcolm's first attempt at a literary work and it already had all the hallmarks of his particular style. He would engage anyone and everyone he could find in lively discussion on the subject in question, note down their legends and folklore, and put the whole lot together in an engaging series of anecdotes. As he put it in his introduction: 'In every research into the general history of mankind, it is of the most essential importance to hear what a nation has to say about itself; and the knowledge gained from such sources has a value, independent of its historical utility. It aids the promotion of social intercourse, and leads to the establishment of friendship between nations.'[33] He was encouraged by Henry Colebrook who, in addition to his job as a judge, was editing *Asiatic Researches,* a scholarly journal of oriental studies. Malcolm's paper – 197 pages long – eventually appeared as *Sketch of the Sikhs* in *Asiatic Researches* in 1809, and was published in book form in England in 1812.

In early January 1807, Malcolm boarded a ship for Madras, leaving Calcutta without regret.

CHAPTER SIXTEEN

Mysore, Love and Marriage, 1807–1808

On the ship to Madras, Malcolm had plenty of time to think. He had hoped to go overland, but the thigh injury from the horse bite of a year earlier was still hurting him, so he could not ride. And he was depressed.

He was depressed about politics in India. Most of the people whom he had served and admired – Sir Alured Clark, the three Wellesleys and Lake – had gone home. He was opposed to the direction of policy under Sir George Barlow, who was trying slavishly to follow the instructions of the Court of Directors in London, based on information that was up to nine months out of date. The Court itself was dominated by Charles Grant, who was strongly opposed to the policy of war and conquest which he associated with the Wellesleys. There were even moves in London to impeach the Marquess.

He was depressed about his career. Here he was, nearly thirty-eight years old, with many years of devoted and, in his opinion, eminently successful service. Yet where had it got him? A Residency at Mysore with no apparent prospect of further promotion. His loyal service to the Wellesleys was held against him.

Finally, on a more mundane level, he was depressed about his financial position. On arrival at Calcutta in mid-1806 he had found that 'though my expenses had been paid (as far as the usages of the service would admit), my fortune was diminished in a considerable degree by the constant extra missions on which I had been employed for these last four or five years – i.e. I possess less than I must have had if I had remained stationary like other Residents.'[1]

He found Madras even less agreeable than Calcutta. The Government was still reeling from the tragedy of the so-called Vellore massacre of six months earlier. The sepoy troops in the garrison at Vellore (where Malcolm had spent the first few months of his Indian service in 1783) had mutinied. Some stupid orders, including the banning of caste marks, had led the sepoys to believe that there was a plot to convert them to Christianity by force. In a foretaste of the circumstances of the great uprising of 1857, they had killed or wounded over 200 European troops. The mutiny had been put down promptly but had left behind a lot of bitterness and recrimination in government circles. Malcolm went straight to see his friend the Governor, Lord William Bentinck, but found him beleaguered. He and his Commander-in-Chief, Sir John Cradock, were blamed for the Vellore disaster, and soon afterwards recalled by the Court of Directors. Lord William felt that he had been made a scapegoat. It is a tribute to his resilience and persistence that twenty years later he succeeded in returning to India as Governor-General.

Pondering what could be done to rescue the Madras Government from the doldrums, Malcolm hit upon the idea of getting Arthur Wellesley appointed as Governor *and* as Commander-in-Chief. In the light of subsequent history this may appear rather far-fetched, but at the time it made some sense. Wellesley was doing nothing more important than commanding a regiment based at Hastings (on the site of the 1066 battlefield) and acting as a modest backbencher in Parliament. Malcolm made his proposal to Wellesley himself, of course, but also to the Marquess, to Sir John Anstruther (former Chief Justice of Bengal) and to several others. Of course all these letters took many months to reach England and the replies just as long to return. Wellesley replied that he did not see the situation in Madras in quite such a serious light as Malcolm. 'I don't think it probable that I shall be called upon to go to India; the fact is, that men in power in England think very little of that country.'[2] By the time Wellesley's reply reached India, the lives of both of them had been overtaken by other events.

What was to become of Malcolm's own career? As he waited for his leg to heal, he took part in the Madras social scene. He wrote to Lake: 'The great rulers treat me as I expected – with much attention, but little confidence . . . the sentiment of my mind is more that of pity than of admiration of some of our first characters here . . . I want to keep clear of all discussions, to draw my salary for eighteen months, and to join you in old England.' Meanwhile, despite his dark mood, he still managed to enjoy himself. 'The races are on the 26th [February]. Grant and I have two horses for the two first maidens, "Marquis" and "Sir Arthur" (all in the family).'[3]

Malcolm's vague idea of going back to England after eighteen months in Mysore was not properly thought through. It was no more than a placebo for his present depression. It took two typically trenchant letters of advice from Wellesley to point out the realities of his situation. In February 1807, Wellesley advised him not to be in a hurry to come to England as 'you could not exist in the way you would like under a much larger fortune than you possess; and, take my word for it, you will lose nothing by staying away from England a little longer.'[4] In October he was even more explicit. 'I strongly recommend you not to return home as long as your health will allow you to remain in India, and as you can retain your office . . . you are not yet sufficiently rich; you will have to return there, and you may possibly find it difficult to get employment in the line to which you are so well suited, and to which you have always been accustomed.'[5] That was in the future. Meanwhile, as Malcolm prepared to travel to Mysore, something totally unexpected happened to him, something that was to change his whole life from that moment on. He fell in love.

It would be astonishing if a man of Malcolm's warm, extrovert temperament and athletic prowess had not, by the age of nearly thirty-eight, had a number of romantic affairs. For East India Company officers in the late eighteenth century, sex was easily available, and not simply with common prostitutes but with delightful courtesans. Indeed, one in three European company servants in 1800 had live-in *bibis* whom they cherished and remembered in their wills.[6] Yet all we get from Kaye's almost contemporary biography is a hardly credible picture of Malcolm's love life. If Kaye is to be believed, 'up to this time Malcolm had carried about with him a heart, the warmest affections of which were given to his mother and his sisters . . . But a life of constant action – of change of scene, of change of society, of varied objects and varied interests – is never favourable to the growth of that tender, but absorbing, passion which, once developed, influences the whole of a man's subsequent career.'[7]

Among Malcolm's friends in Madras were Alexander Cockburn and his wife Olympia (née Campbell). Alexander and his elder brother

Thomas Cockburn were merchants running their family business. Alexander had been Mayor of Madras in 1799, and had married Olympia Campbell in January 1804. Staying with the Cockburns in early 1807 was Olympia's eighteen-year-old younger sister Charlotte.

Olympia and Charlotte were daughters of Colonel Alexander Campbell of the 74th Regiment of Foot. He had been serving in south India since 1793 and was well known to Malcolm. His family came originally from Achallader in the Scottish Highlands but he was serving in south-west England when he met and married Olympia Morshead in 1783. They lived for eight years as tenants of her brother, Sir John Morshead, a local grandee and Member of Parliament, at Trenant Park, St Neots, near Liskeard in Cornwall. There they produced five children (two boys – John and Allan; and three girls – Olympia, Charlotte and Amelia).

Charlotte, born in January 1789, endured a difficult upbringing. Her parents departed for Madras when she was three, and her mother died there in the following year. Her father remained in India throughout her childhood, leaving her and four siblings under the protection of her gambling maternal uncle. Still, Trenant Park was a large country house and a fine healthy place for a child to grow up. But by January 1805, with her uncle having lost all his money at the London gaming tables and on the brink of bankruptcy, it was decided that Charlotte should join her father, elder sister and brother-in-law at Madras. She left England on an East Indiaman on 3 March, suitably chaperoned, and arrived in Madras several months later. Her father was at that time commanding the Mysore troops at Seringapatam, but in 1806 he was transferred to Trichinopoly to command the southern division of the Madras Army. Meanwhile Charlotte stayed with the Cockburns in Madras. Olympia Cockburn had produced a son in November 1804 and a daughter followed in 1806.

Between Malcolm's arrival in Madras on 14 January 1807 and his departure for Mysore on 21 March, there would have been plenty of chances for him to meet Charlotte in the tiny European society of Madras. For once, too, he was not particularly busy. This fresh and lively girl of barely eighteen had a dramatic effect on him. He was smitten. He invited the Cockburns, including Charlotte, to go with him to Mysore and stay at the Residency. Reaching Mysore in early April, they came upon a well-ordered scene. The *Dewan*, Purneah, was a highly competent and honest administrator.[8] Successive British Residents,

Barry Close, Josiah Webbe and Mark Wilks (deputising for Malcolm) were men of considerable ability. The administration was going smoothly and there was not a great deal for Malcolm to do. His Residency correspondence over the next few months included such parochial issues as the recent vaccination campaign, whereby 400 people had been successfully vaccinated against smallpox; and asking the sub-treasurer in Madras to pay 78 Star Pagodas (the local currency) to Mr Benjamin Heyne, the Company's botanist at the Bangalore Botanical Gardens. He was said to have taken Charlotte for a ride on an elephant and whispered a stream of anecdotes into her ear, which had her laughing helplessly.[9] Suddenly the world seemed a happier place.

His undemanding duties at Mysore coupled with the thrill of his new infatuation rekindled his wider imagination. He started to think again about the great political issues of the day, and what should be done about them. The news from Europe was bad. Napoleon was rampant. Continental Europe was almost entirely under his control, and his dream of expansion to the east might be revived. French influence at Constantinople was growing. The Shah of Persia, then at war with Russia, had appealed to Napoleon for help against Russian aggression in the Caucasus. Malcolm's proposed response to this threat was for a Company expeditionary force to attack the eastern provinces of the Ottoman Empire, in other words Basra and Baghdad. He wrote on these lines to Edmonstone in Calcutta at the beginning of May and again three weeks later.[10] There was a strong implication that he personally would be delighted to lead such a force. It was all a bit unrealistic since there was no way that Sir George Barlow, an ultra-cautious civil servant by training, would ever authorise, on his own initiative, the despatch of such a force to Basra, let alone allow a man like Malcolm to command it. Curiously, just as suddenly as he had made this proposal, Malcolm dropped it. Maybe he realised that Barlow would never consent to it, although it is difficult to imagine that Malcolm would ever give up an idea just because he feared that he could not persuade his superiors to agree with him. But in this case, perhaps there was, for once, a more romantic explanation. In May he asked Charlotte Campbell to marry him and was accepted. He wrote to Colonel Campbell asking for his approval and received an immediately positive reply: 'Were the choice of all the men in India in my offer for my daughter, I would have pitched on you.'[11] It was welcome news for the widower Colonel. He must have wondered what he was going to do with his younger daughter, and here was a wonderful 'catch'.

Malcolm was ecstatic. He wrote to John Leyden:

> my mind, my dear friend, has been full of other thoughts than Politics or Literary pursuits for some time past. I have been in love, most desperately . . . I shall be married in a few weeks time to a fair guest of mine, a daughter of your old friend Colonel Campbell. Though you came to be too much in collision with the father . . . to be pleased with him, you would be delighted with the daughter, who is *all soul*, and is as unaffected in her manners and cheerful in her temper as she is graceful in her person and accomplished in her mind . . . I don't care whether you honour my marriage with an *Epigram* or a *Epithalamum* or an *Epitaph*.[12]

Malcolm wrote to Bentinck's Private Secretary to obtain formal permission for the marriage.[13] He wrote, too, to Arthur Wellesley: 'I am on the very brink of matrimony with a daughter of your friend . . . Campbell . . . I shall say nothing about the lady. Mrs Freese[14] (who is staying at Mysore) will wish you all particulars, and Ladies are best at such descriptions.'[15] To which Wellesley politely responded, 'I beg leave to congratulate you on your marriage . . . I beg that you will present my best respects to Mrs Malcolm, to whom I hope that you will introduce me at the first convenient moment.'[16]

Weddings in those days did not attract the hullabaloo that they generally do today. A man would propose to his intended bride, get a favourable reply, obtain her father's approval, and a month or two later a small private wedding ceremony would take place. What mattered was not the ceremony but the marriage, which was definitely for life. In this case the wedding duly took place on 4 July at the Mysore Residency.[17] Colonel Campbell could not come all the way from Trichinopoly, so Charlotte was given away by her brother-in-law, Alexander Cockburn. Also attending was Malcolm's cousin, Charles Pasley.

The Residency records reveal that on the day of his wedding Malcolm wrote three official letters.

Earlier in the year news had come through of the appointment of a new Governor-General (Barlow only had the job on an interim basis).

Gilbert Elliot, 1st Earl of Minto (1757–1814) was Governor-General of India (1807–13).

He was Gilbert Elliot, Earl of Minto. The Elliots of Minto were a prominent family in the Scottish Borders. One of them had married a Pasley, so Malcolm could later claim a distant blood relationship. At fifty-six, Minto was relatively old for a Governor-General. He had had a long and distinguished career as a barrister, a Member of Parliament, Governor of Corsica (1794–6) and Ambassador to the Court of Vienna (1799–1801). He was a highly cultivated aristocrat of cosmopolitan tastes. But he was essentially a diplomat and there were doubts about his resolution when acting in an executive role. On hearing of Minto's appointment, Warren Hastings remarked to his friend Sir Charles D'Oyley that '[Minto's] administration in Corsica made his talents sufficiently well known to be dreaded.'[18] Admittedly Hastings would have been prejudiced against Minto, who had led the prosecution case against him when he was impeached in 1788. Minto was a Whig, appointed President of the Board of Control and later nominated as Governor-General by the Whig-dominated 'Government of the Talents'. But before he left for India, the 'Talents' had been replaced by the Tories, and it was Minto's misfortune that for his whole period in office he was serving a government of his party political opponents. As Sir James Mackintosh put it, he behaved 'too much like a man who, knowing that his superiors are his enemies, seeks above everything else to escape blame'.[19]

Minto's youngest son, John Elliot, had joined the Madras civil service some time before his father's appointment. When Minto got the job, he made John his Private Secretary. William Hickey painted an unflattering picture of young Elliot. 'He seemed to me to be one of the most pert, assuming and forward young coxcombs I ever saw.'[20] Malcolm had got to know him before Minto's arrival, and their friendship was probably quite uncalculated – they were fellow Borderers and distantly related. Nevertheless, when news of Minto's appointment became known, Malcolm was certainly not going to allow any personal failings of the son to inhibit a golden opportunity to use him as an entrée to his father. It is one of the less attractive aspects of Malcolm's character that he ruthlessly exploited any chance of bringing himself to the notice of those in power. In early June he wrote to John Elliot, then in Madras awaiting his father's arrival there, en route to Calcutta, advising him of his engagement to Charlotte (whom Elliot knew). Elliot wrote back offering to introduce Malcolm to his father when he passed through. But Malcolm opted for a more subtle approach, writing that he had no 'intention of intruding myself upon his Lordship', but that since his exertions were being 'neglected' by the Directors in England, he preferred to remain in Mysore for the time being.[21] He thus managed simultaneously to act coy over meeting the Governor-General, while complaining about his previous treatment by the Company. This letter was answered by Minto himself in courtly manner. After thanking Malcolm for his kindness to his son, he went on: 'I am anxious also to assure you in my own hand that nothing would have been more gratifying to me than the pleasure of making your acquaintance, or more profitable than the instruction you are able to afford on the most important branches of our public affairs.'[22]

Flattered by this expression of confidence in his abilities, Malcolm responded with a massive letter, setting out his claims to recognition for his past services and his chagrin at their not being valued by the Court of Directors. As for the future, he offered his services unreservedly. He went on to put his hand up to lead any future mission to Persia, and ended 'I have this day transmitted for your Lordship through Mr Elliot a Memorandum of a very delicate nature. You will, I am assured, acquaint me of any presumption in forwarding this Paper.'[23]

Presumption, indeed! The 'memorandum of a very delicate nature' was no less than thirty-six pages of what amounted to 'staff reports' on the senior figures in the Calcutta Government – on Barlow himself, on his Councillors and several leading members of the Secretariat, including Edmonstone, Adam and Henry Colebrooke. The assessment of Barlow alone occupied twelve handwritten pages. In Malcolm's opinion Barlow was a first-class civil servant, capable of doing any job well, except that of Governor-General. His opinions of the others were equally candid and remarkably perceptive. But they pulled no punches. It was extraordinarily cheeky of him to write these criticisms of his erstwhile boss and colleagues to Minto, a man whom he had never even met. Why did he do it? He must have sensed that the ultra-urbane Minto might well have considered it impertinent. Malcolm had been sulking in April, in love in May, married at the beginning of July, apparently wanting only a quiet life at Mysore; and now by the end of July he was trying, in a very brash manner, to get back into the thick of things. Perhaps these changes in attitude were due to Charlotte's positive influence. Now that he was married, going back to England was out of the question – he needed a steady job and would therefore be likely to look for a more active role in the government of India. An alternative explanation is that Malcolm saw in Minto a man whom he might be able to influence, even to manipulate – to convert to his own ideas of how British India should be run – and he seized this half-chance with both hands. He reiterated his long-held view that the Resident at Mysore (and indeed the Residents at all the Native Courts) should report directly to the Governor-General rather than to the Governors of Madras or Bombay. The departure of his friend Bentinck in August and the interim appointment of Mr Petrie, the senior member of Council, whom Malcolm considered corrupt, added urgency to this plea. Continuing to press his views, Malcolm sent Minto a copy of his paper advocating an attack on the Ottoman provinces which he had submitted earlier to Barlow.[24] Then, in late November, he submitted a long report on Persia prepared by Charles Pasley, who had spent two years there (1802–4).[25]

Meanwhile he was enjoying married life at Mysore. Residents were allowed to choose their immediate personal staff (called 'family') and it was generally considered one of the perks of the job that they could shamelessly select their relations. Malcolm had chosen Charles Pasley as his assistant; but to be fair, Pasley was demonstrably the best man for the job. He appointed Captain Tom Little, another Eskdale man, as the commander of the Resident's Escort, and as *his* assistant, John Little, a young cousin, who had arrived in India in 1804 aged sixteen, and who was serving in the Madras Army. Little's regular letters to his family at Langholm give a vivid worm's-eye view of life at the Mysore Residency in 1807. In October he described his daily routine:

> I get up in the morning about five, mount my horse, which is ready saddled at the door, and accompanied by my Horsekeeper carrying a gun, and my dog Sancho . . . I ride five or six miles and sometimes bring home a duck or a partridge. At eight I return and dress for breakfast, when the whole of the family (consisting of Colonel and Mrs Malcolm, Captain Little, Captain Pasley, Lieutenant Peile and myself) meet together. Almost every day, two or three people come out from Seringapatam and spend the day here. After breakfast we mostly go and take a look at the Colonel's horses (he has only about twenty five and as many dogs). After this I go down home where I find my Moonshee waiting for me; with him I sit and study Persian till Tiffin [light lunch]. And after this I cannot exactly tell you what I do. Sometimes I read, write or draw, sometimes the Col gives me Publick Letters or Papers to copy and sometimes, I am almost afraid to tell you, I go to sleep. But this does not often happen, only when the weather is very warm. At six I dress for dinner and sit till ten, when we all retire home and go to sleep.[26]

Life at the Residency seemed tranquil and easygoing. In early August Malcolm wrote to Tom Munro that 'my plans about going home are a little altered. I have been married a month and yet I, strange to say, am fonder of my *Scotch Wife* than I was the day she gave me her hand.'[27] In September, Malcolm and Charlotte went down to Madras to bid farewell to her father, who was returning to England. There was more correspondence about the Bangalore Botanical Gardens. Charlotte became pregnant.

But Charlotte was to learn, if she had not already done so, that her new husband was never going to be content with a quiet life. The relentless stream of letters to the Governor-General eventually brought results. Shortly after receiving Malcolm's report of 24 November, Minto finally decided that Malcolm should lead a second mission to Persia. He wrote to him on 30 January 1808 instructing him to go to Bombay as soon as possible and await detailed instructions there.

A letter from Calcutta would normally take a fortnight to reach Mysore. Malcolm must therefore have reacted very quickly to Minto's letter. By 15 February he was in Madras with Charlotte in tow, now six months pregnant. Four days later he and Charlotte (and one of his 'family', James Grant) were setting sail on HMS *Culloden*, commanded by Admiral Sir Edward Pellew, the Royal Navy's Commander-in-Chief in the Indian Ocean. They reached Bombay at the beginning of April. A trail of unfinished business was left behind in Mysore for Malcolm's deputy, Mark Wilks, to deal with. There were practical reasons for this hurry; if the mission to Persia had not sailed from Bombay by June, adverse monsoon winds in the Arabian Sea might hold it up for ten weeks or more.

Malcolm had planned to leave Charlotte in Bombay for the imminent birth of their first child. Though eager to press on to Persia, he first had to find somewhere in Bombay for her to live until his return, and in particular, someone to care for her during her confinement in May. He found the answer in Sir James Mackintosh, the Recorder of Bombay and his second wife Catherine. Mackintosh had stayed with the Malcolms at Mysore in November 1807 while on a trip round southern India.

Mackintosh was a truly extraordinary man, an intellectual lion caged uneasily in the tiny provincial Anglo-Indian society of Bombay. Born near Inverness in Scotland in 1765, he read medicine at Edinburgh University, then moved to London. Too interested in politics to stick to medicine, he became an enthusiastic Whig. He made friends with such Whig political luminaries as C.J. Fox and R.B. Sheridan, and in 1791 published *Vindiciae Gallicae*, a tract supporting the French Revolution, in answer to Burke's *Reflections on the French Revolution*. Together with Thomas Paine's *Rights of Man*, it was a best-seller. Not long afterwards, disillusioned with the revolution's excesses, he became an ardent admirer and friend of Burke and also a journalist. He studied law, was called to the Bar in 1796, and became a highly successful barrister and man about town – brilliant, disorganised and extravagant. In 1803 he was rather surprisingly appointed Recorder of Bombay. He claimed that he accepted the post to gain more time for writing, but more probably it was because he had run short of money. He sailed for India in 1804 with his second wife and five daughters (three of them from his first marriage). He also took with him a scholarly young Scot, William Erskine, as his secretary. Finding on arrival that Bombay was, by his standards, a relative intellectual desert, he founded the Literary Society of Bombay, with Erskine as its Secretary.

Malcolm was awe-struck by Mackintosh's vast erudition, Mackintosh by Malcolm's active mind and raw literary talent. The two men got on well. The Mackintoshes and their five daughters were staying at Parel, the Governor's country residence north of Bombay, because Governor Duncan was a bachelor and did not need such a large house. The Mackintoshes took in the Malcolm family at Parel until they could find somewhere else to stay. Many Bombay military families stayed semi-permanently in tents on what is today the Maidan in south Bombay. But except for their temporary stay at Parel, the Malcolm family lived until the end of 1811 at a house called Nonpareil in the vicinity of today's Kemp's Corner, though Malcolm may also have had a tent on the Maidan. Charles Pasley's sister Jean and her husband Dr Gilbert Briggs were also about to arrive in Bombay from Madras, since Gilbert was to be the surgeon to the Persian mission. Jean was heavily pregnant too, and also had to be looked after.

Somehow Malcolm and his mission party got away on 17 April 1808 on HMS *Psyche*, bound for Bushire.

Charlotte, now aged nineteen, and Jean, twenty-one, were thus left in Bombay to wait for their imminent confinements. Neither had lived there before. They knew hardly anybody, and their husbands were going to be away for many months in Persia. It must have been a daunting time for them. Jean's baby came first – a boy, Stephen, on 3 May, and Charlotte produced a girl, Margaret, on 17 May.

Yet Charlotte was no shrinking violet. Less than a month after the birth of her child, with no husband to advise her, she wrote directly to Lord Minto in Calcutta, launching into an energetic proposal for the husband of her friend Mrs Burges 'being appointed a member of the Board of Revenue or Trade – or an Opium or Salt Agency'.[28]

CHAPTER SEVENTEEN

The Second Persian Mission, 1808

Between 1807 and 1811, 'Persia formed the meeting place of Indian and European politics.'[1]

There were five players in this diplomatic game: in Tehran, Fath Ali Shah; in Paris, Napoleon; in St Petersburg, Tsar Alexander I; in London, George Canning, Robert Dundas (son of Henry Dundas) and their envoy, Harford Jones; and in Calcutta, Lord Minto and his envoy, John Malcolm.

Most of these players, most of the time, were far away from the scenes of action. By today's standards, communications were intolerably slow. News from Tehran took at least two months to reach London, Paris or St Petersburg, and three months to reach Calcutta. Ministers and diplomats were forced to make decisions based on information that had frequently been overtaken by events. Modern historians, with the benefit of hindsight, have found it easy to pour scorn on some of the decisions made and actions taken. Yet for some of those players their decisions really did seem like good ideas at the time. Analysis of the motivations and actions of each player, as part of the overall sequence of events, is not easy.[2]

Malcolm played a key role in these events, from start to finish. His actual influence on them tends, however, to be exaggerated; partly because he was such a forceful personality and because, more than most, he committed his thoughts voluminously to paper, but also because, despite his pretensions, he could never be much more than a faithful servant of Lord Minto. He could influence Minto's decisions, but he could not control Minto's method of implementing them.

Back in 1801 Fath Ali Shah had agreed to ratify the Treaty with the Calcutta Government by sending a Persian envoy to Calcutta. But a series of accidents kept postponing the envoy's arrival there. The first Persian envoy, Haji Khalil Khan, had been killed in Bombay in August 1802.[3] Thereafter the British had dragged their feet. With Zaman Shah of Afghanistan no longer a threat to Hindustan, and the French, having been expelled from Egypt, no longer an immediate threat to British India, the British had got what they had urgently wanted in 1800, and were reluctant to involve themselves in the Shah's quarrel with the Russians.

By late 1803 the Russians had started applying increasing pressure on Persian territory in the Caucasus, seizing the Persian fort of Ganja in Azerbaijan, and attacking the Persian army at the gates of Erevan (Yerevan) in Armenia. The Shah asked the Calcutta Government for help, but got no response. So he started thinking about France as a potential alternative ally, especially in view of Napoleon's military dominance in Europe. And if nothing else, a flirtation with the French might galvanise the British. He sent an Armenian emissary to see the French Ambassador in Constantinople, to float the idea of a Persian alliance with France against Russia.

The French reaction to the Shah's overtures was favourable. An envoy, M. Romieu, reached Tehran in October 1805, but unfortunately died shortly afterwards. A second envoy, M Jaubert, arrived in June 1806 and persuaded the Shah to send an envoy to Paris. Accompanied by Jaubert, a Persian Ambassador, Mirza Reza Khan, reached Constantinople, but was then diverted to Poland, where Napoleon was on campaign against the Russians.

Meanwhile, the Shah, still trying to keep his options open, stayed in touch with the British. In mid-1805, three years after the death of Haji Khalil Khan in Bombay, he despatched a second Ambassador, Mohamed Nabee Khan, who finally reached Calcutta in April 1806 (see page 231). The acting Governor-General, Sir George Barlow, finally ratified the 1801 Treaty in late September 1806, but pointed out that the Treaty made no mention of Russia, and that even if it had, the British were bound by their long-standing alliance with the Tsar to abstain from attacking the Russians.

Mohamed Nabee's report about this British attitude reached the Shah in the spring of 1807. For him this was the last straw; the British had let him down. Exasperated, he decided to throw in his lot with the French. At the end of April 1807 Napoleon received the Persian Ambassador at Finkenstein Castle in northern Poland, and the Treaty of Finkenstein was signed there a week later. This treaty was a sort of mirror image of the 1801 treaty with the British. The French undertook to supply the Shah with artillery, infantry officers and engineers, and to organise the Persian army on European lines. In return, the Shah undertook to declare war on the British and expel all representatives of the East India Company from Persia; to encourage the Afghans to invade Hindustan; to grant exclusive right of passage through Persia to a French army en route to India; and to negotiate a commercial treaty. Significantly, the Shah also agreed to cede Kharg Island to the French as a base, but only if and when the Persians, with French help, had succeeded in expelling the Russians from Georgia. All this was to be accomplished with the help of a powerful French military mission to Tehran, to be led by Napoleon's aide-de-camp, General Claude Mathieu, Comte de Gardane.

At the beginning of October 1807 the Persian Government heard from, of all people, its arch-enemy Field Marshal Goduvich, the Commander-in-Chief of the Russian forces in the Caucasus, that in June Napoleon had resumed military operations against the Russians; that the battle of Friedland had cost 25,000 Russian lives; that the Russians had retreated, and that Napoleon and Tsar Alexander had signed a peace accord, the Treaty of Tilsit, on 7 July. Despite France's commitment under the Treaty of Finkenstein to 'make every effort to force Russia to evacuate Georgia and Persian territory', no mention of this commitment had been included in the Treaty of Tilsit.

It was a nasty shock for the Shah. He sent off a new Ambassador to Paris, Askar Khan Afshar, and waited for Gardane, who arrived on 4 December 1807, explaining rather lamely that the Treaty of Tilsit did not necessarily mean that the Russians could not be expelled from Georgia. It would now be done by friendly diplomacy rather than by war. Honey would catch more flies than vinegar. The Shah was not fooled. He realised that he had been cheated. But by now he was committed to the French. He decided to wait and see how things would work out. In February 1808 Gardane brought the welcome news that he had been authorised by Napoleon to act as mediator in peace negotiations between the Persians and the Russians. This was hardly the same as

Sir Harford Jones Bt (1764–1847), British Resident at Baghdad (1797–1806) and British Envoy to Persia 1807–11.

'forcing the Russians to evacuate Georgia', but it was a start.

Back in London, the death of the British Prime Minister, William Pitt, in January 1806, and the appointment of the predominantly Whig 'Ministry of the Talents' had led to a rethinking of the Government's diplomatic policy towards Persia. Hitherto Persia had been seen purely as a pawn in the defence of the East India Company's Indian possessions. Now it was also seen for the first time as a factor in the European war against Napoleon.

British Ministers realised that Napoleon, though thwarted in 1799 in his attempt to march through Persia en route to India, was once again trying to build up French influence in Persia, this time hoping to use alliances with Turkey and Persia as a diplomatic 'second front' against Russia, complementing direct French pressure on Russia in northern Europe. It was time, they felt, for the British Government to become directly involved in Persian affairs.

In arriving at this conclusion they were strongly influenced by Harford Jones, who had recently arrived back in England after being expelled as British Resident in Baghdad by the Pasha in early 1806. In a long letter to the Foreign Secretary he cited a letter he had received from Mirza Bezorg, currently Chief Minister to Abbas Mirza, the Persian Heir Apparent, and an old friend of his, complaining that the Shah:

> has consistently turned French approaches away on the ground that he had a treaty with England . . . If from the negligence of the English, in fulfilling their engagements, his Majesty wishes to establish a friendship between Persia and France, you will please inform me . . . I am astonished, as two years have now passed in open hostility between the Russians and the Persians, which the Persian government has made known to you, that your government has not taken any step to stop these hostilities, either by negotiation or assistance to us. You indeed have made some excuses about the length of the way between Persia and England, but now, as you and I become the medium of communications in this business, it is most sincerely and ardently my task, that nothing contrary to the treaty [of 1801] may take place, and that no alliance or friendship may be formed between Persia and France.[4]

Jones supported this Persian complaint. He proposed that the British Government should send an envoy to Tehran via St Petersburg to mediate between Persia and Russia, and thus remove the need for the French to be involved. He ended, significantly, with the observation that: 'It seems but little necessary to mention that the negotiations must be conducted in the name and under the authority of the King. Neither Russia nor Persia can [now] be expected to treat with a person vested only with powers from the India Company.'[5]

The President of the Board of Control, George Tierney, accepted

Jones's thesis, and the Government decided to send a Crown envoy to Persia via St Petersburg. The next task was to select a suitable envoy. Tierney consulted Marquess Wellesley, who had arrived back in England a year earlier, and was certainly the best informed person on the subject. The Marquess suggested that Malcolm, already the leader of one successful mission, would provide continuity, and would be best able to reconcile the different perspectives of London and Calcutta. As Malcolm's secretary he suggested Harford Jones. But when Tierney consulted the Company's Court of Directors, there was opposition to Malcolm, on the ground that he had wasted the Company's money on his 1800 mission. Moreover, he was regarded as a leading adherent of the Marquess, whose Indian policy was still politically unpopular with the Directors at that time. So Tierney, who knew virtually nothing about India, chose Harford Jones as envoy. He was impressed by Jones's grasp of the issues, his long experience of the region and his language skills. It must have seemed like a natural choice. There were however several drawbacks to Jones's appointment. Although an employee of the Company, he had only spent a short time in India, in the early 1780s, and had never since been back. He had few friends in India, and was known there, dismissively, as 'Baghdad Jones'. More importantly, his character was utterly unsuited to the delicate task of getting on with the Persians while simultaneously serving two masters based in London and Calcutta. He had a suspicious, brooding nature, and all those solitary years in Company outposts, first at Basra, then at Baghdad, had exacerbated its symptoms. He felt, with some justification, that over the years the Company had neglected him, and underrated his talents. As a result he had acquired a huge chip on his shoulder about the Calcutta Government's management. The prospect, therefore, of being able to act in Persia independently of his erstwhile superiors in India must have excited him considerably, but was later to cause a great deal of trouble.

In Britain in March 1807 a Tory Ministry replaced the Whig-dominated Ministry of the Talents. George Canning became Foreign Secretary, and Robert Dundas became President of the Board of Control. This was a great stroke of luck for Harford Jones. Henry Dundas had personally appointed him to the Baghdad Residency in 1796, without reference to the Directors, and Jones had been his protégé ever since. Moreover, Robert Dundas respected his father's judgement.

The news of the Treaty of Tilsit completely changed the diplomatic game for the British Government. Now that the Russians were allied to France, there was no possibility of the British Government acting as mediator between Russia and Persia, or of a British envoy going to Persia via St Petersburg (or even overland via Turkey, since the Porte was also temporarily allied with France). The issue was now much more straightforward – to contain and repel the French influence in Persia. The 'European' element of diplomacy was no longer a major factor. In hindsight, this was the moment when the British Government should have cancelled the Jones mission and passed the ball back to the new Governor-General, Lord Minto. Minto, who was at that moment about to arrive in India, had been President of the Board of Control in 1806 and was therefore well qualified to represent the interests of both London and Calcutta in negotiations with Persia.

But meanwhile, a variation of the original plan had gathered momentum; to send an envoy via the Cape, still in the name of the Crown rather than of the Company. And with Robert Dundas as President of the Board of Control, the envoy was still going to be Harford Jones. To give him status, he was made a baronet. He recorded later that he 'was in a quandary as to whether to accept'. As a further incentive he asked to be made Governor of Bombay. His request was not granted but, according to Jones, Sir Hugh Inglis, a member of the Secret Committee, apparently conceded that 'we should be able to pop you in, in some future opening'.[6] The Secret Committee's instructions were that Jones should now concentrate primarily on combating the French influence in Persia. His final briefing on his status came from Canning. He was to report to 'the Court of Directors, or from their government in India'. Any pecuniary commitments were to be borne exclusively by the East India Company.[7]

In February 1807, just before he set sail for India, Lord Minto had heard of Harford Jones's appointment as the Crown's envoy to Persia, and that he would proceed there via St Petersburg. He shared the worries of other British Ministers about the rise in French influence in Persia, and as he sailed towards India, pondering the problems he would face as Governor-General, he must also have worried about how British policy towards Persia was going to be coordinated between London and Calcutta.

On arrival at Calcutta he found that the irrepressible Malcolm, supposedly settling down to a quiet life in Mysore with his eighteen-year-old bride, was also worrying about policy towards Persia: 'I am preparing a Paper for your Lordship on the subject of Persia. Many circumstances would appear to recommend the improvement of our connection with that State. I had hoped that my claims to be employed if ever a second mission were sent to that Court were of a nature that would make them exempt from invasion, but the personal solicitations of Sir Harford Jones are I find likely to succeed in attaining that appointment.' He then entered into a violent denunciation of Jones (the first of several):

> Without wishing to prejudice your Lordship against a public Officer who may soon be employed under your orders, I cannot refrain from stating that it was not possible I could have suffered a greater mortification than to have the pretensions of this Gentleman brought in competition with my own; and the preference given by His Majesty's Ministers upon this occasion (for they had my claims fully before them) to Sir Harford Jones, will be a lesson to me during life to prevent my ever indulging sanguine expectations where my views are liable to be disappointed by the efforts of personal intrigue or the influence of interested misrepresentation.[8]

Soon afterwards the news of the Treaties of Finkenstein and Tilsit reached Calcutta. Presuming that the plan to send Jones to Persia via St Petersburg must therefore have been abandoned, Minto wondered whether he would still be sent anyway, via the Cape. And if so, what would be his brief? Late in the year Minto became convinced that some urgent action was needed. A British mission of some sort must reach Persia before the French had a chance to consolidate. He decided to assemble a Company mission at Bombay, so that if Jones did not come, or was delayed, an Indian mission could be despatched quickly. The obvious choice to lead it was Malcolm.

In early November Minto wrote to Castlereagh in London, making the case for such action,[9] but did not wait for an answer. On 30 January 1808 he instructed Malcolm to go immediately to Bombay and hold himself in readiness to go to Persia. He was still prudently tentative, worrying about the possible diplomatic complications if Jones's mission also arrived on the scene.[10]

Malcolm responded with alacrity, and had reached Bombay by early April.[11] While at sea between Madras and Bombay he wrote to the Marquess about the Persian mission, arguing that the appointment of Jones, with powers apparently making him largely independent of the Governor-General, was a great mistake, regardless of the personalities involved. He recalled that he himself had suggested to the Marquess several years earlier that the envoy 'should have credentials from the Throne', but that 'it was quite indispensable that he should be placed under the orders of the Governor-General'.[12] He then proceeded to make a vicious character assassination of the unfortunate Jones. To Bentinck he described his chagrin at Jones's appointment in even more lurid terms. He would have felt 'miserable to be superseded by any person – but to make the cup full to the brim it was necessary Sir Harford Jones should be the Man – I should have retired with regret before superior character and talent – but to be obliged to give place to obsequious meanness and specious cunning, combined in a person who professes local knowledge and experience, without either influence or respect, fill me with disgust and indignation.'[13] But he realised that Jones was going to Persia with the approbation of the Crown, and there was not much he could do about it. He wrote in more reflective mood to Arthur Wellesley in England:

> from a knowledge of the character of the King and his ministers, I should have reserved the embassy on which I was empowered to proceed till I had made them pay some attention to those demands which offended friendship had a right to make . . . The Persians, if it should not occur to their own minds (which it readily would), would soon be persuaded by their French friends that the anxiety and humility with which we sought their friendship was a proof of our terror and weakness, and that they had little to fear from hostility with a power that crouched at the very apprehension of hostilities.[14]

Several points can be noted about this letter. First, it was written in the future subjunctive tense; in other words Malcolm doubted whether his potential mission would ever come about. He felt that Jones would arrive at Bombay, and would understandably claim precedence. Secondly, he was familiar with traditional Persian negotiating tactics, developed over the centuries, if not millennia. Typically, the Persian approach was (and still is) to probe, to 'try things on'. If met by a firm rebuttal on one issue, Persian negotiators tend to withdraw, then probe somewhere else. This approach calls for dexterity and suppleness in the negotiator, and a deliberate suppression of that mixture of pride and obstinacy which Westerners call 'spirit'.

On arrival at Bombay Malcolm found three letters waiting for him from Calcutta. One was a public letter from the Governor-General, containing his formal instructions for the mission; one was from Edmonstone (now Minto's Private Secretary), enjoining him to adopt a stance of 'remonstrance' for friendship betrayed, and 'demand' that the Persian Government should adhere to its 1801 Treaty obligations;[15] and the third was a long, rambling private letter from Minto, saying that in view of the uncertainties over Jones's arrival and mission instructions, he could not give precise directions; he could do no more than trust Malcolm to act sensibly, and to get on as well as possible with Jones. What Minto feared most was the arrival in Persia of a French army, and the consequent need to oppose them with an Indian army – he guessed that to overcome 10,000 French troops he would need 20,000 largely sepoy troops from India. But he speculated that the French would probably begin by sending a small force; it was therefore vital that such a force should be thrown out before it had time to establish itself.[16] All this military talk may seem absurdly alarmist. Yet, being unaware of what was actually going on in Tehran, it is not altogether surprising that these fears were sincerely felt by Minto.

By 15 April Malcolm's mission was ready to sail. In addition to 'the gentlemen of his suite', there was a retinue of 300 marines, 100 cavalry, 50 sepoys and two six-pounder 'galloper' guns.[17] The only remaining decision for Malcolm was whether to set off for Persia or to wait for Jones. It was now known that Jones was indeed coming via the Cape of Good Hope, and his arrival at Bombay was said to be imminent. The argument for waiting was that the strategy of the two missions could be coordinated and harmonised, so that the Persian Government would know that it was dealing with a single entity. On the other hand, time seemed to be of the essence, and no one knew exactly how soon Jones might arrive, or how much time it might take thereafter to work out a coordinated strategy, involving correspondence back and forth with Calcutta. Minto's instructions were ambiguous on this point – he left the decision largely to Malcolm's discretion. Admiral Pellew (and others) urged him to go. 'I hurry [Malcolm] every hour to get away before Sir Harford Jones arrives', he wrote to Minto.[18]

While he may well have weighed up the rational arguments for waiting or going, it is apparent that his inner motivation for going rather than staying was that he and Jones, apart from disliking each other personally, had entirely different ideas about diplomatic policy towards Persia. And if he waited, it was almost certain that Jones would be chosen to go, rather than him. He was sure that he could do a better job than Jones. He would take his chance.

So Malcolm decided to sail. It was a highly irresponsible decision.

A mere week later, Jones reached Bombay, and was surprised and annoyed to find that Minto had appointed Malcolm to lead a separate mission to Persia from India, and that Malcolm had already left Bombay, bound for Bushire. He complained, justifiably, to Minto that: 'I think it is to be lamented that Genl Malcolm[19] . . . had not thought it expedient to have suspended his departure hence for a few days, since . . . I presume it might have occurred to him that from my being in possession of the sentiments and wishes of his Majesty's ministers, and the honourable the Secret Committee on the subject of our relations with Persia and the Eastern part of Turkey, the advantage he should have derived from a personal communication with me would more than compensated for the trifling delay in his departure from Bombay which would have been necessary to procure it.'[20] He then went on to strike the first blow in his campaign to make himself effectively independent of the Calcutta Government: 'In closing this letter I am fully determined to pay the most respectful obedience to your Excellency's orders, as far as can be compatible with those I have received from his Majesty's ministers and the Hon the Secret Committee.'[21] In other words I will obey your orders unless I deem that they are incompatible with my orders from London – and I will be the judge of that!

Over the next three years Jones wrote regularly to successive British Foreign Ministers and to Robert Dundas, his sponsor and President of the Board of Control. In a situation where communications were so slow, it was incumbent on all the diplomats concerned to rise above petty jealousies and slights, and to work together as a team. Ostensibly, the tone of Jones's letters was articulate, objective and respectful. Yet below the surface there seems to have been from the outset an agenda, subtly exercised, to paint the actions of the Governor-General and his staff in as unfavourable a light as possible. In writing to Canning, he repeated his complaints about Malcolm, and by extension, Minto,[22] and thoughtfully enclosed copies of selective passages in Minto's instructions to Malcolm to prove his point.[23] No one could deny that Jones had something to complain about. Yet was it necessary to bother the Foreign Secretary in London about it? Jones was emphatically not a team player. He nevertheless very properly agreed to wait in Bombay until the outcome of Malcolm's mission should become known.[24]

As HM frigate *Psyche* sailed out of Bombay harbour, Malcolm was beset by an entirely new and private sensation – the pangs of separation from Charlotte. It was the first time that they had been parted since their marriage nine months before. He was, desperately and overwhelmingly, in love. He wrote to her: 'I found as I lost sight of land that my feelings were different from what they had ever been on similar occasions, nor could all my zeal for my country, nor all my exultation at the distinction I had attained in being called upon in such a crisis, make me forget that I had left a home, in which magic word all my happiness was comprised . . . I have resolved to keep a private record of occurrences . . . in a series of letters to you – and I anticipate the delight with which I shall devote a few minutes of every day to inform you of my proceedings.'[25]

And so he did. Over the next three months he wrote three batches of journal/letters to her, comprising more than 40,000 words. One might imagine that a 39-year-old worldly wise man would tend to patronise or talk down to his nineteen-year-old wife. But he did not. He wrote with boyish exuberance, one day quoting Francis Bacon's essays, another the Persian poets Hafez, Saadi and Ferdowsi; another of meeting Arabs whom he had known on his previous mission eight years before, of showing them his miniature portrait of her and receiving complimentary remarks. And he included endless anecdotes such as the reaction of the locals at Bushire to the arrival of the escort of British soldiers, the first that they had ever seen:

> 'What amazing strong fellows these flesh eaters are', said a poor Arab who had never seen anything but dates and fish;
>
> 'Look at their resemblance to each other, they must all have the same father and mother';

'That cannot be', said another (equally struck by their uniformity of appearance), 'for they must have been all born on the same day':

'They are proper shaitans [devils]', said an old woman.

The *Psyche* and the *Teignmouth* (carrying the rest of Malcolm's 'suite' and the Escort) arrived at Bushire on 10 May, and went ashore two days later. They were received in friendly enough fashion, with due honour and respect for Malcolm's status. Within a week he started to put his plan into action. He despatched Charles Pasley to Shiraz, to the Court of Prince Hussein Ali Mirza (the Shah's third son, still Governor of Fars province), armed with a letter to the Shah's Ministers.

Malcolm's letter reiterated the line which he had taken from the outset, with approval from Calcutta, of 'measured remonstrance and an offended friendship'.[26] Stripped of its abundant *ta'arof* (compliments), it reiterated the offer of subsidies and military help which had been included in the 1801 Treaty, but expressed deep concern that the Persian Government had received a French Ambassador with honour, and allowed French representatives to spy on the British at Bushire and elsewhere. He did not accept the Persian Government's reasons for abandoning the 1801 Treaty (which had covered opposition only to the Afghans and the French, not the Russians) in favour of an alliance with the French. The British had every motive to seek a long-standing alliance with the Persians: for the British, defence of their Indian empire; for the Persians, British command of the seas, which could be used against any future enemies of the Persians (or, it hinted darkly, any allies of the Persians, if they were enemies of the British); for both, trade. On the other hand, the letter claimed, the French were only viewing Persia as a staging post to India; they had few trading ties with Persia; and they had behaved badly, first towards the Porte in relation to their invasion of Egypt in 1798, and more recently towards the Persians, in signing the Treaty of Tilsit so soon after the Treaty of Finkenstein. The letter ended with an implied threat. The Persian Government needed now to choose between the French and the British. If they chose the French, the British might have to respond militarily.[27]

Malcolm was thus burning his boats, hoping his bluff would not be called. But well before his letter could have reached Tehran, a letter came from the Persian Court; and it was not at all what he had hoped for. It asked him to conduct his negotiations for the time being with Prince Hussein Ali Mirza, in Shiraz. His spies told him that the French were firmly in the ascendant at the Shah's Court in Tehran, and that even the Russian Ambassador was supporting the French demand that the British mission should not be received.

The situation thus appeared to be even more serious than he had feared. There would have to be an urgent reappraisal of the whole British strategy towards Persia. He wrote in his journal/letter to Charlotte:

> These circumstances convinced me that nothing short of the adoption of some very strong measures would produce any change in the conduct of a Court which was evidently acting under the influence of our enemies, and it appeared particularly necessary that measures should be of a nature that would remove one impression which the French had endeavoured to produce in Persia, viz. that England had not an ally in the world, was reduced to the last stages of distress, and consequently was soliciting the friendship of the King of Persia from an inability to preserve without his aid its possessions in India. I determined in consequence of these reflections to strike my camp next morning and to go on board the *Doris*, and write to Captain Pasley [who was in Shiraz] to inform the Minister of the Prince at Shiraz why I had done so, impressing them I never should re-land in Persia without he was allowed to proceed to court, and I was assured of being treated with less suspicion and more friendship . . . [The next day] I carried the resolution I made yesterday into effect, to the utter consternation of the inhabitants of Abusheher [Bushire].[28]

He concluded that merely writing despatches was not going to be enough. He decided to go straight to Calcutta in person, to explain to Minto the now critical situation, as he saw it, and participate in working out an alternative strategy.

Meanwhile he waited on HMS *Doris* for news from Pasley, still in Shiraz, of a possible change of heart on the part of the Persian Government. He continued writing letters to Charlotte, making translations of love poems from Hafiz, describing the delicious local figs, and telling endless anecdotes, including one on love sonnets,[29] another on painting his whiskers (with unfortunate results);[30] and another about teasing Jaffer Ali Khan, a Persian, known for his rather unctious compliments:

> He is a perfect gentleman in his manners, which are very mild and prepossessing. He speaks English uncommonly well. His first enquiries were after Charlotte Malcolm, the wife, he said, of his oldest and best friend. He was directed to a picture of Captain Cole's mother (the old lady was about sixty), which hung in the cabin. He appeared evidently puzzled; however politeness prevailed over sincerity. 'It is beautiful,' he said hesitatingly, 'but not quite *so young* as I thought.' Pasley [then] showed him your picture, at which his countenance brightened up at once. 'This is Mrs Malcolm, ay this is proper, she is about eighteen and very handsome.'[31]

On 4 July, the first anniversary of his marriage, in a dead calm sea with the temperature in the nineties, he sat down to write Charlotte a verse tribute in sub-Thomas Gray style, ending excruciatingly:

> My ardent bosom swells for glorious fame,
> That thou may'st hear with Pride a husband's name
> Exulting kiss the prattler on thy Knee,
> And own its absent father merits thee.

Perhaps sensing that this might be a bit 'over the top', he ended, 'If this Effusion is defficient in poetry, my Dearest Charlotte well knows its Sincerity.'[32]

Pasley arrived back from Shiraz in late June, with no favourable developments to report, so Malcolm packed up and sailed from Bushire on 7 July to get water at Kharg [Kharrack] Island. Waiting at Kharg, Malcolm was once again able to indulge his dream of making Kharg a British military base and trade emporium, an idea that he had first taken up in 1800.[33] He finally set off for India on 12 July in the *Doris*, leaving Charles Pasley in charge, assisted by Stewart and Little – all three Eskdale men. After a week at sea they saw a vessel – the *Benares*, from Bombay. Malcolm, like many a prospective father awaiting news of the birth of his first child, was overcome with nerves, and 'retired to a corner of the Cabin and was in vain endeavouring to summon up more fortitude, when my friend Smith, came running and, taking my hand, congratulated me on the birth of a daughter and your perfect recovery . . . I tore open a letter from you – and you may suppose, my dear Charlotte, the emotions with which I read your daily letters from the 21st May to the 6th of June, upon which I can only exclaim, What a wife, What a mother!'[34] There were also letters from Jones, who appeared to be quite happy to hang about in Bombay for the time being,[35] and a longish one from Mackintosh, in his mellifluous style, explaining how things had stood in Bombay in mid-May. Jones had come to visit him, he said: 'to consult me on his conduct; that he had three ways before him; to go immediately, not go at all, or to delay going until September; that the first might occasion divisions injurious to the public service . . .; that the second was impossible without positive disobedience to the King's orders; and that the third seemed to him the best mode of promoting the two grand objects of harmony and expedition . . . As I am the most experienced demagogue here, I have given out the tone to the numerous faction of the Malcolmites to be loud in their commendation of our Envoy's forbearance.'[36]

All this correspondence seemed only to confirm to Malcolm the correctness of his decision to explain the situation to Minto in person, and to persuade him to adopt a clear policy. But he failed to take account of two important factors: first, that Jones was champing at the bit in Bombay, and did not feel himself constrained by any order from Minto to stay there; second, that Minto, not yet fully briefed, had been quite shocked by the way Malcolm had handled the negotiations so far. While he had agreed with, indeed advocated, the tone of 'friendship betrayed' in Malcolm's letter to the Persian Ministers, he thought it wrong of Malcolm to demand the expulsion of the French as a *precondition* of his coming to Tehran. In a letter to General Hewett, the Commander-in-Chief, he wrote:

> I am sorry to say, in strict confidence, that Malcolm has disappointed me exceedingly at the beginning of his mission. Instead of facilitating the commencement of his negotiation, he has begun by creating, I fear, insurmountable obstacles to his own progress . . . the fact is that Persia is puzzled between the two great candidates for her favour, and while the French are well received, the intention was that the English officers should be

> conducted with similar demonstrations of favour to Shiraz . . . Malcolm's peremptory demand for the expulsion of the French mission had left no room for consideration.
>
> The demand cannot be supported on any ground of justice. Persia, as an independent Government, has a right to receive accredited ministers from any other Court, and to enter into any negotiation she may think advisable.

This was the 'dove-ish' argument, expertly marshalled by a seasoned diplomat.

On 12 August, Minto wrote to Jones in Bombay, criticising the 'erroneous principles' contained in Malcolm's letters from Bushire of 6 and 10 June (whereby Malcolm had refused the Persian Government's proposal that he should negotiate with the Governor of Shiraz, rather than proceed straight to Tehran to negotiate directly with the Shah). Minto's opinion was that if Malcolm had already left Persia, Jones could go there straight away; however, 'I suggest to you the expediency of suspending for a time the prosecution of your Mission, and under the circumstances you will I am persuaded feel the propriety of waiting the result of a reference to the Supreme Government [i.e. Calcutta] respecting the most congenial season for your departure for Persia . . . However, this will cause delay, so I leave it to your judgment to act *following* [author's emphasis] receipt of further communications from Brigadier Malcolm.'[37]

Meanwhile Malcolm was steadily approaching Calcutta in the *Doris*. On 1 August, offshore from Bombay, he had thought of Charlotte, but had resisted the temptation to call there. By 20 August he had arrived at the mouth of the Hoogly, and sent a long despatch to Minto.

He was received by Minto 'in a most affable and condescending manner', and was able 'to clear fully to the satisfaction of Government every point on which they had misunderstood my first proceedings, and that I was not only likely to meet with the fullest approbation, but to be solicited to return on my own terms. All this Lord Minto gave me reason to conclude would be the case. I can perceive that I am a favourite . . . I met my friends Colebrooke and Lumsden, the two Councillors, who appeared (particularly the former) overjoyed to see me, as was my excellent friend John Adam.'[38]

Two day later (22 August) Minto sent a hurried note to Jones, saying that he had not had time to read Malcolm's latest despatch, but that he would communicate in a few days, and meanwhile asked him to postpone his departure from Bombay.[39] A further week later, Minto wrote to Jones again, confirming that the reason for Malcolm's return was not because of his demands made to the Persian Ministers, but because the French (and the Russians) had forced the Shah's hand. Minto now approved of Malcolm's actions. 'Every hope of your reception is extinguished . . . Prosecution of this mission would be in direct contradiction of this government'. Despite this, he believed that the Bushire Residency should remain open.[40]

How had this extraordinary change in Minto's thinking taken place – from severely criticising Malcolm on 12 August, to fully supporting him two weeks later? First, Malcolm had been able to point out that whatever one might think of the propriety of his letter to the Persian Ministers in May, it had had no bearing on the Persian Government's decision not to receive his mission in Tehran. Second, Malcolm was able to express, quite sincerely, his belief that back in June the Persian Government had been under the thumb of the French. While he ruled out any kind of military expedition to take on a French army in Persia (an option which Minto had previously considered), he did suggest that a small British military *presence* in the area should be planned for as a contingency, if the French threat continued. Here he introduced his pet scheme of occupying Kharg Island. Third, Minto, a rather irresolute man, was exposed to Malcolm's persuasive charm in face-to-face negotiation. Besides, most of the senior advisers at Fort William were firm Malcolm 'supporters' – especially Colebrooke, Edmonstone and Adam.

Jones had known since early August that Malcolm had left Bushire on 12 July, and was sailing directly to Calcutta, bypassing Bombay. So when he received Minto's letter (on 5 September), he realised that he had got what he had been looking for; a pretext for setting off for Persia, without technically disobeying Minto's instructions. He did so on 11 September. Yet he must have known by then that Malcolm had reached Calcutta. Common sense should still have led him to postpone his departure from Bombay until he received news of Minto's reaction to Malcolm's report, particularly since it must have become clear that Malcolm's mission had apparently been unsuccessful. Plans could then have been coordinated for the Jones mission. Jones's hasty departure was almost certainly made to *avoid* receiving Minto's instructions. It was every bit as irresponsible as Malcolm's departure in April to avoid meeting Jones.

At the Governor-General's request, Malcolm prepared a detailed plan of action.[41] A small military force of about 2,000 men would be assembled at Bombay, and held in readiness to occupy Kharg Island if the circumstances demanded it. The rationale for this strategy was that if a European power decided to invade India via the Middle East, neither the Persian Government nor the *pashalik* of Baghdad could be trusted to oppose it effectively; that Persia and the Ottoman Empire were weak states, which could too easily be destabilised; that though these States would probably be defeated in battle by France or Russia, it was obviously not in France's or Russia's interest to provoke conflict and opposition from them; that on the other hand they might be tempted to share in the plunder of other States attacked by one of these European powers; that if this seemed likely to happen, the Calcutta Government should be in a position to threaten to create internal chaos in that State, and thus dissuade it; and finally, an island in the Gulf, e.g. Kharg, could become a trading emporium, a depot for military operations and a secure base for political activity throughout the Gulf area. This plan needed to be implemented urgently, to forestall any initiatives from the Company's enemies

The plan was instantly approved, and when Malcolm boarded HM frigate *Fox* on 30 September, he congratulated himself on a highly successful six weeks. He had dispelled all the adverse criticism that had been levelled at him before his arrival, and had persuaded the Governor-General to adopt his Kharg Island project, with him in charge. He was now at last going back to Bombay. But, just as he was about to sail, an express boat came alongside the *Fox* at Kedgeree, and delivered a letter from the Governor-General, recalling him to Calcutta. Minto had received a letter from Jones, dated 6 September, in reply to his letter of 12 August, saying he was going to sail to Persia on 11 September – so he must by now have gone. This changed everything, regardless of whether Jones was received at the Persian Court or not. Therefore, 'Karrack [Kharg Island] must be *necessarily* suspended. We cannot commit hostilities on Persia while the King of England is negotiating with the King of Persia.'[42] Malcolm disembarked, and hurried back to Calcutta in gloomy mood.

In retrospect, it seems extraordinary that in all the discussions which had taken place in Calcutta during that September, no one seems to have taken Jones's mission into account. He was not mentioned in any of the letters and memoranda flying back and forth. Malcolm might perhaps have been affected by personal animus for ignoring Jones, but none of the others were. Jones was, after all, as Minto belatedly recognised, representing the British Crown. And up to the moment of his departure for Persia, he had behaved impeccably.

The Calcutta Government's whole strategy had to be thought through anew. It was agreed that Malcolm should still go to Bombay to put together his military contingent, but should wait there until further news was received of Jones's progress in Persia. He was booked to sail on the *Chiffone* on 26 October. Meanwhile he had three weeks of relative ease, living at Government House and enjoying its social round. Once, while staying at the Governor-General's country house at Barrackpore, he wrote to Charlotte:

> I have been employed these last three hours with John Elliot and the other boys in trying how long we could keep up two cricket balls. Lord Minto caught us. He says he must send me on a mission to some *very young* monarch, for that I never shall have the gravity of an ambassador for a prince turned twelve . . . I have often thought of breaking myself of boyish habits; but reflection has satisfied me that it would be very foolish, and that I should esteem it a blessing that I can find amusement in everything, from tossing a cricket ball to negotiating a treaty with the Emperor of China. Men who give themselves entirely to business and despise . . . trifles, are very able in their general conception of the great outlines of a plan, but they feel a want of that knowledge which is only gained by mixing with all classes in the world, when they come to those lesser points upon which its successful execution may depend. Of this I am certain; besides, all habits which give a man light, elastic spirits are good.[43]

This was vintage Malcolm – a bit too pleased with himself, but fun to be with. And this letter was after all written to his wife. Wives must sometimes put up with husbands talking about themselves.

Meanwhile, when Jones arrived at Bushire on 14 October he was favourably received. He wrote immediately to Minto that 'things are not so bad',[44] and were improving. Charles Pasley and Josiah Stewart, whom Malcolm had left behind at Bushire in July, had fled to Basra in early August, after receiving a report that they were to be arrested and held hostage. But now there were apparently no obstacles to Jones proceeding immediately to Tehran. The Persians were eager to resume negotiations on the basis of the terms outlined by Malcolm and Pasley in May.

The explanation for this volte-face in the Persian Government's attitude had little to do with the respective negotiating positions of Malcolm and Jones, and everything to do with timing. There had of course been some dismay in the Persian Court at Malcolm's high-handed approach back in June. They were loath to cut all ties with the British, and there was also a tinge of apprehension at the implied threat of military action if the French were allowed to use Persia as a staging post for an invasion of India. But at least Malcolm's departure had solved one short-term problem – keeping the French happy.

However, as time went on, the French envoy, Gardane, became progressively less convincing in claiming that the French could engineer a Russian retreat from Georgia. All the same, when Gardane told the Shah that discussions between Russia and Persia could be held in Paris, with Napoleon himself presiding, and that meanwhile he could guarantee that the Russians would make no hostile moves, the Shah felt that he had to be patient. But in September came a further blow to Gardane's credibility. The Russians resumed hostilities, laying siege to Erevan and heading for the town of Nakhdjevan, well inside Persian territory. Abbas Mirza, the Heir Apparent and commander of the army, based in Tabriz, counter-attacked, but was repulsed. He was particularly dismayed to discover that, on Gardane's orders, the French military advisers with his army had taken no part in the battle. This was another 'last straw' for the Shah; the French had now let him down, just as much as the British.

Thus, when Jones's mission arrived at Bushire on 14 October, the timing could not have been more opportune for the Shah (and incidentally for Jones). Without bothering to consult the French, the Shah gave orders that this British mission should be welcomed to Tehran, regardless of French susceptibilities. When Gardane heard the news, he objected, threatening to leave Tehran if Jones was received at Court. He pleaded for time to allow news to arrive from Paris of fresh developments in the peace negotiations with Russia. Although the Shah was reluctant to let Gardane leave (he liked him personally), this time he was only prepared to compromise to the extent of keeping Jones waiting for a couple of months.

In November, as Malcolm was sailing back to Bombay from Calcutta, Minto was trying to work out how to deal with Jones. All he knew was that Jones had left Bombay on 11 September. He guessed that he had probably been received with due respect at Bushire, and might even now be on his way to Shiraz. But this did not fit in with the plan which he had worked out with Malcolm for a possible occupation of Kharg Island. In a letter dated 31 October he ticked Jones off, politely, for sailing from Bombay on the pretext that his letter of 12 August had given Jones discretion to sail from Bombay to Persia. Jones must already have received Malcolm's July despatches, and must therefore have known Malcolm's reasons for leaving Persia to go to Calcutta; and he must also have known that Minto had written that letter in ignorance of this. He had no excuse for not waiting to hear the reaction from Calcutta before sailing. Anyway, Minto now felt, the Kharg Island plan should go ahead, which meant that Jones should return from Persia.

To Jones, Minto's letter of 31 October made no sense. Minto and Malcolm clearly had not yet received his letter of 15 October, describing his friendly welcome at Bushire, with intimations that he would be invited to the Court at Tehran without delay. He wrote back, explaining the new situation, and saying that he still intended to proceed to Shiraz and Tehran; it would be foolish to turn back now. While he was thus effectively defying Minto's orders, he felt confident in doing so, not only because he was obviously doing the right thing (which Minto would surely eventually realise, when he received Jones's later letters), but also because of his interpretation of Canning's briefing note in August 1807, which, as he had told Minto in April, was that 'I am on every account, fully determined to pay the most respectful obedience to your Excellency's orders, *as far as can be compatible with those I have received from his Majesty's ministers and the Hon the Secret Committee* [author's emphasis].'[45]

Unfortunately for Gardane, no relieving despatches came from Paris; and he was obliged to admit defeat. On 17 December Jones was allowed to leave Bushire, and he arrived in Tehran on 14 February 1809, Gardane having left the previous day. On 12 March the Shah signed a Preliminary Treaty with Jones, based largely on the terms that had previously been offered in June 1808 by Malcolm. The only significant change in wording from the 1801 treaty was that whereas in 1801 the Persian Government had undertaken to oppose an invasion by a French army, it now undertook to oppose invasion by a European army; thereby implying that its opposition could apply to Russia as well as to France. The speed of the negotiation, a mere four weeks between Jones's arrival in Tehran and the signing of the Treaty (and this despite some delaying tactics by the pro-French faction at Court), illustrates just how keen the Persians now were to make a deal with the British. Two months later the Shah despatched a Persian Ambassador, Mirza Abol Hassan, to London, accompanied by Jones's secretary, James Morier.

Meanwhile Malcolm had arrived back at Bombay on 30 November 1808, after seven months away. He was of course thrilled to be reunited with Charlotte, and to see little 'Maggie' (Margaret) for the first time. But he expected to be off to Persia with his military force within weeks, so he immediately started finalising preparations for the mission. Gradually, however, with the arrival of despatches and other intelligence from Persia, the new reality began to assert itself, as he heard of Jones being successively received at Bushire, Shiraz and Tehran; and finally signing the Preliminary Treaty with the Shah, which he himself had largely drafted.

These developments were galling for his pride. He had been proved wrong in his assessment of the Persian Court's position in June and July 1808, or at least he had exaggerated the degree of control that the French mission had achieved. He had encouraged Minto to adopt a hawkish stance, but, he now realised, even before the news got back to Calcutta, that the new developments would almost certainly mean that his Kharg Island expedition was off. And to cap it all, the main beneficiary was likely to be the despised Jones. His reaction was not graceful. He vented his feelings of frustration on his friends in London. To Colonel Bannerman, a London- based Director, he wrote that he 'should before this have sailed for the Gulf, had not Sir Harford Jones been as successful in getting away from Bushire two days before he received Lord Minto's orders to return, as he was in escaping by twenty four hours the orders of the Supreme Government for him to remain in India.' He then went on to complain bitterly about his treatment by the Company over the previous eight years: 'I am considered, I am told, a friend to Lord Wellesley and his measures. This is my first crime. My second is extravagance of the public money. To the first I plead guilty with feelings of conscious pride. To the second, I say it is false, and that ample proof of its being so will be found on the public record.'[46]

During January and February 1809 he reported to Minto on the progress of Jones's mission in a series of rather sulky letters, all of them bad-mouthing Jones (in one letter he referred to Jones as 'this intriguing reptile'). Minto, meanwhile, was writing back, reluctantly acknowledging the changed political scene in Europe and its repercussions for British policy towards Persia.

Together again as a family in Bombay, John and Charlotte were able to live a relatively normal domestic life. The Eskdale 'Clan' were all around them. Jean Briggs wrote to her half-brother William Pasley in London: 'You will have heard perhaps that I am a mother – the dear Boy is in good health and spirits, thank God, and as fat as a little pig . . . I am residing with General Malcolm and Mrs Malcolm at present.[47] She seems an accomplished young woman; her figure is very elegant and her manner most agreeable. John I am delighted with . . . he is the *drollest* . . . I ever met with – he justly merits the character that people give him, of being everything that is *Manly* and *Great* – in my life I never saw a man so universally esteemed and liked.'[48]

While at Calcutta in September/October 1808, Malcolm had been encouraged by Henry Colebrooke to resume work on his *Sketch of the Sikhs*, which he had begun to write after returning from the Punjab in early 1806. He completed a draft of it during the voyage back to Bombay and sent it off to Colebrooke for inclusion in his periodical magazine, *Asiatic Researches*. He also gave a draft to William Erskine who, since his arrival in 1804, had become a serious oriental scholar, and was to remain a lifelong friend and fellow orientalist.[49] A further copy went to John Leyden, now in Calcutta, with the comment that 'it will meet with more attention from you than it merits'.[50] Malcolm resumed his friendship with Mackintosh, who in September had moved out of Parel to a new house, Tarala, near the Malcolms at Nonpareil.

About this time Malcolm received a surprisingly frank and critical letter from Charles Pasley, then sitting rather disconsolately in Basra. Bearing in mind that Charles, though his cousin, was his subordinate and eleven years younger than him, the letter might have seemed a bit impertinent: 'you must allow me . . . to observe that you are often much too sanguine in your schemes and expectations. In the wide, liberal and extended views which you generally take of every subject, you often forget that there are such obstacles as prejudice, party spirit and misrepresentation to encounter. Hurried away by the magnificence of your conceptions and confident in the purity of your motives, you almost entirely despise and overlook the consequence which may result from the cold plodding operations of the man of form business and intrigue.'[51]

What Pasley had in mind was that in criticising Jones, Malcolm might appear to his detractors to be criticising the Crown itself. Pasley's warning also showed insight into Malcolm's shortcomings. Malcolm's reaction was revealing. Most people, on receiving such a deflating letter, would have quietly filed it. Not Malcolm – he immediately sent off a copy to the Governor-General.[52]

In March, a letter arrived from Minto, finally cancelling the Kharg expedition and telling him that he could return to the Residency at Mysore. The next few weeks were spent dispersing the people and equipment that had been assembled for the aborted mission. When he and Charlotte sailed from Bombay to Madras at the end of April, he was disappointed about the traumas of the last year, but also profoundly relieved that they were over at last.

CHAPTER EIGHTEEN

Mutiny at Masulipatam, 1809

When the Malcolm family (John, Charlotte and baby Margaret) sailed from Bombay back to Madras, they took with them John's brother Tom, his wife Fannie, and their two young sons, George and Duncan. Over the previous few months, Tom had become quite seriously ill. They hoped that a sea voyage would restore his health, but reluctantly conceded that he would have to give up his trading partnership with John Leckie in Bombay and return to England with his family. They also took with them Sir James Mackintosh's second daughter (from his first marriage), Maitland Mackintosh, who was also ill. The sea voyage restored her health and she stayed on in Madras with the Malcolms.[1] The family party arrived at Madras in mid-May.

They found the government in a frenzy over a threatened mutiny by the European officers of the Madras Army. The officers of the Madras Army had some legitimate grievances in 1809. There was the old jealousy of King's Army officers – a King's officer was entitled to supersede any Company officer of the same rank, however senior in age or service the latter might be. Thus a seasoned veteran in the Company's service might be superseded by a newly arrived youth who had bought his commission in England. This anomaly was magnified by the practice in some King's regiments of granting brevet rank (temporary promotion) to its officers when in India.

The reforms promoted by Lord Cornwallis in 1796 had improved allowances to Bengal Army officers but not to officers in the Madras Army, despite the cost of living being higher in Madras than in Bengal. Another factor contributing to their discontent was the rigid application of promotion by seniority, coupled with the rapid increase in the number of European officers. It meant that many newly joined young officers could never hope to rise above Captain, a depressing career prospect for them.

In 1807 and 1808 these smouldering embers of legitimate grievance were fanned into flame by the actions of some stupid and obstinate senior officers. Lieutenant-Colonel the Hon. Arthur St Leger had joined the Madras Cavalry in 1781, and served in many of the wars of the next twenty-five years. After a three-year furlough in England he returned to Madras in 1807. During his absence the post of Inspector of the Madras Cavalry had become vacant and the Government had appointed Colonel 'Rollo' Gillespie, a hero of the 1806 Vellore 'massacre' and other exploits, and, incidentally, a King's officer. But St Leger was senior to Gillespie and on his return he demanded to be given Gillespie's job. Neither the Commander-in-Chief Sir John Cradock nor the Governor, Lord William Bentinck, could persuade him to accept the fact that this was impracticable. St Leger then appealed to the Governor-General in Calcutta, citing his case as an example of the general humiliation of Company officers being superseded by King's officers.

In late 1807 both Bentinck and Cradock had been recalled, being blamed by the Court of Directors for the disaster at Vellore. Bentinck's successor as Governor of Madras was Sir George Barlow, who had ceased to be interim Governor-General with the arrival of Lord Minto in July 1807. Malcolm, still in Mysore at the time, had welcomed the appointment. He saw Barlow as a man of the utmost rectitude, the right person to clean out the corruption and murky dealings of Government officials in the Madras Presidency. He told John Elliot that 'he comes like an angel of light among the heroes of Madras'.[2]

Cradock's successor as Commander-in-Chief was Lieutenant-General Hay Macdowell, a King's officer. On arrival, Macdowell found that, unlike his predecessors, he was not to be given a seat on the Governor's Council. The order had been made by the Court of Directors in London. Taking this as a personal affront, he first talked of going to London to get his grievance righted, then reluctantly agreed to write to London and wait for an answer, which might take up to a year. Meanwhile he sulked. During 1808 more 'memorials' were sent to the Governor (probably instigated by Colonel St Leger) objecting to various government measures for curbing expenditure, most notably the aboli-

Sir George Barlow Bt (1762–1846) was acting Governor-General of India (1805–7) and Governor of Madras (1808–13).

tion of the so-called 'Tent Contract'. This was an arrangement introduced in 1802 whereby commanding officers were given allowances to purchase camping equipment for their regiments. It was a bad system, and following a report by the Quartermaster General, a Colonel Munro, it was duly abolished with effect from 1 July 1808. Sir George Barlow asked Macdowell to send an admonitory address to the memorialisers opposed to the abolition of the Tent Contract. This, formally, he did, but at the same time he wrote Barlow a petulant letter voicing his opposition to 'these disgusting measures'. Furthermore, as he toured the various garrisons, he expressed open hostility to the Government and to Barlow himself. In January 1809 he resigned and, in a farewell address to the Army, related the reasons for his resignation in inflammatory terms. As a parting shot, he ordered that Colonel Munro should be arrested and charged with having impugned the honour of senior officers by his report on the Tent Contract. To save Munro from such a ridiculous and malicious prosecution, the Governor reversed the order. Macdowell, due to sail the following day, then sent out a General Order to all stations regretting that his departure had prevented him from pursuing the prosecution of Colonel Munro, and immediately boarded his ship and sailed for England. He never reached his destination, his ship being lost with all hands in a storm near the Cape of Good Hope.

Up to this point, Barlow had handled Macdowell's childish behaviour with commendable restraint, but now he finally lost his temper. He cancelled Macdowell's General Order and dismissed the two officers who had actually signed the Order on Macdowell's behalf. Understandably, this action provoked uproar in the army. For the first time, Barlow was seen to be in the wrong. Unpopular from the outset, his name from then on was execrated.

Malcolm, waiting at the time in Bombay for possible orders from the Governor-General to set off for Persia, had received the news of these events in Madras with dismay. As an officer himself of twenty-six years' standing, he was immensely proud of the Madras Army. When he had joined, aged thirteen, the Army had acted like a foster-parent to him. He had numerous army friends and kept in close touch with them. In a letter to Colonel Barclay, the Governor's Military Secretary and an old friend, he expressed outrage at General Macdowell's behaviour.[3]

Barlow hoped that tempers would cool, but they did not. There were further acts of defiance. The government decided to take repressive measures. On 1 May the Governor issued a General Order suspending various officers who had been prominent in fomenting sedition. This produced more dangerous excitement, especially at Hyderabad. At Masulipatam, where the Madras European Regiment was stationed, a new commanding officer, Colonel James Innes, arrived in mid May. On his very first night dining in the mess, a mildly seditious toast was drunk to which he took exception. He demanded an apology from the two officers who had proposed the toast, and failing to get one, reported the matter to Madras on the next morning. Back came an order from the new Commander-in-Chief, General Gowdie, punishing the two officers, one being exiled to a remote station, the other being relieved of his job as Quartermaster.

Malcolm, meanwhile, arriving back at Madras in late May, watched the unfolding developments with increasing apprehension. Just before leaving Bombay, he had written privately to the Marquess in England about the situation. He was well aware that the Marquess thought highly of Barlow and had recommended him to be his substantive successor as Governor-General. So he was quite circumspect in describing what he saw as Barlow's failings:

> Whatever justice may be on the part of Sir George Barlow, it will be ten times more difficult for him to settle this question than any other, for the degree of personal dislike which all ranks and classes have of him is not to be described. This may be – and I dare say is – very unjust and very indefensible, but *it exists*, and cannot be changed, and the safety of the State should not be thrown into hazard, if that hazard can be avoided by the adoption of any measures that do not compromise its dignity or permanently weaken its authority. I am quite satisfied of the purity and rectitude of Sir George Barlow's character; the public has never had a more zealous or more laborious servant. He is devoted to his duty and has no enjoyment beyond that of performing it, but his system is cold and inflexible, and proceeds on its course without the slightest attention to the feelings of those for whom it is to operate.[4]

To Minto in Calcutta, he was more direct. On 3 June he reported that Barlow had listened to him, but did not seem to realise the extent of the danger. 'I am satisfied that [the] general spirit of discontent which has long pervaded this army, had never more danger than it has at this moment. I differ with Sir George Barlow upon this point . . . [He] has hopes this agitation will subside of itself. I cannot think so.'[5]

He wrote again to Minto on 12 June voicing his concerns.[6] With John Elliot he was more candid still. He wanted Minto to come to Madras urgently, because Barlow 'has been endeavouring to persuade himself that there was no danger, and even now he tries to think everything will subside, though he knows (for I have told him) . . . it is impossible to convey to men who are calm and think rationally any idea of the state of this army.'[7]

On 18 June Malcolm wrote to Barclay that 'I was at the Admiral's this morning and heard that the *Piedmontese* and *Samarang* were going to Masulipatam to bring some of the 30th to Madras, and to take 100 or more of the European Regiment on board to act as Marines in the fleet.'[8] He warned that this action, though seemingly harmless, would be misunderstood by the officers of the European Regiment. It would be considered as a punishment, and the first step in disbanding the Regiment, rumours of which had been circulating in recent weeks. The Government nevertheless went ahead, reasonably supposing that even if it was indeed about to disband the European Regiment, properly disciplined officers should obey such an order. But Malcolm's prediction turned out to be only too accurate. When they received the order, the officers decided to take drastic action. They formed a committee, called on Colonel Innes to desist from carrying out the order and, when he refused, put him under house arrest. This was on 25 June. The news reached Madras a few days later. It must have come as an unpleasant shock to Barlow and his advisers, and particularly galling to them to discover that Malcolm, with his superior informal intelligence network, had been right all along in his fears.

In the face of a mutiny, a government has two options – conciliation or coercion. In most mutinies, troops are mutinying against their officers and coercion is the usual option. But with a mutiny of Company *officers*, the problem was more complex. To use King's troops against Company officers and to rally their own Company sepoys against them would be a drastic measure of repression. It might lead to a form of civil war and possibly encourage neighbouring Native rulers with a grudge to take advantage of the Company's weakness to attack its territories. There was thus a strong argument for conciliation in such a case.

Barlow called in Malcolm, possibly with gritted teeth, to seek his advice. Malcolm was not short of suggestions. Essentially he was in favour of conciliation, hoping that it would bring the mutinous officers back to their senses, and as always, he was optimistic about his own ability to persuade them. Even if that did not work, he claimed, time would be gained. King's troops could be mustered and sent to the critical places so that if and when repression was needed, the Government would be well placed to enforce it. In relation to Masulipatam, he suggested that a senior officer should be sent there immediately, to take command of the European Regiment and to hold a Court of Inquiry, assisted by two other officers. It was agreed that the obvious person to lead the party would be Malcolm himself. His prestige and popularity could be used to calm the officers and persuade them to return to duty. Later on the same day, a meeting was held at the Madras Army headquarters with other staff officers. When one of them advocated the immediate despatch of a detachment of King's troops to Masulipatam to arrest the ringleaders, Malcolm reacted angrily and got Barlow's support for his more conciliatory approach. Moreover, in considering how to respond to an insolent 'remonstrance' just received from the Hyderabad officers demanding annulment of the General Order of 1 May, Barlow let Malcolm draft a relatively conciliatory reply.

Time was of the essence, so Malcolm was sent off to Masulipatam the following morning (2 July), alone and post haste, without written instructions. This was a bad mistake, because Barlow and Malcolm, both admirable men in their different ways and respectful of each other's talents, were utterly different in character. Barlow was a man of the rule book. To Barlow, the very fact that the officers at Masulipatam had broken the rules was utterly shocking, and the rule book said that a mutiny should be dealt with severely, regardless of the underlying causes. To Malcolm, it was the underlying causes that mattered: settle these and the rest would fall into place.

Malcolm arrived at Masulipatam on the morning of 4 July. The situation he found was daunting if not physically dangerous to him as a lone representative of the Government. The garrison had already made arrangements to march up to Hyderabad to join their fellow mutineers in the Subsidiary Force there, and were in a wild state of excitement. He met the principal officers at once. At first they resisted his authority, refusing to accept him as their commanding officer unless he gave a prior assurance that their various demands would be met. He refused to do so, pointing out that they must first return to loyalty and obedience before any concessions could be considered. The argument went on for five hours before they reluctantly accepted his authority, because, they said, of their regard for him personally.

He dined in the mess that night. After dinner a toast was proposed to 'Friends of the Army' (the same toast which had offended Colonel

Innes some weeks before, since it implied that there were enemies as well as friends). He joined in. The next toast was to 'the Common Cause'. This was definitely inflammatory. For a moment Malcolm hesitated. But then with characteristic boldness he rose, filled his glass, and in a loud voice exclaimed, 'The Common Cause of our Country!' The amended toast was drunk with enthusiasm. Malcolm then rose to leave and as he walked back to the garden cottage which had been provided for him, he heard behind him his own health being drunk to loud acclamation. 'Thus closed', he wrote in his journal, 'the most anxious day I ever passed in my life. May my efforts be successful in reclaiming these men from the errors into which they have plunged!'[9]

Over the next few days he struggled to calm down the officers. The so-called 'Committee' comprised all the officers in the garrison. Their meetings were chaotic affairs. He managed to persuade them to select a small number of the more senior officers to represent them. He also secured the release of Colonel Innes from house arrest.

Meanwhile he bombarded Barlow with reports and proposals (mostly copied to Minto) on an almost daily basis. His analysis was that the situation, not only at Masulipatam but throughout the army, was even more dire than he had anticipated. Thinking that he had persuaded Barlow to adopt a conciliatory approach, he went so far as to send a draft of the sort of General Order which he thought should be issued. It promised, effectively, to recommend to the Court of Directors that the officers suspended by the General Order of 1 May should be pardoned, and a general amnesty given for acts of mutiny and insubordination committed up to that date. The sting in the tail was that it required immediate and complete compliance, otherwise the Government would resort to full repressive measures. He also corresponded widely with officers at other stations, imploring them to come to their senses and to persuade others to do so.

He wrote again to Barlow on 10 July about the dangers of dealing with the men separately from their officers. This, he felt, would drive the officers to 'madness' and would have a deleterious long-term effect on discipline; it should only be tried as a last resort. On arrival he had reassured the officers that there was no truth in the report that the Government was intending to disband the Regiment, and left them to pass the information on to their men. On 14 July, he paraded the whole regiment to witness the sentence of flogging on four soldiers. Malcolm took the opportunity of directly addressing them, and pardoned the convicted men while explaining the Government's position on the recent events.

On 17 July, he received two letters dated 12 July from Colonel Barclay. The first letter stated that the Governor approved of his actions taken so far. The second painted a very different picture: 'Sir George Barlow . . . cannot satisfy his mind of the policy or the course of measures which you have recommended for his adoption . . . and the information which you have now communicated to him, instead of altering these sentiments, has confirmed him in his opinion of maintaining the authority of the Government with unshaken firmness and resolution.'[10] In other words, either he had completely misunderstood Barlow's stance from the outset, or Barlow had changed his mind. The balance of probability seems to be that, at heart, Barlow favoured repression, standing firmly by the rules, but that while still reeling from the shock of the outbreaks at Masulipatam and Hyderabad, he had been half persuaded by Malcolm's powerful advocacy to pursue a more conciliatory policy. Then, when Malcolm was no longer present, he was surrounded by 'hawks' on his staff, and had reverted to his original inclination towards repression.

Whatever the case, this news put Malcolm in a most awkward position. He decided that he must get back to Madras to discuss the situation directly with Barlow to clarify the matter. Either he would manage to persuade Barlow to adopt a more flexible policy or he would retire from the scene. General Pater, the Commander of the Northern Division of the army (which included Masulipatam) was due to arrive on 20 July and could be safely left to deal with the local situation. So he conducted the Inquiry, handed over to Pater, and left Masulipatam on 22 July, travelling to Madras by palanquin. He covered the 290 miles in a shade over three days and arrived on the morning of 26 July.

He went straight to see the Governor, but found to his dismay that during his absence, the repression policy had gained the ascendant. That very day, without waiting for Malcolm's return, Barlow had issued an order calling on all the European officers in the army to sign a declaration of loyalty (later called 'the Test') under penalty of dismissal from all commands if they failed to comply; and ordering all native officers to be assembled and full explanation made to them and their men that their first duty was to the Government, and that they risked destruction if they followed the lead of mutinous European officers. Barlow received Malcolm coldly. He did not appear to be interested in what Malcolm had to report, indicated his disapproval of Malcolm's conduct, and never called him in or consulted him again.

In fact, unknown to Malcolm, by the middle of July, Barlow had already turned strongly against him, and his long letter to Minto of 15 July illustrated the personal antagonism that had developed in Barlow's mind.

> It will be entirely Colonel Malcolm's fault if he does not establish his influence over all the non-commissioned officers and privates of all the European troops in the garrison, in which case the business will be at an end . . . As soon as Colonel Malcolm's presence at Masulipatam can be dispensed with, I shall wish him to return to his station at Mysore. He has too strong a disposition to interfere with what does not concern him, and too great an inclination to take the popular side of every question, and to be led to sacrifice the public interest to that of popularity, to be a fit person to remain among us.[11]

This was a harsh and unfair judgment on Malcolm's conduct, though it did make a valid point about his character.

Malcolm was now 'outside the tent'. Under normal circumstances he would be suffering a terrible setback to his career. But, in fact, as he already knew, he had been lined up by Minto for another important job: to lead a third mission to Persia. Nevertheless, there seemed no future for him with Barlow, and on 1 August he wrote a letter of resignation as Resident at Mysore. He accepted and respected the motives that had led Barlow to adopt a policy of coercion but he could not conscientiously act as an instrument of a policy with which he could not agree. At the same time he submitted the report of his Court of Inquiry at Masulipatam to the Commander-in-Chief, General Gowdie.

Over the next six weeks the policy of coercion proved broadly successful. At the southern garrisons all the officers, including Malcolm himself, signed the Test. Elsewhere, most officers refused to sign, on the ground that the Test held them all up as being untrustworthy. The most vociferous of the mutineers were the officers of the Subsidiary Force at Secunderabad cantonment (near Hyderabad). Barry Close, still

Resident at Poona and perhaps the most respected man in the whole Madras Army, was sent over from Poona to take charge of the situation and implement the coercive policy. He arrived there on 3 August and immediately appealed to the officers to submit. When they refused to do so, he approached the native troops, but they refused to listen to him, and he had to beat a hasty retreat towards Poona. But after his departure, the officers had second thoughts. Motivated, it was said, by the sight of the veteran commander being humiliated, by Malcolm's letter to them of 20 July and by the Governor-General's letter of 21 July to the Commander-in-Chief (but in reality to the Army), they wrote to the Governor-General (but not, significantly, to Barlow) on 11 August, pledging their submission, confirming that all officers had signed the Test, and begging for an amnesty.

At Masulipatam, after Malcolm's departure on 22 July, the garrison remained quiet for a while, but soon became restless again. General Pater reported that their agitation had been increased by their not having heard from Malcolm. It has been inferred from this remark[12] that before he left Masulipatam, Malcolm must have come to an understanding with the mutineers that he would secure a favourable settlement for them; but there is no evidence to support this assertion. Pater, carrying out the Government's order, paraded the troops on 15 August and promised to pardon them if they would submit, but they refused. The following day the officers agreed to submit but the men again refused. Pater, fearing for his personal safety, had to promise a pardon to both officers and men. The officers then signed the Test. After about ten days, word came back from Madras, refusing to confirm General Pater's offer of pardon, but by then the mutiny was effectively over. Only at Seringapatam did fighting break out between mutinous troops and troops loyal to the Government, with up to 300 being killed. But when the news came through that the Secunderabad force had submitted, the Seringapatam mutineers followed suit on 23 August.

Meanwhile Minto, to whom all parties had looked to settle the crisis, was on his way to Madras, but he was held up by monsoon winds, and only arrived on 11 September, by which time the mutiny was largely over. From the outset of the crisis, he and his Council had publicly supported Barlow and the Madras Government. But privately he admitted in a letter to the Court of Directors that Barlow's actions leading up to the mutiny, while legally sound, were not 'politic'. He was greeted on

Charles Grant (1746–1823) was a director of the East India Company from 1794 until his death, and Chairman in 1805, 1809 and 1815.

arrival by a report from Barlow which was understandably massive. He also received from Malcolm a copy of his letter of resignation to Barlow, plus a further 252 pages containing copies of just about all the documents relating to the mutiny, and justifying his own conduct and actions. After wading through all this material and interviewing many of those involved, Minto issued a General Order on 25 September which, while supporting the Madras Government's actions, limited the numbers selected for punishment.

The saga of the mutiny caused tremendous controversy in London as well as in India. Barlow was attacked mercilessly by the partisans of the army officers. Charles Grant, as Chairman of the Court of Directors, and Barlow's main sponsor over the years, stood firm behind him. But when Grant's term ended in late 1810, the new Court of Directors soon recalled Barlow. He retired to his country estate and never took another public job. In early 1811, a great sheaf of papers relating to the mutiny was brought before the House of Commons and published. Barlow's report on the mutiny to the Secret Committee of the Court of Directors dated 10 September 1809 included a scathing indictment of Malcolm's conduct, stopping only just short of accusing him of fomenting mutiny.[13] When the news of this report reached Malcolm in Bombay in mid-1811, he was understandably furious. The report virtually accused him of disobeying orders, a very serious charge against an army officer. But what really incensed him was that Barlow had never made him aware of the accusations contained in the letter which he had sent to the Court of Directors; to a lesser extent this omission also reflected badly on Minto. Malcolm immediately sat down to write a defence of his conduct. He was encouraged to do so by Sir James Mackintosh who had strongly supported his conciliatory approach during the mutiny.

Malcolm's pamphlet, *Disturbances in the Madras Army in 1809*, was published in June 1812. About the same time another anti-Barlow book was published in London by Charles Marsh, a barrister who had worked in Madras and later became a Member of Parliament. *A Review of some important passages in the late administration of Sir George Barlow at Madras* reads like a prosecuting counsel's case, making no effort whatever to appear objective. Malcolm's pamphlet triggered a prompt 'Barlowite' response – a pamphlet published in October 1812. It was anonymous but in fact was written by George Buchan who had been Chief Secretary of the Madras Government until he went home in February 1809, just before the mutiny. Buchan's book was relatively polite. In criticising Malcolm's judgment on the 'causes and progress of the mutiny', it made some telling points. However, in criticising Malcolm's conduct, Buchan was notably less successful. He contrasted Malcolm's temporising approach at Masulipatam in July with Barry Close's determined confrontation in Hyderabad in August. But, as Malcolm later pointed out, the two situations had been entirely different. Paradoxically, Malcolm's early conciliatory approach helped to calm the situation sufficiently for Barlow's coercive approach to succeed, and lessen the risk of disaster – open rebellion and bloody retribution – which such an approach might otherwise have provoked.

There is little doubt that if either Malcolm or Close had been Governor, the mutiny would never have occurred. Barlow did not cause the mutiny, but his rigid attitude and lack of empathy for people certainly brought on the crisis. Malcolm's conciliatory approach was right, but he ignored the vital fact that he was not in charge. He should have seen that a man of Barlow's character would be incapable of carrying out such a policy successfully. When the full crisis arrived, Barlow acted with resolution and courage, but his denunciation of Malcolm to the Court of Directors (especially his failure to inform him of the fact) was shabby and out of keeping with his generally upright character.

Meanwhile, back in Madras, Tom Malcolm's health continued to deteriorate, and he died in early September 1809, aged thirty-nine. Fannie was naturally distraught, but she was lucky to have John and Charlotte with her to sort out the repercussions of Tom's death, and to help her to look after her two boys. Together they sailed from Madras on 15 October, arriving in Bombay in late November. Fannie and her children lodged with the Malcolms, and John helped to negotiate a settlement of Tom's affairs with Tom's business partner, John Leckie.

In the three weeks that John was at Masulipatam dealing single-handed with the mutiny, he also somehow found time to sort out his brother Robert's residual affairs. Robert had lived for many years at Masulipatam and later at Visagapatam, with Nancy and their six children. Late in 1806, when ill health forced him to leave India he did not take Nancy or the children with him. Nor does he appear to have made formal financial provision for her, although in 1804, with John's help, trusts had been set up to provide for the children. He also left behind two properties. He may have intended to give them to his Indian family, but it was John who made sure that the Indian family actually got the benefit of them. When he got back from Masulipatam to Madras, John arranged for further trusts to provide an income for all Robert's children except Anne, who was considered amply provided for through her marriage to John Leckie.

Arriving back in Bombay in late November 1809, the Malcolm family resumed the life that they had led there earlier in the year. But this was to last only a few weeks, as John prepared once again to sail to Persia. Charlotte was heavily pregnant for a second time, and once again he would be leaving her as she was about to give birth. He sailed for Bushire on 10 January 1810, and a son, George Alexander Malcolm, was born on

21 January. But this time the family were well settled in Bombay with plenty of friends, and he had little of the anxiety that had followed Margaret's birth twenty months earlier.

All through 1809, Malcolm had been working on his *Sketch of the Political History of India*. He had started making notes for the book a year earlier, using his sea voyages to write. Now he used the five-week voyage from Bombay to Bushire to complete a full draft. He wrote to Charlotte: 'Five chapters are finished and corrected; and the sixth and last is commenced this morning. I begin now to look forward with great delight to that enchanting word *Finis*. The moment I write it, I will have a jubilee. I mean to dance, hunt, shoot, and play myself, and let who will write histories, memoirs and sketches.'[14] In its final form the book amounted to 531 printed pages – he had researched and written over 250,000 words in less than a year.

His third mission to Persia kept him away from Bombay and his family for the next eleven months.

CHAPTER NINETEEN

The Third Persian Mission, 1810

In late July 1809, while at Masulipatam, Malcolm received a long and thoughtful letter from Minto about Persia. Minto argued that whatever the merits or demerits of the Preliminary Treaty signed by Jones in March might be, he had had 'authentic credentials' for negotiating it; and the Persian Government, by expelling Gardane, had acted in good faith to honour it. It was up to the Calcutta Government to do the same, by paying the promised subsidies and providing the specified military equipment. For this purpose an accredited representative of the Calcutta Government should be sent to ensure that this was done efficiently. But there was a further task for such a representative – the restoration of the reputation and prestige of the Calcutta Government in the eyes of the Persians, which Jones had done so much to lower. This would need Malcolm's special talents. It was not yet clear whether the British Government in London wished to appoint its own Ambassador (Jones or another) or allow Minto to select Malcolm for the role, but either way, it was still necessary for Malcolm to go, to represent the Calcutta Government's interests.[1] Minto was at last beginning to come to terms with reality.

A few days later Minto wrote again, to say that he was on his way to Madras, chiefly to deal with the mutiny, but also to discuss the Persian situation, so Malcolm should stand by in Madras for further orders. He arrived on 11 September, and had detailed discussions with Malcolm about the projected new mission. A supplementary objective was added: to gather information about the geography, economy and political complexion of the Persian region, so that the Calcutta Government would be better informed in the event of future threats to British India from that quarter. Malcolm was to pack up at Madras, return to Bombay, and assemble another mission team.

On 26 October Minto formalised the arrangement for Malcolm's mission to Persia in a letter to the Shah, saying that he was sending Malcolm as the accredited representative of the Calcutta Government. He wrote a separate letter to Jones, with the same advice, reiterating that Jones should retire on Malcolm's arrival, adding what he believed would be a lethal sting in the tail, that: 'no public act of yours in opposition to the orders now conveyed to you will be recognised by this government; nor will any Bills drawn by you, excepting such as are certified to be drawn on account of the indispensable charges of your mission, and incident to your retreat from Persian territories, accompanied by a distinct explanation of those charges will be accepted. I have addressed a letter to the King, repeating my request that on the arrival of General Malcolm, His Majesty will grant you permission to depart.'[2] He clearly still believed that Jones was accountable to the Crown via him, rather than directly.

The feud between Minto and Jones had been simmering for nearly a year, and it had a harmful effect on Britain's relations with the Persian Government. Not long after the signing of the Preliminary Treaty in early March 1809, problems had begun to arise in Tehran, and they seemed to centre round the person of Jones. As a representative of the British Crown, the Shah's opposite number, his status was more acceptable than that of a representative of the Governor-General. Jones, too, was clearly a man of considerable ability, with wide experience of the Middle East, and fluent in Persian and Arabic. But he seemed to the Persians a rather strange, devious character, quite unlike Malcolm or Gardane. And he had a violent temper:

> He has annoyed the Grandees at Court not a little . . . at one conference with Mirza Shaffee [the Prime Minister] and Haji Mohd Hussein Khan [the Minister of Finance] a few days before the Preliminaries were exchanged, he was so enraged at an expression of the former that he rose up and had so little command over himself that he positively kicked down the shades, overset the pelsoozas [pihsuz, oil lamps] and kicked the candlesticks about in great style.[3]

Jones was also reported to be offering lavish bribes, paid in cash or *suftees* [promissory notes] rather than in presents, as his predecessors had paid them: 'the secret service money of which he has permission to make use, pays for this "Shenay Mamoony" [monkey trick]. The Prince of Shirauz received before he [Jones] could leave that place, presents to the amount of nearly 70,000 rupees. He gave a bond also to pay Mirza Shaffee £10,000 sterling if invited up to Court, and it is supposed that he is to pay £30,000 sterling for the letters [sent] to the Ministers in England and the firmaun to himself. Yet, with these erroneous donations, he is abused by everyone, even by those to whom these sums have been paid.'[4]

Nevertheless, in April 1809, it must have been quite a shock to Jones, still basking in the satisfaction of signing the Preliminary Treaty, to see a blockbuster letter from Minto to the Shah, advising him that Jones had been suspended, basically for disobedience, and, much more alarming to the Persian Ministers, threatening that his *suftees* might be 'protested' (dishonoured).[5] How was it, they thought, that a representative of the King of England could be suspended by the Governor-General of one of his provinces? The Shah was understandably appalled, and called Jones in for an explanation. Defending himself energetically, Jones denounced the action of the Governor-General:

> Suppose your Majesty had sent an ambassador, provided with proper credentials, and charged with a letter from your own gracious self to the Turkish Emperor; and he had been received at Constantinople, and negociated a treaty in your Majesty's name; and after that one of your Beglerbegs [provincial Chiefs], started up, and wrote a letter to the Ministers at the Porte, saying to them that you must not credit nor conclude a treaty with the fellow sent by the King, because, in a few days, I shall send you a much greater and cleverer man than he is, who shall be accredited from me, and shall begin his negotiations with you according to the latest rules of established diplomacy; that is, by bringing a large military force with him, and seizing the castles of the Dardanelles![6]

He offered *suftees* on his own bond, and then frantically set about trying to find an alternative source of Company funds to cover them. He succeeded several months later, via the East India Company's agent in Constantinople. The Shah reluctantly accepted this explanation, which nevertheless seemed to demonstrate an alarming lack of teamwork by the British.

All through the summer and autumn of 1809 the Persian Court waited for the arrival of the promised military advisers and equipment, and above all for the funds (called 'subsidies') which the British had promised would come from India. Jones based himself at Tabriz, to assist Abbas Mirza and Mirza Bezorg in negotiating an armistice with the Russians, and hopefully in due course a peace treaty. In early November another letter from the Governor-General arrived,[7] accepting the Preliminary Treaty signed by Jones in March 1809, but still confirming Jones's suspension. Then came Minto's letter advising that he had appointed Malcolm to lead another mission to Persia, the purpose of which would be to implement the East India Company's obligations under the Treaty.

Throughout this period Jones was keeping Canning and Dundas in London regularly informed of his progress. Understandably, he ascribed his remarkable success largely to his own skills as a diplomat and negotiator. He boasted to Charles Grant that 'It appears to me that I have effected what the Governor-General thought impossible.'[8] At the same time he must have had a slightly uneasy feeling about Minto's likely reaction to his instructions being disobeyed. He realised that he must retain London's support in the event of repercussions from Minto. He did so shrewdly, by selective quoting from Minto's letters, to demonstrate how out of touch Minto was with events. Since letters from Persia to London took two to three months, while letters from Calcutta took five or six (and anyway were usually responding to news from Persia which was already three months old), this was not difficult.

Canning and Dundas were dismayed at these clashes between Minto and Jones. They felt that they had made the reporting relationships reasonably clear back in 1807, although inevitably leaving considerable discretion to the individuals concerned. They had urged the parties to work together. In the meantime, unknown to Jones, Canning had became involved in a dispute with Castlereagh during the summer of 1809, which culminated in their fighting a duel (Castlereagh was slightly wounded, and resigned as Foreign Secretary); while Dundas had changed jobs in mid-year to become Secretary for Ireland, though he returned as President of the Board of Control in November. Immediately on his return, Dundas persuaded the new Foreign Secretary, Lord Bathurst, to overrule Minto's suspension of Jones and confirm the Government's support for him.[9] This was really the only practical solution to the problem, even though both Bathurst and Dundas realised that it meant an unfortunate loss of face and authority for Minto and the Calcutta Government in relation to Persia. Appreciating this, both Bathurst and Dundas wrote quite apologetic letters to Minto to explain their decision.

Jones of course was not yet aware of what was going on in London during the second half of 1809; in fact he was still addressing letters to Canning as late as December, and he did not even know that Dundas had been away in Ireland for six months. The strain and uncertainty of his position began to tell on his nerves. When Leadenhall Street refused to pay part of his allowances directly to his wife in England, he decided that he had had enough, and tendered his resignation. In a ten-page letter at the end of October he protested, with some justification, about the refusal of the Company to treat him fairly throughout his career; and in a jealous sideswipe at Malcolm, he complained that the Calcutta Government had given Malcolm a much higher allowance during his Persian missions than he was receiving.[10]

For the next three months Jones, though unaware of what London's reaction would be to his dispute with Calcutta, felt confident enough of his position to write a furious letter of reproach to Minto (copied to Bathurst). Finally, he objected to the recent return of Charles Pasley to Bushire, after five months sick leave in Bombay, which he said was upsetting and confusing the Persian Ministers.[11]

At the end of January 1810, Jones received Bathurst's letter confirming his appointment as Minister to the Persian court, and overruling Minto. Feeling that his conduct was now completely vindicated, he proceeded to take sweet revenge for all the real and imagined slights that he had suffered. He immediately made his secretary, Sheridan, write to Charles Pasley at Bushire, forbidding him to have any further communication with the Persian authorities, and ordering him to hand over any stores intended for the Shah. He then wrote a gloating letter to Minto (copied to Bathurst in London), in which he quoted flattering references to himself from various Persian Ministers, and went on, with what he confidently expected would be the *coup de grâce* for any attempted reappearance at Court by the much resented Malcolm: 'I flatter myself [that] Your Excellency, after perusing these papers, will approve the orders I have given to the Gentleman who has lately arrived [i.e Pasley], or to any other gentleman who may hereafter arrive in quality of your political agent in this country [i.e. Malcolm] . . . I do not wish to conceal from Your Excellency that I have declared most explicitly to the Persian Ministers that I cannot nor will not in any shape act with Brigadier Malcolm in this country. Our ideas and sentiments on Persia are so *essentially* different that such a coalition can lead to nothing but confusion and distraction.'[12]

In a separate letter to Minto, Jones enclosed a *farman* from the Shah. This acknowledged Malcolm's forthcoming arrival at Bushire; noted Jones's objections to it; said that he would take Jones's advice; but also that the Persian Government would have no objection to receiving a delegation from India.[13]

Savouring his triumph, Jones hinted to his staff that he had been offered the governorship of Bombay, though he thought he would turn it down. He preferred the idea of two or three years in Constantinople as Ambassador to the Porte. For the present, the last thing he wanted was to have anyone, let alone Malcolm, muscling in on what he now regarded as his exclusive preserve. This was despite both the British Government and the Shah having stated that they had no objection to a mission from India. It should also have been obvious to him that if the Calcutta Government was going to have to pay for aid given to Persia, it was merely common sense that there should be a representative of that government on hand to ensure that the funds were efficiently procured and spent.

Meanwhile at Bombay, for the third time in ten years, Malcolm was assembling his team of twenty officers to go to Persia. At thirty-nine, Malcolm was easily the oldest; two others were thirty and the rest in their twenties. It was an impressive party of young men, many of whom were destined to become legendary names in the history of British India. They included Charles Pasley, who had been on both previous missions, a brilliant Persian scholar who later succumbed to opium addiction; Josiah Stewart, who later served as Resident at Gwalior and Hyderabad; Henry Ellis, later knighted and British Ambassador to Persia in 1835–37; John Briggs, later a General, a fine Persian scholar who served as Resident at Satara, Nagpur and Mysore; John Macdonald, later knighted and

British Minister in Tehran 1826–1830; Edward Frederick, later a General; Henry Lindsay (only eighteen), later Sir Henry Lindsay-Bethune Bt, who stayed on in Persia for many years; Lieutenant Charles Christie, destined to be killed fighting the Russians in Azerbaijan in 1812; and Henry Pottinger, later knighted as a General, the first British administrator in Hong Kong at the time of the first Opium War and later Governor of the Cape and Madras. They were escorted by five officers and twenty troopers of the Madras Horse Artillery, four NCOs and ten privates of HM 17th Light Dragoons, and six officers, one drummer, one fifer and forty sepoys of the Bombay Army.

Despite his outward enthusiasm, Malcolm was pessimistic about the prospects for his mission. In a letter to the Marquess, he saw himself (and the Calcutta Government) as likely to be humiliated by Jones, who, with the support of the authorities in London, now held all the cards.[14] Johnnie Little was more optimistic, writing from Bombay to his father at Langholm that 'we . . . are all delighted with the prospect of being so soon in a cold climate. Pasley writes that he has been well received, and by all appearances the General [Malcolm] . . . will be permitted to visit the Capital. I hope to God he may.'[15]

Malcolm sent several members of the party in advance on special missions to achieve the third objective of the mission – to find out more about the hinterland of Persia, so that the Calcutta Government would be better able to defend itself against potential future threats of invasion from the French or the Russians, or indeed any hostile power. It is worth recording where they went and what they achieved.

Christie and Pottinger had already been on an exploratory mission to Sind in 1809. They volunteered to explore Baluchistan, Seistan and the southern provinces of Afghanistan and Khorasan. These are wild areas even today; 200 years ago they were wilder still. The outside world knew very little about them. There were no maps, no British consuls or agents to intervene on their behalf if anything went wrong. It was considered too dangerous to travel as British officers; they had to travel in disguise, leaving Bombay in a small native boat, their fellow passengers being the servants of a Hindu merchant with interests in Sind, and a group of Afghan horse dealers. 'We succeeded so well in disguising ourselves,' wrote Pottinger, 'by partly changing the European for the native dress, that although the Uffghans [Afghans] concluded, from our complexions, that we were Europeans, they did not in the least suspect our real characters.'[16]

Landing a few miles north-west of Karachi, they travelled together to Kalat, on the south-eastern border of modern Afghanistan. Here they made the extraordinarily brave decision to split up, so that between them they could cover more territory in the time available, and to meet again at Isfahan. Christie marched north-west, through Helmand province to Seistan, then due north to Herat, Meshed and thence across the Dashti Kavir, the great sand desert of central Persia, via Tabas and Yazd to Isfahan. Pottinger went south-west across Baluchistan to Kerman and Shiraz, arriving there in May, and reporting to Mohamed Nabee Khan at his palace. Mohamed Nabee redirected him to Johnnie Little, whom Malcolm had left behind to look after the mission's interests at Shiraz. He continued to Isfahan with Dr Cormick, the mission surgeon. On their arrival there, an extraordinary coincidence occurred. Pottinger described it in matter-of-fact style:

> Captain Christie arrived in the city [Isfahan] about dusk, unknowing and unknown, and went to the governor's palace to request a lodging, which was ordered, when, by accident, one of the attendants observed that there were two Feringhees in the Chihul Setoon [one of the palaces in which Cormick and Pottinger were allowed to stay]; and that he would possibly like to join their party; he accordingly came up to the palace, and sent up a man to say that he wished to speak to one of us. I went down, and as it was then quite dark, I could not recognise his features; and he, fancying me a Persian from my dress, we conversed for several minutes ere we discovered each other. The moment we did so, was one of the happiest of my life.[17]

Over the previous six months, each man had travelled over 2,000 miles, on foot or on horseback. From Isfahan they rode on northwards together, catching up with the main party on its way out of Persia at Maragheh, sixty miles south of Tabriz, on 31 July.

Captain Grant of the Madras Army had if anything an even more hair-raising journey. He went off on his own from Bombay to the Makran coast of south-eastern Persia. Alexander the Great's Greek army had traversed this route some 2,140 years before, and had been decimated. There were no roads, no maps and very little water.[18] However, he got through to Bandar Abbas in southern Persia, and took a ship to Bushire.

The main party left Bombay on 10 January and arrived at Bushire on 14 February. Malcolm found messages from Pasley who had gone ahead to Shiraz, saying that the Court at Tehran seemed favourably disposed to welcome him. Possibly sensing that Pasley's presence as advance guard in Tehran might well be controversial, and raise the hackles of Jones (Pasley had in any case fallen ill again), he opted to send Dr Andrew Jukes ('Gentle Jukes' as he was known to his colleagues), the resident surgeon at Bushire, to carry his message to the Shah, and to find out how the land lay. Malcolm told Jukes that if he found Jones at Tehran he should withdraw (in fact Jones was still at Tabriz, and stayed there until early June). A few days later news came from England that Jones had been confirmed as Minister. Passing through Isfahan, Jukes reported that Abbas Mirza appeared to be pro-Jones, and so was Mirza Shafee (the Prime Minister), but that Haji Mohamed Hussein Khan (the Ameer ud Dowlah, or Minister of Finance) was pro-Malcolm. Jukes reached Tehran on 25 March and was warmly welcomed. He had a meeting with the Haji the following day, and wrote a detailed report of the meeting. The Haji said that the Shah would be delighted to receive Malcolm, and then:

> seemed perfectly satisfied and pleased with this declaration, and he entered into some little discussion respecting Sir Harford Jones. He said that being the Ambassador of his Britannic Majesty, it was a duty incumbent upon him and his Brother Minister, Meerza [Mirza] Shafee, to treat him as such; that notwithstanding Sir Harford's temper was not the most placid, and his disposition very changeable, they had entered into and concluded a Preliminary Treaty with him for the welfare of both States. 'It is not often', said the Ameer ud Dowlah, 'that we meet with such a man as Sir Harford; he says one thing in the morning, which in the evening he disavows. We have titled him,' said he, smiling, 'amongst ourselves Mr Na Jins' ['Mr Nothing'][19] . . . The Ameer ud Dowlah informed me that Sir Harford Jones had written to him to say, in case you were invited up to Tehran, he would instantly leave Persia and return to England, but he did not know how far Sir Harford would really carry out this threat into execution. 'At all events', concluded the Ameer ud Dowlah, 'if he likes to return to Tehran, we shall be glad to see him. If he

> chooses to remain at Tabriz it is at his own option, and if he proposes returning to England, we cannot help it.'[20]

Two days later Jukes reported on an audience with the Shah, who had stated that: 'I have never seen, among the Europeans who have visited my Court, a man like Malcolm, and as a proof of the regard I entertain for him, I have commanded a *mehmandar* of the first rank and consequence to proceed immediately to Shiraz or wherever he may be . . . and to conduct him without delay to Tehran.'[21]

Malcolm's arrival at Bushire was welcome news to the Shah. He could see that, despite the differences between London and Calcutta, the British were at last on the brink of delivering the promised advisers and equipment, probably in time for a summer campaign against the Russians. He was anxious, too, to receive Malcolm again. He had in fact sent him a *farman* in May 1809 regretting the events of 1808, and saying that he wished Malcolm henceforth to be the channel for all communications and negotiations between India and Persia.[22] Since he had sent that *farman* at a time when he was having trouble with Jones, it is possible that he had also been hoping that he could deal with a more congenial envoy than Jones.

On 8 April Malcolm received a further *farman* from the Shah, welcoming him and inviting him to come to Tehran. He responded immediately with a letter to the Persian Ministers, accepting the offer, and clarifying the status of the two British missions. In explaining the Calcutta Government's view of Jones's mission, he stated that though the Governor-General did not approve of the conduct of Sir Harford Jones, he had immediately confirmed the Treaty which that Minister had concluded, and adopted such measures as he deemed best for carrying the Preliminary Treaty into execution; and as the Shah, 'who always has honoured him [Malcolm] with his favour, and had asked for his return to his court, he was deputed by the Governor-General to confirm and improve the established alliance'. British Ministers in London had heard of the Governor-General's disapproval of Sir Harford's conduct, and his suspension, but they 'nevertheless resolved to confirm the Treaty he had made and to restore him to his powers as Plenipotentiary . . . as they justly considered that not to confirm the Treaty would be to break that public faith . . . and not to restore Sir Harford to his functions as a public Minister might delay the execution of the Treaty.' He pointed out that Persian interests had meanwhile been in no way damaged. As soon as the British Ministers had received a full account of the circumstances they would make a final decision about British representation – this would instantly end all embarrassment, and 'settled on principles which can never again be affected by that Collision to which the most accordant authorities are subject when placed at such a vast distance from each other as England and India'. The Governor-General had told Malcolm to go to Persia, even though he realised that Sir Harford's position as Ambassador might be confirmed. So Sir Harford's recent confirmation did not alter the purpose of Malcolm's mission, which was to represent the Calcutta Government's interests in implementing the Treaty.[23]

Malcolm's only remaining obstacle now was Jones. He had known from the outset that he would have to humour him. Immediately on arrival at Bushire he had written to him, enclosing his instructions from Minto and saying firmly: 'I arrived here on the 14th instant and mean to proceed to court as soon as my preparations are completed',[24] but in other respects his letter was conciliatory, hoping that they could cooperate to implement the Treaty in the most advantageous manner. He wrote again on 10 April, enclosing a copy of his letter to the Persian Ministers. Having had no response from Jones to his earlier letters, his tone became a little sharper. He pointed out that regardless of whether Jones had been confirmed or not as Minister, a mission from India was still justified, since the Calcutta Government was financing the subsidies and equipment provided under the Preliminary Treaty. He had moreover been invited to Tehran by the Shah, and he was accepting that invitation. He warned Jones that no acts of his would be considered binding on the Calcutta Government.

Setting out from Bushire on 15 April, he advanced steadily northwards, reaching Shiraz on 27 April. But on 6 May, while at Persepolis, he received some dreadful news from Rich, the Company's Resident in Baghdad. Two of his officers, Grant and Fotheringham, had been murdered. He had sent them from Bushire to Baghdad and thence via Kermanshah to rejoin the main party at Tehran, with instructions to explore the Luristan country on the way. In Luristan Kulb Ali Khan, a local chief, had enticed them to his encampment, where they had no sooner alighted than he fell upon them. Capt Grant received a mortal wound from a carbine while he was mounting his horse, the rest surrendered. After the Khan had searched the baggage he bound the only Christians of the party, namely Mr Fotheringham, his Armenian servant, a Cook and a Seis [groom] . . . and shot them one after another. The Mussulman part of the escort escaped.'[25] Perhaps surprisingly for a military man, Malcolm was devastated by the news.[26] Nevertheless, he took swift action. He wrote to Rich, asking what could be done to capture and punish the murderers, and sent Edward Frederick to the scene to discover the circumstances of the murder and report back. Frederick moved quickly, reaching Isfahan on 15 May: 'Paid a visit to Mirza Abdul Cassim Wolla, the Soofee. He was very civil, very inquisitive about the object of my journey, and shook his head when I told him I was sent to enquire into the fate of these unfortunate gentlemen. "You know all that already", said he, "What else have you got to do? In short you Feringhees [foreigners, Christians, literally 'Franks'] are all the same, always making enquiries. You want to get Persia as you did India; send Ambassadors first, Armies afterwards."'[27]

Every summer in late May, when the weather became insufferably hot in Tehran, the Persian Court and its camp followers – up to 25,000 people – would travel about 200 km west and set up camp on the plain of Soltaniyeh (then spelt Sultaneah), which had a much cooler summer climate. The plain was (and still is) dominated by the 200-feet high dome of the ruined tomb of Oljeitu, the Mongol ruler who died there in 1317. It was to Soltaniyeh that Malcolm's party were headed.

Malcolm's main party reached Isfahan on 31 May. As spring turned into summer, and the weather became hot during the day, they travelled by night, sometimes covering huge distances. Malcolm wrote on 10 June: 'we marched last night at eight o'clock, and reached our ground this morning about seven – the distance being full forty miles. I rode a mule almost the whole night, and think its paces are rather pleasanter than a horse's, and at night the mule is generally preferred, as being more sure-footed.'[28]

When they were near Kashan (about 250 km from Soltaniyeh) in early June, a letter at last arrived from Jones, but it was addressed to Minto. Malcolm opened it, and found that it contained the interesting rumour, which later proved false, that the Shah had issued a *farman* for Malcolm to be stopped on the road. As Malcolm sourly commented, anyone else but Jones would also have told Malcolm about this.[29] On the contrary, when a later letter came from Jones, its first paragraph contained a strong objection to Malcolm opening a letter addressed to someone else![30] Jones did nevertheless concede that he had, reluctantly, advised the Persian Court to receive Malcolm.

At Qom the party rested from the heat in the luxurious house of an absent Persian nobleman. Sir Robert Ker Porter passed through Qom eight years later, and his description of his visit includes a splendid example of Persian hyperbole:

> I soon learnt that I was not the only European guest who had lodged under their master's roof; and, that the *farangeh* name they so highly honoured, was that of General Malcolm. It was delightful to me, to begin a journey so tracked; for everywhere that I went in the empire, where his mission had led him, still I found his remembrance in the hearts of the inhabitants . . . In many of the villages, the people date their marriages, or the birth of their children, from the epoch of his last visit among them; for, wherever he appeared, his goodness left some trace of himself; and the peasants often said to me, that 'if the rocks and trees had suddenly the power of speech, their first word would be Malcolm!'[31]

All this time, Jones, still based at Tabriz, had done whatever he could to delay Malcolm, and if possible stop him proceeding to Tehran. He wrote to Charles Grant, the current Chairman of the Court of Directors (with copy to Bathurst) on 26 March,[32] quoting Robert Adair, the British Ambassador in Constantinople, to the effect that the Turks 'will also be confused by our having two missions in Persia at the same time . . . I am sorry nothing I have done, nor can do, is capable of pleasing the Governor-General; and I am still more sorry to see the confusion and embarrassment His Excellency's measures occasion in this country; and the superfluous and consequently unnecessary expense they occasion the Company.' He also quoted to Bathurst a *farman* sent by the Shah to Abbas Mirza in Tabriz, which looked as if it had been drafted by Abbas Mirza himself, in response to a threat by Jones to leave Persia if Malcolm were received at Court. Jones wrote a marginal note on this letter: 'After receipt of [Bathurst's] letter of 6 November 1809, I acquainted the Prince Royal [Abbas Mirza] that if the Governor-General's agents were admitted, I would instantly leave Persia.' The *farman* went on to say that the

Shah planned to keep Malcolm waiting until he heard from Mirza Abul Hassan, the Persian Ambassador in London. He would then admit Malcolm to the Court at Soltaniyah, but would follow Jones's advice on how and when this should happen, and would deal with Jones alone on political matters.[33]

In early April news came through from London that a new Foreign Secretary had been appointed – none other than the Marquess Wellesley. Knowing that the Marquess was a Malcolm supporter, this must have given Jones some qualms. Nevertheless, to the Shah's amazement, he still objected very strongly to the Malcolm mission being received at all, threatening to leave Persia, and using every means in his power, (even including, it was reported, bribery of Ministers), to prevent Malcolm being received.

To the Persians, Jones's attitude was petty and patently ridiculous. Despite his earlier expression of readiness to abide by Jones's advice, the Shah now refused to stall Malcolm. In early June he summoned Jones to come to Soltaniyeh from Tabriz to advise him on how Malcolm should be received. Jones now reluctantly concluded that he could no longer prevent Malcolm's reception by the Shah, so he changed his tactics. He advised the Shah that since Malcolm had come so far – defying both the King of England and the East India Company – he might as well be received, with certain 'stipulations'. These stipulations were designed to humiliate Malcolm, and by extension Minto. He would not be allowed to sound trumpets, hoist flags etc, as he had done in 1800; neither he nor his staff should ever have an audience with the Shah or his Ministers without Jones being present, or giving his prior approval; neither the Persian Ministers nor their representatives should ever enter into discussion on political matters with the Malcolm mission; and all presents, equipment etc brought by the mission should first be handed over to Jones, in order that he should be the person to make them over to the Persian Government.

He wrote to Malcolm, enclosing a copy of these 'stipulations', together with a *farman* from the Shah stating that he would be happy to meet Malcolm in the presence of Jones – whatever, in fact, Jones might desire. The letter went on to voice strong disapproval of Malcolm's conduct, concluding with his mantra that: 'I am bound to obey the Governor-General's orders in all cases when these orders are not incompatible with their own [i.e. the Court of Directors].'[34]

Malcolm, still on the road, responded that his approach to the Persian Court had been rapid for one reason only – because the Shah had summoned him. And, at the very least, his mission was justified as the medium for payment of the subsidy and the handing over of the arms to the Persian Government. Regarding the 'stipulations', he had written to the Persian Ministers, that while he accepted that Jones, as the representative of the British Crown, should have precedence over him, he insisted that in other respects he should be treated in the same way as he had been ten years before.[35] The Shah called in Jones, said he agreed with Malcolm, and after what was reported as an acrimonious argument, overruled him.

Over the next three weeks the feud between Malcolm and Jones became increasingly farcical. Malcolm kept a daily journal of events from 18 June, and sent a copy to Charlotte. She showed the journal to Sir James Mackintosh, who, though in a way a 'Malcolmite', owed his appointment as Recorder in Bombay to the British Government rather than the Company. He wrote to Maria Graham,[36] giving an eloquent résumé of this ridiculous episode, ending: 'The bitterness of H's [Harford Jones's] thoughts and feeling, his indefatigable patience in servility and intrigue, his happy indifference to the detection and exposure of his falsehoods, the quickness with which he turns from frowning to fawning, and the insidious court which works some impression on those who best understand him and most despise him, altogether render his character a very curious study. I never knew anyone supply the place of all the high talents so well by the exquisite degree in which he professes all the low ones.'[37]

Realising at last that his stalling tactics had not succeeded, Jones's tone underwent a further overnight change. On 20 June he wrote to Malcolm agreeing that they should meet *privately* and discuss the issues directly. Malcolm arrived at Soltaniyeh on 21 June, and they met the next morning. Malcolm's audience with the Shah was set for 23 June. Jones later recorded in his memoirs that:

> The Shah intimated to me his wish that I should be present at the audience he designed to give him. I answered, that I would most willingly comply with His Majesty's wishes, provided General Malcolm permitted me to present him to the Shah; this being objected to, *on the part of the General*

> [author's emphasis], I considered it my duty to interfere no further in the matter, and on the day on which the audience took place, I made a little party of pleasure, with some Persian friends, to visit and pass the time of day at some beautiful springs issuing from the rock, at the foot of a mountain, a little distance from the camp.[38]

This version of the story is not borne out by contemporary correspondence and records. The fact is that Malcolm gave written consent to Jones to introduce him, and the Persian Ministers were fully expecting Jones to turn up. The more charitable comment on his behaviour is that his memoirs were written twenty-four years later, and that since most of his papers were lost at sea in 1811, time had eroded his memory. The less charitable comment is that he gave way to a childish fit of pique.

The audience went ahead anyway, the Shah saying that he did not need anyone else to introduce his old friend from 1800. When Malcolm arrived, 'with eleven gentlemen of his suite, all in full dress uniform', the Shah was in very good humour, and after the usual *ta'arof* (compliments), asked:

> 'How have you been these many years?'
>
> 'Except for the wish to visit your Majesty, I have been well and happy.'
>
> 'But what made you go back in dudgeon last year, without seeing my son at Shiraz?'
>
> 'How could he, who had been warmed by the sunshine of his Majesty's favour, be satisfied with the mere reflection of that refulgence, through the person of his Majesty's son?'
>
> 'Mashallah! Mashallah! Malcolm is himself again!'

They entered into a long discussion about the organisation of the Indian Army, and what lessons the Persians could learn from it. The Shah spoke with admiration of Bonaparte, asking:

> 'What does he want?'
>
> 'The world'
>
> 'Right,' said the King, 'You are right, Malcolm – but in truth, he is a great soldier'[39]

A few days later, in the confined space in front of the Shah's audience tent, Malcolm exhibited for the Shah the presents which he had brought from India, chiefly the guns, including galloper guns. What particularly caught the Shah's eye, though, was the young artillery officer in charge, Lieutenant Lindsay, nearly seven foot tall, whom the Shah saw as a young Rustum, the great Persian hero.[40]

Meeting again on 24 June, Jones and Malcolm had a nervously amicable discussion. Both were waiting for further news from London. On 28 June Jones left Soltaniyeh to return to Tabriz and, on his way north, at last received news from London, in the form of five letters from the Marquess. The first was a copy of a letter addressed to Mirza Shafee. It supported Jones's actions. The recent embarrassment, it explained, had been caused by misunderstandings resulting from the great distance between London and Calcutta. The British Government had decided henceforth to carry on its diplomatic relations with Persia directly from London, and the King had appointed Sir Gore Ouseley as his Ambassador to the Tehran Court.[41] The second and third, to Jones, acknowledged receipt of all his despatches up to 14 December 1809, and expressed approval of his actions up to that date, both publicly[42] and privately: 'I have received His Majesty's command to inform you that His Majesty has entirely approved your conduct throughout the arduous negotiations in which you have been engaged since your arrival at the Court of Persia.'[43] The fourth stated that Sir Gore Ouseley would shortly sail, and that Mirza Abol Hassan, the Persian Ambassador to Britain, would return with him; and asked Jones to assist him on his arrival at Bushire.[44] The fifth accepted Jones's resignation without comment, merely mentioning that his successor would deliver his letter of recall. Sir Gore's departure date had been postponed to the end of May (in fact he did not leave until the middle of July).

Jones's first reaction must have been a huge sigh of relief. He had known since late January that the Government and the Directors were essentially supporting his defiance of Minto, but he must also have wondered whether this position would be maintained when they came to hear the other side of the story. He must especially have worried about the appointment of the Marquess as Foreign Minister. The Marquess was a known supporter of Malcolm, and when Governor-General had not been particularly impressed by Jones's performance at Baghdad. The news also meant that he was released at last from the need to treat Minto as his putative boss, and Malcolm as his boss's envoy. On the other hand he was miffed that Ouseley was to be given superior diplomatic status to himself – full Ambassador compared to Minister. His future career prospects did not seem all that bright, either. What was he to do after he had been relieved by Ouseley? His resignation letter of the previous November had hinted that he hoped that it would not be accepted. Yet the Marquess had accepted it without comment. He sent on the news to the Shah and to Malcolm, who were still on the road, and met them when they arrived at Oujein, on the open plain south of Tabriz.

When he heard the news, Malcolm realised at once that his own mission was over. It was not the result which he had hoped for, but in a curious way he felt relieved that a clear decision had at last been taken about the lines of authority; also that Harford Jones's days were numbered. He knew of Gore Ouseley by reputation and respected him. Many years before, Ouseley had worked in India, and had recently acted as *mehmandar* to the Persian Ambassador in London, with considerable success. Nevertheless, he felt let down, particularly by the Marquess. It seemed strange that the Marquess had not succeeded, as Foreign Secretary, in getting him appointed as Ambassador. He was not to know the circumstances behind the choice of Ouseley until several months later, when he received a letter from Merrick Shawe, now the Marquess's secretary. Shawe reported that the Marquess had said at the time, 'I have no doubt Malcolm will be angry with me.'[45] He said that if Malcolm had been in England in January 1810, when the appointment was being made, he would have been chosen, regardless of the attitude of the other Ministers or of Leadenhall Street. However, the Persian Ambassador had made plain that the Shah wanted the Britsh emissary to be on the same level as the Ambassador to the Porte. Minto was out of favour at the time, and to heal the wounds of previous dissension between the Government and the Company it was thought right to appoint an entirely new person, known to and paid for by the King. Lord Aberdeen and Lord William Bentinck were approached but were unavailable. Ouseley was strongly recommended by the Persian Ambassador, so he was chosen.[46]

The Shah and Abbas Mirza had hoped to use Malcolm's military experience to advise them in the conduct of the war against the Russians, and were disappointed when he declined, saying that the

Calcutta Government no longer had an official role to play. Also at the back of his mind was the thought that if he stayed he would inevitably be under the thumb of Jones: 'if I remain after my functions have ceased, I become, of course, subject to the orders of Sir Harford, who can, by word or letter, direct me to quit whenever he chooses; and I certainly have not yet confidence sufficient in his character to place myself in such a situation.'[47] He did nevertheless agree to spend a day or two with Abbas Mirza and his army:

> I found him riding alone in front of a line of five thousand new-raised Persian infantry. He received me with great affability, and was delighted with the party of dragoons and gallopers, who exercised and manoeuvred as well as the bad ground we had could permit. He examined the clothing and accoutrements of the Europeans in the most minute manner, and appeared delighted with their equipment. After my review was over, the Prince put his own line of infantry through their firing and some manoeuvring. They had only been raised four months, knew a little of everything, but were evidently grounded in nothing. Abbas Mirza did everything himself, and went everywhere unattended. He was dressed like a soldier, in a plain scarlet coat made in the Persian style, and buttoned tight. After the review was over, the curricle I had brought for the King drove up. He was delighted with it, and in an instant sprang into it. I did the same, and took the reins, and drove off at full trot. His astonishment and delight were equal. Some of his attendants followed. 'You will be tired', said he, 'for I am going to Teheran with Malcolm.' After a short drive I turned round and drove to the front of the troops, where he remounted, and exercised them till dark; he then marched home.[48]

Asked for advice on how to combat the Russians, Malcolm told Abbas Mirza: 'not to attack the Russians in line or in their strong posts, but to keep their newly raised infantry and ill-equipped artillery in reserve, and limit their employment to the defence of forts and difficult passes, whilst they pushed forward every horseman the country could furnish to distress and harass the enemy, whose numbers I understand to be about ten thousand, of which a very small portion were cavalry.'[49] This

Abbas Mirza (1789–1833) was a younger son of Fath Ali Shah but because of his mother's royal descent he was made Prince Royal (Crown Prince) and ruler of Azerbaijan province, based at Tabriz, from 1808.

was a strong echo of Mahratta cavalry tactics against the Company's armies in India. At the insistence of the Shah and Abbas Mirza, and supported by Harford Jones, he agreed to second Christie, Lindsay, and Monteith to Jones's mission as military advisers, and Dr Cormick as physician to Abbas Mirza.

The next day (15 July) Malcolm was back at the Royal Camp at Oujein for his 'audience of leave' with the Shah. As a special mark of favour, the Shah proposed to appoint him a 'Knight of the Sun', a Persian order, as he had done for General Gardane. Malcolm demurred, pointing out that he could not accept a decoration that had been created and first bestowed on a man representing a country with which Britain was at war. Undeterred, the Shah created a new order, of the Lion and Sun, and made Malcolm its first recipient. He also sent him a present of a horse and a sword. The mission party was greeted at the entrance to the audience tent with a *farman* appointing Malcolm a Khan and Sepahdar of the Persian Empire. Entering the tent, Malcolm approached the throne, and the Shah invested him with a diamond star, in the centre of which were the Lion and Sun, the insignia of the new order of knighthood: 'You are now confirmed in my service, in which I know you have been faithful for ten years. I can do no higher honor to anyone than at this moment I have done to you. You will wear this star upon your breast as a proof to all the world of the royal favour of the King of Persia.' Malcolm bowed, thanked the Shah and withdrew. As he made his last salaam, Fath Ali cried out 'Farewell, dear Malcolm, my friend!' – an almost unprecedented gesture on such a formal occasion.[50]

CHAPTER TWENTY

Baghdad and Back, 1810

The route home for the main party was through Persian Kurdistan to Kermanshah, then on to Baghdad, down the Tigris to Basra and then by ship to Bombay.

On the morning of 23 July Malcolm and his party left Tabriz. He wrote, sincerely, portentously, in his journal: 'What a happy man I am to-day. It is impossible to look back without congratulating myself on my good fortune at every stage of my late vexatious and unpromising mission. I have now turned my back, and I hope for ever, on deceit, falsehood, and intrigue; and I am bending my willing steps and still more my willing heart towards rectitude, truth and sincerity. I leave all I hate, and am proceeding towards all I love.' He may have been referring to his relationship with Jones, or with Persia generally. Such sentiments have often been felt, less often expressed, over the centuries, by many a Westerner on leaving Persia. Yet it would be a mistake to conclude that those Westerners disliked Persians. They disliked the intrigues and corruption of Persian governments, but over time were usually charmed and seduced by individual Persians, and Malcolm was no exception.

On 31 July the party reached Maragheh, and there was a great reunion of all the disparate parts of the mission: 'Stewart came across the country to join us with Christie and Pottinger, Frederick and Cormick, and we sate down, fourteen, to breakfast. All the party, except Stewart, were in Persian clothes and had beards as well as whiskers. I should hardly have known any of them, unless I had been prepared for their arrival. Christie and Pottinger have gone through most arduous duties, and have suffered great fatigue and hardship. Their labours will be of benefit to the public service, and, I trust, to themselves. Men who voluntarily encounter such dangers should be well rewarded.' The next day they 'spent a very idle day, eating trout, and talking over wonderful travels. Christie had some capital stories to tell'.

The party was now in the process of breaking up. Charles Pasley had already gone back sick to Bombay from Bushire in late May 1810. Mackintosh wrote at the time, 'He looks very ill, and has come here on his way to England';[1] and later, when Pasley eventually sailed in late January 1811, 'considering the state to which the hookah and beer have reduced him, it will be well if he reaches England alive'.[2] Lindsay, Christie and Monteith were seconded to Abbas Mirza's Persian army in north-western Persia. Macdonald was sent overland to England with despatches. He was robbed in Turkey, and lost the despatches, but when he reached England he was able to report in person on the Persian situation to the main players – to Marquess Wellesley at the Foreign Office, to Robert Dundas at the Board of Control, and to several Directors of the Company. He also sent feedback to Malcolm in Bombay.

The rest of the party stayed at Kermanshah for ten days, and Malcolm was entertained by the Governor, another prince of royal (Qajar) blood. After seven months of stress in Persia, he badly needed a

Claudius James Rich (1787–1821) was the British Resident at Baghdad from 1808 to 1821.

change of scene. The party now crossed the border and made for Baghdad, which they reached on 20 September.

Claudius Rich, the British Resident at Baghdad, with whom Malcolm and his party stayed, was a larger than life figure. Born the illegitimate son of Sir James Cockburn, an Irish baronet, he was brought up in Ireland and Bristol, and became a brilliant linguist. By the age of nine he had learned Latin, Greek and Arabic, by fourteen Chinese, and by fifteen Hebrew, Syriac, Persian and Turkish. At sixteen he obtained a writership in the East India Company, but it took him more than three years to get to India. Shipwrecked in the Mediterranean, he spent three months at Naples, some weeks in Malta, and fifteen months in Constantinople. In May 1806 he sailed on to Alexandria, where he stayed with the British Consul. In early 1807 he set out overland via Syria, Mosul, Baghdad and Basra, arriving at Bombay in September 1807. He stayed with Sir James Mackintosh, to whom he had been introduced in London in 1804. When Mackintosh and his wife went on a cruise to Ceylon in October and November 1807, Rich was left in Bombay with Mackintosh's two grown-up daughters. Mackintosh described what happened next: 'When I went to Malabar, I left him [Rich] at the house of my philosophical friend Erskine, busily engaged with the 'Philosophy of the Human Mind'. On my return I found that this pupil in philosophy was desirous to become my son-in-law. He has no fortune, nor had he then even an appointment; but you will not doubt that I willingly consented to his marriage with my eldest daughter, in whom he had the sagacity to discover, and the virtue to value, the plain sense, modesty, purity and good nature, which will, I hope, make her a source of happiness to him during life.'[3]

They were married at St Thomas's Church in Bombay, followed by a picnic at Malabar Point. Soon afterwards Rich was appointed Resident at Baghdad, aged twenty.

Rich welcomed Malcolm and his party at his summer residence at Garara on the Tigris, three miles south of Baghdad. He had been in his job two and a half years, but was still only twenty-three years old. Malcolm felt 'as if all my troubles were over. I shall here part with all my incumbrances, and sail peacefully down the river. Mr Rich's hospitality is not to be appeased by anything short of living with him while in Baghdad. Twelve hungry men must be a terrible infliction, I told Mrs Rich.'[4] Mary Rich, who was twenty-one, wrote regular letters to her

Bombay-based younger sister Maitland, who had married William Erskine,[5] and had just produced a daughter.

Mary's letters were full of sisterly gossip, but also contained some acute observations about Malcolm during his stay at Baghdad:

> 21 September
> We had the pleasure of welcoming the Genl here yesterday morning, and the moment he saw me, he declared he should have known me for the likeness *between us all*. We are become already very great friends and talking constantly of you, who are a wonderful favourite. He asked me if Erskine and my father were upon good terms again . . . It is impossible to express to you the opinion he entertains of your husband [Erskine], you may be sure it gave us great pleasure to hear justice done to him by one so capable of judging, and whose ideas on that subject so well accord with our own.
>
> I think I never saw one man regard another with such marked love and even reverence as the Genl does my father. He appears to have made it a study to imitate him in all his peculiarities, such as his manner of reading (which by the bye he fails in), his manner of telling a story, of talking, of *eating nuts*, sitting, walking, in short it is impossible to avoid perceiving it, & I was struck the very first day I saw him. He gave me this evening a copy of some lines of his composed at Persepolis on his little girl's birthday, which I desire you to ask him for. *Entre nous* our friend has his good share of *vanity*.
>
> 26 September
> The General talks a good deal to me about the publication my father has lately sent home for him.[6] He says it is all the work of R Smith of Calcutta and my father, and that he shall never be forgiven *at home*! At the same time he evidently demonstrates how proud he feels at the idea of being attacked. He is really a most excellent warm hearted man and a very great favourite of mine, though I find him occasionally rather too boisterous, or to speak more correctly there is too *much* of the boisterous in his character, and he is also too fond of engrossing the whole of the conversation to himself. He talks, and

talks well, but will never listen! In which respect he has entirely lost sight of his *master*. He has astonishing spirits and declares that he is quite a rake at Baghdad, as in Persia he seldom if ever touched wine, and last night, when the servant was pouring him out a glass of port, cried out in *his* voice, fill it up you gee, I am going to get drunk!

28 September
I had a long conversation with your friend Johnny [Johnny Little] . . . He told us Dr Leyden's [John Leyden's] opinion of your husband, which is so true I cannot help giving it. 'There's that fellow Erskine with so much sense and learning if it were not for his d—d modesty, no one would stand before him!' . . . Everyone talks to me of you being so much bustier than I am, but I am the tallest!

4 October
It is impossible to be gayer and merrier than we are at present. Horse racing and *gaming* are quite the fashion amongst us. I say *us* – for you must know I attend the racecourse in the morning and play whist in the evening, and if we had but two or three ladies we would undoubtedly have a dance, which would astonish the weak minds of our friends the Turks, make them stroke their beards . . .

9 October
General Malcolm leaves us to-morrow . . . [he] means to send us up his opinion of Miss Erskine[7] which he says will be the exact one, not dictated by partiality. So if he presumes to differ from you I will inform you and then you must attack him. I never saw any man fonder of his family – he is constantly talking to me of Charlotte and Maggy.[8]

Rich himself also admired Malcolm's force of character, good nature and warmth of heart. But, possibly as a young man in a big job taking himself rather seriously, he claimed to be offended by Malcolm's dispensing with the formality which he had observed towards Harford Jones during his visit to Baghdad in 1801. Malcolm was just as impressed by Claudius and Mary Rich as they were by him.[9]

Johnny Little also wrote to his mother at Langholm:

> in two days we sail down the Tigris to Bussorah [Basra]. From thence we embark for Bombay, and from thence to what part of the world I may be ordered, God knows . . . We are here only a night's ride from Babylon, which I am sorry to say we cannot visit owing to the present unsettled state of the country – as the Pacha has rebelled from the Porte and the two armies are encamped only four hours' march from us, and parties of plundering Arabs are scouring the country in every direction. We however are as safe as we could possibly be at Langholm Bridgend. Both parties wish to conciliate the good opinion of the General, and the plundering parties are too much afraid of our party of Dragoons and Sepoys to venture on our side of the river . . .
>
> The Tigris is a delightful river, and inferior only to the Esk. It is ten times as large, but wants its clearness and the fine scenery on its banks. Here on each side nothing presents itself to the eye but the barren desert; however I am told when it is joined by the Euphrates near Bussorah the scene changes and the banks are covered with trees and verdure . . .
>
> The General remains as he has always been, the kindest and best of friends. Since I have belonged to his family I have done little else but laugh. If I were condemned to cry as much, I should for the time to come have a miserable life.[10]

Malcolm used his leisure time to write an immense (82-paragraph) report to Minto on his mission to Persia. Completing it on 29 September, he turned with enthusiasm to recreation. The Residency was lucky to have Malcolm and his escort on hand during this period. The 'unrest' to which both Mary Rich and Johnny Little referred was dramatic. At the time of Malcolm's visit, the Turkish Pasha of the Baghdad *pashalik* had been in rebellion against the Sultan in Constantinople, who had sent an army under the *Reis Effendi* (a post in the Ottoman Empire equivalent to Foreign Minister) to remove him. The forces met outside Baghdad on 7 October. The Pasha was defeated and fled, but 'was stopt by a party of thieving Arabs . . . about twenty miles from the town, and beheaded; the murderers have taken his head to the Reis Effendi in the hope of a reward'.[11] With the government preoccupied by the civil war, bandits flourished. On one occasion 'a party of Arabs . . . seized one of the chief people of the Residency, stripped him, and plundered five hundred piastres of public money. Malcolm instantly ordered his escort in pursuit of the robbers, who were mounted; and soon his troopers were in hot chase after the Arabs . . . he took horse himself, called on the gentlemen of his family to follow him, and joined eagerly in the chase. After a hard gallop of some ten miles, they captured four or five of the robbers (including one of their leaders), as many horses and ponies, some firearms, and some plundered property.'[12] Not surprisingly, this vigorous reaction had the desired effect; the Residency was not troubled again.

By 10 October the situation had calmed down sufficiently for Malcolm to feel able to let the Residency look after itself. Frederick was left at Baghdad for a few months with some troopers to protect it until the situation returned to normal. The depleted party boarded the Residency yacht and sailed down the Tigris to Basra.

Arriving at Basra on 25 October, Malcolm was entertained by Samuel Manesty at his country house, just as he had been in 1801.[13] Earlier in the year Manesty had been controversially dismissed, and was about to go back to England in disgrace. Two years later he committed suicide. Pottinger was left at Basra, returning to Bombay several months later. The rest of the party boarded the *Ternate* and sailed on 29 October. They stopped for two days at Bushire, enabling Malcolm to inspect the stud of Arab horses which he had set up some years before.

Josiah Stewart was waiting for him at Bushire with a crop of potatoes, having travelled overland via Isfahan and Shiraz. In 1800 Malcolm had noticed that there appeared to be no potatoes in Persia. Thinking this a pity, he brought thirty sacks of seed potatoes with him on the 1810 mission, and planted them at Shiraz on his way north. Now, six months later, 'I was much gratified by receiving from Stewart a dish of excellent potatoes, which he had brought from Shiraz.' He went on to claim that 'I desire the good fame of introducing potatoes to Persia, and look to immortality in the name they have received in that country – "alou-Malcolmeah" [Malcolm's plum].'[14]

This episode was yet again to feature the malevolent ghost of Harford Jones. Twenty-four years later, when Malcolm was safely dead,

Jones challenged Malcolm's claim to have brought potatoes to Persia. In his memoirs he wrote: 'In 1783 I ate potatoes at Bushire at the table of Mr Galley, our then Resident there, who had planted them in the old Dutch garden . . . Long before Sir John Malcolm visited Persia I gave roots of this plant to several Persians.' But apparently they had not liked them: 'When I told [Mirza Bezorg] that potatoes were to us what rice was to the Persians, he playfully tapped me on the back, and said: "You see, God Almighty provides the greatest of all delicacies, and the wholesomest of all food [rice], for the faithful, and leaves you what is fit only for badgers, porcupines and squirrels".'[15] But Malcolm may have had the last word on this. In his 1810 journal (which Jones would not have seen) he wrote:

> in the midst of my labours I was alarmed by a report that they had a vegetable at Ispahan called the 'alou-e-zumeen', which was immediately translated 'pomme de terre', and the merit of introducing this plant was readily given to the French, who had bestowed this benefit on the Persians a hundred years ago; but that ignorant and prejudiced race had since rejected the 'pomme de terre' and treated it as a common weed. These fine conjectures continued in full strength till we reached Ispahan. There, when breakfasting with Hadjee Ibrahim, we sent for the 'alou-e-zumeen', and found it not unlike the potato in form, but no resemblance in taste, being a bitter, useless root.[16]

As the *Ternante* sailed towards Bombay. Malcolm's main activity was to write a 380-line poem for Charlotte, entitled 'Persia', in full Augustan style, beginning:

> From verdant Isles, that near th' Equator glow,
> To where bright Asia's robe is fringed with snow

. . . and so on; though occasionally it comes across quite well:

> Ne'er on that land has freedom shed one ray
> By fate decreed to feel tyrannic sway
> When cruel power provokes th'avenging sword
> The slaves but seek to raise another lord.

More impressive than the poem itself were the twelve pages of notes which followed, demonstrating Malcolm's already deep knowledge of Persian history and poetry.

The *Ternante* finally docked at Bombay on 19 November. Malcolm had been away just over ten months.

From the web of intrigue and diplomacy woven around Persia between 1807 to 1811, what conclusions can be drawn? Why did it happen? Whom to praise? Whom to blame? How did Malcolm come out of it?

For the Shah and the *Persian Government*, it was not a happy period. In their resistance to Russian aggression they had sought help, first from the British, then from the French, then again from the British. They were let down by both; the French simply abandoned them, and the British blew hot and cold at different times, according to their own interests, in both Europe and India. They were encouraged by the British to resist the Russians in 1810–1811, then counselled to make peace in 1812–1813, and so on.

Napoleon's interest in Persia was purely tactical; he wished to use Persia to intimidate, by turns, Russia and Britain. His rapid changes in policy made diplomatic defeat in Persia more or less inevitable. But defeat does not seem to have worried him. And despite his abandonment of the Persians at a crucial point in their war with Russia, they seem to have forgiven him; he remained a hero to them for opposing the Russians and the British.

The British Government may in the end have defeated the French, but no one could describe the events of 1807–1811 as a triumph for British diplomacy. Going back to early 1807, it had stored up trouble for itself by setting up a defective reporting structure. It was understandable that it should appoint an envoy to Persia with credentials from the Crown, to give him more prestige than an envoy from the Governor-General. But in the process it made three crucial decisions which turned out to be mistaken. First, to allow the envoy to operate independently of the Governor-General (or at least to give Sir Harford Jones that impression), yet have the right to make commitments on the Calcutta Government's behalf. With this arrangement the Calcutta Government was bound to be worried about the envoy involving it in commitments which were inimical to its perceived political, commercial and financial interests. It was partly this fear which prompted Minto to appoint a rival envoy from India. Second, to fail to rethink British diplomatic strategy after the Treaty of Tilsit had so completely altered the circumstances, with Persia no longer a factor in the struggle against Napoleon in Europe and reverting to being a factor only in the defence of British India. And third, to appoint Sir Harford Jones as envoy. We will come back to that later.

In assessing *Minto*'s part in the whole affair, it is difficult not to be sympathetic with his predicament. He was not consulted by London, as he had every right to be, about the basis of Jones's mission, nor was he given clear authority to control Jones's actions. He was on the end of a long and slow chain of communications. Despite this, his analysis of the unfolding situation was generally perceptive. It was his decisions and actions which merit criticism. He should have clarified whether Jones was properly accountable to him or not, long before Jones set off for Persia in September 1808. The ticking off of Jones was justified; he should certainly have waited longer at Bombay for a reaction from Calcutta – but Minto's later order that Jones should leave Persia was plain silly, even based on the out-of-date (and subsequently proven erroneous) intelligence that Minto had at his disposal. A more self-confident man would not have worried so much that his authority was apparently being challenged; he would have accepted that events had overtaken his previous order, and that in the new circumstances Jones had done the right thing. He was rightly furious with Jones for lowering the dignity and prestige of the Calcutta Government with the Persian Court, but to some extent Minto's actions created the very situation which provoked Jones into doing so. In particular, his 'protesting' of Jones's *suftees*, thereby putting Jones personally at risk of being held hostage, was inexcusable. It was the reaction of a headquarters man to bad news from the front – blame the messenger.

The main criticism of *Malcolm* was his decision to set off from Bombay in April 1808, when he must have known that Jones was about to arrive there. Malcolm could hardly be blamed for not liking Jones, nor for being mortified by Jones's selection as envoy to Persia. His attempted character assassination of Jones – to Minto, to the Wellesleys and to other influential people – was unattractive. But the vendetta was kept strictly personal. In Persia, he never allowed himself to publicly belittle Jones or the British Government in London. Nevertheless, in setting off from Bombay when he did, he allowed his emotions to cloud his judgement. The sensible approach would have been to wait in

Bombay for Jones's arrival, compare notes with him, and prepare and submit for approval by the Governor-General an agreed plan of action, before either of them set off for Persia.

Malcolm has also come in for criticism for his approach to the Persian Court after his arrival at Bushire in May 1808. His 'Declaration to the Shah's Ministers'[17] demanded, among other things, that the French envoy should be expelled before the British envoy arrived in Tehran. Historians have variously alleged that 'his high handed tone' irritated the Persians, and have accused him of 'losing his temper', of 'impatience', and of 'mishandling the situation'. These observations ignore two relevant facts; firstly, that the tone of Malcolm's 'Declaration' did not affect the Persian Government's decision not to allow him to come to Tehran. For, unknown to Malcolm, the decision had already been made, and requisite instructions had already been sent to Shiraz some time before it received his allegedly offensive 'Declaration'. Secondly, his actions were not thought up on the spur of the moment. The strategy was cleared with Minto several months in advance. His assessment of the Persian character and negotiating technique led him to believe that a 'softly, softly' approach would not work, and that only a 'decided and firm' approach at the outset, followed by flexibility in later 'treating', would have any chance of succeeding. He realised that he was playing a very weak hand, and that there was a strong probability of failure. His private letter to Arthur Wellesley in March 1808, when he was travelling by ship from Madras to Bombay before setting out for Persia, bears out this point.[18]

Malcolm was certainly very unlucky with his timing. Nevertheless, with hindsight, his precipitate withdrawal from Bushire showed a want of judgment. If he had waited patiently in Bushire for a few more months (as he had done in 1800), the situation would have changed in Britain's favour, and he could have reaped the reward which instead went to Jones. On the other hand, during his third mission in 1810, Malcolm handled his difficult diplomatic situation with considerable firmness and propriety. In his letter to the Persian Ministers of 9 April 1810, he explained the background to the apparent differences between London and Calcutta without criticising either of them. Jones could and should have done the same, but chose not to.

This brings us back to *Sir Harford Jones*. Jones's early behaviour while waiting at Bombay in 1808 was impeccable. He very properly agreed to wait there until the outcome of Malcolm's mission became known. But Minto's letter of 12 August 1808 was so loosely worded that it gave him a pretext for setting off for Persia before this happened. Nevertheless, common sense should still have led him to postpone his departure from Bombay until he received news of Minto's reaction to Malcolm's report, particularly since it must have been clear that Malcolm's mission had been unsuccessful. Plans could then have been concerted for the Jones mission. The fact that such plans might well have been wrong ones is irrelevant. Jones's hasty departure was almost certainly made to *avoid* receiving Minto's instructions, and was every bit as irresponsible as Malcolm's earlier departure to avoid meeting Jones.

The timing of Jones's arrival at Bushire in October 1808 was as lucky for him as it had been unlucky for Malcolm in May, for by this time the Persian Government had definitely decided to deal with the British rather than the French. The fact was that the Persians urgently wanted to make a treaty, and Jones had little negotiating to do. And, ironically, Malcolm's 'bad cop' approach in May/June may actually have helped Jones to act as 'good cop' in later negotiations. Not that this implies any particular credit on Malcolm, or lack of competence or shrewdness in Jones – he had both in full measure.

The ill-defined reporting structure put together by Canning and Dundas in 1807 only reinforced the desirability of choosing an envoy who could be entrusted with the delicate diplomatic mission of trying simultaneously to please the Persian Government, the British Government, the Directors of the East India Company in Leadenhall Street and the Governor-General in Calcutta. Whatever his undoubted talents, Jones was the last man who should have been given this role. He lacked neither intelligence nor vision. He had twenty-five years' experience of the Middle Eastern region, and he was a highly competent scholar in Arabic and Persian. But he was a loner, and unpopular with most of his peers in India (not merely the 'Malcolm' faction). If one looks at his whole career, it is clear that he was the sort of person who in the end fell out with just about everyone with whom he came into prolonged contact. It is not hard to see why. He had the sort of personality which can be crudely described as 'all lick up, all kick down'. While in Baghdad he seems to have got on the wrong side of Jonathan Duncan (Governor of Bombay 1794–1811), the most amiable of men. He also upset the Turkish Pasha of Baghdad, who did all he could to get rid of him. This was allegedly due to Manesty, telling tales against him. But why did Manesty hate him so? He managed to enrage the normally urbane Minto. His vindictive and childish behaviour towards Malcolm in 1810 has already been described at length. By mid-1811 his successor, Ouseley, was sending home virulently hostile letters about him. When Jones arrived back in England, he was cordially received by Wellesley as Foreign Secretary, but he was never given another job by the Government or the Company for the rest of his life. Whether this cold shouldering of Jones was fair or not is beside the point. What emerges from the foregoing is that Jones had a continuing capacity to put peoples' backs up, the very last trait required in a British envoy to Persia in 1808–10.

Back for a last word on *Malcolm*. Imagine for a moment that the British Government had appointed an envoy to Persia in 1808 who was working to orders from London but who was accountable to the Crown via the Governor-General; who had the full confidence of the Governor-General and was likely to get on well with the Shah. Can one imagine that the same mistakes would have been made? And who would have been the best candidate for such a delicate diplomatic role? In hindsight, there was one obvious choice.

And finally, the *Tsar and the Russians*. While the other players in the diplomatic game moved back and forth and achieved very little, the Russians steadily extended their territory at very little cost. As Alfred de Gardane, who had accompanied his brother General Gardane on his mission to Tehran, observed: 'Who, then, gained from the withdrawal of France from Persia? Russia alone.'[19] Perhaps Sir James Mackintosh most aptly summed up this whole episode, and Malcolm's part in it: 'Malcolm's introduction of potatoes to Persia will be remembered long after the ridiculous Persian Missions are forgotten.'[20]

CHAPTER TWENTY-ONE

Persian Postscript, 1811–1833

After 1810 Malcolm held no formal post relating to Persia but he was generally considered to be an expert on the subject – he certainly thought so himself – and the publication of *The History of Persia* in 1815 kept him in close touch with the major players, historians and savants.

In the context of British rivalry with Russia in Asia (the 'Great Game'), there were two schools of thought about British relations with Persia. The so-called Bombay school, of which Malcolm was the most prominent advocate, saw Persia as a bulwark against Russian imperial expansion southwards and eastwards towards India. It was therefore thought necessary to support Persia with money and arms to resist the Russians. The other school (later termed the 'Ludhiana' or Punjab school) felt that supporting Persia was a lost cause; it would be more advantageous to defend British India by striking up an alliance with the Afghans; and/or with Ranjit Singh's Sikh kingdom in the Punjab. The weakness of the 'Bombay' strategy was that it involved spending a great deal of money, probably for little perceptible effect on Persia's will or ability to resist the Russians. On the other hand, the 'Punjab' strategy risked allowing Persia to become a virtual Russian protectorate. Also, as subsequent history has amply demonstrated, it would prove almost impossible to make any long-term alliance with an Afghan government.

The logic behind the British Government's decision in 1810 to deal with Persia directly from London rather than through the Governor-General in India was that in the war against Napoleon, Persia had become a pawn of European politics as well as of British India. But with the downfall of Napoleon and the return of peace to Europe, the European threat no longer applied. Early in 1823 George Canning, newly appointed as Foreign Secretary, decided that responsibility for relations with Persia should revert to the East India Company. He was concerned that a direct alliance between the British and Persian governments would greatly complicate Britain's relationship with Russia, which he understandably saw as Britain's most important strategic relationship in European politics. He accordingly wanted the relationship with Persia to be 'wholly Indian, and get rid of credentials from the Crown and correspondence with England altogether'.[1] He was also aware that relations with Persia had recently become rather strained. By the Treaty of Gulestan in 1813, the British had agreed to pay an annual subsidy to help the Persian Government to resist invasion from 'a European power' (in practice Russia). But there were several strings attached, and the British became quite adept (in Persian eyes) at avoiding their obligations. In fact, in 1822 the resident British Minister, Captain Henry Willock, had fled Tehran when threatened with execution unless the arrears of 'subsidy' were paid. Canning thought he could transfer responsibility to Calcutta most smoothly by appointing a 'heavyweight' diplomat to occupy the post during the transition period. His eye fell on Malcolm, his friend and obviously a first-class candidate.

Malcolm, in England at the time, was duly approached. With typical bravado he immediately accepted, writing shortly afterwards to Canning that 'I could not hesitate, for one moment, as to the course which it became me to take. I have therefore, without hesitation or stipulation, informed the Chairman that what remains of me is at the disposal of the Government of my country and the East India Company.'[2] He entirely agreed with the proposition that responsibility should be transferred to the Company which 'must be best able to judge how far our interests in the East (the only interests that can give us any concern with Persia) are affected by the measures that have been or may be adopted by that country. The proximity of the Indian Government is a great advantage, and so is that knowledge which it possesses of Asiatic forms and usages. But above all, it alone can command at all moments competent instruments to employ and furnish them with adequate means to meet cases of emergency.'[3] But he then proceeded to insert a very specific condition to his acceptance – that he should be regarded in Tehran as the representative of the Crown as well as of the Company, 'for . . . the impression given to the Persians must be that the

Crown and the Company are one and the same thing as to interests, and that the representation of both is vested in me'.[4] This was sensible, especially as Malcolm made clear that he did not need to have a direct line to London, as Sir Harford Jones had had in 1808–1811. Nevertheless, Canning refused to budge. He was determined that the Persian relationship should be run from Calcutta alone, fearing that any hint of a connection with the Crown would lead to the British Government in London becoming embroiled in Persian politics. But Malcolm was equally firm in refusing the appointment on Canning's terms.

As Malcolm had foreseen, Canning's strategy of pretending that responsibility for the Persian mission had passed from London to Calcutta offended the Shah, who at first refused to accept the new arrangement, telling John McNeil, an official at the embassy, that 'he had ridden an elephant too long to submit to their setting me to ride a Jackass'.[5] And it had confused and delayed the process of decision making. As Sir Gore Ouseley, Ambassador from 1811 to 1815, later put it, 'the experiment of transferring Persian relations back to Asia and the attempt to put an end to the relations of Persia with Europe have been tried and have failed'.[6]

In the spring of 1826, the British Government sent the Duke of Wellington on a diplomatic mission to St Petersburg. Malcolm had briefed him earlier about the history of Britain's relations with Russia over Persia. He wrote that 'the progress of our political intercourse with Persia has been unfortunate'. His own mission in 1800 had been 'chiefly directed to the object of making a favourable impression of the English nation, which in such a country was deemed . . . of more consequence than any treaty that could be concluded'. Since then:

> the mission of Sir Harford Jones, his disobedience to the Indian government, the measure they took to support their character by sending another representative to Persia, the large pecuniary subsidy granted to the King of that country [the Shah], the deputation of a Persian envoy to England, the appointment of Sir Gore Ouseley as Embassador, his mediation of a treaty between Russia and Persia, his written promise to intercede with the Emperor Alexander for a mitigation of the terms, and the disappointment of the King [of Persia] at his want of success, the negotiation entrusted to Mr Morier and Mr Ellis to modify the

> treaty negotiated by Sir Gore Ouseley, the encouragement given to the formation of a regular army, and the subsequent act of withdrawing almost all of the officers, the protracting beyond the period fixed for the payment of the subsidy, the deputation to the court of Tehran of successive envoys from the King [of England], and then insisting upon all future communications being made through a representative exclusively accredited to the Governor-General of India, whom the King of Persia had for years been taught to consider as a subordinate authority; from a series of measures so contradictory to each other that whatever may be the value of any one of them, they could, as a whole, have no effect but that of conveying impressions adverse to our interests, injurious to our reputation, and destructive to that confidence and reliance which the Persian government was once disposed to place in the English government.[7]

In short, a thorough diplomatic shambles!

Canning, however, was still determined not to become involved, quibbling in a letter to Wellington about whether the wording of the 1813 Treaty (as amended) obliged Britain to come to Persia's aid. When the Duke passed on Canning's letter for Malcolm to read, in confidence, his reply demonstrated once again his understanding of diplomacy with Asian countries.

> Mr Canning appears to me . . . most anxious to shake off Persia. In point of policy I believe him to be wrong; but supposing him to be right, he must take care that he does not, by injuring our reputation for good faith (no matter how or wherefore this faith was pledged) destroy that strength on which we must trust for every stand we may hereafter have to make, from the banks of the Araxes to those of the Ganges, against the encroachments of Russia. And with respect to all questions of faith, as connected with Asiatic states, we must decide them according to their understanding of them when the obligation was contracted. Better for our character to break a treaty at once than to fritter it away with nice distinctions drawn from Puffendorf, Grotius and Vattel, familiar to our diplomatists, but unintelligible to Courts like that of Teheran. Such a proceeding

> would add to the belief of our bad faith an impression of our art and meanness![8]

Following his refusal to accept the post of envoy to Persia for himself, Malcolm successfully persuaded the Governor-General, Lord Amherst, to appoint his brother-in-law John Macdonald, then Town Major in Madras. Macdonald had excellent credentials – he had accompanied Malcolm on his 1808 and 1810 Persian missions, had later travelled through the Caucasus and Persia and had written two relevant books, *A Gazetteer of Persia* in 1813 and *Travels in Asia Minor* in 1818. Moreover, Persian relations with Russia were heavily military in character and Macdonald's training as a soldier gave him an evident advantage over a civilian candidate.

Shortly after Macdonald's eventual arrival at Tehran in September 1826, reports came through of an insurrection within the Caucasian territories occupied by Russia. Abbas Mirza, still the Heir Apparent and commander of the Persian army in Azerbaijan, was unable to resist the temptation to take advantage of these Russian difficulties. He invaded Russian territory and succeeded in getting the Khans of Lenkoran, Kuba and Baku to switch sides. He also massacred a Russian force which had encroached into Persian territory. He thus gave the Russians a *casus belli* which later inevitably resulted in war. The Russians fought back, and by late 1827 had retaken the whole of what is today the territory of Armenia and Azerbaijan and even reached as far south as Tabriz. The Persians were in a state of panic. Macdonald offered his services as a mediator, and was able to persuade the Persian Government to sign the Treaty of Turkmanchai in February 1828, on humiliating terms. The Russians remained, for the time being, in possession of the conquered regions, which enabled them to invade the Ottoman Empire in eastern Turkey. A further disaster for Persian diplomacy occurred in February 1829 when Aleksandr Griboyedov, the distinguished Russian envoy in Tehran, was murdered. He had given sanctuary at the embassy to a Georgian eunuch and two Armenian (Christian) females who had escaped from a courtier's harem. The Shah demanded that they be given up but Griboyedov, knowing what would happen to them if he did, bravely refused, whereupon a Persian mob stormed the embassy and massacred Griboyedov and all his staff as well as the three Armenians. It took a huge effort from Macdonald to prevent hostilities starting up again.

At the time of Malcolm's arrival at Bombay as Governor in November 1827, responsibility for managing relations with Persia lay once more with the Governor-General in Calcutta. But for day-to-day administration, the Persian mission reported to the Bombay Government, so Malcolm had a legitimate excuse to become involved in the Persian mission. And it was hardly likely that such a self-appointed expert on Anglo-Persian affairs would remain satisfied with approving expense claims from Tehran-based staff; still less so in view of the fact that the envoy was his brother-in-law John Macdonald, who had got the job largely through Malcolm's lobbying of the Governor-General four years earlier. Malcolm has been accused of nepotism, of 'packing' the Persian mission with his family.[9] It is true that Benjamin Shee, his brother Pulteney's illegitimate son, occupied a junior position in the Tehran mission, and John Campbell, whose mother was a Pasley, later became an unsatisfactory Head of Mission. But Campbell owed his inappropriate promotion less to Malcolm than to the fact that his father was Sir Robert Campbell, Chairman of the Court of Directors at that time.

From the day of his arrival at Bombay, Malcolm championed Macdonald's cause as envoy, first with the Governor-General in Calcutta and later with Lord Ellenborough at the Board of Control. He knew that there was an anti-Macdonald faction in the Calcutta Secretariat (in 1824 they had advocated the appointment as envoy to Persia of one of their number, a Mr Prinsep) and he felt the need to counteract this, perhaps too much so. 'Macdonald is my connection and I am proud of it, but it is not favour but justice I seek for him.'[10] But there was also a deeper reason for supporting Macdonald. He was a firm adherent of Malcolm's strategy of energetic support to Persia in resisting the Russians as opposed to Canning's strategy of disengagement, which had not worked. Despite the mission being ostensibly under Calcutta's control, Bentinck was understandably reluctant to take decisions without consulting London; and even after Canning's death in August 1827, the British Government continued to take all the strategic decisions. Moreover, Ellenborough was more sympathetic to Malcolm's approach than to Canning's.

Adding to these complications, the British mission fell victim to party political and personal rivalries going all the way back to the days of Sir Harford Jones's mission in 1808 to 1811. Henry Willock had first come to Persia as an assistant to Jones and had stayed on to serve Sir

Gore Ouseley. When Ouseley left in 1815, Willock remained in Tehran as a low-key *chargé d'affaires* until Macdonald's arrival in 1826. To Macdonald, Willock was suspect, first because he was a 'Foreign Office' rather than a 'Company' appointee, and second, because, as a former assistant of Jones, he was suspected of being an adherent of the 'Punjab' policy school. The rights and wrongs of the relationship are not clear. To survive for more than ten years as a diplomat in Tehran must have been quite a feat, and years later Willock became not only a director but Chairman of the East India Company, so he must have been a man of some substance. But he also appears to have been a schemer. He went home on leave in 1826 and came back in 1827, knighted as Sir Henry Willock, via St Petersburg. There he met the Tsar and apparently claimed that he was the British Minister in charge of the mission in Tehran and that Macdonald was simply the representative of the Company. This information reached Macdonald via his wife Amelia (Charlotte's sister), who had gone back to Britain from Tabriz via Moscow and St Petersburg in September 1829, and had been received in audience by the Tsarina.[11]

While Amelia may have been biased in favour of her husband, it seems highly unlikely that she would tell anything other than the truth in a private letter to him. It was understandable that Macdonald should not trust Willock, and he recommended that his presence was no longer required. Ellenborough agreed and Willock was duly recalled. Shortly afterwards, in June 1830, Macdonald died in Tabriz (probably from cancer) and Campbell became first his acting, then his substantive, successor. As Bentinck later put it, 'In no part of the world has party work and clan work run higher than in Persia.'[12]

During Malcolm's time as Governor of Bombay (1827–1830), he had one last fling at what Sir Harford Jones called 'his furious passion for the possession of an island in the Gulf'.[13] This was his thirty-year-old dream of acquiring Kharg Island for the Company and converting it into a combined trade mart and military base, replacing Bushire. As he wrote to the Resident at Bushire, 'an insular position would free us from all that mingling in local disputes and policies . . . which is quite impossible for the representative to escape from so long as he is stationed at Abushire . . . [Kharg] neither has nor can have any value to Persia, and in our hands must early become an emporium of trade.'[14] He wrote on the same lines to the Governor-General and convinced him to write, in a minute on Persian affairs to the Court of Directors that 'an insular position and safe harbour for our marine must be of the greatest consequence. I therefore agree in the recommendation of Sir John Malcolm, that the envoy to the court of Tehran should be instructed to take advantage of a favourable opportunity, if it should ever occur, to obtain a grant of this island.'[15] But the Court let the suggestion pass. British troops did temporarily occupy the island in 1838 and again in 1856, but were soon evacuated, the British fearing that the Russians would demand an equivalent base on the Caspian coast.

In the second half of the twentieth century, Kharg was to became one of the world's greatest oil ports. Not for the first time, Malcolm was ahead of his time.

Plate 1 Burnfoot and Douglen farms in the eighteenth century
Beside the river Esk in the Scottish Borders lay the neighbouring farms of Burnfoot and Douglen. The Malcolm family had the *tack* (lease at nominal rental) of Burnfoot, and as a young man George Malcolm would commute each day on horseback from his father's manse at Ewes to and from the Burnfoot farm.

Plate 2 River Esk, near Burnfoot
In 1761 George inherited the Burnfoot farm from his father, and quickly married 'the girl next door', Margaret ('Bonnie Peggy') Pasley, from Craig, the neighbouring farm across the river.

Plate 3 George Malcolm (1729–1803), father of John Malcolm

Plate 4 Margaret ('Bonnie Peggy) Malcolm (1742–1811), mother of John Malcolm

Plate 5 Douglen Cottage

Between 1762 and 1782 'Bonnie Peggy' produced seventeen children. The first eight, including John (the seventh), were born in this Douglen 'longhouse', before the family moved to Burnfoot House c.1770.

Plate 6 Westerkirk Schoolhouse
The seventeen Malcolm children were educated in this one-roomed Westerkirk school.

Plate 7 Fort St George, Madras, from the sea
In 1781, with the help of local grandees, John, aged twelve, obtained a commission in the East India Company's Madras army. He arrived at Madras in April 1783, still only thirteen years old. This was the scene that would have greeted him on arrival.

Right. **Plate 8 Tipu Sultan, Ruler of Mysore, 1782–1799**
During this period Tipu was the main rival to the British in South India

Below. **Plate 9 Lord Cornwallis and the sons of Tipu**
In the third Anglo-Mysore war of 1791–1792 the Company army defeated Tipu. Under the terms of the Peace Treaty Tipu was obliged to hand over two of his sons as hostages, pending payment of an indemnity. This painting shows the Governor-General, Lord Cornwallis, receiving Tipu's two sons.

Malcolm was one of the British officers attending the event, and is allegedly the third officer from the right in the front row. However, the artist was not even in India at the time, and none of the faces (except that of Cornwallis himself) bears much resemblance to the officers concerned.

Plate 10 Richard Wellesley (1760–1842)
In 1798 a new Governor-General, Richard Wellesley, Lord Mornington, later Marquess Wellesley, arrived in India, with ambitious plans for extending the Company's political control across India

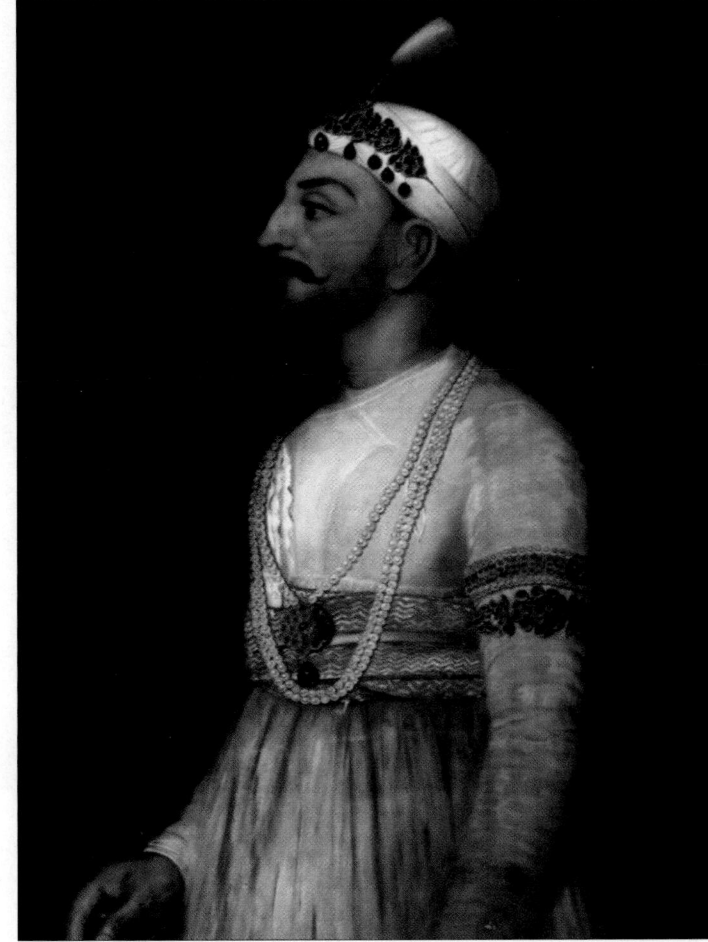

Plate 11 Meer Alam (?1760–1809)
In 1799 the Company again went to war with Tipu Sultan, and was supported by the Mahratta Chiefs and the Nizam of Hyderabad. The Commander of the Nizam's contingent in the allied army was Meer Alam, the Nizam's *vakeel* to the British. Malcolm acted as the Company's liaison officer and military adviser to Meer Alam.

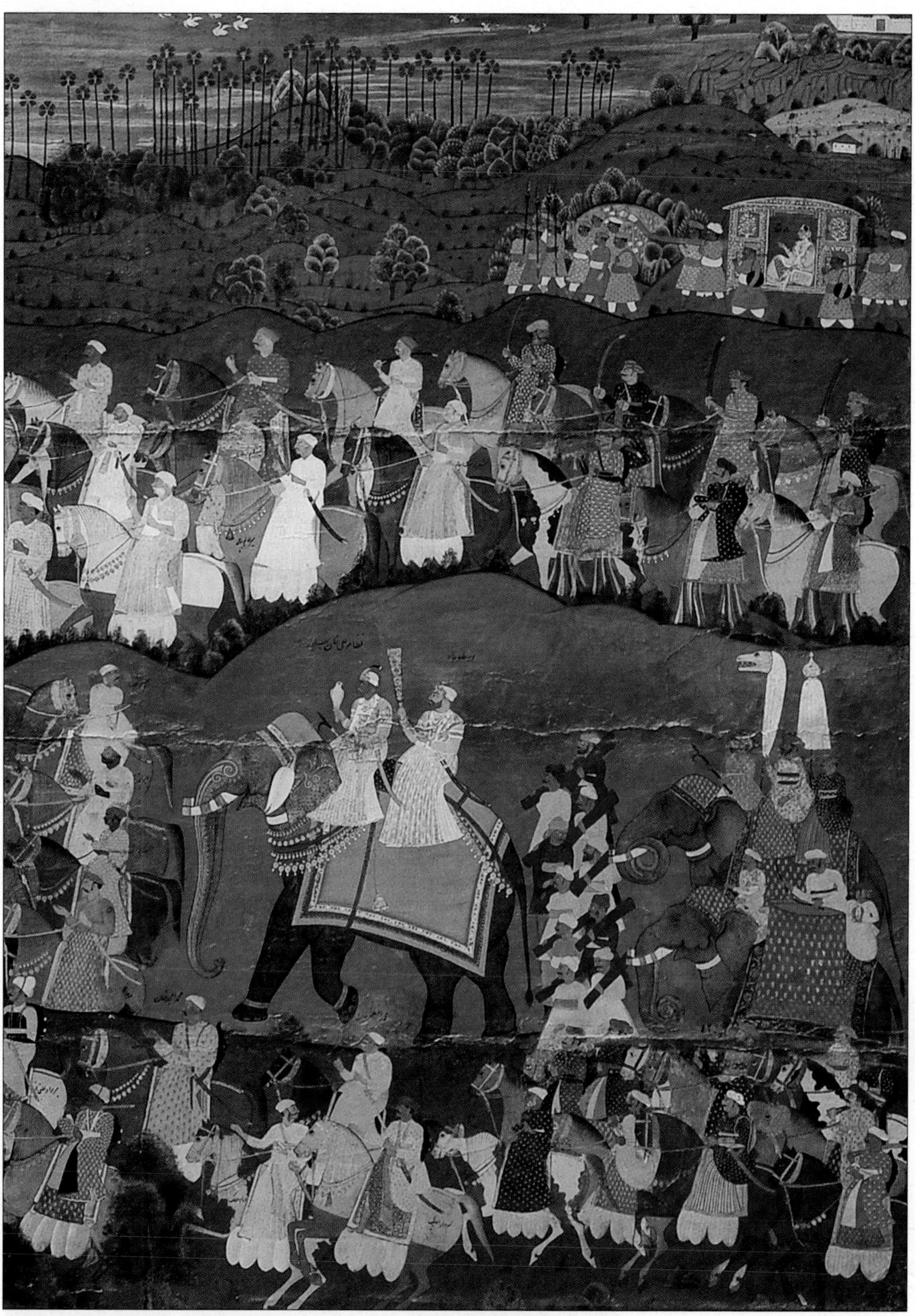

Plate 12 The Nizam and his durbar on a hunting expedition
In the centre of the picture the Nizam is mounted on his elephant, with a hawk on his wrist. Riding behind him is his Chief Minister, Aristu Jah. At the top right in a gilded carriage is the celebrated courtesan and poet, Mah Laqa Bai Chanda.

Plate 13 William Kirkpatrick in Madras, with his assistants and Persian munshis
In late 1799, following the war with Tipu, Malcolm was appointed to lead a diplomatic mission to Persia. His mentor and 'head office' contact was William Kirkpatrick, Military Secretary to the Governor-General.

Plate 14 Persepolis – a contemporary view
In early 1800 Malcolm's Persian mission party landed at Bushire, and reached Shiraz in June. Proceeding north, they stopped at Persepolis to view the ruins of the ancient ceremonial capital of the Achaemenid Empire (c.550–330 BC). At that time the ruins were partially covered by a thick layer of sand.

Above. **Plate 15 Government House Calcutta**
In 1801, on his return from his first Persian mission, Malcolm was appointed Private Secretary to the Governor-General, now Marquess Wellesley. Wellesley was responsible for building this new, magnificent and expensive Government House at Calcutta.

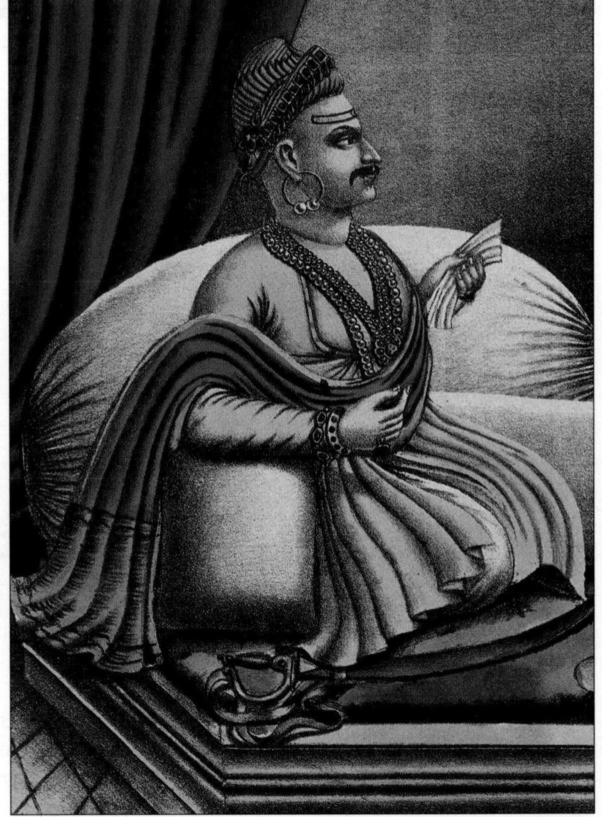

Right. **Plate 16 Baji Rao II, Peshwah of Poona (1775–1851)**
Baji Rao was the Paramount Chieftain of the Mahrattas (though with little control over his subordinate Chieftains, Scindiah and Holkar). Ousted from power by Holkar in late 1802, he signed the Treaty of Bassein with the British, who restored him as Ruler in early 1803. The second Anglo-Mahratta war followed. The Company army was commanded by Sir Arthur Wellesley (later the Duke of Wellington), with Malcolm as the Governor-General's representative and diplomatic agent. Unfortunately Malcolm fell sick, and was unable to participate in Wellesley's great victories at Assaye and Argaum over Scindiah and Raghoji Bhonsle of Berar.

Plate 17 Sir Arthur Wellesley and his favourite charger Diomed
In September 1803, at the battle of Assaye, Wellesley's charger Diomed was shot under him. But four months later, when Malcolm was at Scindiah's camp, he saw the horse at a local horse fair, and immediately bought it. 'The old horse is in sad condition', he wrote to Wellesley, 'but he will be treated like a prince till I have the pleasure of restoring him to you' (see Chapter 12, note 34).

Left. **Plate 18 Dowlat Rao Scindiah (1781–1827)**
In early 1804 Malcolm went to Scindiah's camp and negotiated Treaties of Peace and Defensive Alliance with him.

Below. **Plate 19 Tiger Hunt in India**
The Anglo-Mahratta war dragged on into 1805. By that time both Wellesley brothers had left India. Malcolm was sent to north India to assist General Lake in pursuit of Holkar, who was fleeing towards the Punjab, hoping to form an alliance with the Sikh ruler Ranjit Singh. On one occasion, while Malcolm was negotiating with Ranjit's emissaries, a messenger reported that two large tigers had been seen nearby. Malcolm seized his gun, cried 'Tiger, Tiger', adjourned the meeting and set off in pursuit.

Above. **Plate 20 British Envoys at the Persian Court, 1808–1811.**
In 1807 Malcolm resumed his post as Resident at Mysore, fell in love and married Charlotte Campbell, twenty years younger than him. Later in 1807, a new Governor-General, Lord Minto, decided to send Malcolm to Persia again. This mission was aborted (the British Government in London had sent a rival British mission under Sir Harford Jones). But in 1810 Malcolm was sent to Persia a third time, and clashed with Jones. Eventually, in 1811 a new envoy, Sir Gore Ouseley, was sent from London. This Persian painting purports to show Ouseley, Jones and Malcolm paying court to the Shah. In they attended the Persian Court at different times.

Right. **Plate 21 Lady Charlotte Malcolm and her children in 1815.**
In January 1812 Malcolm returned to Britain with Charlotte and their three children. Two more children were born in the next three years.

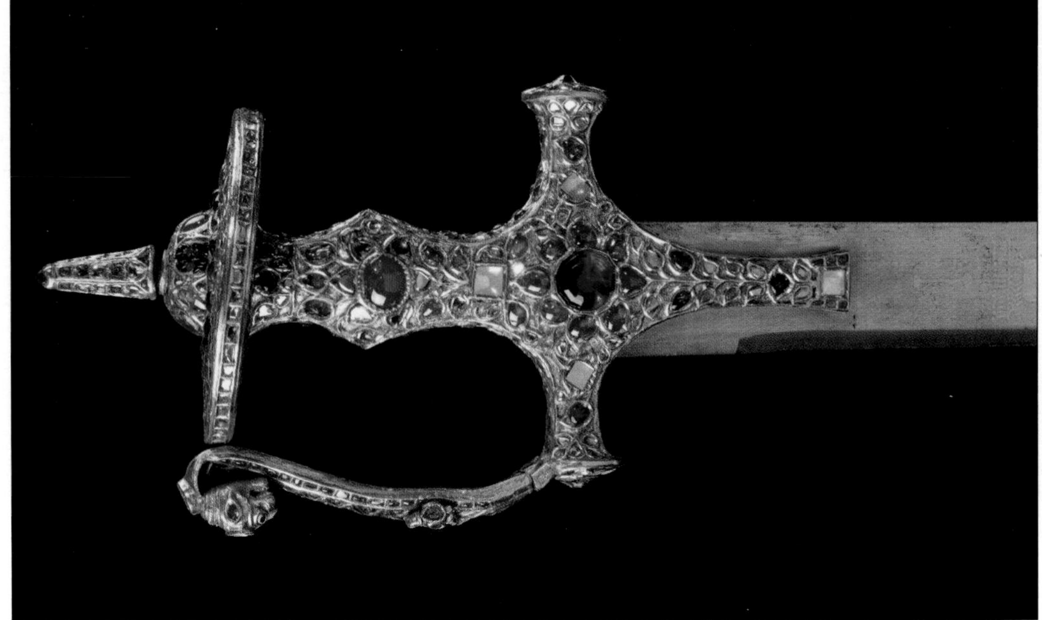

Plate 22 Sword of the Maharajah Holkar
In 1817 Malcolm returned to India (without his family) and served the Governor-General, Marquess Hastings, as his Political Agent and as a General in the Company army fighting the third (and last) Anglo-Mahratta war. In December 1817 the Company army defeated Holkar's forces at the battle of Mehidpoor in Central India. Mysore was allied to the British and the Mysore Horse played a prominent part in the battle, capturing Holkar's ceremonial sword. The Mysore Rajah later presented the sword to Malcolm. In 1888 his last surviving daughter sold the sword to the Victoria and Albert Museum.

Plate 23 The Fortress of Asirgarh
In March 1819 the siege and capture of the fortress of Asirgarh, in which Malcolm played a prominent part, was the final episode in the third Anglo-Mahratta war.

Above. **Plate 24 Nalcha, near Mandu**
From 1818 to 1821 Malcolm acted as the *de facto* ruler of Central India (roughly, today's Madhya Pradesh). He was based at Mhow, south of Indore, but in the heat of the summer he moved to higher ground at Nalcha, near Mandu. Here he stayed in a disused mediaeval building which he termed his 'Summer Palace'.

Right. **Plate 25 Mehmet Ali, Pasha of Egypt (1769–1849)**
In early 1822 Malcolm returned to Britain by the 'overland' route via the Red Sea and Egypt. In Cairo he met Mehmet Ali, an Albanian by birth, who had seized power following the French invasion of 1798, and held it until his death in 1849.

Plate 26 Hyde Hall, Hertfordshire
On Malcolm's return to Britain in 1822, he and Charlotte leased Hyde Hall, near Sawbridgeworth. Here they lived for the next five years.

Plate 27 Malcolm's meeting with Sahajanand Swami
In 1827 Malcolm was appointed Governor of Bombay, covering much of western India, and served there for three years. In February 1830 he visited Gujerat and met a Hindu holy man, Sahajanand Swami, the founder of the Swaminarayan sect of Hinduism. The painting depicts the Swami presenting Malcolm with the *Shikshapatri*, the 'bible' of the sect (see page 506).

Plate 28 The Duke of Wellington, elder statesman
Malcolm returned to Britain early in 1831, and immediately became a Member of Parliament, chiefly as a supporter of his lifelong friend, the Duke of Wellington.

Plate 29 India House, Leadenhall St, London, headquarters of the East India Company
Here, in April 1833, Malcolm made his last public speech, advocating acceptance by the Proprietors (shareholders) of the Government's proposals for changing the Company's charter. A few days later he suffered a stroke, and died on 30 May.

Plate 30 Lady Charlotte Malcolm in 1840
Charlotte lived on until 1867.

PART FOUR

Author

CHAPTER TWENTY-TWO

Bombay, 1811

Sir James Mackintosh recorded in his journal for 19 November 1810: 'At 7 in the morning I heard a salute and at 8 received Packets [letters] from Bagdad. Nothing from England. Went in after breakfast to see Malcolm, just back from Persia. Found him as usual cheerful and bawling. He was twenty days with Rich and Mary both of whom he praises extremely. He particularly speaks of Mary's fortitude during the battles etc which raged around their tents during his stay, and which ended with the deposition and death of the Pacha of Bagdad.'[1]

Malcolm spent a few days settling in with Charlotte and the children

Sir James Mackintosh (1765–1832), doctor, journalist, lawyer and politician. Recorder of Bombay (1804–11).

at Nonpareil, meeting family and friends. Jean Briggs had already left for Madras with her surgeon husband Gilbert and their two children (Jean died in 1811, aged only twenty-four, while giving birth to a third child), but Fannie Malcolm, Tom's widow, was still there with her two boys.

Malcolm then set about dispersing the remaining members of his mission who had returned to Bombay with him. Among them was Josiah Stewart. After Malcolm's precipitate departure from Bushire in July 1808, Stewart had stayed behind with Charles Pasley and Gilbert Briggs. In May 1809, 'on his [Stewart's] return to India the cruiser which carried him was attacked by a French frigate, and though she was completely beaten off after a long and severe action . . . our poor friend lost his right arm during the engagement'.[2] Hanging about in Bombay with the Malcolm family while he waited to return to regimental duties in Madras, he met Fannie Malcolm. As Mackintosh commented, 'Mr Stewart, the sensible officer who lost an arm, has so far lost his senses as to be about to be married to Mrs Tom Malcolm.'[3] The wedding took place on 23 January and shortly afterwards the couple sailed for Madras.[4]

Johnny Little was also sent back to Madras to rejoin his regiment at Vellore. 'From [General and] Mrs Malcolm I parted with the greatest regret', he wrote to his father from his ship near Colombo. 'I had belonged to the family four years and the whole of that time experienced from both, nothing but kindness and affection. When, if ever, I shall spend so happy a time seems to me very uncertain.'[5] [6]

Malcolm, meanwhile, was struggling to finalise the mission's accounts so that he could justify reimbursement of the outlays made from Company advances and his own pocket. Completing expense claims after overseas trips has always been a miserable business. Auditors like to have yardsticks against which expenditure can be compared. But with a one-off diplomatic mission to a virtually unknown country, there were no such yardsticks. In the case of Malcolm's second and third Persian missions this syndrome was aggravated. The outlay of funds was enormous, at £100,000 – more than £6 million in today's money. And there were many outlays in Persia for which receipts were just not available. On top of all this, Malcolm was not a 'detail' man. He was bored with the minutiae of numbers and dockets, and despite his protests to the contrary, he was probably quite cavalier in his attitude to accounts. To accusations of excessive expenditure he replied reasonably enough that both missions were expensive because their original objectives had envisaged a much larger scope than turned out to be necessary. In 1808, a military expedition to Kharg Island had been contemplated; in 1810, a military mission to the Persian army. This had led him to take much larger mission parties than had turned out to be necessary. Correspondence flowed back and forth between Bombay and Calcutta for several months, and was only completed at the end of April when Edmonstone, the Chief Secretary in Calcutta,[7] wrote to Malcolm concluding that in hindsight, it was the government's view that the expenditure had been excessive but that no one held this against Malcolm personally.

While completing this administrative chore, Malcolm considered his next career move. There was no question of returning to Mysore as Resident as long as Sir George Barlow was Governor of Madras – their relationship had remained bitter since their falling-out over the mutiny at Masulipatam in 1809. The general plan was therefore for the whole family to go home to England on furlough. Malcolm was entitled to five years on full pay. But on the voyage back from Persia, a new idea had been forming in his mind. He and his mission party had acquired a vast quantity of material about Persia and its surrounding countries. He wanted to put all these papers in order and write up a memoir while the events were still fresh in his mind. So, ten days after his return to Bombay, he wrote to Minto asking for leave to spend a few months doing so.[8] There was a precedent for this. Mountstuart Elphinstone, after returning to Calcutta from his mission to the Court of Shah Shuja of Afghanistan at Peshawar, had been allowed several months off to assemble his notes. He had been given clerical assistance, but no additional salary. Minto gave his approval[9] and Malcolm started work. He was paid Rs2,000 per month and given clerical assistance.[10] It was an imaginative gesture on the part of Minto, and produced valuable intelligence for the Calcutta Government of a hitherto unknown, but strategically important, neighbouring country.

Malcolm now became a more-or-less full-time professional author. The seed for his literary career had been sown in Mysore back in January 1805, when he had shown his notes on his 1800 Persian mission to the poet John Leyden. By 1811 he had already published *Sketch of the Sikhs* (written in 1806, first published in Henry Colebrooke's *Asiatic Researches* in Calcutta in 1809, and in book form in England in 1812); *Sketch of the Political History of India*, written in 1809–10 and published in England in

1811; and later in 1811 he was to write *Disturbances in the Madras Army* (published in 1812). But these were works completed in his spare time from a busy career. At last, in 1811, when he got Minto's official sanction to spend most of that year in Bombay working on *The History of Persia*, he was able to turn full time to writing.

At the outset, his project suffered a major setback. The *Jehan Banee*, a contract vessel,[11] bringing back some of his servants and most of his papers, English and Persian, and all his drawings, was lost with all aboard in the Arabian Sea.[12] On the other hand, he was lucky to have Sir James Mackintosh, living virtually across the road, as his mentor.

In 1811, Mackintosh's journal letters to his wife (who had returned to England) show that he and Malcolm now became close friends. The following excerpts paint a vivid picture of social life in Bombay over the first ten months of 1811:

> 24/1
> At breakfast employed in laughing very heartily at the gross imposture of the missions to and from Persia, which have cost Mr Bull ['John Bull'] one or two of his spare millions. Malcolm called. He will go home if there be an opportunity in June or July. I should rather like to go with him
>
> 7/2 [Letter to Lady Mackintosh in England]
> Malcolm . . . wishes that we should go together. Since I have sat at the head of the breakfast table I have been struck at his too Scottish mode of dressing and eating. His nails, his spluttering and his use of the napkin. The objection is I find general.
>
> 19/2
> In the morning Mr Elphinstone, just landed, came in with General Malcolm, at whose house he is. He has somewhat of the calm rational manner and awkward appearance of a Scotchman. He is red haired and high cheek boned.[13]
>
> 1/3
> [The Reverend] Mr Martin, the saint from Calcutta, called.[14] He is a man of acuteness and learning. His meekness is excessive

and gives a disagreeable impression of effort to conceal the common passions of human nature.

28/3
Read over with minute criticism Malcolm's poem – *The Persian Traveller*.[15] It has more thought and nerve than volumes of correct and smooth verse . . . Malcolm has been with me two hours, and I have told him all my criticisms, which he has taken well.

30/3
The Crawfords show the same indisposition to take Mrs Malcolm in their ship as before was shewn by Forbes. Malcolm may be kept in this country for some months by his wife's character of bad temper.

4/4[16]
Malcolm continues his friendship – but his company is not so agreeable to me as it was. I know not whether his defects are increased or others have spoken of them more, or I have become more sensitive to them since his good qualities have lost the attraction of novelty. This last is a disposition injurious to happiness and disgraceful to human nature. Both you and I ought to correct it.

Around this time Malcolm rode up to Poona to stay for a week with Elphinstone. They both loved hunting and despite the May heat, spent every day on horseback pursuing wild pigs. 'Not much luck', he wrote one day to Charlotte, 'but hard riding, and no less than seven falls. I did not come off, though very near it.'[17] In the evenings, they discussed their travels in Persia and Afghanistan and the progress of their literary works. Elphinstone had compiled an extensive report on his Afghan mission while in Calcutta, but it was only when he came round to Bombay and Poona and fell under Mackintosh's influence that he was persuaded to turn his report into a publishable book. The pair agreed that Elphinstone would write about Afghanistan and Malcolm about Persia, leaving Henry Pottinger to cover Sind, Baluchistan and Seistan. Mackintosh's journal continued:

28/7
In correcting an mss of Malcolm's, I made an observation which I do not remember to have met in any treatise. A man of vigorous mind conceives original ideas, which, if he be an unpractised or negligent writer, he often expresses in such a manner, that they appear to be commonplace. The new thought may be so near an old one, that it requires the exact expression to distinguish them. This is one of the reasons why men of great talent for active life are inferior to themselves in their writings.

25/8
Malcolm has of late been rather unanimously voted a bore. Though slowly and reluctantly I have been led into the same opinion.'

12/10
Public dinner to me in the evening, at the theatre. About 150 persons. General Abercrombie presided very well and Malcolm kept up a roar. The party (as they say) went off very well. I came away about a quarter past eleven.

Mackintosh's Bombay journal ended on 5 November, and he sailed the next day for England. Malcolm, Erskine, General Abercrombie and Newbolt (his successor as Recorder) came to see him off.

All through the year Malcolm worked on his *History of Persia* (except for a short break in July and August to write his pamphlet on the Masulipatam mutiny). It was a huge job even for someone of his frenetic energy, and it was destined to take him three more years of continuous work to finish it. The manuscript which he showed to Mackintosh would have been no more than a preliminary draft of the first couple of chapters. Nevertheless, Mackintosh's comments and encouragement were of inestimable value to a relatively inexperienced writer.

It was also time for the Malcolms to go, but Charlotte was eight months pregnant, so they waited until she had produced the baby, Olympia, on 10 December 1811.The family – now five of them – embarked on the *Dromedary* in late January. They reached London in July 1812.

CHAPTER TWENTY-THREE

England – Family, Career and the Literary World, 1812–1816

John was delighted to be back. He introduced Charlotte and the three children to the Malcolm family and to close friends living in London. Charles Pasley, now back in England for good, and recovering from illness, found 'the General . . . in the highest possible spirits'.[1] Pulteney's wife Clementina, whom he had married in 1809, meeting John and Charlotte for the first time, wrote enthusiastically to Pulteney, still at sea. They met John's cousin William Pasley at the opera and dined with the Pasley clan at Southgate, north of London. They gave dinners at their temporary lodgings in Baker Street to brother David, back from Spain; to brother James, now commanding a Marine battalion at Chatham; and to sister Stephana, visiting from Burnfoot.

Their first task was to find somewhere to live. With three young children (Maggie aged four, George two and Olympia seven months), they looked for a place in the country. John resisted the Burnfoot family's attempts to persuade them to live in Scotland. He knew that London was where the political action was, and there he was determined to be. Within a month they had leased a small country house, *Claramont*, near Cheshunt in Hertfordshire, probably because it was within a few miles of both the Pasleys at Southgate and the Elphinstones (Clementina's parents) at Enfield. They also rented a town house, 67 Harley Street.

They shared 67 Harley Street with Charlotte's younger sister Amelia and her new husband, John Macdonald, who had accompanied Malcolm on his 1808 and 1810 missions to Persia. Charlotte and Amelia were close as sisters and remained so for the rest of their lives. In January 1813 John

General Sir Charles William Pasley (1780–1861). Eskdale born, Pasley became a soldier, serving in Spain. In 1812 he became the first Director of the Royal School of Military Engineering at Chatham, a post he held until 1841. He has been called 'the father of the Royal Engineers'. During the 1820s he and Malcolm saw a lot of each other.

Macdonald set off to rejoin his regiment at Madras, travelling overland to Baghdad and then on via Bombay. Amelia joined him later in Madras.

As soon as the family had settled in at Claramont, Malcolm set off for Scotland. On the way he stayed for a few days at Nocton in Lincolnshire with Robert Hobart, now Earl of Buckinghamshire, who had recently taken over from Robert Dundas as President of the Board of Control. Malcolm had worked for Hobart when he was Governor of Madras in 1796–1798 and had corresponded with him ever since. In between 'shooting, riding, attending the Lincoln races, dancing at the race-ball, and lionising the cathedral',[2] Malcolm briefed Hobart about the latest situation in India and Persia.

Pressing on northwards, he reached Langholm on 26 September. It was thirty-one years since he had first left Eskdale, and sixteen since he had last visited. He wrote to Charlotte:

> Arrived at Langholm at four, and got out of the chaise at July Murray's, the person by whom I was brought up. The excellent woman was in raptures. Our meeting was disturbed by Mrs Beattie, the keeper of the inn (an old acquaintance), who had

> taken her glass, and came to drag me away from July, who, she said, kept the *driest* house in Langholm. This old woman, who earnestly recommended me some whisky, talked a great deal. I proceeded to Burnfoot. I had been greatly struck with the beauty of the country, from the moment I came on the banks of the Esk, opposite Netherby, all the way to Langholm; but the first burst of Burnfoot surprised me still more (it is greatly improved by the growth of the woods).[3]

At Burnfoot, John found his five surviving sisters and his brother Robert, who had returned from India in May 1807. Their mother had died in November 1811. Pulteney's father-in-law, William Elphinstone, had visited Burnfoot shortly before she died, and reported that 'this is a patriarchal family, of which the old lady [Bonnie Peggy] is the Head. She is weak in Body but strong in Mind. She is looked up to by all with reverence, bordering on adoration.'[4]

John's eldest sister Nancy was a strong character, competent, practical, rather bossy, her father's favourite. She had taken over the management of the farm and the family finances from him in the 1790s. John wrote that 'in cheerful goodness, superior sense, and active benevolence, [she] yields to none of her ancestors . . . she knows the wants and the characters of all, and supplies accordingly.'[5]

The next, Mina, ran the house, but housekeeping was not really her interest or her forte. Outwardly sweet in nature, she was a refined and erudite woman, an intellectual. A nephew later described her: 'Aunt Minnie as she was known in the family . . . was very gifted, with a character blending firmness and piety with considerable literary attainments, which enabled her to enter fully into the large political and social questions which engaged the national attention, and in which her brothers Pulteney and John took such a very prominent part.'[6] There were hints of clashes of personality with Nancy, and later with Robert. In 1804, she built a small cottage not far from the main house at Burnfoot, which she used as her private retreat to get away from the rest of the family. In 1809 the cottage was extended to include a hexagon-shaped room to display her 'Curiosities', chiefly *objets d'art* sent back to her by her family and friends from around the world.[7] Around this time her brothers and cousins in India were producing children whom they sent home to be educated. Mina set up a teaching establishment at

Burnfoot for some of them, using a nearby hut as a school room. From 1810 onwards she taught up to ten children. Fannie Malcolm's sons, George and Duncan, and her daughter Charlotte Stewart, spent most of their childhood at Burnfoot, and looked upon Mina as a surrogate parent and a fine teacher.

The third sister, Margaret had married her cousin, John Briggs, a barrister in London. But he died three years later and she returned to Burnfoot, a childless widow of thirty-eight, in poor health, who nevertheless survived for another twenty-eight years. Little is known of the fourth, Helen, apart from a rather frightening photograph of her in old age. Stephana, the youngest and also the longest surviving (she died in 1861), travelled south quite often, chiefly to act as a companion for ageing aunts and uncles. None of the sisters travelled outside Britain.

John's six surviving brothers (three had died earlier) had all left home while young to earn their living – one to the East India Company as a writer (Robert), two to the Navy (Pulteney and Charles), one to the Madras Army (John), one to commerce (David) and one to become an Anglican priest (Gilbert).

Robert had been welcomed back to Burnfoot in 1807 after twenty-seven years in India (leaving behind his Indian mistress Nancy and his six surviving Anglo Indian children); and as the returning elder son, might have been expected to take charge of the farm and the household. But the sisters were disappointed to receive a rather battered, yellowish complexioned and 'very stout' figure in indifferent health.[8] He was 'unwell through shortness of breath'.[9] Despite joining the Eskdale Farmers' Club in September 1808, he never took an active part in the running of the Burnfoot farm. It had in any case been managed for more than a decade by the highly competent Nancy. A letter from Robert to John (still in India at the time) indicated that Nancy also had reservations about him, in that, 'in the first year I was [with] some Dyse involved . . . and to satisfy her mind there was no Extravagance on my part, I gave her a minute statement of my private expenses, where neither women nor wine out of the house Existed.'[10]

Robert's health continued to fluctuate. By June 1813 he had 'been unwell for six or seven months' and had to 'use the carriage to move about'. Finally, in October 1813, he died.

The prevailing atmosphere at Burnfoot was described, breathlessly, by Sarah Hutchinson (a sister-in-law of the poet William Wordsworth and at one time the mistress of S.T. Coleridge) in a letter to her sister Mary. She and the Wordsworths travelled to Burnfoot to leave the Wordsworth's eleven-year-old son Johnnie to be educated there:

> Pressed on 4 miles beyond Langholm to Burnfoot, Miss Malcolms . . . It was 9 o'clock when we arrived – we found a houseful of company from Edinbro' & I know not where; but we had a truly highland reception – the Miss Malcolms were fit to devour us – there are four sisters – so scotch, so merry, so noisy!! . . . Next morning we assembled a strong party at breakfast – some to tea pobs, some brose [both forms of porridge] some to boiled milk, eggs, ham & all snacks. They were fourteen children I believe – all educated at this Burnfoot in the true highland fashion – and the nephews are sent to their Aunts' house to be educated in the same fashion; there are at present 4 besides a lad of the parish which they make a companion for the first that come – the tutor is a clever young man & they teach Latin most admirably . . . we had a big dinner – scotch soup – sheep's head singed besides many other things spoilt by the cooking – the noise was intolerable, everyone talked at once, at least all the scotch: and we also were forced to seem to be heard . . . at night came the dancing master & all stood up to dance young and old with the Bairns – Lady J[ohnstone], from Westerhall [the next door property], as happy as if she were dancing at Carleton House – all but Wm [Wordsworth] and I & and the old lady who looked on.[11]

John wandered round the district, visiting all and sundry. Talking to Andrew Nichol, an old Burnfoot retainer, he remarked that there had been many changes, and hoped that Andrew still found it a good house to live in. 'Faith', said he, 'it's mair than that – it's the best house to *die* in of a' Scotland.'[12]

After a week at Burnfoot, Malcolm pressed on to Edinburgh. There he met Walter Scott, already famous as a novelist and poet. How the meeting came about is a complicated story. In November 1811, while still in Bombay, Malcolm had heard that his friend John Leyden had died. After being Malcolm's guest at the Mysore Residency in 1805, Leyden had spent a year in Penang studying Malay, then returned to Calcutta, and for the next few years was employed by Lord Minto for several scholarly special projects. In 1811 Minto led an expedition to capture Java from the Dutch, and since Leyden was 'perfect in Malay' (as well as a host of other languages), Minto took him along 'to assist in settling the country when conquered, and as interpreter for the Malay language'. Sadly, 'Leyden's literary zeal took him into an unventilated native library; fever supervened, and he died at Cornelis, after three days' illness, on 28 August.'[13] Malcolm, deeply moved by Leyden's death, wrote a passionate eulogy and some memorial verses which he sent to the local newspaper, the *Bombay Courier*. Knowing that Leyden had regarded Walter Scott as his unofficial literary executor, Malcolm ventured to write a letter to the great man. Introducing himself as 'a fellow Borderer', he told him of Leyden's death, and enclosed his *Bombay Courier* eulogy. 'If you were not a Borderer, I should feel I was addressing a stranger – but a person who was born on the Esk has a prescriptive right to the friendship of every man who inhabits one of the neighbouring Dales. I might also claim some return for the feeling of pride I have always had in your fame . . . In transmitting to you a tribute to our late friend Leyden, I feel assured I am gratifying your feelings while I am indulging my own – and this trifle even will gain importance with you for the love you bear him to whose memory it is addressed.'[14] It was a quite natural thing to do, but the tone of the letter, circumspect by Malcolm's normally bumptious standards, indicates that it must have taken some courage for him to write, out of the blue, to the literary titan of the day. He probably also saw a chance to use this pretext to make his acquaintance and to show off his own writing talents after he arrived back in Britain.

Meanwhile, unknown to Malcolm, Scott had been impressed with the eulogy, and had written to Richard Heber (a bibliophile on a grand scale – at his death his library was said to contain 150,000 volumes) who had introduced Leyden to Scott in 1801: 'Alas for poor John Leyden! His active and indefatigable spirit has at last worn out its clay tenement. I have promised to fulfil an old engagement & to collect his Remains, unless I learn that he has made some final arrangement. General Malcolm[15] has written a very good article in the Bombay Courier with some pretty verses to Leyden's memory. He gives some very interesting anecdotes and touches his character & peculiarities with great truth & kindly feeling. If you have not seen these I will include them in my next.'[16]

When Scott and Malcolm met for the first time in Edinburgh in October 1812, they got on famously. In his journal Malcolm wrote: 'I agreed to drive him home [to Abbotsford, near Galashiels, in the Border country], and we have been together till now [a day later]. A volume would not contain what has passed between us. I am delighted with him, and he says that his feelings are not opposed to mine.'[17] Scott's reaction to Malcolm was even more fulsome. He wrote to his friend John Morrit, an English traveller and classical scholar,

> you missed . . . General John Malcolm – the Persian envoy, the Delhi Resident, the poet, the warrior, the politician and the borderer. He is really a fine fellow. I met him at Dalkeith and we returned together; he has just left me after drinking his coffee. A fine time we had of it, talking of Troy town and Babel and Persepolis and Delhi and Langholm and Burnfoot with all manner of episodes about Iskandiar, Rustam and Johnnie Armstrong. Do you know, that poem of Ferdausi's must be beautiful. He read me some very splendid extracts which he had himself translated . . . To be sure I know him little, but I like his frankness and his sound ideas of morality and policy.[18]

The pair appeared to have little in common. Scott was born in Edinburgh and spent most of his working life there, first as a Clerk of Sessions, then gradually metamorphosing into an increasingly famous man of letters. Lamed by polio at the age of two, he spent part of his childhood on his uncle's farm at Sandyknowe in the Borders. Malcolm, also a Borderer, left school and country at the age of thirteen to seek fame in India. He was six feet five inches tall, fifteen stone, an athlete, the quintessential man of action and adventure. Yet they were both Lowland Scots of the same age; both incurable Romantics, especially about the Scottish Borders and its feudal past. And perhaps each of them saw in the other what he would like to have been himself – Malcolm, to be a famous man of letters; Scott, to be an active hero, not merely a chronicler of heroes. This was the first contact in a friendship which lasted for the rest of their lives. Though they never became intimate friends, their letters exude warmth on both sides and they obviously remained very fond of each other.

After leaving Scott at Abbotsford, Malcolm headed south, calling briefly on Lady Minto, the elderly wife of the Governor-General, at the Minto property near Hawick,[19] and then continuing on to his brother Gilbert's home at Todenham, near Moreton-in-Marsh in Gloucestershire.

Gilbert, six years younger than John, was academically the brightest of the Malcolm brothers. After schooling at the Westerkirk parish school and Edinburgh High School, he won a scholarship to Trinity College, Cambridge. He studied Mathematics, won a BA as sixth Wrangler (mathematician) and was elected a Fellow of Trinity in 1798. John tried unsuccessfully to get him the post of Professor of Mathematics at the newly opened Fort William College at Calcutta. Thereafter he decided to take holy orders and was ordained a priest in the Church of England (Trinity being an Anglican College) in 1801. In 1806 he became a curate at the parish of Toppesfield in Essex, and in the same year married his first cousin Helen Little. In those days 'livings' (i.e. rectorships of parishes), were mostly in the gift of grandees, and John and Pulteney relentlessly lobbied the Wellesley brothers to get Gilbert a living. Eventually their persistence paid off, and Gilbert became Rector of Todenham in 1812, with a living worth, initially, about £250. There he was to stay for the rest of his life – another forty-three years.

What John and Gilbert had to discuss on this occasion was an alarming development – the financial insolvency of their brother David, spelling potential ruin for the whole family. Of all the Malcolm brothers, David's character most nearly resembled his father's – outgoing, charming, but rather reckless with money. Born in 1778, his first job was in an agency business, which entailed going back and forth to Hamburg. In 1806 he went to Spain, making friends with James Duff (later Sir James Duff) who had been shipping wine, sherry and port via Sandemans from the Cadiz region of Spain since 1768. David set up his own wine-shipping business, partly financed by loans arranged by Pulteney. At this time Pulteney was managing John's financial affairs while he was away in India, and he used some of John's funds as well as his own to finance David's business.

In 1808 the Peninsular War came to Spain, and early in 1810 the French army arrived in the south, capturing Jerez and besieging Cadiz. The Cadiz wine trade went into limbo and did not resume until the French were finally repulsed and the siege lifted in 1812. Pulteney wrote to John in late 1810 that '[David's] affairs are a little deranged, but if the siege of Cadiz is raised he may recover, but not otherwise – you and I will be the principal losers.'[20]

Unfortunately, Pulteney's (and David's) hopes were in vain. Over the next few months increasingly desperate letters came from David. Pulteney duly accepted four promissory notes totalling £3,794 payable over a year. Feeling ever guiltier about having lent John's money to David, Pulteney wrote again to John. 'Poor David's affairs are in a very bad way. I tried to save him and have lost most of my small fortune.' By this time Pulteney had given up hope. He wrote to Mina at Burnfoot, 'we cannot arrange David's affairs; he must come home and become bankrupt'.[21] David did finally return home in early 1812, and hung around in London for a time. Despite his financial ruin, he maintained a confident front, charming all – particularly his sisters, who were perhaps less fully aware of the extent of the financial damage that his brothers had suffered on his account. In September 1812 his pious sister Stephana, on a visit to London, wrote home to Burnfoot that 'David dined here . . . on Sunday. I was particularly pleased with his manner.'[22] Not so Pulteney, who wrote to Clementina in July that 'David comes between me and my sleep.'[23]

The full extent of the financial disaster emerged later, when David finally listed his debts to members of the family: £5,750 to Pulteney, £4,340 to John, £650 to Gilbert, £2,725 to Charles, £400 to Archy Little (a cousin); in total, £13,865. It was a huge sum – equivalent to more than £1 million in today's money – and it was a terrible blow to the fortunes of his creditor brothers.[24]

All this time Pulteney had been away at sea. Returning to London in December 1812, he and John were at last able to meet, for the first time in nearly ten years. They agreed that the most practicable solution for David would be for him to go to India and set up in business there on a modest scale. John wrote letters of introduction to his influential contacts, notably John Palmer, the foremost East India merchant in Calcutta at the time. David eventually set sail for India in May 1813, reaching Calcutta late that year; but Palmer could not help.[25] He then sailed on to Bombay and found employment there as a partner in a merchant house. He was to reappear in John's life a few years later.

Although Malcolm was entitled to furlough (paid leave) for up to five years, he still had an appetite for work on the Company's behalf. The Company's twenty-year Charter came up for renewal in 1813, and he was called before various Parliamentary Select Committees to give evidence on the situation of the Company army and other matters. Sir James Mackintosh, back on the London scene, wrote that: 'Malcolm is the next witness to be examined . . . He is to give strong testimony in favour of the Company's favourite argument, that a free trade will lead to an influx of Europeans, which will produce insult and oppression to the natives, and at last drive them into rebellion, which must terminate in our expulsion.'[26] Malcolm indeed strongly supported the Company's opposition to Europeans being allowed free admission into British India:

> I think of all the powers which are vested in the Local Government, there is none more essential to its existence in full vigor and force, than that which enables them to restrain the local residence of every European to particular parts of the empire. If British subjects were allowed to go in the manner described to India, the effects would be various . . . , agreeably to the places to which they went. In the Presidencies[27] where British courts of law are established, there would be no other danger, I conceive, resulting from them, but what might arise from their great numbers, and the changes in the condition of the society, and eventually and gradually of the Government, from that circumstance. But if they went to any ports where there was no established authority to control them, and if they proceeded into the interior of the country, there would no doubt be much mischief arising from those quarrels which must inevitably ensue with the natives, which mischief would vary from a hundred local causes connected with the character of the natives of the places to which they resorted.[28]

These arguments were largely accepted. The Company lost its monopoly of the China trade but was otherwise allowed to carry on much as before for the next twenty-year Charter period.

Another favourite subject, which Malcolm was to keep coming back to throughout his career, was the lower status of officers in the Company's armies compared with the King's armies. He had fought hard for their cause with the British Government as far back as 1794. Much had been promised, but little had been implemented. In the summer of 1813 he wrote a long memorandum to Buckinghamshire [Hobart], with some specific proposals, the gist of which were that Company officers should be eligible for awards and entry to the highest military offices in India. This would not only be fair in itself; it would also attach these officers more strongly to their country of origin. The military establishment should have more senior and fewer junior ranks, which would make it easier for older officers to accumulate enough funds to pay for their passage home and live in reasonable comfort in their retirement. As it was, many old officers had to hang around until they died, of little use to the army and blocking promotion for younger, more vigorous men. Merit should as far as possible replace patronage in the selection and promotion of officers in Company armies, and at senior level, there should be provision for some limited exchange of officers between the King's and Company's armies, and senior Company officers should be eligible for service elsewhere in the British Empire.[29] Unfortunately it took another forty years for these eminently sensible proposals to be fully implemented.

At this time John's assets were worth about £35,000. His furlough pay was about £1,000 per annum and his other investment income about £1,500. His loss of £4,340 on the bad debt from brother David may not seem too serious but it was a cash asset, yielding interest income of 5–6 per cent, or £250. With living expenses of more than £2,000, he was now unable to save; in fact he began living partly on capital.

To add to his problems, his claims for reimbursement of expenses incurred during his various missions in India and Persia were still outstanding. The Calcutta Government had recommended payment of his claims, but the Court of Directors had dragged its feet. He wrote plaintively to a friend: 'You will suppose what I feel when I assure you that the losses I suffered on the sales of my properties (13 in 15 years), the shipwreck of one vessel and the [burning] of another, and charges of agents' commission and interest on public cash, amounted to *£12,000 – eight years ago,* when it was half that [now].'[30]

He had to embark on vigorous lobbying at the India House, and swallow his pride in pleading with people whom he did not like. Chief among these was Charles Grant, no longer the Chairman of the Company, but still wielding immense influence. Twenty years older than Malcolm, Grant had served the Company in India until 1790, then returned to Britain, becoming a director in 1794, and in due course the Chairman. Strongly religious, he was the founder of the evangelical Clapham Sect in 1800. In Parliament, when the East India Company's Charter was being debated in 1812–13, Grant was foremost in including 'pious' clauses enabling Christian missionaries to operate in India with Government support, tabling a tract entitled *Observations on the General State of Society among the Asiatic Subjects of Great Britain with respect to morals, and on the means of improving it*. It proceeded to a thundering climax:

> I most of all suffer from the absurd, malevolent and wicked stories which the weak, the prejudiced, the enemies of Christianity, have poured forth to discredit, to bring into suspicion, to blacken as dangerous and mischievous, the few poor and assuredly harmless efforts which have been made under the British government to introduce the light of the Gospel into India . . . I have for many years considered the question. Caution and prudence are at all times necessary in proposing the truths of Christianity to heathens; there may be particular care when these, and perhaps a degree of forbearance are especially required – but for a Christian nation to say deliberately that they will prohibit the communication of that religion which comes from God to fifty millions of men, sunk in idolatry, superstition, and vice, is a proposition so monstrous and shocking, so contrary to the most rational and probable cause to be assigned for the conduct of Providence in committing so vast an Empire to our care, that I tremble at the thought of it and the consequences it would be likely to produce. The real question depending is, whether the door shall be shut to the entrance of missionaries into British India?[31]

Such a man was unlikely to be favourably disposed towards Malcolm, who in his *Sketch of the Political History of India* had made a strong case against any Government support for the propagation of Christianity in British India. And, as if Grant's differences with Malcolm over religion were not enough, he had also strongly opposed the Marquess's 'warlike measures' in India, and had supported a censure motion against him in Parliament in 1808. Nevertheless, Malcolm felt obliged to seek Grant's support. He wrote to him nervously: 'I have requested Sir Hugh Inglis [a director] to bring on my memorial and subsequent letter in the course of this week, and cannot but feel very anxious that it should meet your support.'[32] Reimbursement – of £5,000 – eventually came in 1815.

These money worries were seriously affecting Malcolm's career plans. In April 1814, Charlotte produced her fourth child, Amelia. By then they had changed houses twice: in April 1813, passing on the lease of 67 Harley Street to Charles Pasley and moving next door to 66 Harley Street; then, in early 1814, moving again to 18 Manchester Street, a larger house. About the same time they bought a cottage in the village of Frant near Tunbridge Wells in Kent. Here – at 18 Manchester Street in London and later at Frant in Kent – the family was based for the next eight years.

The Duke of Wellington, Malcolm's brother Pulteney and his father-in-law, Sir Alex Campbell, had all advised him not to come home until he had accumulated assets of £50,000. He had nevertheless done so, with £35,000, and had now used up some of that. He had hoped for a career in politics. Members of Parliament were unpaid but the valuable contacts made would hopefully lead to other profitable employment. The Duke encouraged him to do so from Spain, with some career advice:

> I have been frequently astonished at the indifference with which public men in England considered the talents of those who had served in India. Although I had long been in habits of friendship with the public men of the day, and had some professional claims to public notice when I returned to England, I believe I should have been but little known, and should not be what I am, if I had not gone into Parliament. I would, therefore, advise you to go into Parliament if you can afford it, if you look to high profile employment. I likewise recommend you not to fix yourself upon Lord Wellesley, or any other great man. You are big enough, unless much altered, to walk alone; and you will accomplish your object soonest in that way. Do not, however, be in a hurry.

Incidentally, this letter was written just after the battle of Vitoria in Spain, 21 June 1813, and ended with typical Wellingtonian understatement: 'You will hear of events here. I have taken more guns from these fellows in the last action than I took at Assye [Assaye], without much more loss, upon about 70,000 men engaged. The two armies were nearly equal in numbers, but they cannot stand us now at all.'[33]

A little later, Malcolm thought of applying for the job of Ambassador to the Porte. Again, the Duke quickly brought him back to earth: 'I do not think I can be of much use to you in any way, and of none in forwarding your views upon Constantinople. That Court is sometimes the seat of important diplomatic negotiations, and at others a seat of splendid retreat for ambassadors. You would be considered an interloper by either the active or the declining diplomat. You had better adhere to your objects in India. Get into Parliament if you can afford it; be nobody's man but your own, and you will soon be known, and get on.'[34]

Meanwhile Malcolm was working away on *The History of Persia*. He had started to work in Bombay in 1811 and continued doing so during the voyage back to Britain in the first half of 1812. But it was a huge undertaking, even for a man of his phenomenal speed of output. He was using largely Persian sources for the first time, including oral history picked up while on the march during his missions. He had an unusual way of working; researching and writing each chapter as a separate stand-alone narrative. Once he had finished a chapter, he seldom returned to edit or rewrite it. All through 1813 and 1814 he worked away on it. Mackintosh, as a newly elected Member of Parliament, was too busy to help. But he continued to use Erskine as a reader, despite Erskine being in Bombay, four or five months' postage time away. It was a mutually beneficial arrangement; Erskine commented on Malcolm's *History of Persia*, and Malcolm commented on Erskine's draft biography of Babur (or Baber as they called him), the first Mughal Emperor. Another friend, Brigadier Alexander Walker, a Persian scholar who had been Resident in Baroda from 1802 to 1810 and was now living in retirement in England, also commented on his draft *History*, and in return Malcolm advised Walker on how to apply to the Court of Directors for a pension, based on his own rather bitter experience.

Malcolm also used his erudite brother Gilbert to read over and edit his drafts, chapter by chapter. Gilbert had already edited the *Sketch of the Political History of India*, which he received in batches from India during 1810, and negotiated with the publishers without being able to refer back to John. He did the same with *Disturbances in the Madras Army* in early 1812, although in that case he was able to get help from Mackintosh, who had brought the draft with him to England.

A further complication for Malcolm was that he had to finance the printing of *The History of Persia*. Pulteney wrote to Nancy at Burnfoot that 'his book will soon be published, that is the first part of it; he does it himself. To publish the whole will cost him £5,000, so my guess of its value, I think it will repay him.'[35] In the late summer of 1814, when the book was nearly finished, Malcolm and his family took a house at Bognor for a few months and he found it agreeable for writing, though he missed stimulating company. As he told Walker: 'In writing, a certain portion of [retirement] is necessary, but the man who leaves society that he may write better commits a great error. In the first place the string of the bow is better from occasional unbending, and in the second, good society is the school. It is where man must both form and try opinions.'[36]

Throughout this period Malcolm's publisher, John Murray, held court at his elegant premises in Albermarle Street with the writers in his literary stable. Here Malcolm met some of the literary lions of the day, including Lord Byron and Walter Scott. John Murray (the second), later recalled Malcolm's first meeting with Byron: 'Lord Byron dined several times at Albermarle St. On one of these occasions he met Sir John Malcolm – a most agreeable and accomplished man – who was all the more interesting to Lord Byron, because of his intimate knowledge of Persia and India. After dinner Sir John observed to Lord Byron, how much gratified he had been to meet him, and how surprised he was to find him so full of gaiety and entertaining conversation. Byron replied, "perhaps you see me now at my best".'[37]

Malcolm had already given Byron a taste of his own literary output. In 1814 he wrote to John Murray 'You will have 225 copies of the latest Poem on Saturday morning. I by your wish send one copy immediately to Lord Byron.'[38] Byron's reaction to Malcolm's poem is not known – probably a mildly embarrassed silence. Nevertheless, Malcolm must have made an impression on him, because some time later Dr John Polidari, who had been Byron's physician but had fallen out with him, wrote a novella, *The Vampyre*, featuring a vampire called Lord Ruthven, obviously based on Byron himself. When Dr Polidari submitted the novella to Murray for publication, Murray wrote to Byron asking him to compose for him 'a civil and delicate declension'. Byron composed some doggerel verses, including the lines:

A party dines with me today
All clever men who made their way;
Crabbe, Malcolm, Hamilton and Chantrey
Are all partakers of my pantry[39]

These literary excursions were gratifying, but the problem of finding a suitable career dragged on. Meanwhile, however, Malcolm found welcome relief for his *amour propre*. He received a knighthood.

Soon after his return to Britain, he had formally applied to the Crown for permission to wear the insignia of the Persian Order given to him by Fath Ali Shah. The Prince Regent gave his permission, and in December 1812 conferred a civil knighthood on him.[40] For a man of such strong upwardly mobile aspirations, this honour of a knighthood was a thrilling event for Malcolm. Mackintosh wrote that at the Regent's Levee: 'he made a conspicuous figure in the insignia of the Order of the Lion and Sun, with a green riband, distinguished from that of the Thistle by the silk being clouded'. He was well aware, however, that it was a personal gift of the sovereign: it did not carry the prestige of the military order, Knight Commander of the Bath (KCB), to which officers of the Company armies were not yet entitled. But just over two years later, the ruling was reversed and on 8 April 1815, he was among the first batch of Company officers to be awarded KCBs. Though already knighted, the KCB gave him great private satisfaction. At last Company officers had been recognised in British military honours, putting them closer in status to King's Army officers in India.

Although John had been the first of the Malcolms to be knighted (in 1812), his brothers Pulteney and James had received KCBs in February 1815, two months before him. Their knighthoods had come about through their part in a remarkable military exploit in America – the raid on Washington and the burning down of the White House in August 1814 during the 1812–1814 war with the United States. Pulteney, by then a Rear Admiral, had led the naval attack force, and James had commanded a battalion of Marines. Pulteney had already had a distinguished career in the Royal Navy and certainly deserved his knighthood. James, on the other hand, had served without great distinction for twenty-five years as an officer in the Royal Marines. He was lucky to have been in the right place at the right time.

The History of Persia was finally published in late June 1815 in two quarto volumes. It was sold for the outrageous price of eight guineas, around £500 in today's money. Nevertheless, it was an immediate success. It was the earliest serious history of Persia in English. Previous works on that country had been derived chiefly from Greek sources, embellished by the travellers' tales of Marco Polo and other Europeans from the twelfth to the eighteenth centuries. Malcolm, by contrast, was at pains to rely as far as possible on Persian sources, despite realising the constraints under which local historians had to operate in a despotic environment. By modern standards the work suffers from inadequate source material, but given the sparseness of material at his disposal and the press of other commitments on his time, it was an astonishing tour de force.[41]

Letters of congratulation poured in. This was all very gratifying for Malcolm who had laboured so long and hard over the previous four years. In June 1815, with publication completed, he was at last unencumbered by work, and could look forward to the gratifying applause of the literary world. And at the end of June, some even more pleasing news reached him – an invitation from the Duke of Wellington to visit him in Paris.

What could have been more exciting than to go at this moment to Paris, where all the crowned heads of Europe were assembling, following the final overthrow of Napoleon; where his friend and host would be the Duke, the victor of Waterloo and the hero of all Europe? Moreover, though few would yet have had time to read *The History of Persia*, the cognoscenti of Europe would know of it. He would be a literary lion. It was any author's dream come true.

Charlotte was pregnant again. John sent her and the children to stay with the Burnfoot family for the rest of the summer. He then set off for France accompanied by a friend, Colonel Allan. He was visiting the Continent for the first time, and on viewing Ostend, wrote that: 'The appearance of this coast is in every respect like Madras – no low sand-hills – all a dead level . . . This place, if it had cocoa-nut trees, would be India all over.' They were put up by Pulteney, now Commander of the Channel Fleet based at Ostend in a magnificent house.

With Napoleon's escape from Elba and restoration to power in France, Pulteney had played a prominent part in the events leading up to the Battle of Waterloo on 18 June. On 15 June he dined with Wellington in Brussels and attended the Duchess of Richmond's famous ball where 'the bugle sounded at midnight'. On the morning of 18 June he was breakfasting at the Hotel d'Angleterre when he heard that there was to be a battle at Waterloo. He immediately set off for the battlefield. On arrival he reported to the Duke, who greeted him warmly and immediately gave him a task – to ride over to Ghent where the King of France (Louis XVIII) was in a state of some panic, to give him a message of reassurance. Leaving the battlefield at 10.30 (half an hour before the battle began), he reached Ghent at 7 p.m., and delivered his message. The next day he rode back to Ostend. In the early hours of the next morning he heard cheers and 'huzzas' in the street and saw an officer giving news of the great victory, and carrying the eagles of two French regiments. He immediately put the officer on a fast sloop to take the news to London. But the sloop became becalmed, so the officer was rowed across the Channel, reaching London late the next day.

Leaving Pulteney at Ostend, Malcolm and Allan proceeded by canal boat to Bruges and on to Brussels, which was full of wounded soldiers from the recent battle. On 19 July they 'went through the hospitals . . . we were met by the surgeons in charge; and saw nearly 2,000 English and French wounded; and no sight could be more gratifying than the care and skill of the surgeons, the cleanliness, comfort and good arrangement of the hospitals.'[42] The next day they rode out to Waterloo and explored the now famous battlefield for three hours before travelling on to Paris.

During his two-month stay in Paris, Malcolm wrote a journal/letter to Charlotte. The original has been lost but it was included more or less in full in Kaye's biography – representing perhaps the most glamorous two months of Malcolm's entire life.[43] It can only be summarised here. As the Duke's guest and close friend, Malcolm was invited to a succession of parades, balls and other entertainments. He dined with the Duke on no fewer than sixteen occasions. He was introduced to the Kings of France, Russia, Prussia and Austria, plus the Prussian General, Prince Blucher, the Russian Count Woronzoff (Vorontzoff) and several of Bonaparte's Generals. Perhaps more significantly, his celebrity as the author of *The History of Persia* enabled him to meet and converse with an array of French savants, orientalists and painters – de Sacy, Humboldt, Denon, Langles, Chardin, Gerard, Volney, Walckenaar, Gais, Chunzy, Henri (who wanted to translate *The History of Persia* into French) and Madame de Staël. By 23 September it was time to go home. Malcolm had a lengthy farewell chat with the Duke, and two days later set off. His stay in Paris had given him a wonderful entrée to the highest society of Europe of that time, and the chance to compare notes with many Orientalist savants.

One of his incidental achievements had been to learn French. Within a week of his first attempts at the language, he was able to carry on a conversation. He took lessons each morning from a tutor, and his progress was remarkable, thanks to his irrepressible urge to engage all and sundry in conversation. The savants advised him that the best way of improving his colloquial French was, in two words, *parlez toujours*, and as he himself admitted, 'you know, that is quite in my way'.[44]

Arriving back in London at the beginning of October, he was reunited with the family. Their visit to Burnfoot had gone reasonably well. The children had loved it. Mina had written to William Pasley in August that 'our sister Charlotte and her dear children do not leave us before Tuesday week . . . I think her a very superior woman. She seems quite contented among us.'[45] Yet this appearance of harmony had a slightly forced undertone. John was desperately keen that Charlotte should like Burnfoot and get on well with his sisters. And the sisters, especially Mina, wanted to please her, too, because they were so fond of John. But there is no record of her ever visiting Burnfoot again, nor of her corresponding with any of the Malcolm sisters. Perhaps she found them too noisy and provincial. She was, of course, heavily pregnant, and gave birth to a daughter, Catherine, at Manchester Street on 31 October. A few days later John left for Scotland, on the way paying another visit to Lord Buckinghamshire at Nocton, where he had 'a pleasant fortnight of good shooting'. Clearly the presence at home of the newborn baby's father was not considered necessary.

Over the next year tributes and serious reviews of *The History of Persia* came from all sides. Among them were letters from Lord Byron, Baron Humboldt and Count Woronzoff.[46]Sir James Mackintosh wrote that Lord Grenville spoke of the first volume 'with a warmth which is often, I verily believe, in his feelings, but very seldom in his language'.[47]

Walter Scott was equally enthusiastic: 'I cannot refuse myself the opportunity of thanking you for the information and amusement I have derived and am deriving from your very interesting account of Persia; a history so much wanted in our literature, and which may be said to form the connecting link between that of Greece and that of Asia. I cannot enough admire the pains which it must have cost you, among many pressing avocations and duties, to collect and compose the materials of so large and important a work.'[48] Scott also wrote to his friend John Morrit: 'Sir John Malcolm's Persia has been . . . part of my winter reading. The succession of so many hard named tyrants through a course of events not strikingly varied, unless when the turbulent tribes emigrated and like a migration of the Solway Moss overran and ruined Indostan, does not sound a very varied or amusing subject. Yet I found it very interesting and I think Sir John has succeeded very well: his own remarks are always naturally and aptly introduced and show knowledge of mankind both in theory and in practice.'[49]

A long article in the *Edinburgh Review*[50] was more a résumé than critical appraisal. But an article in the *Quarterly Review*, written by Reginald Heber[51] was complimentary, stating that Malcolm was well qualified to write the book, though he warned readers to 'beware of the appalling fables by which the earlier chapters of Persian history are occupied and encumbered'. He nevertheless understood why Malcolm had called it a 'Fabulous' period up to the time of the Parthians (third century AD), quoting Malcolm approvingly: 'If we desire to be informed of a nation's history, we must not reject the fables under which the few traces that remain of its origins are concealed. These, however extravagant, always merit attention. They have an influence on the character of the people to whom they relate. They mix, with their habits, their literature, and sometimes their religion. They become, in short, national legends, which it is sacrilege to doubt; and to question the deeds of a Roostom,[52] would raise in the breast of a Persian all those feelings which would be excited in an Englishman, if he heard a foreigner detract from the great name of Alfred.'[53]

Malcolm's point was that legends were genuinely part of the Persian soul. Moreover, talking in parables served a practical purpose in covering up what might be considered a seditious opinion by a tyrannical ruler. 'Where liberty is unknown, and power unlimited, knowledge must be veiled. The ear of a despot would be wounded by direct truths.' He had voiced a similar attitude in the preface to his *Sketch of the Sikhs*. 'In every research into the general history of mankind, it is of the most essential importance to hear what a nation has to say about itself ...' (see page 232).[54] Perhaps this was a rationalisation of his innate love of fables and romance. The character of peoples, as well as of individuals could often 'be better appreciated from anecdotes than from a mere narration of events'.[55]

The book travelled slowly to India, where Malcolm had deputed his brother David to act as his local distributor. There it was reviewed in the *Calcutta Review*.[56] Mountstuart Elphinstone, still Resident in Poona, read the book with his usual assiduity. Knowing Malcolm as well as he did, his initial feelings were a mixture of affection and some misgivings about how his breezy friend would deal with such a tremendous subject. But when he read the book he was pleasantly surprised, and commented that it was 'grave, sober, judicious, philosophical. Not a trace of "Jack" Malcolm in it. It really seems a work of great merit.'[57]

In less than a year from its publication, *The History of Persia* had been recognised both in Britain and abroad as a major work. Johan Wolfgang von Goethe, the great German writer and poet, was fascinated by Persian poetry and Islam. He wrote most of the poems for his *West-Ostlicher Divan* in 1814 and 1815. As Minister for the Arts, Culture and Research of the tiny Duchy of Weimar, he controlled book acquisitions by the Duchy's State Library. He was told about *The History of Persia* by his London agent, Huttner, in February 1816 and arranged for its acquisition shortly afterwards. Two years later he was reading it[58] and the library records show that he took it out three times – 18 September to 20 November 1818, 15–24 April 1819 and 28 April to 19 June 1819.[59] In due course French, German, Russian and Persian editions were printed. Its success was finally crowned by Malcolm's receiving an honorary degree from Oxford University on 26 June 1816. For someone from the Scottish Borders who had left school at twelve, such an honour must have been hugely satisfying.

Still, after more than three years at home, Malcolm was no further advanced in the search for a new career in Britain. When Walter Scott suggested that he might buy 'a very handsome house at Gledswood in the Scottish Borders', he replied: 'You have made my mouth water with a place for sale upon the Tweed . . . but I have too little money and too many children to venture to retire. I must in short for some years to come, do as I have done hitherto.'[60]

'Too little money and too many children': this was becoming increasingly apparent. John and Charlotte now had five children to feed. The cost of living was higher than he had expected, and his capital was diminishing. Despite his excellent contacts, he had not been able to find a suitable paid job in England to go with being, potentially, an unpaid Member of Parliament. He had received £5,000 from the Company, but the additional income from it was still not enough to support his family. Despite his literary output he was not at heart a scholar. His books had been written with a purpose – to influence the course of current events. His real skills were in dealing with people – in negotiating, leading and governing.

Meanwhile his five-year period of furlough would be coming to an end at the beginning of 1817. Time as well as money was running out.

He had high hopes of being appointed Governor of Bombay when the current Governor, Sir Evan Nepean, retired. But there was no immediate prospect of that. Several of his most potent sponsors were dead. Minto had died in 1814, Buckinghamshire in February 1816 (after a fall from his horse in St James's Park). The Marquess was out of office and the Duke was away in Paris.

At the end of June 1816, Malcolm went to stay with Gilbert to talk things over. He would also have liked to talk to Pulteney, whom he had last seen in April at the christening of his youngest daughter, Catherine, when Pulteney and the Duke had stood as godfathers. But shortly afterwards Pulteney had been appointed to command the Royal Navy's Cape Station, which included St Helena. He and Clementina had left for the Cape in May. They were to spend a fascinating year on St Helena where Napoleon was living in exile.[61]

Malcolm also wrote to the Duke, who was always ready with good advice. But the Duke was reluctant to get too involved in the shady business of patronage. He wrote from Paris: 'I have received your letter of the 3rd to which I will give you a very frank answer. I am not at present upon such terms with Lord Liverpool [the Prime Minister] as to ask him any [favour] . . . As for Mr Canning [who had taken over as President of the Board of Control] . . . he is surrounded by needy friends and connections, every one of whom he would think an eligible candidate for the office of Governor of Bombay. The Office could suit them [even] if they could not act the Office. However, if I should go to England I'll see what I can do.'[62]

The Duke was as good as his word. He came to England in early July and went straight to Cheltenham, hoping that the waters there would help him to shake off an attack of rheumatism. He wrote again to Malcolm on 9 July and Malcolm visited him at Cheltenham later in the month. The Duke saw Canning in London in early August, and reported to Malcolm that:

> Mr Canning called upon me the other day, and I spoke to him respecting you. I recommended him to employ you, not less on account of the interest I felt for you than for the public service. He was aware of what your object was, viz to obtain the govern-

> ment of Bombay; and I am quite certain from what passed, not only that there is no disinclination to you, but, on the contrary, every disposition to appoint you if the circumstances should permit. Of course Mr Canning did not make me any promise, or even hint at such a thing; but he spoke highly of you, and of the assistance he had already received from you, and did not appear to doubt your fitness for that or any other high situation.
>
> I now recommend you to let the matter drop, and to turn your attention to the public service only. You may be quite certain that great situations are not obtained in this country by personal exertions and interest. Let a man show that he has talents, integrity, and enlarged views, and he may depend upon it that if employment abroad is his object, he is more likely to obtain it without solicitation than by making the most active exertions.[63]

On the same day the Duke also wrote to a Colonel Allen, an aide to the Marquess: 'I wish to speak to you respecting Malcolm. In my opinion the Company could not do better than employ him in a great situation, such as the government of Bombay, if it should be vacant. He has talents and enlarged views to qualify him for any situation; his integrity and zeal for his employers are undoubted; and it might be desirable to show the military profession in the East Indies that when they produce such a man as Malcolm, the road is open to them to every situation in the service.'[64]

It was time for a decision. As a 'substantive' Lieutenant-Colonel in the Madras Army, Malcolm could eventually expect to 'get a regiment' which would enable him to live in England on full pay. But he did not feel he could risk waiting for such uncertain opportunities to come about. So he reluctantly decided that he would have to return to India. Charlotte and the children would have to be left behind, living at Frant and Manchester Street. There was no question of bringing five children under ten to the uncertain climate of India.

Mackintosh, hearing of Malcolm's decision to return to India, wrote sympathetically: 'Your stay cannot be long, and you will refresh all your Indian politics . . . When I say that I feel concern at your going, it is principally because you wished to stay, and partly because I shall feel more solitary when you cease to inhabit the same island. But it is not at all from dislike of India, to which, on the contrary, I am entirely reconciled by my residence in England. I wish that I had not left India, or that I were now well enough to return, especially with you. But I am better than I have been for these five years.' Walter Scott, too, wished him well: 'I do most sincerely wish you all good things – health, happiness and above all a speedy return to Scotland, not to leave us again. I sincerely hope that this will come to pass before we grow much older, and that you will find a snug corner on the Scotch Border to rest in, after having labored so hard in the public service.'[65]

Malcolm made a short trip to Burnfoot in August, meaning to spend two weeks there, but a rumour that his ship would be sailing shortly had him rushing back south, only to find that the rumour had been false. He now made preparations to settle Charlotte and the children at Frant. Although they had bought the cottage (really a house) in 1814, they had continued to live mostly in London or at *Claramont*.

As the day of departure approached, the prospect of lengthy separation began to affect them, especially Charlotte. A week before the date of departure Malcolm wrote to the ever reliable William Pasley at Chatham.

> I should like to see you again if not inconvenient. I have a further motive. Charlotte accompanies me [to Deal]. If I can anticipate her feelings too much, [I am not] quite comfortable in leaving her alone, with no one to see her over the first stage on her return to her children, but this is a subject on which I have not spoken to her, so therefore if it is not quite convenient – say so – we have a roomy carriage if you are at liberty to join us on the road.
>
> You will be glad to know that my departure has brought all kinds of good feelings to a focus, and I leave my country high in heart except when my family comes across my mind.

Malcolm sailed from Deal on 15 October 1816, on the Indiaman *Charles Mills*.

His four years in England had not been wasted. The frantic activity of his previous years in India had given way to a more leisurely routine. There had been time to think, and to share his thoughts with a wider range of opinion than existed in the parochial Anglo-Indian societies of Bombay, Calcutta and Madras, and the officers' messes of the Company's armies in the field. He had met the great men of the day in England and Europe. At Leadenhall Street, he had made some valuable contacts whom he hoped would help him in his future career. The governorship of Bombay would probably be coming up within a year or two. He was still in his mental and physical prime, but a wiser, maturer man.

And there was work to do in India, destined to test his character and talents to the full.

PART FIVE

Proconsul

of Cheetoo in a perfect state, which they afterwards brought to the English camp.[43]

In February 1818, Malcolm was in exuberant mood. After the humiliations of eleven years before, he felt especially vindicated. He wrote to John Adam: 'The Pindarrees are now giving themselves up by hundreds. Where are now the fools who said we could not do this thing? Never was a more glorious result. The noble views of Lord Wellesley of establishing general tranquillity are now nearly accomplished; and if we have firmness and wisdom to preserve and maintain the great advantages we have gained, India will long enjoy an undisturbed peace.'[44]

In late February he returned to Holkar's camp at Mundassor. He had cautioned Captain Agnew that while his job was 'to exercise that influence over the State which is best calculated to preserve it in peace, and to establish its prosperity on a ground that will promote the interests of the British Government, it is very important that it should be done in a way which would neither affect the temper nor hurt the pride of the Prince or his Ministers.'[45] He was well received and found the atmosphere at the Court to his liking, especially in the thirteen-year-old Prince. He told Charlotte: 'I have lately been with my young *ward*, Mulhar Rao Holkar, and certainly the change of a few weeks is wonderful. The fellows that I was hunting like wild animals are all now tame, and combine in declaring that I am their only friend.'[46]

Perhaps the sight of the young prince prompted Malcolm to write to his own son George, now eight years old:

> You bade me promise to write to you if ever I went to battle. I have been at battle. Mamma will tell you I have tried to behave so that you should not be ashamed of your papa. If you become a soldier, you must recollect this, and behave so that papa will not be ashamed of you . . . I have a little horse not bigger than a mastiff dog. He trots into the tent, and eats off the table, which he can just reach. I take hold of his fore-legs, he rears up, and walks on his hind-legs round the tent. We have a monkey who sometimes rides this pony. It is such fun. I often wish that you were here . . . There are many nice gentlemen who live with me, and play and hunt with me. But not one that is not a good scholar. So take care and be a good scholar, or papa will not let you play and hunt with him.[47]

CHAPTER TWENTY-FOUR

India – Shuttle Diplomacy, 1817

The *Charles Mills* called at Portsmouth and waited there a few days because of adverse winds. Malcolm took the opportunity to dash off letters. He wrote to John Murray, thanking him for a present of books for him to read on the voyage, and for his friendship and assistance. He wrote to Richard Heber about progress in arranging the publication of John Leyden's poetry, ending with a reference to the DCL (Doctor of Civil Law) which he had received at Oxford in June:[1] 'God bless you. I shall not fail to write and entreat you will bear me in remembrance. I have made no friend in England since my return from the East that I value so high – when at Oxford, keep me alive there by speaking now and then of the *Doctor from Persia*.'[2] And he wrote to Charlotte, telling her of his visit to Admiral Lord Keith (Clementina Malcolm's uncle) at nearby Purbrook, where he had played with the Admiral's grandchildren.

But soon they were on their way again. In the Bay of Biscay he was homesick. He wrote a poem to Charlotte:

Far on rude seas our barque is cast,
And mountain waves and howling blast
Make elemental war; . . .
I feel again the parting throe,
And all love's agony of woe,
That proves the passion true[3]

One of his fellow passengers was a Mrs Hall, going to join her husband,

General Hall, commander of the British garrison at the Cape. He showed her a pencil sketch of Charlotte and the children, and finding her a sympathetic listener, wrote her a poem.

Aboard ship his daily routine was to:

> rise at half-past five, and every day, except Sundays, go through my exercises [gymnastics]. I go to my cabin at seven, read in my flannel dress till eight, dress, breakfast at half-past eight, walk the deck till ten, return to my cabin, write . . . At twelve I break off for half an hour, when I commence work again, and leave off at half-past two; good dinner at three, break up at half-past four, walk the deck, read light books, or talk nonsense till six o'clock; drink tea; at seven go to cards – two whist tables for steady ladies and gentlemen, and one for the boys; leave off at ten, and all in bed by eleven. Next day the same course, except Sundays, when there are no gymnastics, no cards. If we have prayers upon deck, Captain C– reads the service; I read lessons and sermon.[4]

At Cape Town he was put up in considerable comfort by the Governor, Lord Charles Somerset. But his five-year furlough officially ended on 1 March 1817 and he needed to keep moving. The Captain of the *Charles Mills* wanted to stay longer at Cape Town, so he transferred to the *Minden* for the second leg of the voyage to Madras. Arriving there on 17 March, he stayed with Amelia and John Macdonald, and caught up with many old friends. 'I am half killed, with returning visits. All seem delighted to see me, and I believe the great proportion are sincere.'[5] His main preoccupation, however, was to line himself up with the Governor-General for a serious job. He wrote immediately to Calcutta, offering his services and enclosing letters of recommendation from Canning and others. Not knowing the Governor-General, he waited with some apprehension for a reply, fearing that he might be fobbed off with some routine regimental posting. 'Nothing but complete employment, and a feeling that I am making progress in advancing both the public interests and those of my own family, can reconcile me to this dreadful separation,'[6] he wrote to Charlotte.

He need not have worried.

The Governor-General was Francis Rawdon, Earl of Moira and

Francis Rawdon, Earl of Moira, later Marquess Hastings (1754–1826), Governor-General of India (1813–23).

Marquess of Hastings. Born into a titled Irish family from County Down, he became a professional soldier, fighting with some distinction in the American War of Independence. He succeeded to his father's title in 1793 and entered the House of Lords as an active Whig politician, joining the short-lived Whig dominated Ministry of the Talents in 1806 as Master General of the Ordnance, a sort of ministry of military procurement. He was a crony of the Prince Regent, and when the Prime Minister, Spencer Perceval, was assassinated in 1811, the Prince invited him to form a Ministry, but he was unsuccessful. The Prince then made him a Knight of the Garter, and late in 1812, through the Prince's influence, he was appointed Governor-General. Although he lacked Marquess Wellesley's intellectual brilliance and soaring vision, he was better at getting on with his masters in London. He was a solid, dependable performer, and as a seasoned professional soldier he was well equipped to deal with the major military challenges that arose during his time as Governor-General. For his services in the war with the Gurkhas he had been rewarded (like Wellesley) with an Irish Marquessate – of Hastings – in February 1817. He was nearly sixty-three years old when Malcolm arrived in India.

In mid-April Malcolm received the Governor-General's reply: 'Your very obliging letter, with Mr Canning's despatch, and the other letters which you announce, have reached me here safely . . . Perhaps you may . . . pay a visit to Bengal . . . I justly appreciate your talents and energy, and I shall rejoice if I find a fit field for their employment.'[7] This letter was music to Malcolm's ears. Not only was it cordial, it also invited him to come to Calcutta as soon as possible. Malcolm embarked on the first available ship and arrived in Calcutta on 30 April. He was warmly received by the Governor-General, and accommodated at Government House.

In 1805, Sir George Barlow's reversal of Wellesley's expansionist strategy had left the country west and south of the Jumna river without a single dominant power. The Peshwah, though a reluctant ally of the British, had no control over Scindiah and Holkar. They, in turn, controlled overlapping areas shared with lesser Chiefs. Each relied on plundering his neighbours to maintain and pay a sufficiently large army to protect his own territory. The resulting devastation of the country meant that there was insufficient revenue to pay regular armies, so they hired freebooters who were paid not in cash but in licences to plunder. The result was a vicious cycle of mutual pillage and extortion.

These freebooters came to be known as Pindaris. Their origins were obscure. They did not come from any particular region or tribe; rather, they resembled robber bands led by petty Chiefs. During the Mahratta Wars in the second half of the eighteenth century they served as mercenaries. Malcolm later wrote that: 'The Pindarries, when they came to a rich country, had neither the means nor inclination, like the Tartars, to whom they have been compared, to settle and repose. Like swarms of locusts, acting from instinct, they destroyed and left waste whatever province they visited . . . [they] were neither encumbered by tents nor baggage; each horseman carried a few cakes of bread for his own subsistence, and some feeds of grain for his horse.'[8]

The Anglo-Mahratta War of 1803–05 had greatly reduced the strength of Scindiah and Holkar. The Pindari contingents in their armies were able to play them off against each other, and increase their own relative strength and independence. But they did have one potentially fatal weakness: 'The Pindarries, who had arisen, like masses of putrefaction in animal matter, out of the corruption of weak and expiring states, had, fortunately, none of those bonds of union which unite men in adversity. They had neither the tie of religious, nor of national feeling. They were men of all lands and all religions.'[9]

During Lord Minto's time as Governor-General the Directors modified their non-interference policy, but Minto was heavily occupied with French activity in Persia, mutiny in Madras and expeditions to Mauritius and Java, leaving little time for dealing with the Pindaris. The early years of Hastings's time were likewise taken up with the Gurkha war. Meanwhile the Pindaris, who until 1810 had not dared to attack British India for fear of retaliatory action, became ever bolder in the absence of it. In early 1816 a Pindari force reached the Bay of Bengal at Masulipatam and plundered over 300 villages in Company territory. Hastings now became determined to annihilate them as a force. Crucially, he at last had the backing of the British Government and Leadenhall Street to do so. Logically, he ought to have been able to call upon the cooperation of the Peshwah, Scindiah, Holkar, and Appa Sahib of Berar. After all, they and their subjects were the main sufferers from the depredations of the Pindaris. But they too depended to some extent on plunder and extortion, and they were wary of British offers of assistance, suspecting a British plot to limit and even reduce what little remaining freedom of action they still possessed. The Mahratta Chieftains' later conduct, which the British saw as evasive and failing to honour agreements, was quite understandable from an Indian perspective, and, in the case of the Pindaris, there was the familiar dilemma that 'one man's terrorist is another man's freedom fighter'.

So the timing of Malcolm's arrival in Calcutta was extremely opportune, not only for him but also for Hastings, who now had at his right hand someone who knew the country and the players, and had been through a similar challenge twelve years earlier. During the voyage to Calcutta Malcolm prepared a long memorandum, to which Hastings responded enthusiastically: 'Your papers have been read by me with great satisfaction, because they justify all my own opinions . . . It is extension of influence, not of possessions, that is the solid policy for us; . . . In this conception I have been solicitous . . . to pursue a course which should promote the stability of even Scindiah's and Holkar's Governments. Were these chiefs, however, to make common cause with the Pindarees, either openly or by covert assistance, they would discard their character as rulers of states, and must be dealt with as predatory aggressors.'[10]

A few days later Malcolm wrote excitedly to Charlotte: 'My appointment is all settled. Governor-General's agent in the Deccan, and Brigadier in the Force serving in that quarter [i.e. Commander of the Third Division]. It will be given me in a few days; and within two months of my coming to India I shall be in good employ on the best allowances . . . You will exclaim, "Now he is happy – now he is in his element, flying about in the thick of work." I will confess that, absent from you, I am delighted to be employed, and above all in a way that is useful to myself, and may, I trust, be also useful to my country.'[11]

The next fortnight was spent finalising strategy and drawing up terms of reference. His first task was to visit the Courts of the major rulers, and try to obtain their cooperation in the campaign from the south against the Pindaris. The 70,000-strong 'Army of the Deccan' would advance northwards in 'a great offensive drive from the south upon a stopping line in the north'.[12] Hastings, meanwhile, would assemble a massive military force to be launched on the enemy simultaneously from the north, as soon as the monsoon was over in October. Hastings himself, as Commander-in-Chief as well as Governor-General, would head the 40,000 strong northern force based on the Jumna river. A third force of Bombay troops would advance east from Gujerat.

At Hastings's request, Malcolm wrote a massive minute setting out the background, the options, the objectives and the recommended strategy for the campaign – what would today be called a strategic plan. Significantly, he warned that while annexation of territory should not be an object of the eventual political settlement 'territorial possession will, in spite of all our efforts to the contrary, come too fast upon us'.[13] His view was that while the British might be able to rely on the cooperation, or at least neutrality, of the Peshwah in Poona and of Appa Sahib in Nagpur, Scindiah and Holkar were uncertain quantities. Scindiah, despite his protestations to the contrary, was undoubtedly the main sponsor of several Pindari Chiefs. The Governor-General should therefore try to neutralise Scindiah. He could best do this by supporting his diplomatic team during the period of negotiations by putting a large military force into Scindiah's Gwalior heartland. Scindiah should be strong-armed into a new and stringent treaty, stipulating at least nominal support for the Company's campaign against the Pindaris. This was in line with the negotiating strategy propounded by Malcolm in 1803 – 'a political officer is never so likely to succeed as when he negotiates at the head of an army'.[14]

Holkar was a different matter. Back in 1806, Jaswunt Rao had been forced by the British to sign a treaty surrendering some of his territory. But neither he, nor his successors after he died in 1811, had ever acquiesced in allowing a British Resident, or a British-officered Subsidiary Force, to be stationed with the Holkar Court at Indore. Besides, the Holkar government was divided and weak. Jaswunt Rao's successor, Mulhar Rao, born in 1805, was still only twelve years old. His stepmother Tulsi Bhai, the Regent, though apparently favouring negotiations with the British, was opposed by the powerful military faction at the Court. There was therefore little chance of the British getting any help from Holkar in their pursuit of the Pindaris. So they needed to adopt a different strategy for limiting the effectiveness of any hostile action by Holkar. The most powerful vassal in Holkar's territory was Jaswunt Rao's General, Amir Khan, a Pathan in origin. In the event of war, he might well sell himself and his army to the highest bidder. So Malcolm recommended that he should be separated from Holkar by an offer to recognise his *jaghirs* as permanent, in return for his support against the Pindaris (and possibly against Holkar too). In other words, for the Company itself to become the highest bidder.

This, then, was the strategy. The aim of the British, as is clear from their internal correspondence at this time, was genuinely limited to extirpating the Pindaris; they had no direct designs on Mahratta territory. Unfortunately, when in due course the Mahratta Chieftains saw the Company's massive military forces being assembled in Central India, they could not bring themselves to believe that the British were not also seeking additional territory for themselves at Mahratta expense. Wars often come about through misunderstanding.

Not all of Malcolm's time at Government House was spent in earnest discussion or writing strategic plans – he still found time for fun and games. One afternoon 'he [the Governor-General] came out of his room in full dress, as he always is; and caught me, without coat or neckcloth, playing billiards with an aide-de-camp in similar costume. He smiled and made a bow. As he was passing on to Mr Seton's rooms, I said, "You will find Mr Seton, who belongs to the Supreme Board, and ought to know better, much worse than us". He did . . . The lord laughed heartily, but made him remain as he was.'[15]

Around 20 May Malcolm embarked on a small ship which struggled southward against the monsoon, taking a month to reach Madras. At Madras he stayed again with the Macdonalds. Recalling former times wistfully, he wrote to a friend, 'Here I am at the old place; but how altered. Where is Close? Where Webbe? Where is everyone?'[16] There he discussed the situation with General Sir Thomas Hislop, the Commander-in-Chief of the Madras Army, whom he found 'a plain, sincere man, without any littleness or jealousy'. He meant to spend no more than a week there but waited a little longer for the arrival of his old friend Tom Munro. 'If the arrangement [i.e. pacification of the southern Mahratta country] is committed to such a *maistry* [skilled workman] as Tom Munro I shall sleep all the way to Poona, and the Commander-in-Chief can proceed as he ought, without another question, to Hyderabad. The Mahrattas will never cheat nor beat Munro, and, besides, he will be the best man in the universe to look after the *Jagheerdars*.'[17]

A fortnight later he set off westward on horseback, accompanied for the first sixteen miles by the Macdonalds, then by *dawk*. Again there was nostalgia. Ten miles from Arcot, 'I got out of my palanquin and dispelled all the fatigues of it by a gallop to Captain Outlaw's, who lives in the house once occupied by our friend Dallas. As I came to this last stage it brought a thousand recollections to my mind.'[18] Among these recollections would have been the gallop over the same ground with Arthur Wellesley in 1799, and again in 1803; and taking Charlotte to Mysore in March 1807 before they were married. At Bangalore he briefed Arthur Cole, Resident at Mysore, on arrangements for a 4,000-strong contingent of the celebrated Mysore Horse to be seconded to the Deccan army. While at Bangalore, he also appointed the 28-year-old Lieutenant John Low as his aide-de-camp. Low's family came from Clatto in Fife and were known to Malcolm. With twelve years' service in the Madras Army, Low had heard of Malcolm's appointment, and back in June had written to him, putting himself forward for a job on his staff. Malcolm, impressed by the young man's boldness, arranged to meet him on his way through Bangalore, and immediately took him on. He had already recruited, as a clerk, George Wareham, a teenage boy who had been a passenger aboard the *Minden* on the voyage to Madras.

He then proceeded to Hyderabad, which was to be the supply base for General Hislop's Army of the Deccan. He discussed with the Resident, Henry Russell and the Nizam's Ministers the setting up of supply depots, provision of carriage bullocks and secondment of a contingent of the Nizam's troops to Hislop's army. It had been fifteen years since he had last visited Hyderabad and he found great changes. For a start, the Residency, once 'the house of a native nobleman, which was pleasant from being surrounded with small gardens and fountains, and had been sufficiently modified by improvements to be rendered a tolerably convenient European residence', had now become 'a palace, for such the present mansion of the British Resident of Hyderabad may be well termed.' He paid his respects to the Nizam, and two days later dined with the Prime Minister, Muneer-ul-Mulk, 'who lives in great luxury and splendour, and was saluted at one point by a guard of female Sepoys.'[19]

> The entertainment was very splendid. I was gratified at meeting my old friend Chanda [Maleeka], the celebrated dancing-girl. I had received several trays of fruit from this lady; and she had also sent me her *picture*, with expressions of regard that were meant, she said, to revive pleasing recollections. The Court of Hyderabad is altered, and the dance and the song no longer prevail. A moody, melancholy sovereign, degraded and dejected nobles, and the impoverished retainers of a fallen Court, offer no field for the genius of Chanda; . . . She commands the principal sets of dancing-girls, and, now that her own bloom is past (she is above sixty), is the first monopolist in the market of beauty at the capital. She danced and she sang for upwards of an hour, but – I know not how it is – the fine tones, the fine acting, the faint, the recovery, the melancholy, the intoxication which she exhibited in turns, as she chanted her Hindustani and Persian odes, did not charm me as they were wont. After all, eighteen years do make some difference in the appearance and feelings both of man and woman.[20]

A week later he wrote, 'I have been very busy. It is now eleven o'clock p.m., and I start to-morrow at half-past three. I ride eighty miles, and go the rest in a palanquin. I expect to travel ninety miles a day, and to arrive [at Poona] within four days.'[21]

Three hundred and sixty-four miles in less than four days! – from Hyderabad, in July, in the monsoon, with an ambient daytime temperature in the thirties. He confined himself to bread and milk twice a day. By early morning on 4 August, he had reached the banks of the Beemah river, about a hundred miles from Poona. There he was met by a detachment of Mahratta cavalry, who escorted him into Poona, galloping the last sixty-four miles in eight hours and arriving late in the evening. 'I was not at all fatigued', he wrote, 'a proof of the health that I am in, and which by the blessing of God, I will by diet and exercise preserve, that I may prove equal to the great duties that are opening upon me.'[22]

He was, of course, well known in Poona and received a warm welcome, above all from Elphinstone, still the Resident and an old friend. They had last met five and a half years before, when they had both been writing books. The Peshwah, Baji Rao, and his Court were away at Mahanleh (Mahuli), a place of pilgrimage about seventy miles south of Poona. Relations between Elphinstone and the Peshwah had reached a low ebb. The problem went back many years, in fact to 1802 and the Treaty of Bassein. The Peshwah had felt humiliated at his ousting from Poona by Holkar in 1802, and no less so at being restored and maintained on his throne since then by the alien British. The fact that Close and Elphinstone, as British Residents at Poona, were both able and utterly reasonable men, only made the humiliation worse; there was so little to complain about in their behaviour. In many ways he was his own worst enemy. As Arthur Wellesley had once so presciently remarked, 'The only principle of [Baji Rao's] conduct is his insincerity.'[23]

The most recent cause of friction lay in the case of Gungadur Shastri, Chief Minister to the Gaekwad of Baroda. In 1815 there was a dispute over accounts between Poona and Baroda, and it was proposed that Shastri should go to Poona to negotiate a settlement. Shastri, knowing Baji Rao's treacherous reputation, was unwilling to go, but after some exchanges and a British guarantee of safe conduct, he made the journey. After several weeks of negotiation he was induced to visit the Peshwah at the temple of Vithoba at Pandharpur. There he was murdered, allegedly at the instigation of Trimbakji Denglia, the Peshwah's Minister (who may also have had accomplices in a faction opposed to Shastri at the Baroda Court). Enraged, the British demanded that Trimbakji should be arrested and handed over to the Resident. After considerable hesitation, Baji Rao eventually yielded, and Trimbakji was imprisoned in the fort at Thana in Company territory near Bombay. But in September 1816 he escaped, possibly with the connivance of the Peshwah. He then sought 'to recover his power' and recruited a force of over 3,000 horse and 300 infantry in southern Mahratta country. Again the British pressed Baji Rao to take action, but he remained evasive. Elphinstone had to threaten all-out war before Baji Rao at last agreed to sign the Treaty of Poona in June 1817, conceding British demands and forcing him finally 'to recognise the dissolution in form and substance of the Maratha Confederacy'.[24]

The Peshwah had thus again been publicly humiliated. Nevertheless, when he heard of Malcolm's approach to Poona, he invited him to come on to Mahanleh. He spoke of Malcolm as 'his last friend among the English'. Malcolm, flattered by the warmth of the invitation, was keen to go, and Elphinstone supported the idea, on the basis that if anyone could succeed in cheering up Baji Rao and inducing him to cooperate against the Pindaris, it would be Malcolm.

The Peshwah asked for Malcolm to come for an evening meeting on 8 August. So, despite having only arrived at Poona after his exhausting ride from Hyderabad late on 4 August, Malcolm set out for Mahanleh late on 7 August, accompanied by Major Ford, a British officer attached to the Peshwah's army and a favourite of the Peshwah. After a stressful journey, they finally reached Mahanleh at seven the next evening, only to find that the Peshwah had gone to bed, saying that he was too tired to meet Malcolm that night.

> The Minister [Moro Dikshit] kept me talking till twelve at night. I was awakened at five o'clock on the 9th, with a message that the Peishwah expected me at six. I was kept by the ceremonies of previous visits from Goklah, and other of the Mahratta military chiefs with whom I was acquainted, till seven, when I went to the Maharajah. Six years, which is the period since I saw him last, had not changed him much, but he looked careworn. He received me with apparent joy, said I was associated with Generals Wellesley and Close in placing him on the Musnud, that I had proved that I still had a warm heart towards him by coming so far to see him, and that he was delighted to have an opportunity

of unburdening his heart to one in whom he had such confidence. I had an interview of three hours and a half.[25]

On his return to Poona the next day, Malcolm reported to Elphinstone on his visit. He believed that Baji Rao was at last being sincere in his protestations of friendship and support for the British campaign against the Pindaris. He had already started to build up his military strength and wanted to do more. Malcolm had encouraged him. He had been flattered to be called a friend, and his persistent optimism made him *want* to believe that Baji Rao was a reformed character. Elphinstone remained sceptical – he had lived too long with Baji Rao's changes of mood to be taken in. The friends agreed to differ.

Malcolm left Poona on 11 August. Whether or not he had cheered up Baji Rao, he had certainly cheered up Elphinstone, who had been depressed and a little miffed at the time of Malcolm's arrival. He was upset that General Hislop had been put in charge, over his head, of negotiations with the Peshwah, and he suspected that this might have been the work of Malcolm, seeking to 'to add everything he could to his own credit'.

However, his mood changed. He wrote on 8 August: 'Malcolm has been here since the 5th, full of good stories, good humour and good sense. We have talked over all subjects, among others, the plan of sending Sir T Hislop to settle with the Peshwa, which was his. It certainly was injurious to me, but I did not know that I had any claim to forbearance.' And, four days later: 'Malcolm is gone. His visit has completely effaced all the bad impressions that remained on my mind. Never was anybody so frank and good-humoured. Considering his time of life, his ardour, his activity of body and mind, his inexhaustible spirits and imperturbable temper, are truly admirable, and all these qualities are accompanied with a sound judgment and a great store of knowledge, derived both from reading and from observation.'[26]

From Poona, Malcolm returned to Hyderabad to complete the supply arrangements for the Deccan army. Here he found that Hislop had fallen seriously ill, so he had to take on Hislop's responsibilities as well as his own. He worked flat out for nearly three weeks 'in an unvaried round of hard work, during which I have been every day employed incessantly from five o'clock in the morning till eight at night, in making arrangements and preparations to put the forces in this quarter in motion'.[27]

When he finally set off northwards towards Nagpur on 4 September with a small escort, he felt a surge of exhilaration. He was relieved to be finished with staff work and relished being on campaign, living in a tent for weeks on end. He had gathered a team around him at Hyderabad. Among them were Josiah Stewart and John Briggs; Lieutenant John Low (whom he had taken on at Bangalore); and young George Wareham. The wet season persisted for several more weeks and the rivers were in flood. The monsoon rains were said to be the heaviest for twenty-five years. Malcolm's party rode mainly on elephants, splashing through the smaller rivers until they reached the banks of the Godavery on 12 September. They got across but were held up four days later by another seemingly impassable torrent. Malcolm decided to cross, and 'for seven or eight hours three of these animals [elephants] kept going backwards and forwards through the stream, loaded with baggage, men, women and children. Besides what were on their backs, half a dozen held on by ropes from them, and other ropes fastened to these animal-bridges hauled over horses and camels. The whole was a scene for the pencil of Hogarth.'[28]

They eventually reached Nagpur on 24 September. Richard Jenkins, the Resident, came out to meet them. So did the twenty-year-old Rajah, Mudhoji Bhonsle, popularly known as Appa Sahib. (Raghuji Bhonsle had died in 1816, and was succeeded by his mentally disabled son Parsoji, with Appa Sahib acting as Regent. But Appa Sahib had soon contrived the murder of Parsoji and taken over as Regent himself.) 'We alighted at one of his gardens, where he gave us a very excellent dinner, and made me the usual presents.' Malcolm described Appa Sahib as 'a good looking young man . . . of pleasant countenance and manners – very inquisitive and intelligent. He is, however, young and inexperienced, and from desiring to rule himself he becomes the shuttlecock of different parties.'[29] Malcolm's task here was similar to that in Hyderabad; to organise supplies and induce Appa Sahib to lend his support. For nine days he haggled with local merchants and courtiers, who realised that the urgency of his situation would enable them to extract extortionate prices. Appa Sahib was friendly and cooperative.

On 4 October Malcolm's party pushed on from Nagpur to join the army, which was assembling on the banks of the Nerbudda river at Husseinabad. The rains had ceased, but the country was still waterlogged and the going was slow. On 19 October, after a march of 'nearly sixty miles through a dreary forest, without a human habitation except one collection of twenty or thirty huts',[30] he reached the Nerbudda. At Harda on 29 October he took command of the Third Division. Here there was more sad news – young George Wareham, whom he had left behind at Husseinabad, had died of fever. 'I weep over his fate, as I would over that of a son.'[31]

As planned earlier, a large military force from Hastings's Grand Army now arrived at Gwalior from the north, and the Company's negotiating team cowed Scindiah into signing a treaty on 6 November, by which he undertook to place his troops at the disposal of the Company in the war against the Pindaris, with a British officer in charge of each division, and to give the Company temporary possession of the forts of Asirgarh and Hindia. Charles Metcalfe, the British Resident in Delhi, had negotiated a treaty with Amir Khan (Holkar's ex-General), guaranteeing him his *jaghirs* in perpetuity in return for disbanding his army, surrendering his guns and assisting in the fight against the Pindaris. Overtures had been made to the lesser rulers who had been victims of the Pindaris. The Rajput Chiefs were assured that they would be freed from allegiance to Scindiah and Holkar, while Malcolm negotiated a treaty with the Nawab of Bhopal. With all these arrangements in place for conciliating, neutralising and threatening the Mahratta Chieftains, the British now felt that they could turn their full attention to dealing with the Pindaris.

The two major Pindari Chiefs at this time were Cheetoo Khan and Karim Khan. Cheetoo had been hired by Raghuji Bhonsle and later by Dowlat Rao Scindiah. By 1814 he had at his disposal 10,000 horse, 1,500 infantry and 17 guns. Karim Khan had been used successively by the Nawab of Bhopal, by Scindiah and by Holkar. His force comprised 6,000 cavalry, 5,000 infantry and 15 guns. Both were formidable and elusive opponents. Hitherto operating independently, the two Pindari forces were becoming increasingly aware of their imminent peril, and the need to stick together, if they could, to survive. By mid-November they were spread out in a line some fifty miles north of the Nerbudda river, running roughly east-west in the hills above Bhopal. The various divisions of the Grand Army were covering the Pindaris from the north, ready to prevent any attempt by them to escape northward in the direction of the Rajput states or the Doab.[32] Concurrently, the Deccan army was assembling at various crossing points along the south bank of the Nerbudda, ready to cross and drive the Pindaris northwards towards the waiting Grand Army.

So far, the objectives which Hastings had decided upon earlier in the year, and the plan which Malcolm had set out in his minute of 17 July, appeared to be working well. The Mahrattas had been neutralised and the Pindaris were being inexorably driven into the closing jaws of the two British armies. But in mid-November some shocking news reached Hislop. On 5 November the Peshwah had suddenly attacked the British Residency at Poona.

In fact, unknown to Malcolm and only suspected by Elphinstone, Baji Rao had been secretly plotting against the British since the middle of 1816. Over the course of the subsequent year he had been in touch with Scindiah, Holkar and Appa Sahib and had posted agents at their Courts in breach of the Treaty of Bassein, which had laid down that he had to inform the Company of any contacts with other states. He had been requested by Scindiah 'to emancipate himself from the English, collect his *jaghirdars* and adherents and after preparing a large army, commence a war . . . I shall be ready to follow your example.'[33] He had written to Appa Sahib that 'We are all pugreebunds, that is we all wear turbans. If I require it, you must send your troops to assist me, or if you require it, I will assist you', to which Appa Sahib had replied, 'I have received your letter and understand its contents. You are my elder brother, have seen and done much and still will. I am your junior. Be perfectly at ease about me. I am yours. The rest you will learn from the verbal communications of Sukharam Punt.'[34] The Peshwah had also promised to lend Holkar Rs150,000 to clear his outstanding debt to his troops, and he had written to the Sikh Chieftain Ranjit Singh of Lahore, while Scindiah had written to the Nepalese Court at Kathmandu seeking their support against 'the English'.

Malcolm now realised with dismay that Baji Rao had thoroughly duped him at Mahanle in August. Elphinstone had rightly been more sceptical. Over the next few weeks following that meeting, Baji Rao had become increasingly hostile, trying (without success) to entice sepoy troops in the Company's Poona garrison to defect. Elphinstone was in a dangerously weak position, because a large part of the garrison troops had been sent north to tackle the Pindaris. The Residency was indefensible and the only Company troops, Colonel Burr's brigade, were stationed at a cantonment some distance away. At the end of October, when the Peshwah started massing his troops at Poona, Elphinstone realised that an attack was probably imminent. He sent urgent word to Bombay for reinforcements, and moved Burr's brigade to the hill at Kirkee (Khadki), about three miles north of the Residency. He himself sat tight, playing for time to allow the relieving troops from Bombay to reach Poona, and judging that the Peshwah would hesitate before attacking the Residency while he was still living there. On the morning of 5 November the Peshwah sent an ultimatum. Elphinstone evacuated the Residency and joined Colonel Burr on the hill at Kirkee. Arriving there late in the day, he could see the Peshwah's troops enter the Residency and set it alight, destroying all his possessions, books and papers.[35]

Now came a dramatic development. A battalion in the Peshwah's army was stationed at Dapuri, a few miles north-west of Poona. It was commanded by Major Ford, the same officer who had accompanied Malcolm to Mahanleh in August. Ford was a Madras Army officer who had acted as assistant to Barry Close at the Poona Residency. In 1812 he had been seconded to the Peshwah, to whom he had sworn allegiance 'except in the event of hostilities with the British'. He considered the present situation to be just such an event, and Moro Dikshit, the Peshwah's General, agreed with him. Moro Dikshit and Ford were great friends and there is a romantic story of an understanding between them. Knowing that they would have to take different sides in the forthcoming battle, and that one of them might die, they agreed that the survivor would maintain the family of the deceased. Moro Dikshit was killed and Ford is said to have kept his word.[36] By bringing his troops with him to join the British, Ford made a material difference to their strength which now amounted to 2,800 men. Elphinstone watched the Peshwah's cavalry move out into the plain below Kirkee: 'the sight was magnificent, as the tide rolled out of Poona. [James] Grant[37] described it as resembling the Bore on the Gulf of Cambay. Everything was hushed except the trampling and neighing of horses, and the whole valley was filled with them like a river in flood . . . this whole mass of cavalry came on at speed in the most splendid style. The rush of horse, the sound of the earth, the waving of flags, the brandishing of spears were grand beyond description, but perfectly ineffectual.'[38]

Realising that static defence against such enormous odds – the Peshwah's army was 30,000 strong against Colonel Burr's force of less than 3,000 – would lead inevitably to their exhaustion and eventual annihilation or surrender, Elphinstone urged Burr to attack. He did so successfully, and as dusk fell, the Peshwah's army retreated to Poona in confusion. British casualties were 86 killed and wounded, the Peshwah's about 500. The next day the Bombay Army detachment arrived at Kirkee, and a few days later the British force was able to march into Poona, only to find that Baji Rao and his army had fled to the south.

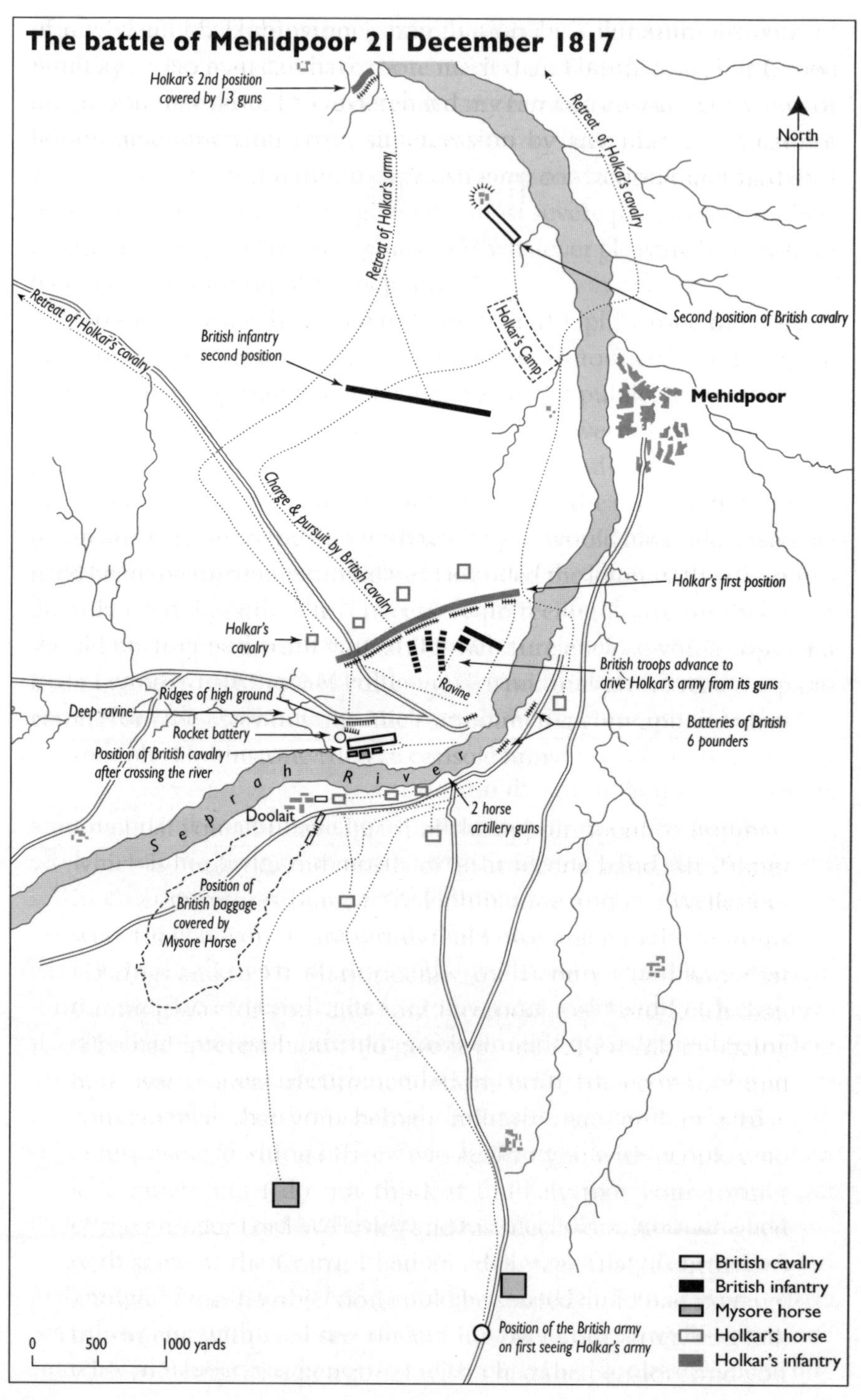
The battle of Mehidpoor 21 December 1817
Holkar's 2nd position covered by 13 guns
North
Retreat of Holkar's cavalry
Retreat of Holkar's army
Retreat of Holkar's cavalry
Second position of British cavalry
Holkar's Camp
British infantry second position
Mehidpoor
Charge & pursuit by British cavalry
Holkar's first position
Holkar's cavalry
British troops advance to drive Holkar's army from its guns
Ravine
Ridges of high ground
Deep ravine
Rocket battery
Batteries of British 6 pounders
Position of British cavalry after crossing the river
Seprah River
Doolait
2 horse artillery guns
Position of British baggage covered by Mysore Horse
British cavalry
British infantry
Mysore horse
Holkar's horse
Holkar's infantry
0 500 1000 yards
Position of the British army on first seeing Holkar's army

CHAPTER TWENTY-FIVE

India – War, 1817–1818

Until the battle of Kirkee, the contest had been a Company campaign against Pindari freebooters. Overnight it was now transformed into a full-scale Anglo-Mahratta War. There were immediate repercussions for Malcolm in Central India. He had crossed the Nerbudda with his Third Division and was already setting out in pursuit of the Pindaris, when he was ordered to halt, in case some of his Madras Army troops might be needed in the southern Mahratta country. But after a few days, with the news that the Peshwah's forces had abandoned Poona, he was allowed to resume his march northwards.

Towards the end of November, Appa Sahib made threatening gestures towards the small British garrison at Nagpur, similar to those of the Peshwah at Poona a month earlier. Jenkins, the Resident, called for reinforcements, and meanwhile concentrated the small British force on the Sitibaldi hills above the Residency to the west of the city. On the evening of 26 November shots were exchanged and heavy firing continued into the night. On the following morning Jenkins found himself surrounded by a Mahratta army estimated at 18,000 men and 36 guns. As at Kirkee, attack was deemed the best form of defence, and the Mahratta force was driven off after eighteen hours of desperate fighting.

The situation at Holkar's Court, which had been confused enough before the Peshwah's attack at Poona, now reached a more extreme crisis. The Regent, Tulsi Bhai: 'was young and beautiful, with more than common ability for public affairs; but she was licentious and vindictive, and her evil passions had rendered her extremely unpopular in the state.

Her chief favourite was one Gunpat Rao, who was associated with Tanteea Jogee [Tantia Jog, the Chief Minister] in his ministry; but almost all real power had passed from their hands into those of the Patan [Pathan] military leaders, who controlled the soldiery; while the Regent and her party were suspected of a desire to betray the state to the English.'[1]

The Peshwah's attack at Poona was a signal that tipped the balance in favour of the 'war' party at the Holkar Court. On 24 November Tantia Jog was deposed by the military faction, which assembled the army and began marching southward from Rampoora (about eighty miles north of Oujein) to Mehidpoor, meaning to continue further south to link up with the Peshwah's army which they understood (wrongly, as it turned out) to be on its way northwards. The size of the army was thought to be about 30,000 horse and 10,000 infantry though a significant proportion of these were later described by Company officers as 'rabble'. The chief problem was that the troops had not been paid for some time; hence the urgent desire to meet the Peshwah and receive the funds that he had promised.

Meanwhile, the Pindaris had retreated northwards, hoping for support from Scindiah, which never came. Malcolm and the Third Division continued their pursuit of Cheetoo, who now veered west, hoping to be protected by Holkar's army moving south. On 13 December Malcolm told Hislop that he had never got nearer than fifty miles from Cheetoo.[2] As usual, a Pindari force, unencumbered by baggage and guns, could move much more quickly than a Company army.

By this time Hislop's First Division had reached Oujein on its way north and Malcolm hurried to join it. He knew that only a combination of the First and Third Divisions would be sufficient to confront Holkar's large army. He arrived there on 12 December, and after two days' rest the two divisions set off towards Mehidpoor, about twenty-five miles to the north, where Holkar's army was assembling. On 15 December two *vakeels* from Holkar arrived at the British camp, with expressions of friendship. Malcolm greeted them, and outlined his terms for a settlement: a demand that Holkar should enter into alliance with the British to destroy the Pindaris, coupled with the sweetener that if all went well, the British would make up the arrears of pay in Holkar's army. The *vakeels* vacillated, bringing back conflicting messages from the Holkar camp. After four days of this, Malcolm concluded that Holkar's Ministers were merely playing for time and had no intention of signing a treaty. He dismissed the *vakeels* and prepared for battle.

Back at Holkar's Court, internal dissension was reaching a climax. On the evening of 19 December, the military faction, still suspicious that Tulsi Bhai and her lover Gunpat Rao were plotting to sell out to the British, seized them both. 'As day broke on the 20th Tilsee Bhaee was taken from the tent in which she had been confined, and carried down to the banks of the Sepree [Sipra] river, where the beautiful head of the unhappy woman was struck from her body, and her bloody remains cast into the stream.'[3]

The Company army spent the night of 20 December camped at Harnia, less than ten miles south of the Holkar camp at Mehidpoor. It was not a quiet night. Knowing that they would almost certainly meet their enemy in battle on the morrow, there were frantic preparations: weapons cleaned, ammunition drawn, scouts sent out to reconnoitre the route, order of march decided upon. By dawn they were on their way. It was a small force, comprising the First and Third Divisions of the Deccan army – two brigades of cavalry, two brigades of infantry, a brigade of horse artillery, some other artillery and a detachment of the Mysore Horse (much smaller than the original 4,000). Apart from the Madras European regiment, plus two companies of the Royal Scots and a detachment of Dragoons, it was a native Indian Army with British officers, numbering no more than 7,000 men. Holkar's army was estimated at about 30,000 men, of whom more than 20,000 were cavalry.

This part of India is flat, open country with a few minor hillocks, interspersed by occasional stands of trees and *nullahs* (dry stream beds). In December the weather is cool and dry. The army made steady progress at marching pace. About eight o'clock Malcolm was approached by *vakeels* from Holkar's *durbar*, bringing letters remonstrating with him about the army's continued advance, and adding that the British should remember that they were 'advancing on the army of Holkar'. This was a veiled reference to the campaign of 1804, when Company armies were given a hard time by Jaswunt Rao Holkar. But Malcolm was too old a hand in Mahratta diplomacy to be diverted by these tactics. He had anticipated the *vakeels'* approach, and the night before he had drafted a suitable response, which he now handed to them and sent them on their way, without interrupting the army's march.

By nine o'clock they were within three miles of the mighty Sipra

The Battle of Mehidpoor, 21 December 1817. The scene looking north across the river Sipra, to the rising ground where Holkar's army was assembled. Note the ravines on the north bank, up which the Company troops climbed on to the plain beyond.

river. Some 300 yards wide, it runs from west to east, then turns north, passing the town of Mehidpoor on its right bank. An avenue of trees ran along the south bank, masking the river. But from the summit of a small hillock, Hislop and Malcolm could see over the trees. There, about 800 yards back from the far side of the river, on slightly rising ground, lay Holkar's army, facing south. It was drawn up in three lines, each about one mile wide. In front were the guns – about seventy of them. Immediately behind them were the infantry. At the back were the cavalry. In the middle, on slightly higher ground, was a ruined village. This was the strong point and headquarters, where young Mulhar Rao and his Generals sat on their elephants. It was an extremely strong posi-

tion, protected on its front and left by the river, and on its right by a deep ravine running down to the river. The ground between the Company army and the south (right) bank of the river was occupied by several detachments of Mahratta horse, which were already starting to harry the approaching Company troops.

Two immediate problems faced the British before they could begin to engage the main body of the enemy: first, how to clear the enemy cavalry from the near side of the river; and second, how to cross it in the face of seventy heavy-calibre Mahratta guns. Hislop gave Malcolm the first task, which did not prove difficult; when challenged, Holkar's cavalry soon faded away. They also gave a useful clue about how to get across the river. There were two fords. Holkar's cavalry all crossed by the nearer one, even though the further one appeared the more convenient.

By midday the Company troops had reached the south bank of the river. Hislop then made the brave decision (at Malcolm's suggestion) to cross by the nearer ford, and immediately attack the enemy line. It was a risky move, because after the troops had crossed the river and assembled on the further bank, they would be extremely vulnerable. But there were mitigating factors. The banks of the river were at least twenty-five feet high, so that during the crossing they would be in dead ground, protected from direct fire from the Mahratta guns. There was also a large sand bar on the north bank where troops could be assembled before they climbed up to the plateau and came under direct fire. The only practical way to reach the plateau was to climb up one of the ravines which ran at right angles to the bank. Luckily for the British, only one ravine, the largest and most westerly, was manned by Mahratta troops.

Hislop now asked Malcolm to lead the river crossing and attack the enemy line. This was a tremendous moment in Malcolm's military career. He had been brought up as a professional soldier, he had seen action as a young ensign in the 1780s and he had been at Seringapatam in 1799. But he had missed Assaye and Argaum in 1803 through illness, and since then he had been a diplomat rather than a soldier. He had listened to the Duke talking about the Peninsular War and Waterloo. Now at last, here was a chance, at the age of forty-eight, to lead troops in a major battle.

A small gun battery was deployed on the south bank to give some covering fire to the troops crossing the river. The first unit to ford the river was the light infantry brigade, followed by the cavalry and a horse artillery battery, which assembled on the sand bar below the left (north) bank. The guns were then pulled up the steep slope on the left of the line. Next to cross was the first infantry brigade. Despite being largely in dead ground, the troops who had already crossed the river were coming under heavy fire and in that confined space there was inevitably a lot of confusion. Also, the British gun batteries on each side of the river had mostly been silenced by the heavier-calibre Mahratta guns, meaning that the British attack would have to proceed without artillery support. At this point Hislop made another crucial decision, again at Malcolm's suggestion. He ordered him to attack the enemy line straight away, without waiting for the second infantry brigade to cross the river. Malcolm immediately sent the first infantry brigade climbing up the bank on the right, the light infantry up the ravines in the middle, and the cavalry up on to a piece of semi-dead ground on the left. Despite heavy fire from the Mahratta guns some 700 yards in front of them, the Company troops were somehow assembled in line. The bugle sounded and the whole line moved forward.

Seven hundred yards! It took only about ten minutes to reach the enemy guns but it must have seemed like an eternity. Without artillery support, the Company troops were cut down in large numbers by roundshot and grape.[4] The dust and, above all, the noise from the booming guns, the whistling and crashing cannon balls, the neighing horses, the cries of the wounded, the shouting of orders, must have been overwhelming and terrifying. Yet somehow, they kept going steadily forward, 'animated by the cheering example of their leaders'.[5] Malcolm led the infantry towards the ruined village at the centre of the Mahratta line. Years later, John Low wrote to him that 'I shall not easily forget your tall figure on your tall piebald horse, cantering about . . . at the head of your division, amidst dust and smoke and grapeshot, surrounded by your numerous staff and friends.'[6] Half way to the target, he raised his hat and led the troops in a loud 'Huzza!' then galloped forward, urging them to follow. Colonel Scott, commanding the first brigade, alarmed by this show of bravado, drew up his horse alongside Malcolm and shouted, 'Oh! Sir John, let us not lose an age of discipline at a time like this.' To which a chastened Malcolm replied, 'I beg your pardon, let us all be composed.' A few minutes later, seeing irregularities in the line, he rode forward in front of the troops, trying to sort things out. His aide-de-camp, Syed Ibrahim, cried out, 'Look at the General! He is in front of the men, who are firing. For God's sake bring him back.'[7] Yet he displayed considerable coolness too. 'Observing a sepoy battalion stop and fire in its advance, he turned round to the men, and said, "My lads, there is little use in that; I think we had better give them the cold iron."'[8] At last the surviving troops reached the guns. They bayoneted and shot the gunners, who had bravely continued to fire their guns until the last moment, and moved on to attack the second line. With its flanks turned, the Mahratta infantry gave way and fled. The few surviving gunners were braver. After their guns had been overrun, they turned them round and fired at the backs of the British infantry. The cavalry on the left of the British line attacked the Mahratta right. Pockets of gunners and infantry held out, but when they saw the second British infantry brigade appearing at the top of the river bank, they too broke and fled. The Mahratta cavalry behaved less gallantly. At the first sign that the battle was going against them, they fled north-westwards. Young Holkar, atop his elephant, is said to have burst into tears. He too fled, leaving sixty-three Mahratta guns in the hands of the British. This action had taken just a quarter of an hour. Of the 1,979 Company troops who had been directly engaged, 510 had been killed or wounded.

It was now early afternoon. The next phase of the battle was the pursuit of Holkar's army, fleeing in two directions: the cavalry and Holkar's Court to the north-west, the remainder to the north-east. As Hislop and Malcolm surveyed the scene from the elevated site of the ruined village, they observed Holkar's tented camp, a mile and a half to the north-east, in low ground near the river opposite Mehidpoor. Malcolm was ordered to capture it with the first infantry brigade. Meanwhile the British cavalry (mainly Mysore Horse) pursuing Holkar to the north-west also noticed the camp and veered eastwards to capture it, arriving there ahead of Malcolm's troops. Finding it abandoned, they resumed their pursuit to the north-west. When Malcolm's infantry arrived at the camp, they came under fire from the remnants of Holkar's infantry and some cavalry, who had set up a new defensive position to the north of the camp, with thirteen remaining guns. But this turned out to be no more than a holding operation, to give their troops time to cross the river.[9] Once again, Hislop turned to Malcolm, ordering him to pursue the fleeing enemy downstream (northwards) along the right bank with a contingent of cavalry and light infantry. But the Company troops were slower than the Mahrattas at getting across the river. Though they continued the pursuit for about eight miles they failed to make up any ground and called off the chase. 'The cavalry and light infantry returned [to the battlefield] about eight o'clock; the pickets were posted as usual, and the troops lay on their arms during the remainder of the night, after having been deluged by as severe a fall of rain as can be imagined in the heaviest monsoon.'[10]

Meanwhile the wounded had been carried back across the river to the site on the south bank where the baggage had been left that morning. Total British deaths were 778, including 38 European and 27 Indian officers. Mahratta losses were thought to be over 3,000. The fate of the wounded was particularly gruesome: 'As the majority of the wounds were inflicted by grape or round shot, they were very severe, if not mortal; and, in fact, over 200 out of 600 wounded men died, not a little through want of proper surgical treatment.'[11]

Mehidpoor was the decisive battle of the war. It was 'the only general action of primary order in India since 1804'.[12] The destruction of Holkar's army resolved the choice of war or submission beyond doubt in the minds of the hitherto wavering Courts of Gwalior and Nagpur, and it removed any hopes that the Peshwah might have had for linking up with the northern Mahratta Chieftains. There were criticisms of Hislop's tactics. Sir John Fortescue, the historian of the British Army, wrote that:

> [The British] had to advance from the apex of the triangle upon its base with no security for their flanks and, viewed in this light, Hislop's attack might be considered sheer madness. If the Mahrattas had occupied the two [more easterly] ravines with infantry in strength, the passage of the river could only have been forced with difficulty, and debouchment upon the plain might have been impossible. If again they had advanced their guns upon each flank, as they actually did upon their left, they might have brought a cross-fire to bear upon the ford and, even if that had been carried, could have enfiladed the subsequent attack from both flanks. Hislop took all these risks, and as he was successful, he must receive credit for his audacity. But such audacity is not far remote from stupidity.[13]

But others, including the contemporary historian of the war, Colonel Valentine Blacker, felt that Hislop had little option. A more cautious approach would have resulted in delay, and delay would have given the Mahrattas, with their overwhelming superiority in numbers, time to harry the British troops, and above all to gain confidence. The psychology of the situation was not dissimilar to that of the battle of Assaye.

For Malcolm, the battle was the summit of his career as a fighting soldier. Although the critical decisions were Hislop's, many of them were made at Malcolm's suggestion. Considering that he was supposed to be acting primarily as the Governor-General's diplomatic negotiator and only secondarily as a divisional commander, and that he had not been on active military service for twelve years, it is remarkable that Hislop chose him to take the lead in every key phase of the battle. Probably his sheer exuberant self-confidence impressed Hislop, indeed overwhelmed him. He was a little reckless, but his boyish gusto had also given confidence to the troops under his command. Certainly the Governor-General, himself a professional soldier of considerable distinction, thought so, asking Hislop 'to impart to Brigadier-General

Sir John Malcolm his Lordship's warm applause of the ardour and intrepidity with which that officer led the attack on the enemy's principal battery. Such an example could not but infuse invincible spirit into the troops.'[14] Hastings also wrote a personal letter of congratulation directly to Malcolm.

He received one other mark of approval which he probably appreciated more than any other. The Mysore Horse had pursued and overtaken Holkar's treasury, capturing 'twenty standards, two guns, one tumbril, seven elephants, 218 camels and a large quantity of very valuable property', including the jewels of Holkar's family.[15] Amongst these was the Maharajah's sword, which the Rajah of Mysore wished to present to Malcolm. The established arrangement in the British and Company armies was that booty should be pooled and shared by the whole army on a predetermined basis, the size of each share being apportioned according to rank. But the Mysore Horse belonged to the Rajah of Mysore's army, and the Governor-General eventually ruled that the Mysoreans could keep the booty, thought to be worth over £1 million, despite Hislop's strenuous later objections. Malcolm quite properly referred the matter of the sword being offered to him to the Governor-General, who ruled that Malcolm could keep it, again despite Hislop's objections.[16]

On the day after the battle, Malcolm wrote an official report to the Commander-in-Chief, providing the bare facts and mentioning the names of officers who had particularly distinguished themselves. At last, on Christmas Eve, he wrote to Charlotte:

> On the 20th, at night, I thought of you and the little ones. On the 21st, if you ever came across my mind, it was only how to prove myself worthy of you; but this even, I must confess, was only for a moment, for I was wholly absorbed in the scene and in my duty. You will see by the Gazette account, and by my report of the attack of which I had charge (a copy of which accompanies this) what my task was. I ascended the bank of the river with proud feelings. I never before had such a chance of fair fame as a soldier; and if the countenances of white and black in this gallant army are to be trusted, I did not lose the opportunity afforded me . . . I have no leisure to write, being occupied with a hundred arrangements; but you need have few

> more alarms, Charlotte. We have taken seventy pieces of cannon, killed and wounded between three and four thousand, and dispersed all their infantry. I hope to proceed in person to-night with the cavalry, as I hear they are within fifty miles, quite broken down and broken-hearted.[17]

Christmas Day was spent in camp, but after four days of clearing up, evacuating the wounded and writing reports, Malcolm was on his way north, called on by Hislop to lead a force of two light infantry battalions, a brigade of Company cavalry, a thousand Mysore Horse and four horse artillery guns in pursuit of the enemy.

Why was there a four-day delay between the battle and this pursuit? Tom Munro later wrote to Malcolm, 'Your battle, while it lasted, seems to have been as severe as Assaye; but I do not understand why you did not instantly follow up the victory, instead of halting four days to sing Te Deum and to write to your grandmothers and aunts how good and gracious Providence had been. We shall talk it all over, some rainy day, in the Strand or Oxford St.'[18] The obvious first answer was that the army had taken very heavy casualties and needed time to regroup. Paradoxically, too, there was not much point in rushing after such a dispersed fleeing force; better to wait until it had partially regrouped, presenting a larger target.

Malcolm pressed on rapidly, hoping to catch up with the remnants of Holkar's army. He heard that they were retreating northwards from Mandassor, a town about fifty miles north-west of Mehidpoor. But on 30 December, when he had reached a point twenty miles north-east of Mandassor, he heard that it had doubled back towards Mandassor to collect its heavy baggage and stores, which were lagging behind the main force. Malcolm immediately sent a detachment of Mysore Horse towards Mandassor. After an overnight dash, they arrived there at dawn on 31 December and in a surprise attack, captured the whole of Holkar's remaining baggage, stores and cattle.

For Holkar the game was up. *Vakeels* were sent to sue for terms. Malcolm now took off his military hat and put on that of the Governor-General's diplomatic agent. It must have seemed for him uncannily reminiscent of 1803–05. He set out the terms required, most of which were accepted on the spot. The following day Hislop arrived with the main body of the army, together with the Gujerat contingent which had joined it two days earlier. 'Malcolm rode out to meet Sir Thomas Hislop and his staff, and taking off his hat, announced that the war with Holkar was over.'[19]

The negotiations were brief. Tantia Jog, the previous Chief Minister at Holkar's Court and now restored to power, arrived at the British camp on 3 January. He had always leaned towards an accommodation with the Company; indeed, that had been the reason for his ousting by the military faction the previous November. The terms laid down by Malcolm were that young Holkar was to become a dependent ally of the British, lose all his territory south of the Nerbudda, and any remaining nominal overlordship of the Rajput princes, while Amir Khan was to be rewarded for his betrayal of his sovereign by being granted his *jaghirs* on a permanent basis. But in other respects, Holkar would be allowed to retain control of his kingdom. The Company advanced four lakhs of rupees so that his army could be paid up and largely disbanded. The formal Treaty of Mandassor was signed on 6 January. In general, the atmosphere was friendly, though some of Holkar's cavalry based at Rampoora (twenty miles north-east of Mandassor) refused to accept the Treaty and made their way south, hoping eventually to join the Peshwah.

The British could now concentrate on chasing down the remaining Pindaris operating in Central India and, of course, take on the Peshwah further south. The Governor-General, who had been waiting at the headquarters of the Grand Army about eighty miles north-east of Mandassor throughout December, now started to make his way back to Calcutta. Hislop returned southwards with the main body of the Deccan army in mid-January. Malcolm was left in charge of the Central India region. This covered the country between the Tapti river to the south, Kota to the north, Bhopal to the east and Gujerat to the west. Within this region lay the old Mughal *soubah* (province) of Malwa proper, bounded by the Nerbudda river to the south and Kota to the north. His immediate task was to finish off the Pindaris and then, in the longer term, to settle Malwa and the adjoining regions of Central India.

Leaving Captain Agnew, his first assistant, as liaison officer in Holkar's Court at Mandassor, he set off northwards. His first quarry was a minor Mahratta Chief, Jaswant Rao Bhao, one of Scindiah's feudal adherents who had refused to accept Scindiah's deal with the British in November. Bhao had fled to Mewar (the Udaipur region in today's Rajasthan) and occupied a large tract of land; he was also said to be harbouring Pindaris. The weather was fine and cold. On the march Malcolm hunted and shot game. A detachment from the Bengal army visited him and he was delighted to find among its officers a son of Robert Burns, the great Scottish poet, 'a very fine young man. We had a grand evening, and I made him sing his father's songs. He has a modest but serious pride of being the son of the bard of his country which quite delighted me.'[20] On 14 February Bhao came into Malcolm's camp. 'This is my lucky year', he wrote, 'Jeswunt Rao Bhao . . . yesterday saved me further trouble by coming into my camp and surrendering himself.'[21]

During December Malcolm had continuously harried both Karim Khan and Cheetoo. He had written to them, offering them terms if they surrendered without delay; they would have to leave Malwa but they would be given land in Hindustan. At the beginning of January Karim, despairing of effective aid from any Mahratta Chieftain but not yet prepared to surrender, abandoned his family and his baggage and turned up at Holkar's camp to offer his services. But Holkar was about to sign a treaty with the British and he was turned away. At last, on 15 February, Karim arrived at Malcolm's camp, 'poorly dressed, looking fatigued and depressed in spirits'.[22] He was exiled to Gorakhpur in Hindustan.

Cheetoo was made of sterner stuff. Malcolm later described his last days: 'His main body was attacked and routed; and his followers, when divided, were everywhere pursued by detachments of the British Army, till they were so broken-spirited, that they became the prey of the petty Rajput Chiefs and village officers, who plundered them with a zeal and activity which was equally prompted by the desire of gain, and a recollection of the miseries they had long endured from these base and cruel freebooters.' Eventually, in desperation, Cheetoo gave himself up to the Nawab of Bhopal. The original offers of exile and a small pension were repeated 'but his alarm, chiefly excited by a fear of transportation i.e. of "*kala pane*" [literally, black water, alluding to the ocean] prevented his accepting them', and he fled, crossing the Nerbudda, and proceeding south to the fortress of Asirgarh. But he was forced to move on. '[He] . . . was now tracked, like a hunted animal, through the jungles, by the prints of his horse's hoofs [he rode a horse with remarkable large hoofs] . . . Cheettoo, while seeking shelter in a deep recess of the forest, was sprung upon and killed by a tiger . . . [a local officer] traced the tiger to his den; and though the animal . . . had left it, they discovered the head of Cheettoo in a perfect state, which they afterwards brought to the English camp.'[23]

In February 1818, Malcolm was in exuberant mood. After the humiliations of eleven years before, he felt especially vindicated. He wrote to John Adam: 'The Pindarrees are now giving themselves up by hundreds. Where are now the fools who said we could not do this thing? Never was a more glorious result. The noble views of Lord Wellesley of establishing general tranquillity are now nearly accomplished; and if we have firmness and wisdom to preserve and maintain the great advantages we have gained, India will long enjoy an undisturbed peace.'[24]

In late February he returned to Holkar's camp at Mandassor. He had cautioned Captain Agnew that while his job was 'to exercise that influence over the State which is best calculated to preserve it in peace, and to establish its prosperity on a ground that will promote the interests of the British Government, it is very important that it should be done in a way which would neither affect the temper nor hurt the pride of the Prince or his Ministers.'[25] He was well received and found the atmosphere at the Court to his liking, especially in the thirteen-year-old Prince. He told Charlotte: 'I have lately been with my young *ward*, Mulhar Rao Holkar, and certainly the change of a few weeks is wonderful. The fellows that I was hunting like wild animals are all now tame, and combine in declaring that I am their only friend.[26]

Perhaps the sight of the young prince prompted Malcolm to write to his own son George, now eight years old:

> You bade me promise to write to you if ever I went to battle. I have been at battle, Mamma will tell you I have tried to behave so that you should not be ashamed of your papa. If you become a soldier, you must recollect this, and behave so that papa will not be ashamed of you . . . I have a little horse not bigger than a mastiff dog. He trots into the tent, and eats off the table, which he can just reach. I take hold of his fore-legs, he rears up, and walks on his hind-legs round the tent. We have a monkey who sometimes rides this pony. It is such fun. I often wish that you were here . . . There are many nice gentlemen who live with me; and play and hunt with me. But not one that is not a good scholar. So take care and be a good scholar, or papa will not let you play and hunt with him.[27]

The self-congratulatory tone of some of Malcolm's letters might appear rather jarring, were it not for their obvious warmth and sincerity. He literally overwhelmed people with the force of his *bonhomie*. By nature an optimist, an enthusiast, he could not resist rejoicing in success. It was also a deliberate attitude. A member of his staff told the story that on his first reporting to the General for instructions, he was told to keep everybody in good humour. 'I need not tell you anything else.'[28]

In mid-March, he set off to quell the Soondees, a hereditary tribe of plunderers who had taken shelter in the forests, mountains and fastnesses of northern Malwa, and could assemble up to 2,000 horse. Within six weeks, many of their strongholds had been destroyed and their lives made so difficult that they came in one after another to submit to the government. In late April Malcolm moved south to the banks of the Nerbudda, between Hindia and Maheshwar, where the local Chiefs had for many years paid what amounted to protection money to the robber bands that infested the forests adjoining the river. As soon as the Chiefs became convinced that the government forces could protect them from reprisals, they proved only too happy to help in the capture of the robber bands.

But at this moment a new challenge faced Malcolm. News came through that the Peshwah and what remained of his army were making their way north towards Central India.

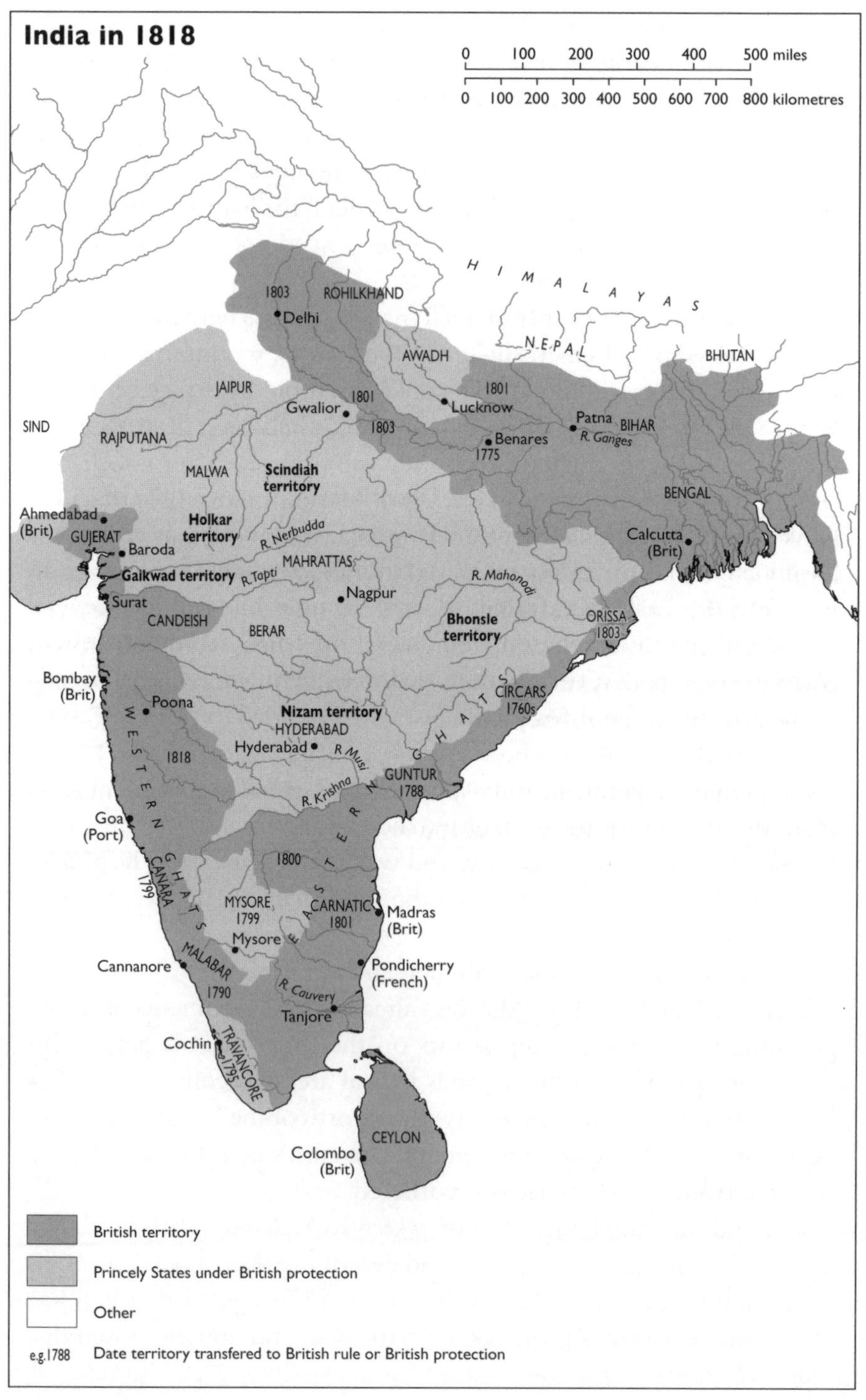
India in 1818
0 100 200 300 400 500 miles
0 100 200 300 400 500 600 700 800 kilometres
HIMALAYAS
NEPAL
BHUTAN
1803
ROHILKHAND
Delhi
AWADH
JAIPUR
1801
Lucknow
Gwalior
1801
SIND
RAJPUTANA
1803
Patna
BIHAR
R. Ganges
Benares
1775
MALWA
Scindiah territory
BENGAL
Ahmedabad (Brit)
Holkar territory
GUJERAT
Baroda
R. Nerbudda
Calcutta (Brit)
Gaikwad territory
MAHRATTAS
R. Tapti
R. Mahonodi
Nagpur
Surat
CANDEISH
BERAR
Bhonsle territory
ORISSA
1803
Bombay (Brit)
Poona
CIRCARS
1760s
Nizam territory
HYDERABAD
WESTERN GHATS
Hyderabad
R Musi
1818
EASTERN GHATS
GUNTUR
1788
R. Krishna
Goa (Port)
1800
CANARA
1799
MYSORE
1799
CARNATIC
1801
Madras (Brit)
Mysore
Cannanore
MALABAR
1790
Pondicherry (French)
R. Cauvery
Tanjore
Cochin
TRAVANCORE
1795
CEYLON
Colombo (Brit)
British territory
Princely States under British protection
Other
e.g. 1788 Date territory transfered to British rule or British protection

CHAPTER TWENTY-SIX

India – Surrender of the Peshwah, 1818

After Peshwah Baji Rao had fled from Poona in November 1817, the Governor-General declared him deposed. Elphinstone was appointed 'Commissioner for the Deccan', the territories conquered from the Peshwah. But the Peshwah still had a large army at his disposal. Several British detachments chased him back and forth around southern Mahratta country. At first he managed to elude them, twice venturing south and twice venturing north, but when he tried to venture east he was defeated in battle. At the beginning of May 1818 he marched north again, hoping to get help from Appa Sahib or even from Scindiah; also from the body of Holkar's cavalry which had refused to submit to the British at Mandassor in January, and was on its way south, hoping to join him. By 6 May he had reached the Tapti river, about seventy miles south of the Nerbudda river. He had 4,500 cavalry and 3,000 infantry, of whom about 2,000 were Arab mercenaries.

Unfortunately for him, Malcolm already had detachments of troops guarding the main crossing points on the Nerbudda, as part of his campaign against the robber bands in that area. Malcolm himself was already at Mhow, only about forty miles north of the Nerbudda, with a substantial force. Meanwhile General Doveton's division was chasing Baji Rao from the south. He was cornered.

In mid-May the Peshwah sent *vakeels* to Malcolm. They brought a letter stating his desire for peace, and describing Malcolm as one of his oldest and best friends. The *vakeels* even tried to suggest that Baji Rao personally had always been averse to the war, and now proposed that Malcolm should come to his camp for discussions. Malcolm refused, first because it might give the impression that it was the British who were suing for peace rather than the Peshwah, and second because, in the event of negotiations being broken off, it would inhibit his ability to direct hostile operations against him. He then laid down his own terms – the Peshwah must abandon his throne and quit the Deccan. He would be allowed to settle in Hindustan and would be given a pension. He proposed that Lieutenant John Low and a small party should visit the Peshwah to convey this message and explain the reasons for it. Low set off on 18 May, and Malcolm moved his camp south to Mandaleshwar on the north bank of the Nerbudda.

On the night after Low left, news came that Appa Sahib had managed to escape from custody. This caused some alarm among the British, who feared that he might be able to stir up dissent, or at least help the Peshwah's cause in some way. After some redeployment of troops, Low was allowed to continue his journey with a larger escort. By now Doveton's force had reached the Tapti, only fifteen miles south of the Peshwah's army, while Malcolm's camp at Mandaleshwar was only sixty miles north of it.

On 29 May Low met Baji Rao, who still seemed to think that he could retain the title of Peshwah and continue to live at Poona. But he did at least consent to meet Malcolm at a village called Khairee (Kyree), which was situated twenty miles south of the Nerbudda and, significantly, about eight miles west of the fortress of Asirgarh.

The meeting finally took place on 1 June at five o'clock, on what must have been a very hot afternoon. Baji Rao, intensely nervous about his personal safety and fearing that the British might try to arrest him, brought an escort of 2,000 men. Malcolm's small party were at first received in open *durbar*, but the two men soon retired to a small tent for a private discussion lasting nearly three hours. Baji Rao used all his eloquence, bemoaning his misfortunes and shrewdly trying to flatter Malcolm, appealing again to their former friendship.[1]

This was, of course, deeply disingenuous. Less than ten months earlier, he had deliberately and comprehensively deceived Malcolm, making a fool of him in the eyes of his British colleagues. Yet here he was, playing the same game again. At this point many men might have become exasperated, but Malcolm remained calm, spelling out the only terms which would be acceptable to the British, and advising Baji Rao to accede to them. He did, however, become more specific about the pension, saying that it would not be less than eight lakhs per annum – a very large sum.[2] Back in 1803, the British had given Baji Rao's half-brother, Amrit Rao, a pension of seven lakhs, in consideration of his retiring quietly from the political scene. So Baji Rao could at least console himself that he had done better than his half-brother. He asked for the discussion to be continued the next day, but Malcolm refused, realising that Baji Rao had still not completely understood and accepted the inevitability of abdication and exile. The meeting broke up at about ten o'clock. Baji Rao returned to his camp at the top of the *ghat*.

Malcolm went back to his tent and immediately wrote out the proposed terms of agreement. He sent them after Baji Rao and gave him just twenty-four hours to accept them and come into the British camp. Yet he was worried. Baji Rao was such a vacillating character. Who knew what he might do next? There was intelligence that he had already moved some of his property into Asirgarh. The fortress belonged to Scindiah and the *killadar* (commandant) of the fortress, Jaswunt Rao Lar, was known to have been a keen supporter of the Peshwah in the past. If the Peshwah were to make a dash for it, he could take refuge there. It was enormously strong and to besiege it successfully would require a major military operation. With the monsoon arriving later in the month, there would be a delay of several months before a siege could even be started. Meanwhile, the very presence of the Peshwah in Malwa, even if holed up in Asirgarh, could stir up plenty of trouble.

No Company man in India knew better than Malcolm what an enormously favourable psychological blow would be struck in the minds of the Mahrattas if the Peshwah were to abdicate voluntarily and retire into relatively honourable exile, rather than be utterly humiliated or even killed. But he also knew that not everyone in the Calcutta Government would have that view. Some would feel that the Peshwah, by his treachery the previous November, had forfeited any claim to leniency. Moreover, the terms which Malcolm had laid down, especially the pension of eight lakhs, were his own idea. There had not been time to get the Governor-General's approval.

The next day, Malcolm wrote to John Adam, 'passed in constant messengers [coming] from the Paishwah, and from his principal officers. The latter, as the crisis approached, became anxious about their individual interests . . . it would fill a volume to detail the particulars of all the intrigues which occurred. I have never, in the course of my experience, witnessed a scene in which every shade of the Indian character was more strongly displayed.'[3]

Now he decided to turn the screw. He summoned Baji Rao's agent who had been allowed to stay in the British camp, and told him to leave. Low reported that Baji Rao had asked for 'another day's delay, as the 3rd of June was, he said, an unlucky day, and he had religious ceremonies to perform of the most indispensable nature, before he could come to my camp . . . I replied it would prove a most unlucky day . . . if he did not come in.'[4]

At two a.m. on 3 June Malcolm ostentatiously posted cavalry around his camp to prevent messengers coming in, then at six a.m. he marched to Khairee, the appointed meeting place, arriving there at about nine o'clock.

These threatening gestures had the desired effect. At eleven o'clock, Baji Rao, together with a force of 4,000 horse, and 3,000 infantry (including 1,200 Arab mercenaries, with another 800 coming in two days later), at last arrived at Khairee to surrender They were an alarming spectacle, especially since many of them were thoroughly discontented. But Malcolm's instinct told him that if they had no prospect of plunder, they would gradually fade away.[5]

This extraordinary assembly, over 7,000 of Baji Rao's adherents escorted by Malcolm's much smaller force, now set off northwards towards Hindustan. For a few days they proceeded smoothly. Malcolm kept his distance, sensing that Baji Rao must be allowed to come to terms in his own way with the disaster that had befallen him. Sympathy would be misplaced. But on the morning of 9 June the Arab mercenaries insisted on being paid the arrears of salary that were due to them. Baji Rao offered to pay them from the time that they had joined his march but they insisted on receiving the whole amount, back to the time when they had first been hired. They surrounded his tent and would not allow him to move. He was terrified, sending messages to Malcolm, crying for help but asking him not to use force to free him, fearing that he might be murdered by the mutineers.

This was a tricky moment for Malcolm, because he had already sent off his main force and his baggage, though he had prudently kept behind a regiment of cavalry and six companies of infantry to deal with just such an emergency. He sent word to recall some of the troops who had been sent ahead, and meanwhile repositioned the troops on hand so that they could, if necessary, attack the mutineers. He waited all day and exchanged messages with the leaders of the mutineers. With only 1,100 cavalry and 700 sepoys plus three brigades of six-pounder guns, he was heavily outnumbered, but his troops were regulars and well-disciplined. The Arabs advanced and even opened some desultory fire, wounding three sepoys but, in a remarkable display of discipline, the Company troops held their fire. Early next morning, the chief Arab officer, Syed Zeyn, perhaps alarmed by the formidable steadiness of the British line, requested a parley. He told Malcolm that their demands had been partially met and they would be prepared to leave the rest to arbitration by Malcolm. With Malcolm assenting, 'he rode back to consult his colleagues. He returned, without effecting this purpose, accompanied by all the leaders. 'These men,' he said to the General, 'must have each your hand given to them that you will not attack them after they have released the Peshwah.' Sir John Malcolm gave his hand to every Jemidar, and the assurance they asked.'[6]

To most, confrontations like this would have been daunting, but Malcolm relished them. He was a master of the impromptu address to a hostile crowd. He had done it several times before: at Hyderabad in October 1798, when the sepoys of the French contingent mutinied; again, on the way to Mysore in February 1799 when part of the Nizam's Contingent mutinied; and again at Masulipatam in 1809, when the European officers mutinied. His enormous self confidence had been sufficient on each occasion to carry the day.

Baji Rao, a man with a low threshold of fear, was profuse in his gratitude to Malcolm, who had probably saved his life. Thereafter he meekly followed Malcolm's advice. Over the next few days the mutinous troops were progressively paid off and sent back to their respective homelands. The northward march continued. The combined party crossed the Nerbudda and arrived at Malcolm's military cantonment of Mhow, about twenty miles south of Indore, in late June. Here Baji Rao was allowed to halt for a month to put his affairs in order before his exile. Knowing Baji Rao's fears, suspicions and mood changes, Malcolm then travelled northwards with him, past Mandassor to the frontier of Malwa, before finally parting company on 17 August. The place chosen for Baji Rao's exile was Bithur, a holy place on the banks of the Ganges near Cawnpore. At Baji Rao's request, John Low was put in charge of the detachment to accompany him on his journey.[7]

The surrender and exile of the Peshwah was a critical event in Indian history: the true end not only of the war, but of the Mahratta Empire itself. The surrender of the last Peshwah, despite all his faults, was lamented throughout Mahratta country. Ninety years later an observer wrote, 'In the Deccan Baji Rao is still remembered. The villagers point out the place where he passed during his flight; and some say that, in the silent watches of the night, they hear the beat of the 10,000 hooves of his myriad horse upon the plain.'[8]

Malcolm was understandably proud of his military and diplomatic achievement. He had organised his troops along a line nearly 200 miles from end to end so that there was no way of escape northwards for the Peshwah. Baji Rao had surrendered to him personally because he had trusted him personally – a vital factor in Indian culture. He had managed to persuade the Peshwah and his force of nearly 8,000 men to surrender with hardly a shot being fired; to get him to go into exile more or less willingly; and, despite a mutiny, to disperse his thousands of followers with hardly a casualty. 'Badjee Rao' he wrote to Adam, 'has unstrung a bow which he can never rebend.'[9]

All this had been done without detailed instructions from Calcutta. Malcolm wrote full reports to the Governor-General, who was still making his way back to Calcutta, and letters to his friends in India and Britain. But, to his dismay, the reaction in the Calcutta secretariat was not approbation but consternation. They were appalled at his offer of eight lakhs as a pension to a man whose previous treachery, they felt, disqualified him from any leniency, and who was in no position to bargain. 'Malcolm's wits are flown', wrote Charles Lushington (Secretary of the Public Department) to Charles Ricketts (a member of the Supreme Council). And in a second letter, 'My mind is fixed on Malcolm's preposterous vanity, his preposterous proceedings and his madness in [settling] Badjee Rao with eight lakhs.'[10]

Hastings was more measured. He warmly praised Malcolm's military dispositions leading to Baji Rao's surrender and his handling of the mutiny among Baji Rao's followers after it. But the grant of eight lakhs 'was much more favourable than he had contemplated'.[11] Baji Rao, he felt, had no alternative but to surrender, and the British Government could have purchased his submission with two lakhs. This stung Malcolm into defending his actions with vigour, and a series of letters passed between him and Adam. He made five points:

First, that while negotiations were proceeding, Baji Rao was within eight miles of the fortress of Asirgarh, the *killadar* of which was prepared to offer him asylum. Scindiah, to whom the fortress belonged, was in secret league with him. Once inside the fortress, with the monsoon about to start, he could have held out for many months, meanwhile creating unrest throughout the Deccan.

Second, that Baji Rao still had 8,000 troops at his disposal, and 'had the power of protracting the war till the next fair season . . . every prince and chief, who had been deprived of their power and possession would have cherished hopes of change', and rallied round Baji Rao.

Third, that the Pindaris had been 'subdued' but not 'destroyed'. In the previous few months, over 12,000 horsemen had offered their services to Malcolm. The rumoured approach of the Peshwah would have 'created a sense of hope and inspiration in them . . . They would at once have reunited under any chief that promised them pay or plunder.'

Fourth, that Elphinstone had told him that Poona and its surrounding territory were in a disturbed state and would remain so as long as the Peshwah was at large. Any further delay would thus have caused trouble for the British forces in southern Mahratta country.

Fifth, that the grant of eight lakhs was linked to the seven lakhs that had been granted to Baji Rao's half-brother Amrit Rao in 1803. Anything less than that would have been considered as 'a degradation' by Baji Rao.[12]

Nevertheless, Adam stuck to his original arguments and Malcolm wrote back to his old friend in some exasperation: 'you continue to occupy every hillock of your original ground, and qualify (like a Scotchman as you are) every sentence of applause'.[13]

Malcolm's friends and colleagues in western India, who knew a great deal more about the Mahrattas than anyone in Calcutta, had strongly supported him on the eight lakhs issue. Elphinstone wrote to him on 10 June: 'I congratulate you on your success with Bajee Row; I must heartily congratulate myself on the same event, which will secure me the peace of this country, and give me more time to think of the important task of its civil settlement . . . I have little doubt of Bajee Row staying with you now you have got him in, but I do not think he would ever have made up his mind, if you had not been so peremptory; eight lakhs is I think a very reasonable provision.'[14]

Tom Munro wrote to Malcolm on 19 June that he deemed the annuity of eight lakhs allotted to Baji Rao 'below what might, under such circumstances, have been given', and observed, 'His surrender is a most important event; it will tend more than anything else to restore tranquillity, and facilitate the settlement of the country. It deprives all the turbulent and disaffected of their head and support.'[15]

And again on 7 July: 'When men's minds begin to cool a little, and Bajee Row's treachery to be forgotten, they will not think eight lakhs of rupees too much for the fallen head of the Mahratta Empire.'[16]

Others who wrote included Sir David Ochterlony (Resident in Rajputana), Richard Jenkins (Resident at Nagpur) and Henry Russell (Resident at Hyderabad).[17] Munro summed the matter up succinctly: he wrote to Elphinstone, that eight lakhs was 'too much for Bajee Row to receive, but not too much for John Company to give'.[18]

Malcolm wrote to Wellington in July that 'I fear Lord Hastings thinks I have given Badjee Row better terms than he was entitled to; but this is not the opinion of Elphinstone, Munro, Ochterlony and others who are on the scene; nor do I think the Governor-General will continue to think so when he receives all the details. You will, I am sure, be convinced that it would have been impossible to have obtained his submission on other terms, and the object of terminating the war was enough to justify all I have done.'[19] It is worth noting in passing that Elphinstone and Malcolm, the two men most betrayed by Baji Rao and therefore having most cause to see him humiliated, were also the most forgiving; and that the men in the Calcutta secretariat were the least.[20]

In the long run, Malcolm's judgment was vindicated, and Hastings had the grace to acknowledge it. Four years later, in a despatch to the Secret Committee, he concluded: 'The importance of Bajee Row's surrender was an advantage I always felt and acknowledged, and the zeal and ability manifested by Sir John Malcolm have invariably received my warmest testimony. Now, after the lapse of four years from the period of Bajee Row's surrender, I am happy to state, that none of the ill consequences I apprehended, from the very favourable terms offered by Malcolm have taken place, except that, perhaps, a larger actual expense has been incurred than would have sufficed to put him down.'[21]. Finally, the Court of Directors themselves, not a body conspicuous in admitting error, conceded that the advantages of an early surrender 'justified the terms that were granted'.[22]

A further consideration that must have crossed Malcolm's mind when determining the size of Baji Rao's pension was his age (forty-three) and the state of his health. He had 'a feeble constitution and debauched habits'; he would surely not last long. Malcolm offered the pension to Baji Rao as an individual, not as the Peshwah; and, like any pension paid to an individual, it could not be passed on to his heirs. But Baji Rao probably had the last laugh on this. He survived for another thirty-three years, dying only in 1851. And there was an eventual sting in the tail. Although much married (eleven wives), he had no surviving sons. In 1827 he adopted a son, Nana Sahib, who achieved notoriety in the 1857 uprising as the villain of the 'Cawnpore massacre', when he was responsible for the hideous massacre of over 200 European women and children prisoners. It has been suggested that Nana's anti-British feelings were at least partly caused by resentment at the Calcutta Government's refusal to continue paying him the pension that it had given to Baji Rao.

Although the surrender and exile of the Peshwah in June 1818 marked the formal end of the Anglo-Mahratta War, there was still a great deal of military mopping up to do. Malwa in particular – 'the rotten core of the predatory system'[23] – had been misgoverned for thirty years and had been in a state of virtual anarchy since 1806. The main Pindari forces had been defeated militarily but there were still robber bands at large – Soondees in the north-east and Bheels to the south and west – who lived to a great extent on plunder. Moreover, the very success of the operations against the Pindaris and Baji Rao's army meant that there were now large numbers of unemployed and unpaid soldiery roaming the country.

Insofar as these bands had any focal point of cohesion, it was now personified in Appa Sahib. In late November 1817, his troops had been fought off when attacking the Residency at Nagpur, and in December, a relieving British force under Doveton had destroyed his army. One might have thought that this would result in his dethronement and banishment, but for reasons of *realpolitik*, the Resident, Richard Jenkins, forgave him, and in January 1818 restored him to power though with diminished territories and tighter British control. But Appa Sahib continued to intrigue and the *killadars* of several forts in his territories refused to submit to Company army detachments. In March Jenkins had him arrested and sent into exile towards Allahabad. But while en route he managed to induce one of the sepoys guarding him to let him escape. He hid in the Mahadeo hills, trying to drum up support and make contact with the Pindari Chief, Cheetoo. In June the Berar

Government, with British support, installed his ten-year-old cousin on the throne. Appa Sahib's efforts to gather support were unsuccessful, and he remained on the run. He eventually reached the fortress of Asirgarh and was taken in by the *killadar*, Jaswunt Rao Lar. Or so the British thought; this was never definitively confirmed and Lar later denied it in a letter to Malcolm: 'I swear by the Maharajah's feet, I gave no protection to Appa Sahib.'[24]

All this time, throughout the cold season of 1818–19, Malcolm was engaged in pacification. He had to deal with a pretender to Holkar's throne; drive out thousands of freebooters from western Malwa; and attend to dozens of minor shows of resistance. Then, in February 1819, came the news that Appa Sahib was apparently sheltering in Asirgarh.

The fortress of Asirgarh, sixteen miles north of the Tapti river, lies in a gap in the range of the Satpura hills which divide the two great valleys of the Nerbudda and the Tapti rivers in western India. Asirgarh's natural defences are formidable. The upper part of it is 1,100 yards long and 600 yards wide and sits on top of a rocky escarpment, 750 feet above the surrounding plain. Thick masonry walls and ramparts cover all approaches that are not actual cliffs. Situated in a vital pass on the route from the Deccan towards Hindustan, it had been of great strategic importance for centuries.

Malcolm marched southwards past Asirgarh to confer with Doveton, who was camped not far from the fortress. After further stalling by the *killadar*, Malcolm wrote to Scindiah in Gwalior, demanding that he order the *killadar* to surrender and hand over Appa Sahib. While the message was on its way to and from Scindiah, the British prepared for a siege. This was going to be a major operation, because the fort's massive guns covered the entire surrounding country. The Company's battering-train, comprising seven eighteen-pounder guns and seven mortars, arrived in Doveton's camp on 1 March, accompanied by 200 men of the Royal Scots and 160 Native Infantry. More troops arrived from other directions. Lieutenant John Shipp of the Bengal army, a soldier of twenty-five years' service, was apprehensive: 'It was a beautiful enough place to look at, but promised to be desperately hard to take . . . the Natives, in their high-flown way, say of this fort that none but the crafty hawk, high-lingering over his prey, or the morning lark soaring and sweetly singing over its young, could ever see inside Asseerghur.'[25]

The messenger from Scindiah returned from Gwalior on 15 March, but the *killadar* still demanded absurdly extravagant conditions for surrendering the fort. On 17 March Malcolm decided to go ahead with the siege under the military command of General Doveton, with himself commanding the part of the force which had come south from Malwa.

The fort was on three levels. At the lower, western end outside the walls was the *pettah* (town or suburb), then came the lower fort and finally, at the eastern end, the upper fort or citadel. The natural sequence of an attack was first to acquire the *pettah*, then the lower fort and finally the citadel. The British quickly occupied the *pettah* without much difficulty or loss, and a gun battery was established in its ruins. The defenders made a sally but were driven back. The battery now set about pounding the lower fort and opened up a breach. Unknown to the British, the defenders actually evacuated the lower fort, but shortly afterwards the powder magazine in the British lines in the *pettah* exploded, killing and wounding nearly a hundred troops. The defenders returned and reoccupied the lower fort. The British then changed tactics: Malcolm's force moved to the north-west of the fort and Doveton's to the east, and both resumed pounding. Malcolm's force was then given the task of storming the lower fort. But the defenders had abandoned it overnight and it was occupied without opposition on the morning of 30 March. The pounding went on for a few more days. The despair of the garrison was increased when a breach was made in the wall of the upper fort.

On the evening of 7 April, the *killadar* finally sent out *vakeels* to negotiate terms for capitulation. The terms were agreed on the morning of 8 April. John Shipp described what happened next:

> at about two o'clock the great man [the *killadar*] started down in his palanquin with three or four followers. All the general and staff officers were ordered to gather at General Doveton's tent to meet him. On his way to us, our people led the Keeladar through the park of artillery, so that he could see for himself that we had at least fifty guns in reserve, above those we were using. The Keeladar was an ugly-looking fellow, a great, fat buffalo of a man, with enormous rolls of flesh about him. When everybody sat down, Sir John said, bluntly, that . . . nothing would do but the surrender of the fort. [After some bargaining

> the *killadar* agreed to] . . . do his best to persuade the men to give up their arms, but he dreaded the result. At last he said that he would guarantee to give up the fort by ten o'clock the next day, unconditionally . . . Under this impression [the defenders] marched out and made their rendezvous under a hill, where a strong party of our men were waiting to march in. There were about seven or eight hundred of the poor, half-starved wretches, some of them almost naked. Sir John, having severely admonished them for their rebellion, ordered them to lay down their arms and property.[26]

That afternoon Shipp went up to examine the fort, and his previous apprehensions were confirmed: 'Every step I took convinced me that we could never have stormed the place . . . they had huge stones piled up on the walls waiting for us, so nicely balanced that a child could have knocked them over . . . It was very fortunate for us that the fort was given up.'[27] As it later turned out, the *killadar* might not have been quite so pusillanimous as the British thought him. Soon after the occupation of the fort, 'a number of letters were found 'in a small writing case' belonging to the *killadar*, in the handwriting of Dowlat Rao Scindiah. One letter clearly instructed the *killadar* on no account to surrender the fort to the British. So, after all, he was acting under orders from his master.[28]

Shortly afterwards Malcolm marched back to his military headquarters at Mhow. Shipp and his Bengal army contingent accompanied him. They went on to Indore, where they were received unenthusiastically by the young Holkar and his Court: 'Sir John however quickly upset their ceremonious gravity, and soon the place resounded with fun. The once frowning Rajah, who was said to be unable to laugh, threw himself back on his cushions and fairly shook with merriment. It was some time before order could be established, . . . and we broke up in a much more friendly spirit than we met.'[29]

Malcolm's outwardly cheerful demeanour at this time concealed an inner turbulence. Back in 1816, when he was setting out for India, he felt that he had a strong chance of succeeding Sir Evan Nepean as Governor of Bombay. Since his arrival in India he had been fully employed in the Pindari and Mahratta War. But after the surrender of Baji Rao in June 1818, with the war virtually finished, he had begun to think seriously about his next assignment. Sir Evan had already advised the Court that he wanted to retire. Malcolm felt that if anything his prospects of the governorship of Bombay had improved. He had played a distinguished part in the Pindari War. He knew that George Canning, the current President of the Board of Control, supported him. It seemed only a matter of waiting patiently. He corresponded light-heartedly with Mountstuart Elphinstone on the subject.

> I will give you a plan for the disposal of your august person the next five years; wait until August or September 1819, when I pledge myself if not appointed to Bombay to go home with you. If I am appointed, I pledge myself to do all you wish about the new conquests, and you can go home in two or three years – see England – marry your cousin Anne Elphinstone or Fanny Callendar, both handsome, sensible and proper cast girls, and return and succeed me as Governor of Bombay. This is a good and a feasible plan, and when it is all fulfilled, I only desire that you will recollect it was me by whom it was projected.[30]

He wrote to Claudius Rich in Baghdad that 'Friends in England tell me that I am certain for Bombay.'[31]

But in mid-March 1819, while he was sweltering among the hot rocks adjoining Asirgarh, some one gave him a copy of the *Morning Chronicle*. It contained the bombshell news that the next Governor of Bombay would not be himself, but Mountstuart Elphinstone.

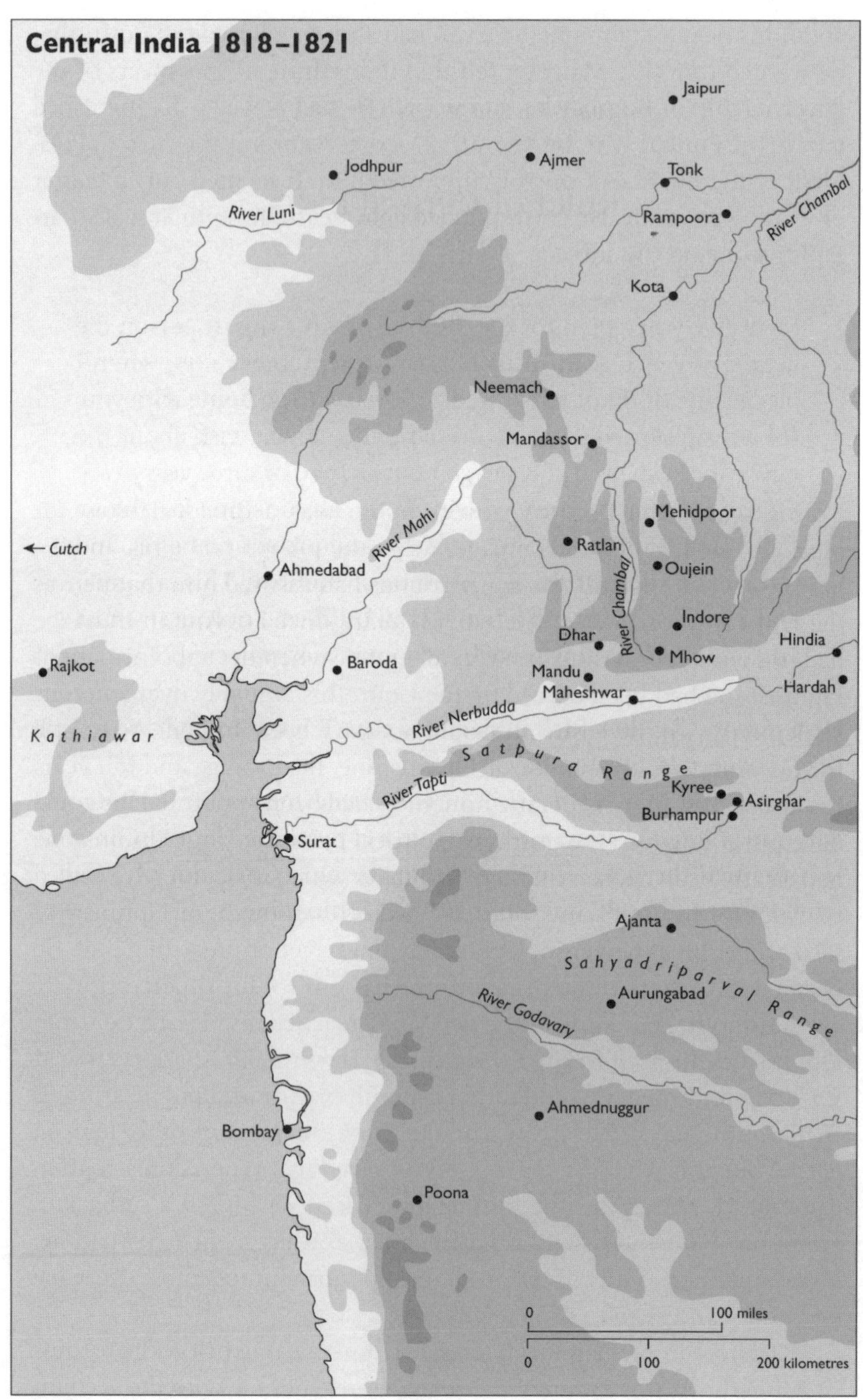
Central India 1818–1821
Jaipur
Ajmer
Jodhpur
Tonk
River Luni
Rampoora
River Chambal
Kota
Neemach
Mandassor
Mehidpoor
River Mahi
Ratlan
Cutch
Oujein
Ahmedabad
River Chambal
Indore
Dhar
Hindia
Rajkot
Baroda
Mhow
Mandu
Hardah
Maheshwar
River Nerbudda
Kathiawar
Satpura Range
River Tapti
Kyree
Asirghar
Burhampur
Surat
Ajanta
Sahyadriparval Range
River Godavary
Aurungabad
Ahmednuggur
Bombay
Poona
0
100 miles
0
100
200 kilometres

CHAPTER TWENTY-SEVEN

Ruler of Central India, 1818–1821

Failing to get the Bombay governorship was a dreadful blow for Malcolm. He had been so confident that the job would be his. In 1816, before leaving England, his many friends had assured him that he was the front runner, and in the last two years since arriving in India, he had not put a foot wrong. In September 1818, when the appointment of Elphinstone had been agreed by the Court, his arguably overgenerous settlement with the Peshwah would not have been known. Worse still for his pride was the choice of Elphinstone, his protégé and ten years his junior. If some aristocratic nonentity had been appointed, he could have put it down to the quirks of political patronage, but Elphinstone had clearly been chosen on merit, a quality which Malcolm felt entitled to claim for himself – in spades. He had often thought of Elphinstone *succeeding* him as Governor of Bombay but never of preceding him. He began to have dark thoughts about the reasons for his supercession.

A rumour, an inkling of the news, had reached him via a letter from Elphinstone himself in late February 1819. He wrote to Charlotte that 'if it is so determined, I would rather on both private and public grounds that Mountstuart Elphinstone had the situation than any other man on earth'[1] but this was just putting on a brave face. When confirmation came on 18 March, it hurt him deeply. Faced with such a setback to ambition, many men might have remained stoically silent. Not Malcolm. He complained loudly of his bitter disappointment to almost everyone he knew – and even to some he did not.

He wrote immediately to Pulteney from his camp below the fortress of Asirgarh: 'At this moment a newspaper reaches me with the account of my friend Mr Elphinstone's nomination, by an unanimous vote, to Bombay . . . No man can have more merit than Elphinstone, but I stood on ground that should have defended my fair and encouraged views of honourable ambition from supercession by any man . . . I cannot conclude this subject without expressing my conviction that this disappointment to me must have given the most severe pain to your father-in-law and my friend Mr W Elphinstone, whatever pleasure he may have had in the promotion of his nephew.'[2] [3]

On the same day he wrote to Mountstuart Elphinstone in Poona: 'I have seen your appointment to Bombay announced, and I again congratulate you upon it, and I congratulate the public, for with all due consideration of myself, I do believe a better Governor than you yourself will make of the settlement could not be found on earth. I wish you joy of the high station you have obtained, with the same sentiments of warm and sincere friendship with which you would have addressed me had I been the fortunate candidate.' He ended the letter with an extraordinarily candid gesture: 'It is necessary no feeling I have on this point should be disguised from you, and I therefore enclose you a copy of a letter I wrote to my brother Pulteney, five minutes after I read the paragraph from the Morning Chronicle announcing your appointment.'[4]

In reply, Elphinstone tried to console him:

> I will tell you all I have heard of the appointment to Bombay, which is but little, and mostly or all at second hand. Mr Palmer in Calcutta writes that Mr W Elphinstone and the Wellesleys were for you. Lord Keith writes that I owe much to the Marquis Hastings and to Mr Marjoribanks, the Deputy Chairman; that Canning was for you, and Lord Liverpool told Lord Keith that, if he had interest he would give it to me . . . I think my being here was a great recommendation, both for economy and convenience; that your being a military man, and an active, enterprising, dashing officer, was against you with people who love quiet; and I do not think it unlikely that your former *offences*, under Lord Wellesley and his successors, have weighed with some at the Court. I had an advantage that, as little was known of me, no objection could be started and I had no envy to contend with . . . I see, on looking over your letter, you talk with contempt of a pension. I wish I had the pension, and you

> the Government. Surely you would rather be at home, with a good fortune, than gaining any addition to your reputation that is to be gained at Bombay.[5]

But in India no one – not even Hastings – knew what had really happened in London during the previous autumn.

Canning had taken over as President of the Board of Control in the summer of 1816. His predecessor, the Earl of Buckinghamshire, had had a hostile relationship with Leadenhall Street, and Canning's first objective was to restore amicable relations with the Court. The choice of Governor of Bombay to succeed Sir Evan Nepean was an opportunity to do this. Canning knew that Malcolm was after the job; before leaving for India in the autumn of 1816, Malcolm had approached him, and the Duke had written in his support. So when the moment came to recommend a new Governor, he put forward three Company men – Malcolm first, then Elphinstone and Munro – knowing that this display of confidence in its own servants would please the Directors. What happened next was described in an apologetic letter from Canning to the Marquess: 'Yesterday I thought that, with the aid of Mr [William] Elphinstone, who has taken a most warm, and I verily believe, sincere part in Sir J M's favour, a prospect of possible success was opened for your friend. But it was a fallacious gleam; and there is, I am truly sorry to say, no chance of his appointment.' He had always believed that Malcolm had overestimated his support among the Directors, and sure enough, that was how it had turned out.[6]

Elphinstone had been unanimously elected on 7 October 1818. That word 'unanimously' seems to have upset Malcolm. What, he thought, had happened to all his friends who had promised to vote for him? The probability is that when they realised that theirs was a lost cause, they closed ranks with their opponents to secure the public impression of unanimity. But none of these reasons really add up to a coherent case for Elphinstone or against Malcolm. The fact was that Malcolm was controversial and Elphinstone was not, and when a large body of men gather to make a selection, they tend to favour the less controversial candidate.

Meanwhile, Hastings had already sent Malcolm a brief letter of sympathy. He was acutely aware of the injustice done to him. In trying to make amends, he floated the idea of making him Lieutenant-Governor of the Deccan, i.e. taking over from Elphinstone when the latter became Governor of Bombay. Malcolm replied that while he was obviously disappointed not to have got the Bombay governorship, he would certainly be interested in taking on Elphinstone's job in Poona.[7]

This produced a longer explanation from Hastings. He denied, sincerely, that he had supported Elphinstone's candidacy, or that Canning had acted against Malcolm. He cautioned Malcolm that 'it would be unwise in the extreme to quit your ground and go home'.[8] At the same time, Hastings was anxious not to upset Elphinstone, and asked him what he thought of the idea of giving Malcolm that job for a short period. This was an embarrassing question for Elphinstone. He had been appointed to take charge of Bombay *as well as* the Deccan; now Hastings was asking him whether he thought it a good idea to give up the Deccan to Malcolm. After first stating that he would be happy to comply, and that no one could do the job better than Malcolm, he went on to suggest that Central India needed a very strong hand: 'It is needless to say that there is no man so well suited to conciliate a conquered people than Sir John Malcolm, and probably there are few whose administration would be of more solid advantage, either to them or to the conquered, from his enlarged views of policy, and his liberal principles towards the natives.'[9] In any case, Hastings's Council in Calcutta strongly opposed this well-meaning but impractical idea, and no more was heard of it. Hastings then floated the even more bizarre idea of making Malcolm Governor of Prince of Wales Island (Penang), and overseeing Malacca, Bencoolen in Sumatra and the new British settlement of Singapore, which had been established by Sir Stamford Raffles in February 1819 (Hastings had a poor opinion of Raffles). But this also came to nought. Malcolm later laughingly scoffed at the idea of his being made a 'Pepper-cloves-and-cinnamon Governor'.[10]

In mid-1819, still nursing injured feelings, Malcolm had been ready to resign. But, consoled to some extent by Hastings's sympathetic attitude, he had taken his advice to refrain from hasty action, and to stay on in India for the time being. He wrote, with a hint of self pity, to Thomas Cockburn in England, that: 'The Directors, whatever I may think of individuals, shall, as a body entrusted with the care of the public interests, find me a Christian knight, whose object is to return benefits for injuries.'[11]

But if he had been completely honest with himself, he would have had to admit that, regardless of status, he should continue to do the Central India job, firstly, because there was a huge amount of work to be done; secondly, because he was the ideal man to do it, and, thirdly, because it was giving him a great deal of satisfaction.

Malcolm now proposed that the person in charge of Central India should become a Lieutenant-Governor, reporting directly to the Governor-General. And of course, the first Lieutenant-Governor should be Malcolm himself. To his disappointment, Hastings did not respond to his letters on the subject. He wrote several letters to Adam and later to Metcalfe, seeking an explanation. But by early 1820 he had given up hope of becoming a Lieutenant-Governor, and was making plans to return to Britain sometime in 1821. Nevertheless, he continued to press the case for someone else to do the job. By mid-1820 he felt that, as no longer a contender, he could be seen to speak with greater objectivity. He put the case most coherently to Hastings in a letter (which, significantly, he copied to Munro in Madras) in August 1820: 'My general opinions regarding the principles on which the administration of this quarter should be grounded have been repeatedly stated. Events (far beyond our control) have forced great and awful duties upon us. There is, among other evils concomitant with our state, a tendency to direct rule, alike arising out of the character and condition of the remaining Native governments and our success in establishing supremacy, which will be difficult, if not impossible, to counteract. But we must try to march slow time if we cannot halt, and to support, at least for a period, what is still left of native rank and power.'

He accepted that the Residents at the various princely Courts were mostly competent men, but their efforts lacked the necessary coordination. He had, he wrote: 'A strong sense of the necessity of there being one head to the whole of Central India, who has sufficient of general views and of local power to keep (under the direction of the Supreme Government) the whole machine right.'[12]

He was himself, of course, already implementing this policy successfully without having the status of a Lieutenant-Governor. But his success was largely due to his own unique personal knowledge, experience and prestige with Indians and British alike. In the longer term a less charismatic character might need some more formal trappings of authority to achieve success. As it turned out, the reason why his proposal was not acted upon had nothing to do with Malcolm, or indeed with the management of Central India. It was that Hastings had become simultaneously unpopular with both the Court of Directors and with Canning at the Board of Control, as Hastings later admitted.[13] But the logic of the proposal could not be denied. In 1822, after Malcolm's departure, the Governor-General appointed Sir David Ochterlony as Resident in Malwa as well as Rajputana, covering much the same territory as Malcolm, and based at Neemach. In 1836 Charles Metcalfe was appointed Lieutenant-Governor of the north-western provinces, with headquarters at Agra. As so often, Malcolm was ahead of his time.

Later in 1819, with the retirement of Sir Hugh Elliot as Governor of Madras, another opportunity for promotion came up, but Malcolm was to be disappointed again. Tom Munro was eight years older than Malcolm and had spent his entire Indian career in south India. Like Malcolm, he was originally a soldier and had fought in all the wars since 1780, but his main activity had been in settling the territories acquired by the Company from Tipu Sultan. He had spent fourteen years (between 1792 and 1807) as an administrator, six years in Britain and four (1814–1818) as a Commissioner appointed by the Court of Directors to introduce to the Madras territories the *ryotwari* settlement system of which he had been the chief architect. He was the Company's acknowledged expert on settlement, and highly regarded, both in London and India. By 1818 he was partially deaf and his eyesight was beginning to fail, and he returned to Britain, reaching London in the summer of 1819. He was therefore on the spot when the time came for the Board and the Court to appoint a new Governor of Madras. He was the obvious choice, and deservedly so.

Malcolm was naturally disappointed, but he accepted the logic of the appointment of Munro: 'Ambitious as I am, and impatient as I have become of slight, I do not know that I should not have had conscience enough to vote against myself.'[14] Nevertheless, he was still bitter about the reasons allegedly given by the authorities for rejecting him for both Bombay and Madras. On hearing of Munro's appointment he wrote to Pulteney that 'I shall not quarrel with the nomination of my excellent friend Tom Munro, but I cannot be pleased or satisfied to be galloped over – even by good horses – in the way that I have been.'[15] To Charlotte, he wrote of his chagrin at the way in which he felt his civilian administrative experience and talents had been belittled: 'Has not my whole life – though I never acted as a judge or collector – been more given to civil than to military duties? Has not the whole Government, in all its parts, been my constant study . . . they shall ere long see this in a Report, which will enable me to ask my friends whether I am, or I am not, fit for civil Government. But let them in the meanwhile take as no slight evidence the condition of these countries, and then ask how much of this remarkable work has been effected by force.'[16]

Being passed over for the Bombay governorship was a turning point not only in Malcolm's career but also in his character. Hitherto he had been too ambitious – he had pushed too hard for recognition and promotion; he had frequently been disappointed, and had complained loudly – but his extrovert character had enabled him to 'offload' his bitter feelings on his friends and quickly recover his cheerful equilibrium. From now on, however, and for the rest of his life, there was a slight tarnish to the shining generosity of spirit which had carried him through so many crises.

Yet, in retrospect, whether by good luck or good management, the Company's deployment of these three vastly gifted Scotsmen – Munro, Elphinstone and Malcolm – turned out to be the best possible use of their respective talents. Each could have done any of the three jobs competently. But in Madras, no one could have matched Munro's ability and steady hard work in implementing and perfecting the *ryotwari* system in south India. In Bombay, Elphinstone's instinctive gubernatorial personality – intellectual, measured and judicious – was coupled with his unrivalled knowledge of the territories of the former Peshwah; no one could have melded the Deccan and Bombay better than him. And in Central India, no one, not even Munro or Elphinstone, could have matched Malcolm's combination of military and diplomatic skills and experience, or his unique ability to get on with all and sundry, to bring peace and relative prosperity to a region that had suffered chaos and devastation for thirty years.

The surrender and exile of the Peshwah in June 1818 marked the end of the Company's war in Central India, first with the Pindaris and then with the Mahrattas. The fall of the fortress of Asirgarh in April 1819 marked the end of any organised military resistance to the supremacy of the Company. Yet the region was by no means pacified, let alone properly governed. Bands of discharged soldiers, many of them mercenary Pathans and Arabs, roamed the countryside in search of food and plunder. Bheels, Gonds, Soondees and other plundering tribesmen, who in more peaceful times had been confined to the hills and jungles, were able to take advantage of anarchy to sally forth into settled areas. The situation was made worse by the fact that, in an area as large as the whole of Britain, there was no single dominant Chief. Nor was most of Malwa under the direct rule of the Company, as was the case in the newly acquired territories in the south Mahratta country, and most of south India. Malcolm had a small army at his disposal but every military operation had to have the consent of the local ruler, often reluctantly given, and sometimes of the governments of Bombay or Calcutta as well.

The southern boundary of Malcolm's direct influence was the Tapti river. Beyond the Tapti lay Candeish, by then Company territory under the direct control of the Bombay Government, but its jungles were a haunt of Bheel tribesman. Fortunately for Malcolm, the British officer in charge there was John Briggs who was an ardent follower of the 'Malcolm' philosophy of governance. To the west lay Gujerat, with some parts directly controlled by the Bombay Government and others by the Mahratta Gaekwad of Baroda. The Gaekwad's government had signed a Treaty of Subsidiary Alliance with the British in 1802. There was a British Resident at his Court and a British-officered Subsidiary Force. But the Gaekwad's government was highly unsatisfactory, corrupt and almost bankrupt. To the east were the relatively stable governments of Berar (at Nagpur) and Scindiah (at Gwalior), both with strong British Residents. But in recent times these Courts had been places of endemic intrigue; they were uncertain allies for the British. To the north were the various small states of Rajputana, including Jodhpur, Jaipur and Udaipur. The 1805–06 treaties which had ended the previous Anglo-Mahratta War had accepted that these Chiefs owed some traditional allegiance to Holkar and Scindiah; and during the last thirteen years without British protection, they had been periodically plundered by these Mahratta Chieftains. They were also vulnerable to raids from the west by the Amirs of Sind, and had various unresolved disputes among themselves. Their relations with the Company were handled by the Resident in Delhi, Charles Metcalfe, succeeded in December 1818 by Sir David Ochterlony, and his agent in Rajputana, Captain James Tod.[17] But Ochterlony and Tod reported not to Malcolm but to the Calcutta Government.

Yet the greatest challenge was in Malwa proper, the country between the Nerbudda river in the south and Kotah in the north. In this region there was no single capital city and no single ruler of a large chunk of contiguous territory. Indore, for instance, was Holkar's base, but Oujein, forty miles to the north, belonged to Scindiah; while Mandassor, a further seventy miles to the north, belonged to Holkar. Holkar had also owned territories to the south of the Nerbudda which he had been forced to surrender to the British by the Treaty of Mandassor. The small states of Dungapur and Banswarra were supposed to pay tribute to the ruler of Dhar, a hundred miles to the south, but he had no means of enforcing payment. Baroda claimed tribute from the Chief of the small state of Lunawada in eastern Gujerat, which was refused. And so on. All these claims and counterclaims had lain relatively dormant during the years of anarchy. But now, with the arrival of the British and the return of a semblance of law and order, the accumulated claims were dusted off and presented for arbitration by the new paramount power. Such was the patchwork quilt of differing jurisdictions and sovereignties over which Malcolm exercised varying degrees of influence and control.

To most men, sorting out this muddle would have been a daunting challenge. To Malcolm it was pure joy. He looked for a site for a military base camp and found it, in June 1818, at Mhow, a flat piece of country about fifteen miles south of Indore. It was strategically positioned to keep a close eye on Holkar's Court at Indore and concurrently cover the western approaches from Gujerat, whence British military reinforcements might come quickly in an emergency.[18]

In 1818/19 the main thrust of Malcolm's activity was to extirpate the remnants of robber bands that had terrorised the country, particularly the Bheels. He wrote to Charlotte in May 1818:

> I have just tranquillised, by beating some and petting others, the most troublesome province in Malwa; and during my operations against the few remaining Pindarees in this quarter, though the country is covered with mountains and forests, though my detachments have marched everywhere, and through countries so infested with robbers and lawless mountaineers, that our troops from past suffering, dreaded them, I have not had a rupee's worth of value stolen, and not a follower wounded. Nadir Bheel, the mountain chief, who has committed

> all these devastations, and is the terror of the country, has already sent his only son, a fine boy, just the age of George, and promises to come himself. I gave the little plunderer a knife with six blades and a nice little Arab pony.[19]

In September: 'I wish you were here to enjoy the blessings I obtain from the poor inhabitants, who all continue to refer their happiness to me; and it joys my heart to find myself the instrument of punishing freebooters, and restoring great provinces to a prosperity they have not known for years.'[20] And to William Elphinstone: 'The countries of that young prince [Holkar] are advancing to prosperity with a rapidity that looks almost miraculous to those who are unacquainted with the patience, industry and attachment to the soil of the Ryots of India. They actually have reappeared in thousands, like people come out of the earth, to claim and recultivate lands that have been fallow for twenty years.'[21]

His unrestrained, boastful enthusiasm was infectious. The officers on his staff praised his achievements, but found him exhausting. In May 1819 one of them wrote from the Mhow cantonment: 'nobody I ever saw or heard of can get over the same quantity of business in the same quantity of time that he does, and his reputation stands so very high with the natives, that his being personally concerned in any arrangements goes further in satisfying them, I believe, than would the interference of any other man on earth . . . for whatever length of time his fame may last in Europe, Malcolm-Sahib will be remembered in Malwah as long as regular government exists.'[22]

Tiring of the May heat at Mhow, Malcolm ventured westwards to the higher ground near the ruined city of Mandu. Situated about sixty miles from Indore and forty miles west of Mhow on a rocky outcrop, Mandu, the 'city of joy', had been the centre of the Taranga (Afghan) kingdom which flourished between the eleventh and fifteenth centuries. Its battlemented walls stretched for twenty-three miles and enclosed (and still do) some magnificent examples of Afghan architecture. Within a few miles of Mandu, at a village called Nalcha, were several smaller ruined palaces which were used to house visiting grandees while they waited for the most astrologically auspicious dates to arrive in the city itself. Malcolm commandeered one of these palaces: '[I] fixed [my] headquarters in an old palace, from which I expelled (I speak a literal fact) tigers. The old ruins of this place, and the celebrated city of Mandoo, have for more than a century been shared by tigers, and Bheels more destructive than these animals in their ravages. The tigers I shoot; the Bheels are my friends, and now serve in a corps I have raised, or cultivate lands.'[23] [24]

To his old friend David Haliburton, now retired in England, he wrote: 'My room is a thoroughfare from morning till night. No moonshis, dewans, dubashes, or even shubdars, but "Char Derwazah Kolah" [literally, "four doors open"], that the inhabitants of these countries may learn what our principles are at the fountain head . . . from the highest ruler to the lowest robber, from the palace in the city to the shed in the deepest recess of the mountain forest, your friend "Malcolm-Sahib" is a welcome and a familiar guest.'[25] He wanted British officials to engage directly with local people – allowing 'four doors open' access to both the greatest and the least in the land – rather than working through

> some artful dewan or fawning munshi whose life is devoted to the discovery of your superior talents, and the treachery and falsehood of the black rascals with whom you have concern . . . the moment we allow khans, pundits, moonshees or any other animals to mix, there is a dabbling and intriguing that gives the work a perfectly new character. These animals fight in our name for their own objects. They are acquainted with our temper and failings and our prejudices; they watch our passions, and study the very moment best suited to the tale that is to make the impression; then charge upon him, whom they desire to depreciate, the faults which their arts have led him to commit.[26]

He told Elphinstone that 'for the last eighteen months I have denied myself a private moment even at meals, and been ready to hear every human being that had a complaint or a representation to make. There is not one in a hundred to whom I can give relief, or interfere in his business; but I explain minutely to all, the causes of not hearing him, and the principles on which our government acts.'[27]

He thus became the fountain head, the oracle of authority, and his statements became accepted and circulated because 'Malcolm-Sahib' had made them. He was responding to the very Indian tendency, as he put it, of 'referring everything to persons'.[28] It certainly was not in line with government systems or legal practice in Britain, but it worked quite well in limiting one of the great defects of foreign rule – the interference of grasping intermediaries.

The Bheels were the largest and most notorious of the wild mountain tribes in Central India, and as Malcolm wrote some time later, 'this extraordinary class of people merit more than a cursory glance'.[29] Mentioned in the ancient Hindu poem of the Mahababharata, 'The plundering or wild Bheels, who reside among the hills, are a diminutive and wretched-looking race, whose appearance shows the poverty of their food; but they are nevertheless active and capable of great fatigue. They are professed robbers and thieves, armed with bows and arrows; they lie in wait for the weak and unprotected, while they fly from the strong.'[30] Malcolm had a disarming way of dealing with these wild tribesmen:

> Once a Bheel broke into his durbar tent, with a dreadful story of robbery and murder, and pleaded that the criminal should be punished.
>
> 'Hold, Hold!' said Sir John, 'Not so fast; the party you accuse shall be sent for, and the cause inquired into forthwith.'
>
> 'What is the use of inquiring? My cattle have been carried off, and one of my sons killed in an attempt to recover them.'
>
> 'It may be so but still I must inquire. Do you know why the Almighty gave me two ears?'
>
> The Bheel looked puzzled.
>
> 'Then I will tell you; in order that I might hear your story with one, and the other party's with the other.'[31]

News of his activities had earlier reached Britain, and Walter Scott wrote to Richard Heber that 'I see our friend Sir Jo. Malcolm is setting up his banners and shouting among the Mahrattas. It is enough to endure him in his loving kindness, but when he roars in wrath Achilles' shout which overturned twelve curricles will be a joke to it.'[32]

Responding to a letter from Scott, Malcolm gleefully recounted an anecdote which he knew would thrill the author of *Rob Roy*:

> The largest tribes are quiet but the difficulty is to keep the *Rob*

> *Roys* under . . . That you may understand how exactly we have *Blackmail*, take the following anecdotes (all of which have occurred during the last ten days) of [my friend] *Nadir Bheel*. This petty chief has his mountain home within eighteen miles of this camp. He rules over the Bheels or hill robbers in the vicinity, and has for ten years laid the whole country above the hills to Indore, and below them to Maheshwar on the Narbudda, under annual contribution. The revenue is independent of the plunder of all who pass near his country, and armies have in vain tried to hunt him down or to guard against his depredations.[33]

Nevertheless, Nadir's days as a Chief were numbered. 'Many of his crimes subsequent to his submission were pardoned; but a deliberate murder of some unarmed travellers, committed by his orders, put him beyond further toleration or indulgence.'[34] In May 1820 Malcolm issued a warrant for his arrest while Nadir was attending the wedding of his son. He was brought to Nalcha and tried before Malcolm and a 'jury' of assembled *Zamindars* and Bheel Chiefs. He received the surprisingly lenient sentence of banishment for life to Allahabad, and was succeeded by his fourteen-year-old son, who had been held and educated by the British at the Mhow cantonment for the previous two years.[35]

From May 1819, with pacification more or less complete, Malcolm was able to resume the task of sorting out the messy arrangements which the Company's takeover as paramount power had produced with the various Chiefs, and between the Chiefs themselves. As an indication of the magnitude of the exercise, between November 1817 and June 1821 the Company signed treaties and made other arrangements with Scindiah and Holkar, and the tribute-paying rulers of Bhopal, Kotah, Tonk Rampoora, Dhar, Dewas, Pertaubgurh, Dungapur and Banswarra. In addition, there were eleven separate agreements with petty Chiefs who paid tribute to different rulers; forty-nine settlements of financial entitlements due to those who had previously been deprived of their land; and forty-five settlements between these parties, through the medium or under the influence of the Company (many of them mediated by Malcolm). Two new Muslim-ruled states were set up: Tonk Rampoora under Amir Khan, and Jowrah (hitherto only Bhopal had had a Muslim ruler). These constitutional arrangements, produced in less than three years, stood the test of time. They were still largely in place when Indian independence came in 1947.

The British did not have it all their own way, however. In one notable field they were frustrated. Opium was a major crop in Malwa, and about seventy-five per cent was exported, making up about half of Malwa's total exports. In theory, this exported opium was consumed in other Indian states. In practice, most of it went to overseas destinations, notably to China. The trade was managed by the merchants of Oujein and Indore, whose profits were used to finance the activities of their governments.

There was a strong demand in China for Indian opium, as a medicinal and recreational drug, and the Company developed a highly profitable triangular trade pattern: tea from China to Britain; cotton and textiles from India to Britain; manufactured goods from Britain to India; and opium from India to China. For Bengal opium, produced mainly in the Ganges valley, the Company created a government export monopoly. It was thus able to maintain relatively high prices and profitability. By the 1820s opium trading was providing about seven per cent of government revenue, and the percentage later rose as high as fifteen per cent Understandably, therefore, the government feared competition from indigenously controlled Malwa opium. In 1818, with the Company gaining suzerainty in Central India, the Calcutta Government set out to destroy the competition. It banned the export of Malwa opium by anyone other than itself, and established a government agency to purchase any opium surplus to Malwa's domestic needs. As a result, Malwa merchants wanting to export opium directly to overseas clients resorted to smuggling. To prevent this, the Company recruited a task force to intercept caravans smuggling opium from Malwa to the western coast.

But implementation of this policy was difficult. In contrast to the situation in Bengal, the Company had no formal authority to intervene in the domestic affairs of a Native State. It could only cajole, persuade or threaten, based on the degree of influence that it possessed over the ruler. In the case of Holkar, this was considerable; in the case of Scindiah, it was much more limited. So the Company's opium policy in Malwa was expensive and only marginally successful. In such an enormous area, most smuggled export consignments got through. Moreover, the Oujein and Indore merchants set up an elaborate system of insurance The insurers hired escorts made up of recently disbanded soldiers (of whom there was no shortage) to protect the caravans from being plundered en route, or from the opium being seized by the Company's enforcement agents. The cost of this insurance was factored into the merchants' costing.

At first Malcolm tried loyally to follow the government's policy. Frustrated by lack of cooperation from Oujein (Scindiah) merchants, he recommended that the influence of Oujein should be lessened and that of Indore (Holkar) merchants increased.[36] But in due course he concluded that the Calcutta Government's approach was self-defeating, because, regardless of fairness, additional revenue gained by a higher price for Bengal opium would be outweighed by failure to get any revenue at all from Malwa opium. He advocated a 'pass' system, whereby Malwa merchants would be allowed to export opium on payment of a duty. Eventually, in 1830, the system of prohibition was replaced by the 'pass' system.

Viewed as the action of a commercial company, the Company's policy was a reprehensible attempt to establish a market monopoly. Viewed as the action of a government, however, it was a perfectly respectable attempt to maximise government tax revenue from the sale of a largely recreational drug. Governments of all political persuasions do it today with liquor and tobacco; in the end, all taxation is anti-market. What really mattered was, first, whether it was the best and fairest way of raising revenue, and second, what did the government *do* with the revenue?

What, one might also ask, was the moral stance of the parties involved towards the opium trade? Opium had long been a recreational drug in parts of western and northern India. Also, until the discovery of aspirin in about 1880, opium (or rather the morphine which it contained) was the only effective painkiller available. This would have given it considerable respectability in most people's eyes. As one Indian historian has commented: 'It would be difficult to locate even a single sentence in official or non-official recordings of indigenous viewpoints on the opium trade that might reveal any moral dilemmas. Outwardly there was not the slightest expression of an awareness that opium was hardly a respectable commodity.'[37]

Soon after his arrival in Central India, Malcolm was struck by how little was known about the region's history and character. He decided to compile a comprehensive report to the Calcutta Government 'for the illustration of its past and present condition'.[38] He started preparing the report in June 1819 and continued working at it with ferocious energy over the next two years. It has been suggested that his motivation was anger at being thought inexperienced in civil administration compared with Elphinstone and, especially, with Munro.[39] While pique may have played a part, his main motivation was almost certainly to acquire and disseminate information. In 1805, after a mere three weeks in the Punjab, he had gathered all the information he could find about the Sikhs, and had written in the introduction to his *Sketch of the Sikhs*: 'In every research into the general history of mankind, it is of the most essential importance to hear what a nation has to say about itself; and the knowledge obtained from such sources has a value, independent of its historical utility.'[40] Before that, he had used a similar approach at the Cape in 1795, and repeated it on a much grander scale in his *History of Persia* in 1815.

At first Malcolm conceived the report as a sort of *Domesday Book* of Central India – a record of its current state in 1817–1821, its population, rulers, government revenue, economy, geology, climate, agriculture, military establishments, treaties and so on. But he was gradually drawn into writing its history and politics as well. He made full use of the various talents of his friends and of the British officers serving under him, a remarkably gifted and dedicated lot. Most of these men had full-time jobs to do, and their contributions to the report were thus made in their spare time. 'Volumes were translated, inscriptions of deeds . . . carefully copied; and a great number of natives of rank and intelligence . . . were minutely examined as to the facts.'[41]

As he finished draft chapters, he would send them off for comment to Elphinstone and Erskine in Bombay, and to John Briggs in Candeish. But the man he was most anxious to impress was Munro, the acknowledged expert on government revenue settlement (i.e. taxation). When Malcolm, bursting with pride, sent him thirteen draft chapters, Munro responded teasingly that 'I could not help thinking, when poising it, as Sancho did when poising Mambrino's helmet in his hand, "what a prodigious head the Pagan must have, whose capacious skull could contain thirteen such ponderous chapters as this!" I look at it with reverence . . . but I must not open it till I can get a little spare time to consider the recondite matter with which it is filled.'[42] But a later letter was more complimentary: 'When I think of . . . your chapters, or volumes rather, on revenue, police etc, I wonder how you have found time for such works. I think that all this must end in your writing a general history, and making all other histories unnecessary.'[42]

The report was sent to Calcutta and was favourably received. Excerpts from it were published in a special edition of the *Calcutta Journal* in April 1822, soon after Malcolm had left India. [44] Back in England it was considered sufficiently important to be edited and published in London in 1823, as *A Memoir of Central India, including Malwa and adjoining provinces, with the History and copious illustrations of the past and present condition of that Country*. The book quickly went to a second edition and became the standard work on Malwa history for over a hundred years. As late as the 1930s, the distinguished Indian historian, Jadunath Sarkar, was complaining that 'Sir John Malcolm's *Memoir of Central India* (1823), written in the infancy of modern historical studies relating to our country and based on imperfect materials handled without sufficient criticism, has remained our only authority on the subject, though it has long been recognised as quite obsolete.'[45 46]

Malcolm boasted about the success of his work in Central India, but his boasts were entirely justified. The economic statistics for the years 1818 to 1821 speak for themselves. In a Malwa population which may be guessed at around three million, about fifty per cent owed allegiance to Scindiah, twenty-five per cent to Holkar and twenty-five per cent to all the other Chiefs combined. In Holkar's territories (where more complete statistics were gathered), of the 3,701 villages, only about fifty-five percent of them were occupied in 1817; while by 1820, occupancy had risen to eighty-five per cent. Agricultural output and government revenue improved commensurately. His name became legendary. In 1824–5 Reginald Heber, the first Bishop of Calcutta, travelled through Hindustan, then turned south, passing through Central India on his way to the Bombay and Madras Presidencies. He wrote a celebrated account of his journey, and when passing through Central India remarked: 'How great must be the difficulties attendant on power in these provinces, when, except for Sir John Malcolm, I have heard of no one whom all parties agree in commending! His talents, his accessibility, his firmness, his conciliating manners, and admirable knowledge of the native language and character, are spoken of in the same terms by all.'[47]

Malcolm had originally planned to go home at the end of 1820. But as time went on, a new factor entered his thinking. He had become so utterly absorbed in his Malwa report that he was determined to finish it before leaving Central India. He came to realise that he could not do so by December 1820 so he decided to stay on until June 1821 and then take a few months of 'local leave' before sailing from Bombay in December, the preferred season for travellers heading west via the Red Sea route, which Malcolm had decided to take. Hastings greeted this decision with relief, since he was beginning to realise how difficult it was going to be to find a suitable replacement. This did not stop Malcolm continuing to badger him. In late 1820 there was a border skirmish in western Rajputana between Company troops and troops belonging to the Amirs of Sind; and some sabre rattling followed. Malcolm heard about it, and immediately wrote to Hastings, volunteering his services if war broke out. But Hastings was too sensible to let this row get out of control, and relations with Sind were patched up peacefully.

As the cold season of 1820–1821 approached and his immediate future became clear, Malcolm began to relax and enjoy himself. On 1 January 1821 he was promoted to Major-General, and, more importantly, he was made an officer of the Grand Cross of the Order of the Bath (GCB) – the first officer of the Company's armies to be given that award. Moreover, Hastings had allowed him to continue drawing his army salary in addition to his civil salary as the Governor-General's agent. He was thus able to save, from the two salaries and interest income on his investments, more than £500 per month. He was, in fact, receiving as much as Elphinstone as Governor of Bombay. As Elphinstone had rather ruefully written earlier: 'you were never better in luck than when you escaped Bombay . . . [I] could not save a farthing; you have Rs 50,000 clear, or nearly so.'[48]

After putting the finishing touches to the draft Malwa report in January 1821, Malcolm set off in mid-February on a tour to the north-west of Malwa and into Rajputana as far as Udaipur. Passing the battlefield of Mehidpoor, he wrote enthusiastically to Charlotte: 'what a contrast has this country known between the three years that preceded and the three that followed that action. Its inhabitants had lost all – even hope; its fields were desolate, and houses roofless. Now we might challenge India – I might almost say the world – to produce a country where there are fewer crimes, or more general happiness and comfort – exempt from domestic and foreign foes.'[49]

By mid-March he was in the jungles of Mewar shooting game, and soon afterwards reached Udaipur. Here he met James Tod, the Company's agent in south and west Rajputana, for the first time. He was a little apprehensive that he would come 'rather in the shape of too large a fish into the sea of his glory', but, somewhat to his surprise, he got on well with Tod. He went on to reaffirm his conviction that a Lieutenant-Governor should be appointed. 'The journey to Rajpootana, and the full communications I have had with Tod and others, joined to my better knowledge of the country and the people, has changed from conjecture into conviction all my former ideas regarding this quarter . . . Sir David [Ochterlony], if he had continued Lord of Rajpootana, might with benefit have had his power extended over western and southern Malwa.'[50]

As we have seen (page 422), Malcolm's advice was heeded. Ochterlony took over command of Malwa as well as Rajputana in 1822.

In mid-April Malcolm returned to his 'summer palace' at Nalcha for the hot weather before the monsoon. Here he devoted himself to writing letters and lengthy 'handover notes'. As his days in Central India were ending, he began to think of his personal legacy. He decided to write a pamphlet embodying his political philosophy, with particular emphasis on the personal relationships of the Company's political officers with the rulers of the Native States. He started writing it at Nalcha in April and completed it on 28 June, while already on his way from Malwa to Bombay. It ran to about 11,000 words, and was rather ponderously titled *Notes of Instructions to Assistants and Officers acting under the orders of Major-General Sir John Malcolm GCB.*[51]

The *Instructions* were included in the Malwa report, and attached as Appendix XVIII to *A Memoir of Central India* (1823), receiving a very favourable notice in the *Quarterly Review*: '[The Directors] could not perform a more effectual service to themselves and their constituents, as well as to their servants in India, and the inhabitants at large, than by making them the basis of a general system of instruction to all their residents at the various courts of the native princes.'[52] In India, in 1825, Munro, as Governor of Madras, wrote in an official minute: 'I have long thought that it would be desirable to have some rules for the guidance of Officers of Government in their intercourse with the natives of India, and it was my intention to have framed them. But this had now been rendered unnecessary by Sir John Malcolm's Instructions . . . in which he states so fully and clearly everything that can be wanted for this object in view, that I think no better course can be followed than to adopt them as far as they are applicable to the general nature of our administration.'[53]

He also took leave of various Chiefs and officials. One of them was Tantia Jog, Holkar's Chief Minister. Born Vithal Mahadev of the Kibe family in Candeish, he came to Maheshwar, the Holkar seat of government in the second half of the eighteenth century, when the celebrated Ahilya Bhai, the daughter-in-law of Mulhar Rao Holkar, was acting as Regent for her handicapped son. She proved to be a model ruler, praised to the sky by Malcolm in his *Memoir of Central India*. Tantia Jog acted as a *gomusta* (agent) for Hari Punt Jog, a prominent Holkar *soucar* (banker) at Ahilya Bhai's Court. He acquired the name 'Jog' when he took over Hari Punt's business. He became rich and increasingly influential at Holkar's Court, despite several political upheavals. Shortly before the battle of Mehidpoor he was arrested and narrowly escaped with his life, but he emerged after the battle as the most powerful man in the state, negotiating the Treaty of Mandassor with Malcolm. Thereafter he and Malcolm became strong allies in running the Holkar State. In short, he was a great survivor. His success as Chief Minister may be measured in terms of the Holkar state's revenue which increased from Rs5 lakhs in 1817 to Rs27 lakhs in 1826, the year he died. But he was also 'on the make' for himself. A current saying went that '*Holkar ka raj, Kibe ka byaj*' (Holkar is the ruler, and Kibe pockets the interest). He was discreetly involved with other Malwa merchants in smuggling large quantities of opium. Shortly before Malcolm's departure from Malwa, Tantia Jog approached him with a request for a character reference, somewhat surprising coming from a Chief Minister. But Malcolm duly obliged, albeit with some careful wording: 'however unnecessary this is to a man whose character is established, and stands so high on Public Record, I cannot refuse compliance with his last request . . . he has been the happy instrument of restoring to prosperity the ruined country of the Prince he serves . . . to conclude, he has hitherto, and will, I make no doubt, continue to merit and receive favor and support from every British authority.'[54] [55]

At last, in mid-June 1821, Malcolm said his final goodbyes to Central India and set off southwards towards Bombay. He was in no hurry, and seven of his team of devoted assistants came along with him. They included Charles Pasley's youngest brother Johnny, now aged twenty-six, an officer in the King's army stationed in India. Johnny was a wild young man, but Malcolm had taken a liking to him in England, and when Johnny arrived in India in 1818, he had made him an ADC. Now he obtained permission for Johnny to accompany him back to England. The party paused for a few days in Candeish to meet John Briggs, who had made such a large contribution to the Malwa report, then pushed on through the monsoon rain to reach Aurungabad on 12 July. Here the party met Charles Metcalfe, newly appointed as Resident at the Nizam's Court in Hyderabad.

Malcolm and Metcalfe had first met in 1805 in General Lake's camp at Muttra (see Chapter 15). From the outset Metcalfe had been a 'political', and remained so throughout his Indian career. He won his diplomatic spurs in 1808 when he led an embassy to Ranjit Singh at Lahore.[56] He served as Resident at Delhi from 1811 to 1819, dealing firmly with the ramshackle Court of the old Mughal Emperor. In 1819 he became Private Secretary to the Governor-General. Malcolm had hoped that he might succeed him in Central India, and Metcalfe was keen to do the job. But a banking scandal occurred in Hyderabad, and Metcalfe was sent there as Resident in November 1820. The two men had not met for many years, but had kept in touch by voluminous correspondence. After a fortnight at Aurungabad, Malcolm's party travelled on southwards, reaching Poona in mid-August, and Bombay on 1 September.

At Bombay he was greeted by many old friends, foremost among them being Elphinstone. It was assumed by everyone, including Malcolm himself, that this was going to be his final departure from India, and for the next two months he was continuously feted. 'My Indian marches are, I trust, over for ever', he wrote to Charlotte. 'I arrived here a few hours ago, after a very quick journey from Poonah. I am uncommonly well – better than I have been for many months. Elphinstone has given up Malabar Point to me – a most delightful residence almost in the sea.'[57] [58]

The first big event was his investiture with the Grand Cross of the Bath. Tom Munro had brought the insignia from London to Bombay more than a year earlier, and the award was made by General Sir Charles Colville, Commander-in-Chief of the Bombay Army. Malcolm wrote to his father-in-law, Sir Alex Campbell, who had recently arrived in Madras

Charles Metcalfe (1785–1846) was a political officer who rose to become acting Governor-General in 1835–6, and was later Governor of Jamaica and Governor-General of Canada.

as the new Commander-in-Chief of the Madras Army: 'Yesterday was one of grand *Tomasha* [commotion], and though with some fatigue, of real gratification to me. Your friend Sir Charles Colville commenced his task at eleven o'clock, and his attentions to his brother Grand Cross did not finish till twelve at night. Elphinstone put off the Governor to attend his friend, and all – ladies and gentlemen – looked as happy as though they had got ribands and stars themselves.'[59]

Another old friend whom he saw frequently was William Erskine.

He acted as godfather at the christening of Erskine's most recent child (the seventh of an eventual fourteen). Erskine was now a judge in the Bombay Recorder's Court, but his real interest was Indian history. Since Malcolm had last met him in 1811, he had translated the memoirs of Babur, the first Mughal Emperor, and Malcolm had sent him numerous draft chapters of his Malwa report for comment and editing. They now continued their discussions face to face. In mid-October they heard the news of Claudius Rich's tragic death (aged only thirty-four) from cholera, while on a trip to Shiraz. Malcolm wrote a quick obituary, and later, a fuller 'Memorial' to Rich while at sea on the way home.

Also living in Bombay was Malcolm's younger brother David. After his bankruptcy and move to India in 1813 he had eventually found a business partner in William Shotton, who ran a commercial agency house. The business became 'Shotton and Malcolm' in 1815. As a 'pure' agency house, working on commission, it required very little capital – just as well, since David had none. In October 1817 David married Maria Hughes, who promptly produced a son, George, but then fell ill and died. Shortly afterwards David went to stay with John at Mhow, and John wrote enthusiastically to Pulteney: 'David is going on as well as his warmest friends can desire – his business which is increasing is of a nature that must make his progress to fortune rather slow, but on the other hand it is certain. His connection with Shotton is in every way happy – the latter is an excellent tempered moderate man, who is fond of David, and rests much upon him.'[60]

Restored in spirits and encouraged, no doubt, by John's contagious joviality, David returned to Bombay, and by October 1821, had found a second wife, Mary Anne Welland, the daughter of a British naval officer. They were married at St Thomas's Church. John attended the wedding, and so did Elphinstone.

As the date of Malcolm's departure became imminent, tributes began to flow in from all over India. The Governor-General in Council issued a weighty statement, of approbation. The tribute of the Governor of Madras (Sir Thomas Munro) was less orotund: 'His career has been unexampled; for no other servant of the Company has ever, during so long a period, been so constantly employed in the conduct of such various and important military and political duties; his great talents were too well known to admit of their being confined to the more limited range of his service under his own Presidency, and rendered him less the servant of any one of them than of the Indian Empire at large.'[61] The officers who had served under him presented him with 'a magnificent silver vase'.

Finally, on 29 November, Elphinstone gave a farewell party for him, 'which went off admirably in all respects. I regret his departure and we shall no doubt miss his spirits and good humor.' Elphinstone often found Malcolm 'egoistic', but all along he had 'reproached myself for want of tolerance of the single defect of one of the first and best of men I knew'.[62]

A guest at Elphinstone's party was a sixteen-year-old Scot, Alexander Burnes, newly arrived in Bombay with a letter of introduction to the Governor. Burnes was destined to become one of the great heroes of British India, eventually being murdered in Kabul at the age of thirty-six, though not before he had killed six of his assailants. As Kaye remarked: 'there must have been something in all this greatly to inspire and encourage the young Scotch subaltern . . . A Montrose man [Joseph Hume] had sent him out to India; an Edinburgh man [Elphinstone] was now at the head of the Government of Bombay; a Glasgow man [Munro] was Governor of the Madras Presidency; and now the son of an Eskdale farmer [Malcolm] was receiving the plaudits of all classes of his countrymen, and returning . . . to his native land, a successful soldier and a successful statesman, amidst a whirl of popularity.'[63] Despite these social rounds, he kept working to the end. On 23 November, just over a week before sailing, he sent off a lengthy memorandum on the Malwa opium trade.[64] Even later, when he was already at sea, he recorded that on a single day he had 'transcribed three public letters'.[65]

On 2 December Malcolm boarded his ship. Many well-wishers came to see him off. As the last of them left the vessel, he thought that he was saying goodbye for ever to India, and to all the people and places he had known for more than half his life. There were so many treasured memories.

PART SIX

Ideologue

Mountstuart Elphinstone (1779–1859) was a political officer. He was British Resident at Poona (1811–18), then Governor of Bombay (1819–27).

Major-General Sir Thomas Munro (1761–1827) was a soldier and political officer, and Governor of Madras (1819–27).

CHAPTER TWENTY-EIGHT

Civil Governance – Three Scots in Western India

Before following Malcolm home via the Red Sea and Cairo, let us pause to look back over the previous four and a half years. During this period the Company had acquired political control, directly or indirectly, over a vast area of western India (and over southern India only twenty years earlier).

In 1817 the Calcutta Government's objectives had been strictly limited – to annihilate the Pindaris, who had been raiding Company territory over the previous ten years, and if possible, to persuade the Mahratta Chieftains to help them to do so. After all, getting rid of the Pindari menace should have been just as much in the Chieftains' interest as the Company's. They did fear, rightly as it turned out, that the Mahrattas would suspect that the Company's operations against the Pindaris were merely a prelude to a Company conquest of Mahratta territory, and this might lead them to take up arms against the Company. But they gave little thought to what would happen if the Mahrattas declared war and were defeated in battle. The Company did not want to acquire any more territory for itself. It was already stretched enough. In the light of subsequent events this policy may seem surprising, but there is no doubt that it was genuine. Again and again it was repeated in the Company's internal minutes and correspondence.

Back in London, Company policy had been even more defensive. There was still a powerful faction of Ring Fencers in the Court of Directors at Leadenhall Street. Minto and Hastings, as successive Governors-General, had repeatedly asked for permission to go after the Pindaris, but had been turned down. The British Government was, if possible, even less enthusiastic than the Court. Only a man with the clout of Canning as President of the Board of Control could overcome this opposition, and allow Hastings some limited authority to attack the Pindaris.

The result was that in June 1818, when the Company found itself in effective military control of the territories of the entire Mahratta Empire, it had to think up, more or less on the run, a system of civil governance. As Horace Walpole had said many years earlier, 'it was easier to conquer [the east] than to know what to do with it'.[1] To compound the problem, few people in the Calcutta secretariat had much knowledge of the politics of western India. Only with the arrival of Metcalfe at the end of 1818 to take charge of the Secret and Political Department was there someone with personal experience, albeit only of Delhi and Rajputana. Furthermore, western India was still a long way away – a message by the fastest *dawk* took at least a fortnight to travel from Calcutta to Poona.

The task of putting together a philosophy of civil governance was thus largely left to the men on the spot. And here the Company (and, one might almost add, India as well) was extraordinarily lucky to have three such outstandingly able men to establish and implement a coherent policy – Sir Thomas Munro, Mountstuart Elphinstone and, last but not least, Sir John Malcolm. It was not easy for them. Between 1817 and 1821 Malcolm and Elphinstone met for a few days in August 1817, before the crisis occurred; Munro and Elphinstone met briefly in southern Mahratta country in early 1818; Malcolm and Munro never met face to face at all. So they corresponded. The constraints were considerable. They had a well-trained army, which had overcome all organised military opposition, but it was largely a sepoy army and had to be handled with care to retain its loyalty. There was no Company police force to enforce the law. There was a great lack of trained civilian administrators familiar with local languages and customs. In the territories conquered from the Peshwah, Elphinstone had only six civilian assistants, some of whom were former army officers. In Malwa, Malcolm had to rely mostly on army officers with little previous experience of civil diplomacy to act as Residents at the Courts of local rulers. So by necessity they had to rule with the overwhelming consent of the governed, to avoid any drastic changes and to apply a very light hand; in effect, to bluff their way. 'We exist on impressions', Malcolm wrote to Munro in July 1818, 'and on occasions like this, where all are anxious spectators, we must play our part well, or we shall be hissed.'[2]

The situation facing Malcolm in Central India was different from that facing Elphinstone in the territories conquered from the Peshwah, and Munro in the Madras Presidency. Malcolm was dealing almost entirely with the rulers of Native States, while Elphinstone and Munro were mostly introducing direct Company government. Yet their underlying philosophies were remarkably similar, and very different from those which had been applied to the governance of Bengal over the previous fifty years.

Malcolm warned against complacency:

> The large work has been done. India is subdued. The very minds of its inhabitants are for the moment conquered; but neither its former history nor our experience warrants our expectation that these feelings will be permanent. We have never, during the whole period of our rule, gained a whole province by our arms in which we have not found a reaction, after the inhabitants were recovered from the stun of the first blow. Can we expect this last and greatest of these strides will be exempt from this evil – that the elements we have scattered, but not destroyed, will perish of themselves? They may; but such a result is against all history and all experience, and is, therefore, not to be anticipated.
>
> Though I foresee danger, I by no means intend to state that we may not prevent, or that we shall not conquer it; but this I will aver, that the Government of India, during the next four or five years, will require more care, more knowledge, and more firmness than it has ever done since we possessed that country. With the means we have, the work of force is comparatively easy. Our habits and the liberality of the principles of our government give grace to conquest, and men are for the *moment* satisfied to be at the feet of a generous and humane conqueror. Tired and disgusted with their own anarchy, the loss of power even is not regretted. Halcyon days are anticipated, and they prostrate themselves in hopes of elevation. All these impressions made by the combined effects of power, humanity and fortune, are improved to the utmost by the character of the first rule established over them . . . But there are many causes which operate to make this period one of short duration. The change from

> it to that of a colder course of policy in our political agents, and the introduction of our laws and regulations into countries immediately dependent upon us, is that of agitation and alarm. It is the hour in which men awake from a dream. Disgust and discontent succeed to terror and admiration. The princes, chiefs and other principal persons who had been supported by the character of our first intercourse, see nothing but a system that dooms them to certain decline. They have, like weak and falling men, deluded themselves with better hopes; but delusion is ever rendered more insufferable by being of our own creation.[3]

Despite his advocacy of direct contact between British officers or agents and the Indian public, he disliked what he called the *zillah raj* system of Bengal. He wrote to Elphinstone that 'The fault I find with what you term the younger politicians (counting yourself a Reish Suffeid, or grey-beard) is not so much that they despise the Natives and Native governments, but that they are impatient of abuses, and too eager for reform. I do not think they know so well as we old ones what a valuable gentleman Time is; how much better work is done, when it does itself, than when done by the best of us.'[4] And in a classic cry of distress of 'the man in the field' railing against 'the man from head office', he wrote to Molony, the agent for the Nerbudda districts, 'Were I to remain in India, I do not think there is a human being (certainly not a Nabob or Maharajah) whom I should dread half so much as an able Calcutta civilian, whose travels are limited to three hundred miles, with a hookah in his mouth, some good but abstract maxims in his head, the Regulations in his right hand, the Company's charter in his left, and a quire of wire-wove foolscap before him.'[5]

Elphinstone had the same instinctive 'hands off' attitude to reform: 'minimum disruption and disturbance of existing ways . . . I shall think that I have done a great service to this country if I can prevent people making laws for it until they see whether it wants them.' His plan, he claimed, 'has this advantage, that it leaves unimpaired the institutions, the opinions, and the feelings that have hitherto kept the community together; and that, as its fault is too little, it may be gradually remedied by interfering when urgently required. An opposite plan, if it fails, fails entirely . . . When it sinks, the whole frame of society sinks with it.'[6]

Malcolm had always been a passionate believer in the principle of indirect rule, of subsidiary alliances with the rulers of Native States, ever since the days of Marquess Wellesley. But he understood the difficulties. 'There cannot be a severer trial to an active, humane and just mind, than to condemn it to associate with those who govern Native States. It requires all the lessons of long experience, combined with a constant recollection of what is good for our general policy, not our local interests, to stand such a trial; and the worst is, that in such situations the best agents of Government are those who make the least show.'[7] He advocated:

> changes . . . in the mode of government, particularly where that new and different species of rule is to be tried, which is to control clusters of states and communities, and to preserve them in temper and in peace, without interfering with their internal administration or arrangements. This is, believe me, under the most favourable circumstances, no easy machinery to conduct, and once out of order, almost impossible to be repaired; yet you have your choice betwixt this and an indent upon Hertford College and Addiscombe[8] for one thousand writers and five thousand cadets, and Feringhy Raj [government by foreigners] all over India![9]

He recognised that Residents at remote Native Courts tended to 'become too local, and feel a partiality for the interests of the Court with which they reside' – in modern parlance, to 'go native'. But he also warned of the danger of too much centralised control. 'If the man of local feelings is too attentive to the personal characters and prejudices of those with whom he resides and associates, your distant powers are often too neglectful of them.'[10]

In a letter to Adam in Calcutta he railed against too much 'tidiness'. He saw how easy it would be for the Company to find fault with Native governments recently brought under its protection.

> Not a day will pass in which the rude Rajpoots, Meenahs, Mhairs, Goojurs and Bheels of Western India will not commit some unpardonable outrage, violate all law, contemn established authority, plunder property under British protection, and compel a moderate and just but firm Government to vigorous

> action to punish and destroy offenders in order that a salutary example may be afforded, and our insulted name and authority vindicated! This is all very fine and proper . . . but the more I see the more I doubt the justice as well as the policy (to say nothing of the humanity) of applying all these flourishing terms and logical conclusions to the poor people to whom they are applied. The great object is to make them sensible of the character of the offence for which they are punished . . . I confess myself (but do not let out the secret to the Lord [Hastings] in Council) a notorious compounder of felony. I consider in my continued collision with rogues, great and small, of every description, that I represent a State which can afford every sacrifice of form, so that the substance of its high name and power is not injured . . . I have persuaded myself that by such proceedings alone the peace can be kept, and our power gradually but firmly established over the minds as well as bodies of the natives of this quarter.[11]

He hoped that indirect rule could be maintained as long as possible:

> Those who are the supporters of a system that leaves a State, which our overshadowing friendship has shut out from the sunshine of that splendour which once gave lustre almost to its vices, to die by its own hand – to perish unaided amid that putrefaction that has been produced by an internal administration consequent to our alliance – can have no rational argument but that the speediest death of such Government is the best, because it brings them soonest to the point at which we can (on grounds that will be admitted as legitimate in both India and England) assume the country, and give it the benefits of our direct rule. But this is the master-evil against which we are to guard. Territory is coming too fast upon us. We cannot prevent accessions, and the period may arrive when the whole peninsula will be directly under our immediate rule; but every consideration requires this period to be delayed, and every effort should be made to regulate a march in which we must proceed. No additional province can now be desirable but as it furnishes us with possible means of supporting that general peace which is

> alike essential for the prosperity of our provinces and the preservation of those whom it is our policy to maintain as rulers.[12]

Direct rule, he acknowledged,

> perhaps, must come at last; but it is the duty of every man who understands the real interests of his country to use all his efforts to avert it as long as possible. The Native Governments are abused as intolerably bad; why, even in this view, the very contrast of their government with ours is strength. Make all India into *zillahs* [administrative districts], and I will assert it is not in the order of things, considering the new sentiments that must be infused – the operation (unchecked by comparison) of that dislike to rule which all human beings have, and that depression and exclusion from all high rank and fame, civil or military, of more than a crore [10 million] of men, which must be the consequence of the establishment of our direct authority – that our empire should last fifty years; but if we can contrive to keep up a number of Native States without political power, but as royal instruments, we shall, I believe, exist in India as long as we maintain our naval superiority in Europe; beyond this date it is impossible.[13]

What astonishing prescience!

Malcolm and Elphinstone largely agreed with each other on the subject of indirect rule, despite the differing situations which they faced during this period. Even though Elphinstone took direct control of the territories conquered from the Peshwah, he actually created a new Native State – Satara – to be ruled by the descendant of the great Shivaji. Malcolm strongly supported him over this:

> we rail at the impolicy of granting power, however limited, to Native Princes, when experience shows they, or their successors, have almost invariably used it against us; we forget the great advantages we have obtained during the period they have submitted to be our instruments. We must be content to purchase these at some hazard; a contrary policy would carry

> our direct authority to the banks of the Indus in three years, and we have not the means for such extended conquest. It is, in fact, my opinion, that when we have ceased to have the faculty of making Indian Princes and Chiefs conquer and govern one another, we shall have obtained the point from which we may date our decline. Your arrangements must depend much upon the disposition and personal character of your Rajah [Pratap Singh, the Rajah of Satara]; but with the sentiments I have expressed, I would raise him as high and make him as useful in independent action as he was capable of being made. If he turned out well, he is in a situation where his power would admit of increase. The Mahrattas have been beaten and bullied into a state of considerable humility. It would be glorious (and the times are favourable to the experiment) to render the descendant of Sevajee the restorer of his race to habits of order and good government.[14]

Munro, on the other hand, was more sceptical of indirect rule as more than a temporary expedient, despite having been deeply involved in the setting up of the subsidiary alliance with Mysore in 1799, and having witnessed at close quarters the successful development of that State. In August 1817 he criticised the 'strategic plan' for the Pindari War which Malcolm had written up for the Governor-General.

> There are one or two things which I do not like. One is the preventing of the Peshwah and other Princes from having vakeels resident with each other. This is an old article of our policy, but, I think, a very useless one; it is worse, it is degrading and insulting our weak allies to no purpose. If they wish to intrigue, they can do so without a public minister at a foreign court, as they can employ private agents. The restraint can therefore have the effect of making them feel their humiliations. Why not let them please themselves with keeping up the forms of independence? The check may be useful with respect to the reception of European agents; because an European cannot conceal himself and act privately.
>
> The other point of which I do not approve is more subsidiary alliances. We have enough of them. It is now more

> advantageous, and certainly more honourable, for us to have no more of them; but when we are insulted, to make war, and obtain reparation either by cession of territory or money.[15]

Munro had of course for twenty years been the great architect of the 'Munro' or *ryotwari* system in south India, where the Company government dealt directly with the headmen of villages, in contrast to the Bengal system of dealing through *Zamindars* and other types of tax farmers. In any case south India always seemed to be a more easily governable region than the rest of India.

The case against subsidiary alliances was succinctly put by Henry Russell, the Resident in Hyderabad from 1813 to 1820: 'By degrees our relations become more intimate, the habit of [Indian States] relying on foreign [i.e. British] support gradually paralyses its own faculties, and in the end it loses the forms as well as the substance of independence. If it is galled by its trammels, and makes an effort to throw them off as the Peshwah did, it only precipitates its own destruction; if it submits, it declines, by degrees, from one stage of weakness to another, until, like the Nizam and the Rajah of Mysore, it expires from exhaustion. The choice is between a violent and a lingering death.'[16] But for better or for worse, subsidiary alliances remained intact until 1947, and only the combined persuasive force of Sardar Vallabhai Patel and Lord Mountbatten brought them to an end.

Three controversial 'governance' topics had long been debated both in India and Britain: first, religion, and the propagation of Christianity in India; second, promotion of Indians in government service; and third, education of Indians (or 'Native education' as it was termed at the time). In western India after 1818, these became highly topical matters, requiring policy decisions.

The three Scotsmen were rather lukewarm Christians – one historian has described them as 'owing much to deism',[17] despite the fact that Malcolm's grandfather had been a Presbyterian Minister, and Munro came from a staunch Episcopalian family in Glasgow. Elphinstone's attitude can be guessed from a letter he wrote to John Adam shortly before he became Governor of Bombay: 'Think of losing a day every week in church and two or three in Council, for I suppose no real business is done there. By the bye, as one must go to church, ought it ever to be [the] Scotch one or is the Govr supposed to be like Horne Tooke, *always of the religion established by law*. Answer this I beg of you. What does Lord Hastings do in this respect? There is some little jealousy between the churches in Bombay.'[18]

All three were implacably opposed to missionary activity being supported by the Company, as had long been advocated by Charles Grant and the Clapham sect faction of the Court of Directors. In September 1820 the celebrated Dr Marshman, who ran the Missionary Society College at Serhampore just outside Calcutta, approached Malcolm to become a patron. Malcolm replied that he would be happy to do so,

> if you think me worthy of the honour after the following explanations.
>
> Though most deeply impressed with the truths of the Christian religion, and satisfied, and were that only to be considered in a moral view, it would be found to have diffused more knowledge and more happiness than any other faith man ever entertained, yet I do think, from the construction of our empire in India, referring both to the manner in which it has been attained and that in which it must (according to my humble judgment) be preserved, that the English Government in this country should never, directly or indirectly, interfere in propagating the Christian religion. The pious missionary must be left unsupported by Government, or any of its officers, to pursue his labours; and I will add, that I should not only deem a contrary conduct a breach of faith to those nations, whom we have conquered more by our solemn pledges, given in words and acts, to respect their prejudices and maintain their religion, than by arms; but likely to fail in the object it sought to accomplish, and to expose us eventually to more serious dangers than we have ever yet known.[19]

It is not clear whether Dr Marshman persevered with his invitation.

Throughout the 1820s, all three men pleaded with the Calcutta Government to do more to promote Indians in government service. Malcolm wrote in 1820 that: 'I regret . . . that there is no opening for natives. The system of depression becomes more alarming as our power extends, but the remedy is not in raising to rank or influence our servants, moonshees etc, however good; we must, or we cannot last, contrive to associate the natives with us in the task of rule, and in the benefits and gratifications which accrue from it. I had hoped to see great advances made in progress to this object, by measures being adopted that would at least lay the foundation of a gradual but real reform in our administration.'[20]

Munro, too, shared his passionate advocacy of 'native advancement', as his lengthy minute to the Court of Directors testifies.[21] But they were largely unsuccessful. Malcolm ascribed the difficulty of doing so to English politics, 'No general plan, however wise and grounded, will ever be able to work its way amid the shoals of prejudice, ignorance and jealousy that exist in what the Persians call the Sea of Power – England.'[22] So reform would have to be on a local case-by-case basis.

Between 1818 and 1821 Elphinstone faced the greatest challenge. In introducing direct Company rule over the territories conquered from the Peshwah, he had only a small team. Remarkably gifted and enlightened, they were able to rule as benevolent dictators, combining the functions of collector of revenue, judge and general father figure. But, like Malcolm, Elphinstone realised that this system sidelined the *Zamindars*, *Brahmins* and other officials of the previous semi-feudal society. He wanted to associate these people with government, while at the same time building up a professional class of native administrator.

The key to this dilemma, Elphinstone felt, lay in the development of Native education. Since the new system of government was tending to render the previous Brahminical system obsolete – 'it had dried up the fountains of native talent' – it was the duty of Government to put in its place an education system (partly at Government expense) that would turn out Indians who could take part in government at senior level. Elphinstone went further, maintaining that the Government had a responsibility to educate the poor as well as the rich, a revolutionary concept which was not put into place in Britain itself for another half-century.

Education of Indians had political implications, too. Many Company men believed that educating Indians in Western concepts would breed insurrection. Here Elphinstone was the undoubted leader of radical reform. John Briggs told of seeing a pile of Marathi books in Elphinstone's tent, and asking what they were there for. 'To educate the natives', Elphinstone replied, adding 'it is our high road back to Europe'. For him there was an overriding moral aspect, the idea that a British Government, like any other government, had a duty to educate its subjects: 'we are bound under all circumstances to do our duty to them'.[23] He wrote to Malcolm in 1819 that:

> the acquisition of knowledge by their subjects may have lost the French Hayti and the Spaniards South America, but it preserved half the world to the Romans, gave them a hold on the manners and opinions of their subjects, and left them a kind of moral Empire long after their physical power was destroyed. Knowledge seems to overturn tyrannical and to maintain moderate governments and it is therefore to be hoped it may strengthen ours; but at any rate the danger from it is distant and uncertain and we have no more right to stifle the growing knowledge of our subjects than Herod had to massacre the innocents because he believed some one of them was to dethrone him.[24]

To Elphinstone's great credit, he persevered. Despite opposition from the Utilitarians (notably James Mill) in Leadenhall Street, and from his own Bombay Councillor, Francis Warden (who wanted government grants to be restricted to schools in Bombay teaching in English), he succeeded in developing some form of government- sponsored education system throughout the Bombay Presidency. In 1824 an English school was set up in Bombay and in 1827, under the auspices of the Bombay Native Education Society, it became Elphinstone College. No less than £30,000 was raised from Indian sources to fund professorships. It survives to this day.

There were, of course, doubters, both British and upper-class Indians, who felt that educating the entire Indian population would cause trouble in the long run. Educated Indians would want to enjoy the liberties which education would tell them they were entitled to. There was nothing sinister about this; it was also the selfish but understandable reaction, many years later, of part of the British upper and middle classes to universal education being introduced in Britain.

Malcolm supported Elphinstone on all these issues. As he put it in his *Instructions*: 'These instructions are grounded upon principles which it has been my constant effort to inculcate [in] all officers acting under my orders; and, at a period when I am leaving Central India (perhaps not to return), I feel it a duty I owe to them, to myself, and to the public service, to enter into a more full explanation of my sentiments upon the subject of our general and local rule, than could have been necessary under any other circumstances.'[25]

The key to success or failure, in his view, lay in the personal relations between the Company's political agents and Indians – both rulers and ruled – in the Native States. 'Our power rests on the general opinion of the natives of our comparative superiority in good faith, wisdom and strength, to their own rulers. This important impression will be improved by the consideration we show to their habits, institutions and religion – by the moderation, temper and kindness with which we conduct ourselves towards them; and injured by every act that offends their belief or superstition, that shows disregard or neglect of individuals or communities, or that evinces our having, with the arrogance of conquerors, forgotten those maxims by which this great empire has been established, and by which alone it can be preserved.' Indian disunity had helped establish the Company Raj. Initially, this would work in the Company's favour but as time went on, the populace would take peace for granted and agitate for increasing autonomy. He advocated that 'private intercourse'

> should extend as much as possible to all ranks and classes, and be as familiar, as kind, and as frequent, as the difference of habits and pursuits will admit.
>
> There is a veil between the natives of India and their European superiors, which leaves the latter ignorant, in an extraordinary degree, of the real character of the former . . . but in private intercourse much may be learned that will facilitate the performance of public duty, and give that knowledge of the usages of the various classes of the natives, which will enable its possessors to touch every chord with effect.

But he warned against British officers 'going native': 'The European officer who assumes native manners and usages may please a few individuals, who are flattered or profited by his departure from the habits of his native country; but even with those, familiarity will not be found to increase respect; and the adoption of such a course will be sure to sink him in the estimation of the mass of the community, both European and Native, among whom he resides.'

In 'official intercourse' he repeated his 'four doors open' mantra – the need for Indians to have direct and easy access to European officers, without allowing native servants to act as 'gatekeepers'. Transparency (or what he called 'publicity') was vital to show that 'there are, and can be, no secrets in our ordinary proceedings'. As an example, in the case of relations with Holkar's Court: 'I chose as a principal native writer an intelligent Brahmin, whose family was attached to that of Holkar. I was conscious of having nothing to conceal, but I knew the importance of Tantia Jog [as Chief Minister] and others being satisfied that this was the case.'

He was keen that officers should beware of 'too much zeal'. 'Men are too apt, at the first view of this great subject [interference in Native affairs], to be deluded by a desire to render easy, and to simplify, what is of necessity difficult and complicated . . . We forget, in the pride of our superior knowledge, the condition of others, and self-gratification makes almost every man desire to crowd into the few years of his official career the work of half a century . . . All dangers to our power in India are slight in comparison with those which are likely to ensue from our too zealous efforts to change the condition of its inhabitants, with whom, we are yet, in my opinion, but very imperfectly acquainted.'

He advocated a generous approach to negotiation with rulers over the observance of treaties, pointing out that they often had a different interpretation to Europeans. Providing that there was no intention to act 'contrary to the spirit of the deed', or of acting 'contrary to pledged faith', the Company should be flexible. 'If in doubt, we should lean to the expectations raised in the weaker than to the interests of the stronger power.' He was concerned that there was such a strong feeling in the minds of the major princes and their Ministers 'of their dependence on the British government that it is almost impossible to make them understand that they are, in the conduct of their internal administration, desired and expected to act independently of it'. He felt that the governments of Native States should be encouraged to do their own work. Whatever their private feelings, British agents should resist the temptation to interfere. If British troops were required to restore order, they should always do so in the name of the local ruler; if they arrested a malefactor they should always hand him over to the local ruler for trial and punishment.

The *Instructions* gave guidance on a variety of other issues – delinquency of British troops or camp followers (severe punishment), *sati* and infanticide (non-interference, disapprobation, no more was possible), employment of natives as Company servants (choose locals where possible), and so on.

They ended with a rallying cry: 'You are called upon to perform no easy task; to possess power, but seldom to exercise it; to witness abuses which you think you could correct; to see the errors if not crimes, of superstitious bigotry, and the miseries of misrule, and yet forbear, lest you injure interests far greater than any within the sphere of your limited duties, and impede or embarrass, by a rash change and innovation that may bring local benefit, the slow but certain march of general improvement.'[26]

Finally, each of the three Scots had his own words to describe his vision.

First, Elphinstone: 'The most desirable death for us to die of should be, the improvement of the natives reaching such a pitch as would render it impossible for a foreign nation to retain the government.'[27]

Next, Munro: 'Your rule is alien and it can never be popular. You have much to bring to your subjects, but you cannot look for more than passive gratitude. You are not here to turn India into England or Scotland. Work through, not in spite of, native systems and native ways, with a prejudice in their favour rather than against them; and when in the fulness of time your subjects can frame and maintain a worthy government for themselves, get out and take the glory of the achievement and the sense of having done your duty as the chief reward for your exertions.'[28]

Last, Malcolm: 'Let us, therefore, calmly proceed on a course of gradual improvement: and when our rule ceases, for cease it must, as the natural consequence of our success in the diffusion of knowledge, we shall as a nation have the proud boast that we have preferred the civilisation to the continued subjection of India. When our power is gone, our name will be revered; for we shall leave a moral monument more noble and imperishable than the hand of man ever constructed.[29]

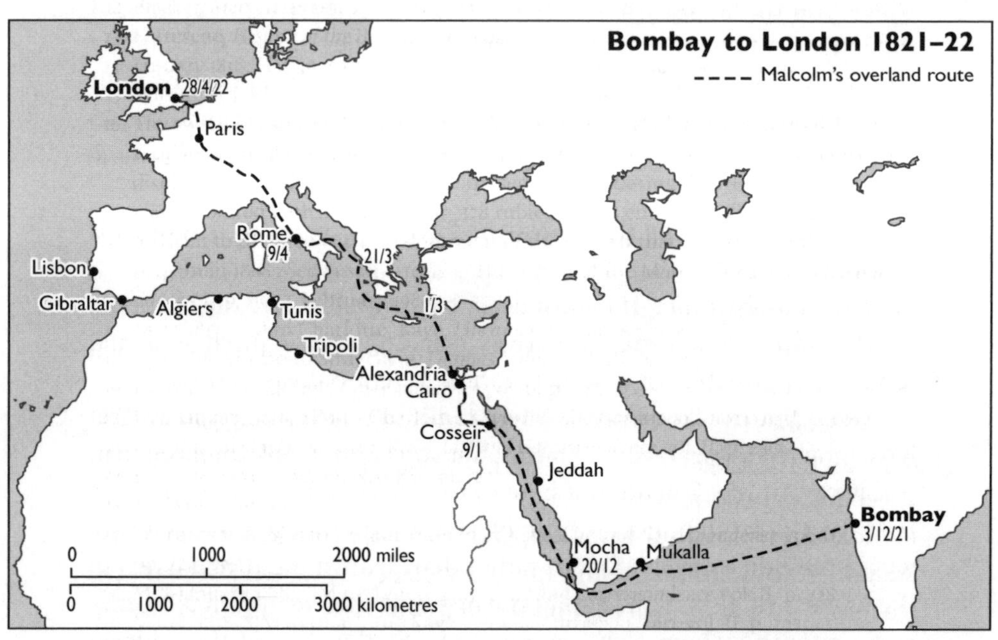
Bombay to London 1821–22
Malcolm's overland route
London 28/4/22
Paris
Rome 9/4
21/3
1/3
Lisbon
Gibraltar
Algiers
Tunis
Tripoli
Alexandria
Cairo
Cosseir 9/1
Jeddah
Mocha 20/12
Mukalla
Bombay 3/12/21
0 1000 2000 miles
0 1000 2000 3000 kilometres

CHAPTER TWENTY-NINE

England – Country Gentleman, 1822–1827

The so-called overland route from India to Europe was at that time novel and quite dangerous. The Red Sea was uncharted and for most of the year northbound sailing ships had to fight strong head winds. The mood of the Egyptian Government was unpredictable, and few foreign travellers ventured down the Nile.

Malcolm's first night at sea was sleepless. But he was not a man to be depressed for long. He wrote in his journal that he was 'well seated in a small but airy cabin, with my good and faithful English servant Charles my sole attendant, four trunks of all my baggage, and an Arabian horse [Sultan] my only animal, with a fair breeze, steering for old England'.[1] On reaching Cosseir, a small port on the Red Sea coast, he mounted Sultan and, with his fellow travellers riding on camels, set off in the cool dry freshness of an Egyptian winter morning. They made their way westwards across a hundred miles of barren *jebel* (hills) to the Nile at Dendera. Here they carved their names on the stone roof of the ruined temple of Hathore, nearly two thousand years old (see image below). Then they bought a boat and sailed down the Nile, which reminded Malcolm of the Ganges, reaching Cairo in mid-February. The Pasha of Egypt, Mehmet Ali, had heard of Malcolm's impending arrival, and called him in for an audience. He had heard that Malcolm had a deep knowledge of Persia, and thought that he might be able to influence British policy towards Egypt. Continuing his journey, he sailed from Alexandria on 25 February, passed through Crete, Corfu, the south-east coast of Italy, across to Naples, Rome, and north to Geneva, reaching Paris on 26 April. He crossed the Channel on 30 April and made straight for London.

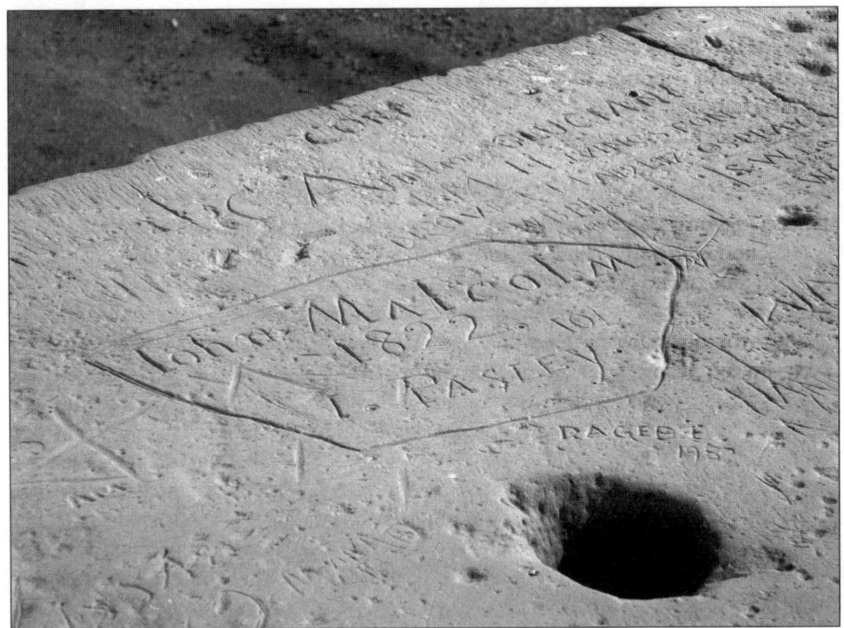

Carving at Dendera, Temple of Hathore, Upper Egypt. When passing through Dendera in early 1822, Malcolm and his young cousin Johnnie Pasley carved their names on the roof.

He was, of course, desperate to get home. The family were waiting for him at Manchester Street. He had not seen Charlotte and the children for nearly six years. Minnie, who had been eight when he left, was fourteen; and Kate, who had been less than one, nearly seven. Since September 1816 the family had alternated between Manchester Street and the 'cottage' at Frant. John wrote to Charlotte regularly and ardently, and she certainly replied. Yet little is known of her life during those years. None of the originals of her letters to him have survived. In the preface to his biography (published in 1856, when Charlotte was still alive), Sir John Kaye wrote that 'the very best biographical materials at my command have been Malcolm's letters to his wife',[2] and he occasionally quoted from them, but he never quoted a word of Charlotte's letters to her husband. Since it was Charlotte who had commissioned Kaye to write the biography, she may not have allowed him to read her letters, or have embargoed their use in the book.

Many years later she wrote to Mountstuart Elphinstone, of 'my poor old cottage at Frant',[3] but today it would be described as a quite substantial house looking out over the village green. Here she lived with her children and a Scottish governess, Miss Manning, taken on shortly after John left in October 1816. The Malcolm family offered her support. Shortly after Pulteney returned from St Helena in late August 1817, he visited Frant and wrote to Clementina that: 'Charlotte and the children all well and very comfortable . . . she is constantly on the move, and rides twenty miles [per day]. Her house is commodious and she has some pleasant neighbours and knows a little of the company at the Wells [Tunbridge Wells] . . . Miss Manning appears an excellent person.'[4]

Charlotte managed her domestic affairs capably, and also found time to do some political canvassing for John at the India House and elsewhere. But she was a worrier, and her worries worried John. He had been kind to Kitty Wellington between 1812 and 1816, when the Duke was away in Spain and Paris. Kitty had spent some time at Tunbridge Wells and had seen Charlotte 'frequently'. In October 1818 John wrote to Kitty confessing that he was 'dying to get home, and I have persuaded my wife of the fact'. And he wrote in May 1820 to Tom Munro, who had been in England in late 1819, that 'My wife met you at Allans (v. grateful for this kindness). It was counsel that she wanted, for she is a bit of a fool in making herself miserable – I take matters quieter.'[5]

Yet she was also self-willed, and showed signs of being difficult She never visited Gilbert in his large rectory at Todenham, where he ran a school for the education of the children of his expatriate brothers and cousins. Burnfoot, too, would surely have been an ideal place for her children to go for the summer holidays; and if she did not want to go herself, she could have sent them in the care of Miss Manning. But after her first visit in August 1815, she never went there again, nor did she let her children go there.

We have three portraits of her: a Hayter sketch of her with her children in 1815; a portrait by Francis Grant in 1840; and a photograph, probably taken in the 1840s. The Hayter sketch shows an idealised, early nineteenth-century look – delicately pretty, large eyed, rosebud lips, porcelain complexion, oval face. Grant's portrait has Charlotte seated at a French desk, writing equipment open, a shaggy little dog at her feet (obviously a pet, a lapdog, not a sporting dog for long walks). She gazes directly, somewhat sadly at the viewer, her regular features framed in a white lace cap, her collar and cuffs setting off delicate hands and pale skin. She is fine-boned, with dark hair and eyes – a lady, no 'braw Scots lassie' like her mother-in-law, Bonnie Peggy. The impression is of someone pampered, well-to-do, a gentleman's choice of wife. John doted on her and shielded her as best he could. She was certainly not 'just a pretty face'. Throughout her marriage she proved quite capable of managing households in both cramped cottages and large rented properties, and of bringing up her five children largely on her own. Her health was a puzzle. She seemed to be healthy enough as a young woman, producing five children before she was twenty-six. But thereafter she became 'delicate', often taking to her bed. John did not complain, but by the late 1820s Pulteney had become exasperated with her, and Charles, on returning from India in 1839, called her 'a great invalid'. Yet she outlived John by thirty years, surviving to the ripe old age (for those days) of seventy-eight.

John had come home sick. Charles noted that 'he is much altered, looks thin and ill',[6] and William Pasley wrote to Mina at Burnfoot that: 'He is a good deal altered, having grown much thinner, and lost a couple of teeth on one side, which has made his face fall in. But, his illness having merely arisen from excessive fatigue in a hot climate, he will soon be himself again.'[7]

He decided to take the (medicinal) waters at Cheltenham, then at the height of its fame as a fashionable spa for the upper classes. He went for a week in early June, then for another week in late June, followed by a day of celebration at Oxford University with his 'brother doctors'. Thence he travelled slowly north to Scotland, stopping for a day or two at Todenham to see Gilbert. He arrived at Burnfoot in early July, still not well, but hoping to recover in the fresh air of the Borders.

From Burnfoot he wrote to Walter Scott, forty miles away. He confessed that he was not yet well enough to come to Abbotsford, and suggested that Scott should come to Burnfoot instead.

> On Monday I go to Netherby Hall and though I do not propose acting the part of Young Lochinvar, I may not be able to get out of the clutches of the Forsters and Fenwicks till Wednesday or Thursday morning.
>
> From that latter day I am (till the 25th) free of all engagements except such as can bend like Easter willows to your convenience. We must have you two days.
>
> My best salaams to Lady Scott and your daughter.[8]

At this period Pulteney and Clementina were living at Irvine, a house on the east bank of the Esk about three miles south of Langholm, which they had leased from the Duke of Buccleuch since 1810. Pulteney was now on half-pay and semi-retired, waiting and hoping for another appointment. John's eldest surviving brother, James, had also arrived in Eskdale during July. He was still a Colonel of Marines based at Chatham, having lost his wife in 1820, giving birth to her sixth child.

Since the three knighted brothers were all in Eskdale at the same time, the locals decided to hold a dinner for them, which was reported in a local newspaper:[9]

> On Wednesday the 31st of July, upwards of Sixty Gentlemen of Eskdale and Ewesdale sat down to Dinner, at the Crown Inn, Langholm, in honour of Sir James, Sir Pulteney and Sir John Malcolm. After the usual loyal toasts, the Chairman, gave in a bumper toast, 'Our Own Three Knights of Eskdale; may they have long life and happiness to enjoy their well earned honours.' The toast was drunk with three times three, and followed by long and repeated plaudits from the whole company – the music played 'Auld Lang Syne'.
>
> Sir John Malcolm then rose, and in the name of his Brothers and himself addressed the company in a speech full of strong feeling and impressive eloquence, the deep and anxious silence of the company (most of whom were moved to tears) while he spoke, was not less striking, than the burst of enthusiastic applause which succeeded.

In all, some twenty-nine toasts were drunk, so it was hardly surprising that: 'it was indeed a night of unrestrained joy and gladness of heart. Within doors and without, one feeling of unmingled delight prevailed. Old and young, the grave and the gay, vied with each other in the demonstration of esteem and admiration of the three knights of Eskdale.'[10]

Another private account gave a less discreet picture of the revelry: 'Barrels of ale and gallons of whisky were expended upon this occasion. A tar barrel and an oil cask formed an excellent substitute for a bonfire, and a dance at the Cross . . . testified the sincerity of feeling.'[11]

By early August Malcolm was back in London. He had decided that

Frant was too small to accommodate the whole family, especially with the children growing up. But Manchester Street was also unsuitable. They needed somewhere in the country. The Burnfoot Malcolms still hoped they might settle in Scotland, but it was too far away from the sort of literary-cum-political life that John wanted to lead, and anyway, Charlotte was against Scotland. He was richer now and could afford to live somewhere more nearly matching his grander aspirations. They settled on Hyde Hall, near Sawbridgeworth in Essex.

> All my books and curiosities, and indeed property, are scattered across the kingdom. So I have been compelled take a good house, as I can only have one. It is called Hyde Hall . . . Its only fault is being too good – that is, being too large; but I got it very cheap. I have thirteen acres of plantations, fifty of park, and I am lord of a manor of 2300, with plenty of game. My lease is for three, five, seven, ten or fourteen years, at my own option; all this at a disbursement of £450 a year. The distance is twenty five miles from town, on the Cambridge and Newmarket road, with dozens of coaches running half a mile from the house.[12]

While waiting to take possession of Hyde Hall, they decided to go to France for a short holiday, taking Minnie with them. They set off in late September, but got no further than Montreuil in the Pas de Calais. Charlotte, who was extremely short-sighted, walked up the slope of a rampart, failed to see that she had reached the top, and fell twenty feet down the other side. She was not seriously injured, but they had to wait several days for her to recover, and then return to England.

In late November they moved into Hyde Hall. Malcolm wrote to Kitty Wellington that: 'both Lady M and myself are in all the horrors of moving into our new house, which we shall not effect before the 28th. We have a houseful at Christmas so there is no hope of being able to pay my respects for some time. Indeed my good Lady has been advised not to move, and I feel as if I could at once be settled, and sign a Penalty Bond never to travel a mile again!'[13] There was more than enough room for the whole family, including Miss Manning, and for all John's 'curiosities' and books. For the first time in his life he was able to 'spread out', with the prospect of staying in the same place for as long as he wanted. Hyde Hall seems to have suited Charlotte even more. She was now the

William Whewell (1794–1866), theologian, Master of Trinity College Cambridge from 1841 to his death.

Adam Sedgwick (1785–1873), was one of the foremost geologists of the nineteenth century.

chatelaine of a grand house, able at last to act as hostess and to cultivate the sort of friendships which she craved.

John and Charlotte enjoyed social life at Hyde Hall. They made several contacts at Trinity College Cambridge (Gilbert's old college). Their first contact at Trinity was Julius Hare. Hare had read law, but in the summer of 1823 he was teaching philosophy, particularly German philosophy. Malcolm brought the German poet/philosopher Auguste von Schlegel, whom he had come across in London, to meet him.[14] Schlegel was said to be 'somewhat egotistical, turgid and opinionated' but under Malcolm's contagious enthusiasm 'soon threw off the lecturer and pedant, and discoursed with pleasant freedom and self-abandonment'[15] At Hare's rooms they also met two other youngish fellows, William Whewell and Adam Sedgwick. Whewell, a scientist and philosopher, later became a distinguished Master of Trinity, from 1841 until his death in 1866, while Sedgwick was to become one of the most distinguished geologists of the nineteenth century.

Over the next few years, these three young dons came frequently to Hyde Hall. All three were delighted with the atmosphere of gaiety and geniality that they found there. They enjoyed talking to the 'old General', whose action-packed life had been in such strong contrast to their academic musings. Hare later gushed that 'he who was always so kind, always so generous, always so indulgent to the weaknesses of others, while he was always endeavouring to make them better than they were'.[16]

They admired Charlotte, in fact they positively doted on her, and continued to do so for many years to come. Sedgwick talked of 'the irresistible charm in her manner', while Hare used to say that 'there is no chance of tearing oneself away when once the hostess appears; one can only fly before she comes down to breakfast'.[17] Perhaps Hyde Hall with its rather rowdy family life was a pleasant contrast to their bachelor existence at Trinity. And Charlotte, still in her thirties, was near them in age. Hare later spent a lengthy convalescence at Hyde Hall, 'a house, which, above all others I have ever been an inmate in, the life and spirit and joy of conversation were most intense . . . a house in which I hardly ever heard an evil word uttered against anyone'.[18]

The Marquess Wellesley had become Lord-Lieutenant of Ireland in 1821. It was a sensible appointment; it pleased the Roman Catholics because he had for many years been a steady supporter of Catholic emancipation, and the Protestants because of his Irish birth and his distinguished career as a proconsul. Malcolm was keen to pay his respects to his erstwhile mentor and hero, and also to see his old friend Merrick Shawe, still serving the Marquess as his Private Secretary. His brother Charles was in Ireland too, as the Captain of the Viceregal yacht, the *William and Mary*. So he decided to make a visit. He set off from London in the Birmingham stagecoach with a travelling companion, Captain Henry Hart, on 19 August 1823. After stopping for a couple of days at Todenham where his son George, now thirteen, was attending Gilbert's school, he went on to Wolverhampton, where he stayed with another friend, and dined with George Canning. He and Captain Hart then travelled in an open coach to Holyhead via Shrewsbury, and though it rained all the way, Malcolm wrote that 'I never enjoyed a journey more. The road is the finest in England – constructed by Telford, an Eskdale man.'[19]

They crossed the Irish Sea from Holyhead to Kingstown (Dun

Laoghaire) in a steamboat, and were met by Charles. Next day Malcolm went on alone to the Marquess's country seat, Woodstock, on the edge of the Wicklow mountains. 'Lord Wellesley was in the very highest spirits, and I could not help feeling with pleasure that my visit was one cause. Walks, dinners, Irish stories, Indian tales, politics, sense and nonsense (which is better) filled up every moment. I was quite sorry to go away.'[20] With Charles and Captain Hart he took in the annual Donnybrook Fair and the Curragh Races, interspersed with lunches and dinners, the Irish gaiety delighting him, then returned for a further two days at Woodstock, where he had 'a serious conversation' with Mr Plunkett, the Attorney-General.[21]

They returned home slowly via Wales, stopping first at Wynnstay near Llangollen, the home of the Wynn family, where they were entertained by Charles Wynn and his brother Sir Watkin. The brothers were both Members of Parliament, and because of their rather thin, high-pitched voices, were nicknamed Bubble and Squeak. Then they went to Powis Castle, near Welshpool, now occupied by Earl Powis's son Robert Clive and his family, and thence to Walcot, to stay with Earl Powis and his wife. Powis[22] was now sixty-eight and a ferociously keen gardener. Here Malcolm achieved a significant literary coup. He had long hankered after the idea of writing a biography of the first Lord (Robert) Clive. During this visit the Clive family invited him to do so, and to make use of the entire archive of Clive papers – a potentially tremendous opportunity, because no biography of Clive had yet been written. For the time being, however, he was heavily engaged on other literary work and was not able to start researching the Clive papers until 1827.

Back at Hyde Hall he wrote a long letter to the Duke, a sort of 'visit report' on his stay in Ireland. He must have known that Wellington, born an Irishman, who had once been Chief Secretary at Dublin Castle, knew infinitely more about Irish politics than he could ever aspire to. He nevertheless waded in with his opinions; though, realising that the Duke's views on Ireland were very different from the Marquess's, he was careful to state that his conclusions were his own.

Sir Henry Colebrooke, one of Malcolm's old friends from Calcutta days, had returned to England in 1814 after a distinguished administrative career in Bengal as writer, judge and member of the Supreme Council, and as an outstanding oriental scholar. Malcolm strongly supported him in founding the Royal Asiatic Society, a forum for Oriental scholars in Britain. Colebrooke was elected the founding director, and Malcolm, a founding Vice-President. The Society met regularly to hear papers given by its members, and it survives to this day. In January 1824 Malcolm read a paper on the Bheels, which was published,[23] and later donated artefacts – 'Hindu sculptures, Indian arms, Persian paintings and Egyptian antiquities' and 'a brass celestial globe made at Mosul in 674 AH [AD 1275] which had been given to him by an Ismaili leader, quaintly described as the 'Archimandrite of the Bohras'.[24] He must also have later had a hand in the award of an RAS diploma to Abbas Mirza, the Prince Royal and Heir Apparent of Persia.

In 1824 Malcolm founded the Oriental Club. Nine years earlier he had been a member of the founding committee of the United Services Club. There had, however, been a certain tension in that Club between the 'British' and the 'Indian' members. Officers in the King's army bought their commissions and their promotions. Officers in the Company armies gained their commissions on merit, though promotions were by seniority. It was a case of Gentlemen versus Players. Those who had seen the Taj Mahal were unlikely to be impressed by the Brighton pavilion. The formation of the Royal Asiatic Society in 1823 had brought a lot of old India hands together, and Malcolm saw the need to form a club where the 'Indians' could meet and talk about India without being thought terrible bores.

In February 1824 he chaired an informal meeting at the Royal Asiatic Society's premises to discuss this idea. Wasting little time, he chaired another meeting a week later, which issued a Prospectus. The objects of the proposed new Club were 'To give to persons who have long resided abroad, the means of entering, on their return, into a Society where they will . . . have an opportunity of forming acquaintance and connexions in their own country . . . and of keeping up their knowledge of the actual state of our Eastern Empire.' There was to be a reading room, with newspapers and periodicals from the east, and a library, chiefly devoted to oriental subjects.[25] Shrewdly, he persuaded the Duke of Wellington to be the first Honorary President, with himself as Chairman. The initial Committee of Management contained many well known names from his Indian past, including Bentinck, Elliot, Alured Clarke, Hislop, Edmonstone, his brother Pulteney, and Robert Campbell. The tone of the Prospectus was brisk. It even had a pro forma letter attached addressed to 'The Secretary of the Oriental Club', effectively containing a standing order instruction to the prospective member's bank.

The results were dramatic. After eight further committee meetings, the first large gathering of members was held on 7 June. In just four months Malcolm had organised an identity, a constitution, a committee and a membership of 540 members (by June 1825 the number had risen further to 744). Admittedly the system of recruiting members was a little haphazard. Malcolm wrote breezily to William Erskine, now living in Edinburgh with seven children to look after, that he had paid his entrance fee and first year's subscription on his behalf, and enclosed a copy of the rules of the club.[26] In July they moved into the Club's first (temporary) premises at 16 Lower Grosvenor Street. Here they stayed for four years while a permanent home was being prepared. At the outset the Duke had given Malcolm two pieces of advice: 'Have a Club of your own; and buy the freehold.' The committee acquired and built new premises on the corner of Hanover Square, and moved there in 1828. By that time Malcolm had relinquished his chairmanship on going to Bombay, incidentally taking with him the Club's first steward, a Mr Pottanco, famous for his unrivalled curry paste recipes.[27]

Early in 1824 news came that Tom Munro was intending to resign as Governor of Madras. Malcolm immediately went to the India House to see the Chairman, William Wigram, and later wrote to Charles Wynn, who had recently replaced Canning at the Board of Control, asking to be considered as a candidate to succeed Munro. He gained Wynn's approval to seek support from the Duke of Wellington, Canning and Lord Liverpool (the Prime Minister) in his application. He realised, however, that there were two potential problems: first that, as in 1818, Elphinstone might also want the job (Madras was considered a more prestigious post than Bombay at that time); and second, that Sir Alexander Campbell, the current Commander-in-Chief at Madras, was his father-in-law. So he put in a secondary request – that if Elphinstone were selected for Madras, he would ask to be considered as Elphinstone's successor at Bombay. In fact, unknown to Malcolm, Elphinstone had already put his name forward for Madras in late 1823, but only because he understood at that time that Malcolm was going as Ambassador to Persia.

The snag with this perfectly reasonable proposal was that the Prime Minister had become involved. Stephen Lushington had served in India many years before,[28] but returned to England in 1807, became an MP and was currently Secretary to the Treasury. Since he had given valuable service to the Government, Lord Liverpool wanted to reward him with an Indian Governorship. Canning and Wellington both thought Malcolm would be a better choice, but since they were members of Liverpool's Cabinet, they felt obliged to support the Prime Minister's choice. Canning told Malcolm that 'I am so peculiarly circumstanced that I cannot take any part or express any wish unfavourable to Lushington's success.'[29] The Duke was more candid. He had advised Malcolm 'not to be too sanguine',[30] and a fortnight later that 'in the contest between Lord Liverpool on the one hand, and the Court of Directors on the other, whatever may be my opinion or wishes of, or in favor of, the individuals put forward by the parties, I can take the side of the Government alone; and I certainly must and will (as is my duty to do) encourage Lord Liverpool by every means in my power to carry his object, and to consent to nothing unless his object is carried.'[31]

At this point there came a further twist in the political manoeuvrings. The Court of Directors had been nettled by a series of rebuffs from the Government. Hearing of dissension in the Cabinet, they took the opportunity to gain some revenge by embarrassing the Government. The Court claimed that it wanted Elphinstone in Madras and Malcolm in Bombay. Since this was obviously a sensible proposal, albeit for the wrong reasons, it was difficult for the Government to find a counter-argument.

As the Duke wrote to Malcolm, 'you are become popular in Leadenhall Street, not because you deserve to be so, but because you happen to be the fittest instrument at the moment to be thrown in the face of the Government and to oppose to them.'[32]

Some weeks later, Wynn called him in, and tried to persuade him to withdraw his application, suggesting that Lushington's supporters at the Court would then support the grant to him of a generous pension. But by now the iron had entered Malcolm's soul. All the bitterness that had been welling up in him over his previous supercessions now came to the surface. He *knew* that he was the best man for the job – for Madras if Elphinstone were not applying for it; for Bombay if he was. While he understood the Duke's dilemma, he was damned if he was going to withdraw his application. Let the Government take whatever decision it liked, and live with the consequences.

There followed an impasse, which lasted through the summer and early autumn. Liverpool stuck with Lushington, but his nerve began to fail, especially when the King told him that 'it will never do to press upon the Directors . . . any person whom they are unwilling to appoint, and more particularly a person so nearly connected with the Government as the Secretary of the Treasury.'[33]

At this point news came from India that war had broken out in Burma, and that Tom Munro felt that in the circumstances it was his duty to remain as Governor. The dilemma was solved. Both the Government and the Court uttered a sigh of relief.

But how did Malcolm feel? The whole charade had made him if possible more bitter than ever. Two years later he poured his heart out in a letter to Gilbert:

> I need not make any observations on the very singular circumstances which have hitherto prevented my advancement in India. Mr Canning placed my name before that of the present governors of Madras and Bombay, in a recommendation for the latter Government. I was rejected by the Court of Directors, who afterwards nominated me Governor of Madras, and I was rejected by his Majesty's Ministers. I found consolation for my first disappointment in the occupation of settling Central India, which, perhaps, considering how all my work has prospered, was a better harvest of fame than I could have reaped at Bombay; but the loss of Madras sank deep in my mind.[34]

Meanwhile, in the autumn of 1824 he consoled himself by going to Scotland for six weeks. He stayed two days at Abbotsford and wrote to Minnie: 'most delighted was my friend Sir Walter to see me. We walked together over all his estate, and looked at all his fine castle. We had a large party and many a tale, and Sir Walter declares that I beat him in legends. But his is the wizard's art of giving them the shape that delights the world.'

In 1825 the British Ambassador in Paris was the Duke of Northumberland, whose wife 'Charly' (daughter of Lord Clive) had known Malcolm in Madras twenty-five years earlier. He invited Malcolm to come to France for the coronation of the new Bourbon king, Charles X, at the cathedral city of Rheims. Malcolm arrived in Paris on the 25 May and dined with the Duke and Duchess that night. 'Nothing can be more splendid than the Duke's hotel and the style of his entertainment.' He went by stagecoach to Rheims, arriving on 29 May, just as the coronation ceremony was starting.

The King, formerly the Duc D'Artois and younger brother of Louis XVI, who had been guillotined thirty-two years before, was already sixty-eight, and had spent much of his adult life as an émigré in England. Malcolm recorded the coronation ceremony in his journal: 'In one line there were standing before me eight marshals of France – Jourdain, Soult, Mortier, Marmont, Oudinot, Macdonald, Lauriston and Molitor.' But what really captured his imagination was the sight of that ultimate survivor, Charles Maurice, Duc de Talleyrand-Perigord and Bishop of Autun, or more simply, Talleyrand, now aged seventy-one and Head Chamberlain of France, 'whose history is more interwoven with the revolution, the wars, the restorations, and the treaties which have disturbed and settled Europe, than of any living being'.

Returning to Paris two days later, he stayed three more weeks with the Duke of Northumberland and was able to enjoy a dizzy round of socialising. At a royal soirée one evening, the King 'was particular in his attentions to me'. He was now more famous as a soldier and as a man of letters than he had been on his first visit ten years before. He met Marshal Soult, the veteran of Austerlitz, Jena, the Peninsular War and Waterloo, and talked with him for two hours, promising to send him a copy of his *History of Persia*. Soult confirmed that 'when Napoleon marched against Russia, it was still England that was his object, and all means that Russia could furnish, had that expedition succeeded, would have been turned against India. We might never have brought back a man from England had we gone over, and our troops might have perished on the road to India, but Napoleon was sincere and earnest in both these projects.' Two days later he took the explorer Humboldt to dinner with the Duke of Northumberland and the next day gave a dinner for him, to which he asked Julius Klaproth (a German Orientalist), Sir George Staunton (a British China scholar), and several British visitors, including Robert Clive.[35]

In the autumn he was off again to Scotland. He passed through Edinburgh and Glasgow and called on various friends, Lord John Campbell and Sir David Baird among them. He spent late August and early

September at Burnfoot and went shooting with Pulteney. On the way back south he took Pulteney's son George with him. In the Lake District they came upon a brace of poets. He wrote to Clementina that 'We breakfasted with Southey[36] at Keswick and dined with the Wadsworths [Wordsworths] at Megadale. We had a beautiful day for the Lakes, and the boys were just wild with joy.'[37]

He was not achieving his goal of a career in Britain, but he was at least playing an active advisory role in several political issues relating to India. The three most important were Britain's diplomatic relationship with Russia over Persia (discussed in Chapter 21);[38] the question of press freedom in India; and the reform of the Company's Indian armies.

Censorship of the press in India was an issue which raised a great deal of controversy in Britain. Effectively there was no 'native' press. The English language press was run by Europeans and intended to serve the European community. With such a small readership it naturally tended towards scurrilous gossip. For many years an informal censorship had been practised, but in 1799 the Marquess had introduced a formal censorship system, justifying his action on the ground that Britain was at war with Napoleonic France. The system worked well enough, but libertarians were naturally shocked that the fundamental English tradition of press 'freedom' was not being allowed in British India. In 1818 Hastings decided to revise the system. He abolished the censorship, and replaced it with regulations prohibiting editors from publishing criticism of the government, or of native religions and usages, or from discussing private scandals. He hoped thereby to encourage not only a degree of public opinion but also the cooperation of local British society with the government. In practice, however, it proved impossible to define the limits of the subjects which were proscribed, and the government became embroiled in frequent rows with editors, especially with the editor of the *Calcutta Journal*, James Silk Buckingham, who showed great ingenuity in evading the new rules. The Court of Directors called for the restoration of censorship, but the Government, although privately agreeing with them, was wary of the trouble which the Opposition in Parliament could cause on such a highly emotional issue, and decided to do nothing. In early 1823, when Buckingham had once more transgressed the regulations, it was left to John Adam, acting as Governor-General in the interregnum between

Hastings's departure and the arrival of his successor, Lord Amherst, to take the brave decision to cancel Buckingham's licence and send him home.

Malcolm had wrestled with this issue for many years. The liberal in him saw the virtue of a free press; the practical in him saw that it could not work in the conditions prevailing in India at that time. In April 1822, while still crossing Europe on his way home, he wrote a seventeen-page memo to the Court of Directors on the subject. In February 1823 he sent a copy of this memo to Amherst, the incoming Governor-General, who received it shortly after his arrival in Calcutta. In July, hearing of the expulsion of Buckingham, Malcolm wrote a letter of support to Adam, telling him that he had consulted Charles Wynn at the Board of Control, and Wigram, the Chairman of the Court, on their views. 'From the former I received a manly and decided note . . . The Chairman seems to approve, but he is a milk and water animal who does not understand the subject in a long view.'[39]

But Buckingham was a fighter, and when he reached England he set about making life difficult for the Government by waving the banner of freedom of speech in Parliament, and for the Company by canvassing the Court of Proprietors (shareholders). Malcolm's opinion, as an expert and relatively impartial observer, was eagerly sought. In a speech in Parliament in May 1824 on the Buckingham case, a Mr J.G. Lambton quoted Malcolm's *Memoir of Central India* to support his case for press freedom, but Malcolm immediately challenged this interpretation of his views, demanding in a letter that 'you will greatly oblige me by informing me to what part of my late work you do me the honour to refer'.[40]

He got his chance to spell out his own views in detail a few weeks later, when the Court of Proprietors held a debate on the subject at the India House. After considerable discussion there was 'a general call for Sir John Malcolm to speak'. He began by observing that Buckingham had been praised, and he wanted likewise to praise his old friend John Adam, a man of unimpeachable integrity. He accepted that a free press was highly desirable in a country where the feelings of the public could be heard. But in England, what constituted the public? Not the military and civil servants of the government; not the nobility and the gentry, who had their own vested interests; not the lower orders, who were uneducated and vulnerable to the siren calls of demagogues and agitators. The public, he asserted, were those who made up the great 'middle' of English society. Did such a public exist in British India, he asked? He went on to describe the composition of society there.

First there was the British population. It mostly comprised the civil and military servants of the government; the rest were a tiny number – not more than 5,000 in the whole of India. It did not therefore constitute a 'public', in the sense that he had defined it. He was a believer in open government, but the fact had to be faced that British power in India was absolute – witness the Governor-General's power to expel a British subject from India without any appeal. Freedom in the English sense was therefore heavily curtailed, even before considering press freedom. Nevertheless there were plenty of checks and balances on the exercise of the local government's arbitrary power. Any local government measure had to be approved in turn, or at least not opposed by, the Court of Directors, the Court of Proprietors, the Board of Control and finally the British Parliament. So, although challenging the Calcutta Government, as William Hickey had once put it, was 'like attacking an elephant', there were plenty of other safeguards for the local British population. Next there was the Anglo-Indian or Eurasian community. This minority community naturally had grievances which needed attending to, but he questioned whether a free press was the best way of doing so. Finally there was the native community, or rather, several communities. Hitherto they had never had a 'free' press, and the idea was quite alien to them. Certainly none existed in the Native States. He wondered what would be the object, for the natives, of such a free press. He feared that the Mohammedans could be rather too easily roused to violent anger by agitators. The Hindus were more pacific, but *Brahmins* were particularly clever at subversive propaganda, aimed especially at subverting the native army of Bengal.

He ended with a typical Malcolm flourish:

> It has often been said, and it has been repeated to-day, that your empire in India is one of opinion. It is so, but it is not an opinion of your right, but of your power. The inhabitants see that [power] limited by law and regulations, and the spectacle increases their confidence; but shew them the person who exercises an authority they deem supreme, [being] braved and defeated by those under him, and the impression which creates the charm will be broken. This, at least, is my view of the subject;

> I am, however, I confess, rendered timid by experience. It has made me humble, and I look with awe and trembling at questions which the defenders of a free press treat as mere bugbears, calculated to harm none but the weak and prejudiced.[41]

He later elaborated these views in his *Political History of India*, in which he repeated the assertion that British rule in India was essentially military and absolute, and that with respect to the freedom of the press, 'as long as the necessity exists for the maintenance of absolute power, it is far better for both the State and for individuals that it should be exercised to prevent rather than to punish'.[42] His defence of censorship and restrictions rested on the undesirability of attacks by locally based Europeans, firstly on Government, which indirectly inflamed the native community, and secondly on native customs and usages, which offended native communities. 'We must necessarily deduce that . . . the existence of a free press, free in the same degree as that of England, is incompatible with a government such as that that we have established in India.'

It is easy enough to denigrate these arguments as a typical government servant's defence of bureaucratic rule – protesting that his motives are pure, and that he should be allowed to get on with government, free from the irritating and sometimes scurrilous criticisms of the press. But at least there is ring of conscience, of acknowledgement that he is trying to defend a system which in a perfect world would be indefensible.

Another political issue which Malcolm continued to press with vigour during his 'Hyde Hall' years was the reform of the Company's three Presidency armies. He had first pursued this subject way back in 1794, when still a Lieutenant.[43] Now, in his *Political History of India*, published in June 1826, he set out his considered views. His major proposal was that the three Presidency armies should be amalgamated into one, with identical conditions of service. He had made the same proposal in 1813, without success. But in his view there was now an even better case for doing so, because the three Presidencies had in the meantime become territorially contiguous. This unified Company army should not, however, be merged with the King's army, as some had suggested, although officers should be able to transfer from one to the other more freely. The Company armies had hitherto been able to avoid the potentially corrupt

King's army practice of patronage, and the buying of commissions. Moreover, the career of a Company army officer was quite different to that of a King's army officer. He was a permanent expatriate, with little opportunity to combine service with a family and a home away from his regiment. There was also the factor of the Company's prestige. If the army in India was seen to be reporting directly to the British Government, the Company would lose face in Indian eyes.

These were radical views. And they were fully supported by Tom Munro in Madras, who at this time carried more weight with the Court of Directors and the Government than even Malcolm. Charles Wynn was impressed by them. He consulted the Duke. But the Duke was sceptical:

> I have read that part of Malcolm's book which relates to the military establishments of the East Indies, and I see that he recommends the amalgamation of the armies, the equalisation of their pay, and indeed the formation of the whole into one. He attacks the opinion which I entertain of the security which is derived from the division of the establishments.
>
> My opinion is not altered by the perusal of Malcolm's. He is a very clever fellow who has considered these subjects more than I have, and knows more of them than I do, and particularly of their present state. But Malcolm, like other men, has prejudices. He thinks the Indian army the first in the world; and of all Indian armies, the army of Fort St George the finest. He knows the pay of the Bengal army cannot be lowered; that of the others must then be raised to the level of that of the Bengal army.

But, he pointed out, the record of the Company armies over the previous forty years – including three mutinies – had not been too impressive. Malcolm himself had written that: 'the natives of the country about Cape Comorin are as unlike those of Hindustan, or of the provinces of Bengal, as a native of Spain or of Italy is to a native of Sweden or the north of Germany or of Russia; and their languages differ as much as their appearance and manners . . . all three armies differ in their discipline, appearance, mode of doing duty etc, not only because they are separate armies and paid at different rates, but because they are composed of people of different nations. This can never be altered. Leave us the rest as it is.'[44]

This was one of the rare occasions when the Duke and Malcolm differed in opinion. Malcolm's proposal to amalgamate the three Presidency armies was clearly logical, and was eventually implemented, while the Duke's argument that troops from one part of India would be ineffective in other parts of India was feeble – he himself had led troops from Mysore into battle in northern Mahratta country. But there was also a wary canniness in his desire to keep the armies separate.

Wynn was still sympathetic to Malcolm's proposal, and told the Duke so, but he dared not override that Olympian oracle of military wisdom. Nothing happened.

Malcolm had come home intending to make a new career in British politics. He looked around for a constituency where he could stand at the next general election. In late 1825 he eyed the seat of Rochester, and approached William Pasley, who was living nearby at Chatham, for local help in securing the nomination. The front runner as Tory candidate was a Mr Campbell, who at first said he would not stand, leaving the way free for Malcolm, but then changed his mind, leaving Malcolm in the lurch. Later, in 1826, the seat became vacant again, setting up a by-election in June. Malcolm was not a candidate, but canvassed for the Tories. He also canvassed for the Tories in June at another by-election campaign, in Hull. But he couldn't find a seat for himself.

This was intensely frustrating. In all the public events since 1822 his role had been no more than advisory. And despite his considerable writing activity, his books were not written for pure literary satisfaction; they were written for a purpose – to influence public policy. But none of this was getting him anywhere personally. In August 1826 he wrote in some anguish to Gilbert that: 'Circumstances have occurred which will early compel me to decide whether I am to be an idle or a busy man. The habits of my past life will probably force me on the latter course, for I already feel the truth of Bacon's observation, that: 'a man who has been accustomed to go forward and findeth a stop, falleth out of humour with himself, and is not the thing he was.'[45] He confessed that being passed over for the governorships of Madras and Bombay 'was taking away from me the opportunity of rendering services to my country that would have opened a prospect of reaching the ultimate object of my ambition, which is to be, ere my career terminates, Governor-General of India.'

His most likely prospect now was to become a director of the East India Company, and combine this with a seat in the House of Commons – easily obtainable for Directors. The Company's Charter was due to expire in 1833, and being a Member of Parliament would enable him to lobby for the interests of the Company when a new Charter was being debated. But this was not as straightforward as it might have seemed. Several of his friends argued that as a director he would be seen as a Company man, and this would lessen his strong existing influence with Government Ministers.

Since 1822 Malcolm had continued to work hard on his literary output. He had converted his Malwa report into book form and published it in 1823 as *A Memoir of Central India* and it was commercially successful, running to a second edition. His *Sketch of the Political History of India*, published in 1811, had told the story of British involvement from 1784 to 1806, ending with the second Governor-Generalship of Lord Cornwallis (and Sir George Barlow). In 1824–5 he wrote up *The Political History of India*, published by John Murray in 1826. To the five chapters of the *Sketch*, it added a further two lengthy chapters to cover the Governor-Generalships of Minto and Hastings, taking the story to 1823, plus some general observations. He must have been sorely tempted to revise the five chapters of the *Sketch* in the light of subsequent events, but, remarkably, he did not change a word. In the second half of 1826 he wrote *Sketches of Persia*, a light-hearted memoir of his several visits to that country. The seed for the *Sketches* may have been the relative success of James Morier's *Haji Baba of Isfahan*. The book was finished in late January 1827 and published by John Murray. It was a considerable success, and ran to several editions. Ahead of him lay the prospect of writing the mighty biography of Robert Clive, using the papers which the Clive family had made available to him in 1823.

One consideration he no longer had to worry about was money. His return to India in 1816 had been partly prompted by the fact that he was running down his capital. He had come home in 1812 with savings of £35,000, but by 1816 these had dwindled to £20,000. Between 1817 and 1821 he was able to draw a Resident's salary (c. £2,500) in addition to his basic Brigadier's salary (c. £800), but he also had large outgoings due to the extraordinary nature of his work, which were only partly allowable as expenses. The Duke, when approached for help, made a remarkably generous comment (by his cautious standards) of what he considered Malcolm deserved:

> from the year 1796 (nearly thirty years ago, and no mean proportion of the life of any man) no great transaction either political or military has taken place in the East in which you have not played a principal, most useful, conspicuous and honourable part; you have in many services, diplomatical as well as military, been distinguished by successes, one of which in ordinary circumstances would have been deemed sufficient for the life of a man . . . But there is one recommendation of you of which I hope you have availed yourself in your communications with your employers . . . and that is your disinterestedness, and consequent necessity of relying upon their liberality and generosity. You have filled many positions in which you might have become rich . . . But the truth is that you are poor.[46]

Eventually, in March 1825, a pension of £1,000 per annum was approved by the Company, and this secured his prospects of living in relative comfort in retirement. But he was still short of capital to enable him to buy a substantial house. Here the issue of the Deccan Prize Fund – the payment of prize money relating to the Anglo-Mahratta War of 1817–18 – was crucial. There was an interminable delay in making a payout, due to a long-running dispute about the nature of the break up of the Mahratta Empire. How much was it a matter of British acquisition of assets on the transfer of political power, and how much was prize money won in battle? And which parts of the Company's and King's armies were entitled to it? Hastings, who had combined the roles of Governor-General and Commander-in-Chief, had decided that prize money should be shared between the Army of the Deccan, under Hislop, coming from the south, and the Grand Army, coming from the north. Hislop objected, on the understandable ground that practically all the actual fighting had been done by the Army of the Deccan. Negotiations had dragged on until early 1823, when the British Government appointed the Duke of Wellington to be the Trustee of the Deccan Prize Fund, and called on him to adjudicate between the parties. By 1826 he had come down strongly on the side of Hastings's interpretation (and incidentally of Malcolm's), and the payment was made. When the Duke asked Malcolm about his financial situation, he replied that his share of the Deccan prize money had made him 'very independent'.[47]

There is no reason to suppose that the Duke was in any way biased in Malcolm's favour. He was celebrated for his total integrity, and was often called upon to adjudicate in disputes for that very reason. He and Malcolm were nevertheless very close at this time. In fact Malcolm was definitely on the Duke's 'A list' of friends. Harriet Arbuthnot, the young wife of Charles Arbuthnot, the Duke's political 'fixer', wrote in her journal about a week-long house party at Stratfield Saye: 'At Stratford we remained a week [1–8 November 1826] . . . We had a very large, gay and agreeable party; all the corps diplomatique, Lievens, Esterhazy, Polignacs, Palmela, Sir John Malcolm, Sir John Keane, Lord Lothian, Clanwilliam etc.'[48]

But as Malcolm's political, literary and social activities drifted on, a new development dramatically changed his situation. Towards the end of 1826, news came from India that Elphinstone intended to retire as Governor of Bombay during 1827. Charles Wynn, still President of the Board of Control, had no hesitation in writing to ask Malcolm whether he 'still retained the disposition to succeed to the appointment which he had felt two years before'.[49]

So now, at long last, he was being offered a Governorship, with support from both Government and Company. In fact, although Wynn greatly valued Malcolm's ability and experience, a year earlier he had been reluctant to select Company servants to Governorships. He thought they would be unfamiliar with politics in England, and would have less prestige than an appointee from Britain; the local British would treat them as 'equals'. But the Duke had reassured him: 'I quite agree with what you say of the employment of the East India Company's servants as Governors etc abroad; but Malcolm is certainly an exception. He has lived much of his life in this country, and to great advantage. He has a thorough knowledge of men and affairs here; and I should say, that if it is difficult to find a proper person out of the Company's service, he is the fittest man in that service who could be found.'[50] Somewhat stunned, Malcolm replied the next day, asking for ten days to consider the implications before giving a definite answer. On the personal front there was the question of his health, and even more so, of Charlotte's health, and of the children's upbringing, if she went with him; and if she didn't go, the prospect of several more years of separation. On the job front, he was no longer particularly keen on the Governorship, as such. What he really hankered after was another go at running Central India, of reviving his old idea of putting Central India under a Lieutenant-Governor, who would report to him. Another enticement, no more than a gleam in his eye, was the possibility, with Lord Amherst expected to retire in a year or two, that he might become the interim Governor-General for a few months until the new appointee arrived at Calcutta.

Pulteney, who was visiting Hyde Hall at the time, was against John's accepting the appointment. He wrote to Clementina that 'I think the Government [of Bombay] will be offered to John, and I hope he will decline it, for I am convinced his health will not stand the climate . . . Charlotte is not well.'[51]

Wynn came to stay at Hyde Hall for a couple of days. Malcolm told him that his acceptance of the Governorship would be conditional on his also taking on Central India, using all the arguments which he had previously used with Hastings back in 1819; that Central India and Rajputana, unlike many other parts of India, had an existing 'aristocracy' of native princes which worked fairly well. This aristocracy should be allowed to continue administering the internal affairs of their States for as long as possible, which would be much more effective than trying to turn Central India into another Bengal. And with his unique experience of settling Malwa in 1818–1821, he personally would be ideally equipped to provide the necessary oversight. Wynn knew little of the minutiae of Indian government, and this radical proposal, no doubt argued with all Malcolm's customary fervour, probably caught him unawares. He reacted favourably, but said that he would have to consult the Court of Directors and his colleagues in the Government before making a decision.

Malcolm followed up a few days later with a long memorandum explaining his views, then went down to London to consult the Duke about the offer. He told the Duke that he had wanted to reject the appointment on the grounds of health, but Wynn's apparent acquiescence over Central India had made him change his mind. A further consideration was that, despite receiving the Deccan prize money, he still could ill afford the £5,000 apparently needed for him to enter Parliament and pursue an alternative career in England. The Duke, like Pulteney, had earlier been against him taking on the job. 'I don't see that anything in India, at present, is compensation to you for the loss of your health.'[52] But he probably sensed that when Malcolm had got the bit between his teeth, there was no stopping him. His only cautionary advice was to doubt whether Malcolm could achieve his aspiration to become temporary Governor-General. In any case the unexpected news of Lord Amherst's resignation, just in, put paid to Malcolm's aspirations – the new Governor-General might arrive in Calcutta before he did, and there would probably therefore be no need for a 'temporary' incumbent.

Wynn reported back that both the Court of Directors and the Board of Control were favourably disposed to the appointment, and on 14 January Malcolm formally accepted, on the understanding that he would control Central India. The appointment of Malcolm to Bombay and Stephen Lushington to Madras was confirmed in an East India Company minute of 18 January,[53] and announced publicly a month later.

At Hyde Hall, at first, there was jubilation. Pulteney wrote to Clementina from Hyde Hall on 23 January: 'I am glad to tell you that I never saw our sister in a better frame of mind. The present resolves are as follows. John sails the end of next month. Charlotte, Minny and George in Italy. Olympia goes abroad with Mrs Hart and if possible the two girls are to be put to school near to where Miss Manning can take a sort of charge of them. I do not see how the last part is to be executed. Nor is there any plan yet suggested for its accomplishment. However it is gratifying to see his mind at rest.'[54] Again, on 7 February: 'John will be the Governor of Bombay next Wednesday – it is understood that he is to have the settlement of Malwa joined to it, which he considers will take him three years – it is possible that he will sail next month for Bengal to advise the Governor-General. He is in great glee, but his family comes over him every hour – how they are to be conveyed is a problem. The Duke advised him to stay at home, and so he would if it had not been Malwa – but that is his hobby.'[55]

In February, however, Wynn and the Chairmen were beginning to backtrack on Malcolm's Central India proposal. They wanted to have more detail: 'Is it proposed that Malwah shall be annexed to the Bombay

Presidency, and that its affairs shall be administered by the Governor in Council at Bombay? Or is it proposed that it shall be placed under your personal and separate charge, acting in a distinct capacity from that of the Governor in council of Bombay, and under the immediate authority and control only of the Bengal (Supreme) Government?'[56] To these questions Malcolm replied, first, that 'it would be highly inexpedient at the present period to annex that country [Central India] to the Presidency of Bombay'; second, that he had hitherto assumed that the only legal basis for him to administer Central India would be through his capacity as Governor in Council at Bombay; but – and here he no doubt saw an unexpected opportunity to achieve what most proconsuls seek, to acquire dictatorial powers without the tiresome business of cajoling a Council's agreement – if the Chairs so wished, he would be more than happy to administer Central India on a personal basis, answering only to the Governor-General. But the Chairs and the Government procrastinated. He wrote to the Duke on 19 April from Cheltenham: 'My health brought me here, and I go to Scotland before I return to London, where I shall remain for five or six weeks before I sail, and I hope to obtain your opinion on some points very vital to our Eastern Empire, which no one understands more completely than you.'[57]

Meanwhile the domestic sky was also darkening. On 18 April Pulteney wrote 'Charlotte is in Town, looking the picture of death. She came to meet her new governess, who had taken herself off to Brighton in the meantime. Miss Manning remains at Hyde Hall with Olympia.'[58] By mid-May it had become clear that Charlotte was too ill to go to India.

John had originally planned to take three ADCs with him to India: his cousin, Captain Alexander Dirom (who dropped out later); his son, George; and Charlotte's nephew, Alexander Cockburn Campbell (the eldest son of Charlotte's sister Olympia Cockburn). George had got a commission in the army as an ensign in the 61st Regiment but was only seventeen, so John accepted William Pasley's suggestion that George should be left with him at Chatham for a few months, rather than go with his father in July.[59]

At this point there was a surprise development. John's eldest daughter Minnie revealed that she was in love with her cousin Alex Cockburn Campbell. In May 1827, she was miserable. She wrote later that: 'I knew my father and Alick were going to India in a very few weeks and that in all human probability I should not see them for three years at the very least. And there was no intention of allowing me to accompany Papa and no apparent possibility of my marrying for a very long time, if ever.'[60] Somehow, either Minnie or Alex must have told her parents that they were in love. John's response was typically decisive. With Charlotte unable to go to India, he would instead take Minnie with him to act as his hostess, but first she should be married to Alex. So the wedding was arranged, and took place, in quite grand style, on 20 June, at St Georges Church, Hanover Square.

On 13 June the Court of Directors gave a valedictory banquet in Malcolm's honour at the Albion Tavern in Aldgate, with about 180 attending. They included many of the great men of the land: the Duke of Wellington, and George Canning, now Prime Minister, though with only two months to live; Charles Wynn of the Board of Control; and Sir Hugh Lindsay, the Chairman of the Court of Directors. But the guest list also included many of the men who had watched Malcolm's long career: the Earl of Powis, who had been Governor of Madras; Sir James Mackintosh, who had been Recorder of Bombay; Lord William Bentinck, who had been Governor of Madras (and was about to be appointed Governor-General); Sir Thomas Dallas, who had met the fourteen-year-old Malcolm in Mysore in 1784; David Haliburton, who as Mayor of Madras had befriended him as a young man in the late 1780s; Thomas Cockburn, the Madras merchant and brother-in-law of Charlotte's sister Olympia Cockburn; and his two brothers Pulteney and Gilbert. The Marquess Wellesley was in Ireland. Sir John Kennaway was still alive, but sadly almost blind, living in Devon. William Pasley, who also attended, wrote in his journal:

> Dine at the Albion Tavern with the Court of Directors to meet Sir John Malcolm . . . The Duke of Wellington in full uniform. Also Sir John. Mr Canning and several of the ministers there; Sir Pulteney and Mr Gilbert Malcolm. Sir John, on his health being proposed by the Chairman makes an excellent speech, alluding to his own service in India, his friends about him, the state of India etc. Mr Canning makes a very elegant speech. The Duke of Wellington an excellent one, distinguished by good feeling and good sense well expressed. Afterwards Mr Wynn makes an excellent speech in affable vein. All complimentary to Sir John. Dinner, wines, attendance excellent. Return with Sir John and

> Mr Gilbert Malcolm. The latter criticises his brother's speech. I differ with him.[61]

Canning said in his speech that: 'there cannot be found in the history of Europe, the existence of any monarchy, which, within a given time, has produced so many men of the first talents in civil and military life, as India has first trained for herself, and then given to their native country.' Charles Wynn spoke of Malcolm's popularity with Indians: 'The affectionate regard in which he is held by the natives of India is the happy result of his own conduct. He did not hold himself aloof from or above them; he mixed in their society, associated himself with them in their hours of recreation, joined in the sports of the field with them, and by such means won their hearts.' The Duke was especially fulsome, concluding that: 'a nomination such as this operates throughout the whole Indian service. The youngest cadet sees in it an example he may imitate – a success he may attain. It is now thirty years since I formed an intimate friendship with Sir John Malcolm; during that eventful period, there has been no operation of consequence, no diplomatic measure, in India, in which my friend has not borne a conspicuous part. He has been alike distinguished by courage and by talent; the history of his life during that period will be the history of the glory of his country in India.'[62]

Such an event would have been flattering to the *amour proper* of just about anyone. For a man of Malcolm's egotistical nature, the cup of joy was filled to overflowing. It was in fact the apogee of his entire career. Typically, he had the grace to remember and toast his two great contemporaries – Mountstuart Elphinstone and Sir Thomas Munro. The next morning he wrote to the Duke that: 'I awoke this morning with the same deep feelings of gratitude with which I went to rest last night. I would not relinquish the testimony you gave me for ten governments. After we broke up from dinner, I learnt more fully the deep impression you had made on all who heard you. It was such as can alone be produced when the head and the heart are in complete union.'[63]

Shortly afterwards he took George down to Chatham and left him with William Pasley. By late June 1827 he was packing and attending to last-minute chores before the voyage, and another lengthy exile. On 1 July he arranged for Charlotte and the girls to visit Apsley House to see the Duke's plate collection. On 3 July he deposited his will with his solicitors, and paid a farewell visit to the Duke. He wrote to John Murray in London and William Erskine in Paris about his literary affairs. Julius Hare came to visit, and 'found Lady Malcolm come up to town determined, in spite of her weakness to accompany him to Portsmouth . . . Lady Malcolm is considerably better, though still very weak and nervous. I sate with her however last night from nine to near one, and she had almost all her wonted life and elasticity of spirits, and talked with much animation and beauty.'[64]

On the morning of 5 July, having just heard that Lord William Bentinck had been appointed Governor-General in succession to Lord Amherst, he postponed his departure in order to have a brief meeting with him, then rushed down to Portsmouth that afternoon. The rest of the Malcolm party – Minnie, Alex and James Little (a new ADC from the Borders and the younger brother of the late Johnny Little) – were waiting for him at Portsmouth. They boarded the *Neptune* late on 5 July and sailed the next day.

After a tearful farewell at Portsmouth, Charlotte made her way back to London and went on to Hyde Hall a few days later. The Trinity dons were kind to her. Julius Hare helped her to catalogue the library at Hyde Hall. Whewell proposed a trip down the Rhine, though the plan fell through. The lease of Hyde Hall was due to expire at the end of October, and since only the two youngest children were still at school, the Malcolms had decided not to renew it. Charlotte was re-established at a rented house in Manchester Square.

There we must leave her for the next three and a half years.

CHAPTER THIRTY

Governor of Bombay – Events, 1827–1830

Malcolm was sailing to India via the Cape for the fourth time in forty-five years; he was an old hand. The *Neptune* was an East Indiaman of 644 tons, built in 1815. Apart from the six officers of the crew, there were twenty-six passengers: Sir John and his 'family' (Minnie and Alex Cockburn Campbell, two ADCs, James Little and a Mr Hamilton); plus three King's army cavalry officers, seven Bombay Army cadets, four writers and six assistant surgeons; and Mr Money, a senior 'civilian' in the Bombay Government.

He had set himself a task for the journey – to write up his biography of Robert Clive. He had arranged for lithographs to be taken of the relevant copies of the Clive Papers, so that he could work on them, first at Hyde Hall, then during the voyage to India.[1]

Among the passengers on the *Neptune* was a seventeen-year-old army cadet, Henry Rawlinson, going to India for the first time. Rawlinson was destined to become a fearless soldier and sportsman, but above all one of the most famous Assyriologists of the nineteenth century. His greatest achievement was to decipher the cuneiform scripts at Bisitun dating from the reign of Darius the Great of Persia (548–486 BC).

Rawlinson wrote a journal of his four-month voyage to Bombay in the form of a letter to his sisters, fascinating in itself but also giving a vivid picture of day-to-day shipboard life in company with Malcolm. At first he was homesick and miserable. But he soon cheered up:

> 11 July: Have been talking to Sir J Malcolm . . . he is a very clever man himself, and often says that everyone's

> promotion must depend on his own talents, and he will never give a place to anyone unfit for it, however strongly recommended.
>
> 15 July: . . . Sir John . . . seems possessed of such a fund of anecdotes that though he had been unremittingly employed in telling stories ever since he came on board, he still goes on at such a rate as to keep the whole table in a continual roar, in which he himself always heartily joins.
>
> 16 July: . . . Sir John goes on laughing, talking and story-telling as much as ever. I intended to have made a collection of his jokes, but I am afraid the task would have been endless. He sometimes however sports rather a stale one.
>
> 24 July: Contrived to make up to Lady Campbell . . . Sir John is very fond of her, but I rather think she bullies him.
>
> 17 August: . . . had a very long talk with Sir John about India, superstition, infidelity, Gibbon, Hume, Voltaire etc. He was defending as usual India and everything relating to her, declaring that he infinitely preferred the superstitious Pagan, who bowed himself before an idol or symbol of the Deity, to the philosophers such as Hume etc, who, elated by the sense of their superior knowledge, worshipped no God but themselves, no idol but their own pride. It was excessively interesting to hear him. He speaks with much eloquence and religion, though he could not help occasionally giving way to his love of humour, and bringing in rather irrelevantly one or two of his interminable jokes.

Malcolm's daily routine was to work away at *The Life of Clive* throughout the morning and early afternoon until dinner at three o'clock, then break off for the day. He would put some of the young men to work copying out excerpts from the Clive papers, turning his horrible handwriting into a form legible to a publisher.[2] On Sundays, following the biblical injunction not to work, he would sit in a corner of the deck and write verse paraphrases of Old Testament stories.

He also took an active part in the production of a play *The Rivals*, put on by the passengers, writing the prologue and epilogue, and finally, as they were nearing Bombay, a farewell address 'from the actors of the Theatre Royal, *Neptune*'.

By the time that *Neptune* sailed into Bombay harbour on 26 October, he had completed 1,000 handwritten pages of *The Life of Clive*.

Malcolm's party were met on arrival by Mountstuart Elphinstone, who was at last going home, after thirty continuous years of service in India. There was some sad news – Tom Munro had died from cholera in July. Malcolm officially took over on 1 November, and for the next two weeks he and Elphinstone attended a round of parties given by the local European and Native communities. Elphinstone, anticipating that he might have to leave Bombay before Malcolm arrived, had set out his thoughts in a long letter, in which he briefed Malcolm about local affairs and local personalities. When Elphinstone told him that he meant to spend at least a year wandering around Europe on his way home, Malcolm wrote out dozens of letters of introduction to the various grandees and savants whom he had met on his own journeys to the Continent.[3] On 15 November, Elphinstone sailed out of Bombay harbour, and Malcolm became the last of the distinguished trio still in India.

Elphinstone had been a great Governor. In the last eight years he had managed to pacify and settle the Deccan territories conquered from the Peshwah with a minimum of bloodshed or ill will. He had done deals with minor Chiefs that had left them with a reasonable degree of local control and self-respect. In Bombay he had introduced a legal code and reforms to Native education. He was scrupulously honest and incorruptible. He was popular among both Europeans and Indians. For Malcolm, he was an easy man to follow. Despite their different personalities, they had similar views. 'The only difference between Mountstuart and I', he reassured the locals, 'is that I have mulligatawny at tiffin, which comes of my experience at Madras'.[4]

But many issues remained unresolved. First and foremost was the need for retrenchment in government expenditure. Successive wars with the Gurkhas (1815–1816), the Mahrattas (1817–1818) and the Burmese (1824–1826), had pushed the Company's finances into serious debt. The unpalatable task for all three Governors was to introduce austerity measures. In the Bombay Presidency Elphinstone had started the process, but it was left to Malcolm to make the major (and most unpopular) cuts. There were opportunities for economic development, but they would take years to mature. In the southern Mahratta country there was the problem of *nazarana*, a sort of inheritance tax levied by Hindu custom when a ruler adopted a son in the absence of a natural male heir. In Gujerat, the Native State of Baroda was in a great financial mess, with a young and erratic Gaekwad and a corrupt government. There was the question of 'Native education' – who should be educated and what should the government do to promote education? What should be done about the expanding Eurasian community? And how far, if at all, should he accede to the demands of the evangelical Christian lobby in Britain for government support for the propagation of Christianity in India? Finally, a confrontation was looming with the judges of the Supreme Court, who reported independently to the Government in London.

But before tackling these issues, Malcolm's first concern was whether he was going to be put in charge of Central India as well as of the Bombay territories. The question had been in limbo since his departure from England in July 1827. While the Court had opposed the idea, the Board, perhaps embarrassed by Wynn's moral commitment to Malcolm in early 1827, insisted on passing responsibility for the decision to the Governor-General in Calcutta. When Bentinck arrived there in July 1828, he found a barrage of letters from Malcolm advocating his case, but a Calcutta secretariat vehemently opposed to it. It was a considerable dilemma for him, since he did not want to let down his old friend, but was not sufficiently in favour of the idea to overrule his entire secretariat. Holt Mackenzie, one of its brightest stars, wrote a minute in late August 1828, admitting that the Bengal Presidency was already too big and unwieldy, and that direct local oversight was required for Central India. But in his opinion it could best be provided by setting up a Governorship or Lieutenant-Governorship at Agra, to cover both Delhi/Agra and the whole of Central India, including Rajputana and Malwa.[5] Malcolm was also probably less aware than he should have been that Charles Metcalfe (now Sir Charles, having inherited a baronetcy from his brother in 1822) was completely opposed to his proposals for governing Central India. They had last met in 1821 at Aurungabad, and although they had remained friends, Metcalfe was now a Councillor, and the strong man of the Calcutta Government. Malcolm may have seen the relationship as it had previously been, with himself as the elder statesman, and Metcalfe as his erstwhile lieutenant. But Metcalfe had matured – he was now forty-three – and had changed. Always a man of rectitude, he had become harder and some would say colder. He was, for instance, sceptical of the Calcutta

Government continuing to acknowledge the nominal suzerainty of the Mughal Emperor in Delhi, which he thought sentimental and pointless. He was probably a stronger character than Bentinck, who at first was rather scared of him. And as Resident at Delhi from 1812 to 1819 he had learned quite a lot about Rajputana. In early September Bentinck advised Malcolm that he had turned down his proposal, and to his considerable relief Malcolm acquiesced gracefully in the decision. Bentinck knew Malcolm well, and always handled him tactfully, flattering his vanity and allowing him to do things in his own way.

In July 1827, when Bentinck was appointed Governor-General, it was made clear to him that his overriding task was to restore the Company's financial position. Since 1814 the Company's operations in India had run at an average annual loss of about £3 million. Only profits on the China trade (mainly through the opium monopoly) had enabled it to pay interest to its creditors and dividends to its shareholders. Moreover, the Company's Charter was due to expire in 1833, and it was widely expected that in any new Charter the China trade monopoly would be removed. So Bentinck was sent off with a clear directive – to get the Company's Indian operations back at least to break even before 1833.

If these austere terms of reference were unwelcome to Bentinck with his liberal reforming and idealistic temperament, they were even more so to Malcolm. His whole career had been based on a philosophy of grabbing 'investment' opportunities when they came up, in the expectation, usually correct, that in the fullness of time they would bring ample returns. Austerity was anathema to him. He was a salesman, not an accountant. He never quite understood that even if a business was profitable, it must also maintain a positive cash flow. And his reputation among the Court of Directors for extravagance, deserved or not, stuck to him until the very end of his Indian career. Peter Auber, the Company Secretary in Leadenhall Street, later wrote to Bentinck 'that Sir John is a distinguished servant we must admit, but at finance he has a reputation still to gain'.[6] Expenditure control in India was lax. Arriving at Calcutta in July 1828, Bentinck quickly set about cutting the cost of government, an understandably unpopular exercise among its civil and military servants.

To understand the task facing Bentinck (and Malcolm), we must first look at the demographic background in the late 1820s. Books about 'British' India in the early nineteenth century tend to include maps shaded in different colours to illustrate the areas ruled respectively by the Company and various Native rulers at different times – typically 1798, 1805 and 1818. But these maps fail to give an accurate picture of the distribution of the population, and the resources needed to govern them. 'British' India comprised roughly the same area as today's India and Bangladesh (i.e. excluding Pakistan and Burma), minus the Native States of Hyderabad, Mysore, Oudh, Travancore and several in Gujerat, Malwa and Rajputana. The population of British India was around 90 million, with a further 10 million in the Native States.

The British armies to control this vast population numbered about 225,000 men. The Kings troops (wholly European) comprised 1,000 officers and 24,000 men. The Company's armies numbered about 200,000, comprising 7,000 officers (3,500 European and 3,500 Indian) and 193,000 men (7,000 European, 186,000 Indian). The entire European civilian population was no more than 4,000, of which only about 1,000 were 'covenanted' Company servants, and no more than 1,000 were women. The population of the Bombay Presidency (an area larger than Britain) was only about 6.5 million, with a relatively larger army (41,000 men), reflecting the less settled state of the newly acquired territories compared with the other Presidencies. There were only 215 covenanted civil servants and fewer than 300 women.

The Bombay Presidency territories comprised three distinct regions: first, Bombay itself and bits of Gujerat, termed the 'Ancient Possessions'; secondly, the Deccan territories annexed from the Peshwah in 1818; and thirdly, the Gaekwad's Baroda territories, over part of which the Company had taken control to enable it to pay off the Gaekwad's debts. The Bombay Government's problem was that for many years after 1818, this greatly expanded territory was not economically self-sufficient. In particular, it needed a relatively large army to impose peace and deal with roving bands of discharged Mahratta soldiers. The scope, therefore, for reduction in government expenditure was quite limited. In the financial year of Malcolm's arrival (1827–28), the Government's revenue was Rs226 lakhs, and expenditure Rs350 lakhs, a deficit of Rs124 lakhs. This deficit was funded, reluctantly, by the Calcutta Government. In July 1828, Malcolm received a stiff letter from Calcutta complaining about the size of its deficit: 'the utmost that can be afforded by Bengal from its regular income to be expended in establishments at Bombay, will be half a crore of rupees [i.e. 50 lakhs]; unless therefore the deficit of the Bombay Presidency can be reduced to this limit, there can be no hope of conducting the management of our Indian empire without an annual addition to the Indian debt, and such a state of affairs can only lead to ultimate bankruptcy.'[7]

Malcolm made a spirited response to this ultimatum: 'we must, with every respect for your superior wisdom and controlling authority, entreat that we may be judged, not by the general results, but by the most minute enquiry into every item of our expenditure.' He pointed out that a proportion of Bombay's outgoings 'should be . . . more correctly brought under the head of general charge.' For instance, the Bombay Marine (later the Indian Navy), although charged to Bombay's budget, acted on behalf of all three Presidencies. He also rejected the argument that each Presidency should necessarily have to become self-sufficient. 'If adopted in the new Presidency of Prince of Wales Island [Penang], Singapore and Malacca, it would be obviously absurd.'[8]

To the surprise of many, Malcolm took up the uncongenial business of cost-cutting with considerable energy, despite realising that, for the first time in his life, it was going to make him unpopular. Reports of Malcolm's cost-cutting activity filtered through to London. John Ravenshaw, a director, and no great admirer of Malcolm, wrote to Bentinck that: 'my friend Lushington [Governor of Madras] has made a melancholy commencement at Madras . . . Malcolm on the contrary is exceeding all expectations formed of him by our court.'[9] Moreover, he largely succeeded. In the next four years the estimated annual deficit was reduced from 124 lakhs to 53 lakhs, very close to the target set by Calcutta in 1828. The main reduction, understandably, was in military expenditure.

Despite their very different personalities, Malcolm and Elphinstone shared the same philosophy of governance for British India. They were both 'Politicals', who had spent much of their careers at Native Courts, and were more sympathetic to Indian ways of doing things than contemporaries who had been confined to Presidency capital cities, administering 'British' forms of government.

But by the late 1820s the philosophy of governance back in Britain was changing. It was the era of Jeremy Bentham and the Utilitarians; of efficiency being the overwhelming catchword in government; of agitation for reform leading to the Parliamentary Reform Bill in 1831–2. In India, the achievement of British hegemony over most of the subcontinent was making the British more confident, more arrogant, that the British approach to government was right, that sensitivity to Indian feelings was mere sentimentalism, that the need was for railways, roads, steam power and industrial development.

Malcolm could sense these changes and was apprehensive about them. He wrote to Henry Wood in Calcutta: 'I fear my views of governing this country are too opposed to the pride of conquerors and the general plans of cold calculation to be much approved, and I conceive that if ever there was a government in which feeling should have a place, it is that we have established in India.'[10]

This was, and remains, a familiar sequence in the evolution of transnational organisations in foreign lands, whether as governments or as commercial entities. First come the pioneers, the soldiers and diplomats and commercial negotiators, who try to understand the languages and the customs of the local people. They have a commitment to the country. Next, when hegemony has been achieved – a political treaty or a major contract signed – come the 'implementors', the engineers and the technicians. They are not interested in the country and the people as such. They come because of their expertise in building roads, railways, industrial plants and training local technicians. When their task is done, they go home. Malcolm could see that in the long run 'British India' should be largely run by Indians. He believed that Company rule should be a partnership between European and Indian, not a dictatorship of one over the other. He perceived the deep conservatism of most Indians, their love of long-established custom, and distaste for radical reform. Not that he was a democrat. He was quite realistic in admitting that the Company ruled India ultimately by the sword. He therefore sought partnership with two particular classes of Indian. First, the Chieftains, for whom he had deep compassion at their 'fallen greatness'. He wanted to leave as much power as he could in their hands, even if it meant some diminution of efficiency in government. This was not mere sentimentality; to run a fully fledged 'Company Raj' throughout the subcontinent would be enormously costly, stretching Company resources beyond their limits. The 'Company Raj' was anyway an enormous bluff waiting to be called. For the time being the prime requirement was to keep everyone as happy as possible, and this was best done through the Chieftains. The second class to be 'conciliated' were the *Brahmins*. They had been the administrators of the Mahratta Empire, who had been displaced, at least in the upper reaches of the civil service, by British Collectors and judges. They were able, educated people and would resent their loss of status and career. It is worth noting that this 'political' class eventually formed the nucleus of the Nationalist movement nearly a century later. They must, he felt, be trained so that they could become senior government administrators. After all, they would be infinitely cheaper to employ than young European expatriate writers, trained at Addiscombe and then taking a year to learn the local languages, and finally needing repatriation and substantial pensions on retirement. The challenge was to introduce *Brahmins* to European methods of government, so that they could combine Western 'efficiency' with local knowledge and local custom. But how was this to be done? It was not going to be easy. He wrote to the Commander-in-Chief, Lord Combermere 'We cannot in a day wean [Indians] from liking [custom] or reconcile them to our regular cold meals'[11]

The answer lay in education. Just about everyone – Benthamites, Tories, liberal reformers and evangelical Christians – agreed about this, but in different forms of education, and for different reasons. With limited government funds available, hard choices had to be made. In the type of students – was it to be comprehensive education for a few, or a smattering (bare literacy) for the many? In the medium of instruction – was it to be in English or in the various local languages? And in content – was it to be in forms of Hindu or Muslim learning, or what the British Utilitarians called 'useful' subjects? A further complication was the hierarchical and caste basis of Indian society. For instance, middle-ranking parents of children living in the Deccan were reluctant to send their sons to be educated in Bombay. When schools were set up there, Malcolm wrote: 'none of any rank could be tempted even by the flattering prospect of future employment in the public service. The Mahomedan and Hindoo mothers are alike averse to part even for a period from their sons. It is to them they look for enjoyment and importance in life; a wife is often neglected; a mother is always respected; in this state of society there can be nothing more hurtful to the feelings than such separation, and the pain is aggravated by the just alarm parents have of their children being brought up in a large and dissolute town like Bombay.'[12]

Malcolm was an enthusiastic follower of Elphinstone's educational philosophy and innovations. Within a month of his arrival at Bombay, he wrote to the Duke about how much progress had been made under his predecessor. He was encouraged by this, because he firmly believed that Indians could be reconciled to British government by participating in it. He preferred that they should be taught in their own languages, since learning English took a long time. He would as far as possible limit government-sponsored teaching to 'practical knowledge'. But he was impressed by the scientific knowledge which *Brahmins* had picked up; some, he wrote, were already as proficient in surveying as Europeans.

His minute on education of 10 October 1829 described the problems he faced. In practical terms, funding could not come from parishioners as it did in Britain, so the central schools would have to be charitable institutions, with those who could afford to pay being given separate (and presumably better) accommodation. He favoured a Spartan existence for boys, and mixing up of Europeans, Anglo-Indians and Indians. The problem here was that however well educated boys from low-born backgrounds might be, the hierarchical state of Indian society would make it difficult for them to get jobs as senior officers in the Deccan. Intriguingly, he also advocated boarding schools for girls – perhaps the first time that female education had been mentioned in any correspondence during this period.

This was pretty radical thinking for the 1820s. In Britain itself, it took another forty years before government-funded universal education was introduced.

Malcolm had an especially soft spot for Eurasians, variously referred to as Anglo-Indians or East Indians, in place of the previously 'offensive' term (as he put it) 'half-castes'. 'When the Eurasians formed themselves into an association for the purpose of aiding respectable persons of their class in agricultural and other pursuits, a grant was made to them of a palace, built by Badgerow [Baji Rao], at Phoolshair, on the banks of the Beemah [near Poona], with forty two acres of land, including a large and productive fruit-garden.'[13] The Phoolshair establishment became a centre for Eurasian advancement. Surveying was a particular skill in which the community excelled. The epic *Trigonometric Survey of India*, started at Madras by the Surveyor-General William Lambton in 1802 and ending triumphantly with the measuring of the great Himalayan peaks (notably Mount Everest, named after Lambton's successor, Sir George Everest, several decades later), was largely the work of Eurasians, who were thought to have greater resistance than Europeans to the diseases of the jungle areas where they mostly had to work.

> A Governor of Bombay cannot . . . perform his duty without frequently visiting the provinces. Those visits [are] . . . attended with considerable expense . . . but no cost that can be incurred will bear any comparison to the benefit produced by such circuits. They give life and animation to all classes; they are a check upon bad conduct, and an encouragement to good. The natives of India refer everything to persons. They are slow to understand the abstract excellence of our system of government. They see in the Governor, when he visits the provinces, the head of the Government. The timid acquire confidence and the turbulent are checked by his presence . . . Besides these impressions upon the native population, the Governor becomes acquainted with the European public officers of the provinces. Removed from the atmosphere and influence of the presidency, [the Governor] learns the characters of those who administer the law or collect the revenue of the various districts, from the feelings and the sentiments of the people. He sees, and remedies, abuses on the spot, and judges in person the value of the proposed improvements. It is by such visits also that he can best determine on measures of economy, and prevent useless expenditure in every department.[14]

On 14 December 1827, less than seven weeks after his arrival at Bombay, Malcolm set off for Poona. A few miles north-west of the city, at Dapuri, he came upon a large house and seventy acres of land. It had belonged to Major Ford, the celebrated British officer attached to the Peshwah's army, who had brought his battalion over to the Company's side before the battle of Kirkee in November 1817. He had died in 1826 and the property was for sale. Malcolm bought it on the spot for 40,000 rupees (about £4,000) and made the house his Deccan headquarters.[15] Dapuri fitted what he perceived as the need for a base for the Government on the Deccan plateau. Being 2,000 foot above sea level, Poona was healthier than Bombay, though certainly not cool. Dapuri's location, some way out of Poona, was not ideal, but it suited Malcolm personally. His habit was to have a public breakfast every morning – a great idea for an extrovert, but tiring for an ageing man. He reasoned that if he were several miles out of town, only people with serious business issues to transact would turn up. The purchase was opposed by his senior civil servants in Bombay, who worried that 'setting up a house in Poona for several months of the year would mean neglecting the seat of Government in Bombay.'[16] To a man of Malcolm's stature and prestige, such concerns were of no consequence. He went ahead anyway.

The property was pleasant, but hardly magnificent. Malcolm turned Colonel Ford's bungalow into a secretariat building, and built a quite modest bungalow behind it to house him and his 'family'. There was plenty of space for the paraphernalia of a Governor's entourage – quarters for the civil servants and officers of the escort, tented lines for the sepoys, stables for the horses. With a typically imaginative flourish he turned the remaining fifty acres into a botanical garden. He appointed as gardening superintendent a Dr Williamson, with an operating budget of Rs500 per month (later reduced to Rs300). He envisaged that Williamson should start a kind of experimental farm rather than a pure botanical garden, and investigate the practicality of growing cotton, coffee, and mulberry trees for silk. Again the civil servants in Bombay protested that in the light of the government's parlous financial position, even 'objects of obvious and useful improvement, such as the formation of a Botanical Garden, should be suspended and not commenced without the Honourable Court's previous sanction'. Again Malcolm pressed on regardless. An official letter advising the Court of the purchase of Dapuri and the setting up of the garden was not sent to London until October 1828.

Malcolm would probably have spent an even greater portion of the year at Dapuri had he not, in April 1828, made a short visit to the Mahabaleshwar hills, about eighty miles south-west of Poona, in the Rajah of Satara's territory. He had probably heard about Mahabaleshwar from John Briggs, who had been the Resident at Satara from 1822 to 1826. Briggs had previously been with Malcolm in Persia in 1810, and was his

ADC in the Pindari War of 1817–8. His idea had been to make Mahabaleshwar into a convalescent station for sick European officers – much cheaper than sending them off to the Cape or to England. Elphinstone had been sympathetic, but no action had been taken. Briggs met Malcolm when he returned to England in early 1827, and came to see him off at Portsmouth in July.

At Mahabaleshwar Malcolm found a clear cool climate and wonderful views. At 4,500 foot above sea level, the hills were the highest point in the western *ghats*. He immediately fell in love with the place. The only major drawback was that in the three monsoon months, up to 300 inches of rain would fall. To test whether it was habitable during these months, he left a detachment of sepoys there, camping in tents through the wet season of 1828. They must have been constantly drenched, but survived without serious health problems.

Throughout his governorship Malcolm had some family support. For the first few months of 1828 Minnie acted as his hostess, but her health gradually deteriorated. After a miscarriage in July 1828, she and Alex moved to Dapuri. But even in the cooler climate of the Deccan her health did not improve, and they were forced to sail for home in October 1828.

Meanwhile, in June 1828, his brother Charles arrived at Bombay as the newly appointed Superintendent of the Bombay Marine, the small flotilla of Company warships which patrolled the sea approaches to western India. He was now a Rear Admiral, having been knighted by Marquess Wellesley after his stint as commander of the Marquess's yacht at Dublin. He was still recovering from the trauma of losing his wife Magdalen, who had died just as he was setting out for India.

Accompanying Charles to Bombay was Malcolm's son George, who had been left in England with William Pasley at the Royal Engineers school at Chatham. At first Malcolm used George as an ADC, but he wanted to get him away from the 'court' atmosphere of Government House. There was a plan to send him to Persia to stay with the Macdonalds in Tehran, and another to accompany the Military Secretary, Captain Graham, to Bengal. Neither came off. George once went boar hunting near the Ellora caves, and wrote dutifully to his father, who responded in familiar paternal manner: 'Thanks for your excellent letter, but to be honest – would the sheet have been filled but for the hogs.

Never mind, I must encourage good actions, and not be too curious as to the motive, so to entitle myself to a Bird's Eye sketch of Ellora, or at least a line to say how the wonders of that place strike you.'[17]

In early 1830 he sent George to Poona, and wrote to the Duke (who had helped to get George his commission) that: 'he joins the Queens (2nd Foot) at Poona, commanded by Colonel Wilshire, a very strict officer and excellent drill'.[18]

Early in November 1828 Malcolm set out on his first major provincial tour, to the Mahratta country south of Poona. He went first to the town of Satara, to meet the young Rajah, Pratap Singh. The Rajahs of Satara were the hereditary descendants of the great Mahratta leader Shivaji. During the eighteenth century although they had been allowed to continue as nominal rulers, their power had been usurped by their *Brahmin* Chief Ministers, the Peshwahs of Poona. Pratap Singh had spent his childhood as a virtual prisoner at Satara. When the British ousted the Peshwah in 1818, they sought to legitimise their new hegemony over the Mahratta territories, and one ploy was to reinstate the Rajah of Satara; to recreate a Native State in a part of the newly conquered territory. As the first British Resident at Satara, Elphinstone had appointed Lieutenant James Grant. Grant acted as a sort of tutor in statecraft to young Pratap Singh for five years, till his health failed and he had to return to Scotland.[19] He was a considerable scholar, and using the materials which he had accumulated during his time at Poona and Satara, he later wrote a massive three-volume history of the Mahrattas. He and Pratap Singh became close friends and continued to correspond for many years after Grant returned to Britain. The current Resident was Colonel Archibald Robertson, a seasoned political officer, who later became a director of the East India Company. Pratap Singh was lucky to have as his early mentors three such able and enlightened men as Grant, Briggs and Robertson.

Malcolm and his party, including Charles, reached Satara on 6 November 1828 and stayed for a week taken up with levees, parades, banquets and fireworks. During the course of this *durbar* Malcolm and the Rajah made a 'handshake' deal whereby the Rajah ceded the nearby Mahabaleshwar plateau to the British in exchange for the village of Khandalla near Wai, then in British territory. A formal treaty was not signed until May 1829 but by that date a sanatorium, several bungalows, a bazaar and roads from two directions up to the plateau had already been built.

Malcolm wrote to friends that he was getting on in years, and could no longer stand the hot weather in Bombay (from April to June). He would happily have spent six months each year at Mahabaleshwar, but since it was virtually uninhabitable during the wet season, he based himself at Dapuri between July and September. In fact, during the whole period of his governorship, he spent little more than a quarter of his time in Bombay – the remainder being equally divided between Dapuri, Mahabaleshwar and on tour to other parts of the Presidency.

With the Governor and his immediate entourage spending so much time there, Mahabaleshwar effectively became the summer seat of the Bombay Government (and remained so throughout the British Raj). As a result it also had the possibly unintended consequence of the sanatorium becoming a hill station as well. Malcolm built a large bungalow for himself, which he called Mount Charlotte, and named various prominent points after his daughters – Mount Minnie, Mount Olympia (later renamed Connaught Peak), Amelia Vale, and Kate's Point – a name which survives to this day. At the Rajah's command, Mahabaleshwar was renamed Malcolm Peth.

Resuming their march southward from Satara, Malcolm's party reached Bijapur at the beginning of December, and Belgaum, their southernmost point, three weeks later. The commander of the army garrison at Belgaum, Colonel James Welsh, who had first met Malcolm in 1803, during the third Anglo-Mahratta War, described the visit:

> At seven o'clock on the 23rd of December, the Governor arrived, when he was received with every honour my means could afford, and delighted everybody with his kindness and affability. He had sixteen gentlemen in his suite, and his camp was pitched on a rising spot near the Eedgah Tope, where he had the most superb canvas habitation I have ever beheld. A large party breakfasted with him at nine, and at noon he came into the fort, and called upon all the ladies; held a Native Durbar attended by many Native Chiefs at two o'clock; and entertained a large party to dinner at half-past three. In a word, he proved the same honest John Malcolm I knew twenty five years ago, in General

> Wellesley's army. All the fire, strength and activity of youth, with those abilities which enable him to transact his business in less time that most other men would take to consider about it. This enables him to appear in company to far greater advantage; not the mere abstracted man of business, but to be a cheerful and entertaining companion. We spent a week in a round of public parties, and when he set out for Colapoor [Kolhapur], his departure threw a damp over our little society, not easily overcome.[20]

The southern *jaghirdar* Chiefs had all previously sworn loyalty to the Peshwah, so that when the British assumed power they had to switch their loyalty to the Company. Technically, therefore, their lands were part of British India, not Native States like those in Malwa or the newly created state of Satara. But to retain their allegiance, the Chiefs had to be handled with delicacy. Their position was similar to that of feudal barons in mediaeval England. They were supposed to supply troops when the government needed them, but otherwise were left to run their internal affairs much as they chose. Neither Elphinstone nor Malcolm was keen to interfere with this arrangement. They had far too many problems elsewhere to worry much about what was happening inside the Chiefs' territories.

One pressing problem exercising the minds of all the Deccan Chiefs, but especially the southern *jaghirdars*, was hereditary succession. It was Hindu custom that if there was no clear male heir apparent, the ruler would adopt a (male) child to ensure a smooth succession. This sometimes involved paying *nazarana*, a sort of inheritance tax, to the Peshwah or to his successor, the Company. The Calcutta Government was not, however, automatically prepared to continue this arrangement. It wanted to retain the right to intervene and, if necessary, place a different ruler on the throne, or to resume the territory and bring it under full Company control. For the Chiefs this was a very worrying risk. It was as if the Company retained the right to disinherit them or, put another way, to apply a 100 per cent inheritance tax on their assets.

Elphinstone had parried this issue. Malcolm had a new approach. He understood the Chiefs' need for certainty, but also rather liked the idea of *nazarana* as a revenue-raising exercise for the government. He suggested that Chiefs should be allowed to continue adopting children as successors, but in all cases where succession was not clearly to a direct male successor of the same bloodline, some *nazarana* should be paid, varying in amount according to the distance of the blood relationship of the proposed heir to the current ruler. In this way the Chiefs would have security of tenure and hence the confidence to make investments in improving their lands, while the government would gain some additional revenue. He sent a minute to Calcutta,[21] followed by a letter, in which he ended: 'We do not want your approbation; we only want your permission.'[22] But the Calcutta bureaucrats had dealt for several generations with the unsatisfactory aspects of the Bengal *Zamindari* permanent settlement system, whereby absentee landlords effectively acted as tax farmers. They were keen to keep all options open. Predictably, they opposed Malcolm's scheme, though in deference to his reputation, they referred it back to Leadenhall Street for a decision. But the 'Old India hands' in London were mostly 'Bengalis' too, and after some to-ing and fro-ing, the proposal was eventually rejected. This was embarrassing for Malcolm, as he had rashly assured any Chiefs he met that it would be accepted.

In the next cold season, of 1829–30, Malcolm decided to go north to visit Gujerat. He arrived at Baroda in late December.

The Gujerati speaking part of western India comprises four distinct regions: South Gujerat, a 200-mile strip of coastline north of Bombay, with Surat, Broach and Baroda being its main cities; North Gujerat, the inland area north of the Gulf of Cambay, with Ahmedabad as its main centre; Kathiawar (today's Saurashtra), the large peninsula jutting out into the Arabian Sea between the Gulf of Cambay and the Gulf of Cutch, with Rajkot, Junagard and Jamnagar as its main towns; and Cutch (today's Kutch or Khhach), a mainly desert area, sparsely populated and isolated from the rest of Gujerat by a large salt marsh, periodically covered by the tide.

In 1818, with the downfall of the Peshwah and the British assuming suzerainty over the whole of Gujerat, there were four fully British districts: Surat, Broach, Kaira and Ahmedabad; in addition there was the Native State of Baroda, and dozens of other Native States in Kathiawar and Cutch owing nominal feudal fealty to Baroda, but in practice, largely administered by the British Resident.

Both the Gaekwad, Anandrao ('a prince in a state of imbecility'), and his brother, the regent Fatteh Singh, had died in 1818, and Elphinstone, the new Governor of Bombay, put the government of Baroda into the hands of their younger brother Sayajee Rao. But when he visited Gujerat in 1820 he found that 'instead of his being (as we thought at Bombay) in danger of becoming dangerous from his overflowing treasury, he [Sayajee Rao] was Rs 12.6 million in debt, his army near three years in arrears and his Government nearly at a standstill for want of money to carry on its current expenses'.[23] To prevent the collapse of the Gaekwad's government, the Company guaranteed its debts.

When Malcolm took over from Elphinstone in 1827, Sayajee Rao was still the Gaekwad, but little progress had been made in reducing his government's debts, (partly because Sayajee was in the habit of siphoning off tax revenue into his private account). The British had not particularly wanted to control the area, but they were being gradually sucked into more and more commitments: trying to assist its nominal overlord, the Gaekwad, to sort out the chaos in Kathiawar and to extend control into Cutch to protect Kathiawar from pirates and raiders coming from Sind, on the north-west frontier of Cutch. For Malcolm it was a delicate situation. There was a temptation either to annex the whole area and assert direct Company control, or to abandon Kathiawar and Cutch altogether. But both these options would militate against two of his most cherished principles: firstly, to bring about reform, especially social reform, by persuasion rather than by force; and secondly, to leave, as far as possible, the existing ruling hierarchies in place, to create and support 'a native aristocracy'. In London the mood was for abandoning Kathiawar and Cutch, which appeared to be causing such constantly recurring trouble without any compensating financial benefit to the Company. The Secret Committee sent a minute asking Malcolm to recommend a plan. He played for time, deciding not to give London an answer until he had surveyed the scene in person.

His negotiations with the Gaekwad were tedious. In some exasperation, he wrote to Sir Sidney Beckwith, the newly arrived Commander-in-Chief: 'I am overwhelmed with work, but I will force my way through it in three or four days, as I am reserved for something better than being killed at Baroda with a negotiation.'[24]

It was vital for the Company's good name that the guarantees should be honoured, but Malcolm stopped short of taking over direct control of the Baroda government. His solution was to insist that the Gaekwad's creditors should be paid, despite the Gaekwad's strong objections, and that the money should be raised by the Company temporarily sequestrating some of the Gaekwad's lands to produce sufficient revenue to do so. He acknowledged that Kathiawar was in a state of anarchy and quite unable to produce sufficient revenue to finance the military contingent stationed there. But he concluded that for strategic reasons it had to be defended against plunderers from Cutch; and Cutch in turn had to be protected from pirates and raiders from neighbouring Sind. Its geographical location was strategically vital, too: 'The extension of the territories of Cutch to Lockput Bunder, and its immediate proximity to the delta of the Indus, give it increased value as a military position, at a period when the two great Asiatic powers, Persia and Turkey, are no longer the formidable barriers they once were considered against the approach of an European enemy to the vicinity of our Eastern possessions.'[25] As so often, his mind was considering issues ranging far beyond the confines of the Bombay Presidency.

But he was not only concerned with political and financial matters. After 1818, the practice of *sati*, the self immolation of widows, caused a great deal of debate in both Britain and India. Among Evangelical circles in London and Christian missionaries in India there was a strong outcry against allowing the practice to continue, at least in 'British' India. The Calcutta Government was inclined to prohibit it by law. But Malcolm, despite his personal abhorrence of the practice, opposed this approach, fearing this would be seen as an interference in Hindu custom, even though it was argued by many that it was not part of Hindu religious practice. He found himself virtually alone in opposing the measure. Visiting Kathiawar in early 1830, he came upon an equally barbaric rite, prevalent among the Jarijah Rajput tribes of Cutch – female infanticide. In 1841 it was reported that: 'the entire Jariyah [Rajput] population of Kathiawar was 5,760 and that of females 1,370; in Kutch there were 2,625 boys to 335 girls.[26] Yet he knew that even if it was prohibited by law, it would be difficult to enforce in such a wild society. Several years earlier he had written that: 'The chief obstruction we shall meet in the pursuit of the improvement and reform of the natives of India will be caused by our own passions and prejudices . . . this theme must be approached with humility, not pride, by all who venture to it . . . We should be humbled to think, in how many points, in how many duties of life, great classes of this sober, honest, kind and inoffensive people excel us.'[27]

Nevertheless, he was still determined to do all he could to stop the practice. What he needed was some sort of moral stick (preferably an Indian one) to beat its perpetrators with. And in Rajkot he found just what he had been looking for, in the person of a 49-year-old Hindu holy man, Sahajanand Swami, later revered as the founder of the Swaminarayan sect of Hinduism. Sahajanand had been born in 1781 at a village near Ayodhya in today's Uttar Pradesh, but had come to live in Gujerat. Basing himself near Rajkot, he had acquired a large following. Malcolm had earlier heard that the Swami had preached against *sati* and female infanticide, and he had sent messages to him inviting him to come to Bombay to discuss the matter. But the holy man replied that he was too sick to travel. So Malcolm travelled to Rajkot. The two men met on 26 (or 28) February 1830 and agreed on a common aim – the abolition of *sati* and female infanticide by moral persuasion rather than by force.[28]

The Swami died later that year, but Swaminarayan Hinduism prospered and spread from Gujerat to other parts of India, and in the late twentieth century it followed the Gujarati diaspora into the western world. Today there are massive Swaminarayan temple complexes in Delhi, Gandhinagar, London (Neasden) and the USA. The meeting of Sir John Malcolm and Sahajanand Swami is commemorated in the iconography of the temples. 'In the stylised paintings Shahajanand Swami, in elaborate dress and with a light shining around his head, is seated on a formal chair surrounded by his ascetic disciples. Governor Malcolm stands before him in black official dress in an attitude of respect along with a few British and Indian officials.'[29] In another Swaminarayan setting Malcolm is depicted as a young man clad in blue and white, a sort of Prince Charming.

Malcolm went on to Bhuj, the main town of Cutch, and held a *durbar* there in early March to meet the assembled Chiefs. Morally fired up, no doubt, by his meeting with Swami Sahajanand, he gave the Chiefs a powerful dressing down and threatened that: 'the crime [female infanticide] is held in such detestation in England that the Nation will not long be reconciled to intimate friendship with a race of men by whom it continues to be perpetrated, in direct breach of their promises and engagements.'[30]

Kathiawar and Cutch had another attraction for Malcolm. Despite the bleakness of the landscape, it was a paradise for hunters of wild game. Malcolm was in good health again and, as ever, boyishly enthusiastic. He wrote to Robert Clive in England that: 'I am just returned from Cutch, in high health, having . . . had glorious hunting and shooting – wild hogs, elks, deer, foxes, hares, black partridges and quails, almost to a surfeit. It has been a great treat. I know not how I shall reconcile myself to your tame proceedings.'[31]

Back in Bombay, he at last faced up to the need for the legal abolition of *sati*. The rite had been practised in Bengal, the Deccan and Rajputana, but was not widespread (even in Bengal no more than 600 widows out of 250,000 were immolating themselves each year). On 4 December 1829, after much debate, the Calcutta Government issued a proclamation outlawing the practice, and the Madras Government had followed suit shortly afterwards. Malcolm took reluctant action to achieve the same effect by 'repealing a short clause of the Regulations which declared [that] assistance at the rites of self-immolation [did not] subject anyone to the penalty of murder'.[32] He still worried that although there might be no immediate repercussions, the prohibition would appear to renege on the Company's pledge not to upset Hindu customs. But the repercussions turned out to be minimal, and Malcolm's caution had proved unnecessary. Nevertheless, these legal measures failed to stop the practice of *sati* entirely. A case was reported as recently as 1987.

The East India Company set up the Bombay Marine during the eighteenth century to protect its merchant ships from pirates operating in the Indian Ocean and also from occasional attacks by the Mahratta navy. Comprising about eight armed vessels, frigates, sloops etc, it became effectively an offshoot of the British Royal Navy, but its existence reduced the need for a constant Royal Navy presence in Indian waters. By the 1820s the Company recognised that the Bombay Marine was doing a useful job in dealing with pirates and in surveying the waters off north-west India and the Gulf. In appointing Sir Charles Malcolm, a Royal Navy admiral, to the command, it signalled its commitment to raising its standards of performance towards those of the Royal Navy.

Throughout the period of Company rule in India, there was persistent debate as to whether there should be a separate Company Navy (like the separate Company armies), or whether the maritime defence of British India should be entrusted solely to the Royal Navy. The need for a locally based and logical chain of command pointed to the former; economy to the latter. Not surprisingly, Malcolm was a strong advocate of a separate Company Navy. Though conceding that it was expensive at a time when the Bombay Government was trying to reduce costs, he pointed out that it was performing a vital service, not just for the Bombay Presidency but for the whole of British India. Also, its local knowledge made it much more effective than the Royal Navy at lower overall cost.

By 1829 the proponents of a separate service had won the day, and the Bombay Marine officially became the Indian Navy in May 1830, with Sir Charles Malcolm as its first Superintendent.

The most revolutionary development in the Indian Navy in this period was the introduction of steam navigation. The 1820s had seen the introduction of steam locomotion in England. At the same time the potential use of steam to propel ships was being actively developed. And three of the Malcolm brothers – Pulteney, John and Charles – were leading advocates. As early as May 1822 Charles's journal described a steamboat excursion with Pulteney off Chatham. And a month later he was having discussions with Admiral Sir George Cockburn on the subject.[33]

The merchants of Calcutta and Bombay also saw the potential for steam to improve the speed of communications between India and Europe. Bombay was better placed than Calcutta to develop steam navigation as a link between Europe and India. There were two potential routes: via the Red Sea to Suez, then overland to Alexandria, and on to Britain; or via the Persian Gulf to Basra, then overland to Aleppo. The Red Sea route was shorter, but the prevailing north winds in the Red Sea had hitherto made the route impracticable for sailing ships for most of the year. Now steam would hopefully overcome that problem.

By happy coincidence, in the crucial period 1828 to 1830, Sir John was Governor of Bombay, Sir Charles was Superintendent of the Bombay Marine/Indian Navy and Sir Pulteney was Commander-in-Chief of the Royal Navy fleet in the Mediterranean. The brothers corresponded frequently, and were in a position to coordinate the process by pulling the right political levers at home. It was Sir John, assisted by Sir Charles, who developed to practical completion the idea of steam navigation from Bombay to Suez.

Malcolm managed to obtain the approval of the Court of Directors to have a steam vessel built at Bombay by the Wadia master shipwrights. So the *Hugh Lindsay* was launched on 14 October 1829 – a ship of 400 tons, powered by two 60-horsepower engines, drawing 11.5 feet, with coal stocks for 5.5 days sailing time. On 20 March 1830 it left Bombay and travelled to Suez and back, a round trip of over 6,000 miles, in 70 days sailing time, with stops at Mukalla, Aden, Mocha, Jeddah and Cosseir (on the return journey) to pick up supplies of coal. The boat chugged along at 6 mph, with smoke billowing and soot everywhere. There were some anxious moments, too, on the way, such as arriving at Aden with coal stocks equivalent to only six hours sailing time. Nevertheless it arrived back safely at Bombay on 30 May 1830. 'The *Hugh Lindsay* has thank God arrived', a relieved Charles wrote in his journal. Meanwhile in the Mediterranean Pulteney had organised a steam packet service between Malta and Britain.[34] John was so excited by the idea of steam navigation that he decided to go himself as a passenger on the *Hugh Lindsay* on its second voyage.

When he arrived back in Bombay from Gujerat on 1 April 1830, Malcolm could measure his remaining time as Governor in months. Despite his outward affability and enthusiasm, he was tired, oppressed by the heat of Bombay and anxious to go home. He went up to Poona as soon as he could, and thence to his beloved Mahabaleshwar. He was happier there, and wrote to Sir Walter Scott in mid-May:

> I must, if not born an enthusiast, be rendered one by my present position. I write by the light of a window through which, from an elevation of 4,700 feet, I have a fine view of the sea – looking over what those, 3,000 feet below, call high mountains. The air in this hottest of our months is such as to give a spring to both body and soul, and were it not for my occupation and absence from those I love, I could be content to dwell amid such scenes as those by which I am surrounded, for the remainder of my existence. But I am toiling from dawn to sunset to bring to a good finish the labors of my public life.[35]

The 1830 rains came and Malcolm retreated from Mahabaleshwar to Dapuri. On 18 June, the fifteenth anniversary of Waterloo, he opened the new bridge over the river at Poona. Charles recorded the event:

> We all started off at half past five o'clock [from Dapuri] to attend the opening of the new bridge at the Sangam. The ladies were placed under a tent on rising ground on the side which commanded a fine view of the bridge and the Procession. We left the adowlat at six o'clock. Sir Sidney Beckwith, Sir James Dewar, Sir Lionel Smith (who got a little testy and stopped before he came to the bridge) and a large congregation of staff, civil and military, with all the prominent natives, attended – in short it was a grand *tamasha*. When we got on the middle of the bridge, Sir John made a good speech in Hindustani that this day fifteen years [ago] the battle of Waterloo was fought by the Duke of Wellington . . . who, 27 years before had entered Poonah, and who was the first man to throw a bridge (a bridge of boats) at this very place, and after a little more talk, to hear which they all crowded round him, he called it Wellesley Bridge – at which we all cheered.[36]

By the end of September, as soon as the rains stopped, Malcolm was back at Mahabaleshwar. Here he settled down to write his final minutes on his governorship. Typically, they were not short: a minute on Kathiawar (36 pages); a minute on Gujerat (31 pages); a minute on the Indian Navy (18 pages); a minute on the Army (21 printed pages); a minute on the government of India (11 printed pages); and a farewell minute (103 printed pages).

In early November he returned to Poona. Thereafter, until the day he sailed from Bombay, he was feted at numerous parties and celebrations. Charles was with him throughout. On 11 November he presided at the opening ceremony of the celebrated Bhore Ghaut Road, near Khandalla, linking Bombay to the Deccan plateau for wheeled traffic for the first time: 'This is, for its length – 6 miles – one of those great undertakings which are so well calculated to astonish with their greatness. It is equal to anything I suppose in the world, and its general utility in opening an easy communication with the Deccan is of the greatest consequence – particularly in a military point of view. Sir John was highly gratified.'[37] A plaque with a suitable inscription was erected at the spot.[38]

Not content with the voluminous minutes churned out over the previous weeks, Malcolm still managed to inflict one last 'farewell note'

THIS GHAUT CONSTRUCTED BY CAPTAIN HUGHES
WAS COMMENCED ON THE 19TH OF JANUARY
AND OPENED ON THE 10TH OF NOVEMBER 1830
DURING THE ADMINISTRATION
OF
MAJOR GENL THE HONBLE SIR JOHN MALCOLM G.C.B
ANNO DOMINI
1830
THE ROAD ON THIS GHAUT WAS CONSTRUCTED
WHICH
BY RENDERING THE TRANSIT OF MERCHANDIZE
ON WHEELED CARRIAGES AVAILABLE
AND
THEREBY FACILITATING AN INTERCOURSE
BETWEEN THE
DECKAN AND THE CONKAN
SECURES TO THE COUNTRY
PERMANENT AND SOLID
ADVANTAGES
ACTIS OEVUM IMPLET, NON SEGNIBUS ANNIS

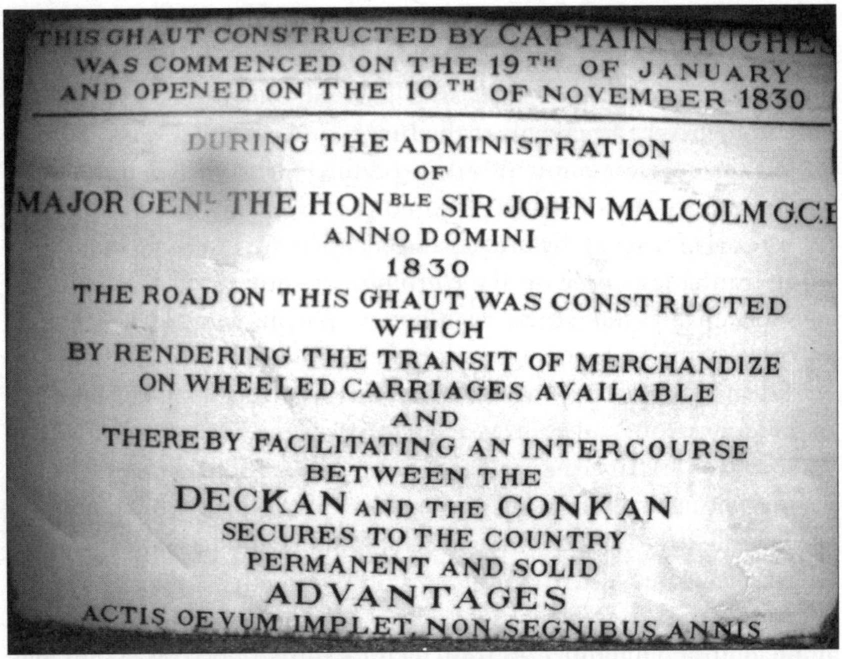

This plaque, still standing beside the Bhore Ghaut freeway (near Khandalla), which links Mumbai (Bombay) and the Deccan plateau, commemorates the opening of the first Bhore Ghaut road by Sir John Malcolm on 10 November 1830.

on Bentinck: 'I sail, or rather go away, to-morrow morning. I have not been able to get all the statements complete for my last minute but they will be soon and the whole will be a complete document. The military reductions will be more than forty lakhs, 29 of which are by orders of this government. The civil reductions are not yet clearly made out but immediate and prospective will be at least five. But the great reduction as your Lordship will discover is in contingencies. It is in that reduction I have personally laboured, and the result has even exceeded my own expectations, with little more than twenty [lakhs] in war expenses.'[39] This letter was so typical. The day before leaving India – this time irrevocably – after distinguished service stretching over forty-seven years, he was still offering his ideas about relatively trivial details of administration, with that same combination of youthful enthusiasm, optimism and self-congratulation.

On 5 December Charles recorded in his journal: 'Sir John left this on his return to England at half past six. He was sent [off] by the Commander in Chief, the Councillors and many gentlemen, both Civil and Military. He walked from them down to the boat between troops. We breakfasted 42 on board the *Challenger*, where he was received with all due honours. He went from there to the *Hugh Lindsay* at half past ten o'clock. She weighed. I went out with a large party as far as the Boy [buoy].'

As an advocate of steam-powered vessels, it was no doubt a thrill for him and his seven fellow passengers (including George) to be travelling for the first time on the *Hugh Lindsay*, but as the ship chugged away, leaving them covered in an increasingly heavy film of coal dust and smoke, the excitement may soon have worn a little thin.

Looking back at his three years as Governor, he had mixed feelings. In some ways he had been very successful, notably in his firm and patient handling of the dispute with the judges (see Chapter 31),[40] and his loyal implementation of fierce austerity measures, for which even Leadenhall Street had commended him. But these measures, coupled with the constant, scurrilous attacks on him by the supporters of the Supreme Court judges among the legal fraternity, had been bruising, and had turned him into an unpopular Governor – galling for anyone, but especially for someone who was used to being loved. And he was no longer young. His management style – using his charisma, warmth and charm to solve problems on a more or less ad hoc basis – which had been so effective in his troubleshooting days, was less effective in the more peaceful era which had begun in 1818. He must have been a trial to his civil servants. As long as he personally was there to sort things out, his style worked. But the lesser men who succeeded him did not have his flair. They needed rules to support them. Charles Metcalfe remarked in a letter to Bentinck: 'I shall not envy Lord Clare, nor anyone who may be Sir John Malcolm's successor; for the duties of the Governor of Bombay will I conceive be very unpleasant.'[41]

This was something which his successor, Lord Clare, was about to find out. John Fitzgibbon, the second Earl of Clare, was an Irish Protestant peer, who had succeeded his father at the age of ten. Educated at Harrow and Christ Church, Oxford, he was a close friend – some said lover – of Lord Byron. He had then managed his Irish estates before becoming active in the House of Lords. He had no knowledge of India when he was appointed Governor of Bombay, aged thirty-eight. He had set out from London in November 1830, and it had been agreed that he and

Malcolm would rendezvous at Cosseir on the Egyptian Red Sea coast, where Malcolm had landed on his way home in 1822, and that Clare and his party would board the *Hugh Lindsay* for its journey back to Bombay. Somehow there was muddle about the agreed date for their meeting. Malcolm had always intended to leave Bombay in early December and reach Cosseir three weeks later. But Clare thought they were to meet at Cosseir in early December, and duly arrived there on time. He then had to wait at that rather godforsaken place for nearly three weeks before the *Hugh Lindsay* turned up.

When Malcolm disembarked at Cosseir, no doubt exuding his usual bonhomie, he was greeted by a furious Clare, who was 'taking it for granted that ocean vessels between Bombay and Cosseir were as easily to be had, if an order were given, as between Dover and Calais'. They met for five hours to talk business, but Clare utterly refused to communicate with Malcolm on a social basis. 'We were neither at the time public men, and had his Irish blood risen a little higher, we might have fought in the desert without reference to what was due to a station which I had resigned, and which he cannot occupy until he reaches Bombay.'[42]

Time did not lessen Clare's rage. On arrival at Bombay he wrote a furious letter of complaint to the Court about Malcolm's behaviour, and later wrote to Bentinck – perhaps unaware that Bentinck was an old friend of Malcolm's – in the somewhat offhand tone of one nobleman addressing another about a social inferior: 'I am happy to say our masters have taken up my cause warmly against him', and went on to complain that 'it is to me very painful to have to carry into execution orders which press hard upon individuals, because Sir John in the wanton exercise of his power thought proper to disregard the orders of the Court'. A month later he was complaining again to Bentinck about *nazarana*: 'no human being, even admitting that his reasoning is correct, can understand how Sir John Malcolm's plan of *nazarana* is to be carried into effect.'[43] He even complained to the Duke of Wellington, of all people, that 'I dare say that prince of charlatans, my predecessor, tells you all he did at Bombay. He wrote long minutes which nobody reads, was a jobber of the first magnitude and has left a bad name behind him. He used me like a dog, and then was surprised that I resented his conduct.'[44] There is no record of a reply to these complaints from either Bentinck or the Duke.

Malcolm remained unfazed by these attacks. He later wrote to Charles in Bombay that 'he [Clare] only does it to get back pay! "A pleasant companion for old women", a noble lord told me, "a judge of good living and pleasant enough in his own way".'[45] Victor Jacquemont, a French aristocrat who travelled around India for four years, and died at Bombay in 1832, was less forgiving about Clare. He wrote in letters to Europe that:

> for the last year the Governor of Bombay has been an English peer of Irish nationality, the companion and butt of Lord Byron at the University, Italian in appearance, and a bit of a dandy. He showers me with politeness in French, and everything in French fashion, to the point of affectation. I far prefer Lord William's [Bentinck's] straightforward and unvarying simplicity. Lord Clare desired to have me as his guest. I declined this inconvenient honour. A newcomer who has only been here a year, and, before coming here, was an exquisite of Naples, Florence and Vienna; who has remained a total stranger to the language of the Indians since his arrival; unaccustomed to affairs and with no natural talent (so it seems to me) for dealing with them; five feet two in height, and as thin as I am – if I were living with him, he would too often cause me to forget that he is the Governor. A Governor should either be old, tall or stout or clever.[46]

And later: 'I have seen Lord Clare, who is far more like an Italian butler in a great house than an English lord. He is full of polite attentions towards me. I do not know what he is really like, but nobody could seem more of a fribble.'[47]

Malcolm and his party travelled to Cairo by the same route as in 1822 – across the desert to Dendera and then down the Nile. As before, he was received there as a distinguished guest by the Pasha, Mehmet Ali, being put up at the Pasha's 'magnificent new palace of the Dufterdar Pasha, the son-in-law of Mahomet Ali. The Pasha's Turkish servants were in attendance, and a complete set of Maltese and Alexandrian servants, with a French cook, were hired to entertain us in the European manner. The plate and china were alike elegant. Every rarity the country produced, or that could be purchased, was in abundance. The wines –

Sherry, Claret, Madeira and Burgundy – were of the best.'[48] Mehmet Ali, although still paying nominal homage to the Porte, was hoping to achieve recognition as a virtually independent sovereign power. He saw an opportunity in Malcolm's visit to point out the desirability for the British of their having a friendly power covering their route to India. Malcolm, of course, had no instructions to act as a diplomatic negotiator, and all he could do was to agree to pass on the Pasha's thoughts to the British Government.

The party sailed from Alexandria on 22 January, called at Malta on 2 February, at Gibraltar on 12 February, and finally reached London on 28 February 1831.

CHAPTER THIRTY-ONE

Governor of Bombay – Quarrel with the Judges

The most notorious episode of Malcolm's governorship (at least to contemporaries) was the clash between the Bombay Government and the judges of the Supreme Court of Bombay. It lasted for almost the whole period of his Governorship.

The Court had been set up by an Act of Parliament in 1823 to replace the Recorder's Court (over which Sir James Mackintosh had presided from 1804 to 1811). The three judges of this Court were directly appointed by the Crown in London, with authority independent of the Governor (and also of the Court of Directors). The object was to give the citizens of Bombay, the Presidency capital, access to English law. But the Act did not make clear what jurisdiction, if any, the Supreme Court would have over the vast additional territories acquired by the British from the Mahrattas in 1818.

The Company had inherited the Peshwah's legal system in the Deccan, whereby the local executive ruler – village headman, *jaghirdar*, ultimately the Peshwah himself – had dispensed justice. As the first Commissioner of the Deccan and later as Governor, Elphinstone had to step into the breach, making ad hoc decisions as problems arose. Elphinstone and his Collectors wisely tried to adhere as far as possible to traditional Hindu and Muslim legal practice. Though messy at first, the arrangement was surprisingly successful. Supported by Indian assistants, usually *Brahmins*, the Collectors dispensed justice rather as their Mahratta predecessors had done. Elphinstone was keen to use *panchayats* (councils of village elders) to settle civil and some criminal cases, and to restrict the activities of Collectors to dealing with appeals from lower courts. But gradually even this became too great a burden on their time, and several full-time European judges were brought in to preside over Company courts.

Inevitably, there were transition problems. The main one con-cerned the so-called 'privileged classes', broadly Chiefs, landlords and religious functionaries. The Company had promised that these classes would be protected from legal attack by their subjects. On the other hand, the natural judicial desire of the Collectors and their Indian assistants was for justice and equality before the law. Gradually a code of regulations was formulated whereby the 'privileged classes' were given certain rights – for instance, not to have to appear in court in person whenever a plaintiff launched a complaint, and to be tried by a specially appointed European judge. Though not logically tidy, it was a practical regime.

However, in 1823, when Sir Edward West, the first Chief Justice, and his two fellow judges took office, they envisaged a much larger role for the Supreme Court. West saw himself 'defending the helpless natives against their more powerful masters'.[1] His first sally against the government came in 1825 over censorship of the press in Bombay, which he considered illegal. Later, gathering confidence, the judges argued that their jurisdiction should extend over the whole territory controlled by the Bombay Government. Most Company officials differed, feeling that extension into the Deccan of the full panoply of English law, with complicated Western concepts such as *habeas corpus*, separation of powers, and equality of all citizens before the law, would be completely unintelligible to the native population. Elphinstone resisted the judges' interpretation, but resolution of the issue was deferred.

In 1827, shortly before Malcolm sailed for India, Wynn had asked him for his opinion on the issue. He replied that regardless of the legalities, there needed to be a political decision clarifying the extent of the Court's jurisdiction; otherwise native perception of division in the British Government would be highly damaging to British interests.[2] On his arrival at Bombay, he found Elphinstone's 'handover note' warning him that his dispute with the Chief Justice had 'certainly weakened both'; the judge's 'suspicious temper' was difficult to deal with, but he hoped that Malcolm's persuasive powers might win him over.[3]

In the first months after his arrival Malcolm used all his charm to improve relations with West. At first all went well, as Lady West recorded in her journal:

> Dec 29 1827
> Sir John Malcolm . . . has sent me some grapes. He evidently wishes to be civil and attentive
>
> Jan 2 1828
> We attended last night the Ball and Supper given by the Governor . . . Sir John Malcolm was remarkably polite and attentive; I went with him to supper . . . [he] is very amusing, though certainly with a large proportion of vanity, and self is not forgotten.
>
> Jan 11
> Edward has written to Mr Wynn to tell him how comfortably we are likely to get on here, as Sir John Malcolm seems to wish to be all that is obliging and friendly . . . We had our party to Sir John yesterday. He was so cheerful and agreeable, the day went off most pleasantly.[4]

In early February 1828 a new judge arrived, Sir John Grant of Rothiemurchus, a Scottish highland laird, London barrister and former Member of Parliament. He came with his wife, two daughters and a son. He had got into financial difficulties in England, and his appointment (arranged by his kinsman, Charles Grant, Lord Glenelg) was used as a means of escaping his creditors. The Grants, too, were welcomed by Malcolm, who saw in Grant a fellow Scot of considerable intellect, and potentially a good friend. He also hoped that Grant might be cajoled into persuading his fellow judges to be more supportive of the government's position. Many years later, one of his daughters, Elizabeth Grant, gave a vivid description of the Grant family's time in India. Two senior officials, one of whom happened to be Lady Grant's brother-in-law, attempted to 'brief' Grant in favour of the government's position, 'telling their own version of Sir Edward West's "mistakes"; but that little wasp, with his King's servants and his pomposity and his flattery of similar weakness, aided by the heavy weight of Sir Charles Chambers [the third judge], got the upper hand of the Civil Service, and enlisted my father in right earnest on their side.'[5]

The Supreme Court continued sitting through the 1828 hot season in Bombay. With the Court session over, the Wests and the Grants travelled to Poona. Malcolm had preceded them. But then West fell ill and died on 18 August. Lady West, heavily pregnant, was supported during the funeral service by the Governor and her brother-in-law. Unfortunately she never recovered, dying in premature childbirth at Bombay a month later. Despite West's opposition to the government, he had been a moderating influence on his fellow judges. Had he survived, an uneasy peace might have been preserved until clarification had come from London about the extent of the Court's jurisdiction.

Now, however, the two surviving judges, Chambers and Grant, were determined to press ahead and bring matters to a crisis. The *casus belli*, as it were, was the case of Moro Ragonath, a fourteen-year-old boy living in Poona and belonging to the 'privileged classes' (or 'privileged *sirdars*'), 'protected' by the Company. Both his parents having died, the boy was living under the guardianship of his uncle, Pandoorang Ramchunder. But his potential father-in-law (i.e. the father of the girl to whom the boy was betrothed), claimed that uncle Pandoorang was exerting a bad influence over the boy, and sought to remove him from his uncle's custody. Since there was no way that this could be achieved under Hindu custom through the local Company courts, he looked elsewhere for advice. He was assured, almost certainly by European lawyers, that the Supreme Court was superior to all other courts, and even to the government itself. He had only to make an affidavit to the Court to the effect that the boy was being held against his will, in a way that was injurious to his health, and the Court would issue a writ (*habeas corpus*) commanding that the boy be brought before it in Bombay. The affidavit was made and the writ duly issued by the judges in early September. This was a direct challenge to the authority of the Company government. It had to be resisted, and Malcolm was determined to do so. He wrote to Charlotte that: 'I am engaged in a battle with the Supreme Court, whose mischievous interference with the inhabitants of our provinces will this day be arrested by my orders . . . If I am not supported, I shall not remain a week to have the Government over which I preside trampled upon, nor the empire to the prosperity of which the efforts of my life have been devoted beaten down, not by honest fellows with glittering sabres, but quibbling, quill driving lawyers.'[6]

Later in September a second case arose. Malcolm immediately came back from Poona to Bombay to consult his fellow Councillors – Mr Sparrow, then a sick man; Mr Romer, a former judge; and General Sir Thomas Bradford, the Commander-in-Chief. With the Council's unanimous agreement, a letter was sent to the Supreme Court on 3 October, intimating that the writs issued in these two cases would not be implemented by government servants, and pleading with the Court to await clarification from London of the extent of its jurisdiction before taking any further action.[7] Chambers and Grant reacted furiously to this letter. Grant in particular took offence at what he deemed a deliberate insult not only to the Court but to him personally. He immediately wrote a personal letter to Malcolm accusing him of trying to outrage his honour, both as a judge and as a man, and ending by stating that he was no longer prepared 'to have any private intercourse with the gentlemen who have thus addressed me'.[8]

The Court met on 6 October, and the government's letter was read out by the clerk. Sir Charles Chambers then spoke of the insult offered to the Court in suggesting that the judges could violate the sanctity of their oaths for political expediency.[9] Sir John Grant was even more belligerent. The clerk was ordered to reply that the Court had received the government's letter, but 'could take no notice thereof'.[10]

Sir Charles Chambers went home, fell sick and within ten days was dead. Grant was now left as the acting Chief Justice and sole judge of the Court, until two replacements could be appointed in London and brought to Bombay. It must have been an unnerving experience for him, sensing that it was his duty to carry on the fight which appeared to have killed his two fellow judges. He did so with considerable, though arguably misguided, courage. He issued another writ of *habeas corpus* (called a *pluries* writ) which imposed an immediate fine of Rs10,000 on any official that might resist its imposition.

Both sides now decided to appeal to higher authority in London. Grant drew up a long petition to the King, citing the insult and injury that had been inflicted upon his Majesty's Court and pleading for protection and redress for this outrage. Malcolm had already sent details of the documentary evidence.

Shortly afterwards came a new twist. Sir Thomas Bradford began to get cold feet. He was a King's officer, 'celebrated for his admirable management of the Commissariat during the latter part of the Peninsular War; a very gentlemanly person, liked by those he took a fancy to, disliked by all those under his command, and quite a despot in his family, but ruled in turn by his very odd wife, a confirmed invalid and a very fanciful one.'[11]

Grant's repeated references to 'His Majesty's' Court had alarmed him and he felt a divided loyalty, as Grant had almost certainly intended. Malcolm wrote rather anxiously to Bentinck (prudently copying the letter to the Duke, who had become Prime Minister) that: 'My civil colleagues are not only my warm supporters on this occasion, and much more irritated than I am with the Proceedings of the Supreme Court, but I regret I cannot say so much of Sir T Bradford.'[12] Bradford was trying to avoid signing the minute stating the government's case. His hesitation became known to the judges, and emboldened them to threaten to issue a further *pluries* writ, ordering Ramchunder to appear before the Court, and if it was refused, to call upon the commander of the military garrison in Poona to support them with troops.[13]

The *pluries* writ was duly delivered to Ramchunder's house in Poona, but Sir Lionel Smith, commander of the garrison and an old comrade of Malcolm's, was not to be intimidated. He even recommended that one solution might be to 'break the catchpole's head'. Although most of the European community sided with the government, the legal fraternity did not. To them, support for the judges was both a matter of principle and in their own interest as a profession. They tried hard to rally the native community to their side of the argument and achieved some success. In this situation Malcolm kept his head. He had the legal power to deport anybody he liked but refrained, limiting himself to prohibiting government servants from publishing articles in the newspapers. Besides, he knew that the charge that Moro Ragonath was being held against his will and being ill treated was a legal fiction. As he pointed out to Bentinck: 'to give you an idea of the extent of the lies (I will not honor them by calling them fictions) the boy . . . who has been sworn to be in a dying state, and to be kept prisoner by a tyrannical uncle who is plotting his death, was last night one of the most lively spectators at a Fancy Ball.'[14]

For the next few months there was a lull in the dispute. Everyone in Bombay was waiting for a response from London. The Court only resumed sitting on 25 January 1829, and the Governor was away on tour until late January. Grant issued a further writ in early March, though rather hesitantly, not really expecting it to be obeyed. It was not, and his temper flared again. On 1 April, the first day of the next session, he announced that he was closing the Court until further notice – a further challenge to the government. Malcolm had gone to Mahabaleshwar a week earlier, but he returned immediately to Bombay to maintain calm and stiffen the resolve of his fellow Councillors. After three stifling weeks he went back to the Mahabaleshwar hills and stayed there until the rains came in mid-June. Meanwhile Grant and his family had also gone to Mahabaleshwar, at the invitation of a Colonel Smith, the commandant of the garrison at Satara, who had been in Bombay on sick leave. So there was the extraordinary situation of both the Governor and the acting Chief Justice being at the tiny new settlement of Mahabaleshwar at the same time, but not being on speaking terms. When in Bombay, Colonel Smith had taken a fancy to Grant's daughter Elizabeth, and this was probably his ulterior motive for inviting the Grants to come to the hills. She recalled the atmosphere:

> The dispute was in full vigour at that time, so we were out of the range of all the Governor's civilities, never asked to meet him either – that is, collectively. I individually was quite his friend, riding with him frequently in the mornings, particularly on the hills, at least till he fancied he might be thought in the way [i.e. of Colonel Smith's courtship of her]. He used to read me the letters he received from his wife and children, sent me their pictures, newspapers, new books, fruit, flowers etc. And when it was known that I was soon to remove to Satara [to get married to Colonel Smith] he . . . wished me joy with all his heart, and . . . told me I was marrying one of the best fellows in the service . . . Only once we got upon the quarrel; he said that if I had been my father's wife instead of his daughter, it would never have got to such lengths.[15]

Soon afterwards relief came for Malcolm. In late May he received a private letter from Lord Ellenborough (Wynn's successor at the Board of Control), stating that he had nominated as the new Chief Justice James Dewar, the current Judge Advocate in Bombay (roughly equivalent to Crown Prosecutor), and a Mr Seymour as the other judge. This was a shrewd move, because although Dewar was only thirty-three, he was well known and popular in Bombay society. Moreover, since he was already living in Bombay, he could take up his appointment immediately. Ellenborough went on to say that although the Privy Council had not yet decided how the problem could best be dealt with, it was firmly on the government's side. He hoped that 'the opinions of the law officers . . . may be sufficient to induce Sir J Grant to revise his notions of law – at any rate, no more mischief can happen, as he will be like a wild elephant between two tame ones.'[16]

Edward Law, Lord Ellenborough (1790–1871) was President of the Board of Control 1828–30.

This letter was music to Malcolm's ears, not only for the decision made, but for its strong expression of support. Later, in early June, came confirmation of the Privy Council's decision to limit the jurisdiction of the Supreme Court to Bombay and its environs. Malcolm's stance had been entirely vindicated. Yet at this moment of triumph, he wrote immediately to both Ellenborough and the Duke, pleading with them not to take too hard a line on Grant. 'I must on this occasion repeat my hope that none of his acts (not even shutting up the Court) should lead to the recall of Sir John Grant. Though I am sorry for this gentleman – and more so that his violence should have hazarded distress to him and his fine family – I state what I now do from no maudlin feeling of pity. The cause must be injured by visiting the defects of the system upon individuals.'[17] And he made light of the whole distressing affair, writing privately a sixty-line doggerel poem, 'The Lawyers Lament', telling the story. It began:

To the East a Judge came
Johnny Grant was his name
In Scotland he's called Rothiemurchus
Though to India quite raw
Yet full of his law
He determined with Statutes to work us

And ended, with a little jab at the Bombay barristers:

Thus Scotch Johnnies, in quarrel
Have reduced to thin gruel
Men used to have plenty in store;
They tremble likewise
Lest clients grown wise
Should employ us poor lawyers no more.[18]

Grant, however, continued to cause trouble. Obstinate and defiant to the last, he boarded a ship to Calcutta on 28 September 1830, and was seen off by more than 400 people. He stayed in India for the rest of his life, working for three years as a barrister in Calcutta, then returning to Bombay as a puisne judge for the following fifteen.

CHAPTER THIRTY-TWO

Last Days, 1831–1833

Malcolm found the family at a rented house in London (8 Hereford Street, off Oxford Street). Back in October 1827, Charlotte had packed up Hyde Hall and moved with her three unmarried daughters, first to London, then to Hastings. In the following summer they went to the Continent, planning to stay there over the winter. But in mid-February 1829 Minnie arrived back in England, still not recovered from her Indian sickness, so Charlotte, 'far from well,' returned to London to meet her. But she spent most of her time at Hastings with Olympia and Amelia, leaving Kate (aged fourteen) at a girls' boarding school in London.

Malcolm was of course delighted to be back with the family. He now looked for somewhere larger for them to live. He needed to be in or near London to pursue his career. But, as he put it in a letter to Alex Cockburn-Campbell (then in Paris), 'Charlotte can't bear Town.' So he compromised, taking 'a delightful house on Wimbledon Common, seven miles from Town . . . where my duties . . . will not prevent my being continually with them'.[1]

As soon as the family were settled in, he set out to meet old friends. In mid-March the Irish novelist Maria Edgeworth wrote that: 'we were fortunately at home when Lady Wellesley [the Marquess's second wife] . . . called, and, thanks to my impudence in having written to him the moment he landed, and thanks to his good nature, Sir John Malcolm came at the same moment, and Lady Wellesley and he . . . talked most agreeably over former times in India and later times in Ireland. . . . Sir John is as entertaining and delightful as his Persian sketches, and as instructive as his Central India.'[2]

At the end of March, Lord Ellenborough gave a dinner for Malcolm, also attended by Mountstuart Elphinstone, who wrote in his journal:

> I dined last night at Lord Ellenborough's in a party to Malcolm at which were the Duke of Wellington, Sir G Murray . . . Sir H Hardinge, Lord Beresford, Lord Camden and some other people distinguished for rank or talent. Malcolm rattled away precisely as he would have done at his own table at Bombay, kept everybody in good humour though he took all the talk to himself, and really commanded my admiration for his ease and independence among a class of people for whom I know him to entertain so excessive a respect. He made no attempt to adapt his conversation to them or to please anybody but himself. The only exception to this was that he constantly went out of his way to bring me forward and to make me as intimate with the company as he was himself. I can now account for his popularity with all people of note whom I have heard talk of him. It could never have been gained by mere courting of favour or sustained by anyone who had less frankness, good humour and talent than Sir John.[3]

But the Wimbledon house did not suit Charlotte, and in June she went to Paris with Olympia and Amelia, to rejoin the still ailing Minnie. John hung on to the Wimbledon house until October, hoping they would return, but they didn't.

Immediately after his arrival in England, Malcolm's patron and mentor, the Duke of Northumberland, offered him one of the two 'rotten borough' House of Commons seats which he controlled at Launceston in Cornwall, and on 14 April 1831 he was sworn in as a Member of Parliament. He rented a small bachelor flat for himself at 12 Abingdon Street in Westminster, to be near Parliament during sittings.

In the British Parliaments of the 1830s, the tightly controlled party machines of today did not exist. Government depended on factions tied to families and patronage. In the unreformed House of Commons of 1830–31, more than one-third of the members had been educated at Eton or Harrow, and one-fifth were the sons of peers. It was an upper-class gentlemen's club.

Malcolm had always called himself a Tory. But he was a special sort of Tory, who had spent most of his adult life in India. His generation of Britons had grown up during the horrors of the French Revolution and the trauma of the Napoleonic wars which followed. They did not need to be hidebound reactionaries to fear the consequences of such a revolution in Britain. And in India, while his philosophy of governance might appear to be highly progressive – advancement of Indians in government, prohibition of European settlement, promotion of Native education, and even emancipation of women – it was also in a way conservative, in its respect for Indians, Indian history and Indian customs. It contrasted with the Whig creed, of government involvement in many aspects of Indian society, in order to bring to the subcontinent the allegedly beneficial fruits of Western-style government. Above all, he was a loyal follower of his great friend the Duke of Wellington. And, like many men of his relatively advanced age, experience had taught him the essentially Tory instinct of being critical of change for change's sake.

At the time of Malcolm's departure from Bombay in December 1830, the latest news from England had been that the Duke was still the Prime Minister of a basically Tory government. But in the meantime, several dramatic events had occurred, in quick succession. The King (George IV) had died, and been succeeded by his brother (William IV), who was more favourably disposed to the Whigs and to the reform of Parliament. The British General Election in August 1830, called as a result of the death of the King, returned the Duke's government on the old franchise, but demonstrated only too clearly the need for electoral reform. The 'July Days' revolution in France, resulting in the abdication of the reactionary King Charles X and his replacement in a virtually bloodless coup by his more liberal cousin, Louis Philippe of Orleans, together with a further revolution in Holland resulting in Belgium becoming an independent country, had greatly encouraged the reform movement in Britain, by demonstrating that reform, even in France, need not necessarily result in bloodshed, chaos and dictatorship, as it had between 1789 and 1793. The Duke's famous (or infamous) speech on 2 November, utterly opposing all reform, had led to the fall of his government in late November, and the appointment of the veteran Whig, Earl Grey, as Prime Minister, with a mandate for reform. On 1 March 1831 (the day after Malcolm arrived back in London), Lord John Russell introduced the first Reform Bill in the House of Commons, and it was passed on its second reading on 22 March by a single vote (305 votes to 304).

Malcolm dived head first into this whirlpool of political activity. The Duke of Northumberland and his wife Charlotte ('Charly') were old friends. Northumberland was against reform, and had forced out one of his two Launceston 'nominated' members, Sir William Morton, for being pro-reform. According to Malcolm, Northumberland did not place any conditions on how he should speak or vote in the Commons, other than on the Reform Bill, to which he was anyway opposed.

He wrote to William Pasley: 'I am no enemy, as you may suppose, to Reform; but that, to be safe, should be very moderate and very gradual. Time, we are told, is an innovator. This is true; but he is an old and slow man. If we march with him we are safe; but if we outstrip him, we rush upon danger, if not upon ruin.'[4]

He made his maiden speech on 19 April, during the debate on the Committee stage of the Reform Bill. He wisely restricted himself to his own area of relative expertise, India.[5] His theme was that India, with its overall population of nearly 100 million, deserved some sort of representation in the British Parliament. It was clearly impractical and premature to introduce a British system of Parliamentary elections. However, the so-called 'rotten boroughs', which the Bill was designed to disenfranchise, had provided, by nomination, a useful sprinkling of Members who had some knowledge of conditions in India, having spent most of their working lives there. In a reformed Parliament such men, having few useful connections in Britain, would have great difficulty in finding seats and getting elected.

In naïve enthusiasm he wrote a pamphlet on the subject of reform, in which he purported to have received a letter from a friend in India objecting to the measures proposed. This earned him a mild rebuke from the Duke, who pointed out that: 'you could scarcely, on 26 May, have received your friend's observations on the discussions of [last] October and November. The Bill was not brought into Parliament and printed till the 3rd of March. Your friend in India and you must have corresponded by balloon if he could have written to you after the publication of the Bill, and you could have received and answered his letter by the 26th of May.'[6]

Not surprisingly, the Bill was opposed by the Tory-dominated House of Lords. The King, upset by the Lords' assault on what he considered his prerogative, prorogued Parliament, and an election was fixed for May. Reform fever was now sweeping the country. There were demonstrations in favour of reform and against its opponents. Even the venerable Sir Walter Scott (a Tory) was stoned at Selkirk, a few miles from his home at Abbotsford. Reform candidates were returned in strength from constituencies which reflected public opinion, and when Parliament reassembled in June, Lord Grey's Whigs were assured of an invincible majority. A second Reform Bill was introduced, and after continuous sittings, was passed in late September by a majority of 136. Malcolm spoke twice on the Bill, on both occasions developing his original theme that a way had to be found for Indian interests to be represented in a reformed House of Commons.

On 5 July he made a lengthy statement of his views. He pointed out that the British public 'and this House' could only obtain 'accurate and minute information' about India from men who, 'from long residence and employment in that country, have become conversant with the character, the institutions and the conditions of its inhabitants'. Moreover, there were now much larger areas to control: 'men who previously had districts are now intrusted with provinces to the extent almost of kingdoms.' A high calibre of man was required; a man who, after spending many years of service in India, could reasonably look forward to a second career in public life in Britain. Pocket boroughs had provided a means for such men to get into Parliament. But 'the present bill will shut the last gate . . . through which those who have spent the better part of their lives in India have hitherto, with a very few exceptions, been able to enter this House'. He concluded that 'The task of preserving India will be found much more arduous than that of conquering it.'[7]

Some notice must have been taken of his arguments because in August, Joseph Hume, the Radical pro-reform member for Middlesex, put up a detailed plan for representation in a reformed House of Commons for three overseas categories of electorate: British India, colonies directly ruled from London, and colonies which had their own legislatures. Malcolm suggested instead that the proprietors of stock in the East India Company should make up a constituency to elect four Members of Parliament, rather like the universities.[8]

But this was a losing battle. Nothing came of either Hume's or Malcolm's proposals. The fact was that, despite some pious statements of support, neither the Ministers nor the members were the slightest bit interested in India. Malcolm was overworked and depressed by this lack of public interest. He wrote to Charles in Bombay that:

> I am alone, working sometimes fifteen hours a day, and always eight or ten. I hope it will be soon over. India and its services are threatened by prejudice, ignorance and the attacks of bodies of men deeply interested in change. The Directors are in a divided state, and the Board of Control new and inefficient . . . As to your affairs at Bombay, your Judges, your petitions from natives, your slave questions, nobody cares one farthing. There is not the smallest borough in England that has been disfranchised or enfranchised that does not excite more interest, and occupy more of the public mind, than our whole empire of India.[9]

As soon as the Parliamentary session was over, he took two weeks off to visit the family in Paris. George was with them, having hitherto failed to get a position with a regiment. He found Charlotte 'very well' and Minnie 'greatly better', but not apparently well enough to come home to England. So he sent Charlotte and his daughters off to Italy for the winter. During his time in Paris the House of Lords had rejected this 'second' Reform Bill, causing uproar in the country. 'A crowd of some thousands gathered in Palace Yard to pelt the Duke of Wellington, and smash the panes of Northumberland House [at Charing Cross].'[10] On his return he wrote to the Duke: 'I called in hopes of seeing you, but found you too busy to intrude . . . I am busy from morning till night preparing for the fight on India [this was for the renewal of the Company's Charter in 1833], but that and everything else depends on the extent of reform. If the Bill passes in its former shape, no Ministers will have power to maintain the interest of the Indian Empire . . . I should (to go from bipeds to quadrupeds) like to have shown you my noble horse Osman before he goes to Warfield; but I shall, when there, not be a distant neighbour, and gallop him over some fine morning.'[11]

'Warfield' was Warfield Hall in Berkshire, about fifty miles west of London, which Malcolm had just bought. It was 'a large three storey mansion, built in the 1730s, with ten bedrooms, stabling, a paddock, an orangery, a well-wooded park with a two acre lake, a fine garden with a terrace, kitchen garden and outhouses',[12] plus 232 acres of pasture land .

A great deal of work had to be done on the buildings and he anticipated that he would not be able to move in for at least a year. This at last, he hoped, would solve the problem for Charlotte who 'could not bear Town', and his having to be within commuting distance of London. He finalised the purchase in late November, and wrote to the Duchess of Northumberland that 'I am now going to Warfield, where my genius must be employed in reforming an old English fabric.'[13] In mid-December he wrote again that he was 'about to commence a Board of Works at Warfield'.[14] Over the next fifteen months he went there frequently, staying in a cottage on the estate and dining at the local inn. He was delighted with the project, recording in his journal one day: 'Remained the day at Warfield House directing a few buildings of brick and mortar; and building at less cost various castles in the air associated with the future enjoyment of this beautiful residence.'[15] But there is no record of Charlotte ever going with him to look over the place.

With Parliament prorogued between 20 October and early December, he went to Scotland, staying with the Burnfoot family, then going on to Alnwick Castle to stay with the Northumberlands. Before setting off for London by stagecoach on 21 November, he promised the Duchess that he would send her an account of his journey – possibly recalling the journal/letters he had written for her mother back in 1799 and 1800, when travelling across the Deccan and Persia. The journal of the four-day trip is vintage Malcolm – relentlessly cheerful, hugely extrovert, engaging all and sundry in conversation.[16]

On 12 December a new Bill – the third Reform Bill – was introduced in the House of Commons, and was easily carried. Parliament was prorogued again, and steps to resolve the crisis were postponed to February 1832.

He spent Christmas with the Clive family in Shropshire. At Ludlow, he was met by Robert Clive and taken to stay nearby at Oakly Hall. On Christmas Day the whole Clive clan gathered about twenty miles further north at Walcot, the grand country house built by the first Lord Clive in the 1760s, and now the home of the Earl of Powis. Over the next few days Malcolm worked on the Clive papers for his biography. He attended two balls at Ludlow, one a 'subscription' ball for the County elite, the other a 'Public' ball. He wrote about the latter: 'All ranks and classes were mingled in true English fashion. There were fine pumps and thick shoes – neat crops and bushy wigs – diamonds and beads –

pale faces and green ribands – and cherry cheeks with yellow ribands. One lady, called the Princess Royal, for she was the acknowledged heiress of the Crown Inn, made tea and negus [a sort of wine cup] one moment for the entertainment of the company, and danced next for her own.'[17]

Early in the new year, he went with the Earl of Powis to visit one of his model farms near Shrewsbury and thence on to see Charles Wynn at Wynnstaye near Llangollen. A few days later he took the coach to Shrewsbury and on to Birmingham. He got into an argument with a fellow passenger, 'a puffy, pockmarked ironmaster, clamorous for Reform'. The ironmaster embarked upon a long tirade against the East India Company, which he accused of being monopolist, justifying its opposition to free trade by claiming that it was its duty to protect, encourage and instruct the millions of fellow creatures under its control. He considered this humbug, and even if it was not, he claimed, what good would it do to Birmingham, Manchester etc? 'The duty of Englishmen, Sir, is to look to England first, and after its interests are taken care of, then attend to your Indians and Chinese, and all the blacks and copper-coloured you like.'[18]

Malcolm was back in London in time for the reassembly of Parliament on 17 January. The third Reform Bill, which had been introduced in December, was passed in the Commons on 22 March. Malcolm opposed it to the end, actually seconding Lord Mahon's proposed amendment to the third reading. There was not much new in his speech; he welcomed some of the modifications made to the Bill, but warned that 'under its operation, no administration will have sufficient strength to carry on the government of this country', much less that of India, and he exhorted the Lords to reject it.[19] This they duly did on 9 April, and a major constitutional crisis inevitably followed. For at least a year the Ministers had canvassed the idea of creating enough pro-reform peers to enable the Bill to pass the Lords. The stumbling-block was the King, who was understandably reluctant to devalue the spirit of the constitution in this way. In the previous December Earl Grey thought he had at last persuaded the King to give way. But when the moment of crisis arrived in April, the King got cold feet at the number of peerages that would need to be created – forty-eight. Grey took this as a challenge and resigned on 9 May. The demand for the Bill had roused the country – there were threats of civil disobedience, a run on the banks, barricades, and for eleven days, the so-called 'May Days', the country was brought to a standstill. As a last resort the King asked the Duke of Wellington to try to form a government of moderate reform, but the Duke could not find sufficient support. The King was now at the mercy of the reformers, and had to agree that he would create the necessary number of peers. Grey resumed his ministry. The resistance of the Lords was now broken, not least through the Duke using his great personal prestige with the die-hard Tory peers to persuade them that further resistance could spark a revolution. The Reform Act became law in England and Wales on 7 June. Bills for Ireland and Scotland swiftly followed, the Scottish Act increasing the number of electors from 5,000 to 60,000. Despite his Scottish roots, Malcolm played little part in the debate on the Scottish Bill.

Apart from his general opposition to parliamentary reform, Malcolm's main objective in becoming an MP had been to fight for renewal of the East India Company's current Charter, which would cease in 1833. Select Committees had been set up in both Houses in 1830, but real progress was not made until 1832. Malcolm was a member of the Commons committee on the renewal of the Charter, and also on the military sub-committee, and he gave evidence to both of them. The committee's report was published on 16 August, the day before the unreformed Parliament was prorogued for the last time. Its contents, historical reviews, appendices and testimony from a host of witnesses, fill many exhausting volumes. Not surprisingly, Malcolm, who had thought so much, written so much and above all achieved so much over the previous half-century on Indian policy, was a key witness. No less surprisingly, he had plenty to say. At one stage he complained to Ellenborough that the chairman of the military sub-committee, Mr Byng, was 'incapable', which sounds credible; but he in turn was criticised by another colleague on the sub-committee that 'he could talk only of himself', which sounds equally credible.[20] Much of his testimony was later quoted in his book *The Government of India* (1833).

At this point he should have given up Parliament with a strong sense of relief. He had done his duty in relation to the Reform Bill and that battle was now well and truly over. Canvassing for the renewal of the Company's Charter was in itself a full-time job. If he had time to spare from that, he could always resume work on his biography of Clive. And finalising the works at Warfield and settling Charlotte and the family there would have been quite enough for most men of his age. In late June he appeared to have made this decision. He wrote to the Duchess of Northumberland that he could get into the reformed Parliament, 'if I would bribe to the extent of from £3,000 to £5,000, or if I would give three or four sound pledges – immediate abolition of Slavery, no Monopoly, no Corn Laws etc. I have rejected all such propositions, and retire the day that Parliament is prorogued, to my country place in Berkshire . . . I have a pretty fair prospect of making a salaam to the old walls of St Stephen's, and of repeating, amid the avenues of Warfield, Goldsmith's lines: "Happy the man who crowns in shades like these, a life of labour with an age of ease."'[21]

But two days later came temptation, in the guise of news that the Tory candidate for the Dumfries boroughs did not intend to stand at the forthcoming post-reform election, likely to take place in December or January. Malcolm immediately wrote to the Duke of Northumberland: 'A proposal has been made to me to canvass the boroughs of my native county, Dumfriesshire, which, on serious consideration, I have thought proper to accept . . . It is thought by the Duke of Buccleuch and others that among those who belong to the county and "hold conservative principles" I have the best chance of success . . . I stand upon my own ground. I belong to a popular family; but I bear the mark of an anti-Reformer upon my brow, and neither mean to brook pledges nor to disburse cash; and with such resolutions it is impossible to be sanguine.'[22]

It was an irrational decision made on the spur of the moment, without consulting anybody. Charlotte had spent the winter in Italy and returned to England at some stage during the summer, going straight to a rented house at Hastings with her daughters. But whether she had arrived by 28 June and met him is unclear. In any case, since he only took two days to change his mind, he could hardly have consulted her seriously. Pulteney wrote to Mina at Burnfoot: 'I fear that John will not be successful. Never mind, the attempt will do some good.'[23]

To a man of his exuberant temperament, being in Parliament at the centre of public affairs was exciting; and the idea of representing his native Scottish Borders appealed both to his romantic nature and his vanity. He remained a genuine Borderer at heart. In January 1832 he had presided (at the invitation of John Murray) at the annual London Burns Night dinner in the Freemasons' Tavern. The guest of honour was James

Hogg, the celebrated Borders poet, known as 'The Ettrick Shepherd', who was on his first visit to London. After Sir Walter Scott's death in June 1832, Malcolm led the drive in London to erect a suitable memorial to the great man, making a public address at the Thatched House Tavern.[24] The Edinburgh 'Abbotsford' Committee had suggested a statue, but Malcolm preferred an alternative idea: 'I have from the first, thought, and continue to think, that making Abbotsford and all its appurtenances a grant from the public to the descendants of Sir Walter Scott, is the noblest tribute we can pay to the memory of that wonderful man . . . by purchasing Abbotsford we shall perpetuate the only fabric he ever raised of perishable materials; it will be a lasting abode to his descendants; and this shrine of genius – for such it is, and will remain – will never pass into the hands of strangers to his blood.'[25]

In the last days of the Parliamentary session Malcolm intervened several times on Indian matters, speaking in support of Sir Lionel Smith's appeal over the affair of the Deccan Prize Fund, which went back to the Mahratta War of 1817–18, and defending Mountstuart Elphinstone and H.D. Robertson against charges that they had 'plundered' the Peshwah's treasury in 1818. Meanwhile on 3 August his much loved sister Mina died after years of illness. As soon as he could get away from Parliament he travelled to Scotland, partly to comfort the Burnfoot clan, partly to test the Dumfries constituency for the next election. The prospects were very discouraging, but as ever he took an optimistic view. 'I labor under every disadvantage in my canvass', he wrote, 'from my opponents having been in the field sixteen days before me; from their promising everything, and giving pledges faster than they are asked; above all, in my having voted against the Reform Bill. Still, all, down to the lowest and most violent are personally kind to me . . . with these feelings I do not quite despair.'[26]

In early December he went back to Scotland to see how things were going at Dumfries. On the journey between Birmingham and Manchester he found himself in the same stagecoach as William Cobbett, the celebrated Radical politician and author of *Rural Rides*. Malcolm entered enthusiastically into a friendly but ferocious argument with the boisterous and abusive Cobbett. 'You may call me a red ruffian of a soldier, and I in turn will call you a demagogue, without any offence.'[27] For six or seven hours they hammered away at each other. By the time they reached Manchester, Malcolm had persuaded Cobbett, a famous horticulturalist, to come to Warfield to advise him about planting apple trees. They shook hands and agreed to differ.

At Dumfries Malcolm found that his prospects were hopeless, so he withdrew his nomination. There then followed an even more bizarre twist – the neighbouring Carlisle Tories invited him to stand there and he recklessly, quixotically, agreed to do so. Carlisle was traditionally Radical, and not surprisingly, he came an ignominious last.

Malcolm was not a success as an MP. Like many military men, he was used to making clear decisions and acting on them. He was unaccustomed to the rather strange customs of the House, the pettifogging procedures, the shifting factional alliances. Moreover, in a place and at a time when oratory was at a premium, when the ability to quote apt Latin tags was an admired art, his rather squeaky voice, and still strong Scottish brogue, were against him. 'Neither voice nor delivery were in his favour.'[28]

After a few days at Burnfoot he returned south and spent Christmas with Charlotte and the family at Hastings. She had been 'in very delicate health' for some time. In the autumn he had written to Nancy at Burnfoot: 'I am pushing Warfield, that we may all be settled. Really this life is very worrying and distracting . . . in this state of my family, I shall, I think, rejoice in the failure of my parliamentary concern.'[29] He knew only too well that he was overworking and neglecting his family, but he just could not bring himself to slow down.

Early in the new year he hurried back to London from Hastings, and now concentrated in earnest on trying frantically to finish *The Government of India*. The Duke of Wellington had written to him in November: 'I heard from your brother the Admiral, whom I saw at Walmer Castle, that you were about to publish something on India. I don't doubt that what you publish will be very creditable to you; but I confess that I don't expect that your writings, or those of an angel from heaven, if they contained truth and reasoning founded on experience and common sense, would have any effect upon the conduct of the Government and the Legislature in these times . . . I declare that I could at times gnaw the flesh from my bones with vexation and despair!'[30]

With the ending of his Parliamentary career he gave up the flat in Abingdon Street, Westminster and took modest lodgings in Princes Street, just round the corner from the Oriental Club in Hanover Square, where he did most of his writing, and no doubt dined frequently with his 'Indian' friends. He had hoped to publish the book early in the year but he was horribly behind.[31] Amazingly, he was also working on his *Life of Clive*, sending draft chapters as he finished them for comment to his old friend from Madras days, David Haliburton, now living at Watford.

The Government of India was published by John Murray at the end of March. It appeared just in time for the final negotiations between the Company and the Board, but in practice it was unfinished. The *Asiatic Journal* called it 'a hasty and indigested compilation'. What was needed for the Charter discussions was a concise compendium of the arguments on each aspect of the Company's Indian government; its proposed relationship with the British Government for the purposes of Charter renewal; and a summing up of his own views. But the book contained no proper table of contents or index; the Appendix took up more than half the volume; and both the Commentary and the Appendix started, confusingly, at page one. Much of it was simply a rehash of his minutes on various subjects written when he was Governor of Bombay. It was, in short, a mess.

It was also the work of an ailing old man. In February he fell ill, a victim of the flu epidemic which was sweeping London at the time. His enormously strong constitution, which had carried him through so many crises in his younger days, had failed, and he unfortunately refused to accept the fact.

There was one last challenge to be faced. The Court of Directors of the East India Company had been negotiating for some months with the Board of Control, representing the government, and had reached broad agreement. Now the Court of Proprietors needed to be informed of the issues on which the Directors had been negotiating, and to be persuaded to accept their recommendations. This was not going to be easy, especially since the current chairs, Campbell Majoribanks and William Wigram, were not highly thought of in Company circles. On 25 March 1833 they distributed to the Proprietors a digest of recent correspondence with the Board on the subject. They then looked around for a proprietor of high standing and prestige, who could put the case for supporting them. Their gaze fell on Malcolm, and despite still being weak from the effects of the flu, he agreed to propose a motion that the Proprietors should approve the Court's recommendations to the Board. The debate, beginning on 15 April, took place in the crowded Courtroom in Leadenhall Street. Since it dealt with the very future of the Company, it was very well attended. Many Proprietors were angry at the way that the Government had appeared to bully the Company during the last few years, and to interfere in its management. They were in touchy and belligerent mood.

There were three major issues at stake. Firstly, the Company's monopoly of trade with China. This was highly profitable to the Company and had more than offset the losses which it was incurring in India. But it was becoming more and more of an anomaly, especially since private merchants from other European countries were free to compete with it. Moreover, in 1830 Ellenborough had made it clear that the monopoly would expire with the current Charter. Second, and following from the removal of the China trade monopoly, was the question of whether the Company should be allowed to continue with its remaining commercial activity in India. If not, and if the Company became in effect a government utility, how would the Proprietors' existing investments be safeguarded? Third, and easily the most important issue, how much power and patronage, and how much responsibility would be left in the hands of the Company to govern British India? In the Charter renewal negotiations of 1813, the Chairs, particularly the older Charles Grant, had mobilised their allies in the City and the 'Indian interest' in Parliament to fight hard to retain the Company's privileges. But this time the Chairs had been curiously apathetic.[32]

This, then, was the atmosphere facing Malcolm as he rose to speak. His tone was, by his standards, rather low key – perhaps through ill-health, more likely a deliberate attempt to calm down his audience, to achieve acquiescence in the inevitable, rather than to rouse them to fight. He spoke as an elder statesman, pointing out that the purpose of the debate was not to approve or reject a particular scheme but to ascertain the Proprietors' feelings about the conduct of the Directors to date, and guide them in future negotiations.

The speech probably lasted about eighty minutes. In his weak state of health 'the exertion was very painful, and when he sate down, he fainted away'.[33] The debate was resumed the next day and, despite his exhaustion, Malcolm dragged himself back to the Courtroom. He had probably intended to say nothing, but who should suddenly appear as an unwelcome ghost from the past but Sir Harford Jones. Still a bitter man, Jones made a short speech opposing the motion, then turned to Malcolm: 'I would here ask one question of the gallant officer, namely, whether the resolution was the consequence of any communication between the gallant gentleman and his Majesty's ministers?' His spiteful implication was that Malcolm was merely acting as the mouthpiece of the Government. Malcolm was immediately on his feet: 'Not in the least. I have not spoken a word to them or to any other person on the subject.'[34]

The debate continued for five more days, and arrangements were made for a ballot on 3 May, at which Malcolm's resolution was carried by 477 votes to 32. Negotiations between the Court and the Government thereafter proceeded quickly. The new President of the Board of Control, the younger Charles Grant, went down with flu, but the negotiations for the Board, both with the Directors and later in Parliament, were handled efficiently by Thomas Macaulay, who had become Secretary of the Board in December 1832. The new Charter became law in August 1833, on terms very similar to those advocated by Malcolm's resolution.

But Malcolm was destined never to know this. He had a recurrence of 'this vile influenza'. On the morning of 28 April he set out from Princes Street in his own carriage, having at last agreed to convalesce with the family at Hastings. With him was his faithful servant Charles Postoure. But when they stopped at Charing Cross to enquire about the stagecoach to Hastings, Malcolm was struck with 'violent paralysis' – almost certainly a stroke. Postoure 'opened the door [of the carriage], and was about to ask for his orders, when he saw that his master had sunk from the seat, and was lying insensible at the bottom of the carriage'.[35] Postoure managed to get him back to Princes Street and call for help. Charlotte came straight away from Hastings; so did Alex Cockburn-Campbell, then living at Teddington, and Gilbert came from Todenham. Pulteney, too, was in London at the time, but had to sail from Portsmouth on 11 May to resume his command of the Mediterranean fleet. All through May Malcolm lay helpless and speechless. At one point there were signs of improvement. Many friends called at Princes Street for the latest news. According to Kaye, 'the Duke of Wellington never failed in his daily visit of inquiry, and was deeply disappointed that the inexorable mandate of the physician forbade him to appear at the bedside of his friend'.[36] But all was in vain. Malcolm died on 30 May, aged just sixty-four.

On the very same day the news came that Warfield – 'a home – the first I ever had' – was at last ready for occupation. He had so looked forward to settling there. But his 'castle in the air' would remain just that, as would his dream that when at Warfield he would mount 'his noble horse Osman and gallop him over [to Stratfield Saye] some fine morning' to see his old friend the Duke.[37] The 'labouring oar', as he had once described himself, had continued to ply, right to the end.

Postscript

Malcolm's funeral took place on 6 June at St James's Church, Piccadilly, and his remains were buried in the crypt.[1]

In the following weeks numerous lengthy obituaries were published. Perhaps the most eloquent eulogy was written by Mountstuart Elphinstone, in his private diary:

> Perhaps no man not entrusted with the government of that mighty province [i.e. the Governor-Generalship of India] ever exercised so great an influence, during his time in India, as Sir John Malcolm. His ascendancy was owing to his natural abilities; for he was entirely self-educated, having come out to India in his fifteenth year, and, long afterwards, led the life of an idle and wild cadet. But he had a quickness of apprehension and a talent for turning what he learned to account, which were not to be acquired by study. In his most careless days he had a quick perception of character, and a ready, though not always accurate insight into affairs. His judgment was soon formed, often sound, and united with a boldness that would shrink at no undertaking; . . . what he resolved, he would enter on with confidence, and generally carry through with success.
>
> In addition to his public merits, Sir John Malcolm possessed, in an eminent degree, the power of gaining the attachment of those with whom he associated, and was, at one time of his life, the most popular man with all classes that ever was known in India. He owed this to his unbounded good nature, to a temper which nothing could ruffle, and spirits which nothing could

> depress, to the relish with which he could join in any amusement . . . and the readiness with which he entered into an intimacy, and the warmth with which he adhered to it when he had the power to assist a friend. To this, at that period, was added a frankness and contempt for all disguise which opened every heart, while it disarmed envy by its inconsistency with every attempt at false pretensions.[2]

Moves were soon under way to erect a monument to his memory. A week after the funeral some friends, mostly Scots, met at Thomas Telford's London house. William Pasley told the meeting that two years earlier Malcolm's Bombay supporters had asked him to arrange for a suitable monument to be erected in Bombay, and that he had already commissioned the distinguished sculptor, Mr (later Sir) Francis Chantrey to do so, for a fee of £2,300. The meeting agreed to erect a statue to stand in London, and £1,600 was raised on the spot. On 1 July another meeting, an altogether grander affair, though with the same objective, was held at Lord Clive's house, with more than thirty gentlemen present. Four Dukes – Buccleuch, Northumberland, Wellington and Montrose – sent their proxies. This meeting appointed Pasley to collect subscriptions. Within two months he had collected £2,288. The Dukes (and Mehmet Ali, the Pasha of Egypt, through his agent) each contributed £100, and the list of the other 106 subscribers included many of the names mentioned in the index to this book. Pasley pointed out that since Chantrey had already made a plaster cast of Malcolm's Bombay statue, this could be used to make a replica for London. The two statues survive to this day: the Bombay statue in the Asiatic Society Library at the Town Hall; and the London statue in Westminster Abbey, flanked by the elder Pitt and, appropriately enough, George Canning. The Oriental Club commissioned a posthumous portrait by Samuel Lane.[3]

Meanwhile the Eskdale community was also planning a local memorial, and once again it was the indefatigable Pasley who coordinated plans. In August he travelled to Scotland, where the locals decided to erect an obelisk on the top of Whita Hill, above Langholm. An obelisk was probably chosen because Malcolm had been a freemason, and there was a strong body of freemasons based in the area, led by Sir James Graham of Netherby Hall. Thomas Telford submitted drawings, and the foundation stone was laid by Graham in September 1835. The obelisk was completed soon afterwards, and remains a landmark in Eskdale to this day, visible from up to thirty miles away.

Charlotte and her three unmarried daughters took up residence at Warfield soon after the funeral. One of her first concerns was how to complete *The Life of Robert Lord Clive*. Malcolm had written the first 13 chapters (out of 19) before he left India in 1830, and finished chapters 14 and 15 after his return. When he died, chapters 16 to 19 remained to be written. Mountstuart Elphinstone suggested that the obvious person to finish the job would be William Erskine, who had read through each of the chapters as Malcolm completed them, and anyway was available, having just finished writing another book. So Erskine took on the job; and the book was finally published in 1836. Although the Preface contained profuse thanks to the person who had completed the book, it did not name the self deprecating Erskine, who had been too much in awe of Malcolm to change a single word of chapters 1 to 15.

The book received mixed reviews, not surprisingly for a book where the author did not have the opportunity to edit and revise the completed draft. But these reviews were in due course totally overshadowed by one of the most famous book reviews ever – Thomas Macaulay's essay on Clive in the *Edinburgh Review* of January 1840, which was ostensibly a review of Malcolm's biography. The essay began: 'Every schoolboy knows who imprisoned Montezuma, and who strangled Atahualpa; but we doubt whether one in ten, even among English gentlemen of highly cultivated minds, can tell who won the battle of Buxar, who perpetrated the massacre of Patna, whether Sujah Dowlah ruled in Oude or in Travancore, or whether Holkar was a Hindoo or a Mussulman.' It did not pull any punches, although accepting that Malcolm could hardly be blamed: 'The materials at the disposal of Sir John Malcolm by the late Lord Powis were indeed of great value. But we cannot say that they were very skilfully worked up. It would, however, be unjust to criticise with severity a work which, if the author had lived to complete and revise it, would probably have been improved by condensation and a better arrangement.' He felt that Malcolm had been too kind to Clive, but he was equally critical of the overly hostile view taken by James Mill in his *History of India*.

Despite siring five children, Malcolm's direct line of descendants eventually died out. His daughters Amelia and Kate died as spinsters; his son George married, but died without issue. His daughter Olympia married Count Guido von Usedom, a Prussian diplomat, and produced a daughter, Hildegard, who died without issue. Minnie's daughter Olympia married a German Count, Frederic von Poellnitz, and produced three children, but all three died without issue; the last, Wolfgang, aged eighty, died in an apartment in Munich in November 1945 – a melancholy place at a melancholy time for a German. Wolfgang left his papers and memorabilia to his housekeeper. In the year 2000, some 138 letters to Malcolm from the Duke of Wellington were sold at auction in Munich.[4] If any other memorabilia survive, they are likely to be found in the home of the descendants of a Bavarian peasant.

What was Malcolm's legacy? Chapter 28 described his vision for Indian governance. Nevertheless he was the servant of an imperial power, and any evaluation of his life must take that into account. In purely philosophical terms the moral basis for imperialism – the rule of an 'Emperor' from one nation over subject peoples of other nations – cannot be defended. But the issue was not quite as clear-cut in relation to the Indian subcontinent of 200 years ago. We need to distinguish between 'colonialism' and 'imperialism'. In the period of Radical philosophical ascendancy which developed during the second half of the twentieth century, these epithets became more or less interchangeable, but they mean different things. Colonialism surely implies colonies, with settlers from the metropolitan power taking up residence in the colonised country. And settlers usually create trouble – modern examples exist in Palestine, Northern Ireland, southern Africa, Kazakhstan, Tibet, West Papua – that is, unless the colonising power has previously taken the precaution of either exterminating or marginalising the indigenous population (as happened in the USA, Canada, Australia and South America). Imperialism, on the other hand is concerned with achieving control – exerting influence over the subject country's foreign affairs and defence, and the main levers of its economy – and might or might not involve colonisation. Who can deny that we currently live in an era of American imperialism? The USA does not have colonies – it does not need to. It exerts imperial power directly in defence matters, and in other matters through UN agencies (over whose actions it effectively has a veto). Today the process is called Neo-colonialism, but a more appropriate term would be 'Neo-imperialism'. The point about British India is that it never became a colony, as defined above, except for the

Presidency cities of Calcutta, Madras and Bombay during the period of Company rule. It was a very special example of imperialism, initially driven more by commercial considerations than by military adventurism or ideological ideas of racial or cultural superiority.

When the East India Company took control of southern and western India in 1818, it was the genius of John Malcolm and his two colleagues, Munro and Elphinstone, to have the vision to leave things in 'British' India largely as they were; to simply *enforce* the existing laws, however deficient they might feel them to be, and in the 'Native States' to refrain from interference, even when they could see that direct Company rule might be more efficient; to prohibit British colonisation – this fortunately became a permanent prohibition; to promote Indians (many of them *Brahmins*) to senior levels in Company administration; to recognise that the moral mandate for British rule in India was temporary; and that its very success would eventually be its undoing.

Munro can justly be described as the father of the *ryotwari* system of revenue collection and civil governance; and of the three men, his ideas were the most readily accepted by the Court of Directors. But his career was largely confined to south India, and Elphinstone's to Mahratta country; Malcolm lived and worked throughout India. In the 1820s, if Munro was the pre-eminent ideologue of civil governance, and Elphinstone the pioneer of 'native' education, Malcolm may justly be described as the leading ideologue of the overall politics, defence and foreign policy of British India.

Looking back from the twenty-first century, the system of governance that Malcolm and his fellow Scots were advocating in the 1820s does not sound too radical. And in many ways it was no more than a natural evolution of the system set up in Bengal and Madras many years earlier. But it was very different from what would have happened if, say, the French, the Dutch or the Portuguese had been the imperial rulers.

Sadly, their ideas were 'forgotten too soon and remembered too late'. By the 1830s the British had become obsessed by the need for 'improvements' in their Indian possessions, and had become confident of their ability to provide them, regardless of the feelings of their Indian subjects. They were overcome by what Malcolm once described as 'the pride of conquerors'. The end result was the uprising of 1857, and the creation of a mutual suspicion which cast a shadow over relations between Britons and Indians for the next ninety years up to Independence in 1947.

A Statue of Sir John Malcolm was subscribed for in 1831 by Bombay residents and stands to this day in the Asiatic Society library in the Town Hall, Mumbai. The above statue, in Westminster Abbey, was a replica subscribed for in 1833 and finally erected in 1838.

This Obelisk on Whita Hill, Langholm, is a monument to Sir John Malcolm.

APPENDICES

1. British Government and EIC Office Holders between 1783 and 1833

British Government

Prime Ministers

December 1783	William Pitt
March 1801	Henry Addington
May 1804	William Pitt
February 1806	William, Lord Grenville
March 1807	William Cavendish Bentinck, Lord Portland
October 1808	Spencer Perceval
June 1812	Robert Jenkinson, Earl of Liverpool
April 1827	George Canning
August 1827	Frederick Robinson, Viscount Goderich
January 1828	Arthur Wellesley, Duke of Wellington
November 1830	Charles, Earl Grey

Presidents of the Board of Control

June 1793	Henry Dundas (1st Viscount Melville)
May 1801	George Lewisham, Earl of Dartmouth
July 1802	Robert, Viscount Castlereagh
February 1806	Gilbert, Earl of Minto
October 1806	George Tierney
April 1807	Robert Dundas
April 1812	Robert Hobart, Earl of Buckinghamshire
June 1816	George Canning
January 1821	Charles Bathurst
February 1822	Charles Watkin Williams Wynn
February 1828	Robert Dundas, Viscount Melville
September 1828	Edward Law, Lord Ellenborough
December 1830	Charles Grant, Lord Glenelg

The East India Company

Chairmen

Chairmen were elected for one-year terms only

Governors-General of India (Excluding Interim Holders)

April 1772	Warren Hastings
September 1786	Charles, Marquis Cornwallis
October 1793	Sir John Shore
May 1798	Richard Wellesley, Lord Mornington, later Marquess Wellesley
July 1805	Charles, Marquis Cornwallis
July 1807	Gilbert Elliot, Earl of Minto
October 1813	Francis Rawdon, Earl of Moira, later Marquess of Hastings
August 1823	William Pitt, Earl Amherst
July 1828	Lord William Bentinck

Governors of Madras

February 1785	Lord Macartney
April 1786	Sir Alexander Campbell
October 1790	Sir Charles Oakley
September 1794	Lord Hobart
September 1799	Lord (Edward) Clive
August 1803	Lord William Bentinck
May 1807	Sir George Barlow
May 1813	Lt. Gen J. Abercrombie
September 1814	The Right Hon. Hugh Elliot
June 1820	Sir Thomas Munro
October 1827	The Right Hon. S.R. Lushington
October 1832	Sir Frederick Adam

Governors of Bombay

January 1785	Rawson Boddam
January 1788	Sir W. Meadows
January 1790	Sir Robert Abercrombie
November 1792	George Dick
December 1795	Jonathan Duncan
August 1812	Sir Evan Nepean
March 1819	The Hon. Mountstuart Elphinstone
November 1827	Sir John Malcolm
March 1831	The Earl of Clare

2. Horses – 'The Khan'

Horse breeding developed quite separately in India, Europe and Arabia. When the British first came to India, immense numbers and a great variety of local breeds of horse were available to them. The main pure breeds (which still survive) were from Rajastan and Sind, the three chief strains being Marwari, Kathiawadi and Sindhi. In 1800, snobbery in horses rivalled snobbery in cars 200 years later. Senior officers competed with each other to be mounted on the most magnificent animal. But the most sought after breed of all – not only in India but in Europe as well – was the Gulf Arab. The 'Darley Arabian' had been brought back to England by Mr Darley, the British Consul at Aleppo, as early as 1704, but very little was known about Arab horses; hardly any Englishmen had ever been to Arabia.

Malcolm was a fine horseman (despite being six feet five inches tall, and weighing nearly fifteen stone). His mission to Persia and the Arab Gulf had given him the opportunity to learn first-hand about Arab and Persian horses. He did so with enthusiasm, purchasing several stallions and mares and bringing them back to India. He bought most of his horses at Bushire so they were probably Persian Arabs, of Arab blood but used for centuries by the Bakhtiari and Qashgai nomadic tribes. Traversing mountains and contending with the extremes of climate in the Zagros range – heavy snow in winter and scorching heat in summer – had made them more sturdy, with greater stamina than the Gulf or Egyptian Arab. But he would also have come across entirely different breeds: in Tehran, the Turcoman horse of the Qajars from north-east Iran; in Muscat and Baghdad, the Gulf Arab. He had, in fact, bought one horse in Baghdad, and Harford Jones wrote to him about it in April 1802: 'Your horse is at grass, but if he and I live he shall go down to you at the end of May or the beginning of June. He was Ally Pasha, my favourite horse. He is five years old, and the Pasha gave him to me one day when he was seized with an uncommon fit of generosity and graciousness.'[1]

When Malcolm returned to Madras in June 1801 he sent a bay Arab stallion that he had picked up in the Gulf to Arthur Wellesley at Seringapatam. Arthur wrote back that: 'The horse has a fine figure, is bright bay and above 15 hands high. You have not let me know what I am to pay for him. I am well mounted upon Arabs, and I don't intend to ask you for any of your stud.'[2] He left most of his other horses in Madras, but brought several to Calcutta; where he sold two to Henry Wellesley and later a fine Arab stallion, Caliph, to the Marquess for Rs4,000. From then on he was considered an expert, a role that he was only too happy to play. The viceregal set nicknamed him 'The Khan'.[3]

Shortly after arriving at Lucknow in August 1801, Henry Wellesley conceived the idea of starting a horse-breeding stud in the Rohilkund area in the north of

Oudh, newly ceded to the Company. Malcolm enthusiastically took up Henry's case with the Governor-General. Though nervous about how the Directors would react to yet another capital expenditure project, the Marquess eventually succumbed to Malcolm's persistent urging, and gave orders for the stud project to be launched. Envious eyes were later cast on the horses Malcolm had left at Madras. After passing through Madras in March 1803 he wrote to Merrick Shawe from Poona: 'My horses were taken out at Madras and my favourite mare seized by Lord Clive to take to the plains of Salopia [i.e. to Walcot, Lord Clive's property in Shropshire]. Had she proceeded to Calcutta she would not have escaped.'[4]

3. Estimated Population of British India, c.1825–1830

	British India			Bombay Presidency		
	Total	*European*	*Indian*	*Total*	*European*	*Indian*
Military						
King's Army (plus European Regiments in Company Armies)						
Officers	1,342	1,342	0	331	331	0
Other Ranks	32,206	32,206	0	7,277	7,277	0
Total	33,548	33,548	0	7,608	7,608	0
Company (Sepoy) Armies						
Officers	7,356	3678	3,678	1,325	662	663
Other Ranks	183,922	0	183,922	32,463	0	32,463
Total	191,278	3678	187,600	33,788	662	33,126
Total Military (incl. Indian Navy)						
Officers	8,698	5020	3678	1,656	993	663
Other Ranks	216,128	32206	183922	39,740	7,277	32,463
Total	224,826	37226	187600	41,396	8,270	33,126
Civil (EIC servants)	11,083*	1,083	10,000*	1,215*	215	1,000*
Civil (other)	89,244,243	3000*	89,241,243	6,210,235	300*	6,209,935
Grand Total	89,480,152	41,309	89,438,843	6,252,846	8,785	6,244,061

* Rough estimate only

Notes to table opposite

- In c.1825–1830 'British' India comprised roughly the same area as today's India and Bangladesh (i.e. excluding Pakistan and Burma), less the Native States of Hyderabad, Mysore, Malwa, Rajastan, Oudh and Travancore, and the Straits Settlements.
- The 'native' population of British India was about 90 million, with a further 10 million in the Native States.
- The Bombay Presidency population was about 6.5 million.
- Company armies totalled about 220,000 men, with a further 25,000 King's Troops.
- European troops (including King's Army) totalled about 5,500 officers and 55,000 other ranks.
- European civilians totalled about 4,000, of whom only about 1,100 were covenanted Company officials.
- Ratio of army officers to other ranks: 1:25
- Ratio of European to Indian officers in Company armies: 1:1

Sources

Main population figures derived from *GOI*, p. 211
Non-EIC European population derived from *PHI* vol. 2, p. 246

4. Finances of Bombay Territories, 1827/28 to 1831/32 in lakhs (100,000 rupees)

Item	*1827/28*	*1831/32*	*Percentage change*
Civil			
Revenue			
Bombay/Gujerat	47	62	+32%
Deccan	145	142	−2%
Baroda	34	32	−6%
Total	226	236	+4%
Charges			
Bombay/Gujerat[a]	−64	−65	+1%
Deccan	−69	−53	−23%
Baroda	−13	−10	−24%
Total	−146	−128	−12%
Gross surplus (+)/deficit (−)			
Bombay/Gujerat	−17	−3	
Deccan	76	89	
Baroda	21	22	
Total	80	108	+35%
Military (charges)			
Army	−182	−139	−24%
Navy	−19	−15	−21%
Building forts[b]	−13	−7	−46%
Total	−214	−161	−25%
Overall surplus (+)/Deficit (−)	−124	−53	

a. Bombay/Gujerat charges included an element of what today would be called ' corporate' or 'head office' charges relating to Deccan and Baroda activities.
b. These charges were presumably capital expenditure.

Note. The table excludes revenues and charges administered directly by semi-independent chiefs (e.g. Baroda). Thus it understates the overall government revenues and charges of the Bombay territories as a whole.

Glossary, Terminology and Spelling

Glossary of Indian, Anglo-Indian and Persian Words and Phrases

abba	cloak
amir, emir	prince, chief, nobleman
arrack	distilled alcoholic spirit
asafoetida	concreted resinous gum smelling of garlic
bakshi	paymaster
banian	Hindu trader, usually Gujerati
beglerbeg	provincial governor
begum	honorific title for Indian Muslim noblewoman
Bheel, Bhil	Central India tribal group
bhishti	water carrier
bibi	Indian wife or mistress
Brahmin	Hindu priestly caste (the highest)
brinjarrie	dealers and conveyors of grain and salt
catchpole	bailiff
chauth	protection money
coss	measure of distance; roughly 4 km
creese, kris	dagger
crore	ten million
cutcherry	government office
daftar	office
dawk	transport by relays of men and horses
deori, deoli	courtyard house of a noble
dewan, diwan	chief minister
dhobi	laundry, washerman
divan	a book, e.g. of poetry
dubash	interpreter/broker between Indian and foreigner
durbar	court or levee; or camp
dyong-frow	young woman (Dutch)
elchee	envoy
estaqbal	welcome ceremony (Persian)
factory	warehouse/godown; not a manufacturing establishment
farman, firman	written order from a ruler
feringhee, firangi	foreigner, mostly European (i.e. Frank)
gadee, gadi	throne (Marathi)
ghat	escarpment, step
Ghurruz, al	the gist
gildee gildee; jildi jildi	quickly
gomusta	native agent/factor (Persian)
havildar	a sepoy non-commissioned officer, a sergeant
hircarrah (harkarrah)	runner, messenger

hookah	water pipe, hubble-bubble
hooley, holi	Hindu festival, in which participants sprinkle each other with red powdered water
jaghir	estate; assignment of revenues by government
jaghirdar	holder of jaghir land
John Company	East India Company
Id, Idd	Muslim festival, the end of Ramadan, the fasting month
khan	title, 'lord' (Turkish and Pathan)
killadar, qiladar	commandant of a fort
Ksatriya, Kshatriya	Hindu warrior caste
lakh	one hundred thousand
lal bazaar	regimental brothel
maidan	city square (Persian)
maistry, mistry	skilled craftsman
masula, mussoola boat	surf boat made of planks sewn together with coir
mehmandar	meeter and greeter, guide
mir	Muslim title, usually indicating a seyyid
mirza	prince or gentleman (Persian)
Moors	Hindustani language
munshi, munshee	secretary, teacher
musnud	throne
nabob (nawab)	English corruption of nawab; applied to returning EIC officers in the eighteenth century
naseeb, nasib	destiny
nautch	Indian dance performed by female dancers
nawab	Mughal title for ruler of semi-autonomous state
nazarana	'inheritance' tax imposed on adopted heirs of rulers of Native States
nazr, nuzzur	symbolic gift, given to a superior
nizam	viceroy or governor of the Mughal emperors
nullah	dry stream bed
omrah	nobleman
palanquin, palankeen	Indian litter
panchayat	council of (five) village elders
pasha	provincial governor (Turkish)
patel, potail	village headman; also a family name in Gujarat; patil in Maharashtra
pelsoozas (pihsuz)	container holding tallow for a lamp
peshkash	an offering to a superior
peshwah	prime minister; paramount chief of Mahrattas
pettah	village, usually adjoining a fort
pindaris	bands of plunderers
poligar	South Indian subordinate feudal chief
pukka	proper, correct
puisne	judge, inferior in rank to chief justice
pundit, pandit	learned man
rangree	barbarian
rasseldar	subaltern of native cavalry

ryot	Indian peasant
ryotwari	land revenue collected directly by government from village headmen
sangan	confluence (of rivers)
sati, suttee	immolation of widows on husband's funeral pyre
sepahdar	army officer
sepoy	an Indian soldier
seyyid, sayyad	a lineal descendant of the Prophet Mohammed
shenay mamoonee	'monkey business'
Shia	one of the two main divisions of Islam, strongest in Iran and southern Iraq
sirdar	a chief or senior officer
shroff	money-changer, moneylender
silladar horse	irregular cavalry, the riders providing their own horse
sirdar, sardar, sircar, sircar	leader or commander
sirdar adoulat	chief court of appeal in a presidency
soucar	banker
sowar	cavalry escort mounted on a camel
subah	Mughal province
subhadur, soubadar	Indian army officer, roughly equal to captain
sudra	Hindu peasant caste (the lowest)
suftees, softees	promissory notes
Sunni	one of the two main divisions of Islam, strongest in Arabia and worldwide
ta'arof	politeness, flattery
tamasha	commotion
vaisya	Hindu farmer, merchant, artisan caste
vakeel, vakil	emissary
writer	junior civil servant in the East India Company
yaboo	Persian horse (not pedigreed)
zamindar	landholder, paying taxes to government
zenana	harem or women's quarters
zillah	administrative district

Note on Terminology

I have generally used the names which were current in Anglo-Indian circles at the time. For instance Persia rather than Iran, Bombay rather than Mumbai.

I have also retained the use of terms which might today be described as offensive, e.g. 'native'. Such words didn't have the negative connotations that they later acquired. For instance, being described as 'a native' would cause no more offence to an Indian living in Poona than it would to a Scot living in Aberdeen.

Note on Spelling of Indian and Persian Names

Two hundred years ago, writers in English were quite casual about spelling; there was little attempt to standardise the spelling of Indian and Persian proper names and place names.

With quotations I have maintained the original spelling. Elsewhere I have used the spelling of that time rather than the present (e.g. Mahratta rather than Maratha).

Spelling of Some Indian and Persian Place Names – Then and Now

c. 1800 Spelling	c.2000 Spelling
Indian place names	
Ahmedabad	Ahmadabad
Alighur	Aligarh
Amboor	Ambur
Baroda	Vadodara
Barrackpore	Barrackpur
Bharatpoor/Bhurtpoor	Bharatpur
Bimilipatam	Beeminipatnam
Bithur	Bithoor
Bombay	Mumbai
Broach	Bharuch
Burhampur	Burhanpur
Calcutta	Kolkata
Cawnpore	Kanpur
Chumbul river	Chambal river
Cutch	Kachchh
Damam	Daman
Gujerat	Gujarat
Hurryhur	Harihar
Hyderabad	Hyderabad
Indore	Indore
Jumna river	Yamuna river
Kathiawar	Saurashtra

c. 1800 Spelling	c.2000 Spelling
Khairee	Kyree
Khandalla	Khandala
Kirkee	Khadki
Kopal/Copoulee	Koppal
Kotah	Kota
Laswarrie	Laswari
Lucknow	Lucknow
Lunawada	Lunavada
Madras	Chennai
Mahanleh	Mahuli
Mandassor	Mandasaur
Masulipatam	Machilipatnam
Murshedabad	Murshidabad
Muttra	Mathura
Mysore	Mysore, Mysuru
Nerbudda river	Narmada river
Oudh/Oude	Awadh
Oujein	Ujjain
Poona	Pune
Rajputana	Rajasthan
Seringapatam	Srirangapatnam
Sind	Sindh
Tapti river	Tapi river
Trichinopoly	Trirchirappalli
Vizagapatam	Visakhpatnam

Non-Indian place names

Basra	Basra, Basrah
Bisitun	Bisotun
Bushire/Aboushehr	Bushehr
Cosseir	Quseir
Erevan	Yerevan
Isfahan	Esfahan
Kerbela	Karbala
Kharg, Karrack Island	Khark Island
Mocha	Al Mukha
Penang	Pinang
Qishm	Qeshm
Ras al Khaimah	Ras al Khaymah
Sultaneah	Soltaniyah

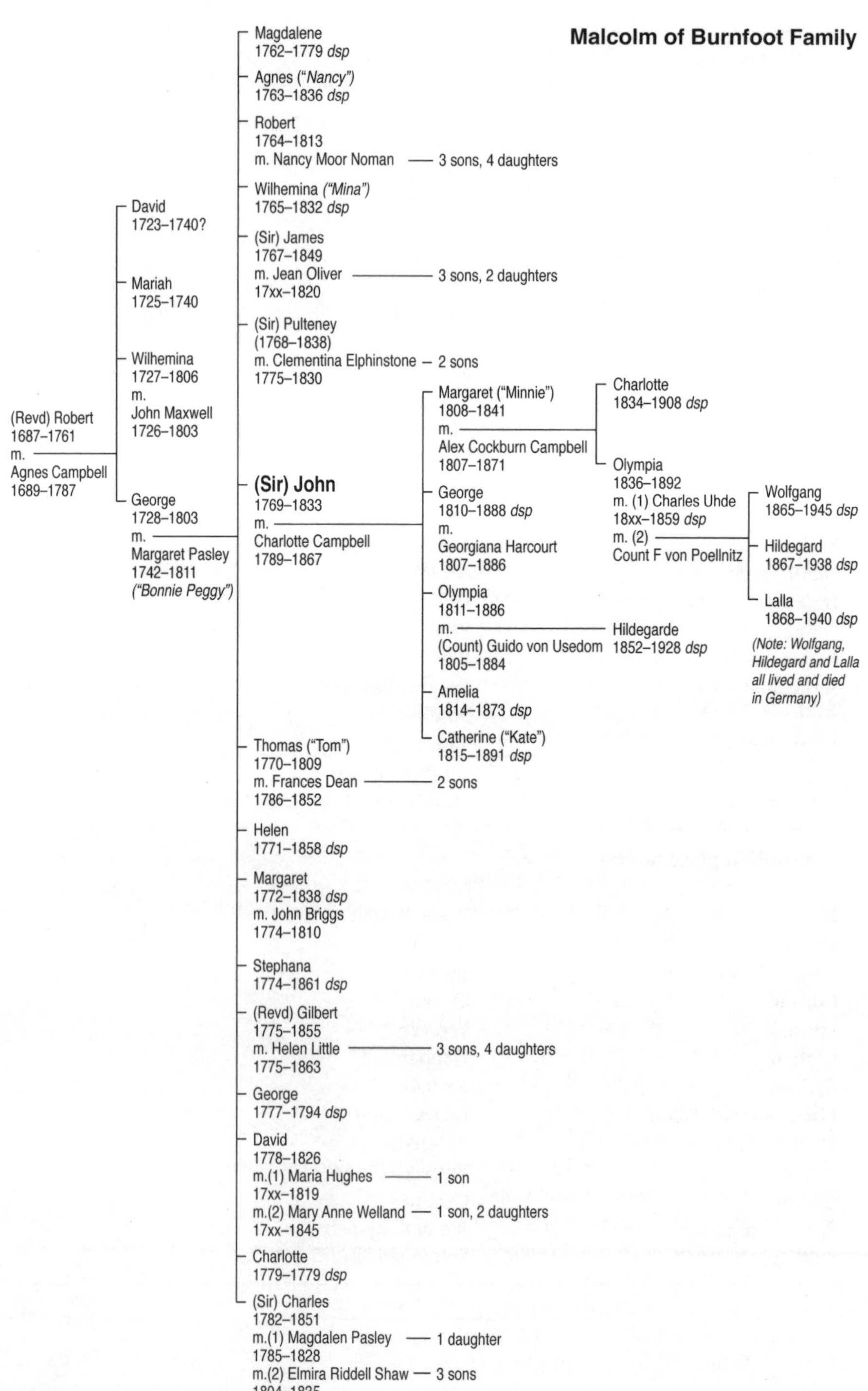
Malcolm of Burnfoot Family
(Revd) Robert
1687–1761
m.
Agnes Campbell
1689–1787
David
1723–1740?
Mariah
1725–1740
Wilhemina
1727–1806
m.
John Maxwell
1726–1803
George
1728–1803
m.
Margaret Pasley
1742–1811
("Bonnie Peggy")
Magdalene
1762–1779 dsp
Agnes ("Nancy")
1763–1836 dsp
Robert
1764–1813
m. Nancy Moor Noman
3 sons, 4 daughters
Wilhemina ("Mina")
1765–1832 dsp
(Sir) James
1767–1849
m. Jean Oliver
17xx–1820
3 sons, 2 daughters
(Sir) Pulteney
(1768–1838)
m. Clementina Elphinstone
1775–1830
2 sons
(Sir) John
1769–1833
m.
Charlotte Campbell
1789–1867
Margaret ("Minnie")
1808–1841
m.
Alex Cockburn Campbell
1807–1871
Charlotte
1834–1908 dsp
Olympia
1836–1892
m. (1) Charles Uhde
18xx–1859 dsp
m. (2)
Count F von Poellnitz
Wolfgang
1865–1945 dsp
Hildegard
1867–1938 dsp
Lalla
1868–1940 dsp
(Note: Wolfgang, Hildegard and Lalla all lived and died in Germany)
George
1810–1888 dsp
m.
Georgiana Harcourt
1807–1886
Olympia
1811–1886
m.
(Count) Guido von Usedom
1805–1884
Hildegarde
1852–1928 dsp
Amelia
1814–1873 dsp
Catherine ("Kate")
1815–1891 dsp
Thomas ("Tom")
1770–1809
m. Frances Dean
1786–1852
2 sons
Helen
1771–1858 dsp
Margaret
1772–1838 dsp
m. John Briggs
1774–1810
Stephana
1774–1861 dsp
(Revd) Gilbert
1775–1855
m. Helen Little
1775–1863
3 sons, 4 daughters
George
1777–1794 dsp
David
1778–1826
m.(1) Maria Hughes
17xx–1819
1 son
m.(2) Mary Anne Welland
17xx–1845
1 son, 2 daughters
Charlotte
1779–1779 dsp
(Sir) Charles
1782–1851
m.(1) Magdalen Pasley
1785–1828
1 daughter
m.(2) Elmira Riddell Shaw
1804–1835
3 sons

Abbreviations

APAC	Asia, Pacific and Africa Collection, British Library
AW	Arthur Wellesley, 1st Duke of Wellington (1769–1852)
AWD	*Dispatches of the Duke of Wellington, 1799–1818* (1834–1838)
AWSD	*Supplementary Despatches of Arthur, Duke of Wellington KG, 1797–1818* (1858–1872)
BL	British Library, London
BRII	Baji Rao II, Peshwah of Poona (1775–1851)
COD	Court of Directors of the EIC
DCM	*Despatches, Correspondence and Memoranda of Arthur, Duke of Wellington KG,1819–1832* (1867–1880)
DNB	*Dictionary of National Biography*, Oxford
EIC	East India Company
GOI	*Government of India* (1833), by SJM
HMMCP	*His Majesty's Mission to the Court of Persia 1807–1811* (1834), by SHJ
HOC	House of Commons, London
HOP	*The History of Persia* (1815), by SJM
IOR	India Office Records, British Library
IOLR	India Office Library and Records, British Library
KPH	Kentchurch Papers, Hereford Record Office
LWB	Lord William Bentinck (1774–1839)
MCI	*A Memoir of Central India* (1823), by SJM
ME	Mountstuart Elphinstone (1775–1859)
NAI	National Archives of India, New Delhi
NLS	National Library of Scotland, Edinburgh
NLW	National Library of Wales, Aberystwyth
OIOC	Oriental and India Office Collection (later APAC), British Library
PHI	*Political History of India* (1826), by SJM
PRO	Public Record Office, Kew
RAS	Royal Asiatic Society, London
RW	Richard, Marquess Wellesley (1760–1842)
RWD	*Despatches, Minutes and Correspondence of the Marquess Wellesley KG* (1840)
SCM	Sir Charles Malcolm (1782–1851)
SHJ	Sir Harford Jones (1764–1847)
SJM	Sir John Malcolm (1769–1833)
SOAS	School of Oriental and African Studies, London University
SOP	*Sketches of Persia* (1811), by SJM
SOS	*Sketch of the Sikhs* by SJM (1812),
SPHI	*Sketch of the Political History of India* (1811) by SJM
SPM	Sir Pulteney Malcolm (1768–1838)
STM	Sir Thomas Munro (1763–1827)
UNPP	University of Nottingham, Portland Papers
UOS	University of Southampton, Hartley Library

Notes

Inroduction

1 Malcolm, John, *Sketch of the Political History of India*, p. 1.
2 Philips, C.H., *The Young Wellington in India*, p. 35.

Chapter 1

1 Coburn, Kathleen (ed.) *Letters of Sara Hutchison*, p. 72.
2 Kaye, J.W., *Life and Correspondence of Major-General Sir John Malcolm* vol. I, p. 5.
3 Wraxall, N.W., *Historical Memoirs of My Own Time*, vol. 3, p. 404.
4 See NLS Acc 10708 and Geddes, Olive, *The Laird's Kitchen*, pp. 71–84.
5 11/12/1795, Bonnie Peggy to Charles Malcolm NLS Acc 6684/27.
6 The kirk was rebuilt in the mid nineteenth century; the school building still exists today, though the school itself was moved across the valley in the early nineteenth century, and was finally closed in the year 2000.
7 Dec 1798, Geotge Malcolm to his children, NLS Acc 6684/27.
8 22/9/1779, George Malcolm to William Pulteney, University of Guelph, Pulteney Papers, no. 1082.
9 6/12/1780, John Johnstone to George Malcolm, Kaye, *Life and Correspondence* vol. I, p. 6.
10 13/7/81, JJ to GM, NLS Acc 6990/6.
11 29/5/81, Sir William Pulteney to John Pasley, NLS Acc 6684/12.
12 11/8/81, JP to Bonnie Peggy, Kaye, *Life and Correspondence* vol. I, p. 7.
13 November 1781, JP to GM, Kaye, *Life and Correspondence* vol. I, p. 8.
14 Kaye, *Life and Correspondence* vol. I, p. 8.

Chapter 2

1 *East India Register of Ships*, p. 96.
2 Dodwell, H., *Nabobs of Madras*, p. 1.
3 Welsh, Colonel James, *Military Reminiscences (1790–1830)* vol. I, p. 5. See also Weller, Jac, *Wellington in India*, p. 29.
4 Welsh, *Military Reminiscences*, vol. I, p. 7.
5 5 July 1783, Mrs Ogilvie to Bonnie Peggy, Kaye, *Life and Correspondence* vol. I, p. 9.
6 Bowring, L.B., *Haider Ali and Tipu Sultan*, p. 99; Dodwell, H.H., *The Nabobs of Madras*, p. 39.
7 Fortescue, Sir John, *History of the British Army*, vol. XI, p. 598.
8 Bowring, *Haider Ali and Tipu Sultan*, p. 91.
9 Wilson, *History of the Madras Army*, vol. 2, pp. 361–362.
10 Roberts, Paul E., *History of British India*, p. 195.

11 *PHI*, p. 40.
12 Callahan, Raymond, *East India Company and Army Reform 1783–1798*, p. 1.
13 Munro, Innes, *Narrative of Operations on the Coromandel Coast*, p. 377.
14 Munro, *Narrative of Operations*, p. 377.
15 Gleig, George R., *Life of Sir Thomas Munro* vol. I, pp. 73–76.
16 Graeme Mercer, quoted in Kaye, *Life and Correspondence* vol. I, p. 20.
17 Quoted in Colebrooke, T.E., *Mountstuart Elphinstone*, vol. II, p. 331.
18 Welsh, *Military Reminiscences*, p. 9.
19 Roberts, *History of British India*, p. 81.
20 26 February 1789, Robert Malcolm to his mother, Kaye, *Life and Correspondence* vol. I, p. 14.
21 Kaye, *Life and Correspondence* vol. I, p. 13.
22 In 1781, the same General Cornwallis, though personally blameless, had suffered the ignominy of surrender at Yorktown in the American War.
23 As could only happen with the (British) Indian Army, that battalion still exists today, in the Pakistan Army. In 1796 it became the 2/11th Madras Native Infantry, in 1824 the 22th Regiment MNI, in 1885 the 22th Madras Infantry, in 1903 the 82nd Punjabis, and finally in 1922 the 5th battalion, 1st Punjab Regiment; and it is still known as 'Dalrymple's battalion'. In 1947, at the time of Partition, the 1st Punjabis were assigned to Pakistan, and the Hindu and Sikh officers and men, who had fought through two world wars beside their Muslim comrades, had to be hastily resettled in India.
24 20 July 1790, SJM to Nancy M., Kaye, *Life and Correspondence* vol. I, p. 15–16.
25 Wilks, Mark *Historical Sketches of South India* vol. III, p. 173.
26 Kaye, *Life and Correspondence* vol. I, p. 14.
27 Mackenzie, Roderick, *War with Tippoo Sultaun*, p. 60.
28 Kaye, *Life and Correspondence* vol. I, p. 15.
29 Kaye, *Life and Correspondence* vol. I, p. 17.
30 28 June 1791, SJM to Sir J. Kennaway, DRO 961M/Add f.73.
31 Kennaway to Binny 27/2/1791, DRO, B961M/Add/B9.
32 n.d., G. Mercer, Kaye, *Life and Correspondence*, vol. I, p. 20.
33 Kaye, *Life and Correspondence*, vol. I, p. 20.
34 Appendix I of Malcolm's *Political History of India*, published in 1826, contains a forty-three page, day-by-day journal of these negotiations, which could only have been written by a participant, almost certainly Malcolm himself.
35 Dirom, Alexander, *A Narrative of the Campaign in India, 1792*, p. 16.
36 ? May 1793 (Kaye says 1792), SJM to family, Kaye, *Life and Correspondence* vol. I, p. 25.
37 Wilkinson, Theon, *Two Monsoons*, p. 3.
38 There was also VD – even Mountstuart Elphinstone once suffered from 'the clap'.
39 SJM to family, c. 1793, Kaye, *Life and Correspondence* vol. I, p. 41.

Chapter 3

1 Kaye, *Life and Correspondence* vol. I, p. 32.
2 14/11/1794, SJM to Colonel Wood, IOR HM 451(2), pp. 243–255.
3 Kaye, *Life and Correspondence* vol. I, p. 35.
4 McLaren, Martha, *British India and British Scotland 1780–1830*, p. 119.

5 22/11/1795, SJM to Gilbert M., Kaye, *Life and Correspondence* vol. I, p. 40.
6 2/1794, SJM to his mother, Kaye, *Life and Correspondence* vol. I, p. 41.
7 28/4/1795, SJM to parents, Kaye, *Life and Correspondence* vol. I, p. 42.
8 14/5/1795, SJM to parents, Kaye, *Life and Correspondence* vol. I, p. 43.
9 12/9/1795, Johnstone to George Malcolm, NLS Acc 6990/6.
10 11/1795, SJM report, OIOC HM 738(1) pp. 1–15 & Kaye, *Life and Correspondence* vol. I, pp. 44–47.
11 10/1795, SJM to Nancy M., Kaye, *Life and Correspondence* vol. I, p. 47.
12 Kaye, *Life and Correspondence* vol. I, p. 54.
13 16/10/1797, SJM to Nancy, Kaye, *Life and Correspondence* vol. I, p. 58.
14 10/1795, SJM to Nancy, Kaye, *Life and Correspondence* vol. I, pp. 47–48.
15 6/2/1796, SJM to his mother, Kaye, *Life and Correspondence* vol. I, p. 49.
16 15/3/1797, SJM to his sister, Kaye, *Life and Correspondence* vol. I, p. 52.
17 *DNB*, vol. H, p. 4.
18 15/3/1797, SJM to his sisters, Kaye *Life and Correspondence* vol. I, p. 53.
19 6/8/1796, SJM to Mina M., Kaye, *Life and Correspondence* vol. I, p. 50.
20 See SPM's report of the exploit, 15/1/1798 NLS Acc 5753.
21 SPM to Mina M., 2 June 1797, NLS Acc 6684/5.
22 15/3/97, SJM to his sister, Kaye, *Life and Correspondence* vol. I, p. 53.
23 Late 1797, SJM to his sisters, NLS Acc 6684/23.
24 15/2/1798, Stephana M. to Nancy M., NLS Acc 6684/23.
25 Dalrymple, William, *White Mughals*, p. 4.
26 Ballhatchet, K., *Race, Sex and Class under the Raj*, p. 2.
27 Ibid., p. 2.
28 2/6/1797, SPM to Mina, NLS Acc 6684/5.
29 15/2/1798, CP to William Pasley, BL Add Mss 41961 f15.
30 16 October 1797, SJM to Nancy, Kaye, *Life and Correspondence* vol. I, p. 57.
31 18 August 1796, SJM to Sir John Kennaway, DRO 961M Add 5/F73.
32 18 January 1797, SJM to SJK DRO 961M/Add5/f73.

Chapter 4

1 29/7/1798, *RWD* vol. I, p. 223.
2 Summarised by Butler, Iris, *The Eldest Brother*, pp. 132–133.
3 6/7/1798, Webbe to Harris, *RWD* vol. I, p. 75.
4 19/4/1798, OIOC Mss Eur F228/85.
5 *SPHI*, p. 225.
6 11/10/1798, *RWD* vol. I, p. 244.
7 April 1798, SJM to Hobart, Kaye, *Life and Correspondence* vol. I, p. 69.
8 OIOC Mss Eur F228/85.
9 The story of Hyderabad and the Kirkpatrick brothers around the turn of the eighteenth century has been marvellously told by William Dalrymple in his book *White Mughals*.
10 14/9/97, JAK to WK, OIOC Mss Eur F228/10, f40.
11 23/8/1798, SPM to Bonnie Peggy, NLS Acc 6684/9.
12 23/9/1798, AW to HW, *AWSD* vol. I, pp. 94–95.
13 2/10/98, AW to SJM, WP 1/1/2, *AWSD* vol. I, p. 117.

14 20/9/1798, RW to SJM, BL Add Mss 13584, f.7.
15 11/10/98, RW to Dundas, *RWD* vol. I, p. 264.
16 1801, ME Journal, OIOC, Mss Eur F88.
17 6/10/1798, JAK to WK, OIOC Mss Eur F228/10, p. 92.
18 Malcolm, *PHI*, I, p. 310.
19 Malcolm, quoted in Kaye, *Life and Correspondence* vol. II, p. 162.
20 ME Journal, 1801, OIOC Mss Eur F88, Box 13/16(b). This building is not to be confused with the new Residency built by Kirkpatrick on the same site in 1803, which survives to this day, and is being restored as a UNESCO project.
21 Various commentators gave different accounts of the numbers in the French Corps, from 11,000 to 16,000, the discrepancies probably being due to the fact that not all of the men were in the Hyderabad cantonments at the time of the action.
22 Kaye, *Life and Correspondence* vol. I, p. 74–75.
23 Kaye, *Life and Correspondence* vol. I, p. 75.
24 *SPHI*, pp. 208–209.
25 Kaye, *Life and Correspondence* vol. II, p. 164.
26 *SPHI*, p. 208–209.
27 22/10/1798, SJM to General Harris, quoted in Lushington, pp. 235–237, and 23/10/1798, Malcolm to Clive, NLW II Corr. 1817.
28 Wilson, *History of the Madras Army* vol. 2, p. 310.
29 22/10/98, JAK to WK, OIOC Mss Eur F228/10 f.112.
30 23/10/1798, JAK to NBE, Kaye, *Life and Correspondence* vol. I, p. 78.
31 23/10/1798, JAK to WK, OIOC Mss Eur F228/10 f.113.
32 8/11/1798, JAK to WK, OIOC Mss Eur F228/10 f.119.
33 Nov. 1798, RW to Hyacinthe, Dropmore Papers vol. IV, p. 384.
34 26/12/98, RW to Dundas, BL Add Mss 13456.
35 November 1798, SJM Memo, *RWD* vol. I, Appendix F.

Chapter 5

1 BL Add Mss 13664, ff.1–59.
2 21/1/1799, SJM to WK, BL 13707, ff.13–14.
3 28/2/99, BL 13664, f.14.
4 22/1/99 BL 13664, f7.
5 14/2/1799, BL 13664, f.19–21.
6 22/2/99, BL 13664, f.23.
7 27/2/1799, BL 13664, f.25.
8 3/3/1799, BL 13664, f.26.
9 Spencer, Alfred (ed.), *The Memoirs of William Hickey (1749–1809)*, vol. IV pp. 190–191.
10 Philips, *The Young Wellington*, p. 25.
11 8/5/1799 AW to RW, UOS, WP/1/14.
12 9/3/99, AW to HW, *AWSD* vol. I, p. 200.
13 Weller's *Wellington in India* and Denys Forrest's *The Tiger of Mysore* probably contain the best descriptions.
14 Kaye, *Life and Correspondence* vol. I, p. 85.
15 4/5/99, BL 13664, f.59.
16 Kaye, *Life and Correspondence* vol. I, p. 86–87.

17 Marshman, J.C., *History of India* vol. II, 1868.
18 4/8/99, JAK to SJM, OIOC Mss Eur F228/53, f.25.

Chapter 6

1 Albeit, as Professor A.K.S. Lambton once remarked, with an 'Indian' accent.
2 22/8/99, SJM to RW, BL 13706, ff 1–19.
3 13/8/99 SPM to Nancy M., NLS Acc 6684/5.
4 10/8/99, SJM to Ross, Kaye, *Life and Correspondence* vol. I, pp. 88–9.
5 10/8/9, SJM to SJK, DRO 961M/Add5/F73.
6 23/8/99, SJM to J. Duncan, Kaye, *Life and Correspondence* vol. I, p. 94.
7 1/9/99, SJM to WK, BL 13707, ff.453–454.
8 Son of Bonnie Peggy's brother, Charles Pasley, the Lisbon wine merchant.
9 See Chapter 3, p. 50.
10 20/7/99, CP to CWP, BL41961, ff.55–56.
11 Son-in-law of Charles Pasley.
12 Love, H.D., *Vestiges of Old Madras* iii, p. 464.
13 Khan, Ghulam Hasan, *Gulzar-i-Asafiya*, pp. 305–315 and Dalrymple, *White Mughals*, pp. 195–196.
14 Dalrymple, *White Mughals*, p. 196, from Shushtari, *Kitub al Alam*.
15 JK to WK, 18/5/00, IO Mss Eur F 228/12, f.42.
16 10/10/99 WK to SJM, BL 13706 ff.71–72 and *RWD* vol. V, pp. 82–90.
17 20/10/99, SJM to WK, Kaye, *Life and Correspondence* vol. I, pp. 99–100.
18 The old city of Susa, in the Khuzestan Province of Persia.
19 17/10/1798, WK to Wrangham, OIOC Mss Eur 228/7, p. 7.
20 Yapp, Malcolm, *Strategies of British India: Britain, Iran and Afghanistan 1798–1850*, p. 24.
21 This *diwan* is now in the British Library, OIOC, Islamic Mss 2768, and contains an inscription in Malcolm's handwriting: 'the Diwan of Chanda, the celebrated Malaka of Hyderabad. This book was presented as a nazr [present] from this extraordinary woman to Captain Malcolm in the midst of a dance in which she was the chief performer on the 18 Oct 1799 at the House of Meer Allaum Bahadur.'
22 A pity, it might have added spice to this story.
23 11/10/99, SJM to RW, BL 13706, ff.20–66.

Chapter 7

1 8/10/1798, RW to Duncan, *RWD* vol. I, p. 286.
2 Duchesse d'Abrantes, *Memoires de la Generale Junot*, pp. 331–332.
3 Amini, Iradj, *Napoleon et la Perse*, p. 53.
4 10/10/1799, WK to SJM, *RWD* vol. V pp. 82–90.
5 300,000 rupees.
6 9/1/1800, SJM to WK, BL 13707, ff.151–156.
7 1/2/1800, SJM to RW, NLW MS4903E, pp. 5–12.
8 Kaye, *Life and Correspondence* vol. I, p. 109n.
9 Wright, Sir Denis, *English Among the Persians*, p. 1.
10 Malcolm, *SOP*, p. 18.

11 *SOP*, p. 22.
12 *SOP*, p. 37.
13 Allegedly – we only have Malcolm's word for this.
14 *SOP*, p. 38.
15 Later Persian envoy to Calcutta – see Chapter 17, p. 46.
16 17/12/1799, SJM to HW, BL 13707, ff.139–140.
17 28/3/1800, SJM to Manesty, BL 13707, ff.223–235,
18 28/4/1800, Manesty to SJM, BL 13707, f.255.
19 *RWD* vol. 1, p. 609.
20 Lorimer, J.G., *Gazetteer of the Persian Gulf, Oman and Central Arabia* vol. I, p. 187.
21 Duncan to MAK, 20/11/1799, IOLR, P381/15, & Wright PAE, p. 19.
22 15/8/1800, SJM to WK, BL 13707, f.335.
23 Kaye, *Life and Correspondence* vol. I, p. 116.
24 Hollingbery Journal, quoted in BL Add Mss 13707, ff.313–324.
25 Milton, John, *Paradise Lost*, Book I, line 710; Hollingbery to WK, 6/6/1800, BL 13707, ff.284–288.
26 This practice, known as *esteqbal* was a normal part of Persian diplomacy.
27 28/6/1800, SJM to NBE, Kaye, *Life and Correspondence* vol. I, p. 122.
28 Kaye, *Life and Correspondence* vol. I, p. 121.
29 Kaye, *Life and Correspondence* vol. I, p. 122.
30 26/7/1800, SJM to NBE, Kaye, *Life and Correspondence* vol. I, p. 123.
31 In 'Persia, a Poem'.
32 17/8/1800, SJM to George Malcolm, NLS Acc 6684/48.
33 Curzon, G.N., *Persia and the Persian Question*, vol. II, pp. 156–7.
34 25/9/1800, SJM to RW, NLW M4903E pp. 445–6.
35 27/9/1800, SJM to John Pasley, NLS Acc 6684/48.
36 *SOP*, p. 199.
37 13/11/1800, SJM to WK, BL 13707, f.424.
38 *SOP*, p. 199–201.
39 Aga Mohamed was a eunuch, castrated as a young man by the Zend ruler.
40 *SOP*, p. 208.
41 ?July 1810, Dr Andrew Jukes to Sir James Mackintosh in Bombay, quoted in Mackintosh, R.J., *Memoir of the Life of the Rt Hon. Sir James Mackintosh* vol. II, p. 48.
42 *SOP*, pp. 209–211.
43 *SOP*, p. 212.
44 *SOP*, p. 213.
45 IOLR G/29/21, quoted by Ingram, Edward, *In Defence of British India 1775–1842*, p. 87.
46 Maister and Fawcett to Duncan, 17/12/1799, Maharashtra State Archives, Bombay; quoted in Kelly, J.B., p. 70.
47 5/5/1800, SJM to RW, NLW MS4903E p. 212.
48 10/10/1800, SHJ to SJM, HRO Item 8381.
49 27/4–14/6/1800, SJM to RW (several letters), NLW 4903E.
50 Kaye, *Life and Correspondence* vol. I, p. 521.
51 *SOP*, p. 223.
52 23/3/1801, SJM to Elgin, NLS 11715.
53 Lord Macartney's much more lavish mission to China in 1792 had achieved practically nothing.
54 Waring, E.S., *A Tour to Sheeraz*, pp. 12–13.

Chapter 8

1 From now on Richard Wellesley, Lord Mornington, will be called 'the Marquess', to distinguish him from his brothers Arthur and Henry.
2 28/4/1800, Butler, J.R.M., *The Passing of the Great Reform Bill*, p. 217, from Carver papers.
3 June 1801, SPM to Stephana, NLS Acc 6684/5.
4 13/6/1801, AW to SJM, *AWD* vol. II, p. 442.
5 n.d. 1801, GM to SJM, Kaye, *Life and Correspondence* vol. I, p. 157.
6 No copy survives, but considering that it contained Malcolm's daily outpourings over about seventeen months, it must have been an enormous document.
7 31/7/1801, NLW, MS4903E, p. 595.
8 28/9/01, RW to SC, Kaye, *Life and Correspondence* vol. I, p. 159.
9 Pearce, R.R., *Memoirs & Correspondence of Richard, Marquis Wellesley* vol. II, pp. 156–7.
10 His niece, Isabella, married the writer W.M. Thackeray, who is said to have used Shawe as the model for Major Pendennis in the novel *Vanity Fair*.
11 14/9/01, BL OIOC Mss Eur J 793, pp. 317–336.
12 In early 1805, the Marquess appointed Colebrooke Professor of Hindu law and Sanskrit at the College of Fort William. He and Malcolm became friends and when Malcolm returned from the Punjab to Calcutta in 1806, he stayed at Colebrooke's house. In 1823, when Colebrooke founded the Royal Asiatic Society in London, Malcolm became one of its three founding Vice-Presidents.
13 19/12/01, SJM to SGB, Kaye, *Life and Correspondence* vol. I, p. 162.
14 Malcolm's Journal, quoted in Kaye, *Life and Correspondence* vol. I, p. 170.

Chapter 9

1 23/5/1800, OIOC Mss Eur F228/83, f.2.
2 Khan, *Gulzar-i-Asafiya*, pp. 305–315, and Dalrymple, *White Mughals*, p. 206–207.
3 26/9/1800, AW to RW, *AWSD*, vol. II, p. 179.
4 11/10/01, SJM to WK, OIOC Mss Eur F228/18, ff.55–61.
5 19/10/1801, SJM to WK, OIOC Mss Eur F228/18, ff.11–13.
6 11/10/01, SJM to WK, OIOC Mss Eur F228/18, ff.55–61.
7 7/10/1801, RW to WK, BL Add Mss 37282, p. 279.
8 8/11/1801, OIOC IOR HM 464(2), pp. 349–355, & HM 464 (11), pp. 357–393.
9 7/11/1801, SJM to JAK, OIOC Mss Eur F228/13, f.266.
10 11/6/1803, JAK to WK, OIOC Mss Eur F228/59, f.1.
11 16/8/1803, JAK to Petrie, OIOC Mss Eur F228/59, f.6–7.

Chapter 10

1 See Chapter 11.
2 9/2/1802, Kaye, *Life and Correspondence* vol. I, p. 175.
3 26/5/1802, SJM to HW, OIOC Mss Eur J 793, pp. 147–149.
4 June 1804, Mackintosh to Sharp, Pearce, vol. II, 283 n.

5 25/4/1802, MS to HW, OIOC Mss Eur J 793 pp. 517–520.
6 August 1802, SJM to Hobart, Kaye, *Life and Correspondence* vol. I, p. 179.
7 31/8/1802, MS to HW, OIOC Mss Eur J 793, pp. 591–595.
8 21/9/1802, SJM to MS, BL 13746, ff.17–18.
9 c.10/10/1802, SJM to Lady Clive, Kaye, *Life and Correspondence* vol. I, pp. 181–182.
10 c.10/10/1802, SJM to Lady Clive, Kaye, *Life and Correspondence* vol. I, p. 183.
11 c.10/10/1802, SJM to Lady Clive, Kaye, *Life and Correspondence* vol. I, pp. 185–188.
12 Mehdi Ali Khan to Duncan, 12/10/1802, OIOC P382/10, quoted in Wright, p. 29.
13 13/10/1802, Kaye, *Life and Correspondence* vol. I, pp. 189–190.
14 11/12/1802, AW to SJM, *AWSD* vol. III, pp. 460–461.
15 Curzon, *British Government in India*, vol. I, p. 43.
16 Valentia, Viscount, *Travels in India 1802–06* vol. I, pp. 61–62.
17 10/10/1801, AW to HW, Brett James, p. 62.
18 9/2/1803, SJM to HW, OIOC Mss Eur J793, pp. 713–719.
19 9/2/1803, SJM to RW, *RWD* vol. V, p. 425.

Chapter 11

1 December 1799, Ingram, Edward, *Two Views of British India, 1798–1801*, pp. 200–201.
2 *RWD* vol. II, p. 359.
3 Marshman, *History of India* vol. II, p.54.

Chapter 12

1 Not to be confused with Jean-Pierre Piron, the French (Alsatian) mercenary officer at Hyderabad in 1798.
2 2/2/1803, RW to Clive, *RWD* vol. I, p. 405.
3 7/3/1803, Clive to Stuart, *RWD* vol. I, p. 419.
4 12/3/1803, Stuart to Clive, *RWD* vol. I, p. 430.
5 From the Coast Army, under Arthur Wellesley.
6 A river in south Mahratta country.
7 16/2/1803, SJM to Hobart, Kaye, *Life and Correspondence* vol. I, p. 206–207.
8 7/3/1803, SJM to NBE, Kaye, *Life and Correspondence* vol. I, p. 210.
9 19/3/1803, *AWSD* vol. XIII, p. 440.
10 This force was commanded, until he fell ill, by Colonel Alexander Campbell of the 74th Foot who was later destined to become Malcolm's father-in-law.
11 Weller, p. 137.
12 3/4/1803, SJM to Clive, *AWD* vol. I, p. 462.
13 15/4/1803, AW to Stuart, *AWD* vol. I, p. 499.
14 21/4/1803, AW to Stuart, *AWD* vol. I, p. 513.
15 24/4/1803, SJM to Clive, *AWD* vol. I, p. 514.
16 27/4/1803, Close to AW, WP 1/48.
17 30/4/1803, Close to AW, WP3/3/45, p. 124, WP 1/48.
18 24/3/1803, SJM to Stuart, Kaye, *Life and Correspondence* vol. I, p. 213–214.
19 10/5/1803, AW to Stuart, *AWD* vol. I, p. 557.
20 22/5/1803, SJM to RW, Kaye, *Life and Correspondence* vol. I, p. 220.

21 18/6/1803, SJM to AW, WP 3/3/70.

22 20/6/1803, AW to SJM, WP 308/15, *AWD* vol. II, p. 20. This letter contains a little PS: 'Buy for me before you leave Poonah blue cotton cloth to make six pair of pantaloons'; and another PS in a further letter: 'The cloth I got from Poonah is very bad. I wish you would send me some superfine Broad (not Lady's) scarlet cloth; and some Lady's cloth, or some blue [illegible] for trousers' (15/9/1803, AW to SJM, WP MS 308/22, *AWD* vol. II, pp. 303–304). The traditional relationship between Poona tailors and British Army officers goes back a long way.

23 11/6/1803, AW to SJM, *AWSD* vol. XIII, p. 131.

24 23/6/1803, AW to Close, WP 3/3/70.

25 30/6/1803, SJM to RW, WP 3/3/70, f.11–17 & BL Add Mss 13746, ff.196–204.

26 4–8/7/1803, SJM to Close, Kaye, *Life and Correspondence* vol. I, p. 224n.

27 Fifteen years later that figure of seven lakhs was to become a crucial issue in negotiations with Baji Rao – see Chapter 26.

28 26/6/03, RW to AW, *AWD* vol. II, pp. 49–53.

29 6/8/1803, AW to DRS, *AWD* vol. II, p. 178.

30 15/7/1803, MS to SJM, Kaye, *Life and Correspondence* vol. I, p. 225.

31 6/8/1803, SJM to MS, BL Add Mss 13746 f.458; Kaye, *Life and Correspondence* vol. I, pp. 227–228.

32 12/8/1803, SJM to ME, BL Add Mss 13746, p. 494.

33 7/9/1803, SJM to AW, WP 3/3/70 f.1, p. 41.

34 Diomed, Wellesley's favourite grey charger, was lost at Assaye. But four months later, Malcolm, writing from Scindiah's camp at Burhampur (about sixty miles from Assaye), reported that 'I was this morning astonished at the sight of old Diomed, whom you lost at Assye. I, however, concealed my pleasure till by hard bargaining I had got him in my stable for 250 rupees. The fellow gave me your Gibson's bit into the bargain. The old horse is in sad condition, but he shall be treated like a prince till I have the pleasure of restoring him to you.' (SJM to AW, 3/2/1804, BL Add Mss 13747 f.42.) Wellesley's response was as cool as Malcolm's had been warm: 'I am much obliged to you for the pains you have taken to recover my horse. I had always understood that he was killed.' (11/2/1804, AW to SJM, D vol. III, p. 64.)

35 26/9/1803, AW to SJM, *AWSD* vol. IV, p. 160.

36 28/9/1803, AW to SJM, *AWD* vol. II, p. 353.

37 October 1803, SJM to HW, Kaye, *Life and Correspondence* vol. I, p. 233.

38 15/12/1803, AW to SJM, *AWSD* xiii, p. 202.

Chapter 13

1 15/12/1803 Kaye, *Life and Correspondence* vol. I, p. 238.

2 Poona Residency Correspondence ii, p. 541.

3 18/12/1803, ME to Strachey, Colebrooke, *Mountstuart Elphinstone* vol. I, p. 107.

4 Welsh, *Military Reminiscences*, vol. I, p. 200.

5 Since Gwalior and Gohad were situated *south* of the imaginary east-west line mentioned above, this was confusing, and was to cause endless trouble later.

6 27/6/1803, *RWD* vol. III, p. 153.

7 There was an ulterior motive in this. A war *started* by the Company would have

been contrary to various Acts of the British Parliament regulating the Company's behaviour.

8 23/12/1803, Welsh, *Military Reminiscences*, p. 200.

9 Many years later, when Malcolm was visiting Wellesley (by then Duke of Wellington) in Paris, shortly after the Battle of Waterloo, he asked Wellington about Talleyrand, reputedly the craftiest statesman in Europe. 'A good deal like Old Brag', was the reply, 'but not so clever'.

10 25/12/03, SJM to MS, BL Add Mss 13602, p. 903.

11 21/1/1804, AW to RW, *AWD* vol. II, pp. 701.

12 18/1/1804, SJM to AW, WP3/3/70, p. 179.

13 20/2/1804, SJM to AW, Kaye, *Life and Correspondence* vol. I, p. 250.

14 11/12/1803, RW to AW, *RWD* vol. III, p. 497.

15 28/2/1804, SJM to AW, WP 3/3/70, f.339.

16 11/2/1804, AW to SJM, *AWD* vol. III, p. 64.

17 17/3/1804, AW to SJM, *AWD* vol. III, p. 155.

18 22/3/1804, MS to SJM, BL Add Mss 13602, f.79.

19 22/2/1804, SJM to AW, PRC, vol. X no. 97, p. 97.

20 7/1/1804, AW to SJM, *AWD* vol. III, p. 634.

21 2/2/1804, SJM to MS, BL Add Mss 13747, f.82.

22 17/3/1804, AW to SJM, *AWD* vol. III, p. 155.

23 22/3/1804, SJM to AW, WP 3/3/72.

24 4/4/1804, MS to JM, BL Add Mss 13602, f.88.

25 8/4/1804, NBE to SJM, *RWD* vol. IV, p. 236.

26 25/4/1804, SJM to AW, WP 3/3/72 & *AWSD* vol. XIII, p. 241.

27 28/4/1804, SJM to Kavel Nyn, WP 3/3/72.

28 4/4/1804, JM to MS, BL Add Mss 13747, f.182–183.

29 Kaye, *Life and Correspondence* vol. I, p. 276.

30 30/4/1804, RW to Resident, *RWD* vol. IV, pp. 59–63.

31 1/5/1804, MS to SJM, BL 13602, f.120.

32 20/5/1804, SJM to MS, BL 13747, f.276.

33 16/4/1804, MS to SJM, BL13602, f.90.

34 20/5/1804, AW to DRS, *AWD* vol. III, p. 303–306.

35 22/5/1804, AW to SJM, *AWD* vol. III, p. 299.

36 AW to HW, 13/5/1804, *AWSD* vol. IV, p. 383–386.

37 30/5/1804, SJM to AW, WP 3/3/72.

38 29/5, 6/6, 9/6/1804, AW to SJM, WP MS 308.

39 14/6/1804, Kaye, *Life and Correspondence* vol. I, pp. 280–284.

40 24/7/1804, SJM to MS, BL 13747 p. 286.

Chapter 14

1 2/11/1804, SJM to Webbe, Kaye, *Life and Correspondence* vol. I, p. 295.

2 SPM to his Burnfoot sisters, 1803, NLS Acc 6684/5 &6684/9.

3 2/11/1804, SJM to Webbe, Kaye, *Life and Correspondence* vol. I, p. 294–296.

4 In 1862 their granddaughter Eliza married her second cousin, Charles Roberts, a grandson of Sir Charles Malcolm, in Bombay.

5 See Appendix 2.

6 20/10/2004, BL 13592/ NLS Mss 11717, pp. 1–131.
7 20/10/1804, Mss NLS 11719.
8 7/1/1804, AW to JM, *AWD* vol. I, pp. 635, 641.
9 1/2/1804, JRH to AW, WP 3/3/70, pp. 315–318.
10 4/3/1804, JRH to Lake, WP 3/3/70, pp. 530–531.
11 4/9/1804, SJM to AW, WP 3/3/72.
12 He wrote four letters to Malcolm between late August and late October 1804, parts of which were deliberately destroyed half a century later by the second Duke of Wellington, with the consent of Malcolm's son. They presumably contained some embarrassing material.
13 14/9/1804, AW to SJM, WP MS308/97.
14 24/11/1804, AW to MS, *AWD* vol. III, p. 555.
15 Stanhope, p. 58.
16 Stanhope, p. 49.
17 For a fine description of some of these buildings, see Mark Bence Jones, *Palaces of the Raj*, 1973.
18 4/1/1805, AW to SJM, *AWD* vol. III, p. 593.
19 3/2/1805, AW to MS, *AWD* vol. III, p. 642.
20 20/2/1805, AW to SJM, *AWSD* vol. IV, p. 493.
21 3/7/1805, AW to SJM, *AWSD* vol. IV, p. 509.
22 20/6/1807, SJM to AW, WP1/170.
23 SJM to RW, 25/12/1804, BL Add Mss 13747, p. 356.
24 *DNB*, p. 215.
25 Undated, Leyden to W. Erskine.
26 Leyden to his father, quoted in Reid, John, *Life of John Leyden*.
27 Nov 1811, SJM tribute to Leyden in *Bombay Courier*, NLS Mss 9848, f.33.
28 25/1/1805, SJM to RW, BL 13747 f.364.
29 Philips, C.H., *The East India Company 1784–1834*, pp. 120–124.
30 Butler, *The Eldest Brother*, p. 352.
31 31/12/1805, AW to RW, Butler, Iris, *The Eldest Brother*, p. 351.
32 2/5/1805, SJM to MS, BL Add Mss 13747, p. 392.
33 3/6/1805, SJM to MS, BL Add Mss 13747, p. 424.
34 6/8/1805, SJM to RW, Kaye, *Life and Correspondence* vol. I, p. 325.
35 *Memoirs of William Hickey*, vol. IV p. 318.

Chapter 15

1 Kaye, *Life and Correspondence* vol. I, p. 343.
2 1/6/05, Metcalfe to Sherer, quoted in Thompson, E.J., *Charles, Lord Metcalfe*, p. 55.
3 4/8/1805, Cornwallis to Lake, in Ross, Charles, *Correspondence of Charles, 1st Marquis Cornwallis* vol. III, p. 535.
4 14/8/1805, Cornwallis to SJM, BL Add Mss 13605, ff.177–180.
5 1/9/1805, SJM to Cornwallis, IOLR, HM738(1), pp. 23–25.
6 15/9/1805, SJM to RW, BL Add Mss 12748, f.24.
7 n.d., Close to SJM, *PHI*, vol. I, p. 384.
8 19/9/1805, SJM to NBE, Kaye, *Life and Correspondence* vol. I, pp. 337–338.
9 6/10/1805, SJM to NBE, Kaye, *Life and Correspondence* vol. I, p. 339.

10 *Memoirs of William Hickey*, vol. IV, p. 322.
11 Thorn, Major William, *Memoirs of the War in India*, pp. 473–475 passim.
12 20/9/1805, SJM to Edmonstone, FSC 48, 20/10/1806.
13 The Treaty of Surji Anjangaon of 30 December 1803.
14 5/12/1805, Lake to Barlow, BL Add Mss 13605, ff.205–220.
15 Thorn, *Memoirs*, p. 480.
16 November 1805, SJM to NBE, Kaye, *Life and Correspondence* vol. I, p. 349.
17 20/11/1805, Barlow to Lake, OIOC, FSP no. 80.
18 Thorn, *Memoirs*, p. 494.
19 The Hyphases of Alexander the Great's time.
20 Thorn, *Memoirs*, p. 495.
21 Thorn, *Memoirs*, p. 494.
22 26/1/06, Metcalfe to Sherer, in Thompson, *Metcalfe*, p. 58. The author was unable to locate a portrait of Jaswunt Rao Holkar. He may have been a reluctant sitter – he was called '*Kana bada mardana*' ('squint-eyed, a great brave warrior').
23 Thorn, *Memoirs*, pp. 497–8.
24 22/2/1806, Lake to SGB, FSC no. 6 of 13/3/1806.
25 14/12/1805, SGB to Lake, FSC no. 12, 16/1/1806.
26 4/4/06, NBE to SJM, Kaye, *Life and Correspondence* vol. I, p. 359.
27 17/4/06, SJM to NBE, Kaye, *Life and Correspondence* vol. I, p. 360–362.
28 August 1806, SJM to RW, Kaye, *Life and Correspondence* vol. I, p. 368.
29 18/9/06, SJM to LWB, UNPP PwJb 32/66.
30 15/3/1810, E. Frederick Journal, OIOC Mss Eur K203.
31 17/8/08, SJM to Charlotte, NLS, Malcolm of Burnfoot papers, unnumbered.
32 August 1806, SJM to RW, Kaye, *Life and Correspondence* vol. I, p. 368.
33 *SOS*, p. 5.

Chapter 16

1 August 1806, SJM to RW, Kaye, *Life and Correspondence* vol. I, p. 368.
2 15/10/07, AW to SJM, *AWSD*, vol. XIII, p. 288.
3 8/2/1807, SJM to Lake, Kaye, *Life and Correspondence* vol. I, p. 379.
4 23/2/07, AW to SJM, *AWSD*, vol. IV p. 590.
5 15/10/07, AW to SJM, *AWSD*, vol. XIII, p. 288.
6 See Dalrymple, *White Mughals*.
7 Kaye, *Life and Correspondence* vol. I, p. 386–7.
8 See Chapter 5, p. 87.
9 Kaye, *Life and Correspondence* vol. II, p. 13.
10 6/5/1807 and 27/5/1807, SJM to NBE, Kaye, *Life and Correspondence* vol. I, p. 382–383.
11 May 1807, Campbell to SJM, Kaye, *Life and Correspondence* vol. I, p. 388.
12 1/6/07, SJM to JL NLS, Mss 3380, f.86.
13 18/6/07, SJM to LWB, UNPP PwJb 32/68.
14 See Chapter 14, p. 205.
15 20/6/07, SJM to AW, WP 1/170.
16 25/2/08, AW to SJM, *AWSD* vol. XIII, pp. 289–290.
17 It was a modest building; the grand edifice being built by the Rajah for the Resident was not completed until the following year. It still stands today, as a

Government VIP Guest House. It has a plaque reading 'This house was occupied by Sir John Malcolm when Resident in Mysore 1803–1807'.

18 30/12/06, W. Hastings to D'Oyley, BL Add Mss 29181, ff.371–374.
19 20/2/08, Mackintosh to Whishaw, NLS 2521, f.135.
20 *Memoirs of William Hickey*, vol. IV, p. 363.
21 28/6/07, SJM to Elliot, NLS Ms 11312, ff.2–9.
22 8/7/07, Minto to SJM, NLS Mss 11282, f.173–175.
23 26/7/07, SJM to Minto, NLS Mss 11312, ff.30–41.
24 6 & 27/5/1807, SJM to Edmonstone, Kaye, *Life and Correspondence* vol. I, pp. 382–383; 13/8/07, SJM to Minto NLS Mss 11715, ff. 2–5.
25 24/11/1807, SJM to Minto, NLS Mss 11715, ff. 50–58.
26 10/10/07, Little to his mother, private collection.
27 2/8/07, SJM to STM, OIOC Mss Eur F151/2.
28 6/6/1808, Charlotte M. to Minto, NLS Mss 11148, f.58.

Chapter 17

1 Ingram, *In Defence of British India*.
2 Heroic attempts have been made, most notably by Professor Savory (*Journal of Iranian Studies*, vol. X, 1972), and Iradj Amini (*Napoleon et la Perse*, 1997 and *Iran* vol. 37, 1999).
3 See Chapter 10.
4 12/10/1805, Mirza Bezorg to SHJ, PRO FO 60/1, ff.13–16.
5 7/1/1807, SHJ to FO (Castlereagh?) PRO FO 60/1 ff.1–8.
6 *HMMCP*, p. 8.
7 28/8/1807, PRO FO 60/1, ff.53–54.
8 26/7/1807, SJM to Minto, NLS Mss 11312, ff.30–41.
9 10/11/1807, Minto to Castlereagh, Minto, pp. 52–54.
10 30/1/1808, Minto to SJM, NLS Mss 11283, ff.195–200.
11 See Chapter 16.
12 23/2/1808, SJM to RW, BL Add Mss 13748.
13 1/3/1808, SJM to LWB, PP PwJb 638/1.
14 Early March 1808, SJM to AW, Kaye, *Life and Correspondence* vol. I, pp. 405–406.
15 7/3/1808, NBE to SJM, IOLR P/BEN/SEC/205/10.
16 9/3/1808, Minto to SJM, NLS 11284 f.30.
17 Savory, *Journal of Iranian Studies*, p. 33.
18 14/4/1808. Pellew to Minto, NLS Mss 11315 f.46.
19 In 1808 SJM was a 'substantive' Lieutenant-Colonel, but was given the 'brevet' rank of Brigadier-General when leading the Mission to Persia. On his return he reverted to Lieutenant-Colonel, but his (extended) family continued to refer to him as 'the General'. He only achieved the substantive rank of Major General in 1819.
20 28/4/1808, SHJ to Minto, PRO FO 60/1 ff.82–85.
21 28/4/1808, SHJ to Minto, PRO FO 60/1 ff.82–84.
22 30/4/1808, SHJ to Canning, PRO FO 60/1 ff.78–80, no. 3 of 1808.
23 11/3/1808, Minto to SJM, NLS Mss 11284 f30.
24 28/4/1808, SHJ to Minto, PRO FO 60/1 f.84.
25 May-August 1808, SJM to Charlotte, NLS Malcolm Papers.

26 15/4/1808, SJM to Minto, NLS 11312, ff.98–115.
27 18/5/1808, SJM to Persian Ministers, BL 37285, ff.150–167.
28 11–12/6/1808, SJM to Charlotte, NLS Malcolm of Burnfoot Papers.
29 21/6/1808, SJM to Charlotte, NLS Malcolm Papers.
30 25/6/1808, SJM to Charlotte, NLS, Malcolm Papers.
31 27 June 1808, SJM to Charlotte, NLS Malcolm Papers.
32 4/7/1808, SJM to Charlotte, NLS Malcolm Papers.
33 See Chapter 7, pp. 118–120.
34 20/7/1808, SJM to Charlotte, NLS Malcolm Papers.
35 13/5/1808, SHJ to SJM, PRO FO 60/1, ff.99–102.
36 17/5/1808, Mackintosh to SJM, OIOC HM 736 ff.135–145.
37 12/8/1808, Minto to Sir Harford James, KPH 8556, no. 6.
38 22/8/1808, SJM to Charlotte, Kaye, *Life and Correspondence* vol. I, p. 27.
39 22/8/1808, Minto to SHJ, KPH 8557 no. 7.
40 29/8/1808, Minto to SHJ, KPH 8558 no. 8.
41 25/9/1808, SJM to Minto, OIOC, Mss Eur D1086/1.
42 30/9/1808, Minto to SJM, NLS 11284, ff.198–201.
43 13/10/1808, SJM to Charlotte, Kaye, *Life and Correspondence* vol. I, p. 443–444.
44 15/10/1808, SHJ to Minto, KPH 8459; also PRO FO 60/1 ff.113–114.
45 28/4/1808, SHJ to Minto, PRO DO 60/1, f.84.
46 7/1/1809, SJM to Col Bannerman, NLS acc 6990/16.
47 See note 19 above.
48 17/1/1809, Jean Briggs to C.W. Pasley, BL Add Mss 41962, f.120.
49 Erskine continued to act as secretary of the Literary Society of Bombay until he left India in 1823.
50 20/2/1809, SJM to Leyden, NLS Mss 3380 f.111.
51 8/2/1809, CP to SJM, NLS Mss 11716 ff.66–73.
52 9/3/1809, SJM to Minto, NLS Mss 11716.

Chapter 18

1 Maitland married William Erskine, who was visiting Madras on his way back to Bombay from a trip to Calcutta, on 27 September 1809.
2 November 1807, SJM to Elliot, NLS, Mss M184, ff.
3 11/2/1809, SJM to Barclay, NLS Mss 11661, f.108.
4 18/4/1809, SJM to RW, BL Add Mss 37285 171–172.
5 3/6/1809, SJM to Minto, ODMA, pp. 71–76.
6 12/6/1809, SJM to Minto, NLS Mss 11655, ff.4–5.
7 15/6/1809, SJM to Elliot, NLS Mss 11655 ff.25–28.
8 22/6/1809, SJM to Barclay, NLS Mss 11667 f.63.
9 Kaye, *Life and Correspondence* vol. I, p. 475.
10 12/7/1809, Barclay to SJM, NLS 11647, f.245.
11 15/7/1809, Sir George Barlow to Minto, NLS 11647 ff.263–274.
12 Cardew, Sir Alexander, *The White Mutiny*, p. 44.
13 10/9/1809, SGB to Secret Committee, NLS Mss 11665 ff.11–16 and ff.132–135.
14 10/2/1810, SJM to Charlotte, Kaye, *Life and Correspondence* vol. II, p. 3.

Chapter 19

1 14/7/1809, Minto to SJM, Kaye, *Life and Correspondence* vol. I, pp. 507–510.
2 26/10/1809, Minto to SHJ, PRO FO 60/3 ff.101–102.
3 17/5/1809, J. Briggs to SJM, NLS Mss 11313, ff.6–15. Since Briggs was considered a 'Malcolmite' this letter might appear to have exaggerated Jones's bad behaviour; yet the story of the kicking down of the shades etc was retold with pride by Jones himself, twenty-five years later, in his book (*His Majesty's Mission to the Court of Persia 1807–11*, pp. 196–197), claiming furthermore that he actually grabbed Mirza Shafee and 'pushed him with a slight degree of firmness against the wall which was behind him'.
4 17/5/1809, Briggs to SJM, NLS Mss 11313 pp. 6–15.
5 30/1/1809, Minto to Fath Ali Shah, NLS Mss 11579 ff.22–25.
6 Jones, *HMMCP* 1807–11, p. 209.
7 20/7/1809 Minto to FAS, NLS Mss 11579 ff.62–67.
8 4/5/1809, SHJ to Grant, OIOC L/PS/9/7.
9 6/11/1809, Bathurst to SHJ, PRO FO 60/2 f.1.
10 30/10/1809, SHJ to Secret Committee, KPH 8895.
11 1/1/1810, SHJ to Minto, PRO FO 60/3 ff.34–49
12 30/1/1810, SHJ to Minto, copy to Bathurst, PRO FO 60/3 f.66.
13 30/1/1810, Fath Ali Shah to Minto, PRO FO 60/3.
14 7/1/1810, SJM to RW, BL Add Mss 13748 f.80–83.
15 9/1/1810, J. Little to his father, Little Papers (private collection).
16 Pottinger, Henry, *Travels in Beloochistan and Sinde*, p. 1.
17 27/6/1810, Pottinger, *Travels*, pp. 242–243.
18 There were still virtually no roads in the late 1960s.
19 Meaning, in Farsi, 'Mr No-thing' – the Persians pronounced Jones 'Jins'.
20 26/3/1810, Jukes to SJM, IOLR HM 733, ff.171–182.
21 28/3/1810, Jukes to SJM, IOLR HM 733 ff.155–162.
22 17/5/1809, Briggs to SJM , NLS Mss 11313.
23 9/4/1810, SJM to Persian ministers, PRO FO 60/3 ff.166–172.
24 16/2/1810, SJM to SHJ, KPH 8598.
25 26/4/1810, Rich to SJM, OIOC, Mss Eur K207/4.
26 6–7 May 1810, SJM Journal, Kaye, *Life and Correspondence* vol. II, pp. 10–11.
27 16/5/1810, Frederick Journal, OIOC, Mss Eur K207, p. 77.
28 10/6/1810, SJM Journal, Kaye, *Life and Correspondence* vol. II, pp. 13–14.
29 8/6/1810, SJM to Minto, NLS Mss 11717 ff.92–99.
30 15/6/1810 SHJ to SJM, OIOC IOLR HM733(5) p. 201.
31 16/8/1818, Ker Porter, vol. I, p. 378–9.
32 26/3/1810, SHJ to Grant (EIC), PRO FO 60/3, f.99.
33 26/3/1810, SHJ to Charles Grant, PRO FO 60/3 f.99 & ff.109–112.
34 19/6/1810, SHJ to SJM, PRO FO 60/3 ff.184–193.
35 20/6/1810, SJM to SHJ, PRO FO 60/3 ff.194–197.
36 An author who later published a celebrated travelogue, *Journal of a Residence in India*.
37 30/8/1810, Mackintosh to Maria Graham, BL Add Mss 78766.
38 *HMMCP*, p. 361.
39 23/6/1810, Kaye, *Life and Correspondence* vol. II, p. 25.

40 Rustum has been immortalised for English readers in Matthew Arnold's 'Sohrab and Rustum'. Incidentally, Arnold based his poem on the Sohrab and Rustum story in Sir John Malcolm's *History of Persia* (1815). This was taken from a seventeenth-century Bengali recension (containing mistakes) rather than from the original in Firdausi's Shahnameh (c. 1010). Sir William Jones, the great Oriental scholar, made the same mistake, so Sir John was in good company. My thanks to Mr Hugh Leach for this information.
41 6/3/1810, RW to Mirza Shafee, PRO FO 60/3 f.355.
42 22/3/1810, RW to SHJ, PRO FO 60/3 ff.1–2.
43 7/4/1810, RW to SHJ, KPH 8583.
44 28/3/1810, RW to SHJ, PRO FO 60/3 ff.8–9.
45 15/7/1810, Merrick Shawe to SJM, NLS Acc 6990/15.
46 15/7/1810, MS to SJM, NLS Acc 6990/15.
47 14/7/1810, SJM Journal, Kaye, *Life and Correspondence* vol. II, p. 33.
48 14/7/1810, SJM Journal, Kaye, *Life and Correspondence* vol. II, pp. 32–33.
49 ?14/7/1810, SJM to Minto, Kaye, *Life and Correspondence* vol. II, pp. 27–28.
50 15/7/1810, Kaye, *Life and Correspondence* vol. II, pp. 33–34.

Chapter 20

1 16/6/1810, Mackintosh Journal, BL Add Mss 52439.
2 17/1/1811, Mackintosh to his wife, BL Mackintosh Papers.
3 Late January 1808, Mackintosh to a friend, Mackintosh, *Memoir* vol. I, p. 366.
4 21/9/1810, SJM Journal, Kaye, *Life and Correspondence* vol. II, p. 40.
5 Secretary to Sir James Mackintosh, see Chapter 16, p. 244 and Chapter 20, pp. 312–313.
6 *Sketch of the Political History of India*, published in 1811.
7 Maitland's daughter Mary Erskine, 1810–1883.
8 20/9–10/10/1808, Mary Rich to Maitland Erskine, Private Collection.
9 Mary Rich was probably the first educated European woman he had talked to for about nine months. In later years the Riches fulfilled all the promise that Malcolm had predicted for them. Claudius explored the remains of Babylon in 1811, and the results of his work were published after his death as *Narrative of a Journey to the Site of Babylon 1811*. In 1820 he made a long journey to Kurdistan and then to the site of Nineveh. In 1821 he travelled to Persepolis and Shiraz, where he died tragically, of cholera, aged only thirty four. Mary, who survived until 1876, edited and published a book of his travels in 1836, entitled *Narrative of a Residence in Koordistan and on the site of Ancient Nineveh*. He was the first man in modern times to excavate and put together on a scientific basis the geological and archaeological remains of Assyria and Mesopotamia, and what's more, he did it in his spare time.
10 5/10/1810, John Little to his mother, Little Papers.
11 8/10/1810, Mary Rich to Maitland Erskine, Private Collection.
12 5/10/1810, SJM Journal, Kaye, *Life and Correspondence* vol. II, pp. 40–41.
13 See Chapter 7, p. 122.
14 November 1810, SJM Journal, Kaye, *Life and Correspondence* vol. II, pp. 46–48.
15 HMMP, note.
16 Kaye, *Life and Correspondence* vol. II, pp. 46–48.

17 18/5/1808, SJM/Minto to FAS, BL Add Mss 37285, ff.150–167.
18 See Chapter 17, p. 253.
19 Gardane, G.A.L., *Journal d'un Voyage dans la Turquie, D'Asie et la Perse*, p. 67.
20 23/8/1811, Mackintosh, *Memoir* vol. II, p. 123.

Chapter 21

1 1824, Canning to Wynn, Kaye, *Life and Correspondence* vol. II, p. 431.
2 16/3/1823, SJM to Canning, Kaye, *Life and Correspondence* vol. II, p. 428 note.
3 April 1823, SJM Memo, Kaye, *Life and Correspondence* vol. II, p. 429 note.
4 Late March 1823, SJM to Canning, Kaye, *Life and Correspondence* vol. II, p. 429.
5 17/10/1824, McNeill to Lockhart, Lockhart Mss 925 vol. III, f. 43.
6 c. April 1832, SGO Memo, IOR Factory Records Persia, vol. 48.
7 16/2/1826, SJM to AW, USAW, WP1/850/4.
8 12/12/1826, SJM to AW, UNPP PwJf2763 & Kaye, *Life and Correspondence* vol. II, p. 455.
9 See Ingram, Edward, 'The Struggle over the Persian Mission' in *Middle East Studies* vol. 17, no. 3, pp. 291–310.
10 3/6/1828, SJM to LWB, UNPP PwJf 2760/3.
11 Amelia Macdonald to John Macdonald, EUL Dk2/37, ff.94–95.
12 16/1/1831, LWB to Ellenborough, UNPP, PwJf 2594 LWBC p. 586.
13 SHJ, *HMMCP*.
14 September 1828, Bombay Government to Resident Bushire, IOR L/P & S/20/C238C.
15 28/10/1828, LWB Minute, UNPP PwJf 2913/1.

Chapter 22

1 19/11/1810, BL 52437 ff.173–174 Mackintosh Journal.
2 18/10/1809, CP to CWP, BL Add Mss 41962, f.175.
3 15/1/1811, Mackintosh Journal, BL Add Mss 52438.
4 After marrying Stewart, Fannie sent her two sons by Tom Malcolm – George, aged six and Duncan, aged four – back to Scotland to be brought up by the Malcolm aunts at Burnfoot. It seems to have turned out well because she also sent her next child, Charlotte (her first by Stewart, born in 1812), to Burnfoot. Curiously, she produced no more children until 1821 then had four in quick succession. Josiah Stewart had a distinguished career as a political officer, acting successively as Resident at Gwalior, Jaipur and finally Hyderabad. He died in 1839.
5 10/2/1811 & 15/3/1811, J. Little to his father, Private Collection.
6 Three years later, Little contracted tuberculosis and died at Mauritius aged twenty-seven.
7 In the absence of Minto, who had set off on an expedition to Java.
8 22/11/1810, SJM to Minto, Kaye, *Life and Correspondence* vol. II, p. 60.
9 12/12/1810, Minto to SJM, NLS Mss 11296, f.196.
10 1811, India House Minute, IOLR O/6/10, pp. 157 ff.
11 i.e. not a Company ship.
12 5/3/1811, SJM to Minto, NLS Mss 11313, ff.26–27.
13 Mountstuart Elphinstone had just arrived by sea from Calcutta. He had recently

been appointed Resident at the Peshwah's court in Poonah, in succession to Barry Close. He stayed with the Malcolms during the few days that he was in Bombay.

14 Reverend Henry Martyn, then aged thirty, had been a Senior Wrangler (mathematician) at Cambridge, and had later gone to Calcutta as Chaplain to the Company in 1805. While there, he helped to translate the New Testament into Persian and Arabic, and was now on his way to Persia.

15 This was the long poem, *Persia*, that Malcolm had written on the boat coming back from Persia to Bombay.

16 Letter to Lady Mackintosh in England.

17 May 1811, SJM to Charlotte, Kaye, *Life and Correspondence* vol. II, p. 66.

Chapter 23

1 26/7/1812, CP to CWP, BL 41963 f.52.

2 Sept 1812, Kaye, *Life and Correspondence* vol. II, p. 71.

3 26/9/1812, SJM Journal to Charlotte, Kaye, *Life and Correspondence* vol. II, p. 72.

4 17/10/1810, quoted by SPM to SJM, NLS Acc 6684/9.

5 30/9/1812, SJM Journal/letter to Charlotte, Kaye, *Life and Correspondence* vol. II, p. 73.

6 Malcolm Family Book, NLS Acc 11800/2.

7 The ruins of this cottage still exist, in undergrowth about 200 metres west of Burnfoot House.

8 19/5/1807 BL Add Mss 41962 f.19 Magdalen Pasley to CWP.

9 28/5/1808 BL Add Mss 41962 f.63 Mina M. to CWP.

10 23/1/1811 Robert M. to SJM in Bombay, NLS Acc 6684/37 p. 14.

11 7/8/1814, Sara Hutchinson to her sister Mary in Coburn, *Letters*, pp. 71–74.

12 Kaye, *Life and Correspondence* vol. II, p. 73.

13 *DNB*, 1st edn.

14 4/11/1811, SJM to Scott, NLS Mss 3881, ff 102–104.

15 At this time Malcolm was a substantive Lieutenant-Colonel, and only a brevet Brigadier.

16 14/5/1812, Scott to Richard Heber, Grierson, H. (ed.), *The Letters of Sir Walter Scott* vol. XII, p. 334.

17 Kaye, *Life and Correspondence* vol. II, p. 74.

18 11/10/1812, Scott to Morritt, Grierson, *Letters of Walter Scott* vol. III, p. 170.

19 Minto himself arrived back in England in May 1814, but died at Stevenage on his way home to Scotland.

20 17/12/1810, SPM to SJM, NLS Acc 6684/11.

21 12/7/1811, SPM to Mina, NLS Acc 6684/5.

22 1/9/1812, Stephana M. to Nancy, NLS Acc 6684/5.

23 10/7/1812, SPM to Clem, NLS acc 6684/2.

24 14/2/1813, David M. to SPM, NLS Acc 6684/11.

25 15/12/1813, Palmer to SJM, Bodleian 40878 C83, p. 215.

26 ?2/4/1813, Mackintosh Journal, BL Add Mss 52452.

27 The capital cities, Calcutta, Madras and Bombay.

28 5/4/1813, SJM to HOC Select Committee, Parliamentary Papers NLS GHC 19/4.

29 Summer 1813: Kaye, *Life and Correspondence* vol. II, p. 77.

30 27/6/1814, SJM to A. Walker, NLS Mss 13721, f.47.

31 n.d. Morris, Henry, *Life of Charles Grant*, pp. 59–60.
32 n.d. 1813, SJM to C. Grant, NLS Mss 14835, f.147.
33 26/6/1813, AW to SJM, *AWSD* vol. VIII, p. 32.
34 18/8/1813, AW to SJM, *AWSD* vol. VIII, p. 196.
35 December 1812, SPM to Nancy, NLS Acc 6684/5.
36 16/8/1814, SJM to A. Walker, NLS Mss 13721 f.63.
37 7 April 1815, Smiles, Samuel, *A Publisher and His Friends* vol. I, pp. 267–268.
38 31/7/1814, SJM to John Murray, NLS Acc 12604/1763.
39 21/8/1817, Byron to Murray, Smiles, *Publisher* vol. 1.
40 *London Gazette*, 15 December 1812.
41 A very full and scholarly modern critique of the book can be found in Professor A.K.S. Lambton's essay, 'Sir John Malcolm and the History of Persia' in *British Institute of Persian Studies* vol. XXXIII (1995).
42 17/7/1815, SJM Journal, Kaye, *Life and Correspondence* vol. II, p. 97–99.
43 Kaye, *Life and Correspondence* vol. II, pp. 100–136.
44 Kaye, *Life and Correspondence* vol. II, p. 106.
45 13/8/1815, Mina to CWP, BL Add Mss 41963 f.195–196.
46 Later lost. Kaye, *Life and Correspondence* vol. II, p. 93n.
47 Kaye, *Life and Correspondence* vol. II, p. 94 and NLS Adv 36.1.7 f.71.
48 Late January 1816, Scott to SJM, Grierson, *Letters of Walter Scott* vol. IV, p. 133.
49 February 1816, Scott to John Morrit, Grierson, *Letters of Walter Scott* vol. IV p. 185.
50 Vol. xxvi, February–June 1816, pp. 282–303.
51 Half-brother of the bibliophile Richard Heber, and later Bishop of Calcutta.
52 See Chapter 19, note 40.
53 *Quarterly Review*, vol. XV, April 1816, pp. 236–291.
54 *Sketch of the Sikhs*, p. 5.
55 *HOP* vol. I, p. xi, quoted in McLaren, *British India*, p. 122.
56 Vol. 26, pp. 285, 388.
57 8/6/1816, ME to Captain Robert Close, Colebrooke, *Mountstuart Elphinstone* vol. I, p. 318; 11/9/1816, Colebrooke, ibid. vol. I, p. 320–322.
58 23/7/1818, Goethe Diary, WA III 3 6 189.
59 I am indebted to Professor Katherina Mommsen for this information.
60 23/2/1816, SJM to Scott, Grierson, *Letters of Walter Scott* vol. III, p. 150n.
61 A book, *Conversations with Bonaparte* appeared later, over the name of Clementina but in fact written by Pulteney.
62 8/6/1816, AW to SJM, UOS MS 308 133.
63 11/8/1816, AW to SJM, *AWSD* vol. XI, p. 458.
64 11/8/1816, AW to Colonel Allen, *AWSD* vol. XI, p. 459.
65 ?August 1816, Scott to SJM, Kaye, *Life and Correspondence* vol. II, p. 140.

Chapter 24

1 Heber was Member of Parliament for Oxford.
2 14/10/1816, SJM to Heber, Bodleian, Mss Eng. Lett d214 41132, f. 252.
3 Malcolm, Sir John, *Miscellaneous Poems*, p. 44.
4 n.d., SJM to Charlotte, Kaye, *Life and Correspondence* vol. II, pp. 145–146.
5 March 1817, SJM to Charlotte, Kaye, *Life and Correspondence* vol. II, p. 149.

6 29/3/1817.SJM to Charlotte, Kaye, *Life and Correspondence* vol. II, p. 150.
7 30/3/1817, Hastings to SJM, Kaye, *Life and Correspondence* vol. II, pp. 150–151.
8 17/7/1818, SJM to Hastings, *PHI*, p.cxxix.
9 *PHI* vol. II, pp. 429–431.
10 6/5/1817, Hastings to SJM, Kaye, *Life and Correspondence* vol. II, p. 155.
11 10/5/1817, SJM to Charlotte, Kaye, *Life and Correspondence* vol. II, p. 156.
12 Fortescue, *History of the British Army* vol. XI, pp. 174–175, p. 92.
13 17/7/1817, SJM to Hastings, *PHI*, Appendix IV, pp. clxxii–ccii.
14 June 1803, SJM to MS, BL 13747.
15 10/5/1817, SJM to Charlotte, Kaye, *Life and Correspondence* vol. II, p. 157.
16 9/7/1817, SJM to ?, Kaye, *Life and Correspondence* vol. II, p. 159.
17 6/7/1817, SJM to John Adam, Kaye, *Life and Correspondence* vol. II, p. 158–159.
18 July 1817, SJM to Charlotte, Kaye, *Life and Correspondence* vol. II, p. 160.
19 These Amazon troops were still around in 1923 according to Bence Jones, *Palaces*, p. 103.
20 Kaye, *Life and Correspondence* vol. II, p. 163.
21 24–31/7/1817, SJM to Charlotte, Kaye, *Life and Correspondence* vol. II, pp. 161–165 passim.
22 Kaye, *Life and Correspondence* vol. II, p. 167.
23 23/6/1803, AW to Close, WP3/3/70.
24 13/6/1817, Chakravorty, U.N., *Anglo Maratha Relations and Malcolm*, p. 109.
25 ?11/8/1817, SJM to Charlotte, Kaye, *Life and Correspondence* vol. II, pp. 169–170.
26 31/7/1817, ME Journal, OIOC Mss Eur F88/370.
27 3/9/1817, SJM to Charlotte, Kaye, *Life and Correspondence* vol. II, p. 173.
28 ?17/9/1817, SJM to Adam, Kaye, *Life and Correspondence* vol. II, p. 177.
29 September 1817, SJM to ? Adam, Kaye, *Life and Correspondence* vol. II, p. 178.
30 19/10/1817, SJM to Charlotte, Kaye, *Life and Correspondence* vol. II, p. 180.
31 October 1817, SJM to Charlotte, Kaye, *Life and Correspondence* vol. II, p. 184.
32 Literally, 'two rivers' in Persian, i.e. the Jumna and the Ganges.
33 n.d. 1816, Rajputana Agency Correspondence, no. 23.
34 30/5/1817, Richard Jenkins to Governor-General, NAI FSC 26/6/1817 no. 70, quoted in Chakravorty, *Treaty*, p. 108.
35 To its credit, the Company later compensated Elphinstone for his loss. 3/4/1820, Metcalfe to Warden, MSA 484(2), 3172–3180.
36 Grant Duff, J.C., *History of the Mahrattas*, pp. 650–651.
37 Captain James Grant, later known as Grant Duff, who was serving in the Residency at the time.
38 6/11/1817, ME Journal, BL OIOC Mss Eur F88/370.

Chapter 25

1 November 1817, Kaye, *Life and Correspondence* vol. II, p. 194.
2 13/12/1817, SJM to Hislop, Kaye, *Life and Correspondence* vol. II, p. 197.
3 20/12/1817, Kaye, *Life and Correspondence* vol. I, p. 201.
4 Grapeshot was small metal balls about the size of large marbles, packed together like pellets in a shotgun cartridge.
5 21/12/1817, Blacker, Valentine, *Memoir of the Operations of the British Army in India during the Mahratta War, 1817–19*, p. 149.

6 21/12/1825, Low, Ursula, *Fifty Years with John Company*, p. 47.
7 21/12/1817, Kaye, *Life and Correspondence* vol. II, pp. 207–209.
8 Prinsep, H.T., *Political and Military Transactions during the Administration of the Marquess Hastings* vol. II, p. 170.
9 Various reports state that Holkar had about seventy guns at the outset but with sixty-three guns abandoned after the charge, and thirteen more captured later, the figures do not seem to tally.
10 Blacker, *Memoir*, p. 151.
11 Fortescue, *History of the British Army* vol. XI, p. 211.
12 Blacker, *Memoir*, p. 153.
13 Fortescue, *History of the British Army* vol. XI, p. 212.
14 January 1818, Hastings to Hislop, Kaye, *Life and Correspondence* vol. II, p. 218.
15 Wilson, W.J., *History of the Madras Army* vol. IV, p. 98.
16 The sword became an heirloom in Malcolm's family until 1888 when his daughter Kate sold it to the Victoria and Albert Museum for £150. To this day it remains on display in the Indian section of the museum. Considering that the hilt of the sword was decorated with 276 diamonds, 378 rubies and 38 emeralds, all set in gold, it is difficult to disagree with the comment of the curator that 'the Museum got a bargain in 1888'. See Susan Stronge, 'The Sword of the Maharaja Holkar', *Orientations* vol. 19, no. 2, February 1988.
17 24/12/1817, SJM to Charlotte, Kaye, *Life and Correspondence* vol. II, p. 216.
18 26/1/1818, Munro to SJM, Gleig, *Thomas Munro* vol. III, p. 308.
19 1/1/1818, Kaye, *Life and Correspondence* vol. II, p. 222.
20 Late January 1818, SJM to Charlotte, Kaye, *Life and Correspondence* vol. II, p. 229.
21 15/2/1818, SJM to Charlotte, Kaye, *Life and Correspondence* vol. II, p. 230.
22 15/2/1818, SJM to Adam, NAI FSC no. 27.
23 *MCI* vol. I, pp. 445–448.
24 February 1818, SJM to ?Adam, quoted in Kaye, *Life and Correspondence* vol. II, pp. 229–230.
25 Mid-January 1818, SJM to Agnew, Kaye, *Life and Correspondence* vol. II, p. 228.
26 March 1818, SJM to Charlotte, Kaye, *Life and Correspondence* vol. II, p. 232.
27 March 1818, SJM to George M., Kaye, *Life and Correspondence* vol. II, pp. 215–216.
28 Kaye, *Life and Correspondence* vol. II, p. 229, slightly edited.

Chapter 26

1 1/6/1818, BRII to SJM, *PHI* vol. II, Appendix IV, p. ccxvi.
2 About £8 million in today's money.
3 4/6/1818, SJM to Adam, *PHI* vol. II, Appendix V, pp.ccxix–ccxxi.
4 4/6/1818, SJM to Adam, *PHI* vol. II, Appendix V, pp.ccxxi–ccxxii.
5 19/6/1818, SJM to Hastings, *PHI* vol. II, Appendix V, p.ccxxiii.
6 *PHI* vol. II, Appendix V, pp. ccxxvii–ccxxviii.
7 Low stayed on at Bithur for the next seven years as an unofficial Resident, keeping an eye on how the Peshwah's pension was being spent.
8 Burton, R.G., *The Maratha and Pindari War 1817–1819*, p. 100.
9 19/6/1818, SJM to Adam, MSA 451/4 4177–4207.
10 June 1818, Lushington to Ricketts, OIOC Mss Eur D1234/6.

11 17/6/1818, Adam to SJM, NAI FSC.
12 24/7/1818, SJM to Adam, NAI FSC no. 22, quoted in Chakravorty, *Treaty*, pp. 118–120.
13 17/8/1818, SJM to Adam, Kaye, *Life and Correspondence* vol. II, p. 261.
14 10/6/1818, ME to SJM, *PHI* vol. I, p. 527.
15 19/6/1818, *PHI* vol. I, p. 532.
16 7/7/1818, Munro to SJM, Gleig, *Thomas Munro* vol. III, pp. 267–268.
17 *PHI*, I p. 527.
18 28/6/1818, STM to ME Gleig, *Thomas Munro* vol. III, pp. 267–268.
19 July 1818, SJM to AW, Kaye, *Life and Correspondence* vol. II, p. 257.
20 15/9/1818, Hastings to SJM, Kaye, *Life and Correspondence* vol. II, p. 263.
21 1822, Hastings to Secret Committee, quoted in *PHI* vol. I, pp. 532–533.
22 October 1822, Court Minutes, quoted in *PHI* vol. I, pp. 532–533.
23 Pasley, R., *Send Malcolm*, p.106.
24 16/2/1819, J.R. Lar to SJM, NAI FSC 13/3/1819, no. 39.
25 Stranks, C.J., *Paths of Glory: the Military Career of John Shipp*, p. 205.
26 Stranks, *Paths of Glory* pp. 209–211.
27 9/4/1818, Stranks, *Paths of Glory*, p. 212.
28 12/4/1819, SJM to Metcalfe, NAI FSC no. 16.
29 April 1819, Stranks, *Paths of Glory*, p. 216.
30 9/8/1818, SJM to ME, IO HM 733 (13).
31 23/9/1818, SJM to C.J. Rich, NLS Adv. 36.1.7 f.79.

Chapter 27

1 26/2/1819, SJM to Charlotte, IOLR HM 733 p. 466.
2 18/3/1819, SJM to SPM, Kaye, *Life and Correspondence* vol. II, pp. 301–302.
3 Despite being Mountstuart's uncle, William Elphinstone had consistently supported Malcolm's candidacy.
4 18/3/1819, SJM to ME, Kaye, *Life and Correspondence* vol. II, pp. 302–303.
5 April 1819, ME to SJM, Colebrooke, *Mountstuart Elphinstone* vol. II, pp. 104–105.
6 3/10/1818, Canning to RW, IO Mss Eur B343.
7 25/3/1819, SJM to Hastings, NLS Acc 6990/16.
8 April 1819, Hastings to SJM, Kaye, *Life and Correspondence* vol. II, pp. 305–306.
9 Late July1819, ME to Hastings, Colebrooke, *Mountstuart Elphinstone* vol. II, pp. 103–104.
10 Late 1820, SJM to Charlotte, Kaye, *Life and Correspondence* vol. II, p. 331.
11 ?May 1819, SJM to Cockburn, Kaye, *Life and Correspondence* vol. II, p. 305.
12 4/8/1820, SJM to Hastings, OIOC Mss Eur F151/62, f.85– 9x.
13 November 1820, Hastings to SJM, Kaye, *Life and Correspondence* vol. II, p. 327–328.
14 n.d. early 1820?, SJM to ?, Kaye, *Life and Correspondence* vol. II, p. 316n.
15 27/2/1820, SJM to SPM, NLS Acc 6684/11.
16 Early 1820, SJM to Charlotte, Kaye, *Life and Correspondence* vol. II, p. 316.
17 Later to achieve fame as the author of *Annals and Antiquities of Rajasthan*.
18 Mhow remains a large military cantonment to this day.
19 May 1818, SJM to Charlotte, Kaye, *Life and Correspondence* vol. II, p. 235.
20 September 1818, SJM to Charlotte, Kaye, *Life and Correspondence* vol. II, pp. 275–276.
21 1/10/1818, SJM to W. Elphinstone, IOLR HM 733 f.365.

22 May 1819, anonymous officer, NLS Acc 6684/48/8.

23 3/4/1820, SJM to Charlotte, Kaye, *Life and Correspondence* vol. II, p. 318.

24 Intrigued by this anecdote, the author set out to locate the 'summer palace' at Nalcha. It was market day. There was an old man squatting on the ground selling biscuits. I asked where I could find the local Patel [headman]. He told me, but then he asked me:

'What are you looking for?'

'A small ruined palace which was once occupied by a *feringhee* [foreign] general.'

'Ah, you must mean koti Malcolm. It is about one mile in that direction.'

He pointed north-west. And sure enough, there it was, still intact, but inhabited now by cattle, rather than tigers – or *feringhees*.

25 ?June 1819, SJM to Haliburton, Kaye, *Life and Correspondence* vol. II, pp. 307–308.

26 Late 1819, SJM to James Williams, Kaye, *Life and Correspondence* vol. II, pp. 376–377.

27 June 1819, SJM to ME, Kaye, *Life and Correspondence* vol. II, p. 367.

28 Malcolm, *The Government of India*, Appendix A, p. 94.

29 *MCI* vol. I, pp. 516.

30 *MCI* vol. II, pp. 179–180.

31 ?December 1818, Kaye, *Life and Correspondence* vol. II, p. 285.

32 27/4/1818, Scott to Heber, Grierson, *Letters of Walter Scott* vol. V, p. 280.

33 26/11/1818, SJM to SWS, NLS Mss 3889.

34 *MCI* vol. I, pp. 524–525.

35 *MCI* vol. I, p. 551.

36 3/3/1821, SJM Memo, NAI, Separate Revenue Br Cons, 23/4/1821:2.

37 Amar Farooqui, *Smuggling as Subversion*, p. 3.

38 *MCI* vol. I, p. iv.

39 McLaren, *British India*, pp. 103–104.

40 *Sketch of the Sikhs*, p. 5.

41 *MCI* vol. II, pp. 305–312.

42 15/10/1820, STM to SJM Gleig, *Thomas Munro* vol. II, p. 75.

43 15/4/1821, STM to SJM, Gleig, *Thomas Munro* vol. II, pp. 75–76.

44 22/4/1822, Adam to COD, OIOC Mss Eur F109/57.

45 1936, Sarkar, Yadunath, *Malwa in Transition*, p. vii.

46 In 1998 the brothers Srikanth and Prematash Zamindar (of a prominent Indore family), told the author that they were using statistics in Malcolm's *Memoir* as evidence in a court case over a land dispute.

47 1825, Heber, Reginald, *Journey through the Upper Provinces 1824–25* vol. II, p. 19.

48 4/12/1819, ME to SJM, Choksey, R.D., *Mountstuart Elphinstone, the Indian Years*, p. 255.

49 24/2/1821, SJM to Charlotte, Kaye, *Life and Correspondence* vol. II, p. 333.

50 End February 1821, SJM to Adam, Kaye, *Life and Correspondence* vol. II, p. 334.

51 *MCI* vol. II, Appendix XVIII. For a more detailed resume of the *Instructions*, see Chapter 28.

52 *Quarterly Review*, vol. LVIII, July 1823, pp. 382–414.

53 15/3/1825, STM Minute, quoted by K.N.V. Shastri, *The Munro System of British Statesmanship in India*, 1939.

54 15/6/1821, Private collection.

55 In 1998 a descendant of the Kibe family showed the author a portrait of Sir John Malcolm, apparently holding hands with Tantia Jog. It looked a little incongruous,

since they were portrayed as the same height, even though Malcolm was 6 feet 5 inches tall and Tantia Jog probably no more than 5 feet 3 inches. In due course this puzzle was explained, when a photo of the original painting which had been on exhibition at the Rajwada (the Holkar palace in Indore until the palace was burnt down in 1984) showed that in place of Tantia Jog, there had been an occasional table. One can only guess that Tantia Jog was added later to a copy of the original painting.

56 While at Ranjit Singh's court in Lahore Metcalfe became romantically involved with a Sikh lady and secretly married her. She bore him three children who were educated in England and came back to India, one of them serving as an ADC to the Governor-General. The fate of their mother remains a mystery.

57 1/9/1821, SJM to Charlotte, Kaye, *Life and Correspondence* vol. II, p. 349.

58 When Malcolm returned to Bombay in 1827, he made Malabar Point his main residence.

59 15/9/1821, SJM to Campbell, Kaye, *Life and Correspondence* vol. II, pp. 349–350.

60 27/2/1820, SJM to SPM, NLS Acc 6684/11.

61 26/10/1821, IOLR O/6/10 p. 399; also Arbuthnott p. 267; Kaye, *Life and Correspondence* vol. II, p. 351.

62 29/12/1821, ME Journal, OIOC Mss Eur F88/453; also Choksey, *Mountstuart Elphinstone* p. 273.

63 Kaye, J.W., *Lives of Indian Officers* vol. II, pp. 10–11.

64 23/11/1821, SJM Memo, NAI SR 18/1/1822.

65 31/12/1821, SJM Journal, Kaye, *Life and Correspondence* vol. II, p. 402.

Chapter 28

1 Horace Walpole to Mann, 27/3/1772, Walpole, Horace, *Correspondence of Horace Walpole (1717–1797)* vol. 23.

2 10/7/1818, SJM to STM, quoted in Gleig, *Thomas Munro* vol. III, pp. 271–272.

3 ?Late 1819, SJM to Josiah Stewart, Kaye, *Life and Correspondence* vol. II, p. 372–373.

4 n.d. Kaye, *Life and Correspondence* vol. II, p. 365.

5 8/4/1820, SJM to J. Molony, Kaye, *Life and Correspondence* vol. II, pp. 335–336.

6 ME, *Report on the territories conquered from the Peshwah*, 1822.

7 ?April 1820, SJM to ME, Kaye, *Life and Correspondence* vol. II, pp. 367–368.

8 These were the two East India Company Colleges in England for training civil servants for India.

9 ?April 1819, SJM to Josiah Stewart, Kaye, *Life and Correspondence* vol. II, p. 371.

10 ?1818, SJM to Adam, Kaye, *Life and Correspondence* vol. II, p. 354.

11 Early 1820, SJM to Adam, Kaye, *Life and Correspondence* vol. II, p. 370.

12 Late 1819, SJM to Josiah Stewart, Kaye, *Life and Correspondence* vol. II, p. 374.

13 ?April 1819, SJM to Josiah Stewart, Kaye, *Life and Correspondence* vol. II, pp. 369–370.

14 1818, SJM to ME, Kaye, *Life and Correspondence* vol. II, pp. 354–355.

15 10/8/1817, STM to SJM, Gleig, *Thomas Munro* vol. III, p. 286.

16 Quoted in Parliamentary Papers, 12/4/1832.

17 McLaren, *British India*, pp. 145–148.

18 8/9/1819, ME to Adam, Choksey, *Mountstuart Elphinstone* p. 257.

19 September 1820, SJM to Dr Marshman, Kaye, *Life and Correspondence* vol. II, pp. 361–362.
20 Kaye, *Life and Correspondence* vol. II, p. 392
21 24/12/1824, see Gleig, *Thomas Munro* vol. III, pp. 319–390.
22 1820, SJM to J. Young, Kaye, *Life and Correspondence* vol. II, pp. 392–393.
23 Colebrooke, Sir E., *Memoir of Mountstuart Elphinstone*, p.72.
24 27/1/1819, ME to SJM, quoted in Choksey, R., *Mountstuart Elphinstone in India*, p. 236.
25 *Instructions*, p. 1.
26 *MCI* vol. II, Appendix XVIII, pp. 433–475; also *PHI*, vol. II, Appendix VIII, pp. 377–407.
27 2 July 1819, in a letter to Sir James Mackintosh.
28 1820s, in a report to the Court of Directors.
29 *A Memoir of Central India*, vol. II, p. 304.

Chapter 29

1 Kaye, *Life and Correspondence* vol. II, p. 398.
2 Kaye, *Life and Correspondence* vol. I, p.vii.
3 1/9/1833, Charlotte to ME, IO Mss Eur F88/85.
4 2/9/1817, SPM to Clementina Malcolm, NLS Acc 6684/2.
5 24/6/1820, SJM to STM, IO Mss Eur F151/62, ff.55–60.
6 8/5/22, SCM Journal, NLS Acc 12150/1, p. 170.
7 17/5/1822, CWP to Mina M. BL 41963, f.270.
8 12/7/1822, SJM to Scott, NLS Mss 3895 f.18. Netherby Hall, near Longtown was (and remains), the seat of the Graham family, and the setting for Scott's famous poem, 'Marmion', including the lines:

O, young Lochinvar is come out of the west,
Through all the wide Border his steed was the best . . .
. . . there was mounting 'mong Graemes of the Netherby clan,
Forsters, Fenwicks and Musgraves, they rode and they ran'.

9 The *Eskdale and Liddlesdale Advertiser*.
10 31/7/1822, NLS Acc 6684/48.
11 4/9/1822, letter to Andrew Little of Langholm, Lynne Bentley archive, Bathurst, New South Wales.
12 ?August 1823, SJM to ?, Kaye, *Life and Correspondence* vol. II, p. 416.
13 4/11/1822, SJM to Duchess of Wellington, Strathfield Saye papers.
14 Auguste Wilhelm von Schlegel (1767–1845) spent fifteen years 'in the house of Madame de Stael', and was later professor of literature at Bonn. He translated seventeen Shakespeare plays into German, as well as Dante, Calderon and Cervantes, and edited the *Bhagavad Gita* and *The Ramayana*.
15 Kaye, *Life and Correspondence* vol. II, p. 418.
16 Hare, J.C. and Hare, A., *Guesses at Truth*, p. 174.
17 Douglas, *William Whewell DD*, pp. 86–87.
18 Hare and Hare, *Guesses*.There may have been another reason for Julius Hare's idyllic memories of the house. As his nephew and biographer Augustus Hare later delicately put it: 'In the family of Sir John Malcolm, lived at this time a governess, a Miss Mary Manning, with whom Julius Hare formed a friendship of mingled love

and reverence . . . In his later life many people believed that Julius Hare had been engaged in his youth to Ma Man, as she was playfully called; but this was never the case.' (Augustus Hare, *Memorials of a Quiet Life*, 1872.)

There was a certain edge to Augustus Hare's praise of Miss Manning. Many years later he wrote that in the 1830s she had married a Dr Alexander in Edinburgh, but he had died, leaving her a widow. In 1848 his uncle Julius found her living in 'a small lodging in Heavitree, near Exeter'. He invited her to stay at the Hurstmonceux Rectory. In 1849 she 'came to Hurstmonceux for three days and stayed three weeks'. In 1850 she 'came for three weeks and stayed five years', in fact until his uncle Julius died.

19 Kaye, *Life and Correspondence* vol. II, p. 424.
20 ?2/9/1823, SJM to Minnie M., Kaye, *Life and Correspondence* vol. II, pp. 424–425.
21 ?9/9/1823, SJM to Minnie, Kaye, *Life and Correspondence* vol. II, p. 425n.
22 Formerly Lord (Edward) Clive, Governor of Madras from 1799 to 1803.
23 RAS Journal, vol. IV, pp. 65–91.
24 Simmonds, Stuart, and Digby, Simon (eds), *The Royal Asiatic Society; History and Treasures*, p. 45.
25 24/2/1824, Oriental Club Minutes.
26 11/6/1824 SJM to Erskine, NLS Adv 36.1.7 f.131.
27 The Club survives to this day.
28 He had married General Harris's daughter at Madras in 1798 – see Chapter 3, p. 48.
29 18/3/1824, Canning to SJM, Kaye, *Life and Correspondence* vol. II, p. 460.
30 19/3/1824, AW to SJM, USAW WP1/753/5.
31 3/4/1824, AW to SJM, USAW WP1/791.
32 3/4/1824, AW to SJM, USAW WP1/1/791.
33 14/10/1824, King to Liverpool, BL Add Mss 38193, f.200.
34 14/8/1826, SJM to Gilbert M., Kaye, *Life and Correspondence* vol. II, pp. 473–474.
35 27/5/1825–23/6/1825, Kaye, *Life and Correspondence* vol. II, pp. 436–448.
36 Poet Laureate at the time.
37 ?16/9/1825, SJM to Clementina, NLS Acc 6684/21.
38 Covered in Chapter 21.
39 5/7/1823, SJM to Adam, IO Mss Eur F109/95.
40 29/5/1824, SJM to J.G. Lambton, NLS Mss 2618.
41 9/7/1824, SJM to Court of Proprietors, *PHI* vol. II, p. ccxlvi.
42 *PHI* vol. II, p. 307.
43 See Chapter 2, pp. 35–38.
44 7/8/1826, AW to Wynn, USAW, WP1/861/6; also *DCM* II, p. 592.
45 Kaye, *Life and Correspondence* vol. II, p. 473
46 March 1825, AW to SJM, Kaye, *Life and Correspondence* vol. II, p. 472.
47 6/2/1827, IO SJM to AW, Mss Eur F151/62.
48 9/11/1826, Bamford, F. (ed.), *The Journal of Mrs Arbuthnot*, vol. II, p. 53.
49 27/12/1826, Wynn to SJM, Kaye, *Life and Correspondence* vol. II, p. 477.
50 25/12/1825, AW to Wynn, USAW, WP1/834/11.
51 ?31/12/1826, SPM to Clementina, NLS Acc 6684/3.
52 8/2/1826, AW to SJM, BL Add Mss 38522 f.103.
53 10–18/1/1827, IOLR HM 455(1), p. 140.
54 23/1/1827, SPM to Clementina, NLS Acc 6684/3.
55 7/2/1827, SPM to Clementina, NLS Acc 6684/3.

56 22/2/1827, EIC Chairs to SJM, Kaye, *Life and Correspondence* vol. II, p. 484.
57 19/4/1827, SJM to AW, Kaye, *Life and Correspondence* vol. II, p. 486.
58 18/4/1827, SPM to Clementina, NLS acc 6684/3.
59 9/5/1827, CWP Journal, BL Add Mss 41985.
60 May 1827, Margaret Malcolm's Journal.
61 13/6/1827, CWP Journal, BL 41985, ff.18–19.
62 *Asiatic Journal*, July 1827, vol. XXIV, pp. 134–138.
63 14/6/1827, SJM to AW, Kaye, *Life and Correspondence* vol. II, p. 492.
64 2/7/1827, Hare to Whewell, Trinity College Library, Add.Ms.a.206.159.

Chapter 30

1 These lithographed copies of the Clive Papers still survive in the National Library of Wales (NLW). They were stored at Powis Castle until 1952 when they were disposed of in an unhappy archival compromise, with the *incoming* papers being deposited at the India Office Library (now part of the British Library) in London (Powis Mss – Mss Eur G 37, 95 Boxes); and the *outgoing* papers (and all of the papers of the 2nd Lord Clive, Earl of Powis) being deposited at the NLW in Aberystwyth (Clive Mss). In 1985 the historian Huw Bowen, noticing that a large proportion of the Papers at the NLW were duplicated, discovered that the watermark dates on the copies were the years 1824–1828; they were clearly the lithograph copies used by Malcolm, which had sometime later been returned to the Clive collection. In 2002 these copies were separately filed and renamed the 'Sir John Malcolm Papers' (GB210JOMALC).
2 As his biographer Kaye ruefully commented, 'I have often thought that if Rawlinson was so employed, it is not difficult to conjecture where he took his first lessons in the art of deciphering strange hieroglyphics.' Kaye, *Life and Correspondence* vol. II, p. 497.
3 Fifteen letters remained unused, and still survive among the Elphinstone papers in the British Library, each in its envelope, each in Malcolm's unmistakable handwriting. 14/11/1827 IO Mss Eur F88/69.
4 Kaye, *Life and Correspondence* vol. II, p. 498.
5 27/8/1828, Holt Mackenzie to LWB, UNPP PwJf2589/1.
6 20/1/1831, Auber to LWB, UNPP PwJf PwJf 250.
7 3/7/1828, Bengal Government to Bombay, *GOI*, pp. 139–140.
8 n.d. Bombay Government to Bengal, *GOI*, p. 140.
9 2/12/1828, Ravenshaw to LWB, UNPP PwJf 1906.
10 21/9/1828, SJM to H. Wood, IOR, HM 734, ff. 517–518.
11 14/12/1828, SJM to Combermere, IOR HM 734, f.566–568.
12 30/11/1830, SJM Minute, *GOI*, Appendix A, p. 78.
13 30/11/1830, SJM Minute, *GOI*, Appendix A, p. 65.
14 30/11/1830, SJM Farewell Minute, *GOI*, Appendix A, p. 94, para 275.
15 Dapuri remained the Government House in the Deccan until 1865, when the then Governor, Sir Bartle Frere, decided that Dapuri was too modest a residence for the increasingly imperial posture which he wished to project, and too far from the centre of Poona. So the government built a much more grandiose structure for £175,000 at Ganesh Khind (now the main building at Pune University).

16 British Library IOR/4/1049 28762.
17 29/7/1829, SJM to G.A. Malcolm, IOR HM 734(2), pp. 669–670.
18 4/4/1830, SJM to AW, USAW WP1/1106/18.
19 The fact that he drank a bottle of port every night might have had something to do with the headaches which he complained about. He later added the name 'Duff', and became generally known as Grant Duff.
20 23/12/1828, Welsh, *Military Reminiscences*, vol II, pp. 339–340.
21 6/6/1828, BL Add Mss 22082.
22 30/7/1828, SJM to Holt Mackenzie.
23 24/3/1820, ME to SJM, IO Mss Eur F88.
24 11/1/1830, SJM to Beckwith IOR HM 734, f.789.
25 April 1830 SJM Minute on Cutch, BL Add Mss 22082, ff.154–177.
26 Williams, R. Brady, *An Introduction to Swaminarayan Hinduism*, p. 28.
27 *MCI* vol. II, p. 154.
28 In the course of their discussions the Swami handed over a copy of his moral and religious precepts – a sort of Bible or Qur'an – called the *Shikshapatri*. Malcolm handed on the volume to David Blane, the acting Political Agent at Rajkot. Many years afterwards, in the 1880s, the descendants of David Blane gave a copy of the *Shikshapatri* (perhaps the same one) to the Bodleian Library at Oxford, where it remains to this day, in the Indian Institute. Understandably, it has become a relic of considerable sanctity to Swaminarayan devotees – it is as if an Old Testament Bible known to have been handled by Jesus Christ himself had suddenly turned up in a local library.
29 Williams, *Introduction to Swaminarayan Hinduism*, p. 5, from which much of the foregoing material is taken.
30 April 1830, SJM Minute on Cutch, para 33.
31 3/4/1830, SJM to R. Clive, Kaye, *Life and Correspondence* vol. II, p. 542.
32 Alluded to in SJM Minute of 30/11/1830, *GOI*, p. 84, para 248.
33 11/6/1822, SCM Journal, NLS Acc 12150/1.
34 3/7/1829, SPM to Clementina, NLS Acc 6684/4.
35 13/5/1830, SJM to Scott, Grierson, *Letters of Walter Scott* vol. XI, p. 409.
36 18/6/1815, SCM Journal NLS acc 12150/6.
37 11/11/1830, Charlotte Malcolm Journal, NLS Acc 12150/6.
38 The plaque survives to this day, halfway up the Ghat, about 1 km above Khandallah at the underpass on the northern (i.e. eastbound) side of the Mumbai–Pune expressway.
39 4/12/1830, SJM to Bentinck, UNPP PwJf 1473.
40 See Chapter 31.
41 18/7/1830, Metcalfe to LWB, UNPP PwJf 1524.
42 29/12/1830, SJM Journal, quoted in Kaye, *Life and Correspondence* vol. II, pp. 555–556.
43 23/6/1831 and 31/7/1831, Clare to LWB, UNPP, PwJf, LWBC letter no. 334.
44 17/7/1831, Clare to AW, WP1/1189/22.
45 14/9/1831, SJM to SCM, IOR HM735, p. 91.
46 1832, Jacquemont, Victor, *Letters from India, 1828–1832*, pp. xxviii–xxix.
47 Ibid., p. 333.
48 January 1831, SJM Journal, quoted in Kaye, *Life and Correspondence* vol. II, p. 556.

Chapter 31

1 *Oriental Herald*, 1825.
2 26/6/1827, SJM to Wynn, USAW WP1/908/8.
3 November 1827, ME to SJM, OIOC Mss Eur F88/9.
4 January 1828, Lady West's Journal, OIOC Mss Eur D888/1.
5 March 1828, Grant, Elizabeth, *Memoirs of a Highland Lady* vol. II, pp. 256–257.
6 9/9/1828, SJM to Charlotte, Kaye, *Life and Correspondence* vol. II, p. 510.
7 3/10/1828, Governor in Council to Supreme Court, Kaye, *Life and Correspondence* vol. II, pp. 513–514.
8 5/10/1828 Grant to SJM, Kaye, *Life and Correspondence* vol. II, p. 514.
9 6/10/1828, Chambers, Kaye, *Life and Correspondence* vol. II, p. 518.
10 6/10/1828, Kaye, *Life and Correspondence* vol. II, p. 520.
11 Grant, *Memoirs of a Highland Lady* vol. II, p. 236.
12 25/10/1828, SJM to LWB, UOS WP1/961/9.
13 Kaye stated that Malcolm 'made up his mind to exercise, in such an extremity, the authority vested in him by law . . . to deport the Commander-in-Chief as he would deport any "free merchant" in the country' (Kaye, *Life and Correspondence* vol. II, p. 525). This is an assertion for which no direct evidence survives. Despite this, the original *Dictionary of National Biography* (published in the 1890s) echoed it, and the recent edition of the Oxford *DNB* (published in 2004), went further still, making the astonishing claim that Malcolm had actually done so, i.e. deported Bradford. The online version has since corrected this obvious howler.
14 13/9/1828, SJM to LWB, IOLR HM734(2), p. 509.
15 May 1829, Grant, *Memoirs of a Highland Lady* vol. II, pp. 257–258. There was a happy outcome for Elizabeth Grant. On 10 June 1829 she was married to Colonel Smith at St Thomas's Cathedral in Bombay by the Reverend (later Bishop) Thomas Carr.
16 21/2/1829, Ellenborough to SJM, UNPP PwJf 1423.
17 7/6/1829, SJM to AW, UOS, WP1/1024/12.
18 1829, BL Add Mss 41964, ff.7 onwards.

Chapter 32

1 15/4/1831, SJM to Alex CC, IOR HM 735.
2 14/3/1831, Maria Edgeworth to Mrs Edgeworth, Hare, Augustus, *Life and Letters of Maria Edgeworth* vol. II, p. 178.
3 28/3/1831, OIOC Mss Eur F88/9, pp. 122–123.
4 25/4/1831, SJM to CWP, Kaye, *Life and Correspondence* vol. II, p. 563.
5 *Hansard*, pp. 1636–7, series 3, vol. III, 1833
6 5/6/1831, AW to SJM, UOS WP1/1188/2.
7 5/7/1831, SJM to HOC, *Hansard* and *GOI*, pp. 276–279.
8 19/9/1831, SJM to HOC, *Hansard* vol. VII, pp. 178–191.
9 6/8/1831, SJM to SCM in Bombay, IOR HM 735, pp. 53–55.
10 11/10/1831, Butler, J.R.M., *The Passing of the Great Reform Bill*, p. 285.
11 14/10/1831, SJM to AW, IOR HM735, pp. 105–107.
12 1840, Barty-King, Hugh, *Warfield, A Thousand Years of a Berkshire Parish*.
13 29/11/1831, SJM to Duchess of Northumberland, IOR HM 735, pp. 118–120.

14 13/12/1831, SJM to Duchess of Northumberland, IOR HM 735, pp. 150–152.
15 21/12/1831, SJM Journal, Kaye, *Life and Correspondence* vol. II, p. 573.
16 29/11/1831, SJM to Duchess of Northumberland, IOR HM 735, pp. 120–131.
17 ?28/12/1831,SJM Journal, quoted by Kaye, *Life and Correspondence* vol. II, p. 574.
18 ?7/1/1832, SJM Journal, quoted in Kaye, *Life and Correspondence* vol. II, p. 576.
19 19/3/1832, SJM speech, *Hansard* vol. II, pp. 425–428.
20 5–8/3/1832 Fisher, D.R. (ed.) *History of Parliament 1820–1832*, p. 322.
21 26/6/1832, SJM to Duchess of Northumberland, Kaye, *Life and Correspondence* vol. II, p. 581.
22 28/6/1832, SJM to Duke of Northumberland, Kaye, *Life and Correspondence* vol. II, p. 582.
23 9/7/1832, SPM to Mina, NLS Acc 6684/6.
24 n.d. ?October 1832, Grierson, *Letters of Walter Scott* vol. III, p. 150n.
25 4/11/1832, SJM to Edinburgh Abbotsford Committee, NLS Mss 6.314 (36).
26 28/8/1832, SJM to a friend, Kaye, *Life and Correspondence* vol. II, pp. 585–586.
27 ?6/12/1832, SJM Journal, quoted in Kaye, *Life and Correspondence* vol. II, p. 593.
28 *Gentlemen's Magazine*, 1833, vol. II, p. 813.
29 29/9/1832, SJM to a sister, quoted in Kaye, *Life and Correspondence* vol. II, p. 588.
30 20/11/1832, AW to SJM, BL Add Mss 38522, f.110.
31 25/1/1833, SJM to SCM, quoted in Kaye, *Life and Correspondence* vol. II, p. 598.
32 15/4/1833, *Asiatic Journal*, July 1833, vol. XI, pp. 4–11.
33 15/4/1831, Kaye, *Life and Correspondence* vol. II, p. 606.
34 16/4/1833, *Asiatic Journal*, July 1833,vol. XI, pp. 4–11.
35 28/4/1833, Kaye, *Life and Correspondence* vol. II, p. 608.
36 May 1833, Kaye, *Life and Correspondence* vol. II, p. 610.
37 14/10/1831, SJM to AW, UOS WP1/1198/42.

Postscript

1 In 1860, SJM's son George bought a vault at Kensal Green Cemetery in north London, with space for seven coffins. The first occupant was Charlotte's sister, Amelia Macdonald, the widow of Sir John Macdonald. In 1861 Charlotte and George arranged for Sir John's remains to be moved from St James's Piccadilly to Kensal Green. In due course the remains of other Malcolms followed – Charlotte herself in 1867, Amelia in 1873, George's wife Georgiana in 1886, George in 1888 and Kate in 1891.
2 1833, OIOC Mss Eur F88/13.
3 It was originally full-length, but when the Club moved into smaller premises in the 1960s the Committee made the extraordinary decision to cut off Sir John at the waist, to fit him into a spot on the main staircase.
4 There is an intriguing story behind these letters. In 1834 Charlotte lent them to the Duke so that some of them could be included in Colonel Gurwood's *Dispatches . . . of the Duke of Wellington*. But six years later, when she asked for them to be returned so that they could be used in a biography of Sir John, the Duke demurred. Only in 1860 did the second Duke, possibly harbouring a slightly guilty conscience, call in Malcolm's son George, and return the letters to him, after getting his prior approval to the destruction of three letters written from Calcutta in late 1804.

These letters (probably) contained details of the Marquess's virtual nervous breakdown at that time. In 1840 the Marquess was still (just) alive, and, not for the first time, the Duke was anxious to preserve the Wellesley family's good name.

Appendix 2

1 2/4/1802, SHJ to SJM, BL 13746, f.274.
2 13/6/1801, AW to SJM, *AWD* vol. II, p. 442.
3 20/3/1802, MS to HW, OIOC Mss Eur J 793, 89, pp. 473–478.
4 June 1803, SJM to MS, BL Add Mss 13746, p. 370.

Bibliography

Manuscript Sources

United Kingdom

Aberystwyth, National Library of Wales
NLW. 4903e, Clive Papers
Aylesbury, Buckinghamshire Record Office
Hobart Papers
Bishop Carr's diaries
Barnstaple, Private Collection
Rich/Erskine/Mackintosh Papers
Cambridge, Centre for South Asian Studies
Edmonstone Papers
Cambridge, Trinity College Library
Whewell Papers
Sedgwick Papers
Cambridge, University Library
Add Mss 7450,7652, Letters of Sir John Malcolm
Dumfriesshire, Private Collection
Little Family Papers
Edinburgh, National Archives of Scotland
CS 228/M/6/15 1783–1789, George Malcolm's Debts
Index of Civil Cases, 1789–1794
Edinburgh, National Library of Scotland
Acc 5753–11800, Malcolm of Burnfoot Papers
Acc 12150, Sir Charles Malcolm Papers
Acc 12604, John Murray Archive
Acc 12935, Sir John Malcolm letters 1808
Adv 36.1.7, Erskine Papers
Mss 578–3903, Sir Walter Scott Papers
Mss 11248–11733, Minto Papers
Mss 13601–13719, 14835, Walker of Bowland Papers
Edinburgh, National War Museum
General Sir Alexander Campbell Papers
Edinburgh, Museum of Royal Scots
Battle of Mehidpoor, 1817
Exeter, Devon Record Office
5991–9491, Kennaway Papers
Greenwich, National Maritime Museum
MS 60/038–040, Sir Charles Malcolm Papers
MS 61/024, Sir Pulteney Malcolm Papers
Hampshire, Stratfield Saye Archive

Duchess of Wellington letters
Hereford, Hereford Record Office
5992–9491, Sir Harford Jones (Brydges) Papers
London, British Library, Asia and Africa Collection
India Office Records
F 1–5, Board of Control
G29, L, N, P, R, Sir John Malcolm, letters from and to
European Mss
B343, Canning Papers
B49, B424, C854, Doyle Papers
C262, Macdonald papers
C562, Hastings Papers
C593, Cole Papers
C961, D1082, Low Papers
D564, D640, D667, Malcolm various
D1086, D1105, Minto Papers
D888, West Papers
D1234, D5556, Ricketts
E176/J793, Henry Wellesley
E216, Arthur Wellesley
E293, Willoughby Papers
F88, Mountstuart Elphinstone Papers
F89,W.F. Elphinstone Papers
F109, Adam Papers
F128, Strachey (Sutton Court) Collection
F140, Amherst Collection
F228, Kirkpatrick Collection
G37, Clive Collection
105 Neg 4391, Dundas
London, British Library, Manuscripts (Add Mss)
13578–13748, Richard Wellesley Papers
20115–22082, Richard Wellesley Papers
36470, Richard Wellesley Papers
37280–37709, Richard Wellesley Papers
41072, Richard Wellesley Papers
29181–29184, Warren Hastings, letters of and to
27541, Sir Thomas Munro, letters to
35918, Hardwicke Papers
37709, Auckland Papers
38193, 38247–38303, Liverpool Papers
38522, Arthur Wellesley Papers
39118, Layard Papers
39781, Flaxman Papers
39945, Erskine Papers
40505, 40573, Peel Papers
41761–41989, Pasley Papers
43070–43209, Aberdeen Papers
52436–52453, Mackintosh Papers

57313, Mackintosh Papers
78765–78766, Mackintosh papers
57315, Wilks Papers
59418–59451, Dropmore Papers

London, Institution of Civil Engineers
Telford Papers

London, Kensal Green Cemetery
Burial Records

London, National Army Museum
6510–6530, Sir Alexander Campbell Papers

London, Oriental Club
Club Minutes

London, Public Record Office, Kew
FO60, 78/19, 249, 705, Foreign Office Archives
PRO IR. 26/1328, Will of Sir John Malcolm

London, Royal Asiatic Society
Rawlinson Papers, Journal 1827–8

Market Drayton, Private Collection
Richard Heber Papers

Nottingham, University Library
Portland Papers

Oxford, Bodleian Library
39966, 39974, John Briggs Papers
40878–40904, 45061, John Palmer Papers
41132–41174, Richard Heber, letters to
41011, Henry Russell Collection
39542–39543, Malcolm's History of Persia
41341, Sir Graves Haughton, letters to
46802, Robert Finch, letters to

Reading, Berkshire Record office
Warfield Hall Records

Southampton, University (Hartley) Library
WP, WP2, WP3, Wellington Papers

Truro, Cornwall Record Office
Morshead Papers

Australia

Adelaide, State Library of South Australia
Malcolm Papers

Bathurst, New South Wales, Private Collection
Eskdale correspondence

Perth, Western Australia, Private Collection
Cockburn-Campbell Papers

Sydney, New South Wales, Mitchell Library
Lachlan Macquarie Papers

Canada

Guelf, Ontario, University Library
Sir William Pulteney Papers

India

Chennai, Tamil Nadu State Archives
General
Delhi, National Archives of India
General
Mumbai, Maharashtra State Archives
Political and Secret Department 1799–1820, 1821–1830
Pune, Deccan College Library
General
Pune, Peshwah Dafter
Maratha Records, Eighteenth Century
Pune, Private Collection
Kibe Family Papers

United States

Ann Arbor, Michigan, University of Michigan (William L. Clements Library)
Sir Pulteney Malcolm Papers
Florida, State University
C.T. Metcalfe, letter to

Printed Sources

Adkins, Leslie *Empires of the Plain (Henry Rawlinson)* (London, 2003)
Aitchison, C.U., *A Collection of Treaties, Engagements & Sunnuds* (Calcutta, 1862)
Alexander, Constance, *Baghdad in Bygone Days* (London, 1928)
Alexander, James E., *Travels from India to England* (London, 1827)
Allardyce, Alexander, *Admiral Lord Keith* (Edinburgh, 1882)
Allen, Charles and Dwiverdi, Sharada, *Lives of the Indian Princes* (London, 1986)
Amini, Iradj, *Napoleon et la Perse*, (Paris, 1995)
Anon. (ed.), *East India Military Calendar, Services of Officers* (London, 1823)
Anon. (ed.), *East India Register and Directory, Annual Register* (Calcutta, 1803, 1809, 1813)
Anon. (ed.), *Fasti Ecclesiae Scoticane* (Edinburgh, 1915)
Anon. (ed.), *Fort William-India House Correspondence* (vols 9–15) (Delhi, 1949–1955)
Anon. (ed.), *Imperial Gazetteer, vol. A, Nagpur District, 1908* (Bombay, 1908)
Anon. (ed.), *Imperial Gazetteer, vol. ii, Central India, 1908* (Bombay, 1908)
Anon. (ed.), *Imperial Gazetteer, vol. xix, Satara District, 1885* (Bombay, 1885)
Anon. (ed.), *Imperial Gazetteer, vol. xxviii, Bombay Presidency, 1885* (Bombay, 1885)
Anon. (ed.), *Opinions of Lords Wellesley & Greville on the Government of India* (London, 1832)
Anon. (ed.), *Opinions of Mountstuart Elphinstone* (London, 1834)
Anon., *Cadets' Guide to India* (London, 1820)

Anon., *Dangers to British India from French Invasion & Missionary Establishment* (London, 1808)
Anon., *History of Mandu* (Bombay, 1875)
Anon., *History of the Shastri Family* (Bombay, ?1860)
Anon., *Malcolm Payt* (Bombay, 1830)
Anon., *Observations on Lieut Col. Malcolm's publication relative to the disturbances in the Madras Army* (London, 1812)
Archer, Mildred, *Company Paintings* (London, 1992)
Archer, Mildred, *Indian and British Portraiture 1770–1825* (London, 1979)
Arfa, Hassan, *The Kurds* (London, 1966)
Arkin, Maurice, *John Company at the Cape* (Cape Town, 1961)
Arnold, Matthew, *Collected Poems* (London, 1964)
Azmi, Rahat, *Mah-e-Laqa* (Hyderabad, 1998)
Baillie, Alexander, *The Oriental Club and Hanover Square* (London, 1901)
Baines, J.E., *Maratha History of Gujerat 1750–1819* (Bombay, 1996)
Bakshi, S.R., *British Diplomacy and Administration in India 1807–13* (Delhi, 1971)
Balfour, Lady B., *Lord Lytton's Indian Administration* (London, 1899)
Ballhatchet, Professor K., *Race, Sex and Class under the Raj 1793–1905* (London, 1980)
Ballhatchet, Professor K., *Social Policy and Social Change in Western India, 1817–30* (London, 1957)
Bamford, F. (ed.), *The Journal of Mrs Arbuthnot, 1820–1834,* 2 vols (London, 1950)
Banaji, D.R., *Slavery in British India* (Bombay, 1933)
Bannerjee, R., *Begum Samru* (Calcutta, 1926)
Basham, A.L., *The Wonder That Was India* (London, 1967)
Basu, Major B.D., *Rise of the Christian Power in India* (Calcutta, 1931)
Bayly, Sir Christopher, *Empire and Information: Intelligence Gathering and Social Communication in India 1780-1870* (Cambridge, 1996)
Bayly, Sir Christopher, *Illustrated History of Modern India 1600–1947* (Cambridge, 1991)
Bayly, Sir Christopher, *Imperial Meridien: The British Empire and the World 1780–1830* (London, 1989)
Bayly, Sir Christopher, *Indian Society and the Making of the British Empire* (Cambridge, 1988)
Bayly, Sir Christopher, *Rulers, Townsmen and Bazaars: North Indian Society . . . 1780–1830* (London, 1989)
Bearce, G.D., *British Attitudes towards India 1784–1858* (London, 1961)
Beatson, Alexander, *The War with Tippoo Sultan* (London, 1800)
Beattie, David J., *Lang Syne in Eskdale* (Carlisle, 1912)
Bell, Evans (ed.), *Memoir of General John Briggs* (London, 1885)
Bence Jones, Mark, *Palaces of the Raj* (London, 1977)
Bennell, A.S., *The Making of Arthur Wellesley* (Hyderabad, 1997)
Blacker, Valentine, *Memoir of the Operations of the British Army in India during the Mahratta War, 1817–19* (London, 1821)
Blackiston, Major General J., *Twelve Years of Military Adventure* (2 vols) (London, 1829)
Blow, David, *Persia through Writers' Eyes* (London, 2007)
Boase, Frederic, *Modern English Biography* (Netherton, 1897)
Bombay Government, *Gazeteer of Satara* (Bombay, 1885)
Bombay Government, *Gazetteer of Nagpur* (Nagpur, 1908)
Boucher, M., *Britain at the Cape, 1795–1803* (Houghton, 1992)

Boulger, D.C., *Lord William Bentinck (Rulers of India)* (Oxford, 1892)
Bowen, H.V., *The Business of Empire* (Cambridge, 2006)
Bowring, L.B., *Haider Ali and Tipu Sultan (Rulers of India)* (Oxford, 1899)
Bradshaw, John, *Sir Thomas Munro* (Oxford ,1894)
Brett-James, A. (ed.), *Wellington at War* (London, 1961)
Briggs, H.G., *The Cities of Gujarashtra* (Bombay,1849)
Broughton, T.D., *Letters Written in a Mahratta Camp, 1809* (London, 1842)
Brown, Edward G., *A Year amongst the Persians* (London, 1893)
Buchanan, A., *A Journey through Mysore* (3 vols), (London, 1807)
Buckland, C.E., *Dictionary of Indian Biography* (London, 1906)
Buddle, Anne, *The Tiger and the Thistle* (Edinburgh, 1999)
Burke, *Landed Gentry, 1825–1925* (London, 1825–1925)
Burke, *Peerage, Baronetage and Knightage, 1825–1925* (London, 1825–1925)
Burnard, Joyce, *Chintz and Cotton* (Sydney, 1994)
Burnes, Alexander, *Travels in Bokhara* (3 vols) (London, 1834)
Burton, R.G., *The Maratha and Pindari War 1817–1819* (Delhi, 1910, 1975)
Burton, Richard F., *First Footsteps in East Africa* (ed. Gordon Waterfield) (London, 1966)
Busted, H.E. *Echoes from Old Calcutta* (Calcutta and London, 1908)
Bute, Marchioness, *Private Journals of the Marquess of Hastings* (2 vols) (London, 1858)
Butler, Iris, *The Eldest Brother* (London, 1973)
Butler, J.R.M., *The Passing of the Great Reform Bill* (London, 1914)
Cadell, P.R, *History of the Bombay Army* (London, 1915, 1939)
Callahan, Raymond, *The East India Company and Army Reform 1783–98* (Harvard, 1972)
Campbell, Major Sir D., *Records of the Clan Campbell 1600–1858* (London, 1925)
Campbell, Margaret D., *Memorial History of the Campbells of Melfort* (London, 1882)
Cannon, Richard S., *Historical Record of the 74th Foot* (London, 1850)
Cardew, Sir Alexander, *White Mutiny* (London, 1929)
Carson, Penelope, *J.S. Mill and the Anglicist/Orientalist Controversy* (Toronto, 1999)
Carver, Lord (Michael), *Wellington and His Brothers* (Southampton, 1989)
Cavaleiro, Rodney, *Strangers in the Land; the Rise and Decline of the British Indian Empire* (London, 2002)
Chakravorty, U.N., *Anglo-Maratha Relations & Malcolm, 1798–1830* (Delhi, 1979)
Chambers, R. (ed.), *Eminent Scotsmen* (Glasgow, 1837)
Chancey, M.K., unpublished doctoral thesis on N.B. Edmonstone (Florida State University, 2003)
Chaudari, K.N, *The Trading World of Asia and the English East India Company, 1660–1760* (Cambridge, 1978)
Chaudari, N.G., *British Relations with Hyderabad* (Calcutta, 1964)
Chaudhuri, Nirad C., *Clive of India* (London, 1975)
Choksey, R.D., *British Diplomacy at the Court of the Peshwas* (Bombay, 1951)
Choksey, R.D., *Mountstuart Elphinstone; the Indian Years 1796–1827* (Bombay, 1971)
Choksey, R.D., *The Peshwa: The Last Phase* (Bombay, 1948)
Choksey, R.D., *The Peshwa: The Aftermath* (Bombay, 1950)
Clark, J.W. and Hughes, T., *Life and Letters of the Reverend Adam Sedwick* (Cambridge, 1890)
Coburn, Kathleen (ed.), *Letters of Sara Hutchinson 1800–1835* (London, 1980)
Cockayne,G.E., *Complete Baronetage & Peerage* (London, 1900)
Colchester (ed.), *Lord Ellenborough's Political Diary 1828–30* (London, 1881)
Colchester, Lord (ed.), *Lord Ellenborough, Political Diary 1828–30* (London, 1881)

Colebrooke, Sir Edward, *Memoir of Mountstuart Elphinstone* (London, 1861)
Colebrooke, T.E., *Life of Mountstuart Elphinstone* (2 vols) (London, 1884)
Colley, Linda, *The Ordeal of Elizabeth Marsh* (London, 2007)
Columbia University, *Encyclopaedia Iranica* vols 1–15 (Columbia, 1982–2011
Conolly, A., *Journey to the North of India* (2 vols) (London, 1834)
Cooper, R.G.S., *The Anglo-Maratha Campaign and the Contest for India* (Cambridge, 2003)
Copland, Ian, *The British Raj and the Indian Princes, 1857–1920* (Bombay, 1982)
Cornwell, E.E., *Songs of Pilgrimage and Glory* (London, 1930)
Cotton, J. S, *Mountstuart Elphinstone (Rulers of India)* (London, 1892)
Crawford, R.G., *Roll of the Indian Medical Service 1615–1930* (London, 1930)
Cunningham, Alan, *Biography & Critical History of Literature of India in the Last 50 Years* (London, 1833)
Curzon, G.N., *British Government in India* (London, 1925)
Curzon, G.N., *Persia and the Persian Question* (2 vols) (London, 1892)
D'Abrantes, Duchess, *Memoires de la Generale Junot* (Paris, 1910)
D'Oyly, Sir Charles, *The European in India* (London, 1813)
Dalrymple, Captain J., *Letters Relative to the Capture of Rachore* (Madras, 1796)
Dalrymple, William, *White Mughals* (London, 2002)
Daniel, Norman, *Islam, Europe and Empire* (Edinburgh, 1966)
Das, S., *Myths and Realities of French Imperialism in India 1763–83* (New York, 1993)
David, Saul, *1857: The Indian Mutiny* (London, 2002)
Davis, H.W.C., *The Great Game in Asia 1800–1844* (Oxford, 1926)
de Lacy Evans, G., *On the Practicability of an Invasion of British India* (London, 1829)
de Moor and Wesseling, *Imperialism and War; Colonial Wars in Asia and Africa* (Leiden, 1989)
Deshpande, Arvind M., *John Briggs in Maharashtra* (Delhi, 1987)
Devenish, James A., *War and Sport in India 1802–1806* (London, 1914)
Devine, T.M., *The Scottish Nation* (London, 1999)
Dictionary of National Biography (Oxford, 1890)
Dirom, Alexander, *A Narrative of the Campaign in India 1792* (London, 1793)
Dodwell, E. and Miles, S.J., *Alphabetical list of the EIC's Bombay Civil Servants* (London, 1838)
Dodwell, E. and Miles, S.J., *Officers of the Indian Army, 1760–1834* (London, 1838)
Dodwell, H. (ed.), *The Cambridge History of India* (Cambridge, 1934)
Dodwell, H., *Muhammed Ali, the Founder of Modern Egypt* (Cambridge, 1931)
Dodwell, H.H., *The Nabobs of Madras* (London, 1926)
Dodwell, H.H., *The New Cambridge History of India* vol. 5 (Cambridge, 1958)
Douglas, James, *Glimpses of Old Bombay* (London, 1900)
Douglas, Mrs Stair, *William Whewell DD* (London, 1881)
Drewett, G. (ed), *Bombay in the Days of George IV: Memoirs of Sir Edward West* (London, 1907)
Durand, H. Mortimer, *Life of the Right Honourable Sir Alfred Lyall* (Edinburgh, 1913)
Dwivedi, S. and Mehrotra, R., *Bombay, the Cities Within* (Bombay, 1995)
Eastwick, R.W., *A Master Mariner* (London, 1891)
Eden, Emily, *Up the Country* (ed. E. Thompson) (London, 1930)
Edwardes, Michael, *Glorious Sahibs* (London, 1968)
Edwardes, Michael, *The Sahibs and the Lotus* (London, 1988)
Elers, George, *Memoirs 1777–1842* (ed. Monson and Leveson-Gower) (London, 1830)
Elliot, Jason, *Mirrors of the Unseen* (London, 2006)

Elliot, Lady & Sir A., *The Elliots – The Story of a Border Clan* (London, 1974)
Elliot, G.F.S, *The Border Elliots and the Family of Minto* (Edinburgh, 1897)
Ellis, Sir Henry, *The East India Question* (London, 1830)
Elphinstone, M., *An Account of the Kingdom of Cabaul* (2 vols) (London, 1815)
Elphinstone, M., *History of India* (2 vols) (London, 1841)
Elphinstone, M., *Rise of British Power in India* (ed. T.E. Colebrooke) (Delhi, 1986)
Elphinstone, M., *Territories Conquered from the Peshwa; A Report* (Calcutta, 1821)
Embree, Ainslie, *Charles Grant and British Rule in India* (London, 1962)
English, Barbara, *John Company's Last War* (London, 1971)
Eraly, Abram, *The Mughal World* (London, 2007)
Erskine, William, *Memoirs of Baber* (Edinburgh, 1826)
Falkland, Lady, *Chow Chow* (London, 1849)
Farooqui, Amar, *Smuggling as Subversion* (Lexington, USA, 2005)
Farrington, Antony, *Catalogue of East India Company Ships' Journals and Logs, 1600–1834* (London, 1999)
Farrington, Antony, *Indian Army – Regimental Titles* (London, 1982)
Fasa'I, Hasan, *History of Persia under Qajar Rule* (Columbia, USA, 1882)
Fass, V., *Forts of India* (London, 1986)
Feiling, Keith, *Warren Hastings* (London, 1966)
Fergosi, Paul, *Dreams of Empire; Napoleon and World War I* (London, 1989)
Fergusson, Niall, *Empire; How Britain Made the Modern World* (London, 2004)
Filor, Eileen, *Global Routes and Imperial Spaces; Burnfoot, Eskdale and the Creation of East India Company Servants* (Warwick, 2012)
Fisher, D.R, *History of Parliament, 1820–1832* (London, 2010)
Fisher, Michael H., *A Clash of Cultures: Awadh, the British and the Moguls* (Delhi, 1987)
Fisher, Michael H., *Indirect Rule in India: Residents and the Ryotwari System, 1757–1857* (Oxford, 1991)
Fisher, Michael H., *Politics of the British Annexation of India 1757–1857* (Oxford, 1993)
Fisher, Michael H., *Visions of Mughal India* (London, 2007)
Fisher, Thomas, *Memoir of Charles Grant* (London, 1833)
Fitzclarence, Colonel, *Across India through Egypt to England* (London, 1819)
Forrest, Denys, *The Oriental* (London, 1968)
Forrest, Denys, *The Tiger of Mysore* (London, 1970)
Forrest, G.W., *Life of Clive* (London, 1918)
Forrest, G.W., *Selections from the Correspondence of Mountstuart Elphinstone* (London, 1884)
Fortescue, Sir J.W., *History of the British Army* (13 vols) (London, 1899)
Fraser, Sir William, *Elphinstone Family Book* (Edinburgh, 1897)
French, Patrick, *Younghusband* (London, 1994)
Frykenberg, R.E., *Guntur District* (Oxford, 1965)
Frykenberg, R.E., *Land Control and Social Structure in India* (University of Wisconsin, 1996)
Furber, Holden, *Bombay Presidency in the 18th century*, (London, 1965)
Furber, Holden, *John Company at Work* (Harvard, 1948)
Furrber, Holden, *Henry Dundas, 1st Viscount Melville* (London, 1931)
Gardane, Alfred, *Mission du General Gardane en Perse* (Paris, 1865)
Gardane, G.A.L., *Journal d'un Voyage dans la Turquie, D'Asie et la Perse* (Paris, 1809)
Gascoigne, Bamber, *The Great Mughals* (London, 1970)

Geddes, Olive, *The Laird's Kitchen* (Edinburgh, 1994)
Ghosh, Biswanath, *British Policy towards Pathans and Pindaris,1805–18* (Calcutta, 1966)
Gibb, Sir Alexander, *The Story of Thomas Telford* (London, 1935)
Gilliat, Reverend Edward, *Heroes of Modern India* (London, 1910)
Gillies, Reverend John, *The Parish of Westerkirk* (Langholm, 1950)
Gilmour, David, *The Ruling Caste* (London, 2005)
Gleig, George R., *Campaigns in Washington, Baltimore & New Orleans, 1814* (London, 1827)
Gleig, George R., *Life of Sir Thomas Munro* (London, 1830)
Goethe, J.W. von, *Noten und Abhandlunger zum besseren Verslandis der West-Ostlichhen Divans* (Tubingen, 1819)
Gorakshkar, S., *Raj Bhavans of Maharashtra* (Bombay, 2002)
Gordon, S., *The Mahrattas 1600–1818* (Cambridge, 1993)
Graham, H.G., *History of the Johnstones 1191–1909* (Edinburgh, 1909)
Graham, H.G., *The Social Life of Scotland in the 18th Century* (London, 1899)
Graham, Maria, *Journal of a Residence in India* (Edinburgh, 1813)
Grant Duff, J.C., *History of the Mahrattas* (3 vols) (London, 1826)
Grant, Elizabeth, *Memoirs of a Highland Lady* (London, 1898)
Grant, James, *History of India* (London, 1898)
Grant, Sir Robert, *The Expediency Maintained* (London, 1812)
Green, Reverend James, *The Parish of Westerkirk* (Langholm, 1836)
Grewal, J.S, *Muslim Rule in India* (Delhi, 1970)
Grierson, H. (ed.), *The Letters of Sir Walter Scott* (12 vols) (London, 1932–1937)
Griffith, P.J., *The British in India* (London, 1947)
Grindlay, *Scenery, Costumes and Architecture, Chiefly on the Western Side of India* (London, 1826)
Gronow, Captain R.H., *Reminiscences and Anecdotes* (4 vols) (London, 1862–5)
Guedalla, Philip, *The Duke* (London, 1931)
Gupta, P.C., *Baji Rao II and the East India Company 1796–1818* (Milford, 1939)
Gurwood, Lt. Col. (ed.), *Dispatches of Field Marshal the Duke of Wellington 1799–1818*, (13 vols) (London, 1834–39)
Guy, Alan and Boyden, *Soldiers of the Raj; Indian Army 1600–1947* (London, 1997)
Halliwell, W., *The Passage to Bombay 1801* (Southampton, 1996)
Hamilton, Walter, *Indian Gazetteer: Description of Hindustan & Adjacent Provinces* (London, 1820)
Hansard (16 vols), 1831–2
Hare, Augustus, *Life and Letters of Maria Edgeworth* (London, 1894)
Hare, Augustus, *Memorials of a Quiet Life* (London, 1872)
Hare, Augustus, *Story of My Life* (London, 1898)
Hare, J.C. and A., *Guesses at Truth* (London, 1847)
Harrington, Jack, 'Macaulay, "Lord Clive" and the Imperial Tradition' (unpublished doctoral thesis), (Edinburgh University, 2006)
Harrington, Jack, *Sir John Malcolm and the Creation of British India* (London, 2010)
Harrison, Michael, *Painful Details* (London, 1962)
Hawes, C., *Poor Relations: the Making of a Eurasian Community in British India, 1773–1833* (London, 1996)
Heber, Mrs R., *The Life of Reginald Heber* (London, 1829)
Heber, Reginald, *Journey through the Upper Provinces 1824–25* (3 vols) (London, 1828)
Hennessy, Maurice, *The Rajah from Tipperary* (London, 1971)

Hollingbery, William, *A Journal . . . during the British Embassy to Persia in 1799, 1800 and 1801* (Calcutta, 1814)
Holman, Denis, *Sikander Sahib: The Life of Colonel James Skinner* (London, 1961)
Holman, James, *Voyage Round the World 1827–1832* (4 vols) (London, 1835)
Holmes, Richard, *Sahib: the British Soldier in India* (London, 2005)
Hook, T., *The Life of General Sir David Baird* (London, 1832)
Hopkirk, Peter, *The Great Game: on Secret Service in High Asia* (Oxford, 1989)
Hoskins, H.L., *British Routes to the Middle East* (London, 1928, 1966)
Hughes, Gillian, *James Hogg, A Life* (Edinburgh, 2007)
Hunter, James, *Picturesque Scenery on the Kingdom of Mysore* (London, 1805)
Hyam, Ronald, *Empire and Sexuality; the British Experience* (Manchester, 1990)
Hyslop, J. & R., *Echoes from the Border Hills* (Sunderland, 1912)
Hyslop, J. and R. *Langholm as it Was* (Sunderland, 1912)
Ilbert, Sir Courtenay, *The Government of India* (Oxford, 1896)
Imlah, Albert, *A Biography of Edward Law, Lord Ellenborough* (Cambridge, 1937)
Ingram, Edward, *Britain's Persian Connection, 1798–1828* (Oxford, 1992)
Ingram, Edward, *Commitment to Empire: Prophecies of the Great Game, 1797–1800* (London, 1981)
Ingram, Edward, *Essays in Honour of Elie Kedourie* (London, 1986)
Ingram, Edward, *In Defence of British India 1775–1842* (London, 1984)
Ingram, Edward, *The Beginning of the Great Game in Asia, 1828–1834* (Oxford, 1979)
Ingram, Edward, *Two Views of British India, 1798–1801* (Bath, 1970)
Ingram, Ellis, *Empire Building and Empire Builders (12 Studies)* (London, 1995)
Jacquemont, Victor, *Letters from India, 1828–1832* (London, 1834)
James William, *Naval History of Great Britain* (London, 1826)
James, Lawrence, *Mutiny in British and Commonwealth Forces 1797–1956* (London, 1987)
James, Lawrence, *Raj: The Making and Unmaking of British India* (London, 1997)
James, Lawrence, *The Iron Duke: Military Biography of the Duke of Wellington* (London, 1992)
Jenkins, R., *Report on the Territories of Nagpur* (2 vols) (Calcutta, 1827)
Jones, Sir Harford, *His Majesty's Mission to the Court of Persia 1807–11* (London, 1834)
Kanungo, S., *Jaswant Rao Holkar, the Golden Rogue* (Lucknow, 1965)
Kaye, J.W., *Life and Correspondence of Charles, Lord Metcalfe* (London, 1854–8)
Kaye, J.W., *Life and Correspondence of Major-General Sir John Malcolm* (2 vols) (London, 1856)
Kaye, J.W., *Lives of Indian Officers* vol. 1 (London, 1867)
Keay, John, *The Great Arc* (London, 2000)
Keay, John, *The Honourable Company* (London, 1991)
Kelly, J.B., *Britain and the Persian Gulf 1795–1880* (Oxford, 1968)
Kelly, Lawrence, *Diplomacy and Murder in Tehran* (London, 2002)
Khalidi, Omar, *British Residents at the Court of the Nizams, 1779–1948* (Hyderabad, 1987)
Khan, Ghulam Husain, *Gulzar i Asafiya*, (Hyderabad, 1891)
Khurana, G., *British Historiography on the Sikh Power in the Punjab* (Delhi, 1985)
Kincaid, Dennis, *British Social Life in India 1608–1937* (London, 1938)
King, P.S, *The British Crown and the Indian States* (London, 1929)
Kinkaid, C., and Parasnis, D.B., *History of the Maratha People* (3 vols) (Oxford, 1918)
Kinkaid, Dennis, *The Grand Rebel – An Impression of Shivaji* (London, 1937)
Kolff, Dirk H.A., *End of the Ancien Regime; Colonial War in India, 1798–1818* (Leiden, 1989)

Kolff, Dirk H.A., *Naukar, Rajput and Sepoy; the Evolution of the Military Labour Market in Hindustan* (Cambridge, 1990)
Kulkarni, A.R., *Life of Grant Duff* (Pune, 2005)
Laine, Jim, *Shivaji Parad* (Cambridge, 2001)
Lake, Edward, *Sieges of the Madras Army 1817–1819* (London, 1825)
Lambton, A.J.S., *Qajar Persia, Eleven Studies* (London, 1987)
Laughton, J.K. (ed.), *The Letters and Despatches of Lord Nelson* (London, 1886)
Lawson, Philip, *The East India Company* (London, 1993)
Lewis, B. and Holt, P., *Historians of the Middle East* (Oxford, 1962)
Leyden, John, *Memoirs of Babur (completed by William Erskine)* (Edinburgh, 1826)
Little, William, *Statistical Account of the Parish of Westerkirk* (Langholm, 1793)
Llewellyn Jones, Rosie, *The Great Uprising* (London, 2007)
Lloyd, Seton, *Ruined Cities of Iraq – Baghdad and C.J. Rich* (London, 1942)
Lockhart, J.C., *A Signal Catastrophe: the Life of Sir Walter Scott* (10 vols) (Edinburgh, 1902)
Longford, Elizabeth, *Wellington, Vol. I: The Years of the Sword* (London, 1969)
Longford, Elizabeth, *Wellington, Vol. 2: Pillar of State* (London, 1972)
Lorimer, J.G., *Gazetteer of the Persian Gulf, Oman & Central Arabia* (Calcutta, 1915)
Losty, J.G., *Calcutta, City of Palaces* (London, 1990)
Love, Henry D., *Vestiges of Old Madras, 1640–1800* (London, 1913)
Low, C. Rathbone, *History of the Indian Navy 1613–1863* (London, 1877)
Low, D.A. (ed.), *Guide to Government Archives in South Asia* (Cambridge, 1969)
Low, D.A., *Eclipse of Empire: Rearguard Action* (Cambridge, 1990)
Low, D.A., *Lion Rampant: Essays in the Study of British Imperialism* (London, 1973)
Low, Ursula, *Fifty Years with John Company* (London 1870, 1936)
Lunt, J., *Sepoy to Subedar, Being the Life and Adventures of Subedar sita Ram, a Native Officer in the Bengal Army* (London, 1970)
Lushington, S.R., *The Life and Services of General Lord Harris* (London, 1840)
Luther, Narendra, *Hyderabad: Memoirs of a City* (Hyderabad, 1995)
Lyall, Alfred, *The Rise and Expansion of the British Dominion in India* (London, 1883)
Macdonald, A., *Memoir of the Life of the Late Nana Furnavees* (Bombay, 1927)
Macdonald, Sir John, *Geographical Memoir of the Persian Empire* (London, 1813)
Macdonald, Sir John, *Journey through Asia Minor 1813–14* (London, 1818)
Macfarlane, C., *Our Indian Empire* (London, 1841)
Mackenzie, Roderick, *A Sketch of the War with Tippoo Sultan* (Calcutta, 1793–4)
Mackintosh, R.J., *Life of the Rt Hon. Sir James Mackintosh* (London, 1836)
Majeed, Javed, *Ungoverned Imaginings, James Mill's History of India* (London, 1992)
Majumdar, Anita, 'Lord Minto's Administration in India' (unpublished doctoral thesis) (University of Oxford, 1962)
Majumdar, R.C., *The History and Culture of the Indian People* vol. 9 (Bombay, 1963)
Malcolm, Clementina, *Diary of St Helena 1816–1817* (London, 1823)
Malcolm, Sir John, *Sketch of the Political History of India 1784–1806* (London, 1811)
Malcolm, Sir John, *Disturbances in the Madras Army* (London, 1812)
Malcolm, Sir John, *Sketch of the Sikhs* (Calcutta, 1812)
Malcolm, Sir John, *History of Persia* (2 vols) (London, 1815)
Malcolm, Sir John, *Malwa Report* (Calcutta, 1822)
Malcolm, Sir John, *Notes of Instructions to Assistants and Officers* (London, 1822)
Malcolm, Sir John, *Memoir of Central India* (2 vols) (London, 1823)
Malcolm, Sir John, *Memoir of Central India* (ed. C.H. Payne) (London, 1922)

Malcolm, Sir John, *Political History of India* (2 vols) (London, 1826)
Malcolm, Sir John, *Sketches of Persia* (London, 1827)
Malcolm, Sir John, *Miscellaneous Poems* (Bombay, 1829)
Malcolm, Sir John, *Revenue and Judicial Administration in the South Mahratta Country* (Bombay, 1829)
Malcolm, Sir John, *Civil Administration of Gujerat* (Bombay, 1830)
Malcolm, Sir John, *Letter to Abbotsford Committee* (London, 1832)
Malcolm, Sir John, *Government of India* (London, 1833)
Malcolm, Sir John, *Speech on the Preliminary Papers Respecting the East India Company's Charter* (London, 1833)
Malcolm, Sir John, *Life of Robert, Lord Clive* (3 vols) (London, 1836)
Malcolm, Napier, *Five Years in a Persian Town* (London, 1905)
Malleson, G.B., *Decisive Battles of India* (London, 1887)
Markham, C. R, *A General Sketch of the History of Persia* (London, 1874)
Marsh, Charles, *Sir G.H. Barlow, Passages in the Late Administration at Madras* (London, 1812)
Marshall, P.J., *East Indian Fortunes* (Oxford, 1976)
Marshall, P.J., *The Oxford History of the British Empire Volume 2: the Eighteenth Century* (Oxford, 1998)
Marshman, J.C., *History of India* (London, 1867)
Martin, R. Montgomery, *The Indian Empire* (3 vols) (London, 1857)
Martin, R.M. (ed.), *Despatches, Minutes & Correspondence of Marquess Wellesley in India* (5 vols) (London, 1834–8)
Martin, Vanessa (ed.), *Anglo-Iranian Relations Since 1800* (London, 2005)
Mason, Philip, *A Matter of Honour* (London, 1974)
Matthews, Noel and Wainwright, Doreen, *A Guide to Manuscripts and Documents in the British Isles Relating to the Middle East and North Africa* (Oxford, 1980)
McLaren, Martha, *British India and British Scotland 1780–1830* (Akron, USA, 2001)
Mehra, P., *Dictionary of Modern Indian History 1707–1947* (Bombay, 1995)
Mehta, Mohana S., *Lord Hastings and the Indian States 1813–1823* (Bombay, 1930)
Metcalfe, T.R, *Ideologies of the Raj* (Cambridge, 1994)
Meyer, K.E., *Tournament of Shadows; the Great Game and the Race for Empire* (London, 1999)
Mill, James and Wilson, H.H., *History of British India* (8 vols) (London, 1818, 1848)
Minto, Countess of, *Life and Letters of Gilbert Elliot, 1st Earl of Minto* (London, 1874)
Minto, Countess of, *Lord Minto in India 1807–1814* (London, 1880)
Mirhusseini, Sayyid Ali, *Biographical Notes on Sir John Malcolm as Historian of Persia* (Tehran, 1965)
Moon, Sir Penderel, *The British Conquest and Dominion of India* (London, 1989)
Morier, James, *A Journey through Persia, Armenia and Asia Minor 1808–09* (London, 1812)
Morier, James, *Adventures of Hajji Baba of Ispahan* (3 vols) (London, 1824–8)
Morris, Henry, *Heroes of Our Indian Empire: Sir John Malcolm, the Ubiquitous Diplomat* (London, 1908)
Morris, Henry, *The Life of Charles Grant* (London, 1898)
Morris, Jan, *Scotland* (London, 1998)
Morton, James, *Memoir of the Life of John Leyden* (Calcutta, 1825)
Morton, James, *Poetical Remains of John Leyden, with Memoir* (London, 1814)
Muir, Ramsay (ed.), *The Making of British India 1756–1858* (Manchester, 1915)
Munro, Innes, *Narrative of Operations on the Coromandel Coast against the Combined Forces*

of the French, Dutch and Hyder Ally Cawn, from 1780 to the Peace in 1784 (London, 1789)
Murphy, V., *Tippoo's Tiger* (London, 1976)
Namier, Lewis, *History of the House of Commons 1754–1790* (London, 1968)
Nelson, Paul D., *Francis Rawdon, Marquis of Hastings* (Madison, New Jersey, 2005)
Nevile, Pran, *Rare Glimpses of the Raj* (Delhi 1998; Oxford; 1971)
Noltie, Henry, *The Dapuri Drawings* (Edinburgh, 2002)
O'Leary, Patrick, *Sir James Mackintosh, the Whig Cicero* (Aberdeen, 1989)
O'Malley, L.S.S., *Modern India and the West* (Oxford, 1941)
O'Malley, L.S.S., *The Indian Civil Service 1601–1930* (London, 1931)
O'Meara, Barry, *Napoleon in Exile; A Voice from St Helena* (London, 1822)
Ondaatje, C., *Sind Revisited* (London, 1996)
Oswell, G.D., *Sketches of Rulers of India* (Oxford, 1908)
Outram, James, *Sinde and Affghanistan* (London, 1840)
Owen, Sidney (ed.), *Selections from Wellesley Despatches* (2 vols), (Oxford, 1877)
Padwick, Constance, *Henry Martyn, Confessor of the Faith* (London, 1922)
Paget, Lady Walburga, *Embassies of Other Days* (London, 1923)
Panikkar, K.M., *The Evolution of British Policy towards the Indian States 1774–1858* (Calcutta, 1929)
Parasnis, D.B., *Selections from the Satara Raja's and Peishawa's Diaries* (Satara, 1906)
Parasnis, D.B., *Poona in Bygone Days* (Satara, 1921)
Parkinson, C.N, *Edward Pellew* (London, 1934)
Parkinson, C.N, *Trade in the Eastern Seas, 1795–1813* (Cambridge, 1937)
Parliamentary Papers (1818), no. 369, *Extracts re Peshwa*
Parliamentary Papers (1818), no. 370, *Extracts re Pindarries*
Parliamentary Papers (1818), no. 370, *Papers re Pindarry and Mahratta Wars*
Parliamentary Papers (1831–32), vol. 13, *Affairs of East India Company and Military*
Parliamentary Papers (1831–32), no. 30, Appendix 2, *Summary Operations in India, 1814 to 1823*
Parliamentary Papers (1834), *Report from Committees, vol. xi, Steam Navigation to India*
Parliamentary Papers (1844), no. 175, *Correspondence re Dowlat Rao Sindhia, 1805*
Parliamentary Papers (1844), no. 175, *Lake to Dowlat Rao Sindhia; and other correspondence, 1805*
Parry, Ann, *The Admirals Fremantle 1788–1820* (London, 1971)
Pasley, C.W., *Military Policy and Institutions of the British Army* (London, 1810)
Pasley, Rodney, *Send Malcolm* (London, 1982)
Pasley, Sir R. (ed.), *Private Sea Journals of Sir Thomas Pasley Bt, 1778–1782* (London, 1931)
Pearce, R.R., *Memoirs & Correspondence of Richard, Marquis Wellesley* (3 vols) (London, 1846)
Peardon, T.P., *The Transition in English Historical writing 1760–1830* (New York, 1933)
Pemble, John, *The Invasion of Nepal: John Company at War* (Oxford, 1971)
Philips, C.H., *The East India Company 1784–1834* (Manchester, 1940)
Philips, C.H., *Historians of India, Pakistan and Ceylon* (Oxford, 1961)
Philips, C.H., *The Young Wellington in India* (London, 1973)
Philips, C.H., *Correspondence of Lord William Cavendish Bentinck* (Oxford, 1977)
Pinney, Thomas (ed.), *Letters of T.B. Macaulay* (Cambridge, 1974)
Pitre, K.G., *The Second Anglo-Maratha War 1802–1805* (Pune, 1990)
Porter, Andrew (ed.), *Oxford History of the British Empire* vol. 3 (Oxford, 1999)
Porter, Robert Ker, *Travels in Georgia, Persia etc 1817–1820* (London, 1821)

Pottinger, Henry, *Travels in Beloochistan and Sinde* (London, 1816)
Prinsep, H.T., *Marquess of Hastings' Political & Military Transactions in India* (London, 1825)
Prinsep, H.T. (trans.), *Memoirs of a Pathan Soldier of Fortune, Nawab Ameer Khan* (Calcutta, 1832)
Pryde, G. S., *Scotland from 1603* (Edinburgh, 1963)
Puryear, V.J., *Napoleon and the Dardenelles* (Los Angeles, 1951)
Pye-Smith, Charlie, *Rebels and Outcasts* (London, 1999)
Qureshi, M.I., *History of the First Punjab Regiment 1759–1956* (London, 1958)
R.G. Shelford Bidwell, *Swords for Hire* (London, 1971)
Ranada, Rekha, *Sir Bartle Frere and his Times* (Delhi, 1990)
Rau, Chalapathi M., *Govind Ballah Pant* (Pune, 1997)
Rawlinson, H.C., *England and Russia in the East* (London, 1875)
Ray, Gordon N., *The Buried Life* (Oxford, 1962)
Reith, John, *Life of John Leyden* (Galashiels, 1885)
Renick, John, *Lord Wellesley and the Indian States* (Agra, 1987)
Rich, C.J., *Memoir of the Ruins of Babylon* (London, 1815)
Rich, C.J., *Journey from Basra to Bushire* (ed. E. Adamson) (London, 1839)
Rich, C.J., *Narrative of a Residence in Koordistan* (London, 1836)
Riches, Hugh, *History of the Oriental Club* (London, 1998)
Rickards, Robert, *The Present System of Our East India Government* (London, 1813)
Ritchie, John, *Lachlan Macquarie* (Melbourne, 1986)
Roberts, Andrew, *Napoleon and Wellington* (London, 2001)
Roberts, Paul E., *India under Wellesley* (London, 1929)
Roberts, Paul E., *History of British India* (Oxford, 1938)
Robins, Nick, *The Corporation that Changed the World* (London, 2006)
Robinson, Andrew, *Maharajah* (London, 1988)
Ross of Bladenberg, *Marquess Hastings, KG* (Oxford, 1893)
Ross, Charles, *Correspondence of Charles, 1st Marquis Cornwallis* (3 vols) (London, 1859)
Rosselli, J., *Lord William Bentinck and the Making of a Liberal Imperialist* (London, 1974)
Rothschild, Emma, *Inner Life of Empires* (Princeton, 2011)
Roy, M.P., *Origin, Growth and Suppression of the Pindaris* (Delhi, 1973)
Roychaudary, Laura, *The Jadhu House* (Calcutta, 2000)
Said, Edward, *Orientalism* (London, 1978)
Sardesai, G.S., *New History of the Mahrattas* (3 vols) (Bombay, 1956)
Sargent, J., *Memoir of Henry Martyn* (London, 1819)
Sarkar, Jadunath (ed.), *Poona Residency Correspondence*, (15 vols) (Bombay, 1937–1955)
vol. 1: *Mahadji Sindhia & North Indian Affairs* (ed. Sarkar, Jadunath)
vol. 2: *Malet's Embassy 1786–97* (ed. Sardesai, G.S.)
vol. 3: *The Allies' War with Tippoo Sultan 1790–93* (ed. Ray, Nirod B.)
vol. 4: *Maratha-Nizam Relations 1792–95* (ed. Dighe, V.G.)
vol. 5: *Nagpur Affairs 1781–1820* (ed. Kalc, Y.M.)
vol. 6: *Palmer's Embassy 1797–1801* (ed. Sardesai, G.S.)
vol. 7: *Close's Embassy 1801–1810* (ed. Sardesai, G.S.)
vol. 8: *Dowlat Rao Sindhia and North Indian Affairs 1794–99* (ed. Sarkar, Jadunath)
vol. 9: *Dowlat Rao Sindhia and North Indian Affairs 1800–1813* (ed. Sinha, Raghubir)
vol. 10: *Treaty of Bassein & Anglo-Maratha War 1802–04* (ed. Sinha, B.K.)
vol. 11: *Dowlat Rao Sindhia's Affairs 1804–09* (ed. Roy, Nirod B.)
vol. 12: *Elphinstone's Embassy 1811–15* (ed. Sardesai, G.S.)

vol. 13: *Elphinstone's Embassy 1816–18* (ed. Sardesai, G.S.)
vol. 14: *Dowlat Rao Sindhia and North Indian Affairs 1810–1818* (ed. Sarkar, Jadunath)
vol. 15: *Selections from Sir C. Malet's Letter Book 1780–84* (ed. Sarkar, Jadunath)
Sarkar, Jadunath, *The Fall of the Mughal Empire* (5 vols) (Hyderabad, 1992)
Selby, W.H., *Memoir on the Ruins of Babylon* (London, 1815)
Seton-Karr, W.S, *The Marquis Cornwallis (Rulers of India)* (Oxford, 1896)
Seton-Kerr, W.S. (ed.), *Selections from Calcutta Gazettes* (3 vols) (London, 1864)
Severn, J.K., *Architects of Empire; the Duke of Wellington and his Brothers* (Oklahoma, 2007)
Shadman, S.F., *The Relations of Britain and Persia 1800–1815* (London, 1939)
Shastri, K.N.V., *The Munro System of British Statesmanship in India* (Mysore, 1939)
Sheik Ali, *Tipu Sultan* (New Delhi, 1972)
Shipp, John – see Stranks, C.J.
Sibbald, Sir Robert, *History of Fife* (Cupar, 1710, 1866)
Siddiqi, Asiya, *Trade and Finance in Colonial India 1750–1860* (Delhi, 1995)
Simmonds, Stuart, and Digby, Simon (eds), *The Royal Asiatic Society; History and Treasures* (London, 1979)
Simpkin, C.G.F., *The Traditional Trade of Asia* (Oxford, 1968)
Sinh, R., *Malwa in Transition . . . The First Phase, 1698–1765* (Bombay, 1936)
Sinha, B.K., *Origins and Growth of the Pindaris* (Calcutta, 1971)
Sinha, H.N. (ed.), *Nagpur Residency Records* (vols 1–3) (Nangpur, 1953)
Skinner, James, *A Concise Account of the People (Tajrish ul Akran)* (Delhi, 1825)
Skinner, James, *A Description of the Princes (Tashirat ul Uman)* (Delhi, 1830)
Sleeman, W.H., *The Thugs or Phausiyans of India* (Philadelphia, 1839)
Smiles, Samuel, *A Publisher and His Friends* (London, 1891)
Smith, George, *Twelve Indian Statesmen* (London, 1897)
Smith, Vincent, *Oxford History of India* (Oxford, 1981)
Smout, T.C., *History of the Scottish People 1560–1830* (London, 1969)
Spear, T.G.P., *Historians of India* (London, 1961)
Spear, T.G.P., *The Nabobs* (Oxford 1932, 1963)
Spear, T.G.P., *Oxford History of Modern India* vol. 2 (Oxford, 1965)
Spencer, Alfred (ed.), *The Memoirs of William Hickey (1749–1809)* (4 vols) (London, 1913)
Stanford, J.K., *Ladies in the Sun: the Memsahibs in India 1790–1860* (London, 1952)
Stanhope, Earl of, *Conversations with the Duke of Wellington, 1831–1851* (London, 1888)
Stapleton, A.G., *Official Correspondence of Canning* (2 vols) (London, 1887)
Stapleton, A.G., *Political Life of Canning* (3 vols) (London, 1831)
Stein, Burton, *Thomas Munro: Origins of the Colonial State* (Delhi, 1989)
Stevens, Sir Roger, *The Land of the Great Sophy* (London, 1962)
Stokes, Eric, *English Utilitarians and India* (Oxford, 1959)
Stranks, C.J., *Paths of Glory: the Military Career of John Shipp* (London, 1969)
Stuart, Margaret, *Scottish Family History* (Edinburgh, 1929)
Studdart, J., *Local Scenery and Manners in Scotland* (2 vols) (London, 1925)
Sutton, Jean, *Lords of the East; the East India Company and its Ships 1600–1874* (London, 2000)
Sykes, Percy, *A History of Persia* (2 vols) (Oxford, 1922)
Taheri, Abolghassen, *History of Iran-British Diplomatic Relations* (Tehran, 1983)
Tajbaksh, Ahmad, *Colonial Policies in Iran* (Tehran, 1983)
Tapper, Richard, *Frontier Nomads of Iran: a Political and Social History of the Shahsavan* (London, 1979)

Taylor, P. Meadows, *Confessions of a Thug* (novel) (London, 1839)
Taylor, P. Meadows, *The Story of My Life* (Edinburgh, 1877)
Taylor, P.J.O., *Indian Mutiny* (Delhi, 1992)
Taylor, Stephen, *Storm and Conquest in the Indian Ocean 1809* (London, 2007)
Teignmouth, Lord, *Correspondence of John, Lord Teignmouth* (2 vols) (London, 1843)
Theal, G.M., *History of South Africa Volume 3, 1795-1834* (London, 1891)
Theal, G.M., *Records of the Cape Colony* (London, 1897)
Thompson, E. and Garratt, G.T., *The Rise and Fulfilment of British Rule in India* (London, 1934)
Thompson, E.J., *The Other Side of the Medal* (London, 1925)
Thompson, E.J., *Charles, Lord Metcalfe* (London, 1937)
Thompson, E.J., *The Making of the Indian Princes* (Oxford, 1943)
Thorn, Major William, *Memoirs of the War in India Conducted by General Lord Lake* (London, 1818)
Thornton, T.H., *Richard Meade; the Feudatory States of Central India* (London, 1898)
Tod, James, *Annals and Antiquities of Rajastan* (3 vols) (ed. W. Crooke) (London, 1829–1832)
Torrens, W.M., *The Marquis Wellesley, Architect of Empire* (London, 1880)
Trevelyan, G.O., *Life and Letters of Lord Macaulay* (Oxford, 1876, 1978)
Trevelyan, Humphrey, *The India We Left* (London, 1972)
Tuck, Patrick (ed.), *East India Company 1600–1858* vols 1 to 6 (reissued London, 1998)
vol. 1: Foster, William, *England's Quest for Eastern Trade*
vol. 2: Marshall, P.J., *Problems of Empire*
vol. 3: Bolts, William, *Considerations on Indian Affairs*
vol. 4: Tuck, Patrick, *Trade, Finance and Power*
vol. 5: Tuck, Patrick, *Warfare, Expansion and Resistance*
vol. 6: Philips, C.H., *The East India Company, 1784–1834*
Tyler, Colonel, C.J., *Life of Sir C.W. Pasley* (London, 1929)
Valentia, Viscount, *Travels in India 1802–06* (3 vols) (London, 1809)
Varma, Sushma, *Mountstuart Elphinstone in Maharashtra 1801–27* (Poona University, India, 1983)
Wadia, R.A., *The Bombay Dockyard and Wadia Master Builders* (Bombay, 1957)
Walia, Urmila, *Changing British Attitudes towards Indian States 1823–35* (Delhi, 1985)
Walpole, Horace, *Correspondence of Horace Walpole (1717–1797)* (London, 1837, 1851)
Waring, E.S., *A History of the Mahrattas* (London, 1810)
Waring, E.S., *A Tour to Sheeraz (in 1802)* (London, 1807)
Warner, Sir W. Lee, *The Protected Princes of India* (London, 1894)
Warner, Sir W. Lee, *The Native States and the West* (London, 1910)
Warner, Sir W. Lee, *The Native States of India* vol. 1 (London, 1910)
Warren, M., *Missionary Movement from Britain in Modern History* (London, 1965)
Watson, R. Grant, *History of Persia 1800–1858* (London, 1866)
Webster, Antony, *The Richest East India Merchant: The Life and Business of John Palmer of Calcutta, 1765–1836* (Woodbridge, 2007)
Weller, Jac, *Wellington in India* (London, 1972)
Wellington, 2nd Duke of (ed.), *Despatches, Correspondence . . . of the Duke of Wellington, 1819–32* (8 vols) (London, 1867–80)
Wellington, 2nd Duke of (ed.), *Supplementary Despatches of the Duke of Wellington 1797–1818* (15 vols) (London, 1868–72)

Wellington, 7th Duke of (ed.), *Conversations of the 1st Duke with G.W. Chad* (Cambridge, 1956)
Wellington, 7th Duke of (ed.), *The Duke of Wellington and His Friends* (London, 1965)
Wellington, 7th Duke, *The Duke of Wellington and His Friends* (London, 1965)
Welsh, Colonel James, *Military Reminiscences (1790–1830)* (2 vols) (London, 1830)
Wheeler, Stephen, *Annals of the Oriental Club* (London, 1925)
Wild, Antony, *The East India Company – Trade and Conquest from 1600* (London, 1999)
Wilkinson, Theon, *Two Monsoons* (London, 1976)
Wilks, Mark, *Historical Sketches of South India* (London, 1810, 1817)
Williams, Captain J., *The Bengal Native Infantry* (London, 1817)
Williams, L. Rushbrook, *The Black Hills* (London, 1958)
Williams, R. Brady, *An Introduction to Swaminarayan Hinduism* (Cambridge, 2001)
Wilson, H.H., *History of British India* (London, 1848)
Wilson, Joan, *A Soldier's Wife: Wellington's Marriage* (London, 1987)
Wilson, W.J., *History of the Madras Army* (4 vols) (Madras, 1882)
Windham, *Wellesley Papers1760–1842* (2 vols) (London, 1914)
Woodruffe, Philip, *The Men who Ruled India* (2 vols) (London, 1953–54)
Wraxall, N.W., *Historical Memoirs of My Own Time* (2 vols) (London, 1815)
Wright, Sir Denis, *The English Amongst the Persians* (London, 1977)
Wright, Sir Denis, *The Persians Amongst the English* (London, 1985)
Yapp, Malcolm, *Two British Historians of Persia* (Oxford, 1962)
Yapp, Malcolm, *Strategies of British India: Britain, Iran and Afghanistan 1798–1850* (Oxford, 1980)
Yazdani, Abdul, *Mandu, City of Joy* (Oxford, 1929)
Yule, Henry and Burnell, A.C., *Hobson-Jobson* (London, 1868)
Zastoupil, Lynn, *J.S. Mill and India* (Stanford, 1994)
Zastoupil, Lynn, *J.S. Mill's Encounter with India: J.S. Mill and Western Culture* (Toronto, 1999)
Zebrowski, Mark, *Deccani Painting* (London, 1983)

Journal Articles

Amini, Iradj, 'Napoleon and Persia', *Journal of Persian Studies* vol. 37 (1999), pp. 109–122
Anon., comment on Sir John Malcolm's *Memoir of Central India* in *Calcutta Review* 95, p. 54 (1856)
Anon., 'Debate at the India House on the Press in India', *Asiatic Journal*, 18 (no. 104) (1824)
Anon., account of degree ceremony, *Oxford Journal 1816*
Anon., account of a dinner to Sir John Malcolm in London, *Asiatic Journal*, July 1827, pp. 135–138
Anon., account of a fete for Sir John Malcolm, *Bombay Courier*, 13 December 1821
Anon., account of a meeting of the East India Company Proprietors on the Charter, *Asiatic Journal*, xi, part 1 pp. 1–297 (1833)
Anon., account of a meeting at Lord Clive's house on 1 July re erection of a statue to Sir John Malcolm by Francis Chantrey, *Gentleman's Magazine* 103, II, pp. 559–560 (1833)
Anon., account of a public dinner to the Malcolm knights at Langholm on 31 July, *Eskdale and Liddlesdale Advertiser* (1822)
Anon., account of a visit to the Mahabaleshwar Hills in May 1834, *Asiatic Journal*, xix, pp. 77–80 (1836)

Anon., 'Press Freedom in India', *Asiatic Journal*, 18 (no. 104), pp. 171–209 (1824)
Anon., 'Knighthood for Sir John Malcolm', *London Gazette*, 15 December 1812
Anon., 'Life of Sir John Malcolm from birth to 1809', *Calcutta Review* 29, pp. 157–206 (1856)
Anon., minute on a visit to the court at Satara, *Calcutta Review* 10, p. 437 (1828)
Anon., obituary of Sir John Malcolm, *Calcutta Review* 12 (1833), p. 353
Anon., obituary of Sir John Malcolm, *Gentleman's Magazine* 103 I, pp. 81–84 (1833)
Anon., report on the death of Sir John Malcolm, *Asiatic Journal* 11, part 2, pp. 81–84 (1833)
Anon., report on the Proceedings of the Military Committee of the House of Commons, *Asiatic Journal* vol 10, pp. 67–69, 209, 224, 348, 359 (1833)
Anon., review of General Gardane's *Voyage to Persia* in *Quarterly Review* 3 (Art xiii), pp. 163–167 (1810)
Anon., review of R. Grant's *The Expediency Maintained* in *Quarterly Review* 9, Art XII, pp. 218–253 (1813)
Anon., review of Sir John Macdonald's *Geographical Memoir of the Persian Empire* in *Edinburgh Review* vol xxii, no. 44, pp. 410 ff, January 1814
Anon., review of John Macdonald's *Geographical Memoir of the Persian Empire* in *Quarterly Review* 9, Art V, pp. 57–58 (1813)
Anon., review of Sir John Malcolm's *Government of India* in *Asiatic Journal* 11, part 1, p. 218, part 2, 203 (1833)
Anon., review of Sir John Malcolm's *The History of Persia* in *Asiatic Journal* vol. 1 pp.155–160, vol 2, pp. 267–272 (1816)
Anon., review of Sir John Malcolm's *The History of Persia* in *Edinburgh Review* 26, pp. 282–304 (1816)
Anon., review of Sir John Malcolm's *Life of Robert, Lord Clive* in *Asiatic Journal* 20 pp. 81–93 (1836)
Anon., review of Sir John Malcolm's *Memoir of Central India* in *Calcutta Review* 14, p. 91 (1823)
Anon., review of Sir John Malcolm's *The Political History of India* in *Calcutta Review* 10, p. 369 (1827)
Anon., review of Sir John Malcolm's *Sketch of the Political History of India* in *Edinburgh Review* 20, pp. 38–53 (1811)
Anon., review of Sir John Malcolm's *Sketch of the Sikhs* in *Quarterly Review* 9 (Art XIV) pp.472–479 (1813)
Anon., review of James Morier's *Embassy to Persia* in *Quarterly Review* 9 (Art V), pp. 57–89 (1813)
Anon., 'Sir John Malcolm and Mr Lushington', *Morning Chronicle*, 21 April 1824
Anon., 'Tarala, Sir James Mackintosh's House in Bombay', *Times of India*, 2 December 1938
Barrett, Alan H., 'A Memoir of Lt. Col. J. D.'Arcy', *Journal of Persian Studies* vol. 43, pp. 241–270 (2005)
Barrow, J., Review of Malcolm's *Memoir of Central India*, *Quarterly Review* 29, pp. 382–414 (1823)
Bennell, A.S., 'The Maratha War Papers of Arthur Wellesley', *Army Records* (1998)
Bennell, A.S., 'Anglo Maratha Confrontation in June and July 1803', *School of Oriental and African Studies Bulletin*, pp. 107–131 (1965)
Bennell, A.S., 'Factors in Marquess Wellesley's Failure against Holkar in 1804', *School of Oriental and African Studies Bulletin* (1962)

Bennell, A.S., 'Arthur Wellesley as Political Agent', *Journal of the Royal Asiatic Society*, pp. 273–288 (1987)

Bryant, G.J., 'Scots in 18th Century India', *Scottish Historical Review*, 64 (1985)

Bryant, G.J., EIC and the British Army Crisis in Madras in 1789. *Journal of the Society for Army Historical Research*, 62 (1984)

Bryant, G.J., 'Pacification in the Early British Raj, 1755–1785', *Journal of Imperial and Commonwealth History* 14 (1985)

Cooper, R.G.S, 'Wellington and the Mahrattas', *International History Review* (February 1989)

Ellis, Sir Henry, review of Malcolm's *Political History of India, Quarterly Review* 34, p. 32 (1827)

Hastings, Marquess of, on his administration in India, *The Pamphleteer*, 24 xlviii, pp. 287–334 (1828)

Heber, Reginald, review of Malcolm's *History of Persia, Quarterly Review* 9, pp. 236–291 (1816)

Ingram, Edward, 'Family and Faction in the Great Game in Asia; the Struggle over the Persian Mission, 1828–35', *Middle East Studies* (1981)

Jeffrey, Francis, review of Malcolm's *Memoir of Central India, Edinburgh Review* 40, pp. 279–297 (1824)

Lambton, A.K.S., 'Sir John Malcolm and *The History of Persia*', *British Institute of Persian Studies* 33, pp. 97–109 (1995)

Macaulay, T.B., review of *Life of Robert, Lord Clive, Edinburgh Review* 70, pp. 296–387 (1840)

McLaren, Martha, 'Scottish Concepts of Asian Despotism in the early 19th Century', *International History Review* 15/3, pp. 442–465 (1993)

McLaren, Martha, 'Ideology of the Company State', *Indo-British Review*, pp. 130–143 (1993)

Malcolm, Sir John, 'Sketch of the Sikhs', *Asiatic Researches* 11, pp. 197–222, (Calcutta, 1811)

Malcolm, Sir John, review of *The History of Persia* in *Calcutta Review* 26, pp. 285, 398 (1815)

Malcolm, Sir John, 'Tribute to Hindoo Character: Asiatics', *Quarterly Review* 13, pp. 238, 389 (1815)

Malcolm, Sir John, 'On the Excellence of Turcoman Horses', *Quarterly Review* 14, pp. 173–186 (1816)

Malcolm, Sir John, review of Williams' *Bengal Native Infantry* in *Quarterly Journal* xviii, pp. 385–427 (1818)

Malcolm, Sir John, letter on the Burmese War and Sir D. Ochterlony, *The Times*, 20 December 1826

Malcolm, Sir John, review of *Life of Robert, Lord Clive* in *Calcutta Review* 95, p. 54 (1836)

Masulipatam Disturbances, *Quarterly Review* 5 (Art viii) pp. 138–203 (1811)

Meredith, Colin, 'Early Qajar Administration', *Journal of Iranian Studies* 4, pp. 64–65 (1971)

Mill, James, review of Malcolm's *Sketch of the Political History of India, Quarterly Review* 6, pp. 454–461 (1811)

Peers, D.M., 'Sepoys, Soldiers and the Lash, 1820–1850', *Journal of Imperial and Commonwealth History* 23, pp. 441–465 (1995)

Peers, D.M., 'The Duke of Wellington and British India, 1819–1827', *Journal of Imperial and Commonwealth History* 17/1, pp.5–25 (1988)

Peers, D.M., 'Soldiers, Scholars and the Scottish Enlightenment; Militarism in early 19th Century India', *International History Review*, 16/3, pp. 442–465 (1994)

Poynder, J., letter attacking Sir John Malcolm re Christianity in India, *The Times*, 11 May 1833

Proceedings of the Bombay Literary Society (3 vols) (from 1804)

Rendall, Jane, 'Scottish Orientalism, from Robertson to James Mill', *Historical Journal* 25/1, pp. 43–69 (1982)

Savory, R.M., 'British and French Diplomacy in Persia 1808–1810', *British Institute of Persian Studies* 10, pp. 31–44 (1972)

Searight, Sarah, 'A Waghorn Letter Book for 1840', *Royal Asiatic Society Journal*, 7.2, pp. 239–248 (1997)

Stronge, Susan, 'The Sword of the Maharaja Holkar', *Orientations* vol. 19, no. 2, February 1988

Thackeray, W.M., review of Elphinstone's *History of India* in *Quarterly Review* 77, pp. 377–413 (1841)

Wright, Sir Denis, 'The Order of the Lion and Sun', *British Institute of Persian Studies* 17 and 19 (1979) and 19 (1981)

Wright, Sir Denis, 'Samuel Manesty and His Unauthorised Trip to Tehran', *British Institute of Persian Studies* 24 (1986)

Wright, Michael, 'Sir John Malcolm and the Battle of Mehidpoor', *Army Quarterly* 109 (2) pp. 203–209 (1979)

Yapp, M., 'Control of the Persian Mission', *Birmingham University Journal* 7, pp. 164–171 (1959)

Yapp, M., 'Establishment of the British Embassy at Baghdad 1798–1806', *School of Oriental and African Studies Bulletin*, pp. 323–336 (1967)

Yapp, M., 'Some European Travellers in the Middle East', *Middle East Studies* 39, pp. 211–228 (2003)

Zastoupil, L., 'The Great Indian Education Debate', *School of Oriental and African Studies Bulletin* (1999)

Index of People

Note: page numbers of 'in-text' illustrations are shown in bold italics.

General Index

Note: page numbers of 'in-text' illustrations are shown in italic.